Bertha Maxwell-Roddey

D1527075

UNIVERSITY PRESS OF FLORIDA

Florida A&M University, Tallahassee
Florida Atlantic University, Boca Raton
Florida Gulf Coast University, Ft. Myers
Florida International University, Miami
Florida State University, Tallahassee
New College of Florida, Sarasota
University of Central Florida, Orlando
University of Florida, Gainesville
University of North Florida, Jacksonville
University of South Florida, Tampa
University of West Florida, Pensacola

Bertha Maxwell-Roddey

A Modern-Day Race Woman and the Power of Black Leadership

Sonya Y. Ramsey

UNIVERSITY PRESS OF FLORIDA

Gainesville / Tallahassee / Tampa / Boca Raton

Pensacola / Orlando / Miami / Jacksonville / Ft. Myers / Sarasota

Publication of this work made possible by a Sustaining the Humanities through the American Rescue Plan grant from the National Endowment for the Humanities.

27 26 25 24 23 22   6 5 4 3 2 1

Library of Congress Cataloging-in-Publication Data
Names: Ramsey, Sonya Yvette, author.
Title: Bertha Maxwell-Roddey : a modern-day race woman and the power of black leadership / Sonya Y. Ramsey.
Description: 1. | Gainesville : University Press of Florida, 2022. | Includes bibliographical references and index.
Identifiers: LCCN 2021054608 (print) | LCCN 2021054609 (ebook) | ISBN 9780813069326 (hardback) | ISBN 9780813068695 (paperback) | ISBN 9780813070100 (pdf) | ISBN 9780813072302 (ebook)
Subjects: LCSH: Maxwell, Bertha, 1930- | University of North Carolina at Charlotte—Faculty—Biography. | African American women college teachers—North Carolina—Charlotte—Biography. | African American college teachers—North Carolina—Charlotte—Biography. | African American women teachers—North Carolina—Charlotte—Biography. | Discrimination in higher education— North Carolina—Charlotte—History. | African American women—Education (Higher)—Biography. | BISAC: BIOGRAPHY & AUTOBIOGRAPHY / Cultural, Ethnic & Regional / African American & Black | BIOGRAPHY & AUTOBIOGRAPHY / Educators
Classification: LCC LC2781.5 .R33 2022 (print) | LCC LC2781.5 (ebook) | DDC 378.1/2092 [B]—dc23/ eng/20220223
LC record available at https://lccn.loc.gov/2021054608
LC ebook record available at https://lccn.loc.gov/2021054609
The University Press of Florida is the scholarly publishing agency for the State University System of Florida, comprising Florida A&M University, Florida Atlantic University, Florida Gulf Coast University, Florida International University, Florida State University, New College of Florida, University of Central Florida, University of Florida, University of North Florida, University of South Florida, and University of West Florida.

University Press of Florida
2046 NE Waldo Road
Suite 2100
Gainesville, FL 32609
http://upress.ufl.edu

This book is dedicated to my mother,
who has been an endless source of support.

Contents

Figures

Preface

In 2008, I was a new faculty member at the University of North Carolina at Charlotte. I had just published my first book, *Reading, Writing, and Segregation: A Century of African American Teachers in Nashville,* and I had just started to investigate possible ideas for my next research project. As a historian of African American gender history who focuses on the experiences of Black women educators, I first became interested in teachers who taught during the era of desegregation while in graduate school. I had the opportunity to be a part of one of the first groups of researchers to travel throughout the state of North Carolina to conduct oral history interviews in Duke University's *Behind the Veil: Documenting the Jim Crow South Project.* During the summer of 1993, I did daily interviews, but the ones I conducted with teachers affected me the most.

Despite being in Charlotte, I didn't get to interview Bertha Maxwell-Roddey during that time. Still, our team did conduct interviews with Kathleen Crosby and Elizabeth Randolph, two of Maxwell-Roddey's administrative peers. After teaching and becoming a public school principal during segregation, Bertha Maxwell-Roddey became one of the first Black women principals of a white elementary school in the late 1960s. I was eager to learn more about her life and discover more about the experiences of African American women educator activists during the 1970s and 1990s.

As an affiliate faculty member of UNC Charlotte's Africana Studies Department, I looked forward to attending the inaugural Dr. Bertha Maxwell-Roddey Distinguished Africana Lecture, named in honor of her contributions to African American and African Studies at UNC Charlotte. When I noticed that the undergraduate members of UNC Charlotte's Iota Rho Chapter of Delta Sigma Theta Sorority, Inc. stood up when Maxwell-Roddey walked into the room, I suddenly realized why her name seemed so familiar to me. I became embarrassed because I didn't stand for her. Why? Even though I had not participated in the sorority for years, I was still a Delta. I should have remembered that Bertha Maxwell-Roddey was a past national president of the sorority.

Participation in most African American Greek-letter sororities extends well after the undergraduate years. Paula Giddings, who joined Delta Sigma Theta's Alpha Chapter at Howard University, expressed her ambivalence as she described her personal experiences within the sorority in the preface of her book, *In Search of Sisterhood: Delta Sigma Theta and the Challenge of the Black Sorority Movement* (1988). As a national officer in Delta Sigma Theta, Maxwell-Roddey and the other members of the sorority's National Executive Board and Membership Intake Task Forces would continuously strive to eradicate some of the practices that affected Giddings's early sorority participation. In a long line of coincidences related to this project, I was initiated into Giddings's same chapter several years after the sorority's implementation of new membership intake procedures. Regretfully, I did not participate in sorority events after graduation for reasons unrelated to Delta.[1]

As Giddings further explained in the preface of *In Search of Sisterhood*, as she attempted to avoid the negative aspects of the sorority, she missed the positive, the sisterhood. I would have a comparable experience when writing about Bertha Maxwell-Roddey. In describing her devoted sister circle and their relentless dedication, I reached a more complex understanding of Deltas' sometimes exasperating hard work as leaders and their immense dedication as community service volunteers. These frustrations can be assuaged when they have the unique opportunity to participate in loving rituals designed by Black women for Black women or when Deltas celebrate friendship and just had fun as part of a loving sisterhood. In effect, by celebrating each other, these Black women could abandon the overwhelming pressures that they faced as African American women, if only for a while.[2]

Although I majored in journalism in college, I had always loved history. I became a devotee of Giddings's book, *Where and When I Enter: The Impact of Black Women on Race and Sex in America* (1984).[3] After working as an entry-level journalist and public relations assistant, I reached a crossroads after being laid off from the Public Broadcasting Station (PBS) where I worked. I finally decided to do what I really loved. I began the often overwhelming, never monotonous, utterly transformative experience of pursuing doctoral studies in United States history at the University of North Carolina at Chapel Hill.

After my mother, the former director of Nashville's Opportunities Industrialization Center, a non-profit, job-training program, moved from my hometown to Dallas, Texas, to become the chief operating officer of the African American Museum of Dallas, I had just decided to return home to live with her for a year to save money while I completed my dissertation. That one-year stint eventually expanded into eleven after I joined the history faculty of the University of Texas at Arlington.

As a Dallas resident and with a family member on its executive staff, I often visited and volunteered at the African American Museum of Dallas. I grew to appreciate how it balanced its role as a Black arts and public historical site with its mission to offer cultural programming that benefited the city's African American communities. I even taught in the museum's afterschool program, where I became painfully aware that I should stick to academic teaching.

As more of Maxwell-Roddey's accomplishments were mentioned at the lecture, I grew excited to learn that she and her colleague Mary Harper started Charlotte's Afro-American Cultural and Service Center in 1974. I loved learning how the Center, now the Harvey B. Gantt Center for African-American Arts + Culture since 2009, has survived decades in an ever-changing urban southern environment, revealing and reflecting how Charlotte's African American communities adapted to urban renewal, the rise of the Black middle class, and the reverse migration of African Americans to the South. As I related to almost every point in Maxwell-Roddey's life, including sharing connections to her hometown of Seneca, South Carolina, which was near my mom's hometown of Westminster, South Carolina, where I spent every summer as a child, there seemed to be one highlight that I wasn't familiar with: her role as founding director of UNC Charlotte's Black Studies Program and her contributions—and that of other early Black Studies practitioners—to the development of the National Council for Black Studies (NCBS). There are excellent works that chronicle the early history of the NCBS, but none that place Maxwell-Roddey at the center. I knew what I had to do. I had to write about her and share her story as an educator and cultural advocate.

Known for sometimes speaking past her allotted time, as Maxwell-Roddey shared her comments after the lecture and as the director tried to get the microphone back, Maxwell-Roddey took the time to thank everyone present and spoke with students. I saw an African American, southern woman who exuded the self-effacing but secure self-confidence of an experienced leader. Even after her non-retirement-retirement from teaching at the University of South Carolina at Lancaster (USC) in 2008, Maxwell-Roddey still wielded significant influence both in Charlotte and nationally as a person who continued to engage in academic, community, and national public service. She established community institutions, such as the Theodore and Bertha M. Roddey Foundation in Rock Hill and Catawba County, SC. Maxwell-Roddey also shared her expertise as a public history consultant at the Historic Brattonsville Cultural Heritage Museum in York County, SC. As a teacher, principal, administrator, and builder of community institutions, or as I say, a modern-day race woman, Maxwell-Roddey's career as an educator underscores the core mission of African American teachers to improve Black children's possibilities during segregation. She and her peers forged new pathways for leadership as desegregation-era urban southern educators.

Since that day in 2008, sitting in the audience of the inaugural "Dr. Bertha Maxwell-Roddey Distinguished Africana Lecture," I have proceeded on a journey where I watched Maxwell-Roddey persevere through and bounce back from several serious illnesses. After ending an almost twenty-year teaching stint at the University of South Carolina at Lancaster in Lancaster, South Carolina, she remains active as a mentor, advisor, and trusted friend as a continuous stream of figures stopped by her home to visit. Whether coming to seek advice, express their gratitude, or just to reminiscence, these visitors often included public figures, like former CMS Board of Education Chair, Arthur Griffin Jr., past UNC Charlotte and USC Lancaster students who sometimes brought their children and grandchildren, prominent scholars and fellow NCBS leaders, such as James Stewart, and her beloved Delta Sigma Theta Sorority sisters who keep her schedule packed with service projects, speaking engagements, and fun, as a revered past national president.

As our bond strengthened—from when Maxwell-Roddey first asked, "Who are you?" to my eventual introduction, "This is the lady that is writing my biography. Give her your records,"—I am aware that this is a nontraditional biography of a unique woman. Notwithstanding her distinctiveness, I found that when I described this project to others, they often responded by sharing recollections of their own "Berthas" or special educators who influenced their lives. I have cherished this writing process that enabled me to further develop as a historian as I uncovered more about Black women's educational activism in the last decades of the twentieth century. I hope that by reading this book, you can uncover the "Berthas" in your lives or become a "Bertha" yourself!

Acknowledgments

As I worked diligently to finish this book, I envisioned writing my acknowledgments as an incentive to spur me on past writing blocks, missing evidence realizations, and life issues. Now, as I start recognizing those people and organizations that supported me as I wrote this biography of Bertha Maxwell-Roddey, I begin by thanking her for agreeing to participate in this process. As she graciously invited me into her home to interview her, I learned so much more than historical information. I had the opportunity to see the inner world of a influential African American woman leader, one who led one of the most powerful African American women's organizations in the world and yet could make anyone feel comfortable.

I remain extremely grateful for the institutional research grants and support I received from the University of North Carolina at Charlotte and Dean Nancy Gutierrez of the College of Liberal Arts and Sciences. From reading drafts to offering words of support as we participated in writing groups and Brown Bag draft-listening sessions, I thank my History Department chair, Jürgen Buchenau, and my UNC Charlotte colleagues for their advice and for taking time from their busy schedules to help. I especially wish to honor Carol L. Higham, whose editing expertise enabled me to transform a very rough draft into a publishable manuscript. I also thank John David Smith for all his unofficial mentorship and help during the years.

I would be remiss if I failed to mention some of my UNC Charlotte original co-conspirators, advocates, motivational guides, and general super sister scholars. My former colleague, Cheryl Hicks, known for her touching cards and gifts and for reminding me of my purpose, and refusing to allow me to sink into self-doubt; Janaka Lewis, a former mentee, gifted writer, and administrator, and future college president, of whom I remain in awe; Minister/Professor Julia Robinson Moore, a true woman of God, whose non-judgmental advice on writing and spiritual matters has enriched my life and this project, and Erika Edwards, another mentee, who I am proud to see fully ascend into her greatness. I'm so grateful for my other friends and former and current colleagues who served as chapter readers: Stefan Bradley, David Goldfield, Christine Haynes, Paula Marie Seniors, and Mark Wilson. Their insights helped to add clarity and substance to my work. I also want to thank Laurie Prendergast for her last-minute editing help.

As I reviewed essential manuscript collections, I must acknowledge the former and current archivists and librarians at the Special Collections and University Archives, J. Murrey Atkins Library at the University of North Carolina at Charlotte who supported this project over the years, including Katie McCormick, Katie Causier Howell, Rita Johnston, Tricia Kent, Lolita Rowe, Dawn Schmitz, and Nikki Thomas. I also express my gratitude to the archivists, librarians, officers, and staff members at the following research repositories and organizations who include Mazie Bowen, Hargrett Rare Book and Manuscript Library, University of Georgia; Bonita Buford, the Harvey B. Gantt Center for African-American Arts + Culture; Shelia Bumgarner, Carolina Reading Room, Charlotte Mecklenburg Library; Meredith Evans and Brittany Parris, Jimmy Carter Presidential Library and Museum; Vann Evans, State Archives of North Carolina; Brandon Lunsford, Inez Moore Parker Archives, James B. Duke Memorial Library, Johnson C. Smith University; Garlenda McNair and Amber Williams, Delta Sigma Theta Sorority Archives, National Headquarters, Washington, DC; and Emily Whitmire Sluder, Seneca Branch, Oconee County Library, Seneca, SC.[1]

Even though I had the opportunity to review several crucial archival collections, much of the written historical sources that informed this project, such as the records of the Afro-American Cultural Center, had been either inadvertently destroyed or remained inaccessible due to their undisclosed locations in private collections. As a result, information garnered from newspapers, published oral history interviews, and recorded phone conversations with historical subjects served as crucial evidence for this project. Unfortunately, there is not enough space to list all the people that I had the opportunity to talk to or interview, but the contributions from Ann Carver, Betty Cunningham, Roberta Duff, Kathryn Frye, William "Bill" Heard, Mary Maxwell, Elaine Nichols, Fabette T. D. Smith, Terry Smith, and Herman Thomas to this project went beyond the actual informational interviews. I relied upon their expertise and experience to do everything from reading the manuscript to sharing information from their private archives. I became more conscious of the remarkable impact that Maxwell-Roddey had on her students and colleagues as Gregory Davis, William King, Alicia McCullough, Harry Robinson Jr., James B. Stewart, and Sheryl Westmoreland Smith continued to provide treasured advice and information. Vanessa Gallman, Maxwell-Roddey's former student, shared Maxwell-Roddey's students' thoughts in a recent publication, *Who Am I? Memoirs of a Transformative Black Studies Program.*[2]

Fabette T. D. Smith deserves special recognition as she provided access to her extensive private Delta Sigma Theta collection, helped me to connect with other members of the extraordinary "Bertha's Girls" group, assisted my search for photo images, and provided invaluable content editing to ensure that I presented information related to Delta Sigma Theta with accuracy.[3] I am grateful to the sorors who shared their insights as interview subjects, supplied research materials and photos, and offered crucial information, including Immediate Past National Presidents of Delta Sigma Theta, Beverly Smith, Marcia Fudge, and Paulette Walker; other national officers and executive committee members; and Charlotte Alumnae Chapter members such as President Melody Harris, Stephaney Crawford, Gwendolyn Marseille, Beulah Moore, Brandi Riggins, Jacqueline Stevens Sanders, and Jodi Douglas-Turner. My fellow Alpha Chapter sorors of Delta Sigma Theta, Odessa M. Archibald, Janeula Burt, Darlene Jackson-Bowen, and Fran Phillips-Calhoun's insights and references also proved to be revelatory.[4]

There's also a great need to express appreciation to the ones whose friendship and guidance helped me to thrive as I undertook this journey. From the members of my writing accountability groups to friends and sorors who let me deliberate on and on about my project or allowed me to rant about my personal life. I first met Prudence Cumberbatch when I worked in Texas, and we have been friends for many years. I could not have progressed as a scholar and completed this project without her enduring support as she provided both personal and professional advice and shared her editing expertise. My "honorary play sister," Deidre Hill Butler knows my struggles and my triumphs and never fails to lift my spirits as we encourage each other professionally and personally. I also want to mention my life-long friends who continue to motivate and inspire me; Sandra Rodriguez (where's my gumbo?) and her talented graphic artist/daughter Simone, Dwight Ferguson, Denise Johnson, and Yeae' Hagler.

As I strove to complete this book, I have appreciated the helpful research suggestions and kind consideration received from so many friends at home at UNC Charlotte and across the nation, including Gloria Campbell-Whatley, Natanya Duncan, Karen Flint, Pamela Grundy, Ramona Houston, Julia Jordan-Zackery, Valinda Littlefield, Gregory and Nellie Mixon, Akin Ogundiran, Heather Perry, Bernadette Pruitt, Ana Y. Ramos-Zayas, Adah Ward Randolph, Debra Smith, and Dorothy Smith-Ruiz; my fellow members of the Association of Black Women Historians; my Women's and Gender Studies Program colleagues; and SEEDS (Sister Educators Eating Dinner), an informal support group that I co-founded with Janaka Lewis for women of color faculty and staff at UNC Charlotte. I also appreciate my students from the freshman to the graduate level. Their enthusiastic zeal for learning both invigorates and sustains me. I especially want to express my gratitude to my Howard University Alpha Chapter Delta Sigma Theta sorors, Michele Fuller and Teri Washington, and my dear line sisters of "Eristic 43," who continue to enlighten and provide emotional support.

As I close this exercise of appreciation, I recognize my family. My mother, Betty Cunningham, enabled me to complete this project by providing endless and untold assistance ranging from serving as an archivist as she discovered important historical documents integral to my research, to repeated chapter editing to eliminate elusive typos, to serving in invaluable child caretaking roles that granted me much-needed research time, to even turning our kitchen into "Miss Betty's House of Beauty," helping me fix my hair in a new low-maintenance style that I saw demonstrated on YouTube. I'm a mama's girl, but I would be remiss if I didn't share how much my father, Charles Ramsey II, and his partner Elizabeth Ann Creecy's wisdom and guidance helped me to succeed. I remain blessed to have both my parents, and I honor them. I can't list all my relatives, but I need to highlight those who facilitated this project in untold ways, my brothers Edward Audain and Charles Ramsey III, aunts Betty Jo Johnson and Jo Ann Johnson, uncle Martin Johnson, and cousins Ann Harbin, Jennifer Johnson, Tammy Burton, and Ron and Requel Reynolds. Through many ups and downs, they continue to exemplify the power of faith in God's abundant love, the grace to overcome obstacles, and the ability to bring peace, patience, joy, and love to my life.

One exciting and a bit exasperating thing that happened almost every time I visited over the years with Dr. Maxwell-Roddey (even though she insisted that I call her Bertha, but I just couldn't) was the fact that she revealed new information at almost every sitting. I realize that even though this book is complete, there are still more stories to share, especially related to current events. Even though I treasured the opportunity to conduct oral history interviews over the years with subjects Kathleen Crosby (as part of the 1993 Duke University Behind the Veil Project), Mary Harper, T. J. Reddy, and Thomas Tillman, who are no longer with us, I sincerely regret that I didn't get to include, contact and/or interview so many others. I apologize in advance if I were remiss in mentioning anyone in this brief statement. Please blame it on my overtaxed brain and not my heart. I also want to express my gratitude to Sian Hunter, who offered patience and guidance as my editor at the University Press of Florida, and her talented colleagues who aided in the publication of this work. In closing, I want to repeat my heartfelt thanks to Dr. Bertha Maxwell-Roddey for granting me the opportunity to share her life and achievements with the world. Completing this biography has been a life-changing experience for me as a scholar and as a person.

Earlier sections of the introduction may be found in "Caring Is Activism: Black Southern Womanist Teachers Theorizing and the Careers of Kathleen Crosby and Bertha Maxwell Roddey, 1946–1986," *Educational Studies: A Journal of the American Educational Studies Association,* 48, no. 3 (May 2012): 244–265.

Note on Surname and Word Usages

African American and Black

To increase readability and reduce redundancy, I use the words "Black" and "African American" interchangeably and capitalize "Black."

Afro-American Cultural Center

The African American Cultural Center was originally named the African American Cultural and Service Center. In 1984, the name was changed to the Afro-American Cultural Center. In 2009, it was renamed the Harvey B. Gantt Center for African American Arts + Culture.

Bertha Maxwell-Roddey's Surname

This book refers to the subject's surname in several ways on a chronological basis. Chapter 1 uses her maiden name, Bertha Luvenia Lyons, until her 1952 marriage to Horace Maxwell.

In chapters two to four and sections of chapters five through seven, I use Maxwell until her 1987 marriage to Theodore Roddey when she started using Maxwell-Roddey.

In chapter 8, she abbreviated her name to Bertha M. Roddey during her Delta Sigma Theta presidency from 1992-1996, and she often used this name in sorority-related matters. In later years, she returned to the name Maxwell-Roddey.

Bertha Maxwell-Roddey uses her current name, Maxwell-Roddey when attributing her direct quotes and offering broad explanations or analyses.

In some instances, I intersperse her first and last names for variety.

Names for Black Studies

As the field of Black Studies developed over the years, it has embraced several titles to describe its evolving theoretical, programming, and pedagogical thrusts. These names include Black Studies, Afro-American Studies, African American Studies, African American and African Studies, African Diaspora Studies, and Africana Studies. Currently, several university programs and departments have adopted the most current description, "Africana Studies." Nevertheless, practitioners still utilize the term "Black Studies" to describe the field, often defying historical conventions for chronological consistency.

UNC Charlotte's Black Studies/African American and African Studies Program/Department

Bertha Maxwell-Roddey's description of Maxwell-Roddey's experiences as the founding director of UNC Charlotte's Black Studies Program and as the founder of the National Council for Black Studies (NCBS) exemplifies these fluid name transitions. For example, in 1971, Maxwell-Roddey began as director of the then Black Studies Program. She worked to change its name to the African American and African Studies (AAAS) Program by the mid-1970s. After her retirement in 1986, the now AAAS Department became known as the Africana Studies Department.

In describing Maxwell-Roddey's work with NCBS, she often associated with other directors whose program names ranged from Black to Diasporic Studies. However, despite the plethora of program names, these practitioners still utilized the broader/foundational term of Black Studies when discussing the field. In summary, chapters four and five of *Bertha Maxwell-Roddey* will discuss the history and development of UNC Charlotte's Black Studies/African American Studies Program and the early history of the NCBS, often simultaneously applying the broad term of Black Studies to discuss changes affecting the field.

Charlotte City Schools/Charlotte Mecklenburg Schools

When Bertha Maxwell-Roddey began teaching in Charlotte, the school system was known as the Charlotte City Schools. In 1960, the municipal governments of Charlotte and its surrounding Mecklenburg County merged. The public schools became known as the Charlotte Mecklenburg School System (CMS).

Delta Sigma Theta Sorority, Incorporated

The book refers to the 2019 Delta Sigma Theta Sorority, Incorporated Writing Style Guide, which calls for using the numerical version of the year, the capitalization of the title National President, and the term "Past" when referring to the formal title of Delta Sigma Theta's national presidents proceeding the person's name. For more information, see www.deltasigmatheta.org, accessed December 22, 2021.

Introduction

In a 1995 *Crisis* magazine article entitled, "Dr. Bertha M. Roddy [*sic*] Just a Reluctant Leader Who Takes the Bull by the Horns," writer Eric L. Clark reported how Roddey, the 20th National President of Delta Sigma Theta Sorority Incorporated,[1] an international women's public service organization of over 350,000 initiated members, claimed that she "never sought out to be a leader."[2] Born in 1930, Charlotte's Bertha Maxwell-Roddey personified the work of untold African American[3] women who strategically forged new pathways to ensure that Black children, women, and families thrived after the collective presence of the civil rights marchers or the fiery speeches of the Black Power activists faded from public view after the 1970s.

As a beneficiary of postwar rights movements, Bertha Maxwell-Roddey used her new social access and political power to enact positive change on the local and national levels from the 1960s to the 1990s. Maxwell-Roddey served as a desegregation trailblazer in 1968 as one of Charlotte's first Black women principals of a predominantly white elementary school. Moving to academia as the University of North Carolina at Charlotte's second Black full-time faculty member in 1970, Maxwell-Roddey later became the founding director of the university's Black Studies Program (BSP) in 1971. There, she extended the reach of the BSP beyond the campus to help Black neighborhoods ravaged by urban renewal and school closings. In 1974 Maxwell-Roddey and colleague Mary Harper co-founded the Afro-American Cultural and Service Center, a local African American community arts institution, now the Harvey B. Gantt Center, Charlotte's premier Black arts space. In 1975, as the BSP director, Maxwell-Roddey worked to institutionalize the broader field of Black Studies and ensure its permanence through the founding of its most prominent professional organization, the National Council for Black Studies.

Even though Maxwell-Roddey, a former 1980 candidate for the North Carolina General Assembly, had explored electoral politics, she was repelled by the negative actions of exploitive, self-absorbed politicians, and she decried these calculating power-seekers who sought top positions through manipulation. In contrast, Maxwell-Roddey became a leader to solve problems. After viewing how racial and economic discrepancies harmed Black children in Charlotte's Black First Ward neighborhood, where Maxwell taught in 1964, she organized the Charlotte Teachers Corps of volunteers to sponsor a summer early childhood education program in the First Ward. The first free program of its kind for Black children in the city, it served as a forerunner to the national Head Start Program. Maxwell-Roddey stepped up to lead on behalf of others, as exemplified when she satisfied the wishes of her local and regional-based sorors by running in 1992 to become Delta Sigma Theta's first national president from the South Atlantic Region. Reluctant yes, as she mentioned in Clark's article, ineffective, no![4]

Charismatic Leadership

German sociologist and philosopher Max Weber defined and described the "charismatic leader" as "one who emerged under great duress to lead with the extraordinary power to persuade his or her followers to act in sometimes extreme measures."[5] As scholars from diverse fields reinterpret Weber's theories, civil rights historians evaluated the influence and role of charismatic male leaders such as Martin Luther King Jr. and other dynamic grassroots activists.[6] By analyzing Maxwell-Roddey's leadership journey, I complicate these historical discussions by offering a much-needed examination of women's executive authority.

As a political biography, this book supplements other recent histories of Black women's charismatic leadership before and after the modern-day civil rights movement, including Prudence Cumberbatch's insightful work on the Baltimore National Association for the Advancement of Colored People (NAACP) heads, Lillie Carroll Jackson and Juanita Jackson Mitchell.[7] Building on the examples set by mentors like Charlotte's Alexander Street Elementary School Principal Jayne Hemphill, Maxwell-Roddey meshed management expert Robert Greenleaf's "servant as leader" concept of accountable leadership with the South African communal leadership philosophies of Ubuntu, meaning, "I am because we are," to become an authentic, compassionate, and inventive leader.[8]

A Modern-Day Race Woman

During the late nineteenth and early twentieth centuries, the term "race man" emerged in the Black press to describe civil rights leaders, such as scholar and philosopher W.E.B. Du Bois and prominent newspaper editor William Monroe Trotter. "Race women" included the National Council of Colored Wome (NACW) president Mary Church Terrell and anti-lynching journalist Ida B. Wells. Over the years, with the onset of the post-1950s civil rights movement, Black people adopted the more action-oriented term of "activist" to describe African Americans who fought for social equality. In this book, I retrieve and modernize the once-dated term "race woman" from the not-so-distant past to describe Bertha Maxwell-Roddey. She and her peers turned hard-won civil rights triumphs into tangible, real-world accomplishments. As Maxwell-Roddey and her contemporaries' post–civil rights era actions remain understudied, describing them as modern-day race women encourages scholars to expand the definitions of activism to incorporate Black women's multifaceted leadership strategies to dismantle discriminatory barriers in the classroom and the boardroom from the 1970s to the 1990s. Immobilized in time, the dominant representations of Black women activists confine them to the front lines of the 1950s–1960s era civil rights and Black Power movements or spiral forward, depicting them as present-day Black Lives Matter protesters. Reconfiguring the term race women promotes the re-envisioning of activists beyond the familiar representations of young freedom fighters to encompass the nuanced images of Maxwell-Roddey and other mid-life African American women educators.[9]

Born in Seneca, South Carolina, a small town in the Piedmont area of the state, during the Great Depression, Bertha Luvenia Lyons, later Maxwell-Roddey, grew up with her grandparents in a home that lacked money, but not affection. Exemplifying the power of education to overcome poverty, Bertha Luvenia Lyons worked her way through school as a dental assistant, eventually graduating from the historically Black Johnson C. Smith University in 1954 in Charlotte, North Carolina, and began teaching in the city's segregated schools. Representing the often lesser-known experiences of Black women teachers during the school desegregation process, in 1966, Maxwell-Roddey broke barriers by becoming the first Black woman to receive a master's degree in Educational Administration at the University of North Carolina at Greensboro. In 1992, at the age of sixty-two, she became the 20th National President of the then 185,000-member African American women's organization, Delta Sigma Theta. In this journey, she assumed the abbreviated title "Bertha M. Roddey" as she moved from a segregated elementary school classroom to become, as *Ebony* magazine stated in 1995, "one of the most influential African American leaders in the United States."[10]

Similar to other Black people of her generation, Maxwell-Roddey often received the title of the "first Black" or "first woman" or "first Black woman" in her professional and public life. *Bertha Maxwell-Roddey* details how Maxwell-Roddey navigated through the minefields of being a "first," reflecting the praxis of intersectionality. As a beneficiary of two powerful social movements, Bertha Maxwell-Roddey's experiences as a "first" call for extending civil rights' chronological constraints to reflect what historian Jacquelyn Hall coined as "the long civil rights movement." Rethinking these fixed-time boundaries allows for more investigation of the nontraditional modes of activism that Maxwell-Roddey and other activists pursued without the involvement of large social justice movements amid the rise of political and social conservativism after the 1970s.[11] Even though Maxwell-Roddey did not lead protest marches, she represents the personal strivings of African Americans who entered former all-white schools, businesses, organizations, and spaces. Historiography discussions define the writings of segregation-era scholars and journalists who promoted African American firsts in education, business, and other areas of public life as a form of contributionist history.[12]

Though modern-day historians now explore the African American experience from multidimensional perspectives of gains and losses, many of the accounts of individual African Americans who desegregated former all-white environments remain untold and unexamined. Whereas some of these "firsts" represented legal or legislative civil rights actions, for Maxwell-Roddey, pragmatic reasons such as economic necessity often spurred her on to become a "first." Little fanfare marked the everyday "firsts" of people like Maxwell-Roddey. However, she received minimal resistance or calls for her dismissal. Possessing a light-brown-skinned complexion, Maxwell-Roddey never attempted to and could not pass for white and did not try to be anything but herself, a Black woman.[13]

Maxwell-Roddey's work experiences reflected how African Americans and Black women, specifically, could sometimes slip through the cracks in the walls of white supremacy and the patriarchy. As a teen and young woman, Bertha often unintentionally secured jobs designated for whites. Working in spaces where her very presence defied segregation's customs and laws, Bertha became an amiable yet sometimes outspoken employee willing to take a stand against discrimination, if necessary. In later years as a professional, she parlayed her influence as a "first" in employment, within social organizations, and on nonprofit boards to push beyond her "token" status to create sustainable opportunities for women and Black people. Within these formerly all-male and/or all-white environments, Maxwell-Roddey's combination of pragmatic affability and social justice advocacy sometimes resulted in uncharacteristic reactions, where challengers resented and opposed Maxwell-Roddey's actions

yet respected her as a formidable adversary. In some instances, Berth´
to champion her cause from positions of compassionate strength,
turned former dissenters into friends or staunch allies. Often these sto..
individual achievement are overlooked by scholars who chronicle large-scale
social movements. The life and work experiences of women like Maxwell-Roddey offer insight into how African American women leaders adapted to and
reformed their surroundings.[14]

Bertha Maxwell-Roddey reveals an underlying factor that explains Maxwell-Roddey's success. Relying on a distinctive form of pragmatic affability or sociability, she formed alliances and friendships with the most unlikely of figures—including Black Power activists, national, state, and local government officials, and corporate CEOs. Often called "down to earth," Maxwell-Roddey possesses the rare ability to make people feel valued, motivating them to act despite their reservations, sometimes to the point of devotion. Whether making allies, confronting adversaries, or just defying critics by supplying overwhelming amounts of evidence, Maxwell-Roddey practiced what I term "charismatic advocacy." She did whatever was necessary, from forming unlikely alliances that crossed racial and class boundaries to confronting adversaries to ensure that as "a first," she would keep the doors open to not be the only or the last one.

Maxwell-Roddey's efforts as a charismatic advocate illustrate the deeds of a cadre of Black women leaders who gained leadership positions from the 1960s to the 1990s. These women employed numerous tactics, from staging traditional civil rights protests to forming powerful coalitions or networks. *Bertha Maxwell-Roddey* exposes how professional Black women, such as Maxwell-Roddey, armed themselves with the unique skills to mount a multifaceted attack on sexism from patriarchal white and Black men and developed responses to overt and insidious versions of hidden racism. As a leader, Maxwell-Roddey promoted participatory democracy by listening and incorporating the ideas of others and advocating for objectives from positions of data-supported strength.[15]

Historiography and Methodology

This work's interpretation of Maxwell-Roddey as a woman who excelled as a trailblazer in the public schools, academia, and within community-based and national organizations complements and expands upon several historiographical works. *Bertha Maxwell-Roddey* provides an extensive analysis of her educational, organizational, and civic activism. By retrieving the turn-of-the-century term, "race women" to describe desegregation-era African American women who dedicated their professional and personal lives to the betterment of Black people, this work builds upon and advances scholar Brittney Cooper's groundbreaking work, which analyzes the writings and concepts of prominent race women throughout the twentieth century. *Bertha Maxwell-Roddey* deviates from Cooper's intellectual historical analysis to explore the complex motivations and exploits of lesser-known but influential race women like Maxwell-Roddey.[16]

As a political biography, this book supplements other histories of twentieth-century African American women's leaders, such as Katherine Mellen Charron's biography of Septima Poinsette Clark, Joyce Hanson's monograph on Mary McLeod Bethune, and Barbara Ransby's work on Ella Baker to illuminate how modern-day race women, like Maxwell-Roddey, overcame intersectional challenges of racism and sexism to forge new avenues for advancement after the advent of the second wave of the feminist movement.[17]

Whether as an educator, Black Studies practitioner, educational and cultural institution builder, or the president of one of the most influential Black women's organizations in the United States, acknowledging Maxwell-Roddey's core beliefs in the promise of education remains vital to understanding her motivations and experiences as a leader. Several histories of African American education by scholars such as James Anderson, Adam Fairclough, V. P. Franklin, Carter Julian Savage, and Vanessa Siddle Walker examine the history of Black teachers and principals as they supported their students and schools during segregation serve as a historiographical foundation for this work.[18] Recent studies and projects by scholars such as Tondra L. Loder-Jackson and Derrick P. Alridge call for a reconsideration of the motivations, goals, and legacies of civil rights–era Black educators. These teachers served as individual activists and encouraged student activism as instructors within the classroom by promoting social-justice-based curricula.[19] By examining Maxwell-Roddey's and other African American women educators' reactions to the gains in access and loss of cultural connections in the aftermath of the civil rights movement, *Bertha Maxwell-Roddey* complements these earlier works by evaluating Maxwell-Roddey's endeavors to fulfill the promise of desegregation within her educational environment and community.[20]

Bertha Maxwell-Roddey is not a comprehensive history of Delta Sigma Theta Sorority, Incorporated. Nevertheless, as a historian writing a biography of one of its national leaders, I reviewed and critically assessed earlier historical works officially sanctioned by Delta. In many ways, the last two chapters of *Bertha Maxwell-Roddey* is a revised history of Delta Sigma Theta that places the endeavors of Maxwell-Roddey in context through her role of charismatic leader and mentor as well as a sister—or soror—and focuses on her strategies for building long-term relationships, institutions, and opportunities for change.

Though an abundance of studies on African American Greek-letter organizations emerging from the fields of education, sociology, and psychology exist, most of these works evaluate the impact of sorority participation on undergraduate college women regarding leadership training, educational success, or hazing concerns. Few focus on African American sorority participation after college graduation. There are several memoirs and self-published books of personal recollections of Delta's national leaders. Paula Giddings's valuable work discusses Delta Sigma Theta's public service and social action initiatives in response to pressing social, economic, and political issues affecting the nation and in relation to the Black sorority movement. Nevertheless, historical studies of the experiences of individual Delta leaders after 1988 have yet to emerge.[21]

One of the main reasons that scholarship on Black sororities primarily remains on a broader, national level is that these organizations restrict information regarding aspects of their private operations and rituals to members only. As a member of this organization, I have gained access to some of Delta's records that would be unavailable to non-members. Notwithstanding these research constrictions, accessible records remain unexamined due to scholarly disinterest or a lack of understanding of the crucial civic and charitable service efforts of Delta and other Greek-letter organizations. Unfortunately, despite Delta Sigma Theta's influence, scholars may have overlooked the efforts of women in sororities due to a perception of exclusivity and stereotypes regarding their frivolity.

Another unique aspect concerning the historiography of African American sororities involves reviewing officially sanctioned histories written by its members before 1998 that promoted the organization's accomplishments and its leaders without providing contextual and critical historical analyses. After acknowledging the purpose of these histories, by recording historical facts and describing members' efforts, these works can still provide valuable and accurate historical information. They continue to be relevant because these histories recount the national achievements of Black women during the Jim Crow era when few professional historians would have acknowledged their existence or chronicled their efforts. Within Delta, these written and oral histories also serve as representations and conveyors of tradition, values, and purpose. Information from these works about Delta Sigma Theta's establishment and its founders continues to be memorized by new initiates, retold at events, and incorporated into songs performed by Deltas.[22]

Drawing from the theories of prominent legal experts and scholars, such as Kimberlé Crenshaw and Patricia Hill Collins, I view the experiences of Maxwell-Roddey and her contemporaries through an intersectional lens of interlocking oppressions of race, gender, and class. *Bertha Maxwell-Roddey* relies on historical sources such as archival data, newspapers, and scholarly writings, but information garnered from oral history interviews became paramount to writing Maxwell-Roddey's biography.[23]

During my bi-weekly interview sessions with Maxwell-Roddey, after several years, I finally became less surprised when she revealed new examples of her leadership at each subsequent interview. Along with utilizing the snowball sampling method to select subjects who interacted with Maxwell-Roddey, I attended several meetings with her former students and teaching colleagues, Africana Studies practitioners, Charlotte cultural programming advocates, and Delta Sigma Theta sisters. Observing how these subjects interacted with Maxwell-Roddey, provided insight into how she influenced their professional and personal lives and led to a greater comprehension of related textual sources. In addition to reviewing documents in public archives, I gained access to personal collections of essential records filed neatly in boxes and placed in the spare rooms, basements, and garages of private homes through persistent inquiry and networking.

As scholars such as Alice Kessler-Harris debate the role and use of biography in historical studies, *Bertha Maxwell-Roddey* represents the critical role of biography and local studies to illuminate or contradict broad historiographical arguments relating to educational desegregation, Africana Studies, and African American women's activism. As a political biography, this work considers pivotal events that have shaped or influenced Maxwell-Roddey's professional and public life.[24] *Bertha Maxwell-Roddey* critically exposes the continuing impact of the civil rights movement and the lesser understood legacies of Black Power by revealing how Maxwell-Roddey and other activists celebrated the gains of these movements while attempting to remedy the losses of community and identity resulting from desegregation.

The first chapter *of Bertha Maxwell-Roddey* focuses on the biographical highlights of Bertha Luvenia Lyons's early life until she graduated from Johnson C. Smith University. At first glance, as a child born to unwed parents, Bertha's family experiences seemed to portray another stereotypical example of a Black dysfunctionality. Chapter 1 delves deeper to dispel this perception as it chronicles how young Bertha grew up well loved and protected in a home and neighborhood where she gained the informal nickname, "the little girl with the big mind." Encouraged by her extended family and community, Bertha parlayed this "cultural capital" to transform from a small-town girl to become a modern-day race woman.[25]

Chapter 2 discusses Bertha Lyons's and later Maxwell's professional career from her early years as a teacher in Charlotte's segregated schools during the mid-1950s to her later administrative work as a principal of an all-white elementary school in the late 1960s. Graduating from Johnson C. Smith University with her Bachelor of Arts degree in 1954, the start of Bertha's professional career coincided with the momentous decision by the United States Supreme Court in *Brown vs. Board of Education* that declared segregation based upon race in public schools was unconstitutional. In addition to exploring Maxwell's relationship with her African American administrative mentor, Jayne Hemphill, who influenced her as a teacher and as a principal, *Bertha Maxwell-Roddey* compares Maxwell's professional trajectory to two other former teachers and principals, Kathleen Crosby, a former principal during desegregation, who became a Charlotte Mecklenburg Schools (CMS) area superintendent and Elizabeth Randolph, another top administrator with CMS. Together, these women represented a small but influential group of Black women educators who rose through the ranks during a period of educational upheaval to become top-level administrators in CMS.

This chapter also explores how African American women educators' responsibilities shifted from helping students overcome segregation's limitations to preparing these children to thrive in desegregated environments from the 1950s to the late 1960s. As Maxwell and her peers engaged in desegregation battles, their professional landscapes were transformed. This was due to expanded federal governmental scrutiny of local education matters following the implementation of War on Poverty initiatives and the enforcement of federal court-ordered desegregation measures. *Bertha Maxwell-Roddey* examines the interactions of these educational race women as they left the classroom to work in desegregated government and nonprofit administrative settings, developed program initiatives, and secured educational opportunities for African American children.

Chapter 3 moves from the public school classroom to the university campus as Maxwell transitioned from working in the public schools to academia from 1968 to approximately 1974. This chapter provides a brief history of the University of North Carolina (UNC) at Charlotte, from its 1946 origins as a segregated learning center for WWII veterans to its eventual emergence in 1965 as one of the few southern public universities established by a woman, Bonnie Cone. As UNC Charlotte expanded its offerings, eagerly claiming its place as the city's only public four-year institution, this chapter examines how Maxwell shrewdly weaved the promotion of the Afro-American and African Studies (AAAS) Program's objectives with the university's plan to promote innovation and growth. As the director of a new program forged out of protest, Maxwell joined other early Black Studies administrators tasked with formalizing Black students' idealistic demands and meeting the bureaucratic curriculum requirements of an often uninformed and sometimes resistant administration. Institutionalizing Black Studies as a new, multidisciplinary area of academic inquiry, Maxwell incorporated the philosophies of Black Nationalism to develop a feasible curriculum that helped her students become confident, self-aware, and pro-Black. Maxwell asserted her power as the only African American administrator at UNC Charlotte and used her networks among the city's civil rights leaders to seek resources for the Black Studies/AAAS Program. Examining how early educators/administrators developed and sustained Black Studies programs remains essential to understanding the institutionalization of this multidisciplinary field of inquiry in the academy.

Chapter 4 continues the discussion of Maxwell's experiences in higher education, chronicling her time as AAAS director during the late 1970s. After securing the AAAS major in 1976, a year later in 1977, Maxwell-Roddey took a position at her alma mater as the first woman vice president for academic affairs at Johnson C. Smith University for eighteen months before returning to UNC Charlotte to lead AAAS in its fight to reach departmental status by 1983. Additionally, as the sole Black female administrator at UNC Charlotte, Maxwell encouraged the formation of the university's Women's Studies Program, directed by her white friend and colleague Ann Carver. This chapter offers a much-needed examination of the critical role of women in the formation of Black Studies.[26] *Bertha Maxwell-Roddey's* gender and regional historical analysis of significant aspects of the formative years of Black Studies contributes to the comprehensive historiographical study of the field and its programs and departments.

In addition to her focus on academic matters, during the 1980s, Maxwell established various programs, sponsored events, and set criteria that laid the foundation for several student support initiatives, such as advising services, first-year minority student orientation, and multicultural student retention programs. Diverging from the discussion of the internal processes Maxwell utilized to sustain the AAAS, this chapter simultaneously explores her instrumental role as the founder of the National Council for Black Studies (NCBS). As an early leader in the Black Studies movement, Maxwell stood alongside influential scholars and administrators such as James Turner, founder of the Africana Studies and Research Center at Cornell University. Nevertheless, the efforts of the pioneering women of Black Studies, and especially those administrators in the South, have often been relegated to short segments or footnotes.

Even though she served as an administrator at a desegregated university, Maxwell maintained her deep-rooted connections to Charlotte's Black communities. Chapter 5 analyzes Maxwell's influential role as a local institution builder from 1974 to the early 1980s. This chapter sheds light on how African Americans transformed the meanings and methods of activism in—what scholar Zandria Robinson coined as "post-soul"—urban New South desegregated cities, such as Charlotte. Maxwell's command to her students to perform community service in Black neighborhoods ravaged by urban renewal and school closings reflected this call.[27] As Maxwell worked on UNC Charlotte's campus to ensure the permanency of the Afro-American and African Studies/Black Studies program by seeking administrative approval for a major and later departmental status, at the same time, she welcomed the opportunity to support and work with her colleague Mary Harper to take Black Studies off-campus and start a Black cultural center. The creation of the Afro-American Cultural and Service Center reflects how Black Studies practitioners like Harper and Maxwell formed campus/community partnerships to create innovative learning opportunities for their students to contribute to the preservation of aspects of Black communities that seemed lost, such as community empowerment and mentoring for African American children.[28]

As race women, Harper and Maxwell engaged in community activism to preserve Charlotte's African American historical and cultural heritage as a response to the detrimental consequences of urban renewal. In 1980, Maxwell's growing community presence and personal introspections led her to throw her hat into the political ring in an unsuccessful bid to win a seat in the North Carolina General Assembly. After winning in the primary, she failed in her quest to become the first African American woman elected to the North Carolina State House. Maxwell turned this apparent loss into an advantage by relying on her amplified public presence as a former political candidate and community leader with a stellar reputation to advocate for the Center.

Chapter 6 chronicles the expansion of the Afro-American Cultural Center (AACC) in the 1980s after its celebrated community-supported fundraising drive and subsequent renovation and relocation to its own site and its 2009 reinvention as the Harvey B. Gantt Center for African-American Arts + Culture. As Maxwell's educational, community, and national organizational obligations expanded, she remained in an advisory role. She relied more on the Center's executive board and administration to manage the institution's daily affairs. As Black middle-class professionals moved to Charlotte as part of the growing reverse migration to the South, they gravitated to the Afro-American Cultural Center. They helped usher in a new modernized post-soul dynamic as the Center became a refuge of artistic beauty and historical reaffirmation of African American culture for discrimination-weary Black professionals. These newcomers' financial donations helped sustain the Center. Its aesthetically attractive structure attracted these Black middle-class patrons seeking culturally relevant artistic experiences. Unfortunately, it also discouraged some working-class Blacks from participating in an institution that Harper and Maxwell originally created for them and their children. During the late 1980s and mid-1990s, the Center gained a reputation in Charlotte as a cultural influencer.

Nevertheless, its outward projection of prominent elegance masked an inward crisis of financial insecurity as it struggled to keep its doors open in the face of dwindling city support and lagging membership rolls. The AACC's journey reflects the expanded movement to establish African American cultural centers and museums across the nation in cities such as Dallas, Baltimore, Chicago, and Detroit. Chapter 6 compares community experiences of the Afro-American Cultural Center to the African American Museum of Dallas, Texas, founded by Bishop College history professor and librarian/archivist Harry Robinson Jr. After their founding in 1974, the AACC/Gantt Center and the African American Museum of Dallas endeavored to maintain ties with established Black communities as they welcomed the new infusion of African American patrons due to reverse migration. Despite having distinct leadership styles, Maxwell and Robinson Jr. played instrumental roles in helping their institutions form public/private fundraising and construction partnerships. These institutions eventually emerged from financial struggle to become the physical representatives of African American progress in the urban New South.

By the 2000s, the Center began to flourish by adapting to the positive and problematic effects of desegregation and reverse migration. Despite its struggles, the Center never deviated from its core mission to educate as it engaged in new artistic endeavors and strove to secure additional funding streams. By 2009, Harper and Maxwell's former one-room grassroots cultural institution had re-emerged as the Harvey B. Gantt Center. As the Center exhibited nationally known artists and sponsored engaging community programming in a brand-new state-of-the-art building, it became embedded within the fabric of Charlotte's urban landscape.

Chapter 7 focuses on Maxwell's experiences as a member of Delta Sigma Theta Sorority from her 1951 initiation to her first election to a national office as a regional director in 1982. This chapter illustrates community-minded sorority women's often overlooked or dismissed actions to encourage and enable local charitable and civil rights initiatives. Emerging as a local Delta chapter president during the height of the civil rights and women's movements, Maxwell led the Charlotte Alumnae Chapter of Delta Sigma Theta (CAC) from 1964 to 1966, a period of turbulent change. This chapter depicts how Maxwell helped CAC reconfigure national Delta service programming directives to formulate local intersectional approaches. Maxwell did this to address the pressing charitable, civic, and employment needs affecting Black Charlotteans.

As the leader of a local chapter and later as the Chair of Delta's National Heritage and Archives Committee, Maxwell helped reaffirm some of the Delta's traditional rituals and policies by adopting innovative business management practices. She incorporated tenets from African American-centered Black Nationalist and South African-based philosophies, such as Ubuntu—"I am because we are"—and the reverence for indigenous African religious practices into the sorority's leadership training activities. By adopting a more expansive interpretation of Black women's activism, this chapter's examination of Maxwell's experiences and leadership within Delta dispels the stereotypical portrayal of charitable but bourgeois middle-class sorority ladies.

Chapter 8 extends the historical discussion of Black women's activism and the Black sorority movement by examining the newly re-married Bertha Maxwell-Roddey's experiences as a regional and national leader in Delta Sigma Theta, primarily from 1982 to 1996. Often deemed an outsider by those within Delta's powerful inner-circles because she belonged to the less populated South Atlantic Region, Maxwell-Roddey turned her status as a member of one of the newest regions into a strength by embracing her identity as a nontraditional candidate. This chapter describes how Maxwell-Roddey, who adopted the title Bertha M. Roddey when she became national president, successfully generated regional and later national support to become the first Delta elected to the presidency from the region. By analyzing her election, the chapter delves into the meanings of political sisterhood, where opposing candidates sometimes wage aggressive campaigns to win powerful offices, only to later join as sisters in service to support the winners after the elections are over.

By looking at Maxwell-Roddey's trajectory in Delta from her induction as a college member to her ascension to the presidency, one can observe how it reacted to significant historical events affecting African Americans after WWII. During these years, Delta's executive leadership offered platforms that expanded its public service efforts and shifted the organization from supporting civil rights organizations to eventually spearheading its own agendas and programs to combat racial and gender injustice. On a more administrative level, each National President had to present an original agenda or service plan for the sorority to implement. These platforms addressed issues influencing education, gender disparities, civil rights, economic issues, health conditions, international concerns, and the future of the arts. During Bertha M. Roddey's four-year presidency, Delta became the first national African American organization to form a partnership with the nonprofit, Habitat for Humanity to build twenty-two homes in the United States and forty in Ghana. After raising over $1.5 million for Habitat from 1992 to 1997, Delta Sigma Theta chapters across the nation continue to volunteer to build Habitat homes.[29]

As a race woman and educator in the Charlotte Mecklenburg Public Schools and later at UNC Charlotte, Bertha Maxwell-Roddey navigated segregated environments without losing her self-esteem or integrity. In desegregated settings, she negotiated with or confronted those in power to ensure equitable opportunities for Black students. During the 1970s and 1980s, as the director of AAAS and as a co-founder of the Afro-American Cultural Center, Maxwell-Roddey performed a balancing act. She encouraged African American students to assume leadership positions as change-makers in desegregated environments while simultaneously creating a cultural refuge for African American children reeling from the erasure of Black spaces as African American neighborhoods and schools fell sway to the economic promise of a progressive urban New South.

Maxwell-Roddey rose to national prominence during the 1970s as the founder of the National Council for Black Studies, an organization whose membership included former activists, radical scholars, and student protesters all working to ensure the permanency of Black Studies as a field. As Maxwell-Roddey worked with some of the leading Afrocentric scholar-activists in the NCBS, she had no qualms later attaching a crimson and cream, pearl, or diamond-encrusted Delta Sigma Theta Sorority pin onto her African-inspired attire. Just as comfortable advocating for change in a classroom, a boardroom, a Delta fundraising gala, or on a dais with prominent political and business leaders, Bertha Maxwell-Roddey personified the category-defying concept of the modern-day race woman, as she directed Delta Sigma Theta to develop innovative public service initiatives that addressed the pressing needs of African Americans facing a new millennium.[30]

1

A "Big Mind," Childhood, and Early Beginnings

When Bertha Maxwell-Roddey talked to students in her African American Studies class at the University of South Carolina at Lancaster or at public events, she often asked how many of them once lived with their grandparents or in a single-parent home and later shared that she grew up the same way. The Frank Porter Graham Distinguished Professor Emeritus and former director of the University of North Carolina at Charlotte's now Africana Studies Department never hesitated to share that she grew up, "P.O. poor." She assured them that she received a wealth of love and support despite lacking material things as a child. Maxwell-Roddey did so to emphasize that she understood their challenges. She assured them that they could still achieve and stressed that she expected them to do their best. Maxwell-Roddey called on her listeners to serve their communities, whether teaching in the classroom or speaking to colleagues, city leaders, or thousands of professional women. Her grandmother Rosa Lyons and other central figures in Bertha's life instilled such a sense of self-worth and respect for others in the young girl that she eventually became comfortable interacting with anyone without feeling inferior or holding any notions of her superiority.[1]

When Luellar Lyons delivered Bertha Luvenia on June 10, 1930, she gave the midwife and Dr. Bryant Sebastian (B. S.) Sharp a fictitious man's name to put on the birth certificate. Despite Luellar's agitated attempt to avoid revealing the father's real identity, her midwife, Lula Austin Earle, recognized the infant's resemblance to one of her family members and boldly announced to Sharp that Luellar's "baby is an Earle!" Now with her secret revealed, the sixteen-year-old mom admitted that Joseph Earle, the grandson of midwife Lula Austin Earle, was Bertha's dad. Despite the drama surrounding her birth, Bertha's great grandmother, Lula, welcomed the new addition to her family. As a young Black woman without economic resources to support her new baby, Luellar brought the new baby home to live with her parents, Rosa Walton Lyons and Wade Lyons, and her toddler son from a previous relationship, George Robert.

Despite growing up as the child of unmarried parents, both sides of her family embraced and cherished young Bertha. The Lyons lived in Seneca in Oconee County, in the upper Piedmont region of South Carolina. Founded in the 1870s, after the Southern Railroad designated Seneca as one of its stops on the Atlanta to Richmond Airline Railway, by the 1930s, it was a small hamlet of fewer than 2,000 residents. Seneca's African American residents primarily worked on the railway lines, farmed, or performed domestic work. The Lyons family lived in Dark Town, named after its predominantly African American population. A prominent Black neighborhood, the enclave served as the home of several local Black landmarks such as St. James Methodist Church and Seneca Institute, a private high school for African Americans.[2]

The Lyons lived on 208 South West 2nd Street in a rented home across the street from St. James Methodist Church. The Lyons's Dark Town neighborhood was close to a nearby white enclave that included one of Seneca's most prominent residents, William J. Lunney, a prominent white pharmacist and drug store owner in the city.[3] Bertha's grandmother Rosa worked as a domestic servant for several prominent white families, including the Morris and Leda Sperling family. They ran the department store in Seneca. Bertha grew up listening to the enthralling stories of neighbor ladies talking with her grandmother. A quiet, soft-spoken woman, Rosa's gentle, receptive nature often led her friends to disclose their secrets with her, to the delight of nosy Bertha.[4]

Luellar Lyons, Bertha's mother, gave birth to Bertha's older brother at fourteen. Luellar never discussed George Robert's father or described him to Bertha. As scholar Darlene Clark Hine contended, some African American women willingly kept their relationships or sexual experiences secret as a form of protection from the disapproval of others or as a reaction to sexual trauma. Rosa, who married forty-six-year-old Wade in 1904 when she was twenty, waited almost ten years for her daughter Luellar's arrival in 1913. She loved children and considered them precious regardless of the conditions of their birth. So, despite Wade's misgivings about his daughter bringing home another baby, Rosa welcomed the new child. Known for her fun-loving nature and sense of humor, Luellar realized that she had to contribute to the family financially and started working as a domestic in nearby Walhalla, South Carolina. Rosa and Wade's shared parenting group included everyone from Bertha's godmother, Carrie Choice Arthur, to her neighbors and co-eds from the Seneca Institute, a Black college down the street from the Lyons's home. Bertha's grandmother Rosa continued this circle of support by giving other young mothers a place to stay or help. When she grew older, Bertha grew aware of her unconventional upbringing, reconfiguring a perceived stigma into a motivator to succeed.[5]

Joseph Earle

In an act of defiance against his father's mandate that he work on the family farm and seeking adventure, Joseph Earle, Bertha's father, ran away to Greenville, South Carolina, when he was only in his teens. Brought home by his father Monroe, Joseph soon left again to avoid incurring the further wrath of his father. Strikingly handsome, he traveled to Florida and had a child there before returning to Seneca, when he met Luellar. With no strong connections, the two had become estranged by the time of Bertha's birth. Eventually, Joseph settled in Washington, DC. Though Bertha had little early contact with her father, her paternal grandparents, Anna Brewer Earle and Monroe Earle and Joseph's siblings surrounded young Bertha with love. Instead of being isolated as the child of a single mother, she grew up surrounded by the Lyons and often spent Saturdays with the Earles. Monroe Earle worked as a farmer and delivery man, and her grandmother Anna, a graduate of the Seneca Institute, worked as a teacher until marriage.[6] With a relative as a graduate, Bertha had strong connections to the Seneca Institute. She lived so close to the school that its students often took her to run errands or stopped by to visit. Enveloped within an environment of learning, Bertha grew up seeing young Black men and women pursue their academic interests.

Learning All Around Her: The Seneca Institute, Bertha's Schooling, and Family Lessons

During the 1886 Sunday School and Baptist Training Union Educational Convention of the Seneca River Missionary Baptist Association meeting, local church member and meeting attendee Catherine Perry donated the first nickel to purchase the land to build a new school for Blacks in Seneca. By 1888, the Association, led by local African American ministers, had raised enough funds from church and community members to purchase and build a three-room building on an eight-acre plot located at the intersections of West South 3rd and South Popular Streets and Scotland Road. When the Seneca Institute opened in 1899, W. J. Thomas, a teacher at the Seneca Colored Graded School, became the chair of the Institute's new board of trustees. Thomas and the other founders of the Seneca Institute joined an African American movement for educational equity after the failed promise of Reconstruction.[7]

Despite the availability of religious leadership in the area, most local African American ministers had few opportunities to obtain higher education credentials. Fortunately, the Association found a local Morehouse College graduate interested in the position. After settling in Seneca, John Jacob Starks became the Institute's first principal. He served as principal for thirteen years, overseeing its growth and development. During his tenure, he served as the minister of Dunn Creek and Ebenezer Baptist churches. His wife, Julia, taught at the Seneca Institute in its early years. During Starks's administration, he stressed that African Americans should control the Institute's growth and finances.[8] As a private college, the Seneca Institute addressed student demands for a liberal arts education and endorsed Booker T. Washington's familiar call for learning industrial and domestic skills. The Seneca Institute offered two tracks, one solely academic and another that included industrial training. The Institute received most of its funds from church missionary association donations and tuition and boarding fees per semester, ranging from forty cents for day students to eight dollars for boarders.[9]

Whereas southern urban cities operated racially segregated schools, validated by the 1896 *Plessy v. Ferguson* "separate but equal" decision that upheld racial segregation, rural Blacks often had limited access to publicly funded schools.[10] In 1876, formerly enslaved minister and Methodist church builder Rev. James R. Rosemond founded Mazyck Chapel, which housed Oconee County's first freedmen's era school. Named after the church's builder and first pastor, Rev. Isaac Mazyck, the school opened with only four students and W. J. Thomas as its teacher. After a fire destroyed the church in 1880, the renamed St. James Colored Methodist Episcopal (CME) Church school relocated to several churches in the area during the early 1880s. Later known as St. James Methodist Church after becoming independent from the CME denomination, its school closed in 1888 when Oconee County opened its first publicly funded school for African Americans, the Seneca Colored Graded School, after the county's newly organized Colored Graded School District received a percentage of property taxes and a donation from the George Peabody Education Fund.[11]

During this period, the rural sections of Oconee County had no schools. Black churches and private donors funded roving teachers who taught children in churches and other settings for six or seven-week sessions per year. Economic conditions affecting sharecropping families hindered African American children's educational access as some could only attend during bad weather and after the harvest.[12] After county and town leaders continued to dismiss African American demands for more schools, Seneca's Blacks pooled their funds and established private institutions, including Norrel Boarding School (1899) and Pine Street Graded School (1921).[13] Historian James Anderson contended that even though Blacks paid taxes to support the public schools, southern states allocated most of those funds to support white schools only. African Americans often had to pay an additional "Black tax" signified in private school fees or financial support to maintain poorly funded public schools.[14]

When the new public Oconee County Training School (OCTS) opened in 1925, it replaced the Seneca Colored Graded School. Led by Columbia, SC minister, Rev. B. F. Stewart, OCTS received over $16,500 from the Peabody/Slater Education Fund and revenues from state and local taxes for its construction. The new building on eight acres on East South 2nd Street in Seneca had eight classrooms and taught grades one through ten, adding the eleventh grade in 1931 and the twelfth in 1947. The opening of the OCTS represented the concentrated efforts of local Blacks to work with philanthropical educational foundations such as the Peabody/Slater and Rosenwald funds and state and local education officials to promote and fund school construction. Often spurred by the encouragement of Tuskegee Institute founder Booker T. Washington, northern philanthropists George Peabody, John F. Slater, Anna T. Jeanes, and Chicago's Julius Rosenwald donated millions of dollars to promote African American educational development in the South after the Civil War.[15] Whether by aiding private Black colleges, sponsoring the hiring of Jeanes teachers to support teacher-training in rural Black schools, or helping to construct African American public schools, these foundations enabled millions of Blacks to further their educational goals. Notwithstanding these philanthropists' contributions in providing greater educational access by working within the confines of local county and state segregated school systems, they failed to address the structural racism embedded within these systems and promoted industrial training. Ideally, a publicly funded school system established to educate the children of its citizens shouldn't require major foundation support just to provide basic educational access for a segment of its school population. The need for the Rosenwald Fund to construct African American schools exposes the glaring racial discrepancies within segregated schools.[16]

In Oconee County, the Rosenwald Fund fulfilled a great need by providing money to construct ten schools, including the only remaining structure: Retreat Rosenwald Colored School on 150 Pleasant Hill Circle. The three-room building, which contained two large classrooms with two teachers who taught grades one through seven, followed the general building plan of the other Rosenwald Schools. Whereas the Rosenwald fund provided financial support, African American communities contributed to the construction and upkeep of these schools and financially supported student activities. African American members of Pleasant Hill Baptist Church donated its land for Retreat's location. Whether providing plots, helping with the maintenance of these schools, or financially supporting student activities, Black Oconee

County residents relied on what historian V. P. Franklin described as "cultural capital" to mitigate some of the adverse effects of a discriminatory education system.[17]

Unfortunately, as African American Oconee County residents welcomed these new public schools, they had an adverse effect on privately funded, fee-based elementary institutions, including the Seneca Institute.[18] Now, in competition for students who could attend OCTS for free, the Seneca Institute expanded in 1926 to become Seneca Junior College, offering a ministerial program and teacher-training courses, with most of its courses now taught by college graduates. Black private and public universities and colleges also benefited from financial donations from these foundations and individual donors, but in some instances, these gifts came with a pedagogical directive to promote industrial education or manual skills training. African American public schools endured by seemingly outwardly acquiescing to the officials' dictates to provide manual instruction to satisfy school board officials. However, after the white school board members' or superintendent's annual visits, these Black principals and teachers covertly offered liberal arts courses under a veil of discriminatory public education rules. Supported by a Black ministers association, the Seneca Institute received little white philanthropic support as its administration expanded the school's mission to train and prepare future teachers and ministers. Unfortunately, this independence as an African American managed school came at a steep cost during the Great Depression when declining enrollments, subsequent funding deficits, and competition for students with the public Oconee County Training School eventually led to Seneca Junior College closing in 1939.[19]

Bertha's grandparents, Rosa and Wade, lived near Seneca Institute as adults, but the two never learned how to read as children due to limited access to teachers and facilities.[20] Even though the Lyons's rented home had only four rooms, it had a toilet in an encased area on the back porch. Reverend James Hicks, a Seneca Institute board member, and administrator, lived near their house and often borrowed water from the bathroom. With no Black hotels in the area or white ones that accepted African American guests, Seneca Institute or St. James officials sometimes asked Bertha's grandparents to host Black dignitaries because the Lyons's house had a bathroom. Bertha remembered that at the age of eight, she helped her grandmother prepare their home for the upcoming visit of Mary Church Terrell. The civil rights activist and former president of the then National Association of Colored Women came to the area to speak at the Seneca Institute. Maxwell-Roddey recalled that "I didn't know it was living history. We had a kitchen, a little dining/sitting room, and two bedrooms. So, when Miss Terrell came, she got the nice bedroom. We cleaned for weeks because 'Miss Terrell's coming.'" Confused, young Bertha recalled wondering, "Who the heck was Miss Terrell?"[21]

Bertha's Big Mind, Family, and Life in Seneca

With encouragement from her father's family, the Earles, and her godmother, teacher Carrie Choice Arthur, Bertha started reading at age four. Rosa often claimed that the young girl had a "big mind." Bertha often read articles from day-old newspapers that her "Ne Ne," her nickname for Rosa, brought home from her work. First, Bertha could only sound out the letters, but eventually, she learned to read the words. Despite having to walk past white children who yelled racial insults at her and her classmates on the way to Oconee County Training School, Bertha loved school. "I was a smart girl," she claimed. Both Bertha's grandparents, Anna, a former teacher, and Rosa, saw the promise of education in Bertha and stressed learning. Influenced by both grandmothers, the confident young girl grew up respecting those who had the opportunity to receive formal schooling and those who did not. Exposed to different types of literacies, from academic to social, Bertha internalized both, and they helped shape her personal and professional world views. Bertha's childhood reflected the fluidity of class among African Americans within her community. Technically, Bertha did not grow up as part of the middle class, but Rosa worked for prominent families in Seneca. Living near the Seneca Institute, an institution of higher learning, granted Bertha unique opportunities to interact with Black professionals in education and the ministry.[22]

After working as a live-in cook for a family in nearby Walhalla, South Carolina, Bertha's mom, Luellar, moved to Charlotte for work, leaving four-year-old Bertha and her brother George Robert with her parents. Bertha's world expanded when she traveled to stay with her mother during the summers and adjusted to city life. In Charlotte, Bertha participated in Friendship Baptist Church's Vacation Bible School program and visited family friends. As historian Leslie Brown explained, Black women moved to cities because they provided more job opportunities than rural areas. Luellar Lyons became part of a wave of millions of African Americans who migrated from rural towns to southern urban cities. "As a single mother of two children, Luellar faced difficult decisions. She missed her children, but she had to relocate to cities to secure enough employment to support them. For women migrants like Luellar, grandparents and other relatives played an instrumental role in their lives, ensuring that their children were protected and loved. Bertha recognized her mother's sacrifices. Although she lived far away, the young girl loved Luellar and looked forward to visiting with her in the city during the summers.[23]

Despite the circumstances surrounding her birth, Bertha received love and acceptance from her paternal grandparents, Anna and Monroe Earle. As she visited the Earles on the weekends, Bertha's father remained a distant figure. This situation changed when Bertha, age eight, would meet the elusive Joseph Earle, her father. When Bertha's teacher called her out of class one day to tell her that her father wanted to meet her, he picked her up from school, and they had lunch at a nearby Black-owned café. "It was like something had fallen out of the sky." Maxwell-Roddey remembered, "You know how you feel things? I could feel all of the love and the admiration of this man." Bearing gifts, Joseph brought her an umbrella and a Bible.[24]

He later invited her to Washington, DC, to stay with him during the summers. Accompanied by her second-grade teacher Gwennie Mae Owens, who promised to watch out for the young child as they traveled to Washington, Bertha boarded the segregated train car wearing a beautiful dress appropriate for meeting her father. When the heat became sweltering on the train, Bertha decided to open a window to get some fresh air. She instantly realized her mistake when instead of receiving a refreshing cool breeze, a cloud of dirt rushed in, enveloping the young girl. Despite her and Gwennie's efforts to remove the soot, when Bertha stepped off the train, Joseph remarked, "Is that my baby?" After appearing as if she had been rolling around in the dirt, she left a very different impression than what she had planned. Bertha lived with her father and several aunts and uncles, who relocated to Washington in a brownstone on New York Avenue. Her siblings increased as Joseph Earle later married and had several more children; Deborah Jean, Elnora, Frank, and Joseph Jr.[25]

Wade and Monroe

Bertha gained insight growing up with her grandfathers, Wade and Monroe, who had vastly different coping strategies as Black men in Jim Crow Seneca. These two men both dispelled common negative assumptions of the experiences of Black men living in the rural Piedmont area of South Carolina. Despite possessing no formal medical training, Wade Lyons often called himself "Dr. Lyons" because he sold homemade African American folk remedies to help people recover from physical disorders and psychological maladies of the heart. Even though sales from his potions seldom produced enough profit to make a living wage, Wade Lyons wore a suit with a vest and used a walking stick, despite having no mobility problems. As a Black man living in the segregated South, Wade Lyons's very appearance could contribute to his demise. If whites deemed him threatening because of their stereotypical "Black beast," imaginings of dangerous African American men, he might have to face a lynch mob. Scholars Shane White and Graham White contend that Black men who asserted a sense of dandyism or fashion during slavery and Jim Crow did so as an expression of resistance to the confining negative perceptions of Black men as either dangerous or docile. By dressing in stylish suits and carrying a walking stick instead of just wearing the plain work clothes that he could probably afford, Wade engaged in a performance of masculinity and respectability to confirm his humanity and assuage fearful whites. "Dr. Lyons" dressed to look the part, even if his appearance didn't reflect the reality that his wife Rosa continued to be the family's primary financial supporter.[26] Maxwell-Roddey later explained, "It was something about him that compelled people to give him some respect when he was just as poor as Job's turkey. That's pretty poor."[27]

Wade Lyons carried himself with dignity in a society where Black men faced lynching for looking a white person in the eye. Sometimes embarrassed by his overly gregarious and non-threatening amateur physician's antics, young Bertha admired his charismatic nature and ability to persuade people. Wade Lyons lived a life seeking the admiration of others. In contrast, Bertha's paternal grandfather Monroe, who owned land and once lived in Detroit, often challenged racial segregation in Seneca. When living in the Motor City, he became a driver for a Black funeral home.[28]

After returning to Seneca, Monroe used his driving skills to get a job as a chauffeur for a local white physician and mortician, James Orr of James Orr Funeral Home. He consistently advocated for Blacks to vote, despite the restrictions that prevented most African Americans from doing so. If Blacks respected Monroe for his advocacy, some local whites considered him arrogant. Nevertheless, Monroe Earle taught Bertha to forge her own path and to fear no one. Wade Lyons survived living in the Jim Crow South by creating a non-threatening, distinguished persona of professionalism that exuded charisma. At the same time, Monroe's brave willingness to speak truth to power and his ability to manage his family's economic conditions successfully garnered him genuine respect from members of Seneca's Black communities. Monroe's inner confidence sometimes evoked fear and resentment from whites who perceived him as a threat. Maxwell-Roddey contemplated, "So, you had a contrast, here I am born with DNA and certain things into a family of whom neither one (Wade or Monroe) wanted to give up what they felt was important to them."[29]

"I was the leader of everything": Bertha During Her Teenage Years

As Bertha's personality emerged, she drew from both Wade and Monroe and the quiet strength of her grandmothers to become someone who could both persuade with charisma and confront with boldness. Both abilities would be useful in her later life. As a child, Maxwell-Roddey learned how to use her leadership skills in positive ways. Known for being well-mannered and polite around adults, when around her peers, another more forceful aspect of her personality surfaced. Bertha acted as a leader among the neighborhood kids, and she fiercely defended her older brother, George Robert, who often refused to respond to petty teasing. Maxwell-Roddey humorously recalled, "Over here, I'd whip boys and girls. My brother, he wasn't like that. Some of the boys would jump on him, I'd go out there and beat them up, and when somebody's jerking (pushing) me around, instead of defending me, he'd say, "Well, you shouldn't have done it." Bertha developed a sort of dual persona where she received praise and accolades when she recited Bible verses in church on Sunday morning and later proceeded to fight her peers if they messed with her brother or her friends. Her ability to meet the criteria of a "smart Black girl," meshed with street savvy, led to an ability to navigate diverse situations and feel at ease. As a child, Bertha often crossed two worlds as she existed as a dutiful and studious granddaughter. Conversely, she acted as a mischievous leader of her friends who exerted power when necessary.[30]

Bertha's neighbors and fellow church members noted her potential and soon became invested in helping her succeed. Since Rosa had to work on Sundays, Bertha's godmother and first-grade teacher, Carrie Choice Arthur, took her across the street from the Lyons's home to attend the St. James Methodist Church. Worshippng in both the Baptist and Methodist churches, Bertha spoke at events and fully participated in church life. Often, she would attend Sunday School, church service, an Epworth League Methodist youth group meeting, and a night worship service. "Church was really all that we had to do." The Black church in the South remained an essential fixture in the spiritual and social lives of African Americans. By encouraging young Bertha to perform recitations and speeches, it provided an educational platform where she felt valued.

A common practice in African American churches involved requiring unmarried pregnant women to stand in front of the church congregation and publicly apologize for sinning. Rosa, who sometimes attended a Baptist church when off from work that did not meet consistently, never made her teenage daughter do that. With Luellar now in Charlotte, Bertha's godmother Carrie

Choice Arthur, a respected teacher, or the Earles took her to St. James. Cognizant of her family status, the prominent church placed no stigma on Bertha as the daughter of a single teenage mother. Instead, it served as a site where Bertha's talents could flourish. As she became known as a talented orator and grew more confident, Bertha's growing faith became reinforced in these settings as she attended church throughout her life.[31]

As word of her oratory gifts spread beyond the Black community, curious whites would go to see the child they referred to as the "little Nigra girl," read out loud. After speaking one day at the local predominantly white Presbyterian church, four-year-old Bertha didn't understand why she couldn't stay for the reception to get some milk and cookies. In this instance, or when Bertha asked to try on shoes in a store or play in the whites-only park, Rosa Lyons seldom explained why she refused to grant Bertha's requests, but the young child knew something was wrong beyond her grandmother's preferences. Despite segregation's constant inference of inferiority, Bertha developed an ability to engage people from diverse backgrounds and social classes without fear or intimidation. The practice of oratory recitations was a widespread practice among African American religious communities in the Jim Crow South. To defy stereotypes regarding African American vernacular language patterns and poor grammar, Black children often had to recite Bible verses at church events and memorize and perform speeches by prominent African Americans in school. Elocution or the ability to speak with perfect diction in a distinguished manner also signified middle-class status.[32]

Growing up in segregated Seneca, Bertha experienced the daily stings of racism and poverty as she worked from age ten to sixteen, cleaning the home of Marie Adams. Bertha's pay of fifty cents a week helped her earn spending money and contribute to the family income. Working in a white middle-class household, Bertha tried to learn as much as possible in this environment as she washed her employer's dirty dishes. Adams taught her how to set the table and other domestic skills. Bertha worked hard, but on some occasions, the young girl mischievously broke some rules, such as taking a relaxing soak in Adams's bathtub, when her boss left. Marie Adams often gave her daughter's old clothes that she had outgrown to Rosa for Bertha. A common practice, Black women domestic workers sometimes relied on these clothing, food, or material donations to offset their meager salaries. Jim Crow etiquette of the day dictated that African American women workers graciously accept these sometimes unwanted gifts to prevent offending or angering their bosses. Ironically, when Bertha wore these expensive discarded clothes to school, her classmates mistakenly thought that she was rich! Technically, Bertha did not grow up as part of the middle class. However, Rosa worked for prominent families in Seneca, lived near an institution of higher learning, wore swanky, albeit used clothes, and often interacted with professional educators. Whether learning from Adams as her domestic helper or her godmother and grandmothers when she accompanied them to church and social events, Bertha learned not to base her opinions on the preconceived class assumptions of others. Historian Elizabeth Clark Lewis explained that Black women domestic workers applied some of the practices they garnered from working in white households in their own homes and social settings.[33]

Though her boss treated her with kindness, Bertha sometimes defied the cultural dictates of segregation. She told a Charlotte magazine reporter, "She (Marie Adams) wanted me to call her child Master Billy. I didn't feel right about that, so I never would call him that. There are certain things that you just intuitively know." In some instances, humanity emerged from within segregation's constrictions, as Adams overlooked Bertha's refusal to address her son in a manner that inferred a hierarchical racialized difference between her Black helper and her younger son.[34]

Bertha and the Southern Negro Youth Congress

In 1937, Richmond, Virginia students James Jackson, Helen Gray, Esther Cooper, and Edward Strong established the Southern Negro Youth Congress (SNYC). This interracial youth version of the National Negro Congress Conference aimed to fight discrimination and support local protests for social justice. As Bertha's reputation as a superior student and dynamic public speaker expanded, she became known as a reliable leader. "I was the leader of everything," Maxwell-Roddey joked. Geneva Sharp, St. James church member and spouse of physician B. S. (Bryant Sebastian) Sharp, lived a block away from the Lyons. Geneva asked Bertha to join the Seneca Chapter of the Southern Negro Youth Congress when Bertha was twelve, and she eventually became its president. In chapters throughout the South, students engaged in labor organizing, boycotting discriminatory establishments, voter registration, and other civil rights campaigns. Young workers and students traveled from high schools and colleges to SNYC conferences to listen to nationally known activists discuss topics ranging from anti-lynching campaigns to labor organizing. South Carolina civil rights activist, former teacher, social worker, and state NAACP leader Modjeska Simkins organized eleven chapters in South Carolina. Demonstrating the more subtle activism of middle-class Black women as Seneca's SNYC Chapter adviser, Geneva Sharp quietly but courageously drove Chapter

President Bertha and the other members to the October 1946 SNYC conference in Columbia, South Carolina.[35]

As the president of SNYC's Seneca chapter and as a delegate, at fifteen, Bertha joined 400 other attendees to listen to presentations by such prominent figures as entertainer/activist Paul Robeson and civil rights leader W.E.B. Du Bois. Mesmerized when Du Bois charged "young women and young men . . . to lift the banner of humanity . . . in the midst of people who have yelled about democracy and never practiced it," in his speech, "Behold the Land," Bertha grew determined to do something to make a difference. Supported by such prominent figures as Mary McLeod Bethune and North Carolina's Palmer Memorial Institute director Charlotte Hawkins Brown, SNYC's general membership reached over 11,000, making it one of the most influential civil rights organizations in the South during the late 1930s and early 1940s. The organization became a target of the Federal Bureau of Investigation as part of its crackdown on civil rights groups under the guise of eliminating possible Communist activities in the South, and SNYC's labor organizing, and voter registration activities attracted criticism from local and state government officials.[36]

As a teenager, Bertha enjoyed going to the SNYC Conference and discussing civil rights issues during their chapter meetings. As Bertha absorbed the information that she learned during these meetings, it further reinforced her need to question the fairness and the "whys" of segregation. She recalled, "I always asked my grandmother why? Why can't I try on clothes in the stores? Why can Blacks attend the carnival on one day only?" Bertha recalled how Rosa struggled against segregation's limitations and poverty to provide pleasurable opportunities for her grandchildren when she bought George Robert and Bertha tickets to go to the carnival on Negro Day, the only day Blacks could attend. As they had fun, Rosa sat outside by the side of the road, unable to purchase her own ticket.[37]

By 1949, the Southern Negro Youth Congress finally succumbed to these damaging attacks. Despite its demise, scholars argue that SNYC served as a forerunner to the civil rights movement by motivating young people to engage in activism. When Sharp took her chapter to the conference, Bertha just thought that these people spoke about fighting for African American freedom. She realized that the federal and state governmental anti-Communist attacks against SNYC masked their motive to dismantle civil rights organizations. Years later, after the Southern Negro Youth Congress's demise, Bertha, as a former member, contemplated if her name might be on one of McCarthy's redbaiting lists as a teenage Communist sympathizer with a bit of pride.[38]

Bertha did well academically, played on the basketball team, and in 1947, her senior year, she won the lead in the school play at Oconee County Training School. Although a teachers' favorite, Bertha sometimes defied authority. Several days before her performance, Bertha disobeyed a teacher's directive to stay seated, and she received a five-day suspension from school. When play officials learned of their lead actress's plight, they pleaded with Principal D. D. Blackman, to allow her to return to perform. Instead of being grateful for their request, Bertha, who thought that her punishment was too severe for just going to sharpen her pencil, used her leverage to demand an apology from Blackman for suspending her. Surprisingly, he did! Maxwell-Roddey often reminded her students that she sometimes acted out and challenged her teachers. She used herself as an imperfect example to tell them that they could overcome past mistakes or poor behavioral choices. When they shared their stories, Bertha responded by claiming, "Don't tell me these things because whatever you have done, I've done it, and I think I've done it better!"[39]

New Beginnings and Losses: Bertha Moves to the City

The year 1947 brought tremendous highs and saddening blows as sixteen-year-old Bertha became the first person in the immediate Lyons family to graduate from Oconee County Training School, and she dealt with her grandfather Wade Lyons's death after an illness. As Bertha grieved for her grandfather, she recalled his complicated role in her family with ambivalence. Wade Lyons outwardly projected a larger-than-life presence but acted differently at home. Maxwell-Roddey recalled that "he didn't share information with my grandmother and would sometimes leave for several months without a word." It took several years after Bertha became an adult to appreciate her grandfather's ability to live his life on his terms. Both her mother and father attended her graduation ceremony. Now the owner of a dry cleaner's shop in Oakland, California, Joseph wanted Bertha to come live with him. Excited at first by her father's proposition to move to California, she had serious concerns because it meant living far away from her grandmother. Rosa liked Joseph, but when Bertha told Rosa, she "could see the hurt in her grandmother's eyes." So, as Bertha considered her grandmother's worries that she would lose contact with her granddaughter and reflecting upon all of Rosa's sacrifices to raise her, Bertha sadly told her dad, "No." Deciding against relocating to California but knowing that she had to leave Seneca to further her education, the sixteen-year-old, recent high school graduate moved to Charlotte to live with her mother, work, and save for college.[40]

In 1945, Luellar married Leroy "Big Man" Baxter. He worked cleaning barrels for a local chemical company and preferred that his wife not work out-side the home. Determined to maintain her financial independence, Bertha watched Luellar as she secretly took the bus and then walked two miles to do domestic work for a family who lived on Providence Road. She returned home before her husband came home from work. Luellar did this for years before Baxter discovered that his wife worked outside the home. During this period, Bertha became closer to her mother. Bertha realized that her mother's desire for independence served as a form of protection for the young woman who had to ask her mother to help her raise her two children. As Bertha worked to save money for college, she wanted to determine her own future.[41]

After graduation from Oconee County Training School, Bertha Lyons joined one of the largest mass migrations in United States history. Scholars often re-count the stories of African Americans who migrated to larger cities such as Charlotte, Atlanta, New York, and Washington, DC. Bertha Lyons shared their experiences as she moved to Charlotte to work. Her migration journey rep-resented the experiences of other African American southerners who moved from rural areas to southern urban cities during the first decades of the twen-tieth century. Whether escaping the harsh physical labor and indebtedness of sharecropping, fleeing from the ongoing threat of racial and sexual violence, or seeking economic opportunities, thousands of Blacks relocated to urban ar-eas. With increased employment options, cities like Charlotte attracted young women like Luellar Lyons because they could work and remain close enough to visit their children regularly. Despite living in the Jim Crow South, these migrants still had some advantages. They could escape the provincialism of small-town life and its pervasive racism but still be close enough to visit with their relatives and friends. In essence, they could go home again.[42]

A "First" or an "Only"

When working in Charlotte, Bertha inadvertently broke several segregation rules when she secured jobs in the whites-only sections of several local business establishments, including the lunch counters at Kress's Drug Store and the City Bus Terminal in Charlotte. Even though Jim Crow laws remained pervasive, Bertha's white employers defied these legal and social mandates to make hir-ing decisions based on their needs and her performance. When Bertha worked at the bus station restaurant in the whites-only section of the terminal, Black women could work as waitresses. However, only white women could hand beverages to white customers at the drinking fountain station. As thirsty and tired patrons poured into the bus station terminal after the Annual Christmas

Parade requesting drinks, Bertha volunteered to assist an overwhelmed white worker by helping her hand out drinks behind the counter, hidden from view. When her supervisor discovered Bertha crouching down, she feared instant dismissal. In retelling the incident, Maxwell-Roddey shared, "Instead, my boss said something very significant. He said, 'If you are going to work the fountain, stand up and do it. Get up off your knees and work!' So, I was the first Black woman to work the fountain in the whites' only section at the bus station." This experience taught Bertha a valuable lesson to take advantage of opportunities no matter where they originated. Her employer told her to "stand up," and she did. Bertha would continue to "stand up" throughout her life.[43]

After working for one year in Charlotte, Bertha moved to Washington, DC to stay with her aunt, and she worked as a waitress in the Walter Reed General Hospital dining room. When she learned that a friend wanted to go to nursing school in 1949, Bertha decided to apply to the nursing program at the then all-white Johns Hopkins University in Baltimore, Maryland. Without fully realizing that she would be breaking a racial barrier, she passed the placement exam! Unfortunately, in 1949, a lack of financial resources prevented Bertha from attending the prestigious nursing school. When Bertha learned that she only had enough funds to pay tuition for one year, she decided to return to Charlotte, live with her mother, work, save money, and reapply to the Johns Hopkins University the following year. As fate would have it, romance intervened and changed her plans when Bertha met her future first husband, Horace Maxwell. He suggested that she attend Johnson C. Smith University and major in education. Bertha listened to Horace's arguments, but she ultimately decided to attend Johnson C. Smith after evaluating her lack of financial resources and her wish to remain near her brother George Robert who also attended Johnson C. Smith. In 1959, more than twelve years after Bertha applied to the Johns Hopkins University's School of Nursing, Gertrude T. Hodges became the first African American to graduate from the nursing program. Bertha's application was not a part of a national NAACP effort to desegregate graduate schools. Nevertheless, her decision to apply to the John Hopkins University sheds light on individuals' still unknown acts to desegregate the nation's schools and universities.[44]

Life as a Johnson C. Smith University Golden Bull: Bertha During Her College Years

After enrolling in Johnson C. Smith University in 1950, Bertha decided to major in elementary education.[45] Initially chartered in 1867 as The Freedmen's

College of North Carolina by the Committee on Freedmen of the Catawba Presbytery as a theological school for men, it was renamed the Henry J. Biddle Memorial Institute later that year after a $1,400 donation from his wife, Mary Henry Biddle. In 1876, the North Carolina Legislature renamed the Institute Biddle University after an eight-acre land donation from Colonel W. R. Myers. After receiving an endowment in 1921 from Jane Berry Smith, the widow of Johnson C. Smith, a wealthy industrialist, the school's board of trustees renamed the school Johnson C. Smith University. By the 1930s, the college had trained many of the state's Black educators and ministers. Johnson C. Smith admitted its first female students in 1941.[46] As an older student with limited finances, Bertha planned to complete her degree in three years, so she immersed herself in her studies by taking twenty-two hours a semester and working. As an education major, Bertha mainly took courses related to teaching, but Johnson C. Smith required students to take other elective courses, including religion. Her religion instructor, Algernon Odell Steele, became a transformative influence on Bertha as he taught his students to gain a deeper understanding of religious philosophy and sound knowledge of Biblical texts.[47]

Bertha married Horace Maxwell in 1952. Her friend and minister, Colemon W. Kerry Jr. of Charlotte's Friendship Baptist Church, officiated the ceremony. A member of Friendship since she participated in the church's vacation bible schools during the summers, Bertha maintained her Friendship ties after joining First United Presbyterian, her husband's church. After moving to 826 East Seventh Street, the struggling newlywed, the now Bertha Maxwell, still had to work to pay tuition and household bills.[48] The need for Maxwell to work outside the home mirrored a common condition for some African American families. An unusual twist for Maxwell involved the fact that she sometimes worked for whites in professional fields denied to African Americans. Horace, then an elevator operator at the Liberty Life Building on 112 South Tryon Street, who later worked for the Charlotte Housing Authority, helped his wife get a job with Henry C. Parker, a prominent white dentist with an office in Horace's building. Maxwell claimed, "Dr. Parker had never had a Black employee or seen the insides of a Black person's mouth until I started working there." As an assistant, she worked helping Parker conduct X-rays and other duties. Over the years, Maxwell often did odd jobs for Parker's wife and visited his family for dinner, where Bertha sat with them at the table as an equal. On one occasion, when Maxwell burst into tears at work, Parker told his nurse to ask Bertha if she could be pregnant. Shocked, Bertha denied being with child. In between sobs, she explained that she lacked the funds to pay the remaining balance of Johnson C. Smith's tuition. Maxwell recalled that Parker calmly replied, "Is that all?" He then proceeded to write out a check to cover the fees.[49]

Whereas Maxwell argued that "Dr. Parker was a kind man," his graciousness did not silence her outspokenness regarding racial issues. When Parker openly condemned Black dentist and civil rights activist Reginald Hawkins for criticizing racist public officials and calling for the desegregation of a restaurant in the newly remodeled Charlotte Douglas Airport, Maxwell confronted her employer and explained, "I told him that you don't see me as a person. How many times have you sent me to go to the segregated Tanner's Snack Bar to get hot dogs or taken your nurse to Ivey's Department Store restaurant for lunch knowing that I couldn't go?" In asking this question, Maxwell reminded Parker that when she ran his errands as part of her job, to whites, she was just a nameless, faceless Black woman. Instead of firing Maxwell on the spot for disrespect, Parker acknowledged her views and stopped complaining publicly about civil rights efforts.[50]

Often when historians discuss the civil rights movement, they examine the ways activists and lawyers encouraged courageous Blacks to risk their lives and livelihoods to desegregate business and large-scale institutions as part of an overall strategy to dismantle legal segregation. Without negating the significance of these actions, countless individuals like Bertha desegregated small businesses and organizations without the backing of national organizations. As historian Robin Kelley argued, working-class African Americans sometimes engaged in small personal protests or individually defied segregation laws. Maxwell relied on these "hidden transcripts" or unwritten, informal acts of resistance to help navigate the conundrum of southern race relations during a time when Emmett Till, a fourteen-year-old Chicago youth visiting relatives in Mississippi for the summer, was brutally murdered for allegedly flirting with a white woman in public. Decades later, his accuser, Carolyn Bryant, recanted her false claim.[51]

If Blacks performed these acts of hidden resistance, African Americans also performed untold racialized negotiations during segregation. Bertha, who risked her position and possible safety to confront her boss and challenge his prejudiced opinions, exposes the complex interrelationships between whites and Blacks. During segregation, proper racial etiquette suggested that even if African American workers had benevolent bosses, Blacks should only exchange polite cordialities with their paternalistic white employers and never complain. When Bertha engaged in an honest and sincere exchange with Parker about how segregation adversely affected her and condemned his racist views, she defied racial hierarchies by talking to her boss as an equal and viewing him as a human being. Unlike other African Americans who suffered terrible consequences for doing the same thing as she did, Bertha's activism paid off in this instance. Instead of firing her on the spot, Parker listened.

When Bertha graduated from college in 1954, she would eventually lead a far different life than she expected, but despite her family's limited economic resources, Maxwell's childhood prepared her to succeed. She learned how to absorb and learn, whether accompanying her teachers, visiting relatives in Charlotte and Washington, or working in environments vastly different than her own. As Bertha shared, "I grew up with a village of people who had a vested interest in my success." Within this world, Bertha learned how to trust in her voice and her value.[52] Bertha's childhood experiences reflected the ways her community used its cultural capital to support and encourage young people to succeed through educational attainment. Girded by her village, Bertha became part of a generation who later fought to dismantle segregation. Growing up wearing hand-me-down clothes from her mother's employers, she often presented herself as someone of note who would attempt to knock down race and class separations as a leader in education throughout the years.

2

"It Was like Putting Diapers on Gnats"

Bertha Maxwell graduated from Johnson C. Smith University only a short time after the influential 1954 Supreme Court *Brown v. Board of Education* ruling. She and her peers reacted to the decision with surprise, celebration, and apprehension; however, Maxwell's immediate concern involved securing her first teaching job. To obtain a position in the segregated Charlotte City Schools system,[1] one had to pass the interview with a committee of African American elementary school principals responsible for making placement recommendations. During her meeting with Biddleville principal Sterleta Perrin Sasso, Double Oaks principal Gwendolyn Cunningham, and Marie G. Davis principal William Howard (W. H.) Moreland, they asked Maxwell, "What do you want to do now after graduation?" Bertha answered flippantly, "Get a job!" Unappreciative of her humor and in response to Maxwell's perceived lack of professionalism, the committee recommended hiring her with "reservations." Maxwell became worried that the "reservations" term could prevent her from receiving a position.[2]

Fortunately, Jayne Wallace Hemphill, the principal of Alexander Street Elementary School on 916 North Alexander Street, where Maxwell worked as a student teacher, came to her rescue. The well-established principal dismissed the committee's concerns and hired the young teacher.[3] This unfortunate episode in public school hiring politics taught Maxwell the importance of having mentors and allies, when and when not to use humor, and the possibilities of severe consequences if she spoke her mind or told the truth. Possessing a disdain for needless formalities, Maxwell's job interview for a position in the Charlotte City Schools reflected her unpretentious personality and future leadership style.[4]

Mentors and Peers: Teaching in Segregated Charlotte's Schools, 1954–1964

Maxwell began her career by teaching fourth through sixth grades at Alexander Street Elementary, located at 916 Alexander Street, a segregated school in

Charlotte's First Ward section. Once an integrated neighborhood during the late nineteenth century, it eventually became a predominantly working-class African American neighborhood by the 1950s. After the city's urban renewal efforts obliterated the neighborhood's properties during the 1960s and 1970s, the former First Ward now lies at the heart of Charlotte's central city Uptown area and serves as the location for the University of North Carolina Charlotte's Center City campus building.[5]

After her unfortunate interview experience, Maxwell was happy to have a job with the Charlotte City Schools. When Cordelia Stiles, the Supervisor of Instruction for Elementary Schools, offered new training workshops at Alexander, Ruth Ezell Kennedy, Maxwell's student teaching supervisor, often asked the young teacher to implement Stiles's pedagogical techniques in the classroom. Stiles, who held a graduate degree from Columbia University in New York, found a willing subject in Maxwell. She encouraged the young teacher to adopt concepts that ranged from allowing the children to sit randomly or in a circle to suggestions for revising curricula. Some of Alexander Street's more experienced teachers grew wary of Maxwell's implementation of Stiles's modern ideas, such as allowing the children to sit in circles because they thought they were impractical. These experienced teachers deemed it necessary to seat children in alphabetical order for attendance and grading purposes. As a young teacher and throughout her career, Maxwell embraced new educational ideas and programs to facilitate learning or to help students. Proud of Maxwell's successful results with students, Kennedy openly praised the student teacher in front of the entire faculty. Resentful, some of the faculty in charge of student placement decided to place most of the children with known behavior problems in Maxwell's class. Distraught and dismayed by the constant battery of discipline challenges, Bertha seriously started to reconsider teaching. She did not realize the uniqueness of her situation until the visiting Charlotte City Schools psychologist Gerald Elston commented that he had never seen so many troubled students in one class.[6] Even though some of her fellow teachers set Maxwell up to fail, she managed to control her classroom and learned valuable lessons about whom to trust. The next year, wiser and warier, she worked with Hemphill to ensure that she had a more balanced class.[7]

All of Charlotte's Black women principals taught before becoming principals. Charged with maintaining positive learning environments, despite the ever-present problems of overcrowded schools, dilapidated structures, and inadequate funding, they maintained strict controls on the one area where they had power, the quality of their faculty. Placing Maxwell's experiences in context with other Black women principals and administrators exposes their varied professional trajectories. As Maxwell's first teaching employer, Jayne Wallace Hemphill (1897–1975) grew up in Mecklenburg County. After graduating in 1917 from Scotia Women's College in Concord, North Carolina, she taught at Fairview School, Charlotte's first all-brick school building for Blacks in Mecklenburg County, until 1929. As a young faculty member at Fairview, she observed her mentor, principal Marie Gaston Davis (1869–1920), who started teaching at age thirteen and served as Fairview's principal for over thirty-three years. In 1948, Hemphill assumed the principalships of Alexander Street Elementary School in the First Ward section of Charlotte and First Ward Elementary from 1961–1964.[8] If Hemphill led Alexander Street, her counterpart Sterleta Sasso (1903–1970) started teaching at Biddleville after graduating from Benedict College in Columbia, South Carolina, in 1925. Sasso became the principal of a four-room elementary school at the intersection of Beatties Ford and Mattoon Roads. In the 1930s, Sasso led efforts to establish a branch of the Charlotte Library for Black children. In 1964, after almost forty years as Biddleville's head, she accepted the principal's position of the newly constructed Oaklawn Elementary School on Oaklawn Avenue. When Gwendolyn Cunningham (1919–2013), a graduate of Bennett College in Greensboro, North Carolina, joined her fellow principals at Maxwell's interview in 1953, she brought a fresh perspective after becoming principal of Double Oaks Elementary on Woodward Avenue. Cunningham later became the principal of Oaklawn Elementary, following Sasso in the early 1970s. As one of Charlotte's four Black women elementary school principals, Beulah D. Moore (1892–1965), the head of Isabella Wyche Elementary School, did not participate in Maxwell's interview. Moore's school was named after Wyche (1871–1906), the first woman principal of an African American public school, the Colored Graded School (Myers Street School) in Charlotte.[9]

As Maxwell's principal, Hemphill served as her administrative supervisor. Later, when she became a principal, Maxwell joined veteran administrators Gwendolyn Cunningham and Sterleta Sasso to manage recently constructed schools in the desegregation era. During the late 1960s and early 1970s, as Maxwell left CMS for academia, two of her peers, Elizabeth Randolph (1917–2004) and Kathleen Crosby (1925–2012), received promotions from CMS Central Administrative Office. In 1967, Randolph, the former principal of University Park Elementary School, became the highest-ranking Black woman administrator in CMS as the director of Elementary Secondary Education Act Programs (ESEA), which included managing the Head Start program. In 1977, Randolph joined a four-member team tasked with managing CMS after the abrupt resignation of its school superintendent. In 1978, CMS promoted her to the position of associate superintendent for curriculum and development, and she served in that role until her retirement in 1982.[10]

Crosby joined CMS's Central Office as an Early Childhood Specialist in 1966, where she held several top management positions in the city's Head Start Program and worked with schools to resolve desegregation issues. During the tumultuous busing era of the 1970s, Crosby served as the principal of Billingsville Elementary (1971–1976). In 1976 she became an Area Superintendent in the CMS system, responsible for twenty-five schools during the 1980s and 1990s.[11] The desegregation process profoundly affected these women's careers as they challenged the color line by moving from predominantly African American environments to desegregated ones, simultaneously gaining positions of power and influence. Once essential leaders in their segregated schools, Black women educators now assumed new administrative positions in desegregated institutions.[12]

As Maxwell gained confidence, Hemphill soon became a trusted mentor to the novice teacher. Bertha observed how her principal earned respect as an administrator who demanded strict adherence to regulations and encouraged new or struggling teachers. Away from school grounds, Hemphill exemplified how Black women principals aided their communities as leaders and supporters in Charlotte's African American professional, civic, and charitable organizations, including the City Teachers Association, the NAACP, the Phyllis Wheatley Branch of the Young Women's Christian Association (YWCA), religious institutions, and Greek-letter sororities. As Maxwell developed her own managerial style, she incorporated some of Hemphill's authoritative management and teaching methods. Maxwell also adopted nontraditional methods, such as the Student Non-Violent Coordinating Committee or SNCC's concept of participatory democracy by encouraging faculty input in leadership decisions. Hemphill retired in 1964, but Sasso and Cunningham worked as principals until the 1970s and 1980s.[13]

When Cunningham and Sasso chided Maxwell for making a sarcastic remark during her interview, they did so to convey to the young applicant that seeking employment as a teacher in Charlotte's segregated schools required a reverence for the process and respect for the position. Black principals maintained influential roles within their schools and communities, but they had less status among white administrators and school board officials. Forced to lobby potentially racist and sexist school officials, African American women principals walked a thin line as principals in a segregated system. They negotiated with white administrators and School Board members to secure financial resources and advocate for faculty and students, often in legally discriminatory environments.[14] They interacted with their male peers in a system that reinforced male administrative authority. During segregation, the elementary school principalship served as one of the few administrative, educational positions available to African American women. In most cases, coveted secondary school positions went to men only. Hemphill excelled in navigating through these pitfalls by adopting an authoritative management style, maintaining strict control, and supporting parents and students. Even as a young teacher, Maxwell acknowledged the positive relationship Hemphill maintained with the school superintendent and learned firsthand that creating positive relationships could reap rewards.

Faced with changing environments after receiving promotions to new administrative positions, Maxwell, Randolph, and Crosby retained the core mission that they learned as college students to serve as role models and present themselves in a manner worthy of respect and admiration. They all graduated from historically Black private institutions of higher learning in North Carolina. Maxwell and Crosby received BA degrees in education from Johnson C. Smith University in Charlotte, and Randolph graduated with a BA in education from Shaw University in Raleigh, North Carolina. As institutions of higher education in the segregated South, these colleges trained their students to act as representatives of achievement and to thrive in a world that consistently dismissed their intelligence and potential. Prepared to work with students on all educational and economic levels, Black college graduates, such as Maxwell, recognized that their duties would often extend beyond their job descriptions to ensure their students' progress.[15]

Elizabeth Schmoke, later Randolph, grew up in Raleigh, North Carolina. Her mother, Pearl Johnson Schmoke, taught in the Wake County Public Schools, and her father worked as a plasterer. After her father's death during the Great Depression, Elizabeth helped her mother take care of her five younger brothers and sisters. Elizabeth's family stressed education, and her mom expected all her siblings to attend college. Randolph explained, "I have always all my life known that I would be a teacher because my mother, from the time that I was able to understand what she was saying, told me that she wanted me to be a teacher. So, I grew up knowing that I would be a teacher, and I never had any desire to be anything else." After receiving a scholarship to attend Shaw University, she graduated in 1936.[16] Randolph began teaching in Asheville, North Carolina, and she taught for six years in the town of Wake Forest before relocating to Charlotte in 1944, where she joined the West Charlotte High School faculty as an English teacher. Randolph first thought she had relocated to a more progressive city but later realized that the school still received fewer supplies and funding. Randolph's students had to use discarded textbooks.[17]

Kathleen "Kat" Neal Ross Crosby grew up in Winnsboro, South Carolina, as one of six children of educator parents. Crosby's father served as principal, and her mother taught at Winnsboro's Fairfield County Training School. After receiving her BA degree in education from Johnson C. Smith University in 1946, Crosby started teaching first grade at Mecklenburg County's Pineville Colored School that same year. Pineville, presently a suburb of Charlotte, was a small town in the late 1940s. Housed in a dilapidated former white school relegated for African American children, Pineville Colored School represented the typical rural Black school during segregation. Teaching fifty first graders with only a potbelly stove for heat was not uncommon for Crosby and her fellow African American teachers. They learned as college students that they had to work in inhospitable environments. Inequities in funding and support remained the norm during segregation; nevertheless, Crosby's reaction to discrimination reflected an early activist spirit. She recalled that the white superintendent of Negro instruction often insulted, criticized, and threatened to fire Black teachers if they spoke out. Crosby recalled, "There were no civil rights. No tenure. If the white man wanted to fire you, he could fire you."[18]

When the superintendent was criticizing Black teachers one day, Crosby responded out loud, "I know he isn't talking about me!" She explained, "The lady behind me touched my arm and said, 'You could lose your job!'" Crosby later experienced repercussions when the superintendent came to her class unannounced with several other white school officials hoping to embarrass her and the students by having her first graders read aloud. When her student confidently volunteered to read, Crosby recalled that the superintendent asked with indignation, "Is that woman from New York? Her children can read!" Crosby explained, "People will intimidate you if you let them. They won't leave you alone." This incident exhibited Crosby's courage in the face of prejudice. "I was never afraid," she contended. Maxwell possessed the same quality of self-assuredness despite her working conditions.[19]

Several prominent historians, such as Valinda Littlefield, Stephanie Shaw, and Vanessa Siddle Walker, continue to analyze the crucial role of Black teachers who nurtured their students and acted as role models during segregation. Other scholars, such as sociologist Tamara Beauboeuf-Lafontant contend that these educators' "caring activism" served as a form of resistance to the constant slights of segregation. As administrators, Maxwell and other Black educators redirected this mandate to serve in newly desegregated schools or office environments. As principals, they mediated racially based disputes among students and teachers and defended the rights of wrongfully accused African American students and faculty. These women's duties ranged from quashing the fears of apprehensive white parents of children zoned to Black schools to planning events to bring faculty and parents from diverse backgrounds together.[20]

Maxwell, Randolph, and Crosby, Teaching in Segregated Charlotte, 1954–1966

Bertha Lyons Maxwell began teaching in the wake of *Brown vs. Board of Education*. Despite this groundbreaking decision, the city's public schools resisted efforts to desegregate fully, instead offering pupil placement plans that allowed white students to transfer to different schools based on race and often denying African American student transfers. In 1957, after little to no action toward implementing desegregation, the Charlotte NAACP submitted repeated appeals and petitions to the Charlotte City School Board to accept the transfer requests of Black students to attend predominantly white schools. Caught between the fears of potential litigation by civil rights leaders and the harsh criticisms of pro-segregationist parents and community leaders, the board agreed for the limited transfer of four Black junior high and high school students. Three of the students, Gus Roberts, who went to Central High School, his sister Girvaud Roberts, who enrolled in Piedmont Junior High School, and Delois Huntley, who transferred to Alexander Graham Junior High, attended school without major problems because the principals and officials of their respective schools issued strong directives that discouraged segregationist protests, thus preventing racial incidents. Frye Gaillard, a former *Charlotte Observer* reporter, recounted, "Central High School Principal Edward Sanders, escorted Gus Roberts through the angry mob and threatened to cancel the football season if members of the football team did anything to disrupt the process."[21]

If Charlotte's school desegregation process seemed to be proceeding smoothly, the horrific treatment of fifteen-year-old Dorothy Counts when she entered all-white Harding High School shattered the city's progressive image. Counts faced a crowd of angry white students who yelled racial epithets and spat at her, and school officials offered her little to no protection. After being hit in the head by an anti-integrationist student, Counts's parents removed her from Harding after a few days of attendance. Despite Charlotte city leaders' promotions, the city's white residents' strong opposition to school desegregation and Charlotte's school officials' recalcitrance toward desegregation revealed the underlying racism embedded within the concept of moderate race relations.[22]

As the fight to desegregate Charlotte's public schools continued, in 1957, Elizabeth "Libby" Schmoke Randolph left her position as an English teacher at West Charlotte High School to be principal of University Park Elementary School, a newly constructed, predominantly African American school. Already possessing a master's degree in education from the University of Michigan, in 1958, Randolph sought to gain more expertise to support her work as University Park's principal, becoming one of the first Blacks to obtain an Advanced Certificate in School Administration from the University of North Carolina at Chapel Hill's Department of Education.[23]

By 1959, desegregation stalled when the School Board refused all transfer requests from Black students. In response, the NAACP filed suit on behalf of eight African American students who did not receive transfers. A part of this new federal court case mandated that teachers desegregate. As the public schools became enmeshed in desegregation conflicts, Charlotte's population growth and push to expand city property boundaries led to County tax losses. To counter the adverse impact of Charlotte's incorporation of former Mecklenburg County neighborhoods on the County's dwindling property tax base and subsequent school funding, in 1960, the Charlotte City and Mecklenburg County School Systems merged, resulting in the Charlotte Mecklenburg School System or CMS.[24]

Though school desegregation battles waged on during the early 1960s, the field of elementary education adopted new pedagogical techniques and programs to help struggling students improve their reading and math skills to diminish economic and racial disparities in education. Without publicly promoting the interracial nature of these programs, they served as early precursors to full desegregation by sending interracial teaching staff to work with students. After teaching at Alexander Street Elementary for six years, in 1960, Maxwell volunteered to work as a corrective reading specialist for CMS. In this unique position, she traveled to different elementary schools, working with children to help them improve their literacy skills. Initially apprehensive, she soon learned that Black and white children faced similar learning challenges. As a reading specialist, she crossed racial lines to meet with teachers and principals and observed a range of teaching and administrative styles as she became more well known among CMS's educational community.[25]

As racial barriers to advancement started to weaken in the 1960s, African American teachers, such as Crosby and Maxwell, pursued post-undergraduate education to better adapt to new teaching pedagogies. Often paid less money than white teachers with the same experience and educational background, African American teachers took additional graduate courses to move up the pay scale. Now Black teachers, like Crosby and Maxwell, pursued further education to prepare them to teach in desegregated environments.[26] After joining the faculty of Charlotte's Lincoln Heights Elementary School in the 1950s, in 1962, Crosby received an invitation from CMS to attend a summer seminar on desegregation at Bank Street College of Education in New York City. One of the foremost institutions in the new field of early childhood education, schools, teachers, and federal Head Start officials adopted Bank Street's innovative curriculum.[27] As Crosby submerged herself to discuss recent scholarship on integration with thirty Black and white southern teachers, she asserted: "That was the beginning of my knowing how little I knew about things." She later decided to pursue graduate study at Bank Street. In 1970, Crosby received her Master's Degree in Early Childhood Education.[28]

Similarly encouraged by her fellow teachers and CMS superintendent Craig Phillips, who promised to fund her graduate education in 1964, Maxwell enrolled in the University of North Carolina at Greensboro's Master's Program in Educational Administration, studying in the summers. After dealing with infertility and health issues, Maxwell and her husband Horace adopted an infant. With no childcare available, Maxwell decided to take her baby daughter, Tawanna, to class with her when she enrolled in UNC Greensboro. Despite her acceptance into the university, most of its residential facilities refused to accept a Black student, especially one with a child, so she often stayed with one of the school housekeepers. Over the years, urban African American teachers often sought master's degrees in universities outside the South. Maxwell joined the small but influential group of Black students who individually desegregated southern graduate schools during the mid-1960s as the program's first African American master's student and the only woman in most of her classes.[29]

Maxwell, familiar with working with white teachers and principals as a reading specialist, did not face overt acts of racism at UNC Greensboro. She quickly learned the mores of attending a desegregated school. White students often greeted and talked with her during class, but these same students seldom acknowledged her in public settings. One exception was an older gentleman named Kenneth, who did speak with Maxwell in public. Maxwell often had friendly chats with him and discussed a range of topics, including desegregation. One day, a fellow student asked her, "Why are you always talking with the Dean?" She realized that Kenneth was indeed Kenneth Howe, the dean of the College of Education. He became an advocate for Maxwell after she received an "A" in a class where most of her fellow students, all school administrators, struggled because they could not understand the instructor's South Asian accent. Eager to learn, she had no problems understanding him. In 1966,

Maxwell received a Master's in Educational Administration degree from the University of North Carolina at Greensboro.[30]

The Charlotte Teachers Corps and the War on Poverty, 1964–1969

Several studies analyze African American teachers and principals during segregation, and others examine women in educational leadership; however, few historical works address the experiences of African American women teachers who transitioned from teaching to administrative positions after desegregation.[31] These women had to adjust to the evolving racial compositions as new desegregation plans sometimes involved busing Blacks and whites from varied socioeconomic backgrounds to their schools. They had to assume the challenging task of heading former all-white schools or encountering new philosophies regarding gender dynamics as they assumed positions once held by male principals.

As administrative forerunners during the desegregation era, their intersectional employment experiences reflect the complexities and nuances of working in sometimes unwelcoming environments. They encountered both resistance and support relating to students and parents from diverse racial and socioeconomic backgrounds. Maxwell and her contemporaries encountered resentful white female teachers, displaced African American male principals, and sometimes patriarchal white male administrators. These women struggled to dispel prevalent and persistent racist stereotypes that promoted Black inferiority, whether in the classroom or sitting behind an executive desk. They fought against sexist misconceptions of women's inability to lead in high-level administration positions. Maxwell and other African American women administrators overcame these limitations by relying upon their past academic successes and self-confidence as influential leaders within their communities to enter their new positions as self-identified equals. Several prominent scholars, including Ange-Marie Hancock and Jennifer Nash, either promote or negate the relevancy and merits of the theories and meanings of intersectionality. Relying on praxis rather than theory, this historical work interprets intersectionality as a means to comprehend how Maxwell and other Black women educators successfully navigated through interlocking systems of oppression related to race, gender, and class.[32]

The passage of the Civil Rights Act of 1964, and the federal government's expansion into state and local education with new educational initiatives such as the Elementary and Secondary Education Act (ESEA) and Head Start, reconfigured the roles of teachers and administrators. ESEA regulations now required local school districts such as CMS to meet federal desegregation criteria to receive federal funding. Teachers and principals now had to adhere to federal and state regulations and guidelines that affected their curriculum design and interactions with students. Amid all these changes, African American women educators faced new obstacles as they traveled to teach or work at formerly all-white schools in the predominantly white structure of higher education administration. As beneficiaries of these educational transformations, Maxwell drew upon her experiences as a teacher to prepare them for future administrative positions. Foremost, their years in this changing school system taught them how to lead and teach students across class and racial lines.[33]

In 1964, the same year Maxwell entered graduate school, President Lyndon B. Johnson declared war on poverty, encouraging the creation of a "great society" devoid of economic inequities and racial discrimination. As scholars still debate the merits and success of his programs, it was a time in the United States where governmental and private foundations attempted to develop and implement innovative methods to eliminate poverty. Johnson's anti-poverty programs, such as the Elementary and Secondary Education Act (ESEA) and Head Start, attempted to create solutions to immense problems such as the lack of adequate health care for the poor and elderly, substandard education, and the negative impact of deindustrialization on African American employment in our nation's urban cities. A year later, in 1965, Congress passed the ESEA, which offered federal funding to help poor children. It had provisions to force school districts to desegregate.[34]

Scholars and public policy experts worked with federal government officials to design programs and policies to uncover the root causes of poverty beyond economic factors. In the 1960s, several scholars from the social sciences and public policy arena contended that pervasive poverty stemmed from cultural deficiencies among the poor, which included flawed family structures, immoral values, and inadequate work ethics. The release of New York Senator Patrick Moynihan's controversial publication, *The Negro Report: A Case for Action* inferred that the matriarchal structure of African American female-led households led to its dysfunction and subsequent poverty, diminishing the impact of systemic and institutionalized racism. Subsequently, an onslaught of rebuttals from scholars and policymakers refuted these arguments stating that poverty among African Americans stemmed from racial and economic injustice and job losses due to deindustrialization.[35]

As scholars and government officials debated the impact and role of federal economic intervention in mitigating poverty, it is worth noting that African American teachers living in the Jim Crow South waged the battle against economic and educational injustice for decades without financial support from the local, state, or federal government. As African Americans formulated new strategies to combat the onslaught of racial oppression and discrimination emerging after Reconstruction, they developed an overall concept of community service or racial uplift that called for middle-class African Americans to serve their communities. This complicated concept reflected class tensions as ideas of service sometimes involved the incorporation of internalized negative stereotypes and directions concerning the behavior and appearance of those who needed help. As educated professionals, urban Black southern teachers engaged in individual and collective efforts to transcend the substandard conditions of their schools and help students economically. Administrators such as Maxwell developed programs and curricula based on their training in new educational methods. They refused to adopt the concept that inferred that their students could not overcome poverty because of their supposed dysfunctional "culture." As Maxwell taught children from meager backgrounds who consistently excelled in their schoolwork despite having a lack of materials and resources, she maintained, "Poor children are not culturally deprived. They are educationally deprived."[36]

Even though scholars continue to debate whether the family's cultural background or institutionalized racism has had the most impact on the cause of poverty, teachers such as Maxwell, who often worked with economically disadvantaged students, strove to educate all their students regardless of socioeconomic class status. Maxwell's principal, Jayne Hemphill, often directed teachers to visit their students' homes to build connections and access their economic and family situations. When Maxwell saw that some of her students slept in boxes or lacked plates for their food, she realized that their frequent dozing resulted from hunger and tiredness. As education officials later began to label poor children as "at risk," Maxwell rejected the predetermined conclusion that there was a direct correlation between childhood poverty and discipline problems, as she taught middle-class students with behavioral issues and those from less affluent backgrounds adhered to strict discipline rules. Maxwell rejected these assumptions because, as a child who grew up in poverty and could be mischievous at times, she thought that these studies neglected to gauge the crucial role of teachers and community support to ensure student success.[37]

Educators such as Maxwell often tried to solve the personal and economic problems affecting their students' academic performances. After learning that Shirley Price, one of her fourth-grade students at Alexander Street Elementary, lived in a three-room house with her mother and six siblings, Maxwell offered to take the little girl home with her for the weekends as a mini vacation. By the time Price reached the 7th grade, she had decided that she wanted to live with Maxwell permanently. Over the years, Maxwell informally adopted Shirley as her other "daughter," and she became an unofficial member of the Maxwell family. Shirley later enrolled in Maxwell's alma mater, Johnson C. Smith University. When a professor told Price that she was not college material, Maxwell firmly told the professor that her "daughter" would not be quitting and insisted that it was the professor's responsibility to ensure that Shirley would be college material by the end of his class. Defying the dire predictions of her professor, Shirley continued to follow in Maxwell's footsteps. After joining Delta Sigma Theta, she graduated with a Bachelor of Arts in Education degree from Johnson C. Smith University. She earned a Master's in Education degree from the University of North Carolina at Greensboro. Like Maxwell, Shirley Price Harris joined the faculties for more than twenty-five years in Charlotte at Cotswold and Devonshire Elementary Schools before passing away from a rare illness in 2006.[38]

Maxwell fought to ensure that all Charlotte's children had equal educational opportunities regardless of race. She strove to provide educational access to children from impoverished backgrounds. Before the onset of the federally sponsored Head Start, Maxwell saw the need to provide early childhood education opportunities for disadvantaged children. As she quietly broke segregation barriers by working with white children at more affluent schools, she became more conscious of the economic disparities between white and Black schools and how poverty impacted children attending First Ward Elementary School. As school systems began to tout the benefits of early childhood education, Charlotte's public school kindergarten program required students to pay a $30 enrollment fee. Cognizant that most parents living in the First Ward could not afford to send their children to this program, she decided to act. Since entering the teaching profession as a young graduate in 1954, she built a supportive network of fellow teachers and Delta Sigma Theta Sorority sisters. She wanted to offer a free kindergarten for the kids in the First Ward, and she needed their help. Her ability to recruit these teachers to give up their vacation or summer work plans to teach for free offers an early example of Maxwell's charismatic leadership style. She recruited twelve teachers to serve as instructors for the six-week program. Bernice Sloan Ferguson, Maxwell's colleague, even volunteered to design the curriculum.[39]

Now that she had the faculty, as part of the newly minted Charlotte Teachers Corps (CTC), Maxwell formulated a development plan that included crossing racial barriers to seek donations and travel support from prominent white religious institutions such as First Baptist Church, Myers Park Baptist, and St.

John's Episcopal Church. The Red Cross donated pencils and safety kits, and the Optimist Club donated funds to pay for daily milk for the kids. She even received funding from an anonymous donor who offered to pay for the kids to have a picnic at Freedom Park.[40] Maxwell secured donations by promoting the CTC in newspapers locally and statewide. After the Charlotte schools let her use an empty school for the location, all Maxwell needed now were the kids. Fortunately, eighty-five kids eventually enrolled in the program.[41]

Maxwell's vision for the program went far beyond teaching children academic readiness skills; she wanted them to fall in love with learning. So, the CTC teachers worked with the children to bring the things that the children learned about in books to life. After listening to a book about planes, the CTC took the children to the airport, and the kids traveled to rural Charlotte to visit the Hunter dairy farm, where they had the opportunity to sit on the tractor and learn about cows. "How many stomachs does a cow have?" Harvey Hunter posed to the children. "Four," they enthusiastically answered. Mary Hunter, a former teacher, and Harvey's wife told the group of five and six-year-olds to "come back and don't you boys and girls ever let me hear of you not finishing school."[42] After the CTC's teachers took the children to visit downtown Charlotte, they grew excited just to ride the elevator. Maxwell recalled that "several of the children had never been downtown before, and they only live eight or nine blocks away."[43] Maxwell hoped that the CTC could ease their transition to school, establish a solid foundation, and prepare them for the first grade, thus preventing delays and eventual student attrition. Maxwell claimed, "These little girls and boys just unfolded like flowers."[44]

Assistant CMS interim superintendent John Phillips praised the CTC's reading readiness program; however, Maxwell's final days working in the program remained bittersweet because she knew that several teachers could not return the following summer due to financial and personal obligations. Fortunately, Maxwell's concern about the CTC's future became moot as the CMS implemented the Head Start Program as part of Lyndon Johnson's new War on Poverty initiative. Maxwell's realization that the federal government would sponsor Head Start epitomizes the broader transformation of local public education systems as it encountered massive changes resulting from federally court-ordered desegregation and the implementation of greater federal government control over local school systems.[45]

Maxwell's vision to create the CTC signified an innovative reaction to the overwhelming economic problems that hindered the kids of the First Ward. This effort drew from a tradition of uplift epitomizing the myriad of ingenious ways Black segregation-era teachers used to promote learning. Maxwell was first encouraged by the implementation of Head Start. She and other Black educators would later react with ambivalence after realizing that anti-poverty programs empowered Black teachers who could assume newly available management positions and diminish the influence of other educators who were now required to adhere to more restrictions in the classroom. Unfortunately, these War on Poverty programs failed to address the fundamental inequities of capitalism, institutionalized racism, and gender discrimination. For example, conservatives in Mississippi and other parts of the South viewed Head Start's hiring of local African American mothers as teaching assistants as a potential threat to white landowners' control over Black labor. If activists considered the War on Poverty programs as legislative and policy extensions of civil rights goals, Head Start's teachers drew from Black Nationalist concepts of self-empowerment as impoverished African Americans formed locally led community service programs.[46]

As historian Crystal Sanders contends, when the Child Development Group of Mississippi's Head Start Program hired residents and parents as instructors, it encouraged Black grassroots activism and helped sever the economic chains of sharecropping. In Charlotte, however, Maxwell's teacher-led program served as the model for Head Start in urban areas as it called for teachers to engage in their efforts to empower children.[47] As educators learned about the CTC, they requested that Maxwell make presentations describing the program. Once, she received a phone invitation from an administrator at Winthrop College in Rock Hill, South Carolina, to make a presentation about the CTC to education students and professors. When Maxwell and her fellow CTC teachers arrived, the white program director was aghast! She didn't know that Maxwell was African American because she did not "sound" Black over the phone. After she made her presentation to a shocked audience, Maxwell and her fellow presenters later laughed at the situation.[48] In August 1999, several former CTC teachers met to reminisce about their summer adventure. Maxwell remembered, "At that particular time, many of the kids had not been exposed to books." She elaborated, "I think it (the Corps) not only created an awareness of what was going on in this community but also of the have and have nots. It truly touched the conscience of some of the people in this community. It really brought a response far beyond our system here."[49]

These new educational initiatives gave women more administrative employment and leadership opportunities as directors of these programs. These experiences prepared them to adapt to a changing school environment. As CMS and local school boards across the nation struggled to adhere to federal court-ordered desegregation plans, the mandate to adopt new state and federal curricula and program initiatives transformed the field of education. For several southern states, Head Start emerged as an offshoot of the civil rights movement because it offered expanded employment opportunities for Black women to work in the program and promoted a culturally progressive curriculum. In contrast, after the passage of the Elementary Secondary Education Act (ESEA), the state of North Carolina allocated Head Start funding to be managed by local nonprofit agencies and school systems. CMS incorporated Head Start as an eight-week summer program as part of its overall funding allocation from ESEA. Financed with almost $300,000 in federal funds, over thirty-two schools housed Head Start Programs helping 2,003 children and employing over 440 teachers, teacher aides, and volunteers.

If Maxwell's CTC served as a local model for Head Start, the federal program also shaped Crosby, Randolph, and Cunningham's professional careers. In 1966, CMS hired Kathleen Crosby to serve as the system's first in-service early childhood education specialist. The Bank Street master's student was hired to train Head Start teachers. Crosby worked under Head Start director and Lincoln Heights Elementary School principal, O. N. Freeman. In 1967, Crosby joined Double Oaks principal Gwendolyn Cunningham as a Head Start Coordinator, establishing four Child Development Centers for Head Start instruction across the city. Already experienced in early childhood education due to her prior experience managing a kindergarten program and as an elementary school principal, in 1967, Randolph received a promotion from CMS to become the director of ESEA Programs, responsible for managing a budget of almost one million dollars in ESEA Title I funds, which included funding for Head Start in CMS.[50] Randolph worked with local entities such as the nonprofit community action agency, the Charlotte Area Fund to distribute and implement ESEA funds. During the 1970s, Randolph worked with other local and state administrators to develop statewide plans for Head Start. The successful implementation of Head Start led CMS to eventually adopt a system-wide kindergarten program for the system's children.[51]

Experienced teachers in early childhood education, such as Crosby and Gwendolyn Cunningham, directed several of Charlotte's Head Start locations. Their responsibilities sometimes included hiring local Black mothers and college students as assistants. Less threatening to white supremacist government officials than Mississippi's Head Start directors, who worked closely with civil rights activists, Charlotte's Black Head Start teachers and directors officially adopted a CMS-approved curriculum. Adept at navigating around segregation's barriers, these educators took advantage of Head Start's innovative structure to develop curricula that promoted the self-esteem of African American children. Despite their experience and qualifications as teachers of children from families with limited economic resources, Black educators, such as Crosby, Randolph, and Cunningham, faced unforeseen challenges as they now had to adapt their teaching philosophies to meet the requirements of new governmental curriculum guidelines that included new assessment measures.[52]

Black Women Administrators during Desegregation, 1966–1996

Business and civic leaders publicized Charlotte progressivism as a New South city by citing its moderate race relations and promising business development. Nevertheless, the CMS school board offered similar delaying and resistance tactics to stall or prevent desegregation as school officials did in other urban southern cities. As civil rights leaders celebrated the success of major legislative gains such as the Civil Rights Act of 1964 and the Voting Rights Act of 1965, strong resistance from local school board members, parents, and pro-segregation community activists stymied all serious efforts to desegregate public schools beyond the token placement of small percentages of individual Black students in white schools.[53]

As Maxwell's CTC looked to supplement some of the racial and economic inequities affecting African American children in the First Ward, her role as an educator would be transformed after the federal government's passage of the 1964 Civil Rights Act, which called for schools to desegregate. A year later, in 1965, the passage of the Federal Elementary and Secondary Education Act (ESEA) offered millions of dollars in aid to develop programs to address the needs of impoverished children and provide funding for libraries but threatened to withdraw its funding if school systems did not desegregate. With the threats from the Civil Rights Act and the ESEA, some southern districts, including Charlotte, finally moved to take concrete steps to desegregate. Nevertheless, it would take the *Swann* ruling to force Charlotte to comply with federal regulations fully.[54]

After graduation from UNC Greensboro in 1966, Maxwell planned to return to the classroom, but education dean Kenneth Howe had other plans for her career. Howe and CMS superintendent Phillips encouraged her to become a principal. When Maxwell adamantly expressed her reluctance, the two powerful administrators delicately mentioned that she might have to pay back her graduate funding if she refused. So, she left the safe confines of teaching to join the administrative ranks just as faculties began to desegregate.[55] By 1967, after working as an assistant principal at predominantly white Villa Heights Elementary, where she often performed the duties of her white principal who was out on sick leave, CMS appointed her to the principal's position at Morgan Elementary School located in the predominantly African American Cherry neighborhood. Education scholars describe an "effective leader or principal" as one who creates a positive school climate, has high expectations for student learning, focuses on instructional planning, and builds parental and community support.[56] Education scholars claimed that women principals tend to have a more democratic leadership style, interact more with students and faculty, and focus more on the curriculum. Maxwell, Crosby, and Randolph's experiences as new principals of their respective schools reflect these characteristics.[57]

As principal, Maxwell eagerly planned to implement some of the programs and concepts she learned in graduate school. Maxwell developed and instituted an open classroom education concept based on her graduate work. In this instruction model, students listened and learned from other teachers working in the same area. She removed some of the dividing walls in classrooms to create open spaces and for student-teachers trained in the open classrooms pedagogy. "She was an innovative principal. I think she was about ten or fifteen years ahead of her time as an educator," said Lorraine Orr, a former member of Maxwell's faculties at both Morgan and Albemarle. She added, "No one was doing the open classrooms concept at the time." Frederick Warren, who taught at Albemarle Elementary, shared, "She (Maxwell) had a participatory management style. It wasn't a lot of directions such as, "you are going to do it this way." As principals of desegregated schools, Maxwell, Crosby, and Randolph, drew from and expanded current leadership models and retained some of their mentors' management techniques to develop their own unique leadership concepts.[58]

As a principal of a segregated school, Maxwell drew from Hemphill's example and sought help from Morgan's neighboring community. Although CMS remained enmeshed in desegregation battles, Black segregated schools still received substandard funding. After CMS denied Maxwell's request for bus transportation for her students required to walk long distances to school, she contacted Phyllis Lynch. Maxwell and Cherry neighborhood community leaders worked together to raise funds from local churches and organizations to purchase a used small blue bus. Lynch volunteered to drive the children. As the principal of Morgan, Maxwell challenged educational inequities by taking students on unsanctioned field trips, which included swimming in the pool of predominantly white Johnston Young Men's Christian Association (YMCA), often shocking the patrons. Charlotte was one of the first cities in North Carolina to desegregate its public recreational facilities, but most privately operated pools, such as the YMCA's, remained segregated. Working with parents, she took Morgan's Black Girl and Boy Scout troops to participate in previously whites-only scouting events.[59]

As the Board of Education developed new desegregation plans to meet federal court regulations, one of its most destructive tactics involved closing seven predominantly African American schools. These closings became a common strategy implemented by school systems to counter hostility from white parents who resisted enrolling their children in Black schools. CMS claimed that it instituted the closings to prevent white parents from pulling their children out of the system or white flight. African American parents protested these closings; instead, they called for the remodeling or construction of new schools in predominantly Black neighborhoods.[60]

Charlotte civil rights leader and Little Rock African Methodist Episcopal Zion Church (AME Zion) pastor George J. Leake III organized the Black Solidarity Committee (BSC) to protest the closings. This Committee submitted a petition with over nineteen-thousand signatures to the School Board. Instead of just closing these schools, the BSC wanted to replace these schools with new ones and send white students to these schools. Even though West Charlotte, one of the city's African American high schools, survived after Black parents and students waged a fierce battle against the school board, most of the predominantly African American elementary schools closed despite the efforts of the BSC and community complaints. This issue became personal for Maxwell. During her second year as principal, Black Central Office CMS administrators James T. Burch and Elizabeth Randolph informed Maxwell that Morgan would close the following year. Educators such as Maxwell soon learned that placing African American children in white schools was just one step in the process to dismantle racial discrimination in education. Although she would eventually lead desegregation efforts, Maxwell's transition from Morgan reflected the ambivalent experiences of African American educators as she lamented the loss of Morgan and saw her colleagues receive transfer notices to report to former predominantly white schools.[61]

The struggle to dismantle segregation, in some cases, led to unforeseen harmful consequences, as CMS and other school systems responded by closing or restructuring African American schools and transferring experienced Black faculty to white schools. As noted earlier, CMS began desegregation by sending African American and white teachers, such as Maxwell, who taught specialized subjects such as art, music, and reading, to travel to work in schools across the system. In 1965, the Department of Health, Education, and Welfare (HEW) ordered school districts to submit desegregation plans that included faculty desegregation to receive federal funding. As a result, CMS submitted volunteer faculty desegregation plans. For those African American teachers who received transfers to white schools, as CMS selected teachers deemed acceptable to whites, issues of colorism emerged as these teachers, though qualified, often had light-brown-skinned complexions.[62]

After only 2 percent of CMS teachers, Black and white, volunteered to transfer to desegregate, Federal District Judge James B. McMillian ordered the desegregation of all teachers by the fall of 1969. In a 1969 survey by the Charlotte Teachers Association of 1,300 African American and white teachers, a majority, 893, voted yes for the simultaneous integration of students and faculties, with 606 no votes. Despite their previous favorable responses, the majority of the teachers surveyed, 851, contradicted the previous result by voting yes to the statement "that the goal of integrated education was not worth all the hardships," compared to 575, who thought that integration was worth all the hardships. This poll revealed that only 196 teachers responded that they would transfer to another school for desegregation. This poll, which only garnered half of the opinions of approximately 3,600 CMS teachers, reflected that most supported desegregation as an abstract principle but were ambivalent when it affected their professional careers. With the sobering results of this study, the failure of volunteer faculty desegregation, and impending federal court legal directives, CMS began mandatory transfers to establish a quota of one minority teacher out of six in every school. Whereas most Black teachers had to transfer, younger or new white teachers received positions at former all-Black schools.[63]

The NAACP battled to end segregation in public education by focusing on students. The process to dismantle segregated education began several decades earlier in the 1930s and 1940s when teachers led the fight for educational equality as the plaintiffs in the NAACP's teacher salary equalization cases. When the NAACP transitioned to focus on full desegregation instead of addressing the hypocrisy of separate but equal facilities, leading up to the *Brown* decision, African American educators faced a precarious dilemma. Charlotte's African American teachers, such as Maxwell, endorsed and participated in school desegregation, which often resulted in the closing of predominantly Black schools. This support often came at a heavy price with the loss of their jobs. A local Charlotte newspaper claimed that more than 182 Black teachers lost their jobs as the city closed Black schools. Statewide, from 1965 to 1967, some 500 African American principals lost their jobs. Approximately one-fourth received demotions to positions of assistant principals at formerly all-white schools. Desegregation's promise of the elimination of racial restrictions enabled Maxwell and her peers Randolph and Crosby to transcend traditional gender barriers. Nevertheless, as new laws preventing hiring discrimination based on gender encouraged women to break the "Black glass ceiling," the concurrent influx of Black high school closings and underlying racism still prevented African American women from obtaining positions in secondary school administration. It would take almost fifteen years for E. Virginia Shadd, a former middle school principal, to become the first African American and the first woman in CMS to serve in the coveted position of principal of Myers Park High School in 1983 and Harding High School in 1986.[64]

By the end of the 1960s, Charlotte's public schools became embroiled in the desegregation process. Maxwell learned that with the closing of Morgan Elementary, its student population would be divided among three upper-middle-class, formerly all-white schools: Eastover, Myers Park, and Dilworth. She considered it her responsibility to protect her students and aid them in the desegregation process. She met with each school principal to discuss their plans for incorporating her students into their schools. Most of the principals stated that they welcomed Maxwell's students; however, the principal of Myers Park Elementary adamantly refused to accept any African American students, despite the board's directives. Extremely frustrated because of Cherry's unique position as an adjoining neighborhood for the African American servants who worked in Myers Park neighborhood, Maxwell sarcastically commented about the situation, "This was very funny, the people that cook and clean house for you (Blacks) and you (whites) won't accept their children." Maxwell told the principal of Myers Park, "These parents work for these people over here at Myers Park. Yes, you're going to take these kids." Maxwell then notified Charlotte's school superintendent, William Self: "I told Bill to get this man straightened out. Don't send me out there when you haven't prepared them."[65] "As the state's rural children already rode buses to schools with no complaints, uproar resulted after the implementation of busing to achieve racial desegregation. Nationally, antibusing reactions helped to re-energize the conservative movement. Charlotte's city promoters later prided themselves as having some of the most racially desegregated schools in the nation. However, Maxwell's experiences placing her students represented African American children's actual struggles.

After the closing of Morgan, CMS assigned Maxwell to work at a white elementary school as an assistant principal. Viewing it as a demotion, she declined the new post. She was not going to take a pay cut and become a victim of the board's one-sided desegregation plan. She responded, "I refused to go to anybody's white school and be somebody's assistant. I earned my degree at UNC-Greensboro." Maxwell also refused CMS's offer to take a principal's position at one of the newly constructed Black schools. She refused to be in the position where she might have to replace Sterleta Sasso, at Oaklawn Elementary and incur negative repercussions from parents, who respected their current principal. So, in 1968, in a bold countermove, CMS asked her to be one of the first Black women principals of Albemarle, a new all-white elementary school in Charlotte. It was such a prestigious offer that she couldn't refuse. Again, Maxwell would become a "first," but in this case, her efforts would not just help her personally. As an African American woman principal of a predominantly white school, Maxwell now served as a change agent in the push to desegregate CMS.[66] Maxwell de-emphasized her role as a forerunner, instead claiming, "Being 'first' is not important to me. This was an opportunity for me to see that every child was able to fulfill his or her potential." Nevertheless, as Maxwell prepared to assume the principal's position at Albemarle amid CMS's busing battles, she realized that the board planned to use her performance as a model for evaluating the success of African American principals in white institutions.[67]

As Maxwell communicated with angry parents and comforted confused students, she wanted to help as many of Morgan's faculty who now faced job losses. As Bertha fought to protect these teachers, her response reflects one of the unique roles of African American principals during desegregation. Unlike Jayne Hemphill, who had to work to maintain a productive faculty at Alexander Street and First Ward to combat segregation's limitations on funding and opportunities, Maxwell's new charge as a Black desegregation-era principal involved helping her faculty navigate potential transfers and job losses. CMS told most principals from closing schools they could only hire up to two teachers from their former schools. Relying on her charisma, friendship with top school officials, and her leverage as one of the first African American women principals of a white elementary school, Maxwell disregarded this edict to successfully negotiate the hiring of eight African American teachers from Morgan and other Black schools. During Maxwell's tenure as Albemarle's principal, the African American student population rose from one to four, with approximately 535 white students. Maxwell and other teachers often transported the few Black students to and from school.[68] Whereas other African American educators who transferred to white schools experienced isolation and a loss of voice, Maxwell endeavored to ensure that both Black and white teachers had opportunities to participate in the life of the school.[69]

Albemarle Road Elementary was a new school nestled in the middle-class white rural/suburban Albemarle neighborhood where some of the students rode their horses with a parent to school. She and several other Black principals, including Wilmore Elementary School principal Natalie Holmes, attended workshops and training in Maine on interpersonal relations. Maxwell looked forward to employing these techniques in these workshops. Determined to make a difference, she developed and implemented several new instruction models and methods and established Albemarle's first Parent Teacher Student Association.[70]

Excited to implement some of the new pedological concepts that she began at Morgan, Maxwell spent the first year developing team teaching plans and non-graded classrooms. She incorporated the open walls or open space teaching concept and encouraged parents and community members to serve as guest teachers of specialized subjects ranging from cooking to auto mechanics to Spanish on Fridays. In commenting on her efforts, she explained, "I believe in the holistic education of the child." Some of these new concepts garnered attention from members of the school board, and she had frequent visitors observe her school. Albemarle's parents seemed receptive to the new initiatives, but after the advent of court-ordered busing, other white parents meshed their disdain for desegregation with a fear of these new changes. Although these disgruntled parents made up a minority, they were vocal and active, writing harsh letters to the school board about the new plans. One parent even claimed that Maxwell's open classrooms promoted Communism! Even though most students embraced Maxwell's new concepts and the school board applauded her efforts, the negative criticism took a toll on Maxwell. She explained in a 1970 *Charlotte Observer* newspaper article, "Maybe I was out there with too idealistic an approach. It was a new school, and I wanted to provide the type of educational experiences I had been trained in."[71]

Unfortunately, Maxwell's successes with new learning initiatives did not insulate her from old ideas of racism and sexism. Her experiences reflected the intersectionality of racism and sexism as shocked parents discovered that their child's principal was a woman and a Black person. Disgruntled white parents who challenged her authority and reported her to the board of education shockingly soon discovered that the board supported Maxwell. In one instance, when she refused to move a child out of a Black teacher's classroom, the angry parent, an alleged member of the Ku Klux Klan, demanded to meet and threatened to report Maxwell to the school board. She responded by inviting the school board to a PTSA meeting at Albemarle at 6 p.m. and invited the angry parent to come to the school at the same time. Before the meeting with the disgruntled parent, Maxwell sarcastically told her staff, "If you find me dead, you know he did it." After meeting with the parent, who was surprised to learn that Maxwell was Black, she told him that since he wanted to meet with the school board, she would bring the school board to him. Firmly and forcefully, Maxwell directly challenged his racism. "Now you can take your daughter out of this school if you want, but I see no reason to take her out of Mrs. Reinhart's class. She is one of our best teachers. I will not remove a student from a class just because the teacher is Black!" After this meeting with the enraged parent, he backed down from his threats. Several days later, the wife of the complaining parent met with her to thank her for "standing up for my daughter."[72]

Maxwell faced new challenges as integration profoundly affected discipline practices in public schools. During segregation, principals and teachers practiced corporal punishment on children by spanking or hitting them with a paddle or ruler. Often parents permitted their children to receive corporal punishment, but after integration and the loss of parent/teacher trust across racial lines, this practice became problematic. One of the most significant issues that arose during desegregation was the implementation of racially motivated, harsh, or unfair discipline toward African American students by white teachers and administrators. On the other hand, white parents vehemently objected to Black teachers spanking their children. New pedagogical theories called for the elimination of spanking as a useful form of discipline. Maxwell did not allow her teachers to spank students, but on the occasion when an African American teacher spanked a white child, Maxwell had to diffuse a very precarious situation. As she recalled, "When Geraldine spanked the daughter of an Albemarle Junior High School teacher because she didn't know her numbers, the parent became very upset and wanted the teacher fired." After careful negotiations among Maxwell, the school board, and the parties involved, the teacher was reprimanded but allowed to remain employed. Maxwell encountered new challenges, such as teachers who were addicted to alcohol and had mental health problems. After two of her teachers unsuccessfully attempted suicide, Maxwell decided to take a counseling course in the Department of Human Development, now the Cato College of Education at the University of North Carolina at Charlotte, to better manage and support teachers who were undergoing mental stress.[73]

During the 1970s, some sixteen schools in the Charlotte area adopted the open space classroom teaching concept; however, when Maxwell implemented these new educational approaches at Albemarle, parents' reactions encompassed more than just concern about teaching plans. Their negative reactions involved their attitudes about the leadership role of their new Black woman principal. Despite her tumultuous experiences, which included death threats from racist community members and frequent challenges by parents who refused to accept her authority as principal, some of Maxwell's progressive teaching methods began to draw positive attention from school officials from across the state.[74] She was even encouraged to serve on a national committee focusing on elementary education within the National Association of Elementary School Principals (NAESP).

Yet, her professional successes did not mitigate the realities of two years of struggle to manage a faculty that had to work under intense pressure and racism. The final straw that pushed her to leave was when community members started racist taunting and harassing some of the children at Albemarle by calling them "n***** lovers." Ultimately, Maxwell grew frustrated with the work of an administrator. She stated, "I didn't want to be a principal anymore. I would sit in my car and cry as I drove home." After learning that Maxwell wanted to resign, CMS superintendent William Self offered her another administrative position at Oaklawn Elementary that was occupied by a popular African American principal, but Maxwell had already decided to leave the system. After Self asked why she wanted to go, she sarcastically expressed her feelings of frustration when she quipped, "It's like putting diapers on gnats!"[75]

The dean of UNC Charlotte's Department of Human Development, John Chase, previously asked if Maxwell might be interested in working as a professor at the university a few years before, but she graciously declined his offer. When Maxwell failed an incompetent UNC Charlotte student teacher from a prominent family who worked at Albemarle, she thought she had ruined her chances to get a job at the university. Now, after suffering through various incidents, she contacted him to ask, "Is that job still available?" Chase hired her, explaining that he wanted someone with the courage to fail a student, if necessary. So, in August of 1970, she joined the faculty of the Human Development and Learning Department at UNC Charlotte.[76]

Crosby, Maxwell, and Randolph: Black Women Administrators in Charlotte

Notwithstanding the emerging historiography analyzing the impact of civil rights educational gains and faculty desegregation on Black women teachers, there still needs to be more studies examining the influence of the women's movement on African American women educators. Black women, who reached top executive positions, such as Maxwell, Crosby, and Randolph, encountered both racism and sexism as participants in school desegregation and as administrators in predominantly male environments.[77] In segregated public schools, African American women seldom received appointments to secondary school principal posts. However, with new legislation and changing attitudes, Black women like Maxwell, Crosby, and Randolph now obtained higher-level administrative positions in schools and in the Central Office, supervising African American men and whites. At these moments, they became entangled in turmoil that challenged their leadership abilities as they guided their schools through the desegregation process.[78]

Whether leaving CMS to work in the college setting or remaining, African American administrators took advantage of the hard-fought gains of the civil rights and feminist movements to secure positions once closed to Blacks and women. Some education scholars argue that the negative consequences of desegregation included the transfer of former Black high school principals to powerless administrative positions in the Central Offices. Although an accurate assessment, the viewing of these transitions from a gendered perspective complicates these assumptions. One of the unintended positive results of desegregation involved the lifting of the barrier of sexism for these women. Suddenly, they became prized because women helped to bring a less threatening African American presence to the administration. While they regretted leaving their principal positions, Crosby and Randolph took advantage of the opportunities in these new administrative positions to gain power and influence in the system supervising both Blacks and whites. As Maxwell sought opportunities in a different educational arena, Elizabeth Randolph's career flourished as a CMS administrator. Kathleen Crosby became enmeshed in the turmoil that challenged her leadership ability as she helped facilitate the desegregation process by working as a desegregation specialist, principal, and administrator.[79]

After successfully implementing innovative early childhood education initiatives and working in integrated settings during the summers, in 1970, the board asked Crosby to serve in a new administrative capacity. She served as a mediator with an integrated team of administrators from the Central Office to solve racial disputes within the system's newly desegregated schools. Crosby recalled, "We were sent to put out fires and talk to children who were tearing up their schools." Vanessa Baxter, a Black student at the formerly all-white Harding High School, recalled Crosby's 1970 visit after some white students started a riot after African American students sang the Black National Anthem during a Black History Month Program performance. She shared, "Mrs. Crosby would come to your school and sit the two groups down and try to talk, and meditate, and resolve conflict, and there was a buzzword back in the day for that kind of thing. I'm thinking the term rap-in was used." Explaining further, Baxter asserted, "It was talking and getting groups to talk where she would get us to see that we had more things alike than we had differences and to help us approach our conflicts and resolve them without fighting and violence."[80]

In 1971, after repeated court challenges by civil rights activists, the Supreme Court ruled in *Swann vs. Mecklenburg County* that busing was necessary to achieve racial desegregation as the city's neighborhoods and its local schools remained segregated by race. Busing became a polarizing question across the nation as antibusing protests rose in major cities. Despite strong resistance to busing by some of Charlotte's white residents, other white Charlotteans realizing that parents and community members should have a more positive role in the implementation of the desegregation progress formed the Citizens Advisory Group (CAG). Led by a white physician's wife and parent Margaret Ray, the CAG's integrated group of twenty-five parents and educators, such as Kathleen Crosby, who spoke out as a parent against the one-sided busing of Black children, as well as community members from the civic, religious, and business arenas, met weekly to submit a feasible desegregation plan to the CMS School Board. Working with CMS, they developed the plan that was eventually approved by Judge McMillian of the Federal Court in 1975.[81]

In 1971, Crosby received a new appointment as principal of Billingsville Elementary School, a former all-Black school in Grier Town, a working-class neighborhood in Charlotte. Billingsville played an instrumental role in the development of the *Swann vs. Charlotte-Mecklenburg County Board of Education* case, as Darius Swann, the plaintiff, declined to send his son to Billingsville after he was rezoned back to the Black school after attending a desegregated white school. When the board refused to send his child to the desegregated school, Swann filed suit in 1965.[82]

After the federal courts forced the board to redraw neighborhood school zones, white children living in upper-middle-class neighborhoods now had to attend Billingsville. Civil rights attorney and *Swann* litigator Julius Chambers and Charlotte's pro-desegregation forces looked to Billingsville to serve as an example of successful desegregation that involved the busing of white students to an African American school. Unlike Maxwell, who encountered resistance as a Black woman serving as principal in a predominantly white environment, when Crosby accepted this new position, she faced overwhelming pressure and controversy from different factions. White parents resented and feared sending their children to what they perceived as a substandard African American school. Black parents, wary of Crosby's ability to represent their concerns, disliked that the board removed a popular Black male principal. At the same time, Crosby's beleaguered new faculty lacked direction.[83]

Journalist Frye Gaillard argued that Crosby meshed the Black community's pride in the rich history of Billingsville, a Rosenwald school founded in 1927 on land donated by Sam Billings, a former slave, with the interests of white parents who demanded the allocation of new resources to the school.[84] Crosby refused to succumb to the pressure and relied on her previous experiences as a teacher and a mediator to turn the school around. She established transparent communication networks among the faculty, parents, and her office to dispel rumors and false perceptions, and she visited every parent and teacher. In a 2005 Public Broadcasting Service (PBS) documentary, "Only A Teacher: Episode Three, Educating to End Inequity," Crosby shared, 'When I came in, I knew I would have to be a principal who loved white kids and the Black kids. And I wanted them to respect each other. Whether they loved each other didn't matter to me, but to respect each other and give each other the benefit of the doubt. I really think that it was only going to work if the parents of the children were involved. Both the Black children and the white children, the African American parents, and the white parents, worked diligently on it."[85]

To protect her teachers and encourage stability, Crosby, like Maxwell, refused to move children from a classroom just because the parent objected to the teacher's race. Moreover, to encourage parental confidence and promote changing attitudes toward discipline, Crosby stopped teachers from using corporal punishment and fired teachers who refused to adhere to her rules. When white parents became the majority of the PTA's members, she persuaded them to integrate the officers' positions. Over the years, her reputation as a fair-minded, straight-talking administrator who put children first helped to dispel controversies, and Crosby's efforts working with teachers helped to improve student test scores. Under her leadership, Billingsville eventually gained a national reputation as a model school for successful desegregation. Crosby received the "Charlotte Woman of the Year" award in 1976 from local television station WBTV, and Billingsville became the subject of several local and national television documentaries. Elizabeth Randolph won the same award in 1978.[86]

As the War on Poverty raged on in Charlotte, one aspect of desegregation seldom discussed concerns the ways that desegregation led to economic class integration. Maxwell and Crosby both served as principals in schools that enrolled children from diverse social classes. Maxwell's new school enrolled predominantly white students who came from diverse socioeconomic backgrounds. In contrast, Crosby welcomed upper-middle-class white children to attend her predominantly African American school in a working-class neighborhood. These administrators mediated disputes based on race and economic class.

After working as a successful principal, in 1978, the school board promoted Crosby to area superintendent, responsible for managing twenty-five schools.

Unlike Randolph, who worked with policy issues primarily, Crosby's position involved interacting with principals and teachers to implement Central Office directives. Although Crosby worked for years in desegregation efforts, she now received resentment from fellow school personnel who, despite her experience, considered her unqualified because she lacked a doctoral degree. Crosby's experiences reflect the complex ways in which the intersectionality of oppressions influenced African American women educators. As an area superintendent, she fought for racial equity, but she encountered gender discrimination from white female teachers who resented her new position of authority. She explained, "It has been the most difficult job of her career. You are on your own, and you either sink or swim." When one recalcitrant principal declined to force his school's music teacher to admit African Americans in his popular music class, Crosby remembered that she politely but firmly told him, "If you won't do it, I will. It's a new day. Black folks can sing. Find a Black person. I know you are going to talk about me when I'm gone, but I know you are going to do it, and they would do it."[87] Though this case was successfully resolved, as area superintendent, Crosby implemented measures to enforce desegregation that sometimes involved making controversial decisions to demote or remove administrators. She retired in 1986 after more than forty years of service to CMS.[88]

At University Park Elementary from 1958 to 1967, Elizabeth Randolph did not have to deal with Crosby's post-*Swann* busing issues as principal of a predominantly Black school. If Maxwell served as the principal of a newly constructed school as well, it was still a predominantly white school. Whereas Randolph did not have to contend with the overt racial conflicts that Maxwell and Crosby encountered, she did face challenges as a former high school teacher in a new leadership role that later included building connections among an integrated faculty. Randolph shared, "I was the principal during the very beginning of desegregation, and my school had some of the first white teachers."[89] Charlotte journalist Frye Gaillard shared, "Elizabeth Randolph was one of the most prominent African American administrators at CMS. Quiet and wise, she had a soft voice, but when she spoke, it was always right." In 2017, the board voted to name an administration building after Randolph and Chris Folk, a fellow administrator who worked with her when she served as part of the interim team that managed the schools.[90]

In reflecting upon the experiences of Black women administrators, they faced challenges as African American women in leadership positions when the governmental policies, the media, and popular culture continued to promote negative stereotypes of African American women as domineering, animalistic and over-sexualized. These women encountered people who were unfamiliar with working alongside African Americans in professional settings. As these women ran their schools and directed programs, they created a new counter-image of the professional Black woman administrator as one who interacted with anyone regardless of race, gender, or class, yet stood her ground, if necessary, in the fight against racism and sexism.

As scholars frequently debated the impact of school desegregation on children and communities, Crosby, Randolph, and Maxwell's careers reflected a paradox, as desegregation's impact on African American teachers and administrators remains complex. Maxwell bore the brunt of hatred and resentment from those against integration; however, she received new exposure as she became a recognized expert on the education of teachers working in desegregated environments, lectured at local colleges, and held a leadership position in the National Association of Elementary School Principals. In 1970, Maxwell's life changed again as she became a leader in a new struggle to educate Black students. When she joined the faculty of the University of North Carolina at Charlotte (UNCC) as an assistant professor, Maxwell came to train teachers. "I did not go to UNCC to do anything in Black Studies. I had just desegregated the Charlotte Mecklenburg Schools."[91]

Though desegregation and the changes wrought from the feminist movement provided new opportunities and options for African American women to advance professionally, Maxwell and Randolph both claimed that they never sought to be leaders. With no Black women role models in administration, it is easy to see why these women neglected to envision themselves in leadership roles. In Maxwell's case, she relied upon the advice of white men, such as Kenneth Howe, Craig Phillips, William Self, and John Phillips all friends and high-level university or CMS administrators who pushed her to assume leadership roles. As Bertha accepted their guidance, she often challenged them to improve desegregation efforts. As Craig Phillips, former CMS school superintendent, shared with Maxwell, "Bertha, you tried to teach us, but we just wouldn't listen."[92]

Whereas Maxwell, who said, "I didn't want to be a principal anymore," decided to seek new opportunities in academia, both Crosby and Randolph left their principal positions to work in the unchartered waters of public school administration. Randolph explained her early ambivalence in leaving University Park Elementary to work in the Central Office in a 1993 oral history interview; she insisted, "This was never anything I aspired to do. I certainly never thought Black people would be hired for this." Randolph described a conversation with a disappointed faculty member: "I remember when one teacher came to me and said, 'I knew that they weren't going to let you stay here; I knew it.' I (Randolph) said to her, 'What do you mean?' She said, 'They always get the good principals and bring them to the Central Office for administration.'" Providing more background, Randolph clarified that, "I had three white teachers and the teacher who told me this was a white teacher. So, I said, 'Good, I certainly wish you were wrong because I don't want to leave, but I have to do what the superintendent says.'"[93]

One can see the importance of having mentors and guides, as most of these women agreed to accept these positions because of the recommendations of others. Although the desegregation process imposed significant changes, it transformed these women's work lives in ways that they never considered previously. One of the biggest challenges Maxwell and other Black administrators faced during desegregation involved constructing their identities as educators. As graduates of segregated institutions of higher learning and as teachers in segregated schools, they sometimes wondered if their educational backgrounds at segregated colleges adequately prepared them to teach in white schools or as Crosby pondered, "attend a white graduate institution." They soon realized that they had adequate training to succeed in an integrated society. In some instances, they possessed additional qualifications, such as graduate degrees, that would help them maintain their confidence during this tumultuous period.[94]

Reflecting on how African American women administrators overcame racism, sexism, and class conflict to create a familial leadership style and form alliances suggests new ways to define women's leadership. Segregation-era administrators, such as Hemphill, led their schools in a more autocratic style. Later administrators, such as Crosby, Randolph, and Maxwell, managed with less hierarchical and more democratic methods that earned respect from faculty, staff, peers, and even their superiors when they challenged their views in sometimes volatile situations. During Crosby's 1986 CMS retirement roast, Bertha Maxwell announced to the audience of some 380 colleagues, family members, and well-wishers that she was presenting her friend with a "distinguished chair." Keeping with the humorous theme of the evening, instead of a formal title, Maxwell gave Crosby a rocking chair with a big blue bow. As Crosby reflected upon her forty-year career, she contended, "I don't advise anybody to be quite as outspoken as I have been. But I would always tell them not to be afraid, to tell the truth, even though it hurts. I don't have any regrets."[95]

During the 1970s and 1980s, Charlotte gained a reputation as the city that desegregated its schools successfully. However, a multitude of people including civil rights lawyers such as Julius Chambers, James E. Ferguson II, George Leake III, and Reginald Hawkins; business leaders such as W. T. Harris; community activists such as Margaret Ray; and courageous students such as Dorothy Counts-Scoggins, contributed to the relative success of school desegregation in Charlotte from the 1960s to the 1980s. Black women administrators like Maxwell, Crosby, and Randolph's dynamic personalities and leadership abilities as administrators helped to quash white parents' fears, promote Black student learning, and offer role models for future African American women in administration. These women all gained national attention as leaders as they diligently worked to promote desegregation and student achievement. Reconsidering their efforts enables us to understand why Charlotte became known as the unique city that achieved the relatively peaceful goal of busing for school desegregation.

3

Planting the Seed

Maxwell came to UNC Charlotte to escape the pressure of working as a principal in a volatile public school environment.[1] As the first Black assistant professor in the College of Human Development and Learning (HDL), now the Cato College of Education, Bertha welcomed sharing her expertise on desegregation with future teachers. Dean John Chase, appreciative of her honesty and on-the-ground administrative experience, soon considered Maxwell a trusted confidant. Maxwell adjusted to academic teaching, worked with Chase and HDL colleagues to design new curricula, and served as a consultant helping public school systems develop desegregation policies to help teachers manage classroom diversity.

Paradoxically, Maxwell joined the HDL faculty just as the Black campus movement emerged in colleges and universities across the nation. In 1969, UNC Charlotte's African American students became a part of this movement when they protested for the inclusion of academic subjects relating to the experiences of people of African descent and official recognition of Black student organizations and initiatives. After negotiating over two years with UNC Charlotte's African American activists, the university decided to offer Black Studies courses and establish a Black Studies Program. Needing a director, UNC Charlotte's Black Studies Committee turned to Bertha Maxwell. So, in 1971, she left her comfortable position to delve into another stressful but innovative environment as the founding director of the university's new Black Studies Program. Charged with developing a sound academic program by university administrators, she realized that her mandate involved creating a supportive environment for African American students.

This chapter first explores Bonnie Cone's founding of the University of North Carolina at Charlotte from 1946 to 1965 from its inception as a school for white veterans to its years as one of two junior colleges, Charlotte College and its predominantly Black counterpart, Carver College, ending with its final iteration in 1965 as a desegregated public university. After providing this unique context and background, I describe the formation and early years of the Black Studies Program (BSP) and Bertha Maxwell's experiences at UNC Charlotte as a professor and as the BSP director from 1970 to 1974. In moving from the public schools to a university setting, Maxwell merged the foundational philosophies of educational racial uplift that she learned as a teacher with new powerful ideas of cultural nationalism to create an affirming Black academic community that extended from the elementary school classroom to the college campus.

Bonnie Cone, Maxwell, and the New University

Maxwell arrived at UNC Charlotte only five short years after its formal opening as a four-year university in 1965. Established in the mid-twentieth century, UNC Charlotte did not retain the venerable traditions of a university created to educate the sons of colonial planters such as the University of North Carolina at Chapel Hill. Nor was it established in the nineteenth century as a land-grant college funded by the federal government's 1862 and 1890 Morrill Acts. The University of North Carolina at Charlotte's origins reflect the transformation and growth of the urban South, as Charlotte, a small city in the Piedmont region of North Carolina, emerged as an important business center.[2]

This new university first began in 1946 as the Charlotte Center, an extension or night school of the University of North Carolina at Chapel Hill for returning white veterans of WWII. Bonnie Cone, a local math teacher, became its director in 1949. That same year in 1949, Carver College, a Black extension school, opened. Over the years, the two schools transitioned to junior colleges. In 1964, the NC General Assembly recommended that Cone's school join the then Consolidated University System of three institutions, the University of North Carolina at Chapel Hill, the Women's College in Greensboro, later the University of North Carolina at Greensboro, and North Carolina State College in Raleigh. The University of North Carolina at Charlotte would be the fourth institution. By 1972, the renamed University of North Carolina System of Universities and Institutions included sixteen universities, colleges, and schools.[3]

Carver (later Mecklenburg) College merged with another school in 1963 to form Central Piedmont Community College in Charlotte. A decade after the *Brown* decision and a year after the passage of the Civil Rights Act of 1964, UNC Charlotte opened its doors as a legally desegregated institution. The University of North Carolina at Charlotte's journey from a small extension school to becoming the third-largest university in the UNC system with over 30,000 students in 2021 reflects the determination and drive of its founder, Bonnie Cone, a staunch supporter of Maxwell.[4]

UNC Charlotte's unique history as the state's only publicly funded university founded by a woman and its complicated relationship with its Black sister school, Carver College, tells a lesser understood story of post–World War II higher educational development in the backdrop of desegregation. Bonnie Cone's ability to form powerful and supportive coalitions with Charlotte's influential educational and business leaders enabled her to turn her vision of a local public university into reality. By developing an innovative Black Studies Program that incorporated academic content with programming to help African American students reaffirm their self-identity and create a sense of belonging, Maxwell reconfigured Cone's original mission by exemplifying a new prototype of the desegregated university: one where Black students felt supported and empowered.[5]

Cone, born in 1907, grew up in Lodge, South Carolina. She graduated from Coker College in Hartsville, South Carolina, in 1928 and embarked on a teaching career. After she had worked in rural South Carolina for several years, in 1940, Elmer H. Garinger recruited her to teach mathematics at Charlotte's Central High School. Garinger, who would later become the superintendent of the Charlotte City Schools in 1949, allowed Cone to work as a roving instructor teaching a variety of math courses. She received her Master's in Mathematics degree from Duke University in 1941 and began teaching summer courses to veterans there. Cone's life transformed again in 1945 when Garinger helped the in-demand master's student get a position working as a statistical analyst, studying mine reports in the Naval Ordinance Laboratory in the Office of the Navy in Washington DC. In 1946, Cone returned to Charlotte and Central High. In addition to her regular courses, she taught night college courses to World War II veterans in an extension program established by the Governor's Commission on Veteran's Education. Administered by the University of North Carolina at Chapel Hill, this program was one of twelve new centers across the state. Known as the Charlotte Center, it was managed locally by the Charlotte City Schools Board of Education, and Garinger, now the associate superintendent of the Charlotte City Schools, served as the representative in charge of its operation.[6]

After Charles Bernard, the Charlotte Center's director, resigned to attend graduate school in 1947, Garinger hired Cone despite his qualms that she may have difficulties as a woman supervisor working in a predominantly male environment.[7] As the director, Cone's new duties included recruiting students, hiring, and supervising the curricula. She endeavored to create a supportive environment for her students by helping them find employment or advising them on academic matters. As a result of Cone's dedication to her students beyond the classroom as an adviser and mentor, some of them began to call themselves "Miss Bonnie's Boys." Yes, Cone sometimes assumed a maternal role, but outside of the school's doors, she became a shrewd negotiator and Charlotte Center advocate, sometimes contending with sexism as she promoted her school. Initially scheduled to close after two years, the Charlotte Center rose to become the largest extension school in the state with 278 white students. The Center was the only local option for students to take college courses at a public institution.[8]

Cone recognized the students' needs for an accessible, low-cost college education and sought additional outside funding to make the program permanent. By 1948, Cone, with the support of Garinger and Charlotte School Board chairman, J. Murrey Atkins, had successfully worked to get the Charlotte City Schools to take over the total operations of the Charlotte Center.[9] In 1949, with the encouragement of Garinger, Cone met with the Charlotte City Council to request additional financial support for Charlotte College. She and Garinger made appeals to leaders in the city's business, religious and civic communities promoting the Center's importance. After they managed to get the Center's funding request placed on an upcoming Charlotte bond initiative, it passed, giving the Center $10,000 of operating funds for five years. The council renamed the school Charlotte College.[10]

Racially segregated in its inception, the nearest extension program for African American veterans was in Asheville, some 150 miles from Charlotte. Despite their courageous fight to end fascism and to save democracy overseas, Black veterans in segregated Charlotte had few options for public higher education. They attended night classes at Second Ward High School on 501 South Alexander Street, and Johnson C. Smith University had a few slots for returning GIs. As a result, these veterans requested access to the same educational opportunities as their white counterparts. Once dismissive of the needs of African American veterans who wished to take courses because the Charlotte Center was operated by segregated UNC Chapel Hill, Garinger had to consider their requests as the new Charlotte City Schools superintendent responsible for managing Carver College. So, in 1949, Garinger proposed that if fifty Black veterans expressed interest in taking college courses, he would open a school. To Garinger's surprise, over fifty vets said yes! Despite the objection of Charlotte NAACP chapter president Kelly Alexander Sr. and other Black leaders who argued against the opening of a separate school and pushed for the desegregation of Charlotte College, the School Board established Carver College, named after

George Washington Carver, located in Second Ward High School with Edward Brown serving as its director.[11]

In that same year, Charlotte and Carver Colleges received additional funding when the North Carolina General Assembly passed the Charlotte Community College System Bill that officially granted junior college status to the two schools with additional funding of $5,000 per year for each. Cone also successfully secured accreditation from the American Association of Junior Colleges for Charlotte College and established an executive board comprising Cone's advisory team and new members, including Atkins, Woodford "Woody" Kennedy, a prominent textile manufacturer, John Paul Lucas, from Duke Power, Charlotte Mobley, president of the Altrusa Club (a professional women's civic organization), and Dick Young, a reporter from the *Charlotte Observer*.[12]

As these two segregated institutions operated during the 1950s and 1960s, most southern school systems and institutions of higher education resisted the Supreme Court's 1954 mandate to desegregate. Unlike these more traditional schools, Cone's Charlotte College unofficially desegregated its student body in 1949 without significant fanfare by accepting African American public health nurses who needed to obtain additional college credits in sociology. Cone recalled in a 1986 interview, "That first year we were operating, the public health nurses asked us to give a course in sociology. They needed to upgrade their certificates or whatever documents they worked on." Thinking more about the best way to help these women take the course that they needed than adhering to the racial mores and laws of the day, Cone revealed, "You know, they were public health nurses, and I didn't question that there were Black ones. We had all of them we could get in sociology five years before the Supreme Court's decision." She even divulged, "When we got through, you know, we wanted to celebrate. We didn't think we were doing anything bad, so we just went ahead and had a picnic. Everybody just had the best time, and I guess that was the first that we had really been out that way with our Black counterparts."[13]

Cone's description of this groundbreaking cook-out reflected both her conciliatory nature and willingness to transcend segregationist customs to support students, and especially women, to succeed without racial designations. This unpublicized instance of desegregation did not appease civil rights activists or invoke strong reactions from segregationists because the event garnered little publicity as Charlotte College continued to accept Black nurses in this specialized course, held at the Charlotte-Mecklenburg Health Center, not on either campus.[14]

Cone worked tirelessly to promote Charlotte College in an environment where she was often the only woman working in conjunction with a predominantly male executive board that made decisions regarding the school. With little power to confront the powerful forces who reinforced segregated education openly, she remained in the background quietly advocating for change. Since the 1930s, the NAACP had waged numerous lawsuits to force southern public universities and colleges to admit African American students in its graduate and professional schools. After the *Brown* decision and repeated NAACP litigation, these schools finally admitted a small number of African American undergraduates. When Blacks, such as Autherine Lucy, legally won the right to attend the University of Alabama in Tuscaloosa in 1956, desegregating public institutions of higher education became an international public media event after mobs of angry, racist students and community members reacted by hurling insults at Lucy and threatening violence. The hostile and recalcitrant reactions of university administrators, faculty, students, and community members to desegregation at the Universities of Mississippi, Alabama, and Georgia also raised debates about the power of individual states to negate federal laws.[15]

In 1957, the North Carolina General Assembly passed the Community Colleges Act, which funded offering additional courses beyond the two years at the two schools. Despite this support, its unequal financial allocation still reflected the inequities of segregated schools, with Charlotte College receiving 70 percent and Carver College getting only 30 percent. This Act enabled the newly formed board of trustees of the Charlotte Community College System to take over the management of the two schools from the board of education. This new board of trustees included some of the most influential business leaders in the city, such as R. S. Dickson and Company president and former Charlotte Schools Superintendent J. Murrey Atkins; Thomas Belk, executive vice president of Belk Department Stores; Linn D. Garibaldi, North Carolina Telephone Company president; *Carolina News* editor Cecil Prince; Addison H. Reese, former president of American Commercial Bank; and Rowe Corporation president, Oliver R. Rowe. In 1957, North Carolina NAACP Director Kelly Alexander Sr. and representatives from the Charlotte Mecklenburg County Parent Commission on Education cited the dual operation of Carver and Charlotte Colleges as part of an unsuccessful petition to call for the Charlotte Board of Education to desegregate the public schools.[16]

After the passage of statewide and county bonds in 1959 and 1960 totaling almost $2.5 million dollars for capital improvements for community colleges, the Charlotte Community College Board proceeded to purchase land and break ground on the construction for Charlotte College's new campus in rural North Charlotte at the intersections of Highways 29 and 49 and Carver College's new campus on Beatties Ford Road.[17] Despite the NAACP's objections, some of Carver's Black students thought that the school provided a rare opportunity. Gershon Stroud, who taught at Carver during the early 1950s, remembered, "The veterans were all mature, and in most instances, married and had jobs. As a result of attending Carver Junior College, they advanced themselves." The principal of West Charlotte and York High Schools added, "During a period of segregation, it was difficult for these young men and women to leave home and go to school outside of Charlotte, especially when schools here in the City should have been willing to accommodate them, but they weren't." Carver College 1961 graduate Marian Ayton, who also earned a degree from Johnson C. Smith, shared that her fellow students "were serious, feeling this is the last stop, you either did it now, or. . . ."[18]

As the Charlotte College board of trustees discussed its construction plans for separate campuses for the two schools in a board of trustees meeting, Ernest S. Delaney Jr. the attorney for the integrated Charlotte-Mecklenburg County Council on Human Relations claimed that building the Carver College campus wasted taxpayer funds because the two colleges duplicated each other and the dual campuses promoted segregation. Although the two school's course catalogs did list similar course offerings, Charles Morris, attorney for the Charlotte College board of trustees, responded by claiming that the two institutions served students on different academic levels: Charlotte College, as a potential four-year university, and Carver, as a school that offered remedial courses to prepare students for acceptance into a four-year college. Morris also reiterated that Charlotte College had no racial restrictions and denied admission to African American students based on their failure to meet academic admission standards, not their race. Later in a March meeting of the North Carolina Advisory Committee on Civil Rights in Durham, Harry Jones, Executive Secretary of the Charlotte-Mecklenburg Council on Human Relations, challenged the board of trustees to work with high schools to help prepare Black applicants to meet the admission standards for acceptance to the predominantly white school, the board's attorney contended that Charlotte College did not have the financial resources to do so.[19]

In May 1961, two African American physicians, Roy S. Wynn, a past Charlotte NAACP chapter president, and James D. Martin filed a taxpayers' suit *Wynn v. Trustees of Charlotte Community College System* in the Mecklenburg County Superior Court for an injunction to cease spending the $267,000 Mecklenburg county tax funds for the further construction of the Carver College campus. The plaintiffs claimed that it was cost inefficient to maintain two separate colleges because they offered similar courses and they argued that operating separate institutions perpetuated segregation. After the Superior Court denied their petition, the North Carolina State Supreme Court dismissed the plaintiffs' claim that the construction of Carver College's new campus was unconstitutional and it upheld the Mecklenburg County Superior Court's decision, stating that the plaintiffs could not provide documented proof that a Black student had been denied admittance solely due to race. Construction continued. Technically desegregated, by 1961 only thirty-two African Americans, including the previously mentioned fifteen public nurses, had received admittance to Charlotte College. In the fall of 1961, the school's expected enrollment reached 900 with four Black students expected to attend.[20]

In a 1974 oral history interview conducted by UNC Charlotte history professor Robert Rieke, Maxwell linked the NAACP's objections to the two colleges since their inception in the late 1940s to the Black student protests at UNC Charlotte during the late 1960s. She contended, "They (NAACP) appeared before the Charlotte City School Board of Education, first of all, Kelly Alexander Sr. (along with a representative from the Negro Council of PTA's [Mary McClain, secretary of the Charlotte-Mecklenburg Parents Committee on Education]), requesting that they do not build the dual system (in 1957)." Describing the plaintiffs' main argument, "that they have one school," Maxwell explained, "When you look at the minutes you will also see that the curriculums are similar, you know, that kind of thing." In retrospect, Maxwell recalled that "There was always a money problem with Carver College, but if the faculty and if the student body had been integrated, desegregated at that particular time, I think it would have not laid the seeds for what happened here in 1969."[21]

Maxwell described the perpetuation of segregated institutions as a paradox whereby Charlotte College won its case by claiming it was non-discriminatory. Yet, the Community Colleges System Board still maintained racially separate schools, and Carver College consistently received less funding and support. That same year, the board decided to give Carver College a more racially neutral name, Mecklenburg College. Again, another desegregation paradox. Despite having a new name, Mecklenburg College's student and faculty populations remained predominantly African American. Maxwell recalled, "There was still this dualism. It was really a very subtle kind of thing like they changed the name from Carver as if changing the name would make it a different institution." Cone, who once welcomed Black students to Charlotte College several years earlier in 1949, did not openly object to the board's arguments in the *Wynn* case; her central focus involved establishing a university.[22]

By the time the board appointed Cone president of Charlotte College in 1961, she had transformed into a super networker who formed coalitions with successful business leaders, the media, and powerful politicians to garner support. Jack Claiborne, explained, "I've heard businessmen say Bonnie would come in and they would steel themselves, ready to say no." The former journalist and former associate vice chancellor of public relations for UNC Charlotte added "Then they'd sit down . . . she'd start talking . . . and then they'd wind up saying yes."[23] Mindful of the need for increased funding and resources, Cone, along with her supporters, wanted Charlotte College to become part of the three-member North Carolina Consolidated University System that included the Universities of North Carolina at Chapel Hill and Greensboro, and North Carolina State University, as a four-year institution. As a Consolidated University member school, UNC Charlotte would receive most of its funding through the State Appropriations Acts. When Cone needed to gain the approval of professors from the Consolidated University System as one of the prerequisites for acceptance, she did so by meeting with groups and sharing her vision of a four-year university that addressed the educational needs of students in the Charlotte area. In 1962, with only a few buildings constructed at Mecklenburg College, the new eleven-building Charlotte College campus opened.[24]

In 1963 the federal government passed the Federal Higher Education Act, which allocated funding to the North Carolina Board of Education to form community colleges. As a result, the Charlotte Community Colleges System Board and the City of Charlotte merged Mecklenburg College with the Central Industrial Education Center, a local predominantly white technical college, to create Central Piedmont Community College (CPCC). The CPCC merger eventually resulted in the demise of the Black junior college as CPCC's faculty and student population became a predominantly white faculty and student population. With a new location in the downtown or "Uptown" area of Charlotte, the board subsequently sold Mecklenburg College's land and buildings.[25] In contrast to the familiar representations of screaming segregationists who openly protested desegregation at southern universities, Charlotte College's elusive race-neutral desegregation claims expose how some southern publicly funded academic institutions subtly resisted *Brown*. Ideally, if the plaintiffs had won their case and forced the board to construct a single desegregated college that merged faculties and students from the two separate institutions on an equitable basis, Charlotte College would have been the most desegregated former all-white Junior College in North Carolina. However, after the actual merger, Mecklenburg College was eradicated, and CPCC became a predominantly white institution.

After the opening of CPCC in 1964, Mecklenburg College director, James Franklin Alexander, received an offer to become the school's new counselor.

Unfortunately, most of Mecklenburg College's instructors received no invitations to join CPCC's faculty. A familiar occurrence in the public schools, Mecklenburg College's African American faculty suffered job losses as a painful byproduct of the desegregation process. Whether in CPCC's case or within the public schools, these desegregation plans often called for closing African American schools. Alternatively, if these schools remained open, they faced changing racial demographics in faculty. In a 1996 oral history interview, former Mecklenburg College mathematics teacher David Hunter described how he shared his fears of unemployment due to the merger with Bonnie Cone. Familiar with his work as a math instructor, Cone persuaded CPCC president Richard Hagemeyer to offer Hunter a faculty position in the Math Department in 1964. After Dora Johnson, CPCC's only other Black instructor, left in 1965, Hunter became CPCC's sole African American professor. Despite being hired as an "only," Hunter later secured top administrative positions at CPCC, eventually retiring as dean of the College of Arts and Sciences in the late 1990s.[26]

In January 1964, Cone's dream became a reality when Charlotte College received approval from the North Carolina General Assembly, the Consolidated System's faculty, and the State Board of Education to become the fourth member of the Consolidated System. Several months later, the University of North Carolina at Charlotte officially opened on July 1, 1965, as a desegregated institution with some 1800 students and ninety faculty.[27] Cone's successful campaign to turn a small extension school into a university served as a model for other junior colleges. In 1969, Asheville-Biltmore Junior College in Asheville and Wilmington College in Wilmington became the fifth and sixth members of the Consolidated University System as the Universities of North Carolina at Asheville and Wilmington. In 1971, the renamed University of North Carolina System of Universities and Colleges incorporated ten other North Carolina junior colleges. Currently, the UNC system comprises sixteen universities and one secondary institution.[28]

Despite Cone's crucial role in establishing UNC Charlotte and her work as acting chancellor, in 1966, the Board of Governors, the decision-making body of the then Consolidated University System, selected Dean Wallace Colvard to be the University of North Carolina at Charlotte's permanent chancellor. Colvard, the former president of Mississippi State University (MSU) in Starkville, left his position after stewarding the university through the tumultuous desegregation process. In 1963, Colvard defied pro-segregationist state officials when he allowed MSU's all-white basketball team to play in the newly integrated National Collegiate Athletic Association (NCAA) basketball tournament. He also oversaw the admission of the university's first African American student, Richard Holmes. For Colvard, the University of North Carolina at Charlotte offered a new start for the experienced administrator. As chancellor, he could help to shape the direction and vision of UNC Charlotte at its inception without the restrictions of formalized segregated traditions.[29]

Critics speculated that the school's founder did not receive the chancellor's position due to arbitrary factors that included sexism, concerns related to her growing power, her lack of a terminal degree, and her inability to delegate. However, the Board of Governors' official reason for hiring Colvard emphasized that the new university needed a chancellor with experience presiding over a four-year university.[30] Cone eventually accepted the position of vice chancellor for student affairs and community relations and served from 1966 until she retired in 1973.[31] Cone explained that "I know other people that felt very differently about it. They felt that this was very bad, you know, some did, and some felt that it was right. I was working to get an institution to serve the people who were not being served. I felt that I had accomplished what I set out to do. The rest of it was okay with me."[32]

During the 1960s, the city of Charlotte rose from a quiet small town to a leading business center. Leaders such as Charlotte mayor Stanford Brookshire and grocery store chain owner William T. Harris promoted the city as a modern, forward-thinking urban enclave that promised a stable environment for business development. Cone joined with these leaders to tout the educational and financial benefits of having a public university located in Charlotte. These leaders presented a progressive counter-image to contrast the public displays of racism found in such southern cities as Birmingham and Little Rock, where state-sanctioned racism and domestic terrorism included dog and water hose attacks and church bombings. Instead, as Charlotte gained a reputation for racial moderation, its political leaders enacted zoning policies and laws that reinforced residential segregation and racial discrimination.[33] Maxwell joined UNC Charlotte's faculty in a pivotal time as the city emerged as a modern-day New South urban business center, and as the fledgling university endeavored to create an identity.[34]

UNC Charlotte's Black Studies Program, 1969–1974: The Early Years

As predominantly white universities began to desegregate after the passage of the Civil Rights Act of 1964, UNC Charlotte, located in rural North Charlotte, officially stated in its catalog and other public documents that it admitted students regardless of race, creed, or ethnic origin. Although there were no visible signs of the vestiges of legal segregation or laws barring Blacks from attending,

UNC Charlotte only enrolled a few African American students, and it hired no Black faculty at its inception.[35] In 1965, most of the instructors from Charlotte College, such as English professor Mary Denney, became a part of UNC Charlotte's faculty. Despite being open to all students who met the admission requirements, it took several years for the university to employ its first African American full-time assistant professor, former West Charlotte High School and CPCC math teacher, Julian Pyles, in 1969.[36]

When Maxwell first came to UNC Charlotte in the aftermath of the 1969 student protests, the growing school faced a broader challenge to address segregation as a member of the Carolina Consolidated System. The university was currently being sued in an ongoing 1964 lawsuit by the US Department of Health, Education, and Welfare (HEW), Office of Civil Rights Division. HEW charged that North Carolina and ten other states operated a dual segregated system of higher education and should develop plans to eliminate it. After years of inaction by North Carolina and six other states, in 1969, the NAACP Legal Defense Fund filed another suit to force the states to desegregate its public universities or deny them federal funding if they did not. The Consolidated University System continued to fight this case for over a decade. It offered plans and resisted edicts from HEW to do student assignments for racial balance or merging schools. Although only indirectly involved, UNC Charlotte argued against forced student assignments or university mergers because of its unique urban location and proclaimed its efforts to support diversity. This atmosphere of national accountability regarding racial inequality in the system's schools provided a context in which Maxwell could later suggest that her Black Studies Program and its Black student orientation and recruitment efforts supported the university's legal response to HEW. Maxwell, friends with prominent Charlotte civil rights attorneys Julius Chambers and James Ferguson, promoted her program with this lawsuit looming in the background.[37]

As building construction continued, UNC Charlotte's administrators and faculty established or expanded academic departments. By the time Maxwell arrived in the fall of 1970, there were seventy-six African American students out of a population of 4,000 students. She would become the university's second full-time Black faculty member. Before Maxwell arrived in 1970, UNC Charlotte's only other African American professors, aside from Pyles, included part-time instructors Hoyle Martin (Economics and Business), Justin Uchenger (History), and Elsie Woodard (English). During this period, it was not an unusual or unique occurrence for Dean John Chase to hire Maxwell directly from the public schools. Several of Maxwell's colleagues in the College of Human Development and Learning (HDL) also came from CMS. Frank

Parker, who joined the faculty in 1972, described HDL and the university as one where programs and departments were evolving. Over the years, UNC Charlotte transitioned from primarily an institution for commuter students to a traditional research-centered university with more formal hiring practices based on scholarly research records and professional academic credentials.[38]

To be promoted to a higher rank and receive tenure, such as the assistant to associate professor level or higher, faculty members received evaluations in three critical areas: research, teaching, and service. As the nation's colleges and universities took their first forays into faculty desegregation, some early Black faculty encountered discrimination when barred from serving on influential service committees. In the desegregation era of the 1970s, Maxwell and other African American faculty faced the opposite problem. As a "first" or an "only," she received an abundance of requests to serve on committees or participate in projects from the departmental to the university level to provide the "Black perspective." Whether motivated by sincere efforts to promote inclusion in Chase's case, or asked by others to serve as a powerless token, these additional, time-consuming service responsibilities placed an undue burden on Maxwell and other African American professors. Facing this dilemma, Maxwell told Chase that she "couldn't be the only Black person to serve on all of these committees and that he needed to get some more Black faculty." Chase responded by hiring CMS math curriculum specialist Almeda Rippy.[39]

UNC Charlotte and the Rise of the Black Campus Movement

The seemingly sudden rise of the field of Black Studies in the late 1960s drew inspiration from the groundbreaking scholarship of Carter G. Woodson, Anna Julia Cooper, W.E.B. Du Bois, William Leo Hansberry, and John Henrik Clarke who taught subjects relating to the African or African American experience or advocated for more faculty of African descent.[40] Charged with excelling in sometimes discriminatory environments, Black students who enrolled in predominantly white universities and colleges during the 1950s and early 1960s encountered courses that promoted racist ideologies or western-based classes that didn't reflect the experiences or actions of persons of African descent.[41]

When the Black Power movement emerged during the late 1960s to challenge African Americans to confront a racist and capitalistic society that refused to grant equality, its student proponents called for the establishment of academic courses and programs relating to the Black experience. College students from historically Black institutions such as Greensboro's North Carolina Agricultural and Technical State University and Fisk University in Nashville remained at the forefront of the civil rights struggle. Now Black Power advocates challenged some of these same students to adopt Black Nationalist concepts. By rethinking European-focused curricula, Black activists demanded courses and programs that focused on their African cultural heritage and history. Once deemed a derogatory word, the adjective "Black" now became celebrated and deemed beautiful. As these activists created a new cultural paradigm, they also started to identify themselves as "Black" instead of "Negro."[42]

In 1968, almost a thousand Howard University students in Washington, DC, staged a five-day takeover of the administration building from March 19 to March 23 to protest the dilapidated living conditions at the school and call for the implementation of a Black Studies curricula. Decades earlier, in the 1930s, Howard University famed attorney Charles Hamilton Houston, established the field of civil rights law. Despite Howard's rich legacy of advocacy and scholarship, Black Power activists called for the prestigious school to transition from a "Negro" University that taught a western-based curriculum to become a "Black" one that promoted instruction and scholarship that examined the experiences of people of African descent. Protests later erupted in other historically Black institutions across the nation, including North Carolina's public universities, Fayetteville State, North Carolina Agricultural and Technical State University, North Carolina Central, and the privately owned Bennett College and Johnson C. Smith University.[43]

African American students at white colleges demanded a more culturally relevant education and the elimination of white supremacist educational theories and practices. In 1968 and 1969, Black student protests erupted on several elite institutions of higher learning across the nation. In May 1968, student activists at Northwestern and Yale Universities held protests and conferences to advocate for establishing Black Studies programs and departments. These activists focused on changing the educational paradigm on campus and, in the 1969 Columbia University protest, they worked to protect the surrounding African American neighborhood from erasure from university expansion.[44]

After negotiations with the administration at San Francisco State University to form a Black Student Union failed in 1969, African American student activists staged a strike that drew support from most of the faculty and students. This conflict, which included an armed takeover of an administration building, gained national attention as the strike lasted almost a year. After the removal of the chancellor, the activists agreed to end the strike, and the first official Black Studies Program began. Professor Nathan Hare became the director of the new program.[45]

After the success of the protests across the nation and the strike at San Francisco State, Black student activism spread like the sit-ins of the early 1960s. Students from across the nation staged protests, which ranged from nonviolent marches and boycotts to armed takeovers of administration buildings in what scholar Ibram X. Kendi described as the "Black Campus Movement."[46] The protests of students during the civil rights years encompassed what scholars describe as a broader Black student movement. However, student campus activism from 1965 to 1972 to reform the curricula and educational practices of the nation's universities and colleges is a distinct movement.[47]

Reluctant school administrators feared the negative publicity and legal consequences if they refused to acknowledge the protesters' concerns. They attempted to meet some of their students' demands by establishing Black Studies programs. Consequently, from 1968 to 1971, some 160 new Black Studies programs emerged during this early period.[48] Historian Peniel Joseph argued that "Black Studies programs remain one of the enduring and outstanding legacies of the Black Power Movement."[49]

As African American students engaged in protests in the elite private universities and flagship public universities of the East, Midwest, and West, the southern Black campus movement emerged where universities openly maintained segregationist traditions.[50] Only a few short years before, during the 1950s and early 1960s, sometimes violent reactions occurred at some of these former all-white universities by anti-integrationists. On the other hand, most student civil rights activists attended historically Black colleges and universities in the South. Within this context, several of the protesters in the UNC Charlotte protest engaged in activism before enrolling at UNC Charlotte. As a teenager, Benjamin Chavis Jr., the son of educators, worked to integrate the public library in Wilmington, North Carolina. He also served as a youth coordinator for the civil rights organization, the Southern Christian Leadership Conference as a student at St. Augustine University in Raleigh, North Carolina, before he transferred to UNC Charlotte.[51]

Thomas James (T. J.) Reddy's family promoted education and activism. A fearless child, at nine, he challenged Savannah's segregated bus system by sitting in the front of the bus and refusing to move. In retaliation for his action, the Ku Klux Klan marched down his street. "Everybody was running, but I just stood there." He later moved to New York to live with relatives, where he became exposed to people from different cultures and found a passion for art, poetry, and literature. Growing up in a household where his grandmother supported the local civil rights boycotts led by Savannah activist Wesley Wallace (W. W.) Law, Reddy later became frustrated at Johnson C. Smith University because of the administration's strict disciplinary procedures governing student behavior.

When he engaged in a rally to protest the dismissal of a fellow student who broke a curfew rule, he remained at the event even when the administration threatened to expel the protesters if they did not disburse. After a philosophy professor advised him to leave Johnson C. Smith for his protection, he started working at Charlotte Urban Ministries, where he met Bonnie Cone.[52] In 1965, Cone became Reddy's ally and asked him to enroll in UNC Charlotte. The history major later met fellow UNC Charlotte student, Benjamin Chavis Jr., who invited him to a meeting to establish a Black Student Union.[53]

Even if they didn't openly adopt Cone's former students' self-proclaimed title "Miss Bonnie's Boys," some of UNC Charlotte's African American students could claim membership in that select group. Humphrey Cummings, one of Maxwell's first Black Studies students, decided to enroll in UNC Charlotte in 1968 because Cone wrote him a warm and inviting letter encouraging him to attend. Cummings, now a prominent attorney in Charlotte, explained, "She made me feel as if they (UNC Charlotte) wanted me."[54] In 1969, David Sanders, another early BSP student, became one of the first African Americans to be named a Bonnie Cone Scholar, one of the most prestigious scholarships granted by the university. Sanders, now a retired human relations executive, formed a close relationship with Cone, who had an open door with students. He even worked with her when she created UNC Charlotte's alma mater song. Sanders often stopped by Cone's office to share his experiences, whether in class or his dorm, as one of the few African American students living in UNC Charlotte's new dorm.[55]

As Maxwell established the Black Studies Program, she did so with the knowledge that she had a powerful advocate in the administration who shrewdly realized that a vibrant Black Studies curricula could attract students to the school. Cone now had help in her mission to recruit Black students. When the Black campus movement reached North Carolina in 1968 and 1969, student protests erupted at universities and colleges across the state, ranging from public institutions, such as the Universities of North Carolina at Greensboro and Chapel Hill, to private universities like Duke. Protesting at some of these predominantly white universities in the South, student protesters faced potentially violent reactions by angry pro-segregationist students, faculty, administrators, and alumni as they challenged their respective universities to establish Black Studies programs and dismantle racism.[56]

UNC Charlotte's student protesters followed in the activist traditions set by earlier protests, but they also reacted to the injustice and violence occurring outside their campus. On February 8, 1968, South Carolina State Highway Patrol Officers randomly fired into a crowd of anti–Vietnam War protesters at

South Carolina State College in Orangeburg, South Carolina, murdering three African American students. This event and the lack of accountability by law enforcement officers saddened and enraged Black college students across the nation. Paring this event with the April 4, 1968, assassination of Martin Luther King Jr., some African American students grew even more disillusioned with the progress of civil rights and the perceived ineffectiveness of nonviolence. Some student protesters embraced aspects of Black Nationalism and called for the development of African American centered courses and additional Black faculty.[57]

One such protest occurred at UNC Charlotte. On February 7, 1969, Chavis Jr., North Carolina Central University transfer Paul Hemphill, Reddy, and a small cadre of African American students boldly lowered the United States flag. They replaced it and raised the red, black, and green Black Liberation flag in a demonstration to commemorate the anniversary of the date of the Orangeburg shooting. Charlotte civil rights activist, Reginald Hawkins, spoke at the event. UNC Charlotte's administration promptly took down the Black Liberation flag and put the US flag back up. Chavis Jr. and the other African American students later released a statement. "We the Black students at UNC-Charlotte, request the immediate replacement of the Black Flag on the campus flagpole at half-mast to continue the mourning of the three African American students who lost their lives in Orangeburg, SC last year."[58] The flag protest represented a turning point for these students who were encouraged by a new wave of Black Nationalist activism that called for Blacks to establish independent institutions and promote racial pride. After UNC Charlotte's administration refused their request, the students continued their protests by calling for the university to approve a Black Student Union (BSU) organization so that, according to its constitution, "it could express the will of Black people on campus and the African American community as well."[59]

On February 26, 1969, after the student legislature failed to recognize and approve the Black Student Union, some twenty students, including Chavis Jr., who would eventually become a nationally known activist and NAACP chairperson, presented Bonnie Cone with a ten-point list of demands. The first demand stated, "We demand an education that relates to the Black student to his true history where the educational requirements are changed to include a Black Studies Program to be controlled by Black students and staffed by Black faculty." Adapted from the Black Panthers' Ten-Point Plan, the students' remaining nine points included the following: increasing the African American student population to coincide with the percentage of African Americans in the state, hiring Black faculty, salary raises for Black employees, a pass-fail grading system for African American students, and denouncing Governor Walter "Bob" Scott's police-state policies.[60] Reddy recalled that he and his fellow activists posted fliers and wrote in chalk on campus structures to the campus officials' dismay. Cone, ever the empathic negotiator and adept politician, reiterated to the activists that she could not personally address their concerns and forwarded their demands to William Hugh McEniry, vice chancellor of student affairs.[61]

After failed negotiations led to the passage of the students' March 3rd deadline with no results, some one-hundred student protesters marched to the administration building. Chavis Jr. described the protest in terms of forced lock-in: "We literally chained the chancellor and the vice chancellor in the building with us. We chained ourselves in the building. We didn't lock them out; we locked ourselves in the building with them." Another student protester, Ronald Caldwell, had a different recollection: "So, we went to the administration building, and we took the demands to Dr. Cone. She welcomed us there. And I remember, 'whatever you want, we'll help you.' So, at no time was there a lock-in or lockout. It didn't happen."[62] Despite the diverging memories about the nature of the meeting, protesters attribute Bonnie Cone for defusing the heightened situation. She offered her support to the students. Chavis Jr. contended that the fruitful meeting let the administration know that "there were some heated words, but they all were toward the end of improving the academic opportunities for all students, and to try and get more African American students on campus. We wanted UNC Charlotte to be a real university in the truest sense of academic pursuit, freedom of speech, and a call for justice in the community."[63] With police snipers ready to attack, T. J. Reddy recalled Cone's diplomatic and tactful manner. Amid the chaos, she smiled and greeted the protesters, "Isn't it a pleasant day today."[64]

On March 5, 1969, only a few short days after the African American students presented their demands to the administration, student activists brought James Farmer, then assistant secretary of the Department of Health, Education, and Welfare and the former head of the Congress of Racial Equality (CORE) to speak on campus. Endorsing the Black students' push for a BSU, Farmer asked the overcrowded room, "If We Are Not for Ourselves, Who Will Be for Us?" In addition to the demand for Black Studies, these students wanted the BSU to serve as an advocacy organization to fight racism. Drawn from the student protesters' Ten-Point List, the BSU demanded the hiring of additional Black faculty and increased recruitment efforts of African American students. The BSU called for a more transparent and fair grading system and an end to alleged racist and stereotypical teaching practices when allegations arose that a biology teacher told students that Blacks were biologically inferior.[65]

As a relatively new university, UNC Charlotte was in a constant state of evolution. Nevertheless, the call for the establishment of Black Studies was unique. Predominantly white universities, including UNC Charlotte, already offered some courses relating to the African American experience in their respective departments in the humanities and social sciences. If the concept of an interdisciplinary program and later field of studies based on the experiences and culture of people of African descent seemed novel, the classic works of such prominent scholars as W.E.B. Du Bois and Carter G. Woodson lay at its foundation. By providing a centralized curriculum, Black Studies programs enabled students to study the works of both prominent and obscure scholars and to conduct research relevant to the African American experience.[66]

Further negotiations with Chavis Jr., Reddy, and other student protesters led to the proposal of the first Black Studies–themed course, "Black African Culture," in the Division of Humanities. By April of 1969, this small group of protesters joined UNC Charlotte's new Black Studies Committee (BSC) to develop a Black Studies Program. The committee now included four administrators, Cone, Mathis, McEniry, and Paul Miller, the director of the Urban Studies Program, five department chairs from the Division of Humanities, two faculty members, seven African American students, including Chavis Jr. and Reddy, and three white students. The university first appointed Division (later College) of Humanities dean William Mathis as its first chairperson.[67]

Ann Carver, a newly hired English professor with a PhD from Emory University in Atlanta, Georgia, later became chair of the BSC. After graduation and her husband's death in a car accident, Carver decided to stay in Atlanta and applied for a job at Morehouse College, a historically African American male-only institution. As a young white woman who grew up in the mountains of western North Carolina, Carver realized that she knew little about African American literature and engaged in self-study to prepare herself to teach. Carver enjoyed working at Morehouse, but the young professor wanted to do more to eliminate racism by encouraging more understanding among whites. She then started applying for jobs at other universities and colleges. After being interviewed by English Department chair Robert Wallace, Dean William Mathis, and Chancellor Colvard, UNC Charlotte hired Carver. Although her department chair and the English search committee knew that she was white, when Carver joined her first full university-wide faculty meeting, they reacted with shock to learn that the new professor from Morehouse was a young white woman. In addition to chairing the Black

Studies Committee, Carver became a dedicated supporter of Black Studies and friend and confidant to Bertha Maxwell.[68]

When David Sanders arrived at UNC Charlotte in the fall of 1969, the administration was still reacting to the protest by African American students that past spring. Some Black students feared rumors that the administration had implemented a rule that restricted African American students, forcing them to only walk in groups of three or less. When Sanders encountered Maxwell walking across the campus a year later in 1970, he was excited to learn that there was another Black professor on campus in addition to math professor Julian Pyles. After a few cordial pleasantries, he decided to test Maxwell by boldly asking her, "So what are you going to do for us?" She responded by telling him to, "Wait and see!" Maxwell soon learned that her responsibilities would always go beyond those of a traditional academic. Despite Maxwell's previous service commitments, she agreed to serve as a member of the Black Studies Committee. If being a "first" meant that she received an overabundance of committee service requests, it also enabled her to join a historic new Black Studies Committee where she could help African American students and gain more insight into the inner workings of the university administration.[69]

Even though student activists served on the university's newly formed Black Studies Committee, most, if not all, of the administrative and faculty members had little familiarity with Black Studies. Nevertheless, they were responsible for approving the program's curriculum. So, first, the committee researched published articles and books on Black Studies and reviewed programs and curricula from other universities and colleges. The committee then had to select a program director who could balance the formation of a new program that met the demands of the student protesters for more inclusive courses and meet university curricula standards maintained by a sometimes-skeptical group of professors and administrators.[70]

After further negotiations on November 26, 1969, UNC Charlotte's administration and student legislature finally approved the Black Student Union as an official student organization and Paul Hemphill became its first president. Chancellor Colvard responded by relating, "The university had been working toward furnishing appropriate Black Studies courses for some time but conveyed that the curriculum is the responsibility of the faculty."[71] UNC Charlotte's student protest, while tense at some points, did not result in violent interactions. Fortified by their victory, Hemphill and the BSU defied administrative restrictions to hold a Martin Luther King Jr. Day celebration and continued to work for the creation of a Black Studies program. Bonnie Cone's reputation as an advocate for students and the protester's willingness to work with Cone to find consensus eventually led to the formation of the Black Studies Committee and the creation of the Black Studies Program.[72]

After reviewing information, the committee's next step involved hiring a chairperson or director for the program who could meet students' demands and contend with a sometimes recalcitrant faculty and administration. Finally, in 1971, after a failed search where most male candidates either declined the position or were rejected due to apprehension concerning their activist reputations, the Black Studies Committee decided to look inward and asked Maxwell to direct the program. If the administration possibly considered her less threatening because of her public school educator's background, CMS superintendent William Self warned the committee, "If you want Black Studies, then hire her. If you don't want Black Studies, then you better not hire her because she's going to get it!" Self, who befriended Maxwell during her years as a principal in CMS, made it clear that if the university planned to hire a director with the expectation of failure or to just serve as an ineffectual place holder, Maxwell, known for her resolve and tenacity, was not the right choice.[73] In a 1971 letter to William Hugh McEniry, Black Studies Committee chair Ann Carver recommended that Maxwell be hired for the director's position and be granted academic tenure and leave time for her to pursue further graduate study. Due to her unique position as an administrator, Maxwell did not have to subscribe to the standard requirements for promotion to tenure, receiving it based upon her prior administrative experience. First hired as an assistant professor in the College of Human Development and Learning, she made the significant climb from assistant professor to the administrative director of a program and later an endowed chair position.[74]

What Is Black Studies?

As the first Black administrator at the university, Maxwell had the daunting task of designing an innovative, interdisciplinary program of study based upon themes that her colleagues may have questioned. Well-informed of current educational concepts and experienced in administration, Maxwell now had to immerse herself into the scholarly and theoretical literature of Black Studies to develop a sound curriculum of culturally relevant courses.[75] In a meeting with some of the BSU members, Bonnie Cone told them that she wanted them to work with a new faculty member who could address their demands, Bertha Maxwell. A skeptical group, they promised to meet with her. While she only agreed to serve as the director based upon student approval, some were apprehensive. Maxwell explained, "They thought I was a handkerchief head n*****, but I told them that I have something that you all don't have. I have the skills to run this program."[76] Explaining Maxwell's incendiary phrase, of the handkerchief, as a reference to the stereotype of the fearful, accommodating slave, the students thought that the former school principal possessed the views of some African American civil rights supporters who disagreed with the tenets of the Black Power movement including its disavowal of nonviolence. As supporters of educational desegregation, some of these activists voiced their concerns about the establishment of Black Studies programs and courses at white universities. They claimed that these programs marginalized African American students even further by creating alternative racially segregated spaces, separating Black and white students.[77]

These students soon learned that behind the conservative, professional demeanor of their new director, lay the soul of an activist who had no problem confronting anyone from parents to school superintendents, without pretentiousness or concern for reprisal, to increase the educational opportunities of Black children. They also underestimated Maxwell's ability to maneuver and negotiate in white settings and openly promote her agenda.[78] Despite the students' misguided perceptions, she created an academically sound program where she incorporated the tenets of Black Power into a feasible curriculum that taught African American students academic subjects while helping them to become self-aware Black students. In her interpretation, this was the practical application or praxis of Black Power.[79]

Maxwell drew from her experience as an educational administrator and professor to develop the structural foundation of the program. Hired to create a new curriculum, she came directly from an environment of creativity where her colleagues in the College of Human Development and Learning looked at new and innovative ways to improve the educational experiences of children. Maxwell's HDL colleague, Frank Parker, explained that these nontraditional academics also espoused theories where students engaged in intellectual exploration, contesting truths and facts, and designed curricula that explored self-identity.[80]

Maxwell then merged this structural foundation with the tenets and theories of Black Cultural Nationalism, such as Maulana Karenga's promotion of Kawaida philosophy. This theory suggested that persons of African descent must first develop a positive self-identity as an African American person living in an oppressive and demoralizing environment. Then they can work toward dismantling oppressive structures. Soon after her appointment, Maxwell took a group of her students to visit Vincent Harding, the director of the Institute of the Black World (IBW). Located on the campus of Atlanta University, in

Atlanta, Georgia, the IBW was an early research center for African-centered intellectual thought and Black Studies.[81]

After arriving and learning that Harding would not see Maxwell and her group of students until the next day, she was shocked when he informed her that she would have to pay a $2,000 fee. Maxwell remembered Harding said, "Your first lesson is that when you represent white institutions, you have to pay." Shocked, she responded, "I said, that's good, but I'm representing Black people. These young Black students that you see here, that's who I'm representing. I just happen to be on a historically white campus, and their budget and their thing isn't any better off, and they're not getting but so much." Maxwell then made herself clear: "So, I want you to know, no, I'm not going to pay you two thousand dollars for whatever it is that you think you're going to tell me. But I came to interact with you to get some information so that I can help these people develop what it is that they're trying to get to do."[82]

Surprised by her frankness, Harding waived his fee, and eventually, the two formed a friendship. Maxwell later crafted her own sabbatical traveling on the weekends to Atlanta to the IBW, where she studied African American history and philosophy.[83] As Black Studies scholar, Perry Hall, explained in his work, *In the Vineyard: Working in Africana Studies,* the purpose of Black Studies included the following: the dissemination of knowledge relating to the experiences of persons of African descent, the promotion of cultural nationalism; and as promoters of social change. Maxwell established a Black Studies Program that incorporated all those themes.[84]

Black Studies Curriculum Development and "The Block"

Working in conjunction with the Black Studies Committee, in 1971, Maxwell helped to design the university's first official Black Studies course, the "Black Experience."[85] When she could not find an experienced academic, she decided to reach out to African American professionals in Charlotte. She proceeded to ask James Ross and Jim Polk, co-owner of one of Charlotte's first sensitivity training consulting firms, to co-teach the course with her. Prominent city leaders, Ross, Polk, and CMS administrator James Burch previously worked to improve relations between the Charlotte Mecklenburg Police Department and African American communities and to desegregate Charlotte's businesses.[86] The Black Experience course called for students to engage in sensitivity training and laid the groundwork for Maxwell's overall educational philosophy. David Sanders, recalled, "that one of the exercises involved self-identifying and explaining why they called themselves, "Black," or "African American," or

"Negro," to gain an understanding of what these terms meant within their own lives." T. J. Reddy, another student in the course, remembered that Maxwell pushed students to think beyond protest, which was a crucial first step. She now wanted to impart "the necessity of teaching African American students how to use education to increase their intellectual abilities, but also to learn how to thrive as a Black person."[87] As the nation's schools remained engulfed in the desegregation process, several of UNC Charlotte's Black students participated as the first Blacks to desegregate the public schools in their hometowns or came from racially segregated environments. Cognizant of the positive and negative impact of school desegregation, Maxwell created this innovative and self-reflective curriculum to help students succeed academically in a predominantly white institution.[88]

Black Studies directors and scholars debated whether their programs should promote a nationalist theme or encourage integration. Maxwell refused to see a division between the two and incorporated both philosophies into the Black Studies curriculum. When she set out to design the curriculum, she included courses that reflected the Black experience, such as African American history and literature courses.[89] Maxwell wanted to develop a self-reflexive curriculum that expanded traditional academic content to help students form positive self-identities as African American students in potentially unsupportive environments. She knew that since this program arose from the protests of students, she had to respect and address their concerns. In 1971, she developed a group or Block of courses that explored the following themes: *Awareness,* which meant becoming conscious of the factors which shape individual and racial sensibilities; *Catharsis,* the removal of barriers that prevent ideas and feelings from being brought to the level of reflection, *Black Functioning,* applying their knowledge to working in the community, and *Liberation.* The Black Studies Block consisted of four components. Phase 1: *Who Am I?* Phase 2: *Why Am I Here?* Phase 3: *Where Did I Come From?* and Phase 4: *Where Do I Go from Here?*[90]

One of the most crucial aspects of the emerging Black Arts Movement, which represented the artistic dimension of the Black Power movement, was the development of the concept of a "Black aesthetic." First explained by theater scholar and poet Larry Neal in his groundbreaking 1968 article in *The Drama Review,* this new "Black aesthetic" called for visual and performing artists and writers to create pieces that focused on the Black experience. These artists no longer emulated white artists or writers or desired that their work be evaluated by them. Instead of producing art for whites, they created works for their communities. In 1971, Maxwell wanted to offer a course titled the "Black Aesthetic," which would focus on the writings, artistic works, and dance performances of artists of African descent, including artists of the Black Power movement.[91]

To offer a new course in the BSP, Maxwell had to receive administrative approval. After submitting the proposal to Dean William Mathis, Maxwell recalled that he responded by stating, "there was no such thing as a "Black aesthetic!" So, she decided to meet with Mathis, BSP faculty Ann Carver, Mary Harper, Beverly Ford, and student Humphrey Cummings to explain the origin and meaning of the "Black aesthetic," and discuss the course's content. After the dean still refused to grant approval, she realized that she had to adopt alternative tactics. Mathis often had lunch meetings with faculty, and Maxwell stopped attending these occasions because she felt that he sometimes ignored her responses. After relying on Beverly Ford's informal psychological assessment that the dean found Maxwell to be daunting, yet still sought her friendship, Maxwell then decided to make more of a conciliatory effort. She invited Mathis to lunch and shared how much the students needed the course. As director of a Black Studies program on a predominantly white campus, Maxwell faced the daily challenges of determining when to negotiate or cooperate with faculty and administrators or when to protest. In this case, she realized that the dean could be persuaded to accept change. Mathis later approved the course.[92]

In 1971, Mary Harper and Ann Carver co-taught an introduction to Black American Literature course that became deeply divided by race. Carver and Harper applied some of the teaching methods that they learned as Black Studies instructors, where they met with students for two weekends in Carver's apartment to have intense workshops. In these meetings, they discussed racism, stereotypes and worked to help students establish new positive perceptions of each other. After those sessions, the class ran more smoothly. These encounter sessions eventually led Maxwell to work with Harper and Carver to develop a course on Human Relations, which later morphed into a three-day workshop. Carver and Harper's class reflected the willingness of some faculty to do nontraditional things as they helped to create the character of a new university.[93]

In the Human Relations Laboratory workshop, students learned about the racial climate on campus and engaged in personal development, led by BSP faculty and community leaders, including desegregation expert, assistant director of public instruction for the State of North Carolina Dudley Flood.[94] During these workshops, Flood, Maxwell, Carver, Ford, and other professors had students form "encounter" groups where they taught a concept called "Black mindfulness," which promoted intellectual and cultural growth and community service. Former student Dorothy Dae recalled in a 2004 interview,

"Talk about some great history now. She was it. The Black Studies Department and through that department, we got more African American representation. We got Mary Harper, Bev Ford." In retrospect, she affirmed, "But it started with Bertha. Bertha, Bertha would have encounter sessions. And all the Black kids on campus would go to those encounter sessions."[95] Attendance was mandatory for BSP students at these workshops. After students led the charge for Black Studies, Maxwell incorporated theoretical concepts into the BSP curriculum.[96]

As the women's movement called for the nation to acknowledge gender discrimination and to remedy it, Maxwell exemplified African American women who engaged in feminist practices but did not necessarily identify with the perception and goals of the feminist movement. For some other Black women, interlocking oppressions of race and gender often prevented them from aligning with white feminists who sometimes dismissed or overlooked their own acts of racism and class discrimination. On the other hand, some African American men demanded racial solidarity at the expense of African American women. Nevertheless, during the 1970s, Maxwell often used her platform as director to advocate for Black women's rights. In 1971, she participated in a lecture series where she presented two lectures entitled, "The Role of the Black Woman in Modern Society," and "Paradox Without a Promise." Drawing on some of the foundational tenets of the Black Studies curriculum, she told the audience that Black women in the future would base their cultural foundations on African indigenous cultures. However, she told the audience that they must first undergo a four-step process based on the BSP Block that included self-awareness, catharsis, giving back to the Black community, and self-liberation.[97]

In 1972, the Black Studies Program offered the first year of the new Block curriculum, including the Human Relations Workshops and the Black Aesthetic course.[98] Maxwell's path-breaking model of incorporating components of self-identity development within her curriculum parallels a growing movement among psychologists and scholars of the Black experience, such as William Cross Jr. He and other scholars coined this process "Nigrescence." This theory describes the process of developing a racial identity as a Black person. Maxwell's mission to help her students formulate positive self-identities as African Americans did not emerge from the perception that they had low self-esteem. Maxwell created the Block to help promote self-awareness in her students to help them overcome negative factors ranging from isolation to racism or develop, as scholars Kristine S. Lewis and Stephanie C. McKissic called, "critical resistant navigational skills." She wanted the Block to serve as a unifying force helping African American students develop a sense of belonging and connection with the university.[99] In the early years of the program, Maxwell formalized the welcoming process for Black students by establishing a freshmen orientation program and booklet for incoming students. In this booklet, she introduced the program, talked about African American organizations, including the Black Student Union, fraternal organizations, and cultural groups such as the student gospel choir, *Children of the Son.*

Supporting Her Vision: Maxwell and the Faculty and Staff

Since Maxwell became director and strove to expand the program, she knew that an innovative curriculum would be ineffectual without qualified faculty. As a program, Maxwell worked with departments to form faculty affiliate partnerships, where faculty members taught courses in both their home departments and in the BSP. Former Black Studies Committee chairperson and English assistant professor Ann Carver taught in the BSP and helped to promote and explain the concept of Black Studies to her colleagues who were unfamiliar with the field. Maxwell even claimed that some of the administrators asked her not to bring Carver to meetings because she sometimes pushed them to address their racism or privilege. A staunch advocate for racial justice before working in Black Studies, in 1969, Carver wrote a letter to Senator Ted Kennedy to decry the murder of Black Panther activists by police where she posed, "Whether or not this is a calculated plan to annihilate the members of the Party, I do not know." She expressed her fears of fascism when she argued, "I do know that the killing (in "self-defense") of large numbers of one group of people, and the justification of such killing simply by attaching the group's label to the murdered individuals-I know this is too reminiscent of Nazi Germany's mass murder of the Jews to be ignored." [100]

Other core faculty hired during this period included: Mary Harper, an assistant professor in English; Herman Thomas, a local minister and professor from Religious Studies, who later became assistant director; Beverly Ford, an instructor from the Psychology Department who played an integral role as a confidant and adviser to Maxwell by applying her counseling experience to help Maxwell navigate the pitfalls of academia; David Frye, a white minister of a local Presbyterian church with a predominantly African American congregation who taught sociology classes, and Geraldine Dillard, a UNC Charlotte alumna, who had the responsibility of managing the Block program.[101]

In 1973, Maxwell recruited her friend, Roberta Duff, to manage the office as an administrative assistant. Duff, a former assistant to CMS Area superintendent James Burch, knew Maxwell when she was a principal. Familiar with some of the issues that Maxwell faced at Albemarle Elementary, Duff would alert her when an angry white parent came to Burch's office to complain about the "Black" principal. When Burch left his position, Duff asked Maxwell if there were any available positions at UNC Charlotte. When Maxwell's secretary resigned, she asked Duff to join her. Knowing Duff was used to working in a very formal setting, Maxwell warned her that it was not a traditional office setting when Duff first arrived at UNC Charlotte. Even though Duff was unfamiliar with the concept of Black Studies, she and Maxwell had the same mission to provide opportunities for African American students that they did not receive themselves. Duff was key in making the BSP office, housed in the Rowe Arts Building, a "home away from home" for the students. In this office, which later moved to the Macy building in the late 1970s, students could use Duff's typewriter, watch soap operas on the office TV, and eat their lunch. Years before the advent of relatable student counseling and multicultural support programs, Duff and Maxwell's academic oasis melded perfectly with the core mission of Black Studies to go beyond academics to help students thrive.[102] Maxwell considered her students like family. She asserted, "You reprimand and punish family, but you don't abandon family."[103]

The BSP office served as an informal Black cultural center. James B. Stewart in his book chapter, "Bridging Time, Space, and Technology: Challenges Confronting Black Cultural Centers in the 21st Century," claimed "Black Cultural Centers, particularly during the early years, functioned as a bulwark against the forces creating the type of identity crisis that W.E.B. Du Bois described in his pioneering work, *The Souls of Black Folk*." Although some professors and departments looked at the informality of the BSP office with disdain, Maxwell and Duff worked together to provide a safe and comfortable space for African American students.[104]

As Duff and several of Maxwell's core faculty, such as Ann Carver, played essential roles in the development of the program, Assistant Director Herman Thomas, who came in 1973, played an instrumental role as an adviser and confidant to Maxwell and as a supporter of her mission. A Greensboro, NC native, Thomas engaged in civil rights activism as a college student when he participated in the sit-in movement. Thomas continued his activism as one of the first Black students to receive a Master of Theology degree from the Divinity School at Duke University in 1969. As the former director of the Black Studies Program at Springfield College, in Springfield, Massachusetts, he joined Maxwell to help her develop the program and to be closer to home.[105]

The BSP may have been a nontraditional academic program; however, it did reflect the core philosophies of the field of Black Studies. In addition to academics, it offered emotional support for students as well. Beverly Odom Ford, a former high school teacher and counselor, who taught in the Block and the Psychology Department, had the responsibility of advising and counseling students. While support is a foundational proponent of Black Studies, this concept of expanding teachers' roles beyond the classroom walls also emanated from Maxwell's core educational philosophies as an educator in the era of segregation and during desegregation.[106]

Despite the support of some of her colleagues, Maxwell still faced the lack of funding to hire tenure-track faculty or lecturers with graduate degrees. There was also a shortage of available professors with terminal degrees. In these early years, Black Studies programs either drew academic talent from historically Black universities or sought to hire recent graduates from white institutions. In demand, many of these scholars either preferred to remain at their historically Black schools or wished to work at a more established university. During this early period, some Black Studies programs received criticism from university administrators for hiring nontraditional inexperienced instructors with limited academic credentials.[107]

In addition to designing the curriculum, Maxwell had to ask faculty from other departments to give course seats or cross-list their courses so that BSP students could take their courses. This process could be sensitive because department chairs did not have to participate. In these instances, one can reflect upon Maxwell's confident leadership style. A charismatic personality, she was able to form coalitions with her fellow administrators to help the program, yet she made sure that the nationalist curriculum remained. She also asked departments that if they did not offer any relevant courses, to develop some and hire African American instructors. Justin Uchenger, a faculty member from Barber-Scotia College in Concord, NC, taught African history before the establishment of the program.[108]

Maxwell, Students, and "the Block"

In the early years of the program, Maxwell formalized the welcoming process for African American students by establishing a freshmen orientation program and developing a booklet for incoming students. In this publication, she described the program, talked about Black organizations, including the Black Student Union, fraternal organizations, and cultural groups such as the student gospel choir, Children of the Son.[109] Sheryl Westmoreland Smith, the first student to graduate with a BA in English and a concentration in Afro-American Studies in 1977, claimed that when she entered as a freshman as one of sixty-three African American students in 1973, "Bertha Maxwell, Herman Thomas, and Ann Carver met us at registration and encouraged us to enroll in the Freshman Block. They assured us that they would take care of us. There was strength in numbers."[110]

While Maxwell was an experienced administrator, she did not subscribe to the status boundaries so prevalent in academia. When a student had a good idea or exhibited leadership abilities, she welcomed it. As a BSP student assistant, David Sanders helped write drafts for descriptions for block courses. When he asked Maxwell why UNC Charlotte didn't have an African American counselor and recommended that she hire Beverly Ford, his former high school counselor, she then persuaded the administration to hire Ford who earned a bachelor's degree in psychology from Talladega College in Alabama. She later received a Master's in Counseling Education from UNC Charlotte. Sanders later had administrative duties and taught in the program when he was completing his master's degree at UNC Charlotte.[111]

Although African Americans made up a small percentage of the students at UNC Charlotte, those enrolled in the Block took most of their courses together. In this way, the Black Studies Program helped students build support networks to combat the feelings of isolation sometimes experienced by Blacks in predominantly white institutions. When moving into the dorm at UNC Charlotte as a freshman, Winnie McNeely Bennett remembered her feelings of unease, "All I saw to the left of me, all I saw to the right of me, were white people." Concerned about their reactions, McNeely Bennett thought, "What have I gotten myself into?" When she heard laughter down the hall, she happily discovered that Brenda Stedman, another African American student, lived on her floor. After discovering that her new friend was from the small community of East Bend, North Carolina, Winnie decided to call her "East Bend," and it remained her nickname for many years. Black students who lived on campus at UNC Charlotte sometimes experienced racism before even entering the classroom. In the dorms, some white parents demanded transfers for their children after learning that they would have an African American roommate. Turning this indignity into a positive, they now had the privilege of having private rooms.[112]

As other universities provided remedial courses to help underprepared students adjust to the rigors of college curricula, the Block's academically intensive course load became one of the most rigorous at the university. It only offered student-led tutoring for incoming first-year students. One of the Block's main objectives involved helping to create a sense of personal self-confidence and awareness among students. The Block stressed more than just guidance on how to survive college; it emphasized how to lead. It also reinforced the concept that Black students belonged at UNC Charlotte and that the university was a safe space for learning. Terry Smith, one of the first students to enroll in the Block in 1972, remembered how taking courses in the Block helped him to become more self-confident and self-aware. Smith recalled how his teachers and Maxwell helped to reinforce the concepts of the Block in their interactions with students. "She gave me a boost of self-confidence to embrace my talent." Smith argued that Maxwell "reminded him of his grandmother, whom he lived with in high school," because of her support and encouragement.[113]

Maxwell supported her students, but she had no problem chastising them if necessary. When Elaine Nichols threatened to quit school in anger, Maxwell responded by telling the honor student to go ahead, then helping Nichols after she had calmed down! Nichols, now a prominent curator at the Smithsonian, not only remained at UNC Charlotte but became a student leader at the university.[114] The Black Studies Program offered courses and programs that focused on the African American experience, but white students, such as Tony Watson, were encouraged to participate. He told a reporter in a 1974 *Charlotte Observer* article, "I was attracted because of the personal tutoring available in the program. I'm majoring in psychology, so I think that this will be helpful to see the Black person's point of view."[115]

When L. Diane Bennett decided to attend UNC Charlotte, it was not because of the university. She knew little about the school, but as the daughter of a veteran, she won a coveted scholarship, and her godfather, a prominent minister in Charlotte, told her, "God would bless her if she went to school in the city." Brought up in a strict religious environment, Bennett's immediate family encouraged her academic pursuits, but she always felt that she was an "outlier." When she first arrived in the gym to register for her classes, she soon saw Maxwell and Herman Thomas beckoning her over to their table, where they suggested she enroll in "the Block's" core courses. The Block helped students to form connections and friendships based on shared interests. She and her fellow students soon "became a family" as they bonded. As the thirty entering students created a community, Maxwell encouraged them to try new things, such as joining the orchestra or research project, to avoid isolation. For Bennett, the very image of Maxwell was awakening. She explained, "To really see firsthand, a strong African American woman thrive in a predominantly white and predominantly male environment was something. She was a bad somebody."[116]

As the director of a program in a new field of study, Maxwell knew that her students would face criticism. She realized that the program had to be academically rigorous, so she implemented an honors thesis program for her students applying the tenets of Black Studies to their majors. She knew that one of the best ways to ensure that her students survived the isolation and sometimes racism they encountered as African American students would be to help them to develop confidence. "Dr. Maxwell told us that we had to sit in the front of the classroom." Westmoreland Smith also remembered that they learned to speak up in class and always be prepared or face the consequences of their Block teachers."[117]

By creating a welcoming place for African American students, Maxwell helped to ease some of their transition from segregated high schools to a de-segregated university by helping them to build a community. As Maxwell en-deavored to seek approval for the program and implement the BSP curricula, she often relied on her ability to be a charismatic advocate for the program, likable but also steadfast in securing what she needed. When others did not succumb to her dynamic personality, Maxwell had no problem resorting to confrontation if necessary. "She demanded respect. I think they were a little scared of her." Phaedra Berry-Holley, a former student, claimed.[118]

Students knew that Maxwell would serve as an advocate. L. Diane Bennett recalled one instance when Maxwell stood on a table to express her concerns when the administration seemed reluctant to appoint Black students to student arbitration meetings. Bennett remembered, "I look around, and she is standing on the conference table, shouting, "Damn it, I know what I am talking about! When an administrator told her, "'Don't get upset,' she replied, 'I'm not upset. You haven't seen me upset!'" The administrator then helped her down and promised to appoint African American students to the all-white committee.[119] Maxwell created a cocoon-like environment where Black students felt some of the same experiences as students who attended predominantly African Ameri-can institutions within a white environment. Students took core courses for the major, including methods courses, and presented a senior project.[120]

Following the practices of civil rights–era African American teachers who endorsed student activism through curriculum instruction, and as examples, Maxwell encouraged students to engage in activism without seeking permis-sion from the administration.[121] In 1971, Connie Tindall, a Wilmington NC student protest leader, called for a boycott of the city's public high schools. The protesters, located in Gregory Congregational Church, wanted to bring attention to some of the gross inequities affecting African American students in Wilmington's newly desegregated high schools. Unfortunately, their peace-ful protest soon evoked violence when the Rights of White People (ROWP), a white supremacist domestic terrorist group, started shooting at the church.

With little police response, boycott supporters formed an armed guard to protect the students. In the chaos, several nearby white-owned businesses became engulfed in flames, including Mike's Grocery Store. Two deaths resulted from the confrontations when the police shot Steve Mitchell, a reportedly unarmed student leader. In self-defense, protesters shot Harvey Cumber, an armed white person trying to enter the church.[122]

Although not a part of the original protest, as a prominent community organizer in Wilmington, Chavis Jr., along with nine other activists, received indictments for conspiracy and burning down Mike's Grocery. When several BSP students decided to go to Wilmington to protest and support Chavis Jr., Maxwell encouraged their activism. Westmoreland Smith exclaimed. "We felt like we were Angela Davis. You couldn't tell us we weren't activists!"[123] Collectively sentenced to 282 years in prison, the trial verdicts of the now Wilmington Ten garnered national attention as the trial spurred investigations that revealed widespread examples of prosecutorial misconduct. Pardoned after five years by North Carolina Governor Jim Hunt, a federal appellate court overturned the Wilmington Ten's verdicts in 1980.[124]

As a former educator and administrator in predominantly white public schools, Maxwell sometimes mediated racial disputes with white parents and African American teachers and protected Black students in crisis. Unlike chairs of traditional academic departments, as a modern-day race woman and as the director of the BSP, she knew that one of her core duties involved helping African American students thrive despite their circumstances. Directed by the Black Studies mandate to bring knowledge to the community, in 1972, Maxwell and Ann Carver secured a grant from the Department of Vocational Rehabilitation in Cooperation with the Department of Corrections in Charlotte for work-release inmates from the Charlotte Advancement Center to take classes at UNC Charlotte. A year after the 1971 Attica prison uprising in New York and during the rise of antibusing reactions, Maxwell and other early Black Studies directors looked to see how Black Studies courses could help empower African American people beyond the campus, whether it was within African American communities or in prisons. Maxwell wanted to use her position as director to equip incarcerated people with the knowledge to secure gainful employment or empower themselves intellectually.[125]

So, from Monday through Friday, a white bus would transport inmates from the Advancement Center to UNC's Charlotte's campus for classes. Refusing to differentiate between the inmates and more traditional students, the classes were open to any eligible work-release student. Maxwell enrolled most of the inmates in the Block program. Accounting major Larry Horne shared in a 1974 newspaper article written by UNC Charlotte Black Alumnus, James Cuthbertson, "At first, I thought that someone would look at me odd or strange, but I found out that people here at (UNCC) accept you for what you are. It's a phobia that you develop by being in prison." Maxwell wanted to share the vibrancy of the university experience by taking them to lectures and events on campus. Cuthbertson reported that Sociology major Greg Davis* (not BSP professor and minister Gregory Davis) shared that "the study release program is an opportunity for freedom. He likes going to UNCC so much that he hates to see the end of the day come."[126]

Classes ran mostly without incident, except for one student who stole textbooks and attempted to re-sell them to students. When Bertha reprimanded this student using a few expletives, he grabbed her by her shoulders, picked her up, placed her outside of the Black Studies office, and shut the door. Stunned, Roberta Duff remained in the office as she and Maxwell were screaming at him to open the door. He later let Maxwell back in the office, and she gained control of the situation.[127] After the student apologized and the incident passed, Maxwell did not remove him from the program. Later, the student sarcastically promised Maxwell that if he ever graduated, he would run down the street naked, carrying her on his back. She retorted that if he graduated, she would run naked down the street, carrying him on her back! Neither Maxwell nor this student followed up on their threats.[128]

After the student left the program, he later graduated from Central Piedmont Community College. In 1974, when UNC Charlotte's administration became aware that the university had allowed work-release inmates to take courses alongside students for over two years without prior administrative approval, they reacted with shock. When Vice Chancellor of Academic Affairs William Hugh McEniry voiced his frustration, Maxwell and Carver feigned ignorance, "Were we not supposed to do that?" Expecting a reprimand for inadvertently signing a contract that had the potential to expose the entire UNC system to liability, Maxwell and Carver were shocked to learn that McEniry would have approved the program. Carver explained that he just wanted them to inform him before they initiated any new projects and programs. Maxwell sarcastically explained, "If a Black Studies program does what it is supposed to do, you sometimes have to take a risk; you might end up in jail."[129]

Maxwell often encouraged Black students to engage in protest on campus. In 1974, when *The Sanskrit*, UNC Charlotte's literary magazine, published an essay with the offensive title, "F**king a N***** on a Saturday Night," which described raping a Black woman, African American students conducted a silent march in protest and burned several issues of the magazine. Westmoreland

Smith remembered, "When Black students learned that a writer for the magazine used the word n***** in an article, we had had too much encouragement from our mentors to let that ride. Teachers were not included. We met in the basement of one of the dorms. We could not let them think that it was OK to use that word." About eighty Black students, wearing black armbands, staged a silent march across campus from the Belk Tower, which at that time was the center of campus, to the Student Union, which housed the magazine's office. Westmoreland described her feelings, "It was very unnerving at the time. White students who were our friends spoke to us, but we had to keep our focus and ignore them. They didn't understand what we were doing." She sadly recalled that "It affected some of our relationships. We became seen as a threat. We demanded a retraction from the magazine, and they apologized for using language so explosive. It was one event that I will never forget."[130]

Unlike many of the directors of Black Studies programs, Maxwell did not come from an academic or traditional activist background, but she had a history of desegregating the public schools. She defied the usual image of Black Studies directors as young male activists from the Ivy League or prominent schools in the Midwest. By engaging in continuous campaigns to explain and justify the need for Black Studies courses, developing student support programs, and encouraging the hiring of African American faculty, and administrators, Maxwell expanded the role of the desegregated university beyond the admittance of a few token individual African American students. By granting students opportunities to assume leadership roles or supporting their advocacy, Maxwell reconfigured and expanded the roles of both students and professors to adapt to a desegregated campus environment.[131] Reddy explained, "She was more of a revolutionary than all of us."[132]

4

Aluta Continua! The Struggle Continues!

Looking Outward to Strengthen Within

Seeking more stability for the Black Studies Program (BSP) in 1973, Maxwell asked the Black Studies Committee (BSC) to form a special task force of current members and new faculty unfamiliar with the BSP. Not satisfied with just offering a series of classes or curriculum, Maxwell now wanted the BSC to develop a proposal for the BSP to offer a major and to change the program's name to Afro-American and African Studies. The field of Black Studies emerged from the public protests and demands of African American students but establishing and maintaining a Program involved more than addressing student concerns.

As the director of a program within a publicly funded, UNC system member school, Maxwell had to seek multilayered approvals from the task force of the BSC, the Division, later the College of Humanities, the vice chancellor of academic affairs, and the chancellor in a seemingly endless process of bureaucratic administrative protocols. In these often behind-the-scenes negotiations, Maxwell had to interact with faculty and administrators whose procedural holdups or denials masked their apprehension, reluctance, or racism as they either misunderstood or dismissed the need for Black Studies courses and programming. As she sought to expand the BSP, programs at other universities succumbed, due in some part to their failure to maneuver around these administrative pitfalls. Maxwell overcame these hurdles by ensuring that the BSP met strict academic standards, but she had no problem working around some of the rules to benefit Black students or sustain the program. Students led the charge for Black Studies programs. However, the actual establishment and expansion of these programs at predominantly white universities like UNC Charlotte depended upon a director's mastery of administrative and negotiation skills.

The stories of Maxwell and other early Black Studies directors' attempts to maintain their programs despite facing both internal and external obstacles may not be as dramatic as the accounts of daring Black student administrative building takeovers. Nevertheless, understanding how these administrators carved out intellectual and physical spaces to accommodate the formation of a new Black Studies paradigm remains a lesser understood but fundamental dimension of the Black campus movement. As the sole African American woman administrator on UNC Charlotte's campus responsible for managing a controversial new field of study, Maxwell overcame a multitude of challenges from frustrating encounters with oblivious administrators and faculty to intersectional affronts of racism and sexism to lead the BSP to permanency. Cognizant of the power of community engagement, she looked outward from her campus office to construct networks as a "first" or "only" Black woman member of the executive boards of several of Charlotte's influential educational and nonprofit organizations. Sensing a need for mutual support, Maxwell eventually established a national organization to support Black Studies directors and ensure the stability of the field.

Maxwell developed a curriculum based upon Black Nationalist principles, but she realized that advocates of the Black Studies Program could be of any race or gender. College of Human Development and Learning Dean John Chase remained her friend. College of Humanities dean William Mathis, skeptical of her curriculum suggestions at first, later backed her program ideas. Lloyd Witherspoon, the chair of the Religious Studies Department, spoke with the administration on behalf of the BSP. At first, Newton Barnette, dean of the College of Engineering, balked at Maxwell's invitation to join the Black Studies Committee. He told her that he didn't believe in Black Studies. Maxwell responded to the experienced administrator's dismissal by explaining that his disbelief was the main reason she wanted him to join. Maxwell appreciated and welcomed supporters, but she often asked detractors or those unfamiliar with Black Studies to join the Black Studies Committee to sway colleagues who had different perspectives. At first, Barnette served begrudgingly, but when he learned more about the BSP, he realized its vital role in supporting Black students, including African American engineering students. Maxwell recalled that during a budget request meeting with Dean Mathis, Barnette challenged the dean by stating, "How long will Bertha have to bend at her knees? Give her the money!" She was shocked. In another instance, a skeptical math professor asked her about the Block's curriculum catharsis process, by repeatedly posing the question, "What is a catharsis?" Maxwell, frustrated, crudely responded by asking him if he had ever been constipated and felt relief after going to the bathroom? Shocked when he said, "Yes," she replied, "That experience was a catharsis!" After that, her embarrassed colleague never raised that question again and voted to approve Maxwell's requests.[1]

As southern women, Bonnie Cone, Ann C. Carver, Alice Lindsay Tate, and

Bertha Maxwell overpowered the toxic legacies of Jim Crow and elitism that resulted in friction between Black and white women to fashion their own feminist collaborations in a desegregated environment. Despite their differences, Maxwell formed deep and lasting friendships across racial and class lines with these women. Their support enabled Maxwell to manage and maneuver the pitfalls of working as a female administrator at UNC Charlotte. Going beyond the premise of basic allyship, Bonnie Cone was a trusted supporter of African American students until her retirement in 1973. BSP faculty member Beverly Ford recalled, when Maxwell encouraged her to get her doctoral degree, Cone, a staunch supporter of women's advancement in higher education, secured a grant from the local Lion's Club to pay Ford's tuition.[2] Cone and Ann Carver, who was a core member of the BSP faculty, contributed to the formation of the Black Studies Program as accomplices in distinctive and effective ways.

If Cone offered administrative support and Carver worked alongside Maxwell in the trenches of the BSP, Alice Lindsay Tate, grandniece of former North Carolina Governor Thomas Michael Holt and a member of one of the most prosperous textile manufacturing family dynasties in North Carolina, provided a financial foundation to undergird the BSP's survival. By the early 1970s, Black Studies programs across the nation faced elimination as their directors vied to secure course approvals and funding from sometimes adversarial administrators, only a few short years after their emergence. As Maxwell worked to build the BSP, she never worried about the elimination of the BSP due to UNC Charlotte's fear of losing Alice Tate's financial donations. In 1967, Tate, an aspiring opera singer who moved from Charlotte in the 1930s to live in New York City, donated over $275,000 to help fund scholarships for Black Studies students. First named the John Austin Tate-Lindsay Tate Culbertson Scholarship Fund from 1967 to 1969, the scholarships were later renamed the William Edwin Holt and Robert Lindsay Tate Scholarships. Tate donated funds in 1969 to establish an endowed chair position, the Frank Porter Graham Professorship in Black Studies. This donation was the second largest gift to the University at the time. This financial backing enabled Maxwell to reaffirm the relevance and permanency of the Black Studies Program.[3]

As a philanthropist, Tate supported causes that helped better the lives of African Americans, including UNC Charlotte's Black Studies Program, several years before Maxwell's appointment as director. Tate's support of social justice movements ranged from donating to civil rights organizations, such as Martin Luther King Jr.'s Southern Christian Leadership Conference in the mid-1960s, to writing impassioned letters in the early 1970s to NC political leaders calling for the pardon of nationally known imprisoned African American people, such as Joan Little and former UNC Charlotte students, Benjamin Chavis Jr. and T. J. Reddy. When Maxwell became BSP director in 1971, she invited Tate to meet the scholarship winners so that they could thank her personally. Tate appreciated meeting the students, and a friendship grew between the two. Often addressing each other as "Dear Friend" or "Sister" in their letters, Maxwell and Tate's bond extended beyond the campus as Tate even stayed at Maxwell's home with her family on a visit to Charlotte instead of staying with her relatives. In a letter to Maxwell, Tate shared, "How can I convey what it meant to me to partake of your Black Studies in action, to be allowed in sacrosanct rooms, and to be accepted? It was an event in my life I shall cherish always, also, the warmth and beauty of the Maxwells' Shangri-La and all the people in it."[4]

Tate and Maxwell's friendship offers a counter to predominant historical discussions about the complicated relationships between white patrons whose financial donations to support African American organizations or causes sometimes became wrought with paternalism and attempts to exert control. Maxwell's relationship with Tate did not solely rely on Tate's support of the BSP. Tate's decision to donate to educational initiatives, including Religious, Judaic, and Black Studies, sometimes caused tensions with her family members who expressed concern as to why Tate, a southern white woman of the Protestant faith, made such large financial donations to these fields. Dispelling the stereotype of the vacuous wealthy southern belle, Tate, an intellectual who lived in a modest apartment before receiving her inheritance, cherished her independence. Tate appreciated Maxwell's charismatic personality and nonjudgmental attitude. Maxwell welcomed Tate's kindness, and the BSP became the vehicle in which Tate could physically express her desire to help. Often when people ask what they could do to help improve race relations, Maxwell's BSP provided a platform for Tate to see the tangible impact of her philanthropy. Maxwell accepted Tate's friendship not just as patron and benefactor, but as an equal.[5]

In 1974, Maxwell became the first person to receive the Frank Porter Graham Endowed Chair in Black Studies at UNC Charlotte, funded by Tate, which cemented Maxwell's status at the university as an administrator who could garner funding if necessary. As an Endowed Chair, Maxwell became another "first" as the only person to be named as an endowed chair in the field of Black Studies at that time. As a devotee to scholarly subjects related to African history, Tate later worked with Maxwell to donate her extensive collection of books on African and African American history and world religion to Johnson C. Smith University.[6]

In a campaign to foster race relations in the 1970s, the Ford Foundation began to offer grants to Black Studies scholars or programs at leading private universities and colleges. Some scholars contend that the Ford Foundation's emphasis on the production of scholarly publications resulted in a shift away from activism. Smaller and less prominent Black Studies programs at schools in the South, such as UNC Charlotte's BSP, either received public funds or had fewer opportunities to secure these foundation grants. Maxwell's BSP held a unique and coveted position because Tate's support came with no restrictions or demands.[7]

Building Communities: Boards and Conferences

Maxwell's job as a UNC administrator garnered her entry into Charlotte's leadership class. She continued to serve on nonprofit boards that focused on African Americans and received invitations to serve on boards where Maxwell often became the first African American or Black woman member. Historians continue to examine the experiences of Blacks in management or as entrepreneurs, but few works examine the role of African Americans on the boards of former all-white cultural organizations, charitable, and nonprofit boards, or commissions. Maxwell's service on these boards helped her to build connections with local organizations that eventually led to educational or career opportunities for her BSP students. She used her presence and voice on these boards to push for increased services for African Americans and women. Board participation helped Maxwell engage with the broader Charlotte community, expanding her presence as an educational professional beyond UNC Charlotte's campus. Her efforts to fight against discrimination enabled her to use her token status to enact real change as part of what Historian Jacquelyn Hall described as the "long civil rights movement."[8]

Once reserved for whites only, corporate, or nonprofit organizations appointed influential persons who provided financial support or shared their expertise. By the early 1970s, a few male African Americans, such as the president of Johnson C. Smith University, prominent ministers, and attorneys, received invitations to serve on the City's nonprofit boards. As one of the few Black women to serve on the boards of predominantly white women's organizations, Maxwell formed lasting friendships with a wide array of people that enabled her to promote a plethora of civic and educational initiatives and goals. Established in the 1920s, the Charlotte League of Women Voters (CLWV), a chapter of the National League of Women Voters, reorganized in 1947 after several years of inactivity. Subsequently, Charlotte's reconstituted chapter played an integral role in educating citizens about voting issues. Segregated at its inception, in 1954, the CLWV opened its membership ranks to African American women that included principals Sterleta Sasso and Gwendolyn Cunningham and the city's first African American public health nurse, Thereasea Elder.[9]

Maxwell, as a past president of the Charlotte Alumnae Chapter of Delta Sigma Theta, joined the CLWV in 1966. As CMS grappled with desegregation, the CLWV offered statements in support of desegregation. In 1971, Maxwell became one of the first African American women to serve on the CLWV's Board of Directors. As the CLWV Board reacted to pressing issues, such as urban renewal and education, Maxwell shared her opinions and learned firsthand how the organization supported local, state, and national electoral processes. Even though Maxwell participated in African American women's organizations such as Delta Sigma Theta Sorority, serving on the Board of the Charlotte League of Women Voters represented the less examined but meaningful actions of African Americans who desegregated women's organizations after World War II. These clubs, comprised of local leaders or the spouses of prominent men, influenced election outcomes and a range of city government operations affecting education, civic life, and the arts. Maxwell's appointment to the CLWV's Board enabled her to ascend beyond token status to help the CLWV shape its policies and procedures. Unfortunately, as other professional responsibilities arose in 1974, she resigned from the League.[10]

Maxwell first gained prominence in Charlotte from her past reputation as a sound administrator in the public schools during desegregation and the close alliances she developed with several CMS school superintendents. As an HDL faculty member and later as director of the BSP, she continued to lead desegregation workshops for teachers and school systems across the nation. In 1972, Maxwell joined the Charlotte Chamber of Commerce's Quality Education Committee (QEC).[11] The Chamber established the QEC to respond to African American civil rights leaders' complaints of racial discrepancies in the degree and frequency of disciplinary measures in student conflicts in CMS. Chaired by former Chamber of Commerce Public Education Committee Chair Charles A. Hunter, the QEC included non-chamber members from the educational and religious fields. Other board members included leaders, such as Kathleen Crosby, from the educational and religious communities.[12]

After several months, the QEC became independent from the Chamber and worked with CMS administrators and similar groups in other cities to set clear, non-discriminatory discipline regulations or to develop what the QEC chair called "a climate of learning." Maxwell joined with Crosby again in 1972 to participate in "Let's Make Tomorrow Together," a child development conference sponsored by Charlotte's Child Development or Head Start Centers. In this workshop of some 200 attendees, Maxwell drew upon her experience in CMS to lead a workshop on parent-child relationships, stressing the importance of communication. Maxwell considered her participation in these influential boards and workshops as a form of service to ensure that the objectives or demands of activists came to fruition. CMS administrators Kathleen Crosby and Elizabeth Randolph also received invitations to serve on governmental and nonprofit boards, with Randolph becoming a member of the Charlotte Mecklenburg Library board of trustees and Crosby serving on the Charlotte Mecklenburg Charter Commission and was appointed to the North Carolina Board of Governors in 1977. From the 1970s to the 2000s, Maxwell served on over fifty influential civic, nonprofit, and educational boards in the city.[13]

As Maxwell formed local networks, she recognized the importance of building coalitions with other Black Studies Program Directors in the region. In 1973, the BSP program sponsored "Black Studies: Catalyst for Change?" a conference to "open lines of communication concerning Black Studies among all campuses of the UNC system." At this Conference held on UNC Charlotte's campus, Maxwell wanted to build coalitions with Black Studies administrators, faculty, and students from public and private institutions across the state. She designed workshops based on the themes of the Block program, expanding its themes of, "Who am I? Why am I here?" to examine Black Studies programs. The two-day conference included university officials, Colvard, McEniry, and Mathis. By incorporating the views of these high-level administrators, she wanted to hold them accountable. In order to learn about issues affecting other programs, she included academics and students from several UNC colleges and universities. She invited community leaders such as prominent civil rights attorney Julius Chambers to show the impact of the BSP program on Charlotte's African American communities.[14]

Professional Triumphs and Challenges

Despite securing approval for the BSPs curriculum in 1972, Maxwell learned after discussing her plan for the major that the BSP never received official approval from the administration. Shocked, in 1974, Maxwell decided to address both issues by submitting a formal proposal to offer the Afro-American and African Studies Bachelor of Arts degree and reaffirmed the request to change the program's name. In the proposal, Maxwell described new programming thrusts and provided additional statistical data regarding curriculum and faculty. Despite having Mathis's support, the chancellor and the Academic Council refused to submit any of the six proposals from the College of Humanities, which included Maxwell's BSP proposal, as part of the university's long-range plan to the Board of Governors. When Maxwell asked for an explanation, UNC Charlotte's Administration cited the following: Black Studies programs at other universities failed, lack of clarification regarding the program's expenses, and the unsubstantiated view that other majors would be more beneficial in preparing African American students to get jobs.[15]

With the support of Dean Mathis, Maxwell responded to these concerns by claiming that UNC Charlotte's program was not just a rushed response to student demands explaining that she and the faculty developed the curricula over several years. She solicited student reactions. Benjamin Chavis Jr. explained, "UNCC has one of the strongest African American, African studies programs in the whole United States. Why? Because of the way it was set up to be a permanent part of the university. Not as some of those special programs where you throw a few dollars at it." He emphasized, "You know, that's not what we wanted. We wanted a degree conferring department where you could major in African American and African Studies."[16]

Maxwell worked to submit supplemental data to address the administration's concerns and supplied additional statistical data about the efficacy of the program. Fortunately, African American student enrollment almost tripled after the advent of the Black Studies Program. In 1968, only forty-seven Black students were enrolled full-time at UNC Charlotte. By 1973, over 339 full-time African American students attended the university. Most of these students registered with the Black Studies Program or had taken at least one Black Studies course.[17] "Three years ago, before the program, their grades (African American students) averaged around a low "C," claimed BSP faculty member, Beverly Ford, citing data from a survey. She added, "During the two years of Black Studies, their grades have risen to a low B average." Ford added that more African American students took the full fifteen-hour course load. Maxwell even recruited members of the Black Student Union to work with the admissions office to contact Black applicants to encourage them to attend UNC Charlotte.[18]

Maxwell became adept at responding to the unsubstantiated claims of administrators to sustain her program. However, in 1974, she decided that securing a terminal degree would benefit her professionally and meet the growing administrative demands of faculty expertise for the program. As a former principal, Maxwell did not pursue the traditional scholarly path to academia to engage in her research agenda. Instead, she wished to obtain a PhD to become more knowledgeable about the philosophical foundations of Black Studies in order to develop a sound and sustainable program. Maxwell decided to enroll in the Doctoral Program in Education at the University of South Carolina at Columbia to study the influence of the educational philosophies of Booker T. Washington, W.E.B. Du Bois, and the French West Indian philosopher Frantz Fanon on the development of Black Studies. Unfortunately, she soon learned that the school had no professors available to advise and help her write her dissertation. Faced with a dilemma, one of her professors suggested that she leave USC and enroll in the Graduate Program of The Union of Experimenting Colleges and Universities instead. A collaboration of universities located in several locations, including Cincinnati Ohio, and Sarasota Florida, this university catered to professionals who wished to get advanced degrees by offering courses during the summer. As a student at Union, Maxwell exerted much more control over the implementation of her program than traditional doctoral students. When she realized that some students attended classes solely for their personal fulfillment in perpetuity, she told her professors that she wanted to finish her degree in a timely manner.[19]

When Maxwell learned that Union had no African American professors, she demanded that the university hire Black Studies practitioner Andress Taylor, an English professor at the then Federal City College, now the University of the District of Columbia, to direct her dissertation. Used to Union acquiescing to her demands regarding the direction of her graduate program, Maxwell decided that she wanted to write the script for a documentary based on the Black Studies Program instead of completing a traditional dissertation. Despite Maxwell's efforts to get Taylor hired as her adviser, to her shock, he dismissed her novel idea and insisted that she write a dissertation. So, she stubbornly decided to do both. In 1974, Maxwell successfully defended her written dissertation, *Black Studies: Paradox with a Promise?* Soon after she received her Doctor of Philosophy in Curriculum Development and Educational Administration, Maxwell worked with WBTV, Charlotte's CBS Network affiliate, to air the documentary, *Black Studies: The Invisible Man Confronts the American Dream, A Documentary on the Black Studies Program at UNCC,* based on her script, featuring Black Studies student Terry Smith.[20]

By airing this documentary, Maxwell shrewdly looked to promote the program beyond the campus to the entire city of Charlotte. Featured on-camera, Maxwell explained, "When I created this program, it was not in the paradigm that most people on that campus were accustomed to." She elaborated, "They needed something that would help to reverse 200 years of historical dehumanization and result in mental survival and liberation." Maxwell told the viewers, "I think that it is out of this basis of which we try to reestablish this personhood, which has been void in the educational processes for Black people because educational systems in this country have not addressed itself to the needs of Black people, period."[21]

As Maxwell grappled with the administrative and bureaucratic complications, she worked to build coalitions with other Black Studies directors who struggled with similar issues. When Maxwell served as a principal and later as an assistant professor in HDL, she worked with several Southern Association of Colleges and Schools (SACS) accreditation teams as an evaluator of public school systems. By the 1960s, in order to receive state and federal funding, most colleges and universities required that their academic departments and programs undergo an accreditation process through independent agencies, such as SACS to ensure that the institutions were fiscally sound and offered rigorous academic programs with qualified faculty.[22] Maxwell knew that a proposed African American and African Studies major would have to meet SACS accreditation standards, but as a new field of study grounded in the experiences of people of African descent, how would these Black Studies programs be evaluated and who would serve as its evaluators? Sensing the potential problems of accreditors with no familiarity and or interest in the merits of the field of Black Studies responsible for its approval, Maxwell wanted Black Studies experts to have the power to accredit other Black Studies programs and more African American administrators in powerful accrediting positions on the college level.[23]

As a program at a public institution, Maxwell had to justify the BSP's strengths and that its faculty and academic standards were adequate. This process was during a period when Black Studies programs across the nation faced criticisms of lack of scholarly merit and curricula rigor. Securing SACS approval would help to undergird Maxwell's proposal for the major. Unlike the growing field of American Studies that emerged from well-established disciplines, such as history and English, Black Studies required an accrediting body to evaluate a field based on the study of persons of African descent as subjects rather than as objects.

So, Maxwell began a journey that would take her beyond the campus grounds to form a national organization where she worked with some of the leading theoreticians and activists in the field. When she called for the establishment of the National Council for Black Studies (NCBS) as an entity to help accredit Black Studies programs, Maxwell eventually became a leader in helping the field to define itself and sustain its existence. She had already gained stature as an administrator at UNC Charlotte. In 1975, Maxwell received national attention as the organizer and first chairperson of the National Council for Black Studies as she worked to secure the Afro-American and African Studies major for the BSP program.[24]

Fortunately, a thriving community of historians and Black Studies scholars continue to chronicle the history and impact of the National Council for Black Studies. In discussing the early formation of the organization, one must discuss the rise of the field itself. Scholars such as Abdul Alkalimat, William King, Charles P. Henry, and Jonathan Fenderson place the origin of the NCBS within the context of the history of Black Studies. However, they don't provide an in-depth examination of Maxwell's pivotal role during the formative years of NCBS. Her practice of allowing others to step to the forefront may have led to scholars underestimating her influence. Maxwell worked to establish the NCBS's organizational structure and advised members on curriculum and procedural processes.[25]

As one of the early women directors of Black Studies programs, she had few women role models to emulate, but she and her fellow female directors developed vital support networks. Few historical works analyze the experiences of African American women directors. However, Emory University professor Delores Aldridge and San Jose State University professor Carlene Young's groundbreaking work, *Out of the Revolution: The Development of Africana Studies,* chronicles the efforts of Black women directors. Historian Claudrena N. Harold's history of the University of Virginia at Charlottesville's Afro-American Studies Program and its director, Vivian Gordon, informs this work.[26]

After the success of the North Carolina Conference, Maxwell decided to move forward to create a national organization. She drew upon her experience organizing conferences and events as a former educator and as a participant in civic and Greek-letter organizations. She knew that she needed help from the BSP faculty and staff first. Maxwell possessed the ability to persuade her faculty to go beyond their stated work descriptions to support her vision. So, BSP faculty and staff, Herman Thomas, Roberta Duff, Mary Harper, and Beverly Ford, who later served as the NCBS secretary, and countless students agreed to help form an organization that could ensure the survival of the BSP and Black Studies in general.[27]

With the help of the BSP faculty and staff, Maxwell set up a committee and proceeded to invite fellow Black Studies practitioners to a conference to discuss forming an association. To publicize the conference, Maxwell placed an ad in the March 1975 issue of *Black World Magazine,* formerly titled the *Negro Digest,* a national news magazine published by John H. Johnson publishers.[28] Maxwell drew from the title of her dissertation, *Paradox With a Promise?* to name the conference. The national ad announced, "The National Conference for Black Studies," with the upcoming keynote speaker Nick Aaron Ford, author of the book, *Black Studies: Threat or Challenge?* The ad promoted the conference's workshops on establishing a "National Association for the Evaluation and Accreditation of Black Studies Programs."[29] She and Herman Thomas asked other prominent African American directors or chairs of Black Studies programs or institutes to participate, such as James Turner, director of Black Studies at Cornell, and Ewart Guinier of Harvard. The participants at this conference agreed to form a national organization.[30]

When Maxwell first encountered her future allies in the founding of NCBS, she stood out as several of the program directors/former student activists were just a few years older than her students. Maxwell soon realized that as she worked to create the NCBS, scholars, such as Molefi Kete Asante, John Bracey Jr., Perry Hall, Leonard Jeffries, Maulana Karenga, William King, James B. Stewart, and James Turner, were constructing the theoretical foundation of Black Studies. These intellectuals passionately debated the philosophies of Pan Africanism versus Cultural Nationalism or the role of Black Studies practitioners within Black communities. Maxwell countered their continuous debates by offering a pragmatic perspective. She realized that the NCBS could eventually serve as a supportive organization that enabled these scholars to sustain their own Black Studies programs and departments. Self-taught as a Black Studies educator, Maxwell welcomed these scholars' research contributions and shared her management advice with them. Maxwell drew upon her supportive upbringing to develop a fearless personality, with little deference to class and the ability to overcome racial perceptions. She felt at home, whether it be in the BSP office meeting with students, in a nonprofit board of directors meeting, or surrounded by scholars at an NCBS conference.

As Maxwell ran the meetings of these Black Studies directors and former participants in the Black student movement, she relied upon her expertise as a desegregation activist and skills as a master teacher to earn their respect. Even though Maxwell now worked in an academic setting, she never severed her ties with Charlotte's educational community. Maxwell called her friend, William Harris, a former elementary school principal, now an executive with the Educational Testing Service (ETS) to see if the ETS could host a follow-up meeting later that year, in 1975.[31] Harris knew Maxwell when she started the Charlotte Teachers' Corp in the mid-1960s. They attended Brooklyn Presbyterian Church together. As complaints of racial and class biases in testing arose, and ETS worked to address minority concerns, Harris and his colleague, Joseph E. Williams, sensing a welcoming climate, successfully gained approval from ETS to host Maxwell's new organization for no costs. So, from July 16 to 18, Maxwell invited Black Studies practitioners to join her at ETS headquarters in Princeton, New Jersey. Harris remembered, "It was easy to work with Maxwell; she was so organized. She told me what was needed when she needed it and how it was to be deployed. Then I could take it from there."[32]

At this pivotal meeting, Colorado State Black Studies Director William

King coined the name the National Council for Black Studies, and they elected Maxwell as its first chairperson. During this meeting, the group addressed accreditation issues and raised broader questions relating to "what Black Studies was?" Maxwell listened to these meaningful theoretical discussions, but she held no allegiances or impetus to promote one theory over another. Maxwell's primary purpose involved finding ways to support her program. James Turner, retired director of Cornell University's African American Studies Department, asserted during those early meetings, "Dr. Roddey was task orientated. We were not just going to have a conversation. There were all these internal debates between Pan-Africanists, Cultural Nationalists, and those who followed the beliefs of Malcolm X." Dr. Roddey had the command to tell us to "Be quiet. Let's do this now," and all of these virile, strong young brothers would say, "Yes, Ma'am, All right, Sister Bertha." Turner explained, "She didn't carry any internal baggage because she came from the outside of the Black Student movement. She was a neutral broker. To give her credit, she built respectful relations with all those people."[33] As a former public school principal trained in administration, she formed a bond with the NCBS members, wherein she sought their expertise regarding theoretical and scholarly materials to develop the intellectual foundation of her program. Maxwell, in turn, helped the young activists-scholars run their programs in sometimes hostile environments.[34]

As a mature professional woman working alongside younger male activists, Maxwell created an environment where she commanded respect within masculine spaces. When some of her fellow members asked her to show some cleavage to an administrator at The Ohio State University to secure funding, she jokingly dismissed these younger men's crass suggestions to use her sexuality to sway this official. On the other hand, Maxwell had no problem chastising them or using an occasional swear word to make her point or defend herself. As these educational activists formulated the intellectual foundations of Black Power, they sometimes inadvertently or purposely promoted patriarchal concepts of masculinity. In response, African American women simultaneously had to confront their sexist colleagues in the struggle and fight against white supremacy. This intersectional battle affected Maxwell, but she previously worked in educational environments where women held leadership roles as principals. She had a sense of accomplishment that she brought with her to the organization as an experienced administrator. Maxwell soon learned to pick her battles when interacting in this masculine space of the early NCBS. She may have overlooked incidents of subtle sexism, but she never let these men disrespect or dismiss her.[35]

The NCBS subsequently met in Atlanta at the Annual Meeting of the Association for the Study of African American Life and History in October 1975, where the group appointed Joseph Russell of Indiana University at Bloomington as the executive director, responsible for managing the day-to-day operations. William King, of the University of Colorado at Boulder, the second president after Maxwell, offered to host the next meeting in November of that year in Boulder, Colorado, where the group became an official organization.[36] As more Black Studies programs and departments joined the NCBS, Joseph Russell and Herman Hudson of Indiana University received funding to host the NCBS Constitutional Convention in 1976, where they officially formalized the name, The National Council for Black Studies. The group presented the organization's three major goals. 1. To promote Black Studies courses, programs, and departments at all levels of education. 2. To develop and disseminate classroom-usable materials for the various separate and interdisciplinary subject areas that constitute Black Studies. 3. To determine national standards for the certification of Black Studies teachers and instructional programs.[37] During this meeting, Maxwell became chairperson of the newly formed executive board. In 1977, William Nelson Jr. helped to sponsor the NCBS's first academic conference at The Ohio State University.[38]

As the founder of the NCBS, Maxwell had no problem letting others assume leadership positions if it could help further negotiations and help the organization move forward. Her main goal was to ensure that the NCBS remain successful, not retain power. With the NCBS on a steady path, Maxwell stepped down from her position as chairperson in 1978, but she still served on the NCBS Executive Board. As an experienced administrator and manager, she helped to formulate the foundation by developing the structure and objectives of the NCBS. James B. Stewart wrote "In many respects, Maxwell played the same type of catalytic role in advancing Black Studies as Mary McLeod Bethune performed for the ASALH (Association for the Study of African American Life and History) during her presidency." Maxwell's expertise in alliance building, which led to the formation of the NCBS and her call to disseminate Black Studies scholarship in public schools, reflected Bethune's efforts as the first woman president of ASALH (1939–1952) when she popularized the organization's *Negro History Bulletin,* a condensed version of its scholarly journal designed for classroom teachers and created events and programs to encourage youth participation.[39]

Constructing the Afro-American and African Studies Major

With the successful formation of the NCBS, Maxwell continued to seek the major. In 1975, the UNC Charlotte's administration finally included the BSP in its long-range academic plan to submit to the Board of Governors. In 1976, with support from top UNC Charlotte administrators, including Colvard and Vice Chancellor Philip Hildreth (who replaced McEniry), Maxwell's proposal finally received formal approval from the board to offer the major and to change the BSP's name to Afro-American and African Studies (AAAS). Maxwell knew that if she could get the proposal to her friend and Board of Governors member, attorney Julius Chambers, he would help to get it approved. As Black Studies programs continued to struggle, Maxwell's journey to secure a major reflected her well-earned lessons in managing the now AAAS Program within the confines of a predominantly white university.[40]

The year 1976 marked another first for Maxwell when she took students on the AAAS Program's first study abroad trip to Africa. Working with the New York-based In-Africa Student Study Abroad Program, Maxwell and three UNC Charlotte students, L. Diane Bennett, Sheryl Westmoreland, and Robert "Bobby" Flowers joined nineteen faculty and students from historically African American universities to study in three African countries, Ghana, Togo, and Benin for six weeks. Receiving little funds from the university, Maxwell sought help from Alice Tate and raised almost two thousand dollars from local churches to cover the student fees for two students, with another securing his own funding from his parents. After traveling to Ghana, and two other countries, Maxwell realized that African scholarship primarily promoted a colonist perspective and that AAAS students needed to learn African-related subjects from a Black Studies worldview. This trip helped to reinforce her earlier decision to rename the BSP, Afro-American and African Studies.[41]

The Bachelor of Arts in African American and African Studies included the four phrases of the Block curriculum and courses from other traditional subjects, such as English, History, and Sociology. Instead of the Human Relations Workshops each fall, incoming students now had to take the Human Relations Lab, where they learned study skills and how to adapt to the university.[42] Maxwell considered community service a central component of her program. Therefore, in 1976, she implemented an internship program with Beverly Ford as the director. In this program, students volunteered in area hospitals, public schools, nonprofits, and charitable agencies that served the African American community. These internships gave students opportunities to apply knowledge learned in their classes to real-world situations. It also helped them to establish networks to help them gain future employment. Some seventy students participated in the first year of the internship program.[43]

Community service encouraged students to apply their academic knowledge to improve the social and economic conditions of African Americans and dismantle white supremacy. Yale Black Studies Department Director John Blassingame discussed some of these critiques of Black Studies in a chapter in *New Perspectives on Black Studies.* The prominent historian contended that students could not make relevant contributions because they had little knowledge of the actual needs of local African American communities. Maxwell's background as a former educator and community activist, along with Ford's support, enabled her to disprove Blassingame's assessment as she helped Beverly Ford place students with previously established contacts in nonprofits, hospitals, and government agencies.[44]

Historically Black colleges' foundational directives to their graduates to serve by precept and example served as a forerunner for this new concept of student learning by interacting with their surrounding communities. The modern-day term *service-learning* emerged in the 1960s stemming from early student volunteer programs, including Volunteers in Service to America or VISTA and the Peace Corps, which were reorganized in 1971 as ACTION, a federal domestic service agency under the Nixon administration. By the 1970s, university service-learning or experiential programs could range from oral history to environmental clean-up projects.[45]

Expanding upon the historical legacy of racial uplift endorsed by African American leaders during segregation, Maxwell combined the concept of student volunteerism with the Black Studies's call for community engagement. Whereas in the past, the concept of racial uplift often became intertwined with the quest for respectability and approval from whites, Maxwell designed the AAAS to encourage students to exemplify the core values of Black Nationalism as they shared knowledge to help African American communities thrive. She sponsored volunteer programs that ranged from tutoring to volunteering at nonprofits. By the 1980s, Black Studies began to focus more on establishing itself as a field or as a discipline by promoting scholarly and theoretical research and analysis that would be recognized and adopted by larger academic communities.[46]

As Maxwell supported some of the new directions in Black Studies, she did not adopt this change and continued to promote community service. She thought service-learning helped to connect students to local African American charitable and arts agencies and nonprofits. Maxwell believed that as desegregation provided educational access, she had to ensure that students developed pride and a sense of responsibility to their communities by doing service. Whereas some current Africana Studies programs and departments no longer emphasize community service and activism, the concept that students' academic experiences would be enriched by doing service off-campus remains a legacy of Black Studies.[47]

Ever conscious of the criticism concerning the potential for AAAS majors to secure employment after graduation, Maxwell's Bachelor of Arts in Afro-American and African Studies integrated humanities and social science curricula with practical applications. Students had the option of a double major in a traditional discipline and AAAS. Before students could graduate with an AAAS major, they had to complete a senior honors thesis project relating to their other major. Patterned after a masters' program, students had to form a defense committee of faculty and defend their thesis in a formal meeting. When parents or others asked Maxwell, "How are students going to get a job with a Black Studies degree?" She sometimes flippantly replied, "Look for one like everybody else." However, she prepared majors to complete a capstone thesis that could represent their academic skills to be used either as writing samples for graduate or professional school applications or to show potential employers. As Black Studies promoted community involvement, this push to take students beyond the campus walls helped to create new innovative connections between universities and their communities that later evolved into standard academic honors programs and colleges.[48]

As an administrator, Maxwell sought out exceptional students and fostered their skills in leadership by including them in administrative meetings or giving them influential roles as volunteers in community organizations. Maxwell sent students to visit the chancellor's office several days a week at 2 p.m. to ask when UNC Charlotte planned to hire an African American person in upper administration. In addition to exposing students to the inner workings of the administration of the university, she required students to assume leadership roles as volunteers or as student workers. When students, such as Sanders and Westmoreland Smith, who worked at the AAAS office, typed, and filed, they saw how Maxwell, Duff, Thomas, and the rest of the faculty established organizations and institutions, such as the National Council for Black Studies.[49] In this manner, they learned the inner methodologies of activism at a desegregated institution. In turn, the administration became aware of the students' widespread support, which reinforced her stance. After these repeated efforts and other student actions, the university eventually hired its first African American administrator on the executive level, Robert Albright, in 1981 as vice chancellor of student affairs. Albright would later become president of Johnson C. Smith University in 1993.[50]

With the field of Black women's history just gaining ground, Maxwell looked to contribute by teaching her students in her own fashion as a community builder. In 1976, Maxwell created one of the first African American women's history courses taught at a predominantly white institution in the South. Her course, "Black Women in America," chronicled significant events and important figures in African American women's history, adding a specific focus on eleven local African American women leaders in Charlotte. These leaders included Barber-Scotia College president, Mabel McLean; Kathleen Crosby, CMS; Mildred Baxter Davis, president of Black Presbyterian United Council, now National Black Presbyterian Caucus; Phyllis Lynch, director of the Charlotte-Mecklenburg Youth Council, and community leader Anita Stroud. After the class presentations, Maxwell provided lunch so that the speakers could talk with the students. Maxwell's course garnered local news coverage as a *Charlotte Observer* reporter, Vanessa Gallman, a former BSP student, wrote articles on each speaker. By presenting herself and these women who achieved, "despite the odds," Maxwell shared examples of women who exhibited the praxis of intersectionality and womanism with the class's predominantly Black female student population. By discussing the impact of the double jeopardy of racism and sexism that affected Black women, Maxwell encouraged students to formulate their definition of justice and apply it to situations affecting local college students and African American communities.[51]

During the 1970s, Maxwell often spoke about women's issues at local events and workshops. In 1976, she participated in a lecture series at Queen's University. After previously being denied part-time employment at Queens University, she commented, "My qualifications were two degrees, plus maximum experience. My barrier was being Black. But I finally made it there as a lecturer!" Maxwell took advantage of this opportunity to inform the Queens University audience about the experiences of African American women, adding, "It's only when it happens to you that you can relate what happens to Blacks daily." She explained, "My goal with this is to develop some level of empathetic understanding, even if it is a low one." She questioned why Queens had African American students but no Black instructors and no Black Studies program.[52] Maxwell supported Ann Carver's quest to establish a Women's Studies Program at UNC Charlotte. In 1976, Carver applied the organizational skills that she learned from working with Maxwell in AAAS to form a task force to help organize a Women's and Gender Studies Program.[53]

"You Can't Go Home Again?": A New Opportunity in a Familiar Setting

Instead of basking in success after securing the major in 1976, Maxwell decided to do the unexpected. She left! "I felt a need to get away from something that I had been immersed in for so long." Maxwell further explained, "I was exhausted from the many efforts that went into the conceptualization, experimentation, and implementation and finally getting the AAAS Program approved as a major. I also had my own personal life pressures that had to be dealt with." In 1977, Maxwell accepted the position of vice president for academic affairs at Johnson C. Smith University (JCSU), her undergraduate alma mater. In another first, Maxwell welcomed the opportunity to serve as Johnson C. Smith's first woman executive administrator. AAAS faculty, Beverly Ford, also left UNC Charlotte to work at JCSU.[54]

Responsible for managing the Departments and Programs in Alumni Affairs, Federal Regulations, Institutional Research, Public Relations, and Community Relations, at the university, JCSU president Wilbert Greenfield charged Maxwell with developing a system-wide master plan for growth for the then 110-year-old university. After Maxwell and her assistant, Carolyn Mason extensively reviewed all academic operations for the first year of the plan, Maxwell placed Mason in charge of working with Smith's administrative and academic units to develop specific criteria to measure leadership goals or objectives based on the Management by Objectives (MBO) System. This MBO system, popularized in the 1950s by Peter Drucker in his book, *The Practice of Management,* eventually emerged as a leading management process by the 1970s.[55] Maxwell then utilized aspects of the MBO process to develop a five-year, "The Year 2000" plan, where she promoted recruiting nontraditional students to increase enrollment and expanding Smith's role within its surrounding neighborhoods by building affordable housing units for residents and students. To support her strategic plan, Maxwell established a forty-member community advisory board comprised of educational and business leaders such as Joe Martin, president of North Carolina National Bank.[56]

Although excited to return to her alma mater and work at a historically Black institution, she faced other unexpected challenges. Maxwell now found herself in an environment where some of her fellow administrators expressed a reluctance to implement her ideas. Maxwell's relationship with Greenfield also grew more antagonistic after he made unprofessional jokes at a gathering of influential officials at Maxwell's 2000 master plan meeting.[57]

When she first accepted the position, she told Greenfield "If you have a problem with my leadership, tell me directly. Don't go behind my back." As a female executive working among primarily male counterparts, Maxwell wished to ensure that her boss would support her authority as a leader. When she learned that the president denied a raise that she had allocated for one of her staff members who had worked at Johnson C. Smith for years without notifying her, Maxwell promptly offered her resignation. She later explained why she returned to UNC Charlotte in a 1984 *Charlotte Post* interview, "My perception of me is that I am a professional activist. I have to make waves, and I can never be satisfied with the status quo, but I never dealt with negativism. At Smith, I knew that I could not be that professional activist. I was doing what was best for my alma mater and myself." Claiming that it just wasn't a good fit, Beverly Ford resigned the same year as Maxwell. She later opened her own training company.[58]

Viewing this situation from an intersectional focus, one sees the ways that Maxwell navigated and managed racism as an African American administrator at UNC Charlotte and sexism as a high-level female administrator at JCSU. Even though she loved Johnson C. Smith, in this case, a lack of respect for her authority that led her to stifle her vision left her demoralized. As Maxwell attempted to implement her plans, she propelled her fellow administrators to undergo a process that called for units to meet measurable outcomes. As often as the only woman among her fellow male executive-level peers, she eventually realized that the resistance to the adoption of her innovative management techniques whether motivated by sexism or just apprehension would be her biggest challenge to overcome. "Maxwell was just ahead of her time," Mason claimed. Fortunately, her position was still open at UNC Charlotte, and despite being in the process of conducting a national search, her former employers welcomed her return. Maxwell received a small raise and reclaimed her endowed chair position. UNC student Larry D. Springs welcomed Maxwell back, claiming, "Dr. Maxwell will be to the University of North Carolina at Charlotte what Harriet Tubman was to the Underground Railroad." Maxwell attempted to escape some of the problems facing Black administrators on predominantly white campuses, but her struggles at Johnson C. Smith led her back to UNC Charlotte, a university so receptive to her return, that she now had even more leverage to accomplish her administrative goals.[59]

Just as her professional life took a different path when she assumed a new position, Maxwell went through a very tumultuous turn in her personal life as she ended her twenty-four-year-old marriage to Horace Maxwell. For Bertha Maxwell, whose social and cultural life revolved around the interactions of married couples, it became challenging when she lost several friends. Maxwell had the difficult task of explaining the divorce to her teenage daughter, Tawanna. In one of the most painful situations of her life, she permitted her daughter to live with her father. After Tawanna had difficulty adjusting to high school, Maxwell enrolled her in Boggs Academy, an African American private boarding school in Keysville, Georgia, where Maxwell served on the board of directors. As Maxwell encountered obstacles at work and difficulties at home, she relied upon close friends, her sorority sisters, and family members for support. When she had to purchase a new home, she sought the advice of a fellow UNC Charlotte administrator who helped her locate a townhouse in South Charlotte. The same neighborhood where her mom once worked as a domestic. She gained new independence as she learned that she could not only survive as a single mother but thrive as well.[60]

Now, Onward to Departmental Status

As Black Studies programs across the nation faced a myriad of challenges to their autonomy, such as being folded into other disciplines or even elimination, Maxwell knew that securing accreditation and departmental status would ensure AAAS's autonomy. This push to gain some control over the sustainability of the field of Black Studies may not seem as controversial as the ongoing theoretical debates or the expansion of Black Studies to include the diaspora or the study of gender. However, none of these pertinent developments would have had the space to occur without structurally sound Black Studies programs.

One of the promises made to Maxwell when she returned was that the AAAS Program would receive support to become a free-standing or independent department. Before her departure, she encountered resistance from some university administrators, who thought that AAAS should remain an interdisciplinary program with cross-listed courses and no dedicated faculty. When Maxwell rejoined UNC Charlotte's administrative ranks and submitted a request for AAAS to a department in 1980, the university's administration had experienced several leadership changes. E. K. Fretwell Jr. replaced Colvard as chancellor in 1979. In 1980, Sherman Burson Jr. became the dean of the newly formed College of Arts and Sciences, which combined the Colleges of Humanities, Social and Behavioral Sciences, and Science and Mathematics. James H. Werntz became vice chancellor of academic affairs in 1981.[61]

She faced several administrative obstacles, such as obtaining funding lines to employ tenure-track faculty. The administration interviewed AAAS faculty, who candidly discussed the benefits of department status, including more support for research and additional colleagues and the fear of increased committee work and publishing pressures.[62] As a nontraditional academic administrator, Maxwell did not follow conventions; she remedied her hiring and funding dilemmas by employing former students to teach introductory courses. These students graduated from a program, led by an experienced trainer of teachers. Maxwell knew her students' intellectual and teaching abilities. Gregory

Davis became one of her most significant hires. Maxwell taught Davis in the 4th Grade. After losing his sight as a child, Davis attended the North Carolina School for the Blind. A determined and exceptional young man, he defied racial prejudice, poverty, and discrimination because of his vision impairment to enroll in Carolina Piedmont Community College, where he eventually became the school's first Black student body president. Davis knew little about Black Studies, but Maxwell encouraged him to enroll in UNC Charlotte and take AAAS courses. After receiving a BA degree in Religious Studies from UNC Charlotte, in 1979, he willingly joined AAAS to teach and eventually direct a section of the Block Program.[63]

By the 1980s, the faculty now included Douglas Davidson. Maxwell encouraged other Black faculty, such as Gregory Davis, Beverly Ford, Mary Harper, and Julian Pyles, to obtain doctoral degrees from Union. Reflecting broader trends in the field or discipline of Black Studies during the 1980s, Maxwell's self-reflective Human Relations Lab met with resistance as the newly established UNC Charlotte counseling center and the Psychology Department sought to manage all student mental health services. Black students now had more access to professional counselors and mental health services, but they lost access to the AAAS informal counseling services.[64]

Lyman Johnson, a retired UNC Charlotte history professor, who served on the BSC Faculty/Staff review committee responsible for evaluating AAAS's request for departmental status, recalled that most of UNC Charlotte's faculty were in support of AAAS but had reservations about it becoming a department due to Maxwell's unique position as department chair. Johnson recalled that some of the faculty thought Maxwell's permanent status as chair limited faculty governance and promoted a top-down leadership structure. Despite these challenges, Maxwell's negotiation strategy, presentation of AAAS curriculum and student enrollment data and statistics, along with upper-level administrative support, enabled AAAS to secure university approval in 1982 and approval from the NC Board of Governors in 1983. AAAS then joined some 150 other Black Studies departments in colleges and universities across the nation as part of 525 Black Studies programs in operation.[65]

African American Women and Black Studies

Maxwell grew even more acutely aware of the travails of Black women administrators after her sobering experience at Johnson C. Smith. In 1979, she engaged in a fierce campaign to help the University of North Carolina Chapel Hill's director of the African American Studies Curriculum Sonja Hayes Stone, in her fight for promotion to the rank of associate professor with tenure at UNC Chapel Hill. Maxwell and Stone, a member of the NCBS Executive Board, first met in 1974 when they both worked to develop Black Studies curricula at their respective schools. Stone participated in Maxwell's first North Carolina Black Studies Conference in 1973. Maxwell added, "We were both in the belly of the whale. I just had a chancellor that was just a little more compassionate. At the same time, my sister was just struggling on this campus to have this discipline acknowledged."[66]

Stone was a mesmerizing teacher and dedicated mentor, and in 1977, UNC Chapel Hill's Black students petitioned the university to create an Afro-American Cultural Center in her name. Beverly Ford recalled that Maxwell organized the National Council for Black Studies to serve as an influential collective body that advocated on behalf of members in adverse situations like Stone's tenure fight. To support her friend and colleague, Maxwell sent out threatening letters on NCBS letterhead, portraying the fledgling organization as a powerful entity that would retaliate if Stone did not get promoted. Unlike Maxwell's unique experience of receiving tenure as part of the position as AAAS director and the Endowed Chair's position, Stone encountered promotion issues that affected Black professors at other predominantly white universities. Despite Stone's extensive service record and stellar teaching evaluations, UNC Chapel Hill's promotion committee and administrators did not consider Stone's record worthy of tenure.[67]

Along with Maxwell's NCBS battle, in 1979 over 200 students staged a campus protest in support of Stone. In an unprecedented move, in 1980, UNC Chapel Hill's board of trustees reversed its decision and approved Stone's formal appeal. Her successful tenure fight received national attention, and she received numerous awards, including a NAACP award. After Stone's untimely death in 1991 from a stroke, students waged a national campaign to rename the Black Cultural Center after her. Students later petitioned the university to construct the free-standing Sonja Hayes Stone Center for Black Culture and History, which opened in 2004.[68]

In 1981, Maxwell contributed to the emerging field of African American women's history by serving as a consultant to help develop a Black Women's Studies curriculum at the University of Alabama at Tuscaloosa, sponsored by the US Department of Education.[69] The project's goals included developing curriculum materials for teachers on African American women's history. Years before the frequent use of the term intersectionality, Maxwell argued that "too often teachers don't look at the total Black experience." By discussing African American women's history before 1619, Maxwell added "You get the total background, moving up then to indentured servitude, slavery, Jim Crow segregation, and sexism. Then that progression must be looked at in light of the economic, political, and social conditions of the time and how Black people responded to them."[70]

As Maxwell offered courses in African American women's history and lectured on the topic, as the only Black woman administrator at UNC Charlotte, she grew more aware of sexism's impact. "African American women were at the bottom of the totem pole in society," Maxwell explained. "If all the racists on the face of the earth decided to be kind, I still had to face sexism."[71] At UNC Charlotte, Maxwell continued to support Ann Carver's Women's Studies task force as it conducted studies, researched other programs, and engaged in repeated negotiations with the administration to establish a Women's Studies Program. Carver and the task force, which included current UNC Charlotte Department of Political Science Chair Cheryl L. Brown, UNC Charlotte's first African American woman assistant professor in the Political Science Department, finally gained administrative approval in 1984 to offer classes in the new Women's Studies Program. Carver contending that "knowledge and research about women and their contributions to society are legitimate areas of study," drew from Maxwell's AAAS Block curriculum themes to argue that "This program will help male and female students better address the question of "Who am I?" Building upon Maxwell's organizational work with the NCBS, Carver became one of the founding members of the Southeastern Women's Studies Association and participated in the National Women's Studies Association.[72]

As the founder of NCBS, Maxwell worked with other women Black Studies directors, such as Valerie Edmundson of Fayetteville State University, who participated in Maxwell's North Carolina Black Studies Conferences. During the 1980s, women NCBS directors managed the organization as the field of Black Studies faced conservative political attacks and internal divisions. These women founded Black Studies programs at their respective universities. Carlene Young, the director of the African American Studies Program at San Jose State University, served as NCBS director from 1982 to 1984. Dolores P. Aldridge, the director of Emory University's Department of African American Studies, led the NCBS from 1984 to 1988.[73]

Maxwell and the Transformation of Black Studies: 1980s

When talking with other academics, Maxwell often liked to kid pretentious colleagues by remarking that "she was no scholar, but . . ." Nevertheless, as a savvy administrator, she successfully established a thriving department at UNC

Charlotte that met strategic academic and programming goals. The diminishing role of the educator/director reflected a turning point in the development of the field of Black Studies as it started to veer from the student-focused/protest model to focus on developing a scholarly theoretical foundation for the field or discipline in its second decade. James Turner argued that by forming the NCBS, Maxwell provided a supportive environment where directors could address the practical business of Black Studies, such as the formation of institutional curricula, pedagogy, academic support services for students, and faculty recruitment. In the second decade, most of these issues dissipated, and scholars now asked more theoretical questions.

Maxwell secured departmental status for the AAAS by relying on her negotiating skills and using the data to support the program's efficacy when the field of Black Studies faced mounting challenges, including academic budget cuts to the humanities and social sciences. Maxwell enacted several measures, such as the dual major, where students could major in a traditional discipline and AAAS, to attract more students.[74]

Black Studies programs faced challenges to their original missions of community service during the 1980s as financial support for African American cultural or community centers waned, and academic pressures led programs to adopt more traditional standards for academic validation that diminished the value of community service. Black Studies scholars Charles E. Jones and Nafeesa Muhammad argued, "First and foremost, disciplinary vigilance to the two-fold mission of Africana Studies suffers from the absence of external forces which undergirded the saliency of community outreach."[75]

If Maxwell refused to abandon AAAS's commitment to community service, it did subscribe to globalization, another predominant research development in the field of Black Studies. Maxwell first sensed the necessity for Black Studies to encompass the study and experiences of people of African descent from an international perspective by first changing the name of the BSP to AAAS. In the late 1970s, Maxwell hired Myriette Ekechukwu as its first dedicated full-time faculty member to teach African Studies and, in 1981, AAAS sponsored its first annual Africa Day conference to provide a platform to discuss issues affecting UNC Charlotte's African students and provide panels and lectures on topics ranging from African history to economic development, and international politics. Africa Day featured prominent speakers, such as scholar Ivan Van Sertima and Carole Collins of the National Campaign to Oppose Bank Loans to South Africa, who encouraged students to support the South African Anti-Apartheid movement by calling for disinvestment by US banks and other companies.[76]

In 1984, Maxwell and the AAAS Department hosted the 10th Annual NCBS conference in Charlotte. A decade after she sent out her first announcement to form an organization, the NCBS had become the premier organization for the field of Black Studies.[77] Despite its continued growth during its first decade, the NCBS never realized Maxwell's aim to be the main accrediting body for Black Studies programs/departments. As the field of Black Studies moved toward more traditional scholarly pursuits, they could receive the same evaluations as other liberal arts programs by the Southern Association for Colleges (SACS).

Maxwell successfully secured departmental status for AAAS, but she now faced increased demands to recruit academically credentialed faculty with terminal degrees without the increased funding to support these new faculty positions. Maxwell faced mounting new pressures from the university and the broader field of Black Studies to restructure AAAS to reflect a more traditional academic model. In 1986, she decided to resign from the Department at the age of 56. A reporter from the *Carolina Journal* recounted Maxwell's views, "The past fifteen years have been an uphill climb, and a constant struggle for her, the climb and the struggle were well worth making, but they have left her very tired."[78] After retiring from UNC Charlotte, Maxwell reduced her responsibilities with the NCBS. "All they do is read papers," she sarcastically sighed when talking about the NCBS conferences. Cognizant of the importance of scholarly research, Maxwell, a teacher and activist at her core, grew discontented that the NCBS had yet to fulfill its potential to promote Black Studies in the public schools and the community.[79]

When Maxwell left, several of the AAAS faculty decided to seek new opportunities as well. Herman Thomas resigned from the AAAS after establishing the University Transitions Opportunities Program or UTOP. Thomas and Maxwell first encouraged freshmen students to enroll in the Block, as Coordinator of UTOP. Now he directed a formal orientation program for students located in the Office of Minority Services. After serving as the UTOP coordinator from 1986 to 2001, Thomas later retired in this position and as a professor of religious studies in 2005.[80]

Gregory Davis also worked with Thomas to design UTOP as an assistant director in 1986. He later became an academic adviser for minority students in the Educational Support Services Division of the university. He later held more administrative positions in advising, eventually becoming director in 1995 of the Office of Minority Academic Services. He created the Student Advising for Freshmen Excellence or the (SAFE) Program. Despite having years of experience working with students and obtaining several advanced degrees, one administrator questioned Davis's management capabilities because of his vision impairment. Davis recalled, "I was so angry. How could they go outside? I was right there." Fortunately, the university later hired Davis, and he served as the director of the SAFE Program from 1995 to his retirement in 2008.[81]

After Maxwell resigned, Mario Azevedo, a Tanzanian scholar from the University of Notre Dame served as the AAAS director from 1986 to 2006. He restructured the department to reflect a more standard academic curriculum, placed more focus on the African diaspora, and renamed the department Africana Studies. From 2006 to 2008, English professor Malin Pereira served as interim director. Akinwumi Ogundiran, an archaeological anthropologist and cultural historian, who received his PhD from Boston University, became the director in 2008. In the fall of 2009, the Africana Studies Department sponsored the first annual Dr. Bertha Maxwell-Roddey Distinguished Africana Lecture series. Julia Jordan-Zachery, who obtained her PhD from the University of Connecticut, and whose research focuses on Black women and public policy, became the director of the Africana Studies Department in 2018. In the fall of 2021, African American Religious and Intellectual Historian Chris Cameron (PhD, UNC Chapel Hill) became interim director.[82]

Whereas more than fifty years have passed since the inception of the field of Black Studies, scholars have just begun to explore its lasting legacies. Maxwell's student-centered, educational focus led to the development of many core programs and the making of the modern university. Her innovative pedagogical constructs to help bolster the psychological well-being of her students led her to offer programming and encounter sessions that eventually resulted in the establishment of multicultural student services. The creation of community internships is now called service-learning, and Maxwell's student orientations eventually led to the development of broader student orientation programs. Gregory Davis maintained, "Talk about Learning Communities; Bertha was doing that in 1975. We wouldn't get that idea until the 2000s." He added, "as a university administrator, everything that I did all pointed to my experience with Bertha. Everything that I did, from creating scholarships to the SAFE Program, the foundation was based upon what Dr. Maxwell taught. She laid the foundation. It all pointed back to that."[83]

A New School, A New Beginning

When Maxwell decided to leave UNC Charlotte, she had no plans to go back to work immediately. Tired of all the administrative pressures, she just wanted to rest. Maxwell had left the AAAS Department in good standing, and she wanted to do something different. After a brief encounter with John Arnold, dean of the University of South Carolina at Lancaster, who invited her to teach whatever she wanted, Maxwell changed her mind. USC Lancaster was a small community college in Lancaster, South Carolina. Maxwell decided to join the faculty as a lecturer in Africana Studies. Returning to the classroom might have seemed like a step back for some, but the former director realized that after years of administrative work that she missed interacting with students. Unhindered by any university or departmental dictates regarding curricula, Maxwell had the freedom to design her African American Studies courses as she saw fit. She began her broad sweeping African American Studies course looking at the lives of people of African descent before the birth of Christ to the present, incorporating Cultural Nationalist theories with a strong emphasis on community activism. As a self-taught public historian, she took her curricula to the public, setting up exhibits for her class and designing an African American history exhibit for display at the local mall.[84]

At USC Lancaster, she continued to connect sometimes isolated students to African American communities. After Billy Wireman, the president of Queens University, heard her do a presentation based on Maya Angelou's book, *I Know Why the Caged Bird Sings,* he asked her to teach a Black Studies course. To help her students better engage with the local African American communities, Maxwell asked them to visit a local African American church. This outing did not go as planned because the minister and some of the church members dismissed a churchgoer who seemed intoxicated. Upset by the harsh way the church officers treated the impaired visitor, the students complained to Maxwell. She attempted to remedy the situation by inviting the minister to speak to her students to share his point of view. As she advised UNC Charlotte's student activists years before, Maxwell's benign plan to expose her students to Charlotte's African American institutions motivated them to stand up and to speak out when they saw injustice, even if it meant chastising a local authority figure.[85]

Maxwell, later Maxwell-Roddey after her remarriage in 1987, also continued serving on local and national boards. Facing the negative impact of the end of court-ordered busing, Maxwell-Roddey also co-chaired the Future Schools Task Force to look at the educational issues affecting CMS in 1997. Appointed by former student and fellow educational activist, CMS Board of Education chairperson Arthur Griffin Jr., Maxwell-Roddey worked diligently with her co-chair John Kramer to help provide statistical data and evidence that the end of court-ordered desegregation plans would have a detrimental impact on the city's efforts to provide equitable educational opportunities for all public school students. Unfortunately, the task force's findings could not overcome widespread community disinterest in desegregation only a few short years after Charlotte proudly claimed to be a city that successfully desegregated its schools. Whether as a professor at USC Lancaster, supporting the educational programs at the Afro-American Cultural Center/Harvey B. Gantt Center for the Arts + Culture, or designing leadership initiatives for educators and her Delta Sigma Theta sisters before, during, and after she was its national president, Maxwell never stopped working as an educational advocate. Despite having to retire from teaching due to illness in 2008, she still takes time to advise and support former students and colleagues.[86]

In 2013, a national survey of Black/African American/Africana Studies programs listed out of 1,777 four-year colleges and universities surveyed, some 366 schools had either a formal Black Studies program or department, and 999 institutions offered courses. Southern institutions had fewer formal programs, but some 87 percent of these schools offered Black Studies courses.[87] Over the years, the development of Maxwell's AAAS eventually led to the framework to develop other interdisciplinary studies programs at UNC Charlotte, based upon gender, ethnicity, or subjects such as urban and film studies.

At the NCBS's 40th Anniversary Conference in 2016, Maxwell, UNC Charlotte's Gregory Davis, Herman Thomas, and NCBS scholars Leonard Jeffries and Maulana Karenga joined a roundtable discussion to discuss Maxwell's impact and legacy. They reminisced about how this former elementary school principal enabled the creation of a new discipline. Not afraid to tell these powerful young men and women to shut up, if necessary, she respected their scholarly vision to create a field. James Turner once claimed, "that Maxwell should be considered a modern-day race woman in the tradition of Rosa Parks and Ella Baker. She followed in a long tradition of women who had the civic courage to stand up to racism and work to advance her race. She didn't run away."[88] Maxwell refused to be intimidated by anyone, whether they were school administrators, young activists, or city business leaders. As she emerged as a Black Studies leader, Maxwell would simultaneously expand its reach by serving as a local community institution builder.

Artist re-creation from a photograph of Bertha as a child wearing a dress made by her paternal grandmother Anna Brewer Earle. Courtesy of T'Afo Feimster.

DELTA SIGMA THETA SORORITY

OFFICERS

MAMIE RUTH ELLIS	President
ROSE RAWLINS	Vice-President
MARY JONES	Recording Secretary
EVELYN DAVENPORT	Corresponding Secretary
CATHERINE GIBSON	Treasurer
NANNIE McCLURE	Dean of Pledgees
LEATRICE ROBERTS	Journalist
NATALIE COWAN	Historian
FRANCES McADAMS	Sergeant-at-Arms

MEMBERS

SADIE ALEXANDER	EVA M. JONES	BILLIE MARIE MITCHELL
MARY CHILDERS	GERALDINE JONES	CLEMENTINE RIGGSBEE
ESTHER CREWS	REMONIA LEVANT	JEANNETTE RIVERS
JOAN DAVIS	BERTHA LYONS	AZALIA REYNOLDS
NORMA FUGATE	BERNICE McQUAIGE	BESSIE SIGLER
LOUILYN FUNDERBURKE	ELLEN J. MARTIN	JEAN STERLING
NEVADA JOHNSON		MARY E. WILLIAMS

Gamma Lambda Chapter Delta Sigma Theta, 1952 Golden Bull Yearbook, p. 67, Johnson C. Smith University. Maxwell is on the second row, second from the right. Courtesy of Inez Moore Parker Archives, Johnson C. Smith University.

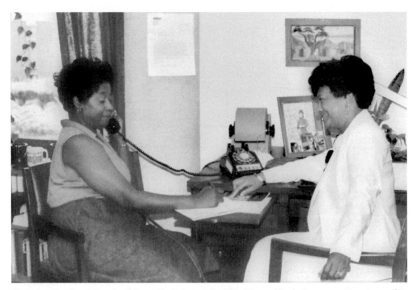

Roberta Duff and Bertha Maxwell sitting at Bertha Maxwell's desk, 1970s. Courtesy of J. Murrey Atkins Library, UNC Charlotte.

Reception for UNC Charlotte's Afro-American and African Studies Program director Bertha Maxwell's Black women's history class that honors Charlotte African American women leaders for their "achievement against the odds," December 1976. Held at the Afro-American Cultural Center, Spirit Square, honorees include, *left to right*, Alice Diamond, Mildred Baxter Davis, Bertha Lewis, Sarah Stevenson, Anita Stroud, Phyllis Lynch, Kathleen Crosby, Dorothy Counts-Scoggins, Carrie Graves, and Julia Harshaw. Courtesy of *Charlotte Observer* Photograph Collection, RSCR, Charlotte Mecklenburg Library.

Ann C. Carver teaching a class in the Afro-American and African Studies Program, 1976. Courtesy of J. Murrey Atkins Library, UNC Charlotte.

Rev. Jesse Jackson Sr. and Bertha Maxwell at a Wednesday, October 8, 1980, rally at Johnson C. Smith University for Maxwell's 1980 campaign to win a seat in the North Carolina General Assembly. Courtesy of Bertha Maxwell-Roddey.

Afro-American Cultural Center, 1986. Courtesy of Charlotte Mecklenburg Corporate Communications and Marketing Organization Records, J. Murrey Atkins Library, UNC Charlotte.

Picture of the Harvey B. Gantt Center on opening day, October 24, 2009. Courtesy of Mark Clifton. Source: https://www.flickr.com/photos/37063827@N02/4040794999. Attribution-ShareAlike 4.0 International (CC BY-SA 4.0).

Mary Harper, Mayor Vi Lyles, and Bertha Maxwell-Roddey at a reception in honor of the naming of the Harper-Roddey Grand Lobby at the Harvey B. Gantt Center, Wednesday, August 22, 2018. Courtesy of Sonya Ramsey.

Group photo of the National Presidents of Delta Sigma Theta Sorority, Inc. taken at the Eastern Regional Conference, Buffalo, NY, 1995. *Left*: Bertha M. Roddey, Eastern Regional Director Guessippina Bonner, Eastern Regional Representative Pamela Hall, and the National Presidents of Delta Sigma Theta from 1958 to 1992, Jeanne Noble, Geraldine Pittman Woods, Frankie Muse Freeman, Thelma Daley, Mona H. Bailey, Hortense Canady, and Yvonne Kennedy. President Lillian P. Benbow is not pictured. Courtesy of Guessippina Bonner.

Campaign ad for Bertha M. Roddey for the office of National President of Delta Sigma Theta Sorority, Inc., 41st National Convention Workbook, Baltimore, MD, 1992, p. 101. Courtesy of Bertha Maxwell-Roddey.

National Executive Board Meeting at the home of 14th National President Frankie Muse Freeman, St. Louis, Missouri, 1994. National President Bertha M. Roddey is at center left. Courtesy of Gloria Bryan Banks.

Bertha M. Roddey and sorors at the St. Louis Blitz Habitat Build Site, July 1994. Courtesy of Bertha Maxwell-Roddey.

Maxwell-Roddey and her husband Theodore Roddey Jr. were invited to dine with President Jimmy Carter and Rosalynn Carter at the 1995 President's Day Weekend at Habitat for Humanity International Headquarters in Americus, Georgia. Courtesy of Bertha Maxwell-Roddey.

Bertha Maxwell-Roddey and Congressman John Lewis at the Arch of Triumph Gala, April 20, 2013, sponsored by Johnson C. Smith University, Charlotte, NC. Lewis received an award at the event. Maxwell-Roddey is a 2010 recipient of the prestigious award for service and achievement. Courtesy of Johnson C. Smith University.

Bertha's Girls at the 2004 Delta Sigma Theta Sorority, Inc. National Convention in Las Vegas. *Seated*: Michel Vaughan, Ella Goode Johnson, Bertha M. Roddey, and Fabette T. D. Smith. *Standing*: Roselle Wilson, Ann McMillon, Dorothy White, Rose Marie Swanson, Oscar Faye Williams, Faye Clark, Patricia Alford, Doris Greene, Lucille Webb, Claudia McKoin, Sara Smalley, and Lois Gilder. Courtesy of Gloria Bryan Banks.

Six of thirteen Iota Rho (IP) charter line members of Iota Rho Chapter, Delta Sigma Theta Sorority, Incorporated, UNC Charlotte. *Seated, left to right*: Claudia J. Jordan (Sergeant-at-Arms), Bertha Maxwell-Roddey, Jacqueline Stevens Sanders (President). *Standing, left to right*: Barbara A. Washington, Cynthia Mullen Stewart, Patricia Hubbard Marsh (Treasurer), Phaedra Berry Holley (Vice President). Courtesy of Jacqueline Stevens Sanders.

UNC Charlotte Alumnae, 1981, Donnie Koonce, Masherrill Fant Koonce, Bertha Maxwell-Roddey, Herman Thomas, and Gregory Davis attending the 2014 UNC Charlotte Alumni Association Green Tie Gala. Courtesy of UNC Charlotte Alumni Association.

Charlotte Alumni Chapter, Delta Sigma Theta Sorority, Inc. members, and Bertha Maxwell-Roddey at reception for new Dorothy Height US Postal Service Stamp at Friendship Missionary Baptist Church, Charlotte, NC, March 27, 2017. Courtesy of Beulah Moore, photographer.

UNC Charlotte Black Studies/AAAS students. *Seated*: Dr. Bertha Maxwell-Roddey. *Standing, left to right*: David B. Sanders, unknown, Jacqueline Stevens Sanders, Phaedra Berry-Holley, T. J. Reddy, Humphrey S. Cummings, Paul E. Hemphill, Ronald R. Caldwell, and Octavia Walker Caldwell. Courtesy of Jacqueline Stevens Sanders.

5

Retrieving What Was Lost, Building New Beginnings

At 10 a.m., on a bright sunny day on October 24, 2009, Charlotte mayor Pat McCrory cut the ribbon on the beautiful new building to commemorate the official opening of the Harvey B. Gantt Center for African-American Arts + Culture. This $18 million structure would feature exhibits of regionally and nationally known artists. Located at 551 South Tryon Street, the new Gantt Center joined several of Charlotte's other major arts institutions as part of an Uptown arts and entertainment cluster that included the Bechtler Museum of Modern Art, the Mint Museum Uptown, and the Knight Theater.[1] The Center's namesake, former Charlotte mayor Harvey Gantt, gushed, "This beautiful awesome building is far beyond my wildest dreams," as he and other prominent dignitaries celebrated the opening.[2]

During the ceremony, as Gantt President and CEO David Taylor, thanked the predominantly male crowd of city officials and generous corporate benefactors for all their contributions, he recognized the efforts of the Center's two women founders, Mary Harper and Bertha Maxwell. Thirty-five years ago, in 1974, Mary Harper asked Maxwell to help establish an Afro-American Cultural and Service Center (AACSC) in Charlotte. This chapter recounts how Maxwell drew upon her established community networks to transform Harper's dissertation proposal concept into a thriving arts center from 1974 to 1986. The following chapter explores the internal and external challenges that Maxwell and the now Afro-American Cultural Center's (AACC) staff encountered as they struggled to sustain the Center during the late 1980s and 1990s to eventually evolve into the Harvey B. Gantt Center for African-American Culture + Arts in 2009.[3]

Harper originally planned for the Center to serve as a repository for local African American history and culture. However, over the years, with limited financial resources to employ an archivist and no location to house materials, the Center evolved into a community arts institution.[4] As director of UNC Charlotte's Black Studies Program, later known as Afro-American and African Studies, Maxwell agreed to help Harper start the Center. As Maxwell and Harper worked to establish UNC Charlotte's Black Studies Program's presence in Charlotte, a year later, in 1975, Maxwell's educational influence would expand beyond UNC Charlotte's campus to establish the National Council for Black Studies.

One of the lesser publicized roles of African American administrators like Maxwell at predominantly white universities involved supporting Black faculty during the promotion process. Harper, who joined UNC Charlotte's English faculty in 1970, after teaching at Johnson C. Smith University and in local public schools, had taught in the Black Studies Program since its inception. By serving as the adviser for Harper's Union School Graduate School dissertation project (also titled as a Project of Purpose by Union) and developing the Center, Maxwell endorsed Harper's doctoral research. She encouraged Dean Mathis and Harper's English department to expand the European-centered evaluation criteria to recognize the research contributions of Harper and other faculty whose innovative scholarship examined aspects of the Black experience.[5]

As scholars such as Rhett Jones examine the impact of Black Studies apart from academia, Harper, and Maxwell's unique premise to locate a university student-involved cultural center in Charlotte reflects the combined contributions of the civil rights and Black Power movements to the development of African American museums and cultural centers.[6] During segregation, Black historians, archivists, and art collectors diligently struggled to preserve African American material and cultural sources. Limited in space and resources, they often located collections or exhibits in high schools, historically Black cultural and religious institutions, and in private homes. African American historians and artists of the 1960s civil rights era pressed for inclusion after exposing the pervasive segregation that plagued predominantly white history museums and the art world. Concurrently, others like Chicago art historian Margaret Taylor-Burroughs, co-founder of the DuSable Museum of African American History in 1961, established independent cultural and historical institutions. The Black Power movement called for institutions to embrace a new Black aesthetic and to display the broad scope of African American and diasporic historical experiences in response to shifting urban sites. This direction led to the formation of museums like Detroit's Charles H. Wright Museum of African American History (1965). Later African American historical and cultural entities, such as Baltimore's Reginald F. Lewis Museum of African American History and Culture, which opened in 2005, emerged as a reflection of African Americans' growing entrepreneurial and political power in the post–civil rights era.[7]

Harper and Maxwell's decision to open the Center reflects the changing role of local African American women cultural activists in desegregated-era Charlotte. Maxwell and other modern-day race women in Charlotte, such as CMS school administrator Kathleen Crosby, who helped establish the Charlotte chapter of the National Urban League in 1978; Thereasea Elder, the city's first Black public health nurse and neighborhood activist; Sarah Stevenson, the first Black woman president of the Charlotte-Mecklenburg PTA Council in 1978, and the first African American woman to win a seat in 1980 on the CMS Board of Education; and neighborhood activists Mildred Baxter Davis and Phyllis Lynch, secured decision-making positions in education, health care, and nonprofits. In the 1970s, writers and scholars, including Alice Walker and Clenora Hudson Weems, presented a more expansive interpretation of African American women's feminism, called womanism. Unlike some white feminists who cited the patriarchy as the central force of oppression affecting their lives, African American womanists strove to eliminate the racism, classism, and sexism affecting their families, their communities, and themselves. Womanists continued to build upon the historical legacy of the race women of the past, years before Walker's seminal 1983 publication of *In My Mother's Gardens,* where she suggested, "Womanism is to feminism like purple is to lavender."[8] As modern-day race women, Maxwell and her contemporaries' actions utilized their influence as community activists and institution builders to establish a womanist power base within Charlotte.[9]

Maxwell assumed a leadership role to help create the Center because it reflected her values concerning community service. In 1964, she formed the Charlotte Teachers Corps to provide free kindergarten classes to neighborhood children. Now, Maxwell saw the need to protect Black children from the negative consequences of urban renewal and one-sided desegregation. After working as a pioneer during school desegregation, she meshed the call for modern-day uplift with the Black Studies's mandate to support Black communities by establishing a Center to help children after the decimation of several of the city's Black neighborhoods and the closing of predominantly African American schools.

Since the end of slavery and the advent of Jim Crow segregation, housing discrimination and poverty often relegated African Americans to living in neighborhoods that contained substandard housing. Segregated by race, but not by class, these enclaves served as the home of people from all socioeconomic levels. Urban renewal efforts began in Charlotte during the 1930s and across the nation as part of Depression-era recovery efforts. It peaked in Charlotte in the 1950s and 1960s as the city used local and federal funds to "eliminate blight" or tear down dilapidated structures. The Brooklyn neighborhood, or Charlotte's Second Ward, formerly known as the Logtown community for enslaved people, had re-emerged as Brooklyn by the 1880s. The thriving segregated neighborhood had some run-down areas. Still, several of Charlotte's African American doctors and teachers lived in Brooklyn, and it served as the location for influential Black churches and businesses, including the Second Ward High School and the Hotel Alexander, the city's only African American hotel, and barber and entrepreneur Thad Tate's Afro-American Insurance Company. As director of the Mecklenburg Investment Company, he and several other Black leaders in Charlotte constructed the Mecklenburg Investment Company Building, the first Black commercial office building in Brooklyn.[10]

Sold as a positive process to beautify the city by its proponents, urban renewal destroyed all the structures in the proposed area with no regard for its economic worth or historical significance. The closing of African American schools, coupled with urban renewal, led to the virtual annihilation of Brooklyn and several other African American neighborhoods in Charlotte. Its residents, now forced to relocate to new areas, had to do so without relying upon established businesses, churches, and cultural institutions. Maxwell experienced this dislocation firsthand as she witnesses the closing of Morgan Elementary School, where she served as principal, and her mother had to relocate due to urban renewal.[11] Maxwell shared her view in a 1997 newspaper article: "You have to look at the businesses that were destroyed, the restaurants, the theaters, and the things that gave an identity to the Black community." She asserted, "The facilities weren't equal, but you had a sense of community. You wonder how long had this destruction been planned? And why couldn't this Black area have been incorporated into the master plan?[12] Harper and Maxwell watched with disappointment as urban renewal efforts continued in the early 1970s after Charlotte's Redevelopment Commission looked to demolish African American neighborhoods in Charlotte's First and Third Wards, including Maxwell's former home in the First Ward. These wards comprised Charlotte's Center City area.[13]

After clearing this now very profitable land, the Charlotte Redevelopment Commission sold it to businesses as part of the city's economic development efforts. To attract new residents, the commission allowed developers to construct high-end housing units in these now exclusive and often renamed neighborhoods. A 1970 promotional brochure written by the Real Estate Commission of the City of Charlotte claimed, "Available for sale in the Inner City Urban Renewal Area are fifty-one acres of prime land for commercial development. The Redevelopment Commission of the City of Charlotte will pay the real estate broker's commission."[14] Ironically, as city boosters promoted Charlotte's new city center as a representation of a thriving, business-friendly New South urban area, it did so by erasing African American neighborhoods. A 1970 report, "The Brooklyn Story," written by the Charlotte Redevelopment Commission, described the obliteration of the neighborhood in the following way, "Charlotte's is-was-Brooklyn, 238 acres of blight beyond repair, next door to downtown and at the back doorstep of City Hall and the County Courthouse. Today—Urban redevelopment is wiping the old Brooklyn from Charlotte's face." The commission followed by making the bold statement, "Today, new landmarks are beginning to rise from the rubble of demolished slums. In the months ahead of the dreams of many years, a gleaming new governmental center complex will start to come to life, replacing the squalor that is no more."[15]

By the early 1970s, Black Charlotteans had grown painfully aware that city officials neglected to adequately compensate displaced Brooklynites for their residential and business relocation costs. African Americans, including community activists like Greenville neighborhood's Thereasea Elder, Cherry neighborhood resident, Phyllis Lynch, and the Third Ward's Mildred Baxter Davis, engaged in sophisticated battles ranging from legal actions to public-private development partnerships to grassroots activism. As these women and other activists fought to keep their localities intact, Harper and Maxwell established the Center as an entity to help children and Black Charlotteans retrieve what was culturally lost.[16]

Mary Harper planned for the Center to inform Black Charlotteans about local African American history. She explained, "Black people themselves were not valuing their artifacts, not preserving their heritage by casting off family relics for trash." Harper elaborated that "she realized that many Black people living in Charlotte did not know the Black history of their hometown."[17]

As some of Charlotte's Black neighborhoods disappeared as part of urban renewal by the late 1960s, CMS's desegregation plans included closing several African American schools to stem the possible white flight of parents who may be apprehensive about sending their children to former Black schools. Often the settings for meetings and events during segregation, these African American institutions served as community centers in their neighborhoods. By 1971, school desegregation in Charlotte reached national headline news with the controversial *Swann vs. Charlotte Mecklenburg County Board of Education* ruling. CMS now had to revise its desegregation plan to incorporate transporting children by bus outside their segregated neighborhoods. As Black Charlotteans endured the loss of their communities and schools, Maxwell and Harper decided to open an Afro-American Cultural Center.[18]

The efforts to establish an Afro-American Cultural Center reflected African

Americans' collective efforts to alleviate some of the negative consequences of desegregation and urban redevelopment on Black communities. Maxwell developed the Block curriculum to promote self-identity development and a sense of purpose among African American students at UNC Charlotte. As a desegregation activist, Maxwell understood that African American children's understanding of self-identity could be detrimentally affected by the following: school closures; faculty desegregation that transferred African American teachers to white schools; and the busing of Black children to predominantly white schools. She supported Harper's concept of a cultural center that would help Black children learn about Charlotte's African American history and visual and performing arts. Maxwell hoped that the Center would provide a supportive space for African American visual and performing artists, educators, and cultural activists to interact with the public and build a thriving cultural community. In recognizing Harper's concept, Maxwell realized that the Center could serve as a physical manifestation of her community outreach efforts at UNC Charlotte. She claimed, "The structure of the culture of the people in the First, Second, and Third Ward areas is gone. So, you need some semblance that they existed." She further explained, "that the only institutionalized programs regarding African Americans in the Queen City in the early 1970s were from the AAAS and what was going on at UNCC."[19]

Building Community and the Formation of the Afro-American Cultural and Service Center, 1974–1984

Whereas Harper envisioned the original concept for the Center, Maxwell assumed a more leadership role by chairing committees, recruiting a board of directors, helping to secure locations, and working to obtain funding. Busy with internal administrative duties and working to establish the NCBS, Maxwell never sought out to manage the daily operations of the Center. However, she continued to serve in advisory roles. Following formal academic procedures, Maxwell and Harper first established an advisory committee to develop the Center, including Herman Thomas, Beverly Ford as secretary, David Frye, and university officials, William Mathis and William Britt, the Vice Chancellor for University Development. During these meetings, Maxwell and the committee drew from Harper's dissertation to develop a formal proposal with objectives and a budget.[20]

One of Maxwell and Harper's goals involved creating an Executive Board to manage the Center. Maxwell's considered the AACC as a natural outgrowth of her educational philosophy of community engagement. As longtime residents of Charlotte, Maxwell and Harper relied upon previously established networks to look for potential members. Maxwell invited former Alexander Street Elementary School Teacher Mamie Brewington to serve as the Center's first board chairperson. Maxwell and Harper solicited member recommendations from prominent Charlotteans such as Fred Alexander, the first Black member since the late 1900s elected to serve on Charlotte's City Council in 1965. He later became the first African American to serve in the North Carolina State Senate.[21] Maxwell asked her neighbor and friend, Mary Maxwell, a local insurance executive (no relation to Bertha Maxwell) to help contact members for meetings. Bertha Maxwell consulted with the board as it formed the bylaws for the institution, sponsored fundraising initiatives, and developed the broader management vision for the Center.[22]

With the support of Harper, Maxwell took a leadership role in helping to establish and advise the Center, but the board would have the actual responsibility for managing it. The original board of more than fifty members included some of the most prominent African Americans in Charlotte, such as future mayor Harvey Bernard Gantt and Maxwell appointed several current and former students. Sitting among prominent ministers, educators, community activists, and business leaders were students Humphrey Cummings, David Sanders, and married couple, Jerry and Brenda Hogue Springs, who had full voting rights, and Maxwell expected them to participate as equal members.[23]

Maxwell's laissez-faire leadership style did not discriminate based on age or experience. If she thought students had talent and skills, Maxwell appointed them. Imbued with the motivation to create a Center that engaged with the African American community, these younger members pushed the Center and its board to emphasize programming that included more of a cross section of Charlotte's African American community to attract working-class residents. Maxwell's students only made up a small fraction of the board, but they had no problem voicing their views to other members. Even though they respected these revered figures, as students working with Maxwell, they learned the value of their self-worth and allowed no one to intimidate them. Jerry and Brenda Springs worked hard to recruit other younger board members, eventually helping to reconfigure its population and membership.[24]

Now that the Center had the approval of UNC administrators to create the Center, how would it make its presence known in Charlotte? First, Harper suggested an oratorical contest, and Maxwell proposed that they have a choir recital or concert. Center Board Member Clara Lowry Williams, the first Black woman broadcaster at WBTV television and director of Public Affairs, wanted to do something more distinctive and proposed sponsoring an outdoor arts festival for people across class and racial lines. Excited, Harper and Maxwell decided to go with Lowry Williams's innovative idea adding that she wanted the festival to be free and open to all. Lowry Williams shared her recollections in a 2008 oral history interview, "The Afro-American Cultural Center was the idea of Drs. Bertha Maxwell and Mary Harper. It was really funny because they'd say, "Okay, we got this idea. But how are we going to let folks know that we're here? (She said.) Let's do something different and have a big festival." Lowry Williams continued, "With my skills again, I was able to put together a twelve-hour art and cultural festival right downtown at Marshall Park called the Afro-American Cultural Festival, which was really exciting. As she described the event, she touted, "People came from everywhere. We had art exhibits. We had all kinds of choirs and blues singers and everything down there. I'm really proud of it."[25]

August 31 was a beautiful sunny day, perfect for the Center's Festival in Marshall Park. First of its kind in Charlotte, the festival announced the presence of the Center, marking a new visibility by displaying Charlotte's African American culture in its Center City area outside of segregated environments. The festival included dance and musical performances by prominent local artists and groups such as the gospel group, the Miracle Voices, who sang the popular song, "Oh Happy Day." The festival had a variety of artistic dance presentations. It attracted hundreds of visitors and brought much-needed public awareness of the Center.[26]

Reflecting a principal aspect of Maxwell's community service-oriented pedagogy, the Black Studies Program, later the Afro-American and African Studies Program, offered internships at the Center as part of the BSP/AAAS's service-learning course offerings. Maxwell placed students in management positions at the Center to prepare them to assume executive positions at arts and cultural institutions and expose them to the works and efforts of African American artists and arts educators, thus reinforcing some of the core tenets of Black Studies.[27]

Elaine Nichols, one of Maxwell's former students, currently serving as a curator at the Smithsonian National African American Museum in Washington DC worked managing the festival for several years. Always unorthodox, Maxwell entrusted Nichols to manage this significant event because she recognized her leadership potential and believed in granting students opportunities to excel outside of the academic arena. Responsible for securing artists for the festival, Nichols often persuaded skeptical visual artists to show their works. With Maxwell's support, she successfully coaxed up-and-coming local artist, Tommy Robinson, to display his work at the festival. After attendees purchased several pieces, the now nationally known artist became an active participant in the Center's activities. Nichols's youthful energy and fearlessness enabled her to manage this event with supportive older volunteers successfully.[28]

The Center now had a board of directors and a direction for the future, but it still had no operational space. Maxwell's friend, Center supporter *Carolina Israelite* newspaper editor, and UNC Charlotte professor, Harry Golden, offered to donate one of his homes for the Center to use. Maxwell graciously declined due to concerns that the Center's performances and activities might be disruptive in a residential area.[29] Maxwell then decided to utilize her community networks. Before the inception of the Center, Maxwell served on the advisory board of influential community activist Phyllis Lynch's Charlotte Mecklenburg Youth Council, an organization working to decrease student school withdrawals. As a member of the council's board, she helped the organization apply for funding from the Emergency School Aid Act of the Department of Health Education and Welfare. In an example of the rising power of Black women to support each other professionally, Maxwell now turned to Lynch for help with the Center.[30]

In response, Lynch agreed to provide space for the Center in the Youth Council's location on 916 Morehead Street. Friends since the mid-1960s, Maxwell's friendship with Lynch grew after she came to Maxwell's rescue by securing a school bus for her Morgan Elementary School students to take on field trips after the CMS refused to allocate funds for a bus. Lynch, a community activist in the Cherry neighborhood that included Morgan, raised money to purchase a bus for the students. In later years, Lynch worked tirelessly to prevent Cherry's extinction due to urban renewal. She rose to become a political power broker in the city as a reliable vote-getter, influencing local, state, and national Democratic party politics. Having Lynch's support helped to provide more recognition and standing among the city's influential nonprofit and charitable leaders.[31]

After the festival's success, the Center became known as the leading African American arts institution in Charlotte. The festival continued throughout the 1970s and 1980s as the Center found a permanent location and expanded its services. Over the years, the festival became an annual event in Charlotte's Uptown area. It brought African American artistic endeavors to the forefront, attracting visitors without regard to class or racial designations, free of charge, and without the need to wear certain types of attire. Its presence cemented the Center's place as the umbrella representative of African American arts in the city.[32]

UNC Charlotte's administration encouraged Harper and Maxwell, but it provided no long-term financial backing for the off-campus Center. They depended on the volunteer efforts of colleagues, such as Herman Thomas, but realized that securing outside funding would be necessary to sustain the Center. So, in 1975, Harper and Maxwell filed the necessary governmental incorporation documents to designate the Afro-American Cultural and Service Center as a nonprofit institution. During these early years, the Center received funding from the Arts and Science Council (ASC). Formerly the United Arts Fund (UAF), the reconstituted Arts and Science Council looked to restructure the city-sponsored organization. Since its inception in the late 1950s, the former UAF only funded seven arts organizations, and none of them reflected the diversity of the city's population. To encompass more arts institutions and broaden its funding base, the new ASC submitted a more inclusive, Cultural Action Plan to the Charlotte City Council for approval.[33]

The Arts and Sciences Council started the same year as the Center's founding in 1974, and it became the only African American arts institution to receive funding from the ASC. This funding from the ASC provided the Center with more financial stability. It helped validate its existence in the city as it became the primary representative of African American cultural offerings in Charlotte. In 1974, ASC President William H. Williamson III invited Maxwell to serve on the board of directors comprised of community advocates, business executives, former mayors, and cultural and civic leaders. As the co-founder of the AAASC, her appointment represented the necessity of including African American arts institutions in the city's arts funding and operational structures. During Maxwell's tenure, she made the passage of its Children's Arts Program, which worked with CMS and local artists to expose children to the arts, one of the biggest goals of the new ASC.[34] Over time, Maxwell adapted to the ASC's board culture, learning the intricacies of how an entity of its type funded arts institutions. She worked to build networks and alliances on the board in the same way that she did as an administrator at UNC Charlotte. She served along with several prominent business and civic leaders, including Charlotte City Council Member, Pat Locke Williamson.[35]

The Center was little more than a concept in 1974; Maxwell relied upon her negotiating skills to assure the other committee members that the Center would become the leading Black arts institution in the city. She used her presence to argue that by supporting the Center, the new ASC could counter some of the criticisms that it only funded elite, white arts institutions. Serving on the ASC helped Maxwell realize that despite the ASC's attempts to remake its image, it still offered most of its support to established arts organizations, leaving the Center to seek additional funding opportunities. In 1975, the Center petitioned the City Council to receive a portion of the federal Comprehensive

Employment and Training Act (CETA) Grant of $6,972 to pay the salary of James (Jim) Jeeter, its new executive director, who replaced volunteer director, Jim Hoard.[36]

As a board member, one of Maxwell's strategic goals involved persuading the ASC to include the Center in its long-range cultural development plan. This request to the City Council included remodeling Charlotte's First Baptist Church on 110 East 7th Street, now vacant, into a building to house performing spaces and offices for local arts groups called Spirit Square. If successful, Maxwell could find the Center a new home.[37] With the endorsement of Maxwell's friend, WBTV Community Affairs director, and prominent philanthropist, Loonis McGlohon, she managed to secure a location for the Center in the new Spirit Square building. Opening on October 2, 1976, in an office on the third floor, the Center offered music appreciation and Black history classes taught by AAAS interns and Arts and crafts storytelling for children.[38]

The year 1976 also marked another critical change for the Center as married former UNC Charlotte students Jerry and Brenda Hogue Springs helped reorganize the board by reducing it from fifty to fifteen members. Jerry and Brenda Springs thought that its large size led to redundancy and a lack of interest by some members. Jerry explained in a 1976 newspaper article, "The reorganization gave it some stability, and as a result, it functions better. The new members are more dedicated, and we have more participation." When she first helped to form the board, Maxwell invited a large group to ensure that it would have enough members. Trained by Maxwell to act, her student members may have misinterpreted others' more methodological or private efforts as actual inaction. Confident and dedicated in their mission to support the Center, Maxwell's students had no qualms about asking members, some of whom even held prominent positions in the city, to step down to streamline the board.[39]

Maxwell's plan to ensure that students participated in the Center at all levels led them to exert their influence far beyond the usual position of a student intern or volunteer. Just as she established orientation programs and the Block curriculum to help African American students adjust academically and create a sense of community and connection with the university, Maxwell wanted students to realize that they served an essential role in the Center's survival and success. These students and their allies' successful actions to reconstitute the board demonstrated their power to shape its direction. Chairperson Mamie Brewington suggested that the AACSC's new "energetic young board members should receive credit for the Center's rededication to community service." It now had its first operating budget of $6,000. It included $2,500 from the Arts and Science Council, $2,500 from Charlotte's City Council, and a $1,000 grant from the North Carolina Council for the Arts.[40]

With a new location, a paid director, and a budget, the Center emerged from its festival roots to become a vibrant center for Black culture. As its staff expanded, Harper remained involved but became less enmeshed in the AAC-SC's daily operations to encourage more community involvement. Maxwell remained in a core advisory role. She balanced helping the Center with her work to establish the National Council for Black Studies and her transition to working at Johnson C. Smith University. During the late 1970s, Maxwell connected UNC Charlotte's AAAS Program to the Center by hosting special events, like the reception to accompany her 1976 Black Women in America course. Maxwell and the Center sponsored speaking events on behalf of African American organizations, such as Johnson C. Smith's Student Government Association and UNC Charlotte's Black Student Union's Black History Month Program in 1978 that featured the sixties activist Stokely Carmichael (Kwame Ture). With Jeeter's management, the Center sponsored an exhibit and a fifty-page pictorial essay describing the Brooklyn neighborhood chronicling its history. It offered arts and historical programs for children, dance, and jazz performances, and became the host of the theater group the Ebony Players. Jeeter and volunteers established lasting relationships with other institutions like Johnson C. Smith University to provide additional space to sponsor art exhibits. The Center worked with CPCC to host adult education courses with African artistic themes. Soon on its way to becoming one of the preeminent African American cultural institutions in Charlotte, by the end of the 1970s, its push to create vibrant programming initiatives masked the somber reality that the Center faced severe funding deficits.[41]

Although a college administrator, Maxwell often ignored status or titles and related to people based on their talents and skills, not their background or behavior. T. J. Reddy, Maxwell's former student who helped stage the UNC Charlotte flag takeover and worked with her to establish the Black Studies Program, remained incarcerated when Maxwell contacted him to ask him to work as the artistic director for the Center. The newspaper reporter, poet, and political prisoner responded, "Bertha, I am in jail!" Maxwell did not see his situation as an obstacle. A talented visual artist and poet, she thought Reddy could do the job as soon as he gained release.[42]

In 1968, suspected arsonists burned down the stables of the Lazy B Ranch, and fourteen horses died. In 1972, informants told the police that Reddy and two others burned down the stables because of the Lazy B owner's segregated policies. The police arrested Reddy, Jim Grant, and Charles Parker for arson and other charges. Later that year, the defendants, now known as the "Charlotte Three," received harsh sentences. Grant had to do a twenty-five-year sentence, Reddy, twenty, and Parker, ten. The case received national attention as local and national prison and civil rights activists, including AAAS's Maxwell and Ann Carver, and public figures demanded their release when new information surfaced that the prosecutors failed to disclose that the informants received payments. After years of local and national protests demanding the release of the Charlotte Three, in 1978, the Charlotte City Council passed a resolution commuting their sentences, and a year later, North Carolina governor Jim Hunt followed suit, and the Charlotte Three were free. Reddy started working at the Center shortly after his release.[43]

When Herman Thomas joined the BSP faculty in 1974, he already had previous experience as a director of a Black Studies program as the founder of Springfield College's Black Cultural Center in Springfield, Massachusetts. As AAAS director, Maxwell often asked faculty to participate in non-academic or nontraditional community or cultural programs. Despite working at UNC Charlotte for one year, Maxwell thought Thomas a natural choice to be director based on his experience and leadership abilities. He agreed to work at the Center after he completed his doctoral studies. Following Real Estate Broker Sam Young, who served as board chairperson from 1977 to 1979, Thomas fulfilled his promise by becoming chairman of the Center's board of directors in 1979 after obtaining his PhD in 1978 from Hartford Seminary Foundation. Over the years, Thomas balanced teaching, serving as a minister, and serving in crucial leadership positions like chairman of the Center's board of directors for several terms from the 1970s to the 2000s. As she made the transition back to working at UNC Charlotte from Johnson C. Smith University, Maxwell depended on Thomas and credited his leadership as one of the crucial factors in maintaining the Center's survival during pivotal moments in its history, including dire funding crises and successful relocations.[44]

In 1979, the Center's CETA grant that funded Executive Director Jim Jeeter's salary ended, he subsequently resigned. With no director and mounting funding issues, the Center's future looked dim as it had to negotiate a $981 per month payment plan with Spirit Square after neglecting to pay rent for over a year. During that same period, Shirley Farrar, an education administrator and a recent transplant from Virginia, started volunteering at the Center. When other volunteers suggested that she contact Bertha Maxwell, she was intimidated to meet such a prominent figure in the city. Surprised to learn that Maxwell was so down to earth, Farrar recalled that the AACC co-founder told her about some of the Center's funding and personnel issues and gave her a copy of the Center's long-range plan for development. Sensing a need and with her then-husband's support, Farrar resigned from her stable job as an educational professional and applied to become the Center's new executive director. Reflecting Maxwell's leadership philosophies again, Maxwell overlooked Farrar's lack of experience managing a nonprofit arts institution to see her leadership qualities and dedication to service, which became apparent when Farrar agreed to work for the Center without a guarantee of a permanent salary![45]

During her tenure as executive director, from 1979 to 1984, Farrar established and re-activated several critical educational initiatives and artistic programs such as the Guest Artists and Visual Arts Program and led the Center to seek a new permanent location in the mid-1980s. Despite funding woes, Farrar, with the support of Thomas and a small staff that included Maxwell's former student, artist T. J. Reddy, and a cadre of dedicated UNCC student and community volunteers, helped create a dynamic cultural space. The Center sponsored everything from oral history and genealogical workshops to local events honoring Charlotte's early Black business leaders to jazz symposiums. Developing a Guest Artist in Residence Program, Farrar often invited national performing and visual artists like local jazz musician Billy Porter to do side workshops or performances when they appeared at other venues. When Farrar learned that visual artist Romare Bearden was in town, she first tried to reach the nationally known artist by phone to no avail. The determined director then just went to Bearden's hotel, where she pleaded with his assistant for him to visit the Center. Happy to learn that Charlotte had an African American arts center, the Charlotte native and internationally known artist generously agreed to stop by the Center to talk with patrons for no fee. Farrar worked with CMS to establish the first Building Bridges program, where visual and performing artists taught afterschool programs at schools in several low-income neighborhoods. Under Farrar's leadership, the Children's Arts Program, a Saturday arts program for kids, began in 1978. By the mid-1980s, this one-day event expanded to run almost the entire school year, meeting every Saturday at the YMCA on Trade Street from 10 a.m. to noon, from October to June.[46]

An Election as an Escape in 1980

Maxwell served as Farrar's support system that involved advising the new director and helping her fundraise by calling for the Center to organize a women's patrons' group. Having a mutual bond, Maxwell depended on Farrar to efficiently run the Center because, in 1980, the Center's co-founder decided to embark on a new venture that would draw her away from the daily concerns of the Center. While Maxwell continued to work with the Center as a board member and as a fundraiser, major personal tragedies helped her embark on a new endeavor. Not one to turn inward, Maxwell had several crises in her private life as she experienced a job change, divorce, and the illnesses and subsequent death of her brother, George Robert Lyons, at age fifty-one. Maxwell also had to face the terminal cancer diagnosis of her mother.[47] After Luellar's husband, Leroy Baxter, passed in 1963, Maxwell became her mother's sole caretaker.[48]

In an unusual move, she decided to run for a seat in the North Carolina House of Representatives to escape her grief. Motivated for personal reasons, she also decided to run because of the lack of African American women's leadership in state politics. Maxwell transformed her sadness about her family into a public campaign to enter public office. Some naysayers might have scoffed at the idea of a Black woman college administrator's candidacy as just some type of lark. By relying on established networks of people from diverse circles of Black Studies practitioners, white allies, and her sorority sisters, Maxwell pushed through her sadness to energize her campaign and impress potential voters as she waged a valiant attempt to win. Albeit running for the House seemed to be an odd choice for the educational administrator, Maxwell did have prior experience in the political realm as African American city councilperson Ron Leeper recommended her appointment to the Charlotte City Planning Commission in 1978. Unfortunately, Maxwell lost to UNC Charlotte Political Science Professor William J. McCoy in a close run-off vote. [49]

One of the first hurdles Maxwell faced involved securing permission from the University of North Carolina's Board of Governors to run for the Democratic primary without taking a leave of absence. She balked at this requirement to seek the board's approval because she thought that white professors routinely ran for office without undergoing this process. The board permitted Maxwell to run for the primary during the spring term, with the caveat; she may have to take unpaid leave to run in the general election.[50] It was a crisp, chilly morning on Friday, January 25, 1980, when Maxwell formally announced her run for the Democratic primary for one of Mecklenburg County's eight seats in the North Carolina State House of Representatives. Maxwell spoke to over forty well-wishers at the event held at the Mecklenburg County Board of Elections Office. Maxwell explained, "Running for the State House will be an uphill battle. It will not be something easy to accomplish." Nevertheless, she claimed that "the community would support her because she represented diverse perspectives and would offer accountable leadership."[51]

Maxwell's campaign platform included promoting diversity in government and developing legislation on various topics, including education, employment, inflation, energy, conservation, problems of the aging, and health care.[52] On April 18, the same day that she welcomed civil rights activist Rosa Parks to speak on campus, Maxwell's public endorsement by the North Carolina Association of Educators made the city's newspaper headlines.[53]

After campaigning for several months, Maxwell and her supporters eagerly awaited the results. When the last precincts reported that Maxwell won, finishing 7th with 16,929 votes out of thirteen candidates, in the May 6 Democratic Primary election, a *Charlotte News* journalist quoted one of Maxwell's supporters, who exclaimed, "Praise the Lord!" as she hugged the candidate. This unexpected win shocked Maxwell, whose poll numbers had her in a losing position of 10th place. As she thanked her campaign staff and supporters, Maxwell reiterated that she met her goal to get more Blacks involved in the political process, "raising consciousness because that was what it was all about." With six incumbents winning, Maxwell and optometrist Joe Black, who secured the eighth place with 16,706 votes, were the only newcomers to win. Her campaign now looked ahead to the general election when Maxwell and seven other Democratic candidates faced eight Republican candidates in the battle to win Mecklenburg County's eight available seats in the NC House.[54]

Maxwell's efforts to strengthen ties between AAAS students and the local community and her work with the Center allowed her to build powerful networks with influential organizations and businesses in Charlotte. Despite being the only African American woman candidate in the general election, Maxwell's ability to connect with diverse sections of the community resulted in her receiving endorsements from entities ranging from the NAACP, *the Charlotte News,* the Fraternal Order of Police, and her UNC Charlotte colleagues.[55]

During her campaign, Maxwell participated in community events, ranging from parades to meetings. Even though she campaigned for votes, Maxwell did not hesitate to speak her mind regarding controversial issues. On May 17, the first major urban riot or uprising in the US since the 1960s occurred in the Liberty City neighborhood of Miami, Florida, after an all-white Tampa, Florida jury acquitted four white police officers of the killing of Arthur McDuffie, a thirty-three-year-old Black insurance salesman. The police claimed McDuffie died in a December 1979 crash after a car chase with the officers. However, forensic, and other evidence later revealed that the police beat the unarmed Black man to death with their flashlights. After peaceful protests of the verdict and previous incidents of police brutality erupted in a three-day violent uprising, ten Blacks and eight whites lost their lives.[56] The police made 800 arrests, and the rebellion accrued over $100 million in damages. Several weeks later, in June, Charlotte Police Chief J. C. Goodman invited Maxwell and twenty-one prominent African American ministers, politicians, and educators like Sarah Stevenson and Kathleen Crosby to discuss improving relations between African Americans and law enforcement. Goodman wanted the group to establish measures to prevent future incidents in Charlotte, like the one that happened in Miami.[57]

When police officials asked the group if they thought a similar uprising could happen in Charlotte, several participants responded that no city was immune due to the adverse effects of rising unemployment and inflation. Maxwell remarked, "You going to tell me that you won't get mad if you didn't have any money?" During the two-hour meeting, they made the following suggestions. The police force should be responsible for prevention. Hire more African American officers in leadership positions. Require officers to undergo sensitivity training to prevent police harassment and institute a civilian review board to review complaints against the police. After the meeting, Maxwell commented, "If there's a plan of action that follows what he (Goodman) heard, then I think it's fantastic. If nothing happens, we could have stayed home." Sarah Stevenson added, "I think one thing that most of the people in that room felt is that we were going over things that had been discussed as much as ten years ago. While we've made some progress, we haven't made as much progress as we would like to see." Maxwell reiterated, "They say we have to wait, but we have waited 300 years." Even though Maxwell could face public scrutiny as a candidate for political office, as the director of UNC Charlotte's African American and African Studies Program and a community activist, she refused to sugarcoat her thoughts regarding the systemic racism and poverty that led to the uprisings.[58]

As a candidate, Maxwell looked to increase her presence in Charlotte's community by participating in programs like the community policing workshop and holding campaign events. Out of the candidates running for the House, Maxwell had a unique advantage. As the founder of the National Council for Black Studies, she attracted nationally known figures to support the campaign and help her fundraise. Maxwell welcomed over 700 students and supporters at a Wednesday, October 8 morning campaign rally at Johnson C. Smith University's church with civil rights leader, and Operation PUSH (People United to Save Humanity) Director Jesse Jackson Sr., and the director of the US Department of Labor's Women's Bureau, Alexis Herman. After Maxwell's AAAS student Gaile Dry-Burton drove Jackson to the event, he energized the enthusiastic crowd in a group chant saying, "I am somebody! I may be poor, but my mind is a pearl! I can learn anything in the world! If my mind can believe it, I know I can achieve it! The White House isn't the biggest reason to vote. Who's on the board at the schoolhouse: At the statehouse? At the courthouse?" After Jackson Sr.'s stirring message roused the crowd, Maxwell's campaign arranged for other prominent public figures in education and politics to hold four additional prayer meetings and events that included an October 11 prayer rally at JCSU with former Morehouse College President Benjamin Mays and Bill Owens, Massachusetts's first African American State Senator also spoke at a November 1 event.[59]

Unlike her previous individual experiences at being a "first" or an "only," Maxwell's ability to attract these prominent figures to her campaign reflected its national impact as she could be the first African American woman elected to the North Carolina House of Representatives.[60] Her fellow educators realized that if Maxwell won, she could promote Black Studies's tenets of self-pride, activism, and community support to a much wider audience. Black Studies would now have one of its own in a powerful political office. Unfortunately, the publicity did not transfer to substantial financial donations. Maxwell explained that "these politicians contributed their time, not their money." In addition to holding traditional events, earlier, on October 7, Maxwell's campaign sponsored a disco music dance party at the Excelsior Club, one of the oldest and most prominent African American-owned entertainment venues in the city. With most of the donations given by individual members of Maxwell's sorority, Delta Sigma Theta, she graciously thanked everyone for gifts of any amount, remarking that "money has come in from the little people who care," Maxwell acknowledged that the campaign was not wealthy. For the primary, she raised over $10,148, but her expenses totaled $11,751.[61]

The whirlwind of campaign events and work occupied most of Maxwell's time when her mother died in late October. Maxwell's world stood still as she suddenly had to manage the campaign and make funeral arrangements, only a few short weeks before the election. With the support of her mother's informally adopted son, Robert Wearing, and her family, Maxwell attended her mother's funeral. The support of her mother, a former domestic worker, enabled Maxwell to thrive. Luellar had the opportunity to see Maxwell interact with national figures in a life that she could have never imagined for her daughter.[62]

With the election soon approaching, Maxwell reduced her campaign stops to devote more time to family concerns. Shortly after her mother's death, Maxwell learned that despite endorsing her in the primary race in the State House election, the *Charlotte Observer* newspaper decided to back Jim Black. The latter finished after Maxwell in the primary. The editorial board wrote, "We didn't recommend Mr. Black in the spring primary. We believed the background, training, and experience of Bertha Maxwell would better complement the strengths of the incumbents, but since last spring, Mr. Black clearly has done a lot of homework and shown an impressive ability to grow and learn." The newspaper writers claimed, "His point of view has broadened considerably, and he now displays a better understanding of issues than Ms. Maxwell."[63]

The inference that Black, an optometrist from Matthews, NC, who had only voted twice since 1976, knew more about the issues affecting Charlotte than Maxwell, a seasoned community activist, reflected more about the editorial board's opinions than the facts. The board's writers graciously gave Black the benefit of the doubt, commending him on his ability to learn the issues, but it did not grant Maxwell the same privilege. Notwithstanding whether this slight reflected the editorial writers' doubts in Maxwell's abilities or the biases of its writers, Maxwell still held the endorsement of the city's rival newspaper, *Charlotte News*. With passionate rebuttal letters from citizens and Maxwell's associates decrying the *Charlotte Observer's* switch, Maxwell proceeded on with the campaign.[64]

Before her mother's passing, Maxwell's campaign had gained more momentum raising more than $18,227,05 by October. Despite the conservative wave sweeping the nation, Democrats still won most of Mecklenburg County's House Seats in the November 4 election. She received 57,876 votes overall, with high vote counts from predominantly African American precincts, but it would not be enough to win. She finished in ninth place after incumbent Gus Economos, with 60,017 votes.[65] Jim Black's fundraising efforts paid off when he also won a seat in the NC House of Representatives. By soliciting $1,000 donations from his optometrist colleagues, Black raised $36,000, which was almost twice as much as Maxwell's campaign did. Ambivalent, she told a reporter from the *Charlotte Observer* that she thought that she ran a good campaign despite the "lag from her mother's death two weeks ago. I wouldn't have done anything differently. I think I ran an impressive race."[66]

Despite failing to garner enough votes to secure a House Seat, Maxwell didn't regret running as her campaign served as a distraction as her mother became progressively more ill. She experienced another loss as her paternal grandfather, Monroe Earle, passed later that October. Maxwell's campaign propelled her to greater prominence within the city as she continued to engage in the civic life of Charlotte by working with local African American politicians such as city councilperson Fred Alexander and Charlotte mayor Harvey Gantt. Maxwell's impressive results finishing a close ninth showed that Black women did have the potential to win. This race helped open the doors for Anne Brown Kennedy of Forsythe, North Carolina, to become the first African American woman in 1983 to win the election to the State House. Maxwell didn't make history as a first in this instance. Nevertheless, her remarkable venture into local and state politics as the director of UNC Charlotte's Afro-American and African Studies Program in a southern city demonstrated the growing acceptance and influence of Black Studies as an extension of the Black Power movement by a cross section of Charlotte's citizens less than ten years from its inception in 1971 as an educational program of study. As the first local African American woman to make serious inroads with her candidacy, Maxwell harnessed the growing organizational power of Charlotte's African American communities to encourage Black Studies's tenets of community empowerment, educational equity, and cultural advocacy.[67]

The Center at Spirit Square, 1979–1984

One of the seldom examined effects of the civil rights and women's movements' efforts to eliminate gender and racial employment discrimination was the opening of leadership positions to African American women in Black and white nonprofit institutions. The experiences of women directors and board chairs reveal the impact of interlocking oppressions. They encountered sexism as they interacted with male employees, artists, and staff and internalized gender discrimination from other women. Women directors dealt with structural racism as they sought donations from the broader community and vied for funding allocations against predominantly white organizations. These women contended with the complexities of class as the Center struggled to provide inclusive programming that appealed to both working-class African Americans and Black professionals. Its directors had to confront these issues and face the harsh reality that failure to meet proscribed fundraising goals could result in their termination.

When Maxwell first began to select board members for the new Center, she invited several prominent Black ministers to join. Even with the advent of desegregation, most of Charlotte's religious institutions remained segregated by race, and African American ministers still held significant influence in Charlotte's Black communities. Maxwell knew she had to get their support for the Center to succeed. Over the years, ministers served on the board, sponsored fundraising campaigns, and encouraged their members to volunteer. Maxwell knew several of these ministers from interactions at her church, Friendship Baptist, at other community events as a member of Delta Sigma Theta Sorority, or as friends and advisers. Even her colleague Herman Thomas was a minister at First Baptist Church-West in Charlotte. As a growing New South city,

Charlotte attracted Black migrants. Some long-term residents, including some of the Center's board members, still attempted to determine a newcomer's, like Farrar's, possible class status, and even their racial "authenticity" through their church and organizational memberships. Despite having to raise funds to cover her salary, Farrar discovered that some board members questioned her dedication, even going so far as to ponder if Farrar was "Black enough" because she didn't belong to one of the more influential African American churches in the city, attending a more mainstream church instead.[68]

Aside from some board members' seemingly intrusive non-work-related presumption, others thought the executive director's religious affiliation limited her ability to make important contacts with African American religious leaders on behalf of the Center. They doubted the possibility that Farrar could eventually foster new connections with predominantly white churches. Membership in one of Charlotte's more influential African American places of worship could lead to more opportunities to solicit donations, recruit volunteers for the Center, and promote its membership drives. When Maxwell encouraged the Center to hire Farrar, she saw a woman who agreed to run the Center without knowing if she would ever get paid because she believed in its mission. Maxwell never doubted Farrar's "Blackness." She had no problem with Farrar's religious preference.[69]

One of the pressing issues affecting the Center concerned how to remain dedicated to Harper's and Maxwell's original vision for the local site for community empowerment with alternative ideas of the Center as a space to bolster African American economic progress. As a newcomer to the city, Farrar had little knowledge of the hidden guidelines regarding social class among Black Charlotteans. Farrar received praise from the board and Center members for securing grants from CMS to fund the Center's educational programs. However, when she proceeded to recruit children from Earle Village, a local public housing project, to participate in the Center's Saturday Children's Art Program (CAP), she unknowingly sparked the ire of some of the Center's members who had children in the program. The rise of poverty and the emergence of the crack drug epidemic during the 1980s led to increased violence and had a devasting impact on African American families in low-income neighborhoods.[70] Scholars continue to examine the effects of the increase in the surge in gun violence, including state-sanctioned actions on African American communities and the mass incarceration of Blacks for nonviolent crimes. Fewer historical studies analyze the impact of these issues within diverse African American communities.[71]

The Center's members' criticism exposes the complexities of African American middle-class life as they navigated through the pitfalls of living in a desegre-gated society. On the surface, some of the CAP parents' resentment smacked of "bougieness" or elitism that resurrected historic chasms among African Ameri-cans based on class and internalized racism. Sociologist Karyn Lacy argued that as some middle-class Blacks preferred to live and work in white spaces for status and economic reasons, they practiced a form of "strategic assimilation" carefully selecting Black spaces for their own escape from the isolation and racism within these white environments. African American middle-class parents enrolled their children in Black cultural spaces like CAP to interact with other African Ameri-can children to ensure that they "remembered where they came from," or to sustain their Black self-identities. When their children participated, whether it was an invitation-only exclusive social organization like Jack and Jill, or in the Center's Children's Arts Program, these Black professionals expected their chil-dren to learn about Black history and culture.[72]

Knowledge of aspects of African American culture, like music, art, and lit-erature, then becomes a sort of measuring tool to determine one's Blackness. As Lacy contended, as these parents embraced these Black spaces even though some of them originally came from meager beginnings, they distanced them-selves from working-class Blacks, adopting the negative stereotypes of laziness, immoral behavior, and criminality surrounding economically disadvantaged African Americans. Like other Black professionals, some of the CAP parents even succumbed to the proliferation of the harmful and pervasive "thug or child predator" stereotypes in the media and promoted through governmen-tal policies. Consequently, these CAP parents may have considered housing projects like Earle Village or other low-income areas, danger zones. Whether affected by an actual incident of physical violence or merely making assump-tions based on negative stereotypes of the "project kids," some of the CAP's middle-class parents possibly feared that their children might get bullied if they interacted with the kids from Earle Village.[73]

Although these parents' criticisms reflected their seemingly classist appre-hensions, their reticence reflected a desire for the Children's Arts Program to serve as a supportive community for their children who possibly experienced isolation as Black children attending predominantly white schools. Similar to Jack and Jill of America, Inc., which was established in 1938 to create oppor-tunities for Black children living in white neighborhoods to interact, some of these parents viewed the CAP as an enriching space, where their kids could connect with other Black children who potentially had the same values and backgrounds. Sociologist Patricia A. Banks suggested that Black middle-class parents placed their children in arts programs to help them engage in a cultural socialization process to appreciate African American visual artistic culture. Charlotte's Black middle-class parents enrolled their kids in the CAP program because they wanted them to learn aspects of African American visual and performing arts culture not taught in their schools.[74]

On the other hand, some of the parents from Earle Village feared that the other kids might not accept their children. Even though some of the Center members' perception of the Children's Arts Program conflicted with Farrar's directives, the kids in CAP formed friendships. They enjoyed the program despite their parents' opinions. The Center's children's education programs may have served a purpose for middle-class parents, but Harper and Maxwell's original purpose and intent involved helping all Black children. Eventually reshaped by the complex influences of school desegregation and a crime epidemic, by the 1990s, the Children's Arts Program had transitioned to the Building Bridges afterschool program designed to serve the children from Earle Village specifically. Located in several low-income neighborhoods across the city, the Building Bridges program served as a much-needed educational resource for parents who wished to broaden their children's environments by uncovering new artistic and cultural worlds. On a more practical level, the program's structured environment reassured working parents that their children could thrive and be safe in a teacher-supervised cultural refuge, protected from the potential dangers that their children could encounter. This CMS-funded program addressed current concerns and fulfilled Maxwell and Harper's overall mission of the Center to expose Black children and especially those from low-income families to the arts.[75]

Fortunately, other board members supported Farrar, but she sometimes grew disillusioned from these conflicts and sought Maxwell's guidance. Maxwell served as Farrar's encourager, adviser, and support system. She helped the director in numerous ways, including sharing tips to manage Farrar's interactions with the board and calling to secure funding from a reluctant donor after the director received a denial. When the director expressed her frustrations, Maxwell listened with a sympathetic and pragmatic ear, telling Farrar, "Don't let them drive you away." She encouraged the director to remember that she played an instrumental role in the survival of the Center. Maxwell's mentoring advice enabled Farrar to continue working despite disappointments and dilemmas.[76]

One of Farrar's main dilemmas included the constant struggle to secure funding. In a February 1980 newspaper article, the director explained that "the Center is running on a 'vicious cycle because it wanted to expand its programming to attract new members but needed more fee-paying members to fund these new offerings. Farrar had to request a payment plan arrangement to pay the Center's overdue past rent to Spirit Square's building managers. In February, the Center only raised $24,000 of its proposed $64,000 budget. The Arts and Science Council's funding allocation included monetary support for the Center's affiliated arts groups. Over $2,700 of the ASC's $9,000 allotment to the Center went to the Ebony Players and the Performing Arts Ensemble, PAGE, a group of poets, musicians, and dancers. To draw more community support, Farrar co-sponsored the Broadway musical *Ain't Misbehavin'* with the Charlotte Section of the National Council of Negro Women. Held at Charlotte's Owens's auditorium, the Black History Month event raised almost $4,000 from ticket sales. The director worked with another African American women's public service organization, the Charlotte Chapter of The Links Incorporated, to sponsor an enrichment program where PACE performers worked with teen girls.[77]

In June, Board Chair Herman Thomas supported Farrar's efforts by requesting additional funds for the Center from the Charlotte City Council. In Thomas's 1980 presentation to the council, he contended, "Black people constitute about one-third of the Charlotte population. It seems only fair that it (the Center) should receive more than the amount previously allocated and the currently recommended amount to operate effectively and efficiently." Thomas reminded the council members of the Center's vital role, "as the only Black cultural organization, which seeks to preserve not only Black culture but caters to the general population." In Thomas's persuasive description of the Center as an influential arts center that welcomed anyone regardless of race, he illuminated its continuous pursuit of equity and recognition as a vital arts institution in the city. Thomas received $10,000 in 1980.[78]

In Thomas's subsequent 1981 request to the council for a funding increase to $15,000, he touted the fact "that the Center's main objectives include educating the Charlotte community about the "integral part of which minorities have played in Charlotte and in American culture." Thomas reiterated, "these minority contributions have already been walked over and obscured in the educational processes as it is." He acknowledged "that white organizations received continuous funding even though, traditionally recognized organizations will never be able to have the ability to handle this need. The Center, nevertheless, is serving an assortment of needs, and its services are in great demand, as evidenced by the letters of requests to visit by school principals, teachers, students, and community persons, both Black and white." Despite Thomas's well-reasoned plea, the council denied the Center's request for additional funds. Thomas's appeal to the council symbolized the precarious position of local African American cultural organizations like the Center that depended on local governments to bolster their budgets. These government entities endorsed the Center and other African American organizations as part of its promotions of Charlotte but neglected to provide adequate funding to sustain its operation.[79]

Maxwell and Farrar attempted to supplement the limited funds that the Center received from the Arts and Science Council and Charlotte's City Council by continuing to apply for financial and programming grants and work with volunteers to build a patrons' fundraising network. No novices to fundraising, these volunteers, who included Mary Maxwell, spearheaded capital campaigns. They supported other African American institutions, such as Johnson C. Smith University, or charities like the United Negro College Fund. This national non-profit organization offered scholarships and raised funds for historically Black universities and colleges. These volunteers contacted influential business leaders, African American churches, fraternal organizations, and potential individual donors interested in supporting the arts.[80]

During Farrar's first year as director, in 1979, Bertha Maxwell reached out to several volunteers, including Vivian Williams and Mary Maxwell, to ask them to organize a patron group of people interested in supporting the Center. Williams, an education administrator, and former boutique owner was the spouse of Warren C. Williams, the first Black physician to gain hospital privileges at a white hospital in Charlotte. Williams shared that "Bertha contacted me and told me that they are in the process of organizing a membership drive for the year and said that they hadn't gotten the financial support that they needed." So, Williams contacted other volunteers, including fellow founder Adeline Hunt, to meet to establish the Friends of the Afro, short for Afro-American Cultural Center. Williams added, "We have to get out there and get involved. The Center is a viable and visible part of Charlotte Mecklenburg." On Sunday, July 29, 1979, the Center's resident performing arts group, the Ebony Players, sponsored An Evening of Ebony Entertainment as the Friends of the Afro's first event. The $13 ticket price to attend included a free membership to the Center. Williams told a newspaper reporter that the Center hoped that subsequent events and initiatives would add more than one-thousand new members to its current membership of slightly under 200 members. After the success of their event to raise funds and attract donors, the Friends of the Afro group continued sponsoring fundraising initiatives.[81]

Most of the women who participated in this group already belonged to other women's groups or civic organizations. Working to help support the Center offered them opportunities to build new friendships and alliances outside their familiar circles. For those women who recently moved to Charlotte, joining the Friends of the Afro helped them meet new friends with similar interests. During segregation, organizations ranging from small neighborhood groups to national entities played a vital role in the social, civil, and cultural lives of African American women by providing leadership opportunities and spaces to engage in acts of personal enjoyment. In 1980s Charlotte, the rise of groups like Friends of the Afro reflected Black women's economic progress and new intersectional challenges. As they moved to exclusive predominantly white neighborhoods or reached the executive level in corporations, they struggled against new, more subtle reconfigurations of racism and sexism from chilling isolation to piercing microaggressions. Building on a historical tradition of women's organizing, for some of these women, joining the Friends of the Afro, helped them to build a sense of community, form powerful networks, and use their influence to help the Center prosper.[82]

By 1981, the forty-plus Friends of the Afro, now renamed the Friends of the Arts, sponsored the first Jazzy Christmas Luncheon, a semi-formal musi-cal event at a room in Efrid's Department Store at 120 North Tryon Street to raise funds for the Center. Once again, Maxwell called on Loonis McGlohon to perform at the luncheon for free along with another local performer and artist in residence at the Center, Michael Porter. In subsequent years, Black-owned McDonald's Cafeteria on Beatties Ford Road hosted the annual Jazzy Christ-mas Luncheon that featured entertainment and offered awards and recognition to influential artists, sponsors, and volunteers for a moderately priced ticket. Williams organized and managed the luncheon that became a main fundraiser for the Center until she stepped down in the mid-2000s.[83]

As Maxwell encouraged organizing community fundraising groups, she worked with the Center's executive staff to lobby local public officials for their support. Fortunately, one of Charlotte's most influential African American pol-iticians, Harvey B. Gantt, served on the Center's board. Active in civil rights since high school, in 1965, Gantt became the first African American person to graduate from Clemson University in Clemson, SC. He later received a Master of City Planning Degree from the Massachusetts Institute of Technology in 1970 and relocated to Charlotte to join the Odell and Associates architecture firm. In 1971, Gantt co-founded the Gantt Huberman Architects and Associates with Jeff Huberman in Charlotte. When Center Board Member Fred Alexan-der decided to vacate his city council seat to run for the North Carolina State Senate in 1974, he asked Maxwell if Gantt, who also served on the board, would be the right person to fill his seat. She told her friend that she thought Gantt would be a good choice. Of course, Maxwell's approval of the rising political leader likely had minimal influence as Gantt later won his election to the City

Council. Though Maxwell failed in her bid to gain a seat in the North Carolina House several years later in 1980, this behind-the-scenes conversation with Alexander emphasized her growing political influence and the hidden power of Black women community actors to shape the local political environment. As a Center board member and later as a City Council member, Gantt helped to promote the interests of the Center. In turn, in 1983, when Gantt ran for mayor of Charlotte, the Center's volunteers participated in his successful campaign.[84]

Maxwell, the Center, and the Community

During the 1980s, Maxwell led the AAAS Program to secure departmental status, served on the Executive Board of the National Council for Black Studies, held national elected office in Delta Sigma Theta Sorority, and continued to serve as an adviser to the Center. Despite all these responsibilities, Maxwell, an administrator at an integrated university, never severed her connections to Charlotte's African American communities. She did not hesitate to respond to a plea from Loonis McGlohon to help civil rights icon Septima Poinsette Clark, 1898–1987. After moving to Columbia, South Carolina, in the early 1930s for a higher paying position, the Charleston native and civil rights activist rose to prominence after participating in the NAACP's Columbia teacher salary equalization campaign. In South Carolina, on average, Black teachers received 2.4 percent lower salaries than white teachers. African American teachers with advanced degrees and years of experience often received lower salaries than entry-level white teachers. In 1945, Clark worked with NAACP lead attorney Thurgood Marshall and local lawyers to courageously ask Black and white teachers to share their personal salary information. The teachers' pay stubs exposed the blatant salary inequities and served as evidence in the NAACP's successful *Thompson v. Gibbs* case, which eventually led to the state equalizing salaries later that year. Now Clark led teachers to fight the state's new tactic of basing teachers' salaries and employment on testing scores. With limited access to professional training, African American teachers suffered job losses under the plan. Later fired because of her affiliation and activism work with the NAACP and denied her pension, in the 1950s, Myles Horton of the Highlander Folk School in Monteagle, Tennessee, invited Clark to teach workshops. In her classes, students like Rosa Parks learned the meanings of citizenship and civic activism. After Tennessee revoked Highlander's charter in 1959, Clark returned to South Carolina, where she and her cousin, civil rights activist Bernice Johnson Reagon, and Esau Jenkins developed over thirty-seven citizenship schools in the Sea Islands and throughout the state. Tapped in 1961 to join Martin Luther King Jr.'s Southern Christian Leadership Conference (SCLC), she eventually established over 800 citizenship schools to train teachers in voter education methods and civics. Called the "Mother of the Movement," by civil rights leaders, in 1972, Clark won a seat on the Charleston School Board.[85]

Maxwell interacted with Clark over the years when she arranged for the activist to speak at UNC Charlotte and the Center. In 1979, when Clark came to Charlotte to promote WBTV's documentary on her life, "What's It Like Being Septima Poinsette Clark?" Maxwell organized local speaking events for her, and a few years later, in 1982, she and Farrar arranged for the former Charleston School Board Member to speak at the Center and UNC Charlotte when Clark returned for the re-airing of the 1979 documentary on her life. After learning about Clark's financial troubles, Farrar even invited Clark to stay at her home because the Center could not afford a hotel.[86]

Several years later, in 1985, when McGlohon realized that Clark's home was in disrepair, he organized a letter-writing campaign to solicit funds for the activist, raising some $300. Due to her participation in the NAACP's teacher salary equalization case, the state of South Carolina denied Clark's teaching pension in 1956, only to reinstate a small lump sum payment of $3,600 in 1976.[87] Similar to civil rights activist Rosa Parks, whom Clark taught at the Highlander Folk School, these women sacrificed their economic status and often family connections to serve on the front lines of the civil rights movement. Fans often bestowed Clark with accolades, but she needed tangible financial support.[88] In economic distress at the time of the fundraisers, Clark, 87, had limited physical abilities to do speaking engagements.[89]

After working with Clark when the station aired its 1979 documentary based on her life and experiences, McGlohon learned that Clark needed financial help to repair her damaged roof. He promptly contacted Maxwell and admonished her for "letting her heroes be treated this way," and asked what she could do. So, Maxwell went to work. With support from WBTV, the Center, and African American women's groups, she organized *Herstory Day,* a reception and luncheon at the Excelsior Club, honoring Clark and other local Black women leaders. With tickets set at $12, some 200 people attended the gala affair with entertainment provided by McGlohon. After receiving almost $3,000 in proceeds from the events and other donations, Maxwell and McGlohon helped Clark financially and brought attention to her plight, generating later support. Again, Maxwell's friendships with people like Alice Tate or Loonis McGlohon transcended the typical one-sided, generous benefactor, thankful recipient relationship example to form mutually beneficial alliances. Maxwell's enriching presence in McGlohon's life enabled him to feel comfortable enough to openly shame her as a representative of her people when he learned about Clark's plight. McGlohon knew that Maxwell would resolve the issue and trusted her judgment. In 1980, the city of Charlotte remodeled the sanctuary of the former First Baptist Church at Spirit Square and renamed it the McGlohon Theater. McGlohon and Maxwell both overlooked preconceived class expectations or gender or racial stereotypes about people to form friendships based on character and not their status. Despite being an internationally known musical artist, McGlohon often performed for free or at a low cost at the Center.[90]

As a modern-day race woman, Maxwell relied on her cultural capital or influence to honor a woman who sacrificed so much to better the lives of African Americans. In celebrating Clark's service, Maxwell used this opportunity to bring attention and recognition to Charlotte's Black women activists. Herstory Day honored seven other local educational and political activists including civil rights activist Aurelia Henderson, the first Black woman to manage a Post Office Branch in Charlotte in the 1950s; school desegregation forerunners Fannie Waterman Berry and Delois Huntley Miller; voting rights advocates Calvene Ross and Laura Malone, organizers of the 1960s' voter registration and desegregation nonprofit, Mecklenburg Organization on Political Affairs (MOPA); Virginia Stepteau, a promoter of voter registration and the city's first African American female voting precinct registrar; and Grier Town neighborhood community activist Naomi Drenan. The success of this event epitomizes Maxwell's ability to connect people from disparate backgrounds to celebrate or to enhance African American women's lives. Although not trained as a formal historian, Maxwell's efforts reflect her sense of dedication to commemorating and preserving African American women's history.[91]

The Center Faced a New Decade of Change

During the 1980s, Charlotte's downtown area became known as "Uptown." Initially coined by nineteenth-century traders who shortened the phrase "up to town" to Uptown, Charlotte's city leaders promoted the name change to draw attention to its new vibrant city center.[92] In 1982, Farrar successfully petitioned the ASC to provide its allotment on an annual basis, which provided more financial stability. Despite this achievement, the Center still faced funding limitations. After serving as director for four years, Farrar became adept in maintaining the Center's ambitious programming offerings with limited budgets. As a result, its increased presence in Charlotte now mandated that the institution find a larger space.[93] As it evolved into a local arts center, it abbreviated its name to just the Afro-American Cultural Center by 1984. Harper originally wanted local Black Charlotteans to run the Center. Although she remained in an advisory role, her involvement in its daily affairs lessened over the years.[94]

Once a small southern city in the shadow of Atlanta, Charlotte began a process of economic growth that eventually led it to become the third-largest banking center in the world by the early 2000s. Charlotte's business leaders, such as Bank of America CEO Hugh McColl Jr., had formed influential alliances with the city's political leaders to build artistic institutions and sports venues to attract potential employees and tourists.[95] Within this context of urban renewal and global growth, Mary Harper and Bertha Maxwell created the concept for an Afro-American Cultural and Service Center.[96]

6

Charlotte's Afro-American Cultural Center and the Rise of the New South, Post-Soul City

In the early 1970s, urban renewal, interstate construction, and the closing of inner-city schools had decimated African American neighborhoods in Charlotte and other cities across the nation.[1] In response, educational and cultural advocates, like Mary Harper and Bertha Maxwell, created programs, organizations, and institutions to remedy the growing sense of displacement and cultural loss among Black Charlotteans. Despite having to contend with funding shortages, by 1986, the Center embodied Harper and Maxwell's vision of a Black arts center after its relocation to the historic Little Rock African Methodist Episcopal Zion Church on 403 North Myers Street. The church relocated to a new building nearby on 401 North McDowell Street. This chapter scrutinizes the evolution of Harper and Maxwell's vision for the Afro-American Cultural Center as it expanded its presence in Charlotte. Now, as one of the city's most influential arts institutions, it reconfigured its cultural mission to adapt to growth while simultaneously grappling with stark financial realities from the 1980s to the 2000s.

Several scholars of Charlotte, such as Thomas Hanchett, David Goldfield, William Graves, Heather Smith, Gerald Ingalls, Isaac Heard Jr., and Steven Samuel Smith chronicled Charlotte's history and its rise as a pro-business progressive, New South, global city. Historians first used the term "New South" to analyze the efforts of southern cities and the business elite to describe economic actions to rebuild the South in the aftermath of the destruction from the Civil War. During Reconstruction, southern business leaders reconceived the image of the old, slavery-based South to emphasize the rise of a New South. This new concept emphasized diversifying southern economies by encouraging business and manufacturing development and downplayed the rising implementation of Jim Crow segregation of African Americans. In the post–World War II, post–civil rights era, Charlotte emerged as a prototype of the modern New

South city that encouraged non-agricultural businesses and promoted moderate race relations.[2] Scholars, including William Frey and Carol Stack, and Zandria Robinson in such diverse fields as history, geography, demography, sociology, and cultural studies, continue to analyze the reverse migration of African Americans to southern cities, like Charlotte, in the aftermath of the civil rights movement.[3]

Looking beyond the outward perception of Charlotte as a New South city, "that made busing work," one can see that the decimation of Black neighborhoods through urban renewal and gentrification lies at the root of the development of the new Uptown or Center City. Scholars of the post-integration Black middle class, including Patricia A. Banks, argue that members of the Black middle class supported African American art to reaffirm their collective self-identities. These patrons wanted to use their economic power to advance Black artistic expression.[4] Whether describing Charlotte as a New South, global or post-soul city, these scholars investigate how the promise of improved economic opportunities and the perception of less overt racism led African Americans to influence and reshape Charlotte and other southern cities.

Charlotte's reputation as a New South city did not just attract businesses to the "Queen City," African Americans saw the growing area as a location where Blacks, like Maxwell, could progress economically and socially.[5] Following her mother's relocation in the 1930s, Maxwell moved to Charlotte in the 1950s to work and later enrolled in college. Recent scholarship by historians such as Bernadette Pruitt and Luther Barnes, whose works on Black migration to urban southern cities from communities in the rural South continue to expand the traditional understandings of African American migration. Historians still need to thoroughly analyze the return or reverse migration of Blacks to the South and especially southern urban cities since the 1970s.[6]

Cultural critic and writer Nelson George's *Post-Soul Nation: The Explosive, Contradictory, Triumphant, and Tragic 1980s, as Experienced by African Americans, Previously Known as Blacks and Before that Negroes* offers a poignant, personal exploration of the significant events that shaped African American urban life after as Nelson explained, the "soul" era or height of Black cultural consciousness (soul music, soul food, etc.) of the late 1960s and 1970s. In *This Ain't Chicago: Race, Class, and Regional Identity in the Post-Soul South*, Zandria Robinson reconceptualizes Nelson's concept of the post-soul era to discuss how new African American migrants helped to transform southern cities, like Memphis, into "post-soul," urban enclaves that outwardly welcomed middle-class African Americans. Blacks in Charlotte, Raleigh, Atlanta, and Dallas envisioned these cities as locations for progress and innovation.[7]

Both the African American Museum in Dallas (AAM) founded by Bishop College (Dallas, Texas) librarian and history professor Harry Robinson Jr. and Charlotte's AACC opened in 1974. Charlotte's AACC and Dallas's African American Museum stemmed from the visions of educators affiliated with colleges and universities. Harry Robinson Jr. first opened the African American Museum of Life and Culture in Dallas as part of the Special Collections of Zale Library at Bishop College. After Bishop's closing in 1988, the Museum relocated to the WRR Radio Station Building in the Fair Park section of Dallas. First, a site for the Texas State Fair, in 1936, the 277-acre Fair Park site received refurbishing when the federal government and the city constructed new art deco buildings as part of the Texas Centennial Exposition World's Fair. National and local civil rights leaders successfully received federal funds to construct the Hall of Negro Life at Fair Park, the first inclusion of African Americans in a World's Fair. With exhibits describing African American achievements in business, education, art, and health, over sixty-thousand visitors attended the Hall of Negro Life. After the Centennial, in a harsh example of the reinforced disrespect of racial segregation, the city demolished the majestic building and put a whites-only swimming pool in its place. Visitors continued to come year-round to Fair Park to visit the music hall, museums, and the Cotton Bowl football stadium. After the passage of a $1.2 million city bond in 1985, Robinson Jr., successfully secured additional private donations to construct a $7 million African American Museum in 1993. The 38,000-square-foot structure opened on the site of the former Hall of Negro Life Building.[8]

The AAM in Dallas and the Afro-American Cultural Center/Gantt Center both began as community engagement efforts arising from their respective schools to later emerge as influential arts institutions. Comparing the development of the Afro-American Cultural Center with the African American Museum in Dallas contributes to the much-needed historical discussion of Black cultural institutions in the post–civil rights era urban South and supplements the scholarship of historians, including Andrea Burns, by examining the history of the African American Museum movement. Southern cultural centers and museums, such as Charlotte's AACC, Dallas's AAM, and Atlanta's Hammond House Museum (1988), along with those in smaller southern enclaves, need further examination.[9]

As this chapter looks at the myriad of ways Maxwell engaged with her community as an educator, community citizen, and social activist, it addresses the question: How did the efforts of Maxwell and other cultural activists drive Charlotte to actualize its New South image? This image of the progressive New South city helped to attract thousands of African Americans. As these newcomers relocated to Charlotte, they shaped the meaning and dimensions of the city's African American communities. New residents represented a growing demographic trend of reverse migration as more and more African Americans relocated from urban areas in the East, Midwest, and West to the South.

Experienced community activists, such as Maxwell, now faced new obstacles working with the "Black community," when traditional African American enclaves, such as Charlotte's Brooklyn neighborhood, either disappeared or its residents moved to former all-white areas. During the subsequent years, Charlotte's dispersed African American communities became even more diverse due to the influx of African Americans from different regions relocating to Charlotte. This reverse migration of Blacks to Charlotte since the 1970s exposed the growing class divisions between rising African American professionals seeking new economic opportunities and struggling working-class African Americans stymied by employment losses due to deindustrialization and the lack of affordable housing options. Maxwell and her fellow activists' reaction to these changes would redefine the role of the African American cultural activist in a desegregated, evolving urban environment. What is the impact of releasing one's vision into the world? The Center's tumultuous journey to becoming a nationally recognized arts institution reflects both the lasting influence of Maxwell and the effect of her diminished role in later years.

By the 2000s, Charlotte's political and business leaders' push to reaffirm the city's forward-thinking, pro-business image, coupled with the reverse migration of African Americans to the city, shaped the direction of the Center. The story of its journey from its beginnings as a cultural festival to its current reiteration as a regional arts center, on the one hand, tells the story of how Maxwell turned Harper's original vision of an Afro-American Center into a reality. On another level, it represents a broader, more complicated, dual-story of community loss and symbolic achievement in the post–civil rights era, urban South.

The Afro-American Cultural Center's Big Move, 1975–1986

Harper and Maxwell set out to establish the AACC to offset the losses from urban renewal. By the 1980s, the Center would challenge new gentrification efforts as Charlotte expanded. In contrast to the widespread destruction of urban renewal, city officials worked with property developers to rezone residential areas for commercial use. Or builders purchased inexpensive lots to construct expensive housing units. Even though these locales technically remained intact, redevelopment efforts drove up property taxes and forced out long-term residents. As the Center became one of the prominent African American arts institutions in Charlotte, its progress came with the reality that the notion of a "sole homogeneous Black community" no longer existed as they now lived in dispersed neighborhoods. Still struggling to reach those African Americans who remained in Charlotte's historic Black neighborhoods, Maxwell and the Center's administrators became determined to find a location where African Americans from different socioeconomic classes could visit easily with public transportation. Maxwell wanted the AACSC located near Black churches and other institutions. In 1979, it planned to renovate the former Mount Carmel Baptist Church at 412 Campus Street near Johnson C. Smith University to serve as an additional space to host the Children's Arts Program and other events. After the council failed to fund the project, the Center learned from Charlotte assistant city manager Don Steger and community development director Jay Walton that the city wanted to sell Little Rock African Methodist Episcopal Zion Church, in the First Ward. Excited to consider the purchase, Center officials later learned that it faced demolition as part of the city's ongoing urban renewal plans. If they could save it and buy it, it would be a perfect location.[10]

Several years before, in 1975, Little Rock AME Zion Church sold its building to Charlotte's city government for $155,000 and began construction on a new church building nearby on 403 N. McDowell Street, relocating in 1981. The council, under the First Ward Urban Renewal Area Plan, wanted to demolish the old Little Rock Church, close surrounding streets, and open the area for new business and housing development. After facing criticism from residents concerned about the destruction of their neighborhood and the loss of their homes, Little Rock AME members petitioned the city council to include affordable housing in their redevelopment plan on their behalf.[11]

Now that it decided that the Little Rock Church would be a perfect new home, the Center had a big problem. First, Maxwell and the AACSC had to save the church from destruction as part of the city's urban renewal plan. In 1982, Maxwell worked successfully with Thomas, Farrar, UNC Charlotte history professor Dan Morrill, who chaired the Charlotte-Mecklenburg Historic Landmarks Commission, and a local architectural firm to get the church, constructed in 1910, designated as a historic landmark to prevent its destruction.[12] Now that the church had protection, Maxwell's next step would be to work with Farrar, along with Board Director Herman Thomas, to convince the city council to curve a section of 7th Street around the old church, saving both the street and the church. The Center called on Mayor Harvey Gantt to help. Maxwell, Morrill, Thomas, and Farrar, convinced the council that the Little Rock Church, with a congregation that first started meeting in the 1880s, played a vital role in the history of African Americans in Charlotte, and it was worthy of preserving as part of the First Ward neighborhood.[13]

Maxwell's ability to sway the council reflected her growing reputation as a community leader. She convinced these council members that keeping this road helped the AACSC and bolstered Charlotte's image. As a city that sometimes neglected its rich history in the push to encourage economic innovation and growth, Maxwell's success was no small feat. With the support of the Center's officials and Gantt, she ensured the council that having the AACSC housed in a stately, newly remodeled African American historic building in an ever-disappearing Black neighborhood was the perfect way to display the rich history of Black Charlotteans. The state-of-the-art Center promoted Charlotte's future as a welcoming locale to African Americans.[14]

Now that the threat of demolition ended, it had to figure out how to make the dream of a stand-alone building a reality. With the move to the Little Rock Church building a potential possibility, Farrar decided to step down for family reasons. During the early 1980s, as a new conservative wave swept the country, Farrar constructed an organizational foundation that prepared it to ascend to a higher level. As Maxwell bid farewell to her friend, she knew that the Center must proceed. In 1984, Maxwell encouraged the board to hire Vivian Nivens, a public affairs director at WCPG radio station in Charlotte, who once worked with Maxwell at Johnson C. Smith as the Center's new executive director. The architectural firm, Dalton Morgan Shook & Partners, told Center officials that the church structure needed substantial renovations, such as building a theater in the attic to make it suitable. After several years of negotiating with the council, in 1984, Maxwell and the executive staff reacted with muted optimism when they learned that the city council approved $540,000, directing the Center to raise an additional $800,000 needed to purchase and renovate the building.[15]

One of the significant downsides to this offer was that the Center just had thirty days or one month to secure the funds. After failing to obtain funding to renovate Mount Carmel Church, the now AACC realized that it had to expand its financial development networks to solicit funds from large donors and corporations in its first capital campaign. Ten years after its opening, it began this monumental undertaking by appointing co-chairs, Sam Johnson, the first African American owner of a car dealership in Charlotte, and Rolfe Neill, the publisher of the *Charlotte Observer*. As manager of the capital campaign, one of Nivens's first tasks as a new director became one of the Center's most important endeavors. Working with the project coordinator, Dee Dee Murphy, and a team of volunteers, they solicited donations from Charlotte's philanthropists. Recently elected Mayor Harvey Gantt lent his name for a fundraising letter-writing drive to religious institutions, businesses, and even Sammy Davis Jr. With no contribution too small, the AACC welcomed hundreds of individual donations. Board Chair Herman Thomas even asked UNC Charlotte interns and students to make a $1 to $3 weekly contribution to the Center. Nivens remarked, "To move from cramped quarters at Spirit Square into the restored and renovated Old Little Rock Church was a dream come true. That dream was realized because of hard work and dedication."[16]

On the evening of Friday, August 3, 1986, an enthusiastic audience of donors and supporters at an event at Johnson C. Smith cheered and reacted with waves of applause. The Capital Campaign chairs just announced that the Little Rock Restoration Project exceeded its original $800,000 goal, receiving over $1.1 million! So, after extending the campaign an additional month, it received pledges and donations that included $200,000 from the Mecklenburg County Commissioners and $50,000 from Mecklenburg's County's state senators. It received contributions from over fifty businesses, thirty religious institutions, and 300 individuals and organizations. Throughout its existence, Maxwell, the board, students, and executive staff debated whether to adhere to the Black Studies's directive to run a Center, supported exclusively by Charlotte's African American communities or demand that the city's businesses, as corporate citizens, should donate to African American institutions. It resolved this issue by aggressively seeking donations from any person or entity who wished to sign a pledge card, regardless of race. African American donors gave over $224,000, exceeding the campaign's goal to secure $200,000 from Charlotte's Black communities. The ability to garner individual donations from church volunteers to substantive pledges from members of the Black professionals represented the rising power of African American Charlotteans and their desire to support a Center that symbolized their history and presence in the city. In the past, the AACC's fundraising efforts included events like parties, concerts, and dinners. Maxwell, Nivens, and Thomas now realized that the Center's development plan must look beyond membership drives and governmental funding to seek corporate donors.[17]

After helping to manage the Capital Campaign, in 1984, Thomas stepped down from the board chair's position. Maxwell, the board of directors, and Nivens decided to grant him the new title of chairman-emeritus for his tireless dedication and service. On another high note, UNC Charlotte promoted the professor and minister to the rank of associate professor with tenure in 1983.[18] Thomas remained on the Center's board of directors. Retired West Charlotte principal and CMS assistant superintendent E. E. (Edwin Elbert) Waddell served as the new chairperson.

After taking two years to complete the renovation, on March 15, 1986, Maxwell, Harper, Nivens, Waddell, and past and present city officials celebrated the grand opening of the Afro-American Cultural Center's new home on 401 North Myers Street. The three-story, 11,000-square-foot structure included a visual arts gallery, a lecture hall for classroom space, offices for artists-in-residences, and a 180-seat Attic Theater with dressing rooms for actors. With its beautiful new theater, the Center now served as the resident host of the GM Productions theater group, directed by Defoy Glenn, and managed by Carolyn Mason, and the Afro-American Children's Theatre, led by Barbara Ferguson.[19]

The white owner of the city's two major newspapers, Capital Campaign chairperson, Rolfe Neill proclaimed "This was a church for seventy-five years, a temple of the Holy Spirit, and I can't help but think of this church as a place to nurture Black people when the whites turned their backs on them. Today we re-consecrate this place to the human spirit."[20] The basement, once the location for Sunday School classes, now displayed the works of local artists such as T. J. Reddy and Tommy Robinson. As a board member, Maxwell remained instrumental in helping to raise funds for the Center by staging events, such as lectures by Africana Studies leader and founder of Kwanza, Maulana Karenga, and prominent entertainers. Now with more classroom space, it expanded its educational programs. Maxwell's Delta sorors served on fundraising committees.[21]

Since its inception, UNC Charlotte's AAAS students served in integral roles in the Center from volunteering to holding management positions. Harper and Maxwell's plan to incorporate student involvement as experimental learning led to these young people gaining exposure to new employment opportunities in arts administration, like Elaine Nichols and T. J. Reddy. If Maxwell heard the familiar question, where would someone with a degree in African American and African Studies get a job? She could now confidently respond, "at the Afro-American Cultural Center!" The AACC utilized the talents of Maxwell's former students, who sought careers in arts management and as professional artists. Former AAAS student, poet and playwright, Ruth "Makeba" Sloane, became the first full-time artistic programming director in 1986. Instrumental in developing educational and artistic programming for the Center, Sloane later applied the skills that she learned to get subsequent leadership positions in arts education at CMS and in the Children's Theater of Charlotte.[22] By the late 1980s and early 1990s, despite serving as a national officer in Delta Sigma Theta Sorority, which included attending functions and meetings at its national headquarters in Washington, DC, Maxwell kept abreast of the Center's happenings and served as an adviser. In the tradition of activists like Ella Baker, Maxwell strove to enable others to lead to ensure its stability. However, she remained just a phone call away if needed.[23]

Facility Rich–Finances Poor: The Center Struggles to Find Its Place, 1986–1992

Despite its initial success, the AACC became a victim of the perception that it needed less support when it required more funds because of increased operating costs. Much of the monies raised in the Capital Campaign supported the renovation costs and spanned a three-year pledge period before the Center could receive all the funds. Now located in this expansive structure, the AACC's maintenance and programming costs expanded. For example, after receiving over $60,000 for operating expenses from the ASC in 1986, the following year, citing the Center's need to secure outside funding, it only allocated $37,000.[24]

By the last decades of the twentieth century, a new generation of young African Americans who benefited from the new laws and policies stemming from the Civil Rights Act of 1964 and affirmative action joined Charlotte's rising management class seeking new residences. Older Blacks, who once felt compelled to leave the South in search of increased employment opportunities and an escape from racial terrorism, joined this out-migration wave seeking to retire or settle in the refashioned South of their youth. From 1965 to 1970, some thirty-thousand Blacks left North Carolina. Twenty years later, from 1995 to 2000, the state now attracted over fifty-thousand new African American residents.[25]

Charlotte became a city, along with others, like Atlanta and Houston, that attracted African Americans from other regions. Harvey Gantt, Charlotte's new African American mayor from 1983 to 1987, represented the changing South, as the city attempted to publicly cast off the visible perceptions of its racist legacies of lynching and water hoses. The rising crime statistics in the 1980s, due to the growing crack cocaine epidemic, which further decimated working-class African American neighborhoods in the North pushed Blacks to this imaginary, idyllic new South that was safe from the ravages of urban blight. This younger generation, who attended desegregated schools, did not have the tragic memories of the segregated South of their parents. They did, however, see the rising rental and housing costs and compared them to the relatively low cost of living in southern cities, such as Charlotte. Its reputation as a New South city attracted new residents as the city took pride in its success in busing and celebrated the election of its first African American mayor, Harvey Gantt. African Americans flocked to Charlotte, but not to its traditional African American neighborhoods. They wanted to live in the suburbs, such as the University area in North Charlotte.[26]

This influx of migrants shaped Charlotte and the Center. Over the years, the AACC welcomed them as they visited and gave it a valuable financial infusion. Migrants such as Civil Rights Attorney Geraldine Sumter and Bank Executive Isaiah Tidwell shared their expertise in business, law, and the health care fields as part of a new African American professional class to support the Center. As African Americans with no local ties and unrestricted mobility, they had a lesser vested interest in maintaining local African American community connections. Even though they acknowledged the racialized past of these southern cities, they wished to escape the rising crime, police brutality, and the high cost of living in large urban cities of the East, Midwest, and West. Seeking a simpler life, they, along with older Blacks, flocked to Charlotte to reinvent themselves as professionals unencumbered by urban blight and a lack of opportunities.[27]

The Center's new permanent location led to unexpected problems as some patrons grew less interested in attending outdoor events. In 1987, the AACC would hold its last festival for several years due to dwindling community interest and lack of funding. The three-day event included a presentation by artist and activist Yolanda King, Martin Luther King Jr.'s daughter. Facing a financial crisis, the Center's administrative staff and board refocused by promoting outreach efforts. Similar to other nonprofit arts organizations, the AACC continued to raise funds by holding traditional fundraising events like parties, galas, banquets, and entertainment, where donors interacted with each other.[28]

After the ASC reduced its financial allocation, the quest to secure funding became paramount. Drawing from the earlier cultural nationalist sentiments of Maxwell's students, Laura McClettie, then chair of the board's Ways and Means committee, thought that African Americans should control and support their institutions and sought to generate more donations from Charlotte's Black population. In May 1987, she created the "Queen of the Nile Extravaganza," which promised to take the audience back in time to ancient Egypt to learn more about the lives and experiences of the ancient queens of Egypt, including Hatshepsut, Tiye, Nefertiti, Maheda, Candace, and Cleopatra VIII. Seeking to find Charlotte's own imagined version of an Egyptian queen, the Center featured eleven women, including community activist Charlotte Mecklenburg School Board Member Sarah Stevenson who adorned Egyptian dress, regalia, and make-up, as they vied for the title Queen of the Nile."[29]

Patterned after African American scholarship pageants where the winning contestant raised the most donations, the woman's team that donated the highest amount would receive the coveted "Queen of the Nile" title. Held at the Charlotte Convention Center, tickets for the event cost $25 per couple and $15 for individual tickets and raised over $9,000. Laura McClettie explained, "Our goal is to raise funds for the Afro-American Cultural Center and to have fun doing it by reaching out to Charlotte's communities." After a fun-filled evening, businesswoman Vonda Frazier won the crown, stating, "We were all queens. We won because the Center won.[30]

The next month, McClettie, Board Chair Sharon Waters (1987–1989), and *Charlotte Post* managing editor Jalyne Strong organized a three-month campaign, Show Our Strength in Dollars (SOSID). From June to August, volunteers solicited Black Charlotteans to donate one dollar to support the Center and other Black organizations, such as the Urban League of the Carolinas and the Sickle Cell Anemia Foundation. Unfortunately, SOSID only raised around $3,000 by the end of the campaign in August. With limited publicity and volunteers to promote SOSID and a short time frame to collect donations, McClettie's plan to attain more African Americans' support for Black organizations fell short of its initial goal to raise $80,000 from Charlotte's 100,000 African American residents. Despite garnering mixed results from her development efforts, the Center selected the business executive and entrepreneur McClettie as its new board chair in September 1987.[31]

That same year, Herman Thomas, now chair of the Center's Shotgun Restoration Committee, worked with Nivens and McClettie to purchase the two remaining shotgun houses left on West Bland Street in the former Blandville neighborhood in Charlotte's Second Ward. Named because their straight structure enabled one to fire a shotgun straight through the front of the house, and it would come out the back without hitting a wall, these shotgun houses represented examples of the housing structures in many southern African American communities and Charlotte. These small houses reflected the poverty endemic within Charlotte's working-class African American communities, as the city tried to eradicate dilapidated homes in Black neighborhoods without alleviating the economic conditions that resulted in inadequate housing and limited financing relocation efforts. They served as a visual symbol of the journey of Black Charlotteans to gain economic parity in a city that promoted itself as progressive. Now, historical representations, these homes epitomized the progress of the rising African American middle class who now viewed these shotgun houses as tourist sites rather than as part of their neighborhoods.[32] By 1989, its goal of renovating the houses clashed with the reality of limited funding for remodeling. Besides, these houses were not immune to poverty issues when homeless people attempted to sleep in the shotgun houses. Thomas talked with the squatters and agreed to let them stay in the homes if they didn't damage them.[33]

In 1988, Nivens and McClettie faced the stark realization that the Center would have to reduce staff after the ASC cut its funding more than half to $22,000. Nivens worked to raise more capital, but with programming cuts, only 12,000 people visited. She elaborated, "If you took any arts organization and moved it from one room to a large facility, there would be many adjustments to make. It is extremely difficult to raise funds to renovate a facility and raise money for operations, especially with a small staff and no development person." In 1988, Maxwell said goodbye to another friend when Nivens resigned to manage public relations for Charlotte's YMCA. Despite being a former board member himself, in 1989, Gerald Johnson, the editor of Charlotte's Black newspaper, the *Charlotte Post,* shared his frustration. "The board is not successfully raising money, which leaves the Center underfinanced, which keeps it understaffed, which prevents it from reaching people."[34]

Subsequently, in January 1989, as the AACC marked its fifteenth year, it named Vanessa Greene as its first executive director with arts administrative experience. Promoted from an interim director's position, Greene explained, "The first thing a sick organization has to do is admit that it is sick." Charged with increasing membership, Greene launched a major membership drive to get 3,000 new or reinstated members. Local media personalities Sonja Gantt, at WBTV and the daughter of Harvey Gantt, and Charlotte WPEC radio host, Skip Murphy, chaired the campaign of over fifty volunteers to solicit memberships that started at $10. Confidence in Greene's abilities to increase patrons' support and secure non-governmental funding, the ASC increased its funding to $30,000.[35]

Even when conservatives swept national and state politics during the 1980s, Harvey Gantt managed to hold two terms as mayor of Charlotte. In 1987, Black Charlotteans finally felt the impact of the conservative political ascendancy in another historical election when Gantt lost his bid for a third mayoral term to republican Sue Myrick, Charlotte's first woman to hold the position. As the director of an organization located in a predominantly African American neighborhood where some residents faced the spectrum of growing poverty and rising gun violence, Vanessa Greene adapted Harper and Maxwell's vision of the Center's mission to serve a community under siege. Greene elaborated on her philosophy, "You use the arts not just to entertain but to empower people. To give them a sense of self-worth. Community development means nothing unless you give people a sense of self-worth."[36]

Greene attempted to make the Center a more welcoming and inclusive place by using its educational programming as a tool to attract working-class parents. If Harper and Maxwell created the AACC to mitigate the detrimental effects of urban renewal and school closings, Greene wanted it to serve as a protective space for Black children to prevent them from falling prey to the "streets." She expanded the Building Bridges program to sponsor additional afterschool programs in the Cherry and Double Oaks communities. Greene elaborated, "Children are our number one on our priority (list) because that's what the community wants. If we're not losing them outright to gangs, they're getting pulled into drugs and violence."[37]

Her new budget plan called for reducing high-cost performances and focusing on community-oriented programming. In 1992, Thomas, as head of the Shotgun Restoration Committee, worked with the Center to secure grants to complete the renovation of the two shotgun houses purchased some five years before. Their efforts, with the support of community volunteers, including Kenneth Bridges of First Baptist Church-West, Peggy Campbell, William (Bill) Pickens, and James McCullough from Friendship Missionary Baptist Church, to protect these structures embody Maxwell and Harper's guiding mission to preserve local African American history and a remnant of Charlotte's African American neighborhoods. However, its struggles to obtain the actual funding reflect the Center's difficulties during this period as it attempted to engage with the community while dealing with funding crises.[38]

The Center during the 1990s

After two years, Greene explained that when she first became director in 1989, the Center "had the rap of being sort of a country club for middle-class Black women." Unpacking this criticism that suggested that it had abandoned its mission to serve a diverse group of Black people calls for a more introspective discussion of the gendered meanings behind Greene's assertion. When Harper and Maxwell, both members of national Black women's Greek-letter organizations, founded the Center, they wanted to provide a cultural resource that would help African Americans regardless of gender or class, not another women's group. For Maxwell, dedication to the Center's goals remained a requirement for leadership, not factors such as gender or race. However, as an administrator herself, she appreciated women's leadership capacities in the context of some of the issues that they had to overcome. This statement both dismissed the vital importance of men like Herman Thomas, Isaiah Tidwell, and later, David Taylor, as they served in crucial roles in the Center's development. The perception also denigrated women's contributions as volunteers, members, and donors. This critique unintentionally illumined the growing influence of Black women in executive positions who financially contributed to the Center and attended its events.[39]

By 1991, Greene had successfully reduced the AACC's deficit from over $60,000 to $43,000. She enacted strict cost-cutting measures, like reducing staff to one additional person, hiring part-time staff, and relying more on volunteers. Greene knew that her vision for the Center depended on its fiscal soundness. During her tenure as director, Laura McClettie stepped down with Civil Rights Attorney Geraldine Sumter assuming the position in 1989. She served for two years. In the past, most chairs only served one-to-two-year terms, except for Isaiah Tidwell, who became board chair in 1991. The recently appointed regional vice president of Wachovia Bank, now Wells Fargo, worked with Greene to develop a two-year plan to implement a conservative budget to eliminate the Center's deficit. Tidwell worked with the executive director directly to help the AACC restructure its debts, increase donations and memberships, and attract more patrons.[40]

In 1991, Maxwell, now Maxwell-Roddey after her 1987 marriage, entrusted Tidwell, and Greene to guide the Center to fiscal solvency as she balanced her time as the National First Vice President of Delta Sigma Theta Sorority. She remained apprised of the AACC's happenings as a board member, but her input lessened as the board made more independent decisions. After she became the 20th National President of Delta Sigma Theta Sorority, Inc. in 1992, Maxwell's new position required frequent travel throughout the US and internationally. Though inundated with the immense tasks of managing a national organization, Maxwell remained a trusted adviser.

Former Center board chairperson Geraldine Sumter credited Greene with rebuilding the Center's funding and membership bases. However, the director's success in regaining the confidence of entities like the Arts and Science Council and local corporations came at a cost. When Greene focused on securing corporate underwriting grants to exhibit the works of nationally known artists such as John Biggers to attract patrons, local artists received less support. Her strict cost-cutting measures, like discontinuing the Center's jazz music series, to get it back on a solid financial footing also garnered mixed reactions. When Greene and Tidwell limited payments to local artists' exhibits, it threatened to damage the relationship with one of its local core units. In 1992, visual artist Tommy Robinson and a group of visual and performing artists formed Umoja Sasa (Unity Now). They complained to the media that Greene reallocated money designated to pay artists to fund staff salaries. Even though the board eventually cleared Greene of these allegations, the beleaguered director resigned several months later.[41] Tidwell worked with incoming executive director Wanda Montgomery to help rebuild its operations and reputation after this crisis.[42] The Center mended its fraught relationship with local artists. Nevertheless, Umoja Sasa's complaints that AACC neglected their interests revealed the unfortunate consequences of the Center's need to build economic stability by focusing on publicly funded educational programming and sponsored regional and national artists. Wanda Montgomery explained that "artists represent just one of the Center's constituencies, "What some people don't realize is that, because of our history, we're also serving communities around the country."[43]

Some twenty years after Harper and Maxwell-Roddey decided to create a Center that helped all Black children, dwindling individual donations and low membership revealed the complex consequences of success. The growing prominence of the AACC both attracted Black professionals and simultaneously made some working-class African Americans feel unwelcome. Even though Charlotte's burgeoning Black middle class flocked to the area, in 1987, only 8 percent of African Americans worked in top-level management positions in Mecklenburg County.[44]

To survive, the Center needed help from Blacks from across the economic divide and corporate donations support. Once the only venue for African American arts, during the 1990s, the AACC faced new competition for patrons from other cultural organizations like the Levine Museum of the New South and the Charlotte Symphony, which started sponsoring African American themed programming. As its programming expanded, the Center still faced administrative instability as several executive directors left after only a few years in their positions. Hired for their business and fundraising experience, most of these new directors came from large urban areas. Faced with mounting challenges to secure funding and promote the interests of the Center, some of them just failed to accomplish the substantial tasks given to them.

When Wanda Montgomery took the helm as executive director in 1993, the experienced arts executive and former ASC employee worked diligently with Tidwell to increase the Center's budget by 62 percent. Under her leadership, Montgomery hired former South Carolina Arts Commission executive, Henry Harrison as the new program director, reconnected with local artists, expanded the Building Bridges educational program, and secured national art exhibits and international performers. By 1994, the AACC now operated in the black, and the completed shotgun houses were open for public viewing. After helping to lift the Center out of a downward spiral, Tidwell left his position as chair. As it celebrated its 20th anniversary in 1994, Montgomery and new board chair, attorney Frank Emory Jr., cited several years of deficit-free growth. The Center flourished under Montgomery's direction as she secured national sponsorships from the Seagram Company and federal grants. Unfortunately, after helping the AACC realize five years of consecutive growth, Montgomery had to resign due to illness in 1997. She later succumbed to breast cancer in 1998.[45]

In 1995, Hugh McColl Jr., CEO of NationsBank, successfully raised over $26 million to fund Charlotte's Arts and Science Council Endowment.[46] Two years later, in 1997, the endowment would come in handy after a group of conservative city council members voted to cut the ASC's budget because it funded the local performance of the Broadway play, "Angels in America," because of its queer themes and frank discussion of HIV-AIDS.[47]

Maxwell first interacted with McColl Jr. when she sought donations for the Center. Over the years, she grew comfortable talking with the dynamic banking leader, even suggesting that his bank divests from South Africa during the late 1980s, Maxwell-Roddey humorously recalled that "he didn't speak to me for a while, but he got over it." Over the years, NationsBank donated funds and even sent an executive to work on behalf of the AACC for free. In 1998, McColl Jr. purchased the Vivian and John Hewitt African American Art Collection and donated it to the Center. Laura Foxx, president of the NationsBank Foundation, managed the transaction with AACC officials. Containing over fifty-eight pieces from nationally known artists such as Romare Bearden, John Biggers, Elizabeth Catlett, and Henry O. Tanner, the Hewitts possessed one of the most expansive collections of African American art in the world. Owning this collection reflected the Center's entrée into the level of national art museums. Unfortunately, it lacked the space and funds to house and maintain the collection. The Center negotiated with Foxx to send the collection out as a traveling exhibit to museums in other cities for five years and to later house it in the Mint Museum of Craft + Design in Uptown Charlotte.[48]

Now it became imperative that the Center expand by either remodeling the structure and expanding it by purchasing adjacent land or building a new structure at a new location. In 1998, the new board chair, business owner Sharman Thornton, who followed banking executive Edward Dolby, Herman Thomas, and builder Anthony Hunt, petitioned the city council to purchase land adjacent to the AACC.[49] Despite its positive negotiations with the council to secure the additional property, the cultural organization received a severe blow when the council denied its request, selling the land to developers instead. Shocked after learning that the Center failed to secure the property transaction that previous board members and executive staff negotiated, Maxwell grew incensed. After her Delta presidency ended in 1986, she spent her time teaching at the University of South Carolina at Lancaster and serving on boards in Charlotte and her second area of residence, Catawba County, South Carolina. Maxwell, who once negotiated with the city to curve a street to protect the Center some ten years ago in the 1980s, realized that as the AACC grew in prominence, its relationship with the city's political leaders weakened. By the end of the 1990s, the Center's funding problems resurfaced, causing arts manager and Center Executive Director Cynthia Schaal to resign in 1999. Unfortunately, the directors' turnovers continued as they left seeking more lucrative employment, faced possible firing, or resigned after neglecting to meet the board's expectations.[50]

The Center's tumultuous journey toward becoming a nationally recognized arts institution reflected the lasting influence of Maxwell-Roddey's guidance as she trusted the AACC's staff to manage the institution efficiently. In 1999, Center board member and Delta soror, attorney Michel Denise Vaughan sought Maxwell-Roddey's help after the sudden departure of its executive director. Originally asked to serve for six weeks as the Center's interim director, she eventually stayed six months.[51]

As co-founder of the Center, Maxwell-Roddey now had the daunting responsibility of working with the board to restructure its management directives. Complaints by artists and disgruntled staff forced Maxwell-Roddey to make personnel and leadership changes. She formed a separate advisory board that included Carolyn Mason and Kathleen Crosby to help her develop a strategic plan for the Center. Seeking help from someone she trusted, Maxwell-Roddey asked her friend Herman Thomas to help. As board chair during its early days at Spirit Square, he led the board when the Center moved to Little Rock, and now he had to manage it in a new aspect of its growth.[52]

Moving Uptown: The Center during the 2000s

The Center maintained its programming goals despite funding deficits for several years, but the lack of space for expansion and dwindling membership numbers persisted. After the failed 1998 attempt to expand at its present site, the AACC decided to work collectively with Charlotte's other arts institutions and the ASC to fight for funding and bond packages. This joining of forces helped place it in a more powerful position as part of the city's arts community and as just an independent institution. The Center's status later became more complicated when city leaders proposed an Uptown arts center.[53]

By the 2000s, Charlotte had emerged from its small-town Piedmont regional roots to become a world banking center and the home of several national banks, including Wachovia and Bank of America. In 1998, Hugh McColl Jr.'s Nations-Bank merged with Bank of America. Now, he set out with several other business CEOs, informally titled "the Group," such as Belk's Department Store head, John Belk; First Union Bank's Ed Crutchfield; Duke Power CEO, Bill Lee; real estate developer John Crosland Jr.; Lance Foods' Alfred F. "Pete" Sloan; and *Charlotte Observer* newspaper publisher, Rolfe Neill to build Charlotte's cultural infrastructure to attract top business executives and clients to the city. He led Bank of America to donate funds to support the symphony, sponsor NBA and NFL teams and founded the McColl Jr. Center for the visual arts. Maxwell looked to McColl Jr. for support.[54]

From the Campus to the Community: Two Black Cultural Institutions in the Post-Soul New South

Created in the context of rising New South cities, both the Afro-American Cultural Center and the African American Museum of Dallas faced challenges securing funding and attracting patrons across class lines. In contrast to Maxwell-Roddey's more advisory role, Harry Robinson Jr. currently serves as the president and CEO of Dallas, Texas's African American Museum. Maxwell-Roddey and Robinson Jr. became adept in making connections with wealthy benefactors to secure the necessary funding, but they differed in leadership styles though Maxwell-Roddey's role as an adviser limited her ability to make critical hands-on decisions as the Center expanded. Robinson Jr. could continue to maintain control and influence the policies of the Dallas Museum as its president. As he welcomed new Black residents to Dallas and the African American Museum, Robinson Jr. worked to maintain relationships with local volunteers, including some of the Museum's most reliable supporters, members of Black Greek-letter and other service and civic organizations, and churches. Robinson Jr. constructed a supportive volunteer community by becoming adept at helping Black Dallasites commemorate their collective past. Like the AACC, Robinson Jr.'s AAM relied on educational programming like summer camps, school tours, and afterschool programs to connect families from diverse economic backgrounds to the Museum. Although the AAM offered diverse programming from children's art activities to the Texas Black Rodeo, it still had problems attracting some working-class people to its offerings. Betty Cunningham, former executive vice president of the museum and chief operations officer, suggested that "Even with free admission, some nearby Blacks either had no interest in the Museum's offerings or unfortunately, thought that

that the AAM only catered to professional African Americans or the 'wine and cheese crowd.'"[55]

As Dallas emerged as another favored New South destination for Black professionals, Robinson Jr., balanced the Dallas Museum's programming offerings to appeal to both local and new residents from different economic backgrounds. The AAM sponsored events, such as traditional teas and banquets to celebrate the achievements of Texas athletes from the high school to the professional level and a Black rodeo event with a low-cost admission. It also sponsored lectures by local African American scholars and receptions to celebrate the naming of galleries and even chairs after donors. The Museum's extravagant black-tie gala secured donations from corporate and prominent city leaders. During this event, patrons could bid in a silent auction of high-ticket items and listen to musical artists like the Four Tops, Ashford and Simpson, and Earth Wind and Fire. By the 2000s, the AACC looked to multiple funding streams to support the Center's activities, including private donations and corporate sponsors. The now Jazzy Gala reflected this progression and the financial development trajectories of other local arts organizations as it transformed from a business-type luncheon to a formal evening gala with nationally known performers and corporate sponsors.[56]

Over the years, the AAM and Charlotte's AACC had to adapt to retain and attract new members within an evolving urban landscape. The Afro-American Cultural Center established in response to urban renewal, eventually became a part of Charlotte's urban revitalization efforts. Dallas's AAM, located in the expanded Fair Park area, contended with the area's complicated relationship with neighboring Black Dallasites. Shortly after the end of the Exposition, Dallas city officials demolished the beautiful Negro Hall of Life and opened a white-only swimming pool. During the 1950s, civil rights activist Juanita Craft led protests to end segregated "Negro Day" at the State Fair.[57]

In 1969, the Dallas City Council issued an eminent domain order that forced the residents living in Fair Park's surrounding predominantly Black neighborhood to sell their homes so that the city could demolish them to build a parking lot near the Fair Park grounds. City leaders also wished to appease potential white visitors who expressed apprehension about going to visit Fair Park because of its urban location. So, the city decided to engage in its own version of urban renewal to erase the Black presence from the Fair Park area to attract more white visitors. Dallas civil rights activist Peter Johnson demanded that the city increase its meager offer to the residents of $1 per square foot to $3.75. After negotiations with the city stalled, Johnson, a former member of the Student Non-Violent Coordinating Committee (SNCC), responded by alerting

Dallas city leaders that if they didn't meet the residents' demands, He would lead a protest march of over 600 neighborhood residents to block the entrance to Fair Park preventing football fans from entering the Park's Cotton Bowl Stadium on the day of an annual televised game. The city acquiesced and agreed to purchase their homes at a higher price equal to the amount previously offered to white residents.[58]

Robinson Jr. struggled to ensure that Black patrons would be welcome in Fair Park. Both the Center and the AAM had to balance the financial needs of their staff and local artists with the push to display the works of nationally known artists to attract corporate sponsorships. The AACC and the AAM managed to overcome financial issues that ranged from donor recruitment to addressing discrepancies in funding to Black and white organizations by their respective city cultural organizations to survive and sometimes flourish for decades. In the 2000s, the Center would undergo another reinvention.[59]

In 2003, Charlotte's Arts and Science Council requested $88 million from the city council to fund a new arts cluster to expand and renovate the AACC and several other cultural institutions. Despite the Arts and Science Council's assurances that the plan's funding would come from tax rebates and private donations, the city council denied the project, citing a lack of funds.[60] When David R. Taylor, a former financial services business owner, became the Center's board chairman in 2004, he realized that fundraising needed to become a top priority for the AACC's survival. In 2006, the Charlotte City Council passed the Wachovia First Project. Wachovia Bank, now Wells Fargo, asked if the Center wanted to join several other major arts institutions in an arts cluster in Uptown. The AACC would relocate to the corner of South Tryon and Stonewall streets in a former Wachovia parking lot in Uptown. Wachovia's First Street Project included the Bechtler and Mint Art Museums, the Knight Theater, a forty-eight-story office tower, three hundred condos, and an underground parking garage. Tom Wurtz, Wachovia's chief financial officer, and the bank's real estate division worked with Charlotte's city council in an innovative public-private partnership where the bank would construct the buildings in the complex. The city would then purchase the finished arts cluster buildings for approximately $126 million with an estimated $58 million garnered from city and county property taxes from the Wachovia complex; $58.5 million from increased car rental taxes; and $10 million from Bank of America and the Arts and Science Council. With guarantees that Wachovia would continue to pay property taxes on the tower and condos, and other buildings in the new complex for at least $4.6 million for twenty-five years. Charlotte's city council agreed to support the plan.[61]

After receiving approval from the AACC board, Taylor accepted Wachovia's offer. The only African American institution included in the project, its expanded relocation space now enabled the Center to house its prized Hewitt Collection. After Taylor stepped down in 2006, the new board chair, Earl Leake, AACC president and CEO and former Chicago consultant company owner Deon Bradley, and development officer Patrick Diamond launched a successful three-year $3.5 million Founders Society endowment campaign to raise funds to support the relocation and worked to develop a relocation plan.[62] After Bradley resigned in 2009, Taylor returned as the Gantt Center's new president and CEO. The Center worked with the city council to sell the Little Rock Church building back to its members for $600,000, with $590,000 of the proceeds going to the Gantt Center's endowment fund.[63]

Once founded upon a vision to alleviate the losses from urban renewal, now the Center benefited from new urban revitalization efforts. As it outgrew its current location, the AACC now had an offer that it could not feasibly refuse. Whereas the Mint, North Carolina's first art museum, would maintain two separate locations, with the original site on Randolph Road and its Uptown site opening in 2010, the Center lacked the financial ability to sustain two operations. Albeit sometimes with tensions, the AACC remained a central host for local visual and performing artists. A reliable and dedicated group of sometimes skeleton staff, volunteers, and donors remained vital to the Center's survival during these years. Looking at the evolution of Harper and Maxwell's founding vision of a community cultural institution as it expanded from its small office in Spirit Square to its location in a beautifully restored church is not just a history of the AACC. It reflects how African American urban cultural institutions like the Center reconfigured their mission to adapt to an ever-changing "African American community," no longer defined and connected by shared location and facing expanding pressures relating to economic class. Now Maxwell and Harper's vision would be transformed again by the complicated implications of progress as the AACC and African American culture emerge as a prominent part of the city's center.[64]

The relocation of the Center to Uptown to become part of an expanded arts cluster reflected its growth as a major arts institution. It served as a reflection of these new residents' contributions whose success supported the AACC while also drawing it away from its community roots. As these successful Black Charlotteans supported the AACC, it grew to represent more middle-class or regional interests. The Center no longer had a theater as part of its arrangement with the city and the other arts institutions to prevent an overlap with other Uptown theater venues. As a result, local performing arts groups no longer called the AACC home, as it now welcomed nationally known visual artists.[65]

The Center's officials discussed naming it after Bertha Maxwell-Roddey, but she didn't want the title. She wanted to name it after founding board member North Carolina State Senator Fred Alexander because of his vital support of the AACC. After further discussion, the board decided to call it the Harvey B. Gantt Center for African-American Arts + Culture. The decision received approval from the city council in April 2007. Gantt had supported the Center for years as a board member and helped it move to the old Little Rock Church.[66] They hoped Gantt's prominent name would help in fundraising and support.[67]

When the Harvey B. Gantt Center opened in 2009, the beautiful 49,000 square-foot facility represented African Americans' progress in Charlotte and the loss of the AACC's local small community focus.[68] A little over ten years later, after McColl, Jr. purchased the Hewitt Collection in 1988, it found a permanent home in the new Gantt Center.[69] With a collection that rivaled those of more established African American museums, the Gantt soon became one of the most influential African American arts institutions in the South. It marked its place among other prominent African American arts museums and centers in the US, including nationally known museums in Baltimore, Dallas, Detroit, Los Angeles, and Chicago. As an African American arts institution with the capacity to mount major exhibits, it joined these other Black museums as they sought to show the works of major Black artists and pushed for parity with their white counterparts. These Black museums had to compete with formerly segregated white arts institutions, which now looked to diversity by recruiting these same artists.[70]

By the 2000s, reverse migration and gentrification led to a modern-day reconfiguration of Maxwell-Roddey's and Harper's vision to meet Black newcomers' demands living in the millennial era. Even though Maxwell-Roddey expresses pride when discussing the Gantt, she lamented the loss of community cohesiveness after the AACC's relocation, as the Gantt represents the gains and losses of African American communities in the reinvented new South. Despite her ambivalence, Maxwell-Roddey realized that the Gantt Center now has the influence to shape the cultural landscape of the city as it represents African American artistic achievement to Charlotteans and visitors from around the world.[71]

Charlotte's reputation as a mecca for African Americans had reached new heights as the city now rivaled Atlanta as a popular destination for African Americans of all social classes. Unfortunately, as Charlotte emerged as a world banking leader, city leaders engulfed in development projects neglected to plan for the rising need for affordable housing for its working-class residents, often displaced due to urban renewal and later gentrification. The dream of Charlotte as a progressive center became a mirage or nightmare for some, as working-class Blacks faced a city with inadequate low-cost housing and substandard schools. In 2013, a Harvard University study ranked Charlotte last among American cities in economic mobility. As the Gantt became the visible symbol of the influential rising Black middle class, its perpetual lack of funding and inability to fully attract Black working-class patrons also reflected the growing class divide among African Americans in the city.[72]

During the 1990s, Maxwell-Roddey served on several desegregation committees and task forces to review issues affecting African American children and how to prevent the growing segregation of CMS's schools. Years earlier, in the 1970s and 1980s, Charlotte's business and educational leaders joined to promote busing and school desegregation to encourage the city's business-friendly progressivism. Unfortunately, by the 1990s, McColl Jr. and some of the city's business elite offered limited reaction to the 1999 *Capacchione v. Charlotte-Mecklenburg Schools* case where a conservative US Federal District Judge, who was once active in antibusing measures, ruled to rescind the federal court's desegregation order, which eventually led to the resegregation of the city's schools. In effect, with Charlotte's New South image intact, at this time, city leaders moved away from the promotion of desegregation as a measure to boost the city's economic growth.[73]

Formed over forty years ago to stem the adverse effects of urban renewal and school desegregation, Harper's and Maxwell-Roddey's Gantt Center still acts as a guiding force. With a renewed purpose to expose Charlotte's children, now mainly attending resegregated schools to African American art regardless of race, the Gantt Center sits at the corner of East Stonewall and South Tryon, two streets named to honor Confederate General Thomas Jonathan "Stonewall" Jackson and North Carolina's slave-holding Colonial Governor William Tryon, illustrates the conundrum that is the New South.[74] This modern, majestic structure celebrating African American art serves as a visual site of resistance against the municipal endorsement of slavery as it serves as the structural embodiment of African American achievement. Yet, it is only a short walking distance from where fans cheer on the National Football League's (NFL) Charlotte Panthers football team in the Bank of America Stadium. Decades before Hugh McColl Jr. helped to bring an NFL Team to Charlotte in 1996, the voices of the African American doctors and nurses of Good Samaritan Hospital rang from its halls. Demolished years before in the urban renewal destruction of

African American neighborhoods in the Third Ward, a plaque marking its existence remains on one of the stadium's walls. As urban renewal or redevelopment efforts erased the physical structures of Charlotte's central city, African American neighborhoods, The Gantt, UNC Charlotte's Africana Studies and History Departments and J. Murrey Atkins Library, and the Levine Center for the New South strive to reclaim the history of voices of their former residents.[75]

The Gantt's very physical presence reflects the shaping of a new dynamic as African Americans stake their claim as part of Charlotte's history and future. With the continued support of the ASC and corporate sponsors, the Gantt now had the means to bring in prominent speakers and sponsor arts workshops. By continuing its role as a site for community dialogue, the Gantt Center provides a powerful platform to honor the once-silenced historical voices of local African Americans and examine relevant issues affecting today's Black Charlotteans.

As the Gantt prepares to celebrate its upcoming 50th anniversary in 2024, it has weathered the storms of economic recession to become a central part of the city's urban creative landscape. The Center maintains its regional arts focus, offering new programming that bridges class divides relating to pertinent issues facing African American Charlotteans, such as urban poverty, gentrification, and police brutality. It offers a myriad of children's arts and educational programming. With new access from the nearby light rail, the Gantt Center hopes to increase its grassroots presence and attract new volunteers. In 2017, the Charlotte Alumnae Chapter of Delta Sigma Theta Sorority held an event at the Center to commemorate the chapter's 75th anniversary and raise funds for a Johnson C. Smith University scholarship in honor of Bertha Maxwell-Roddey, its former chapter president and past national president of Delta. Throughout her years as director of the BSP/AAAS Department, when she worked with the NCBS and the Afro-American Cultural Center, she simultaneously traveled on a parallel trajectory as a regional and national leader of Delta Sigma Theta Sorority. Often acting as a change agent on behalf of the sisterhood, Maxwell-Roddey shared her expertise and knowledge in a succession of executive positions.

7

What Does It Mean to Be a Delta?

As a small eight-year-old child, Bertha had the extraordinary opportunity to pin a flower corsage on the lapel of Mary McLeod Bethune when she visited St. James Methodist Church in Seneca, South Carolina. A larger-than-life figure, Bethune was a prominent member of the Roosevelt administration and president of the National Council of Negro Women (NCNW). Bethune also belonged to another major African American women's national organization, Delta Sigma Theta Sorority, Inc.

Delta and the other African American sororities, Alpha Kappa Alpha, Inc., Sigma Gamma Rho, Inc., and Zeta Phi Beta, Inc. are nonprofit public service organizations. Members support their communities in educational, economic, and cultural service endeavors. Most of their members are African Americans, but these multi-ethnic, international organizations welcome women of any ethnicity or race. Inspired by Bethune as a college student, Maxwell decided to join the organization of her heroine and thousands of other African American women. In 1951, Maxwell became a member through the Gamma Lambda Chapter of Delta Sigma Theta at Johnson C. Smith University. She now shared a collective identity as a member of a national sisterhood that involved promoting academic excellence, engaging in public service, participating in bonding ceremonies and artistic performances, or fellowshipping.[1]

For Maxwell, participation in Delta became an extension of her educational vision to empower people with academic knowledge, promote self-identity development, and foster leadership opportunities that she developed as a teacher, principal, and director of African American and African Studies at UNC Charlotte. From its inception, women in Delta's national leadership ranks often held positions of authority and influence in their professional careers, through public service leadership, and within their communities as clubwomen, entrepreneurs, and activists. Gains from the civil rights and women's movements led to the dismantling of some of the gender and racial barriers affecting Black women as they pursued careers in higher education, employment, and politics.

Delta's top leaders reflected this change as they emerged from the top ranks of these arenas to implement innovative management practices while in office.

Maxwell's story reveals the rarely discussed ways Black women exercised their power in female-centered political settings after World War II. Delta and the other three African American national sororities provided an arena for Black women to become leaders and power brokers in a political and cultural environment of disenfranchisement. Even if they could vote, African American women had few opportunities to assume positions of elected political leadership. Some Deltas immersed themselves in the political process or "political sisterhood" by campaigning for sorority offices and constructing powerful support networks. During segregation, the field of education remained one of the few avenues where African American women could become professionals and secure middle-class status. During segregation, Black men dominated the secondary school and college higher administration ranks. Within Black sororities, like Delta Sigma Theta, Black women could rise as high as their ability and networking capability.[2]

One of Delta's main goals was to encourage scholarly achievement by providing college scholarships for women; however, participation in sorority life helped Black women teachers expand their support beyond their students' direct academic needs to promote their cultural awareness and affirm their creative talents. One of Delta's signature programs, Jabberwock, a youth talent variety competition first created in 1925 by Marion Hope Conover, a member of the Iota Chapter of Boston, began as a youth variety talent competition for prizes with the proceeds supporting scholarship funds. After its formal adoption by Delta's Grand Chapter in 1947, the Jabberwock scholarship and community service project fundraiser was implemented nationally. It has expanded thematically to include cultural enrichment activities, children and youth talent shows, scholarship pageants, and artistic competitions.[3]

What does it really mean to be a Delta sister or soror? Referring to dictionary entries, the definition of the term "sister" includes the female relation to daughters and sons of the same parent or defines a female member of an organization or female religious order. Some African Americans use the term "sister" as an address or informal greeting to African American women. According to Delta's Constitution, Delta women receive the title *soror* after joining. Deltas use that title as a greeting, for example saying, "Hello, Soror Jones." For Deltas and the members of other African American sororities, the word soror represents a woman enjoined in a bond with her fellow members that mimic blood relations.[4]

Delta sorors may have personal differences or conflicts with each other, but as members of this organization, they must still work with each other to do public service. Delta does not require that its members assume leadership roles. Nevertheless, the organization enables women to become leaders in an environment unhindered by racism or sexism. Whether seeking an elected office in a chapter, region, or nationally, sorors must offer an individual platform of ideas and implementation strategies consistent with the sorority's guidelines and mission. Within Delta, collegiate, city or county-based graduate or alumnae chapters, regional (grouping of collegiate and alumnae chapters by area), and national leaders are responsible for directing the organization and implementing its initiatives. Unlike partisan politics, these women can challenge or debate programmatic priorities and/or the firmly held convictions of another soror and still embrace each other as sisters. These leaders have the responsibility of disciplining Deltas who violate its constitution and bylaws.[5]

Delta Sigma Theta's electoral processes resemble traditional political elections only to the extent that individual sorors must campaign for votes. Even though candidates often receive support when campaigning from other Deltas from their respective local city chapters or when they run for regional or national office, Delta Sigma Theta office seekers run as individuals, not as representatives of a political faction or party. Candidates can share their qualifications for office, experience, and interests when running, but they don't need to announce their formal national agenda until after the election. The new president's plan detailing her ideas regarding the sorority's service and internal growth initiatives does not require membership approval. For these reasons, Delta's elections expose the complex dimensions of a political sisterhood, where candidates vying for office recount their experience and abilities and emphasize how sisterly they are and their dedication to upholding the sorority's ideals.

As a national officeholder in Delta, Maxwell adeptly navigated this unique political process to win elections by firmly advocating for her objectives and valuing the collective emotional support garnered from belonging to a national sisterhood. As a national officeholder, she established organizational and leadership initiatives that led the sorority to become more transparent, improve efficiency, confront hazing, and expand its public service efforts. Her experiences within Delta reveal a complicated story of power, service, and sisterhood that dispels prevalent negative perceptions of sorority women as frivolous, anti-intellectual, shallow, and over-sexualized. Maxwell's story rejects the perceived presumptions of pettiness and elitism that stereotype members of African American Greek-letter women's organizations.[6]

As sororities encouraged Black women to do charitable service, participation sometimes served as an avenue for class reinforcement and identity reinvention. These women joined clubs and organizations that secured their position in the Black middle class. As an African American woman who grew up in meager surroundings with unmarried parents and had to work her way through college, Maxwell defied the characterization of the elite, upper-class sorority member.[7]

Her charismatic personality enabled her to form alliances and friendships with fellow sorority members allowing her to cast away class distinctions and attain their support. As the founding director of a successful African American and African Studies department and as the founder of the preeminent organization of its field, the National Council for Black Studies, during the 1970s and 1980s, Maxwell supported many of the tenets of Black Cultural Nationalism. She designed a curriculum to help her students reinforce their Black identities within a predominantly white institution. If she donned an African head wrap when speaking to students at a Black History Month class event, later that weekend Maxwell might wear a beautiful evening gown to a Delta fundraising gala. The visual image of a Black Studies advocate donned in classic evening wear seems in direct conflict with societal assumptions of an activist and what one should look like. These constricting perceptions portray Black women activists as only angry, anti-establishment, afro-wearing Black militants, in direct contrast to the negative representation of the stuck-up African American sorority woman, as a card-carrying member of the Black bourgeois who emphasized socializing over activism. These stereotypical designations fail to acknowledge the fluidity of class among African Americans and overlook the varied examples of activism within African American communities. Maxwell's refusal to be labeled enabled her to traverse these seemingly conflicting worlds with authority and ease.

After offering a brief history of Delta Sigma Theta Sorority, Incorporated, this chapter discusses Bertha Maxwell's experiences as a member of Delta Sigma Theta with particular emphasis on her early leadership journey, beginning in 1964, when she became president of the Charlotte Alumnae Chapter and concluding in 1981 after Maxwell served in her first national position as chair of Delta's Heritage and Archives Committee (H&A). Appointed by Delta's 17th National President Mona Humphries Bailey, Maxwell worked with H&A to gather, analyze, and store historical information related to the sorority. Chapter eight focuses on Maxwell's entry into the Delta Sigma Theta national electoral process and describes her successful campaigns beginning with her election to her first national office in 1982 as the South Atlantic regional director through her ascension to the national presidency in 1992.

The Birth of the African American Sorority Movement

As the United States entered the first decades of the 20th century, African Americans struggled to combat disenfranchisement and racialized violence. After the rise of Jim Crow practices and legislation, Black leaders such as Booker T. Washington and W.E.B. Du Bois promoted strategies for progress that called for educated African Americans to engage in community service or "racial uplift" to help less fortunate Blacks achieve. Bound by shared oppression and universal negative stereotyping, helping other African Americans to achieve inevitably benefited the race as a collective. In 1896, Mary Church Terrell became the first president of the National Association of Colored Women (NACW), an umbrella organization of Black women's civic, educational, and charitable clubs. With the motto, "Lifting as We Climb," the NACW, later renamed the National Association of Colored Women's Clubs (NACWC) in 1914, mobilized to address mounting problems affecting African American women and families. Whereas white club women engaged in community service to help the unfortunate, Black club women realized a shared connection with other African Americans because of their collective experiences as oppressed people. Racial uplift work eventually became a signifier of middle-class status and respectability.[8]

Prominent honorary Deltas, Mary Church Terrell and Nannie Helen Burroughs, and other late nineteenth and early twentieth-century African American women leaders advocated for and promoted what historian Evelyn Brooks Higginbotham called in her seminal work, *Righteous Discontent, The Women's Movement in the Black Baptist Church,* the "politics of respectability." This concept suggested that if Black women acted in respectable ways, they could challenge or dispel prevalent negative stereotypes of African American women and thus avoid or prevent racial and sexual harassment. They endorsed this approach to gain some sense of control over their lives in an atmosphere of pervasive Jim Crow segregation and racial and gender discrimination with no legal avenues for redress. Unfortunately, the politics of respectability's emphasis on presenting positive representations of Black womanhood sometimes reinforced patriarchal, religious-based concepts of moral respectability and placed the onus of preventing discrimination on its victims, who had little to no protection. Reflecting their understanding of the complicated limits of this strategy, most Progressive Era Black women leaders also engaged in acts of civil rights activism. For example, journalist and anti-lynching activist, Ida B. Wells Barnett actively used the power of the pen as a writer and journalist to publicize the horrors of lynching and protest sexism and other acts of racial injustice.[9]

When historians of the African American experience write about the Progressive Era, their work often revolves around the efforts of notable figures such as W.E.B. Du Bois and Ida B. Wells, the leaders of the Black women's club movement or the rise of African American national civil rights organizations, such as the NACWC and the National Association for the Advancement of Colored People (NAACP). Yet, in this same period, the emergence of African American Greek-letter public service organizations receives less attention. Incorporating the founding of these fraternities and sororities within the historiographical discussions of Progressive Era African American institution-building and activism exposes how Black Greek-letter organizations emerged as a response to racism and a reflection of the power of the Black middle class.

In 1906, seven African American students at Cornell University formed Alpha Phi Alpha Fraternity. Two other Black fraternities emerged in 1911, with the establishment of both Kappa Alpha Psi at Indiana University and Omega Psi Phi at Howard University. Howard became the founding home for Phi Beta Sigma in 1914. Several decades later, in 1963, at the height of the civil rights movement, twelve students formed Iota Phi Theta Fraternity at Morgan State University.[10] These organizations had similar organizational structures to their white counterparts; however, African American Greek-letter organizations promoted the concepts of racial uplift and social responsibility so prevalent at the time as a definer of middle-class status among African Americans.[11]

The Black sorority movement emerged within this environment. Sororities provided a social outlet for Black women barred from participation in organizations due to their race or gender. Howard University became the founding location for the first three African American sororities, Alpha Kappa Alpha in 1908, Delta Sigma Theta in 1913, and Zeta Phi Beta in 1920. Butler University in Indianapolis, Indiana, served as the home of Sigma Gamma Rho in 1922. Like their male counterparts, these organizations provided leadership opportunities and created spaces for fellowship and support. They also reflected an intersectional perspective, as these women encountered isolation as a select group of students on Howard's predominantly male populated campus, with only twenty-five female graduates out of 4,238 in 1910, or encountered racism as Black women on Butler's campus..[12]

The Howard University women who founded Delta Sigma Theta represented the ideal of proper respectable young ladies, yet these high-achieving college students risked public reproach to engage in activism. They would jeopardize their reputations and even their lives to join NACW leader Mary Church Terrell in the 1913 Women's Suffrage March. Demonstrating their respect for the diverse aspects of Black women's leadership that included advocating for respectability and public activism, they asked Burroughs, Terrell, and later Mary McLeod Bethune to become honorary members.[13] Delta Sigma Theta and the three other African American national sororities that are members of the National Pan-Hellenic Council would provide an arena for college-educated Black women to become leaders and power brokers in a political and cultural environment of disenfranchisement.

Over the years, as several sororities, including Delta Sigma Theta, marked the passing of a century since their inception, they continue to maintain their core mission of advancing academic excellence, supporting sisterhood, and engaging in public service. Scholars need to consider the rise of the Black sorority movement as a means for African American women to practice mutual support, encourage leadership, and alleviate the negative impact of intersectional discrimination by literally forming a sisterhood.[14] The remainder of this chapter is not an official history of Delta Sigma Theta Sorority, Inc. Instead, it supplements the official histories sanctioned by Delta. In addition to my review and critical assessment of some of these historical works, as a member of the organization, I secured access to some of its records and personal collections of materials that would be unavailable to non-members. The analysis and incorporation of information from these records within these chapters offers a more comprehensive and nuanced understanding of Delta's significance in the development of charismatic leadership and advocacy.

In 1944, former National Secretary and Official Delta Historian Edna Johnson Morris wrote, "Delta: Its History and Development," one of the first comprehensive histories of Delta Sigma Theta Sorority, Inc. This manuscript discussed Delta's history from its inception to the 1930s. Ten years later, in 1954, Durham, North Carolina Central University professor Helen G. Edmonds (1911–1995) wrote a comprehensive, well-researched monograph that placed Delta Sigma Theta's history within the broader context of African American history during the first half of the twentieth century. During Edmonds's illustrious 36-year career at North Carolina Central University, she served in several administrative roles, including dean of the College of Arts and Sciences as the first woman to do so. An active participant in the Republican Party, Edmonds became the first African American woman to second the nomination of a presidential candidate when she cast her vote for Dwight D. Eisenhower at the 1956 Republican Convention.[15]

One of the first Black women to obtain a PhD in History from The Ohio State University in 1946, Edmonds's monograph offered a rich, detailed historical analysis and continues to remain a lost contribution to African American historiography. Edmonds completed the manuscript, and it was under review by Random House Press. Even though her book placed Delta's history at the center of the discussions of pivotal events and experiences in African American history, the National Executive Board of Delta Sigma Theta asked Edmonds to revise the manuscript to only focus on the sorority's history. Edmonds, a professional historian, declined to do so, and the board failed to grant final publishing approval.[16]

In 1965, Mary Elizabeth Vroman, an accomplished screenwriter and the first Black woman to become a member of the Screen Actors Guild, wrote *Shaped to Its Purpose: The First Fifty Years* for Delta Sigma Theta's fiftieth anniversary. Published by Random House Press, this publication focused primarily on the sorority's national officers and programs. Delta Sigma Theta's sanctioned histories eventually evolved to incorporate more contextual non-Delta related information.[17]

In later years, Delta Sigma Theta sanctioned an official history that reflected more of Edmonds's comprehensive historical perspective and incorporated more contextual historical and current information about non-Delta related events or issues. Historian and journalist Paula Giddings's authorized history of the organization written in 1988 to commemorate the 75th anniversary of its founding and historian Deborah Gray White's 1999 study of African American women's organizations both provide a historical context for examining Maxwell-Roddey's experiences as a member and leader of a prominent women's organization.[18] In the last two decades, other works by Tamara L. Brown, Lawrence Gross, Gregory S. Parks, and Clarenda M. Phillips have concentrated on Delta Sigma Theta's history, national policies, and projects.[19]

In 1908, with the support of Howard University Faculty Member Ethel Robinson, Ethel Hedgeman Lyle organized eight of her fellow co-eds to form the first African American Greek-letter women's organization, Alpha Kappa Alpha Sorority, Incorporated. Originally designed to be the female counterpart to the Beta Chapter of Alpha Phi Alpha Fraternity, Alpha Kappa Alpha promoted academic excellence, performed charitable service, and sponsored beautification projects such as planting ivy plants on campus.[20] As a new class of young women joined Alpha Kappa Alpha, they ushered in a new spirit of activism spurred by the establishment of the NAACP and the prominence of the national movement for women's suffrage. Sensing the need for change, these students wanted to transform their organization. In 1912, Madre Penn (White) shared her bold idea to reconfigure the organization to become an independent entity with AKA president Myra Davis (Hemmings). Penn and

Davis wanted Alpha Kappa Alpha to reinvent itself by discarding its name, colors, and rituals, adopting the Greek letters Delta Sigma Theta as its formal name and creating new ceremonies. Penn encouraged the newly reinvented organization to seek legal incorporation to allow for it to expand by encouraging women to charter chapters at other universities.[21]

Beverly Smith, the 26th National President and CEO of Delta Sigma Theta, shared her thoughts in a 2016 newspaper article, that "Delta Sigma Theta Sorority, Inc. was founded as an organization on Howard University's campus in 1913 by a group of twenty-two collegiate 'rebels' who broke ties from one of our other sister organizations because they had a thirst for more involvement in social action and decided to take the 'road less traveled' that Robert Frost would write about a few years later." Offering additional clarification, Smith assured the membership that, "They saw nothing wrong with the organization from which they came and loved but, because they differed in their focus on social action, they broke ties to form another sorority of those with like minds."[22]

Astonishingly, twenty-two members, almost a complete majority, had voted in support of this drastic reformation. At this time membership ceased after graduation. After receiving detailed information explaining the sorority's reorganization, most former AKAs agreed except for past AKA president and recent Howard graduate, teacher Nellie Quander. She adamantly objected to the massive changes and demanded that Alpha Kappa Alpha retain its original name and colors. After the new members of Delta Sigma Theta denied Quander's request, she then contacted six Howard alumna and former AKA members and they decided to reconstitute Alpha Kappa Alpha Sorority.[23]

The one sorority, now split into two, became separate organizations. The members of the proposed Alpha Chapter of Delta Sigma Theta submitted their application for a charter in December of 1912. To the Deltas' dismay, Howard's board of trustees waited until after the Christmas break on January 13, 1913, to approve it. This is the day that the sorority considers its official Founders Day. A month later, on February 18, 2013, the board granted Delta Sigma Theta a certificate of incorporation, making it an official university-recognized organization. As African American sororities engaged in friendly rivalries and competitions, Alpha Kappa Alpha, Delta Sigma Theta, and the other national Black sororities, Sigma Gamma Rho, and Zeta Phi Beta share more commonalities than differences. As these organizations tout their public service records or promote their members' scholastic and career accomplishments, they motivate each other to continuously strive for excellence. Though Black Greek-letter sororities may challenge each other, they still share a common purpose to promote scholastic achievement, perform public service with a primary focus on helping African American communities, and encourage social action or activism.[24]

The Women's Suffrage March 3, Washington, DC, 1913

When the Fifteenth Amendment granted African American men the right to vote during Reconstruction, Black women, according to historian Elsa Barkley Brown, remained involved in the political process and saw voting rights as crucial to the progress of African American communities. In a desperate attempt to recruit white southern women, suffrage leaders turned to racist claims that white women's vote could ensure white supremacy. In response to this discrimination, some Black voting rights activists, such as Ida B. Wells Barnett, who formed the Alpha Suffrage Association in Chicago, became even more determined to secure the franchise.[25] As the suffrage movement rose to prominence across the United States, some white college women joined the fight to obtain the vote.

After learning of a national suffrage march to be held in Washington, DC in the spring, members of the newly established Delta Sigma Theta responded with curiosity and support. Alpha Chapter member Osceola Adams suggested that Delta Sigma Theta participate in the march as its first public act. The new chapter agreed. A controversial decision indeed, because it generated adverse reactions from their parents who feared for their safety and from Howard University's administration, which recoiled at the notion of respectable college ladies marching in the streets. Reluctantly, the Howard administration agreed, but only if they had a male professor as a chaperone. Fortunately, theater instructor, T. Montgomery Gregory, who later became a prominent playwright, African American veteran's advocate, and an Atlantic City, New Jersey, public school principal, agreed to accompany them. The Deltas also asked former NACW president Mary Church Terrell, wife of Howard Law School professor and judge Robert Terrell to accompany them on the march. Later as an Honorary Member of the sorority, Terrell would write Delta Sigma Theta's oath in 1914.[26]

These young women faced controversy from several sides as they defied the wishes of their parents and teachers. They challenged the racist views of some of the march planners who specifically asked Black women not to march or remain in the back, fearing the ire of southern white suffragettes. In response, some Black voting rights activists refused, in protest, to participate in the proposed segregated national parade. Anti-lynching activist and voting rights advocate Ida B. Wells Barnett defied the directives of white suffrage leader Alice Paul and some white Illinois suffragettes, by walking alongside her state contingent as a representative of the African American, Alpha Suffrage Club. Despite Alice Paul's instructions for them to remain racially segregated and march in the back, Mary Church Terrell adeptly negotiated with white suffrage activist and labor attorney Inez Milholland to let the Deltas march with their fellow white student protesters in the education section. The Deltas, dressed in caps and gowns, courageously proceeded. These situations reflected the intersectional dilemma of fighting for voting rights in a racially discriminatory environment.[27]

On March 3, 1913, Osceola McCarthy led the way as the Deltas encountered disapproving looks from their white participants and jeers from racist and sexist white onlookers. As they marched, the Deltas disobeyed their concerned parents' orders and faced the disapproval of worried Howard University officials. The young sorority members proceeded on despite intense opposition on a multitude of fronts that included critiques by some Blacks concerning their reputations to outward racist taunts because they wanted to participate in an organization that promoted Black women's early political activism. In an excerpt from a 1996 Presidential Address, Roddey shared an excerpt from a 1913 article from the *Washington Times*: "The young women of the newly organized Delta Sigma Theta Sorority, which is located on the campus of Howard University, participated in the high feminist demonstration here in the District of Columbia today . . . The Deltas were reminded that they, as Negro women had dual reasons for demanding the ballot."

Roddey affirmed, "When they established their sorority, they envisioned an organization 'for the concerted action in removing the handicaps under which we as women and as members of a minority race, labor, and for promoting social and race betterment.'" Roddey proclaimed, "still today that mission holds true for us as Deltas. As we remember the zeal, the vision of our founders in their initial struggles as we continue to fight for the liberty and betterment of African American women through social action."[28] In her address, the 20th National President represented the views of Delta's members who revered the twenty-two founding members and respected these young women's courage to confront both racism and sexism in a daring feat of activism. As the sorority expanded, Delta chapters hold annual events and performances to honor the founders.[29]

Delta Sigma Theta Chapter Expansion and Development

In subsequent years, Delta Sigma Theta organized chapters at other universities and colleges, including its second, the Beta Chapter at Ohio's Wilberforce

University, in 1914. In these early years, Delta developed its organizational structure, procedures, and service objectives that enabled it to endure and flourish for more than a century. During this period, Delta accepted African American women who met its membership criteria, which involved grade average requirements, letters of reference from professors and community members, and service involvement. Delta did accept some women who didn't attend college in its early years, but most of its members joined through undergraduate chapters on their college campuses. Granted the rare privilege to study at an institution of higher learning, these sorority women strove for academic excellence and endorsed the call for public service. However, they existed in a unique collegiate environment that could serve as a symbol and an incubator of elitism that prevented most working-class women from participating. As college students, they stood apart from the rest of their counterparts, who could not attend high school, much less college. Notwithstanding issues related to exclusion, the campus environment enabled the formation of a cohort of professional Black women primed to assume leadership roles and promote the interests of African American women.[30]

As Delta Sigma Theta established uniform criteria for accepting new members, which included evaluating a candidate's interest statements and interviews, scholarly achievement, public service efforts, and references, unfortunately, some sorors disregarded these standards. Instead, they disregarded Delta's bylaws and admission procedures to determine acceptability based on personal preferences or subjective requirements like class status. Colorism, where African Americans discriminate against each other based on the degree of darkness of their skin remains a pervasive problem that stemmed from the internalization of racism. Delta Sigma Theta had to contend with the colorism of some members, which was reinforced by the predominance of lighter-skinned college students due to colorist acceptance policies at historically Black institutions.[31]

Over the years, with the advent of the civil rights and Black Power movements, more African Americans now had more opportunities to attend integrated colleges. Not unlike their peers, some Deltas absorbed the Black Power movement's "Black Is Beautiful" call for African Americans to celebrate their natural features including hair and skin tone. The continued enforcement of standard acceptance criteria based on factors such as grades, references, and service commitments with the approval of Delta's regional director led to the abating of favoritism and unfair acceptance practices, including colorism.[32]

Just as traditional families work to resolve conflicts, the Delta sisterhood continues to enact measures to promote inclusivity and fairness. Delta is an organization that requires members to learn about its history and the inner workings of the sorority. This intake process allows women to make connections with each other and with their "big sisters" or as Deltas suggest, form a "bond." This connection is the foundation of the sisterhood. As Deltas reinforce this concept in their public actions, events, and performances, as they collectively sing, "Join the Delta girls," the sorority attracts other women who wish to be in a supportive environment.[33]

During the 1920s and 1930s, Delta Sigma Theta expanded by chartering new undergraduate, alumnae, and combined undergraduate and alumnae chapters in schools and cities across the nation. As it expanded nationally, Delta Sigma Theta recognized the need to establish a Grand Chapter with executive officers and organize by region. It became incorporated as a national body in 1930. Delta Sigma Theta now endorsed a national agenda of service projects and management practices for individual chapters to implement. Chapters had the power to adapt these national directives to serve their local communities best.

As African American sororities expanded to charter alumnae chapters of graduate members across the nation, Delta Sigma Theta and the other African American women's Greek-letter organizations faced critiques of elitism from other Blacks for sponsoring tea parties and galas. Nevertheless, proceeds from these social events often supported scholarships and charities. For Maxwell and other Deltas employed as teachers during segregation, regardless of their middle-class status as professionals, they often worked in dilapidated, one-room schools or overcrowded substandard buildings. By veering past the outward representation of bourgeoisie frivolity, the funds generated from these social events provided opportunities for Deltas to surround themselves with festive beauty. Notwithstanding the sometimes-valid criticisms of exclusivity and shallowness, over the years, as Deltas focused more on social action and addressing problems within African American communities, a stronger devotion to service and activism emerged.[34]

As a public service nonprofit, Delta Sigma Theta's national initiatives during the 1920s and 1930s included helping women secure safe and meaningful employment and increasing the amount and number of college scholarships given. With segregation's racial restrictions barring Blacks from attending public libraries and inadequate funding for school libraries, some African American children had limited access to books. In 1937, Delta initiated the National Library Project, which began in Franklin County, North Carolina. This traveling library brought collections of books to Black teachers to share with their students. The organization continued to support civil rights efforts to end lynching and secure voting rights.[35]

The 1940s marked the expansion of Delta Sigma Theta into Charlotte, North Carolina, with the formation of the Beta Xi Sigma Chapter (later known as the Charlotte Alumnae Chapter) in 1942.[36] It sponsored several charitable events such as the Jabberwock talent show to raise funds for scholarships and supported African American institutions and organizations such as the NAACP and the Good Samaritan Hospital, the city's only African American hospital.[37]

Adopting the slogan Delta Dynamic for Defense, the sorority also sponsored drives to purchase defense bonds and hosted United Services Organizations (USO) lounges and entertainment events for African American troops during World War II. On behalf of Delta Sigma Theta, Mary McLeod Bethune, director of the Division of Negro Affairs of the National Youth Administration, and Delta National Presidents Helen Elsie Austin and Mae Wright Downs (later Mae W. Peck-Williams) called for the desegregation of the women's armed forces. On the home front, Delta supported the establishment of the Federal Employment Practices Commission. In 1945, as the nation adjusted to life after World War II, Delta consolidated its service initiatives under a central organizational framework at its 18th Convention, with the theme "Design for Living in a New Age." National President Mae Wright Downs presented Delta's new Five Point Program, centered on education, employment, housing, race, and intercultural relations. Later known as the Five Point Programmatic Thrust, some of the titles of primary service areas would change, but the five points service theme has become a permanent organizational platform for Delta Sigma Theta's public service initiatives.[38]

The sorority donated to the NAACP and several Deltas including Founder Jessie McGuire Dent in Galveston Texas and Jackson Mississippi teacher Gladys Noel Bates became plaintiffs in the NAACP's teacher salary equalization cases during the 1940s, which served as a crucial step toward *Brown*. Gladys Noel Bates and her educator husband, John, lost their jobs and met with personal danger when terrorists fired guns into their home and later burned it down. After rebuilding and later relocating to Colorado in 1960, Noel Bates continued to engage in local civil rights efforts.[39]

As scholars discuss Dorothy Height's rise to become one of the most influential women civil rights leaders in the United States as the president of the National Council of Negro Women, her prior leadership within Delta Sigma Theta as its 10th National President, from 1947 to 1956, coincided with the advent of the Cold War. A mentee of Bethune, Height applied her experience as an organizational leader of the branches of the Young Women's Christian Association (YWCA) in Washington DC and New York City to expand upon the

NCNW president's model of charismatic leadership. Height encouraged Delta Sigma Theta members to engage in social action efforts within the US and she wanted to advance its international presence on the world stage as a prominent Black women's organization. Under her administration, Delta engaged in discussions centered around the intent and purpose of the creation of the United Nations' Founding Charter and worked to bring awareness to the plight of impoverished women in India and other countries who were engaged in anti-colonialism efforts. In 1950, Delta established its first international chapter in Port-au-Prince Haiti. In 1957, after her tenure as Delta's president ended, Dorothy Height became the fourth president of the National Council of Negro Women.[40]

Gamma Lambda Chapter, Johnson C. Smith University

When Bertha Lyons enrolled in Johnson C. Smith University in 1951, her soon-to-be-husband, Horace Maxwell suggested that she join Delta Sigma Theta because he was a member of the Omega Psi Phi Fraternity, Inc. Maxwell often kidded that Horace only married her to make sure that she returned the $125 that he loaned her to pay Delta's membership fee. Jokes aside, Horace may have encouraged Maxwell to become a member of his fraternity's unofficial sister organization because he recognized that she could benefit from participating in Delta and for his own social reasons. Nevertheless, Bertha already planned to join Delta Sigma Theta because of its service programs and her respect for several prominent members, including Terrell and Bethune. In 1951, she became a member of the new initiates or pyramid club of Gamma Lambda Chapter of Delta Sigma Theta. As an initiate, Maxwell learned about Delta's history, participated in service projects, and learned more about her "Big Sisters" and fellow initiates. Creating a lifetime bond with her sorors, Maxwell grew to cherish her friendship with her Delta "mother," Gamma Lambda president, Mary Louise Massey Jones.[41]

As a new Delta, Maxwell wanted to participate in Gamma Lambda's service projects and events, such as May Week, which was devoted to promoting educational excellence and academic achievement, but her work schedule limited her availability. Her commitments to work, school, and her family, meant that Maxwell could not take on a variety of leadership positions. Yet those roles that she did assume, such as when she served as the event coordinator, securing materials and supplies for Gamma Lambda's float for the Johnson C. Smith University homecoming parade enabled her to hone her skills of negotiation and organization. Delta provided a space where Maxwell could emphasize her new identity as a successful co-ed. Buoyed by the support of a bevy of new sorors, Maxwell soon adapted to the rigors of college life and the social customs.[42]

As Gamma Lambda sorors worked collectively in public service efforts, for Maxwell, participation in scholarship or charitable benefit events reflected the class diversity within her chapter as some members joined as daughters of the Black elite and others like Maxwell, came from more economically modest backgrounds. When she learned that most sorors wore fur coats when attending formal occasions, she faced a dilemma because she lacked the money to purchase a fur coat. Maxwell supported her college career by working. Her Great Aunt Elouise loaned her the money to purchase a fur stole, telling the anxious Maxwell, "If you need a fur, you will have a fur."[43] The wearing of fur coats or stoles became a symbol of middle-class economic achievement and femininity among African American women who may not have had access to other visible signs of material success such as cars or homes. In Maxwell's case, it represented the ways Black women supported each other in performing middle-class constructions, as Maxwell often allowed other Deltas to wear her stole on special formal occasions as an undergraduate and throughout her life.[44]

Public Service and Social Action

Encouraged by the activism of Delta National President Dorothy Height, Delta Sigma Theta and five other African American Greek-letter organizations joined to form the American Council on Human Rights (ACHR) in 1952. The ACHR, an umbrella organization created to utilize the collective power of its members in civil rights activities, sponsored letter-writing campaigns, and lobbied public officials. The ACHR also developed reference guides detailing its position on critical civil rights issues such as desegregation, voting rights, and the dismantling of apartheid in South Africa to share with public officials. Run by the four African American sororities and Phi Delta Kappa, a professional sorority of African American teachers, by the late 1950s the ACHR's goals and tactics seemed to overlap with the growing civil rights movement and its focus on direct action. The ACHR established a Student Emergency Fund to provide financial support to student activists and called for the sororities to stop holding free formal dances and donate the fees from these events to the Fund. In 1963, Delta Sigma Theta withdrew from the ACHR to support Delta's 10th National President Dorothy Height's National Council of Negro Women's projects. The 1960s marked a new era in the sorority as it encountered the onset of the modern-day civil rights movement.[45]

A unique aspect of African American sorority life is that membership continues after college graduation. Indeed, for many, this stage just marked the beginning of their Delta journey. Women can join as a college student through an undergraduate chapter or become a member as a college graduate through a city-based, alumnae or graduate chapter.[46] Bertha's Delta membership followed this trajectory. So, after teaching for two years at Alexander Street Elementary School, Maxwell joined Charlotte's then Beta Xi Sigma Chapter of Delta Sigma Theta in 1956, only a year after civil rights attorneys sought remedies for continued segregation in *Brown v. Board of Education II*. Delta's leaders and some of its educator members reacted to the *Brown* decision in a variety of ways. Some had serious concerns that school desegregation would result in job discrimination or elimination. Others thought that the push to achieve educational equality was worth the genuine risk of job loss. As desegregation efforts rose to the forefront, Delta sorors, like Maxwell, now reconsidered their personal philosophies toward desegregation and civil rights and the sorority's role in this era of change. As a member of Beta Xi Sigma, Maxwell could work through these complex issues in a warm, supportive environment of women who understood the frustrations that Black women educators faced during segregation.

Maxwell joined Beta Xi Sigma during the last year of Dorothy Height's tenure as Delta's national president. She looked up to Height as a leader who expanded its national presence and directed the sorority to increase its participation in civil rights organizations as a national entity and as individual sorors. As Delta responded to the impact of the civil rights movement by social justice and school desegregation efforts, under Dorothy Height's leadership, it began to strengthen the direction and structure of its service goals and projects. Out of these discussions, in 1955, it incorporated more public service programming to expand its Five Point Programming Project, which included library service, job opportunities, volunteering for community service, the international project, and mental health awareness. Aside from sponsoring national service initiatives under the Five Point Programming Project, Delta chapters had the flexibility of adapting this new programming structure to their own local concerns.[47]

In addition to promoting academic achievement by providing scholarships to high school and college women, after *Brown,* the Delta's educational mission now included protecting and supporting students who desegregated the public schools, like Charlotte's Dorothy Counts (later Scoggins). In 1956, Delta Sigma Theta's 11th National President, Dorothy Harrison (1956–1958), directed members to donate funds and clothing to support the efforts of

Little Rock civil rights activist, journalist, and publisher Daisy Bates who guided the nine Black students who desegregated Central High School in Little Rock, Arkansas. Delta Sigma Theta recognized Bates's courageous actions to spearhead this endeavor by voting to make the newspaper owner an Honorary Member.[48]

In 1958, Columbia University education doctoral student Jeanne Noble became the youngest national President of Delta Sigma Theta at thirty-four. A Howard University graduate, she would later break ground as the first Black woman to become a tenured professor at New York University. Noble drew from her mentor, former National President Dorothy Height, and the Delta members' own interests to direct the almost fifty-year-old organization to reaffirm its central role as a public service organization. As the civil rights movement emerged across the nation, the Delta Sigma Theta sponsored a national study of its undergraduate members to learn that some 35 percent participated in the 1960s sit-ins and other civil rights activities as individuals. In shifting to supporting civil rights as an organization, during Noble's tenure as president from 1958 to 1963, Delta established the Teen Lift mentoring program for young girls, and chapters tutored and supported children in areas like Prince Edward's County, Virginia, where the school board closed the public schools in retaliation to desegregation. Delta Sigma Theta funded voter registration drives and worked with other civil rights and women's groups to provide financial support for activists who faced firing or incurred legal costs. [49]

Delta Sigma Theta aligned and contributed to African American organizations, such as the National Council of Negro Women, the National Urban League (NUL), and the National Association for the Advancement of Colored People (NAACP). While individual Deltas belonged to these organizations and personally supported their respective goals, its affiliation as a group allowed it to join publicly with the campaigns of other organizations. In 1960, Delta Sigma Theta joined with sixteen other national women's organizations to form the National Organization of Women (NOW) for Equality in Education. Led by Eleanor Roosevelt, this group served as the predecessor to later interracial, female-led civil rights efforts, such as Jewish civil rights activist Polly Cowan and Dorothy Height's Wednesdays in Mississippi coalition of women's groups who supported women activists during the 1964's Freedom Summer campaign.[50]

During its three-day conference in New York, NOW for Equality in Education published a national survey of 10,000 high school students as part of a research study project conducted by H. H. Remmers of Purdue University. The study found that 80 percent of the northern, midwestern, and western students supported integration, with one-third or 33 percent of southern students in favor. The dissemination of this poll and NOW's lobbying efforts evoked an angry response from Georgia Senator Richard Russell Jr. He irrationally argued that by sponsoring this study, NOW purposely wanted to spark a race riot with the hope of garnering sympathy and propel the passage of the Civil Rights Act. As the only African American sorority in the organization, Delta Sigma Theta joined with the National Council for Negro Women and the National Association of Colored Women's Clubs in the interracial group of fourteen thousand members of women's civic, charitable, and religious organizations.[51]

As Delta National President, Jeanne Noble emphasized the sorority's outward public service and social action missions in her administration. She also worked to enact measures to strengthen connections to ensure that Delta retained its unique soul as a sisterhood as it expanded with the establishment of new chapters across the nation and internationally. In 1960, sensing a need to address some of the potential logistical and communication growth-related issues facing the chapters in the states of the Southern and Eastern Regions, Noble led efforts to establish a new South Atlantic Region comprised of former Eastern Region states, North Carolina and Virginia, and the Southern Region's South Carolina. The new South Atlantic Region included the now renamed Charlotte Alumnae Chapter (CAC). The Bermuda Alumnae Chapter became part of the region in later years.[52]

As the civil rights movement continued to engulf the nation, Delta Sigma Theta Sorority marked its 50th Golden Anniversary at its 27th National Golden Jubilee Convention in New York City from August 11 to 17, 1963. During the convention, Delta presented NAACP civil rights lawyer Constance Baker Motley with the Mary Church Terrell Award for her part as a key strategist on the *Brown v. Board of Education* legal team representing the plaintiffs. Noble motivated Deltas to become more involved to support women activists when she participated in civil rights campaigns in her hometown of Albany, Georgia. At the convention, delegates representing Delta's 280 chapters decided to participate in the National March on Washington for Jobs and Freedom on August 28, 1963. Delta chapters and individual members marched and supported civil rights leader and immediate Past National President Dorothy Height. In 1964, President Lyndon Johnson appointed Jeanne Noble to help plan the Women's Job Corps, a female counterpart to the War on Poverty's Job Corps Program.[53]

Charlotte Alumnae Chapter President, 1964–1966

With over 9,675 active collegiate and alumnae members, Delta Sigma Theta became further interlinked within the civil rights movement. Along with collegiate sorors, Delta leaders such as Mary McCleod Bethune, Mary Church Terrell, and Dorothy Height, had participated in the sit-ins, civil rights campaigns and endorsed the passage of the 1964 Civil Rights Act.[54] While national figures drew attention to Delta's national participation in the movement as an organization, on the local level, its members also worked to challenge racial discrimination even as employed professionals. By 1964, Maxwell had taught for over eight years. Maxwell broke a personal and racial barrier by enrolling in the Master's Program in Educational Administration at the University of North Carolina at Greensboro, taking classes in the summer.

Still, an active member of Delta Sigma Theta, the now experienced teacher belonged to the Merry Makers and other social groups. African Americans created their own cultural worlds that included social clubs like Charlotte's Merry Makers in response to a restricted segregated society.[55] Established in 1947, the Merry Makers sponsored social activities and charitable events like its annual fundraising luncheon and card party, where the proceeds went to charity. Maxwell's acceptance into a private group like the Merry Makers that had a membership limit of sixteen only further solidified her inclusion into Charlotte's Black middle class. Though Maxwell sometimes transcended segregation's barriers, she also participated in Charlotte's African American middle-class life fully without ever forgetting her small-town Seneca roots.[56]

During this period, Maxwell remained an active member of the former Beta Xi Sigma, now renamed the Charlotte Alumnae Chapter (CAC), but she expressed little interest in becoming an officer. Maxwell had even skipped the CAC's important election meeting to hang out and play cards with her Merry Makers group. Maxwell's charismatic personality led her fellow sorors to do the unexpected. Despite not being on the official ballot, members of the CAC overlooked the requirement that candidates be present at the meeting and elected Maxwell to be the president! This unexpected opportunity opened a new path for Maxwell. As the youngest president of the Charlotte Alumnae Chapter of Delta Sigma Theta at thirty-four, she began an unplanned and surprising ascension to executive leadership as chapter president from 1964 to 1966.[57]

The Debutante Cotillion

One of the first challenges Maxwell faced was the Charlotte Alumnae Chapter's lack of financial assets. The chapter's financial coffers were close to empty. Maxwell knew that she needed to raise funds. Using her own money to purchase stamps, Maxwell sent out notices to members encouraging them to pay their dues and donate funds. Meanwhile, fellow CAC member Grace Solomon, suggested to Maxwell that they do a popular fundraiser in the African American community, a debutante cotillion ball. Maxwell agreed, and Grace Solomon served as the first chair of the Cotillion Committee.[58]

The concept of the cotillion stems from a formal ceremony where white women who reached marrying age would be "presented" or "come out" to society. In contrast, African American cotillions reflected Black women's attempts to redefine their image and perceptions in a society where derogatory images of African American women remained pervasive. Unlike their white counterparts, these events did not mark the beginning of the courting season. From outward perceptions, debutante cotillions could signify the exclusivity of the Black middle class as the young women dressed in beautiful ball gowns to attend a fancy gala. Yet, scholarship cotillions like the CAC's demonstrated a type of inclusivity because the criteria for acceptance focused on applicants' academic potential and community service endeavors, not their appearance, perceived family connections, or class status. Part of the proceeds from these events enabled young students to fulfill their dreams of attending college. Unlike traditional cotillions, each participant had to secure individual donations from family and friends and get sponsors to purchase ads on behalf of the debutante for placement in the cotillion souvenir program booklet. The deb who raised the most funds received the crown as the queen of the cotillion. The proceeds from the cotillion replenished chapter funds and enabled it to offer more scholarships, donate more to charities and organizations, and sponsor community events.[59]

Another crucial component of the cotillion experience included self-transformation. The young women had opportunities to interact with each other as the Deltas planned a series of free classes and programs for the participants. They learned about a variety of topics ranging from proper etiquette to viewing fine art. The debutante participants performed community service and attended events with prominent speakers of the day. During the actual evening of the cotillion, each debutante enters a beautifully decorated room with her father after hearing her name announced. The debutantes later performed waltzes with their fathers and escorts and presented choreographed group dances in front of a crowd of well-wishers. As the first African American Greek-letter organization-sponsored cotillion in Charlotte, the event attracted high school students from across the city. At the gala affair, Grace Solomon and Maxwell announced that Etta Davidson, a senior at West Charlotte High School, received the crown, CAC's first "Miss Debutante."[60] In 1981, Maxwell's eighteen-year-old daughter Tawanna participated in Delta's seventeenth cotillion. The popular event continues to be a scholarship fundraiser for CAC's nonprofit organization, the Deltas of Charlotte Foundation.[61]

When does a debutante cotillion become an engine for civil rights protest? When Maxwell strategically used the cotillion to confront the discriminatory treatment of African American women in the local press. Her actions challenge the negative critique by scholars, such as E. Franklin Frazier, who portrayed the Black middle class as self-absorbed elites, satisfied with the status quo.[62] When Maxwell looked to publicize the cotillion, she used this occasion to push for greater inclusion of African American women's events and achievements in the city's white newspapers. She met with the editor of the *Charlotte Observer* several times to ask why the publication didn't mention African American women's bridal announcements and participation in events, such as the cotillion. Maxwell thought that the newspaper should cover Black women's social activities in the same or equal way as news about white women's social activities. During segregation, white newspapers often portrayed African American women only as workers or worshippers in religious settings or as victims or perpetrators of crime. Coverage of other aspects of African American women's social culture remained limited or non-existent.[63]

Though seemingly trivial in comparison to the civil disobedience protests of civil rights activists, by demanding that Charlotte's mainstream newspapers provide equal coverage of all aspects of African American women's lives, Maxwell confronted segregation's ability to render Black women invisible. After her repeated requests, the newspaper agreed to cover these events, which later resulted in the hiring of more Black reporters and provided more publicity for CAC and other African American organizations' charitable fundraising events.[64] When Maxwell left office, the Charlotte Alumnae Chapter could boast that it now provided more scholarships and donations to charities due to the success of the cotillions.

The Five Point Programmatic Thrust

In 1964, when Maxwell assumed the presidency of the Charlotte Alumnae Chapter of Delta Sigma Theta, she took the lead during a tumultuous time. As the civil rights movement reached new heights with the passage of the 1964 Civil Rights and 1965 Voting Rights Acts, it did so during mounting social unrest among African Americans. Sensing the need for the CAC to respond to these pressing issues as a public service organization, Maxwell worked to place the Charlotte Alumnae Chapter at the forefront of enacting social change. First, she drew on Delta's updated National Five Point Programmatic Thrust to examine some of the problems affecting African Americans in Charlotte and develop solutions that the chapter could address. Delta Sigma Theta had introduced the renamed program several years ago, but it did not mandate that individual chapters enact programming to address all the points. Merging her sense of history and respect for Delta's programming initiatives with a spirit of innovation, Maxwell re-envisioned and expanded the CAC's service programs to become its first president to lead the chapter to develop initiatives that encompassed all the Five Points.[65]

To address the points related to library service and volunteerism, the chapter formed a volunteer network to support the Red Cross, local libraries, and the NAACP voter registration drives. Members also served on the boards of local and state human relations councils. Relating to educational issues, the CAC sponsored an education and employment clinic for students at J. T. Williams Junior High and presented scholarships to high school and Johnson C. Smith University students. In the area of international awareness and health, the CAC donated funds to support the Delta-sponsored Thika Maternity Hospital in the newly independent country of Kenya, and they promoted greater mental health understanding in a volunteer door-to-door information campaign.[66]

The immense responsibility of tending to the day-to-day organizational needs of one of the largest Black women's organizations in Charlotte fell to Maxwell as she soon realized the chapter needed more organization and structure. Despite being known for her unorthodox teaching style and relatability, Maxwell respected the need to adhere to Delta's traditions and protocol. So, she directed CAC officers to start wearing ceremonial robes when leading certain rituals and events instead of business dress attire. Maxwell enjoyed talking with her sorors at the monthly meetings, but as president, she insisted that members focus on Delta work. One of the greatest benefits from her role as chapter president involved having the opportunity to honor and celebrate Delta's history by inviting one of Delta's founders, Jimmie Bugg Middleton, to the chapter's Founder's Day celebration. Soror Middleton had strong North Carolina ties as the driving force behind the chartering of Shaw University's Alpha Rho Chapter in 1934 and the Alpha Zeta Sigma (later Raleigh Alumnae Chapter) in 1938. An educational administrator, Middleton served as the dean of girls at Washington High School, Raleigh's first Black secondary school.[67]

Ironically, Maxwell's longing for the CAC to have more of an activist and service presence within Charlotte only happened because proceeds from the cotillion financed the chapter's programming agenda. In a period where some activists critiqued or dismissed Black sororities for their elitism, Maxwell's intention to use the proceeds from the cotillion to foster community service and engagement reflects the need to re-evaluate the use of the often clichéd and oppositional labels of the "bougie" sorority member and socially aware activist. For Maxwell and other African American women, the two designations meshed and called for a more nuanced analysis of the role of Black middle-class women during this period. As she grieved the loss of her paternal grandmother Anna Brewer Earle in December of 1964, Maxwell rose to leadership as Delta's service agenda now included extensive efforts to support social action or protest. Maxwell later incorporated the tenets of cultural nationalism of positive Black-self-identity formation into her vision as a leader.[68]

The 28th National Convention, August 1965

As CAC president, Maxwell had the responsibility to serve as a voting delegate at the 28th National Convention in Los Angeles from August 10–15, 1965. First established in 1919, the national convention draws delegates from every Delta chapter who are often chapter presidents or elected representatives, to learn more about new initiatives, vote on policies and procedures, and elect executive officers and national committee members. It is an opportunity for other members from across the nation to meet and fellowship, attend elegant affairs, and listen to speeches by nationally known public figures. The convention also serves as a safe place for women to foster and exhibit leadership skills and interact with the executive officers. In a 1996 newspaper article, Maxwell emphasized the serious purpose of the convention: "It's not like most people think of a sorority, where you have a little tea party."[69]

With thousands of Deltas in attendance, the convention provides a site for collective self-affirmation, where Black women can achieve on their own shared terms without the negative influences of racism or sexism. Paulette Walker, the 25th National President of Delta Sigma Theta, explained the unique role of the convention in a 1986 newspaper article when she was president of the Tampa Bay Alumnae Chapter. "We don't get that feeling every day. We work in isolation. It's like when you walk into this building, and you see all these people wearing this red and white, there's a linkage. That is our legacy."[70]

Concerned about the costs of traveling to Los Angeles to attend the 1965 National Convention, Maxwell decided to organize a bus trip for sorors from the South Atlantic Region to travel to the convention. As a working mother and graduate student at UNC Greensboro, Maxwell faced the dilemma of child-care. After her husband seemed reticent about babysitting the toddler alone, Maxwell invited him along. So, she, Horace, and toddler Tawanna boarded the bus for the month-long trip. On the way, they stopped to see the sights in Utah and Colorado. After finally arriving in Los Angeles, Maxwell received a dinner invitation from a friend and former Charlotte resident, who now lived in the Black middle-class Baldwin Hills neighborhood of Los Angeles. After dinner, the group decided to go outside and received a shock when it seemed as if flames engulfed the entire city! Unbeknown to Maxwell at the time, she witnessed the fires stemming from the Watts uprising.[71]

With physical and metaphorical flames of racial unrest engulfing Watts, as sorors attended meetings during the Delta Convention, they grew painfully aware of the pressing need for the sorority to continue its support of the civil rights movement. Drawing on its unique strengths as a public service sorority, Delta expanded its national Teen Lift Program, where chapters mentored girls from economically underserved areas, offered academic tutoring, and took them on trips to large US cities to visit colleges and landmarks. Several Teen Lift participants spoke at the convention.[72]

In addition to their convention activities, Delta sorors engaged in social action efforts with their chapters and as individuals by marching in local, state, and national civil rights protests. They joined civil rights organizations like the Student Non-Violent Coordinating Committee (SNCC) and supported Mississippi's Womanpower Unlimited organization. Delta worked with African American NAACP lobbyist Clarence Mitchell Jr. to advocate for civil rights measures with Delta's "March to the Mailbox" letter-writing campaign to public officials.[73]

As Delta's sorors looked to enact change, one could see how the civil rights movement's call for racial and economic justice led Delta to question some of its own allegiances. Two years before, at the 1963 Delta National Convention in New York, some sorors criticized the national executive board and convention planners for inviting political leaders like Robert Kennedy to speak and for enthusiastically clapping after his address. Instead, these young soror-activists wanted to hold Kennedy and other political figures accountable by questioning them on their civil rights stances. In contrast, two years later at the Delta National Convention when Sam Yorty, the mayor of Los Angeles, mistakenly assumed that the Delta convention attendees agreed with his condemnation of the Watts riots, sorors reacted to his remarks with silence and icy stares. On the other hand, the visit of Martin Luther King Jr. energized the crowd. Delta Sigma Theta selected activist Myrlie Evers, the wife of slain Mississippi civil rights activist Medgar Evers to be an Honorary Delta.[74]

As Maxwell left the convention, a new shift became evident as Delta Sigma Theta grappled with how the venerable organization, ensconced in an environment that promoted the politics of respectability, would now respond to acts of nonviolent protest and the impending rise of the Black Power movement. As some of Delta's members reaped the academic and economic rewards resulting from the dismantling of southern Jim Crow laws, other African Americans grew more frustrated with the slow progress of the civil rights movement in their areas. The juxtaposition of the eruption of a Black uprising as the ultimate reaction to systematic oppression and police brutality, while Delta sorors, dressed in beautiful evening attire attended receptions and banquets, represents the dichotomy of the Black community. On the way back to Charlotte, Maxwell's bus had to travel through the night, taking a shorter, less scenic route to bypass southern states to avoid possible racial and/or sexual harassment. Maxwell, cognizant of the changes that were coming, would later build a hypothetical bridge between the advocates of Black Nationalism and the beneficiaries of the civil rights movement as the director of the AAAS Program at UNC Charlotte.[75]

Informing the Community and the Region: CAC, the War on Poverty, and Supporting Civil Rights Organizing

As an educator and the past director of the Charlotte Teachers Corp early childhood education program in the summer of 1964, Maxwell thought that the CAC could serve its community by disseminating information about War on Poverty programs, like Head Start and other federal initiatives. Under Delta's National President Geraldine P. Woods's (1963–1967) administration, it established the nonprofit Delta Research and Education Foundation (DREF) to provide fundraising and grant writing assistance to Delta chapters to facilitate service initiatives. In October 1965, the Charlotte Alumnae Chapter sponsored a community forum to discuss the War on Poverty. Relying on contacts that Maxwell made as a teacher and as a graduate student at UNC Greensboro, she joined a panel with Assistant CMS Superintendent John Phillips; O. N. Freeman, director of Project Head Start; Ernest Russell, Charlotte Bureau of Employment Training and Placement director; John

Zuidema, director of the Charlotte Area Fund; and Maurice Kamp, County Health Department director. The speakers shared their experiences working with anti-poverty programs and praised the success of Head Start and other programs. As president of CAC, Maxwell's interest in the War on Poverty inspired Deltas to offer proposals on how the chapter could develop initiatives to support or align with anti-poverty programming. By expanding the influence of Charlotte Alumnae as an organization engaged in social action, she gained more public recognition, which eventually led to her becoming a cultural institution builder and an influential figure among African Americans in Charlotte.[76]

Almost a month after the Charlotte Alumnae Chapter's successful War on Poverty forum, an act of cruel terrorism shook the city to its core. On the night of November 22, 1965, bombs erupted at the homes of four local civil rights leaders: Charlotte City Councilmember Fred D. Alexander, his brother, NAACP State President Kelly Alexander Sr., attorney Julius Chambers, and dentist Reginald Hawkins. No one was hurt, but the bombings shocked the city and disputed Charlotte's claim as a progressive, New South city. As president, Maxwell authorized the CAC to donate $65 to an Anti-Terrorism Fund sponsored by the *Charlotte Observer*. Receiving donations from businesses, churches, and individuals, The Fund raised over $8,000. Charlotte mayor Stan Brookshire, the city's community relations committee, a group of prominent Black and white city leaders, and the *Charlotte News* contributed over $4,000 to find the bombers. Unfortunately, the bombers remain at large.[77]

As the civil rights movement gained even more prominence and Charlotte looked to reassert its progressive image after the bombing, in February 1966, Maxwell's CAC organized a regional workshop to help Deltas develop more programming under the Five Point Programmatic Thrust. The all-day workshop focused on current civil rights legislation and public school desegregation, featuring local civil rights leaders, such as dentist Reginald Hawkins; Little Rock African Methodist Episcopal Zion Church Minister George J. Leake III; Jim Kiser, associate dean of Piedmont Community College; CMS School Board Member Betsy Kelly; and Charlotte City Council Member James Whittington. With delegates from forty-four Delta chapters of the three-state South Atlantic Region in attendance—North Carolina, South Carolina, and Virginia—the participants learned about subjects relating to the Five Point Programmatic Thrust. As Maxwell explained to a local newspaper, at the regional meeting, "chapters attending will learn ways to develop and carry out programs, which will help them solve community problems in the areas studied."[78]

Maxwell's Charlotte Alumnae Chapter Legacy

Choosing not to run for a second term, in April 1966, Maxwell served as a voting delegate to Delta's South Atlantic Regional Conference in Durham, North Carolina. Besides learning more about the region's service programs and current political and social issues such as, the Voting Rights Act, from special assistant to the US attorney general Wiley A. Branton and other African American leaders at the regional conference, Maxwell met popular entertainer and civil rights activist Lena Horne. An Honorary Member of Delta Sigma Theta, Horne discussed her new autobiography, *Lena*.[79]

The outgoing CAC president also met current and former Delta presidents and executive board members, including current Geraldine Woods; National Treasurer and future National President Thelma Daley; Jeanne Noble, and one of Delta Sigma Theta's founders, Jimmie Bugg Middleton. As Maxwell intermingled with these leaders, she had no clue that she would one day join their ranks. Through her interactions with these national figures, she would later gain a mentor in Jeanne Noble. As Maxwell observed and learned from their leadership styles, these officers observed a dynamic local chapter president whose innovative ideas, keen management skills, and dedication marked her for further leadership opportunities.[80]

As CAC head, Maxwell gained valuable organizational and leadership skills as she worked to improve the chapter's service programming. She did all of this while employed full-time, pursuing a master's degree, and parenting a toddler. Charlotte Alumnae's reputation as a service organization dedicated to social action expanded as Maxwell directed the initiatives under the Chapter's Five Point Programming Thrust. During her tenure, Maxwell became known among social justice activists and community leaders, as she worked internally to ensure the financial stability of the CAC. Some sorors may have balked at the changes, but others recognized her leadership potential.[81]

Advising in a New Age: Iota Rho

By the time Maxwell started working at the predominantly white Albemarle Elementary in 1968, the overwhelming duties of a school administrator during desegregation often prevented her from participating in Delta activities. When Maxwell's fellow principal and Charlotte Alumnae Chapter President Sterleta Sasso chastised her for missing meetings, Maxwell told the venerable and respected principal that she did not understand the pressures that Maxwell faced as the head of a white school. Sasso then backed off. Despite Maxwell's concerns, when the South Atlantic regional director Louise Reddick asked her to advise the Gamma Lambda Chapter at Johnson C. Smith University, she agreed. As an adviser, Maxwell worked with the sorors of her former chapter, offering guidance when they implemented programming and brought in new members.[82] Although the past CAC president purposely decided to step back, after a few short years, she would be called back into action. In 1972, after only one year in her new position as director of the UNC Charlotte's Black Studies Program, several undergraduate women asked Maxwell to help them establish a chapter of Delta Sigma Theta on campus. Louise Riddick also made this request to Maxwell.[83]

Even though UNC Charlotte's predominantly white sororities did not openly discriminate or segregate, these young future Deltas thought that these organizations did not fully address their need to create community as young Black women. Delta Sigma Theta had collegiate chapters on predominantly white campuses since the founding of the Gamma chapter at the University of Pennsylvania in 1918. The sorority now saw avenues for more expansion as African American women attending recently desegregated southern colleges and universities sought to participate. Delta undergraduates who attended predominantly white schools during the era of segregation supported each other as they faced social isolation and discrimination. Decades later, UNC Charlotte co-eds wanted to belong to an organization that represented their perspectives and campus goals.[84]

Local graduate chapters of Alpha Kappa Alpha Sorority allowed some UNC Charlotte students to join in off-campus ceremonies, but no African American sorority chapters existed at the newly established university. This absence left a void that UNC Charlotte student Jacqueline Stevens (Sanders) hoped to fulfill. First, Stevens and a group of friends created an informal sorority-like group, Soul Phi Soul, but they soon realized that they wanted to belong to a nationally recognized organization. Although Riddick encouraged Maxwell to lead the process of chartering a Delta chapter on UNC Charlotte's campus, she hesitated because of her busy schedule and the concern that Delta would be the only Black sorority on campus. Maxwell refused to subscribe or engage in petty sorority rivalries. She respected the other African American sororities as sister public service organizations. Maxwell also did not want students to feel forced to join Delta Sigma Theta because they had no other options.[85]

After meeting with Stevens and the other interested students, Maxwell contacted her Afro-American and African Studies colleagues and Alpha Kappa Alpha members Mary Harper and Beverly Ford and learned that Alpha Kappa Alpha would be chartering the Kappa Chapter on campus. Maxwell agreed to work with the Charlotte Alumnae Chapter members to charter the Iota Rho Chapter and serve as its first adviser. Maxwell's actions to help establish Iota Rho and her advisory position served as an extension of her role as the director of UNC Charlotte's BSP/AAAS. Maxwell and the AAAS helped students built supportive networks connecting them with each other, to the school, and beyond the campus.[86]

As AAAS director and founder of the NCBS, Maxwell associated with some of the leading activists and scholars of the Black Studies movement, including chair of the Department of Africana Studies at California State University, Long Beach, Maulana Karenga, and University of Massachusetts-Amherst Department of Afro-American Studies chair John H. Bracey Jr. In some ways, Maxwell's presence offset the criticisms by activists in the Black Power movement who sharply criticized other African Americans for ascribing to traditional concepts such as the politics of respectability and integration. Maxwell defied these arbitrary categories. As a former educator who worked in both segregated and desegregated institutions, she never strayed from her original mission to help African Americans, and her belief that all children thrive and learn in a supportive environment. As a Black Studies practitioner, she strove to create a safe and welcoming space for Black students to succeed at a predominantly white institution. Maxwell incorporated some of the tenets of Black Power, such as African ethnic group traditions and indigenous religious beliefs in her work as director of Black Studies/AAAS and as a Delta.[87]

As the rise of the Black Power movement and its campus counterpart the Black campus movement emerged on college campuses nationally, collegiate Deltas reacted in a myriad of ways that included joining Black student activists, sponsoring innovative programming to honor African traditions, exposing students to the artists of the emerging Black Arts Movement, and supported Black community empowerment. These changing currents also engulfed Delta's national leadership. Under Delta Sigma Theta's 14th National President (1967–1971), Frankie Muse Freeman's administration, the sorority contributed as an organization and as individual sorors to the Poor People's Campaign led by Martin Luther King Jr. and the Resurrection City anti-poverty initiative. During Freeman's presidency, Delta was considering the future direction of social justice movements. Delta's leaders and members deliberated whether the organization should retain its integrationist stance, as younger members argued for change. Even Maxwell jokingly threatened to join the Black Panther Party when some sorors questioned her activist positions. Despite making this threat partially in jest, Maxwell understood that some Deltas seemed hesitant to accept the fast-changing world around them. So, she tried to act as a generational bridge, helping Iota Rho and other young Deltas launch initiatives, such as supporting former UNC Charlotte student activist T. J. Reddy, whose harsh imprisonment as a member of the Charlotte Three sparked national protests, which reflected Iota Rho's perspectives as activists.[88]

In 1972, after participating in several workshops and other events, Maxwell and the Charlotte Alumnae Chapter welcomed the thirteen founding members of the new Iota Rho Chapter of Delta Sigma Theta on UNC Charlotte's campus. With Stevens serving as president, Iota Rho worked hard to gain a reputation as one of the most prominent and positive organizations on campus. In addition to addressing campus concerns, they volunteered in the community helping patients and staff at the Green Acres Rehabilitation Hospital. They also welcomed and hosted Delta Soror and Democratic Presidential Candidate Shirley Chisholm when she visited UNC Charlotte's campus.[89]

As a new chapter, Iota Rho fashioned their initiation process within this new setting. Although the collegiate chapter did not have a sorority house, they still found ways to fortify their new sisterhood by sharing rooms in the new residential dorms or visiting with sorors who lived off the campus. Iota Rho's chapter members strove to adhere to Delta's constitution and bylaws, maintain high grades or GPA's, engage in charitable and civic public service, and for fun, participate in regional and later campus step dance shows and other events.[90] Maxwell's advisory role continued beyond the formation of the chapter as she was one of its staunchest supporters. Indeed, the support engendered through sisterhood extended both ways. After Rosa, Maxwell's beloved seventy-two-year-old grandmother passed in 1973, she received compassion and sympathy from her sorors.[91] Maxwell and the members of Iota Rho formed a deep bond as she not only served as their educational mentor; she became their soror.

Delta Encounters the Second Wave, Womanism, Delta Style

When Delta National President Frankie Muse Freeman led the sorority, she called for Deltas to evaluate the sorority's purpose and role within the context of the emergence of the Black Power and the feminist movements. Delta Sigma Theta received grants to sponsor programs to rehabilitate women in federal prisons and help school dropouts. Before lawyers and scholars defined the term "intersectionality" and discussed its meanings, African American women throughout history embodied this concept as they contended with racial, gender, and class oppression. Beginning with Delta's founders who participated in the 1913 suffrage march, to its efforts to create job opportunities for Black women, to the securing of grants to support equal rights for Black women, Delta Sigma Theta used its unique advantage as an organization of college-educated women to combat the ways that racism, sexism, and class discrimination hindered African American women's progress by offering an array of programs related to its Five Point Programmatic Thrust.[92]

As Maxwell encouraged her students to discover "Who am I" in the Block program, she urged sorors to embrace their cultural heritage as African American women. When some Deltas stopped straightening their hair and began wearing afros, Maxwell understood that it embodied a new concept of beauty and self-love and their growing interest in activism. As Maxwell worked with the members of the Iota Rho Chapter, the co-eds could now look to Delta's 15th National President Lillian P. Benbow (1971–1975), as the first president to wear her hair in an afro style. To promote artistic expression, the Michigan former housing director and poet established the Arts and Letters Committee to develop the arts and arts education programs, inspiring Delta chapters to support the arts within their communities.[93]

In reaction to the Nixon administration's conservative policies, Benbow openly criticized the US president's attack on school desegregation and busing. Benbow's administration promoted Black economic ownership, or entrepreneurship, and the adoption of technology. The new Delta Resource Bank used computer technology to facilitate better communication among chapters. Delta's DST Telecommunications disseminated taped video recordings of panel presentations that addressed issues of sexism and racism. Delta Sigma Theta became the first Black Greek-letter organization to finance a feature film when DST Telecommunications produced *Countdown at Kusini,* starring actress and Delta Soror Ruby Dee, which opened in 1976 in the United States and Nigeria. Even though the film did not reap the expected financial rewards and positive critical attention, Benbow's vision for Delta to utilize its resources and power to produce a feature film helped to increase its international reputation as an innovative organization.[94]

During the 16th National President Thelma Daley's administration from 1975 to 1979, Delta continued to support efforts from the Benbow administration to pass the Equal Rights Amendment. President Daley's platform focused on rededication to Delta's traditions and public service efforts. She called for Delta Sigma Theta to update its Five Point Programmatic Thrust, which now consisted of Educational Development, Economic Development, Community and International Involvement, Housing and Urban Development, and Mental Health. The sorority opened Life Development Centers, where Delta Alumnae Chapter houses would serve as community service centers. Daley also called for economic support for historically Black colleges and universities with donations to the United Negro College Fund and funding for Delta's first Distinguished Professor Endowed Chair position for Black universities.[95]

An iconic artistic representation became one of the most lasting legacies of the Daley administration. In 1979, the members of the Alpha Chapter of Delta Sigma Theta unveiled *Lady Fortitude* at Howard University. Created by James King, this beautiful Corten-steel sculpture is 12 feet × 6 inches in height, with an arm span of 12 feet. It depicts a lady pushing forward, slightly lunging, with her arms outreached. Dedicated to Delta's founders and with the purpose of inspiring women, *Fortitude* symbolizes strength, love, courage, and determination. Beloved by Deltas, the image of *Fortitude* now represents an iconic visual representation of the sorority, where the image appears on Delta-inspired clothing and is recreated in jewelry and home décor. Some sorors even physically imitate the statue's position of strength in performances. Sorors often journey on January 13 to Howard University to gather at the statue to commemorate Delta's Founders Day. Howard's past and present-day Alpha Chapter members often hold gatherings and performances at the base of *Fortitude* and consider the statue as part of their legacy.[96]

Now with *Lady Fortitude* serving as a permanent marker of Delta's presence on Howard University's campus, the Daley administration reinforced its "Back to Basics" administrative theme by calling for expanded collegiate and alumnae service efforts. As a nonprofit public service organization, it sought federal funding to implement new initiatives. In 1979, Delta Sigma Theta secured a one-year $134,000 grant from the US Department of Education to sponsor ten regional conferences to examine the impact of racial and gender discrimination on Black women. Named the Women's Educational Equity Training Project, or WEETAP, national director Delores Thomas, a former equal opportunity specialist for the Maryland Department of Education, explained the conference's intersectional focus: "To have a career is not something new for Black women, but for Black women, it has long been necessary to work to help their men. We want to develop a broad base of understanding who we are and why we are." By referring to the interlocking oppressions that affect African American women, Thomas contended, "The Black woman is stuck with the old double jeopardy act of racism and sexism in employment. We want to develop skills to foster change."[97] Sorors of the Charlotte Alumnae Chapter had the responsibility of sponsoring the first WEETAP conference in their area. Soon after Maxwell returned to UNC Charlotte after her brief stint as an administrator at Johnson C. Smith University, members of the Charlotte Alumnae asked her to replace the resigning coordinator. Maxwell agreed to organize the WEETAP conference "The Dual Barriers of Black Women in America: Racism and Sexism." Some 300 people attended the event that featured prominent civil rights, education, and political figures including Julius Chambers, lead attorney in the *Swann vs. Mecklenburg County Board of Education* case on busing and racial integration in public schools and later president of the NAACP Legal Defense Fund. Other participants included Kathleen Crosby, CMS area superintendent and recently appointed member of the UNC Board of Governors, and North Carolina State Senator, Fred D. Alexander. Calling for the passage of the Equal Rights Amendment, the workshops discussed strategies to address inequalities in education, media, employment, housing, politics, healthcare, and aging.[98]

The Year 1980: A Year of Campaigns, Committees, and Change

After participating in Delta Sigma Theta's programming and service projects for decades, it was now time for Maxwell to ask her sorors for help. In 1980, when Maxwell decided to run for a seat in the North Carolina General Assembly, she turned to her sorors and community members for support. Although Delta Sigma Theta is a non-partisan organization, in Maxwell's case, she needed assistance as an individual Delta. Charlotte-area Deltas from the Iota Rho, UNC Charlotte, the Charlotte Alumnae, and other local chapters along with Deltas from the South Atlantic Region donated money and volunteered for the campaign. Maxwell's platform promoted educational development and diversity. Even though they had little experience running political campaigns, Maxwell asked Charlotte Alumnae Sorors Lucille Batts, a CMS librarian and bookstore owner, E. Virginia Shadd, a fellow CMS teacher, and administrator to manage her campaign based on their reputations as educators and entrepreneurs and their willingness to help. These women also gained experience in a powerful political management position previously unavailable to Black women. Batts explained why she volunteered, "I knew I was smart, why not? Why couldn't I do it?" Fortunately, her campaign managers could build upon Maxwell's prominence in the community as an educator and co-founder of the Afro-American Cultural Center, which gave her an advantage over less known candidates. Despite losing in the general election, Maxwell's experiences in the campaign prepared her to be a stronger candidate for regional and national offices within Delta.[99]

Service to Delta's National Heritage and Archives Committee

Maxwell may have failed in her bid for statewide office, but her political journey within Delta Sigma Theta had just begun. After serving as the president of the Charlotte Alumnae Chapter in the 1960s and as the adviser of the Gamma Lambda and Iota Rho Chapters during the 1970s, Delta's 17th National President, Mona Humphries Bailey (1979–1983), appointed Maxwell to chair Delta's National Heritage and Archives Committee (H&A) in 1980. As head of the H&A, she now served on Delta's powerful National Executive Board, which consists of the following officers: National President; National First Vice President who is the chair of Scholarship and Standards Committee; the National Second Vice President, who is an undergraduate member; the National Treasurer; National Secretary; and the regional directors and the regional representatives, who are undergraduates for the seven geographical regions of Delta, and the chairs of national committees.[100]

The executive board provides administrative guidance and direction when the national convention is not in session. Deltas must be elected to most national committees. As in Maxwell's case, however, the national president can appoint members to national committees or task forces. Administered by the national president and national executive board, which consists of elected and appointed officers, Delta Sigma Theta's Grand Chapter also includes all dues-paying members. Though the Grand Chapter oversees and sets national policies, members of the collegiate and alumnae chapters can initiate chapter-specific service projects that address the concepts of the Five Point Programmatic Thrust. Over the years, as Delta created guidelines for serving in leadership roles, it established regulations to ensure that women seeking elective office possessed experience serving in leadership roles and knew the inner workings of the organization. One of the ways that members gained knowledge included serving on a national committee.[101]

Even though Maxwell remained extremely busy as the recently returning chair of UNC Charlotte's AAAS Program, with her advisory role at the Center, she continued to conduct desegregation workshops and serve on local nonprofit and educational boards, she could not refuse an opportunity to do what she loved, helping Delta honor and preserve its history. The mission of the H&A included preserving and promoting Delta's written and material history and historic buildings and landmarks. In a "Message from the Chair" Maxwell described her committee as follows: "The members of the Heritage and Archives Committee sees its major role in promoting our sisterhood by passing on the customs and traditions of our ancestors." She assured sorors that the H&A would achieve its archival goals "by continuously organizing and preserving our records that hold information and vital history of our sorority as well as safeguarding the history of Black women throughout the world."[102]

For some sorors who wished to gain experience in a quest to seek higher office, securing the chairmanship of a national committee could be considered a wise political move. Maxwell used her new position to delve into the emerging field of public history. As Delta expanded as an international organization, Maxwell and her fellow committee members that included Delaware State University Educator Allie Miller Holley and Jean Blackwell Hutson, curator and chief of New York's Schomburg Center for Research in Black Culture wanted to chronicle and collect the rich accounts of Deltas serving in their chapters to better their communities to preserve these histories. Even though sorors previously chronicled Delta's national history, Maxwell wanted to conduct a historical examination of the sorority at its grassroots by chronicling the efforts and leaders of Delta regions. As someone who deeply respected the importance of history, she discovered a general lack of awareness regarding the importance of preserving the records of collegiate and alumnae chapters. She used tactics from persuasion to chastisement to promote the previous committee's efforts to solicit chapter histories. Delta's national programs often received widespread media attention. Maxwell thought that the innovative program ideas and efforts of individual chapters needed to receive historical recognition. Maxwell realized that by neglecting the histories of local chapters, the true story of Delta's impact remained incomplete.[103]

The H&A committee sponsored archival training workshops at the convention to help sorors learn how to preserve their own chapter records for safekeeping. The Heritage and Archives Committee created and distributed a booklet that explained how to preserve and archive historical records. The committee developed long-range plans to provide stability and to create public history exhibits and programs.[104] This work resulted in the Heritage and Archives Committee staging the 1981 traveling exhibit, *Delta's Heritage: The First Decade 1913–1923* at the 36th National Convention in Washington, DC.

As chair of the Heritage and Archive Committee, Maxwell also sponsored a reception for Delta's founders and Past National Presidents at the 36th National Convention. Throughout her journey as a national officer in Delta, Maxwell would strive to honor the remaining living founders and other prominent Deltas. They helped establish the sorority's core rituals and practices. Maxwell's respect for her elders stemmed from her childhood and growing up with her grandmother. She grew to deeply appreciate African American history and leaders after she established the Black Studies Program at UNC Charlotte and co-founded the Afro-American Cultural Center.[105]

When Maxwell learned that the executive board planned to eliminate the Heritage and Archives Committee and distribute its responsibilities to office staff, as chair, Maxwell argued vehemently against this decision and for Heritage and Archives to continue as a permanent standing committee. Her reputation as a renegade grew as she openly questioned the lack of transparency surrounding the board's decision. Maxwell ruffled feathers, not by proposing radical ideas but by calling for adherence to Delta's established procedures. From her role as chair of a national committee, Maxwell engaged in efforts that disrupted the status quo by advocating for more organizational structures, greater transparency in the selection of sorors for committees, and the implementation of measures to provide uniformity in policies. As some sorors applauded Maxwell's efforts, others saw the call to standardized practices and procedures as cumbersome and thought that she overstepped her bounds or demanded too many changes too fast.[106]

Maxwell applied her management by objectives style that she honed as a university administrator to revitalize the Heritage and Archives Committee. Despite being successful in her first foray as a chair of a national committee, Maxwell's sometimes blunt manner endeared some and annoyed others who were reluctant to change. Maxwell had no problem voicing her concerns to the sometimes dismay of her fellow Delta sisters. Even though Maxwell had a successful term as Charlotte Alumnae Chapter's president and further defined the purpose and objectives of the Heritage and Archives Committee, and after a failed attempt to be elected to the National Nominating Committee in the 1960s, she had little interest in seeking other executive positions. Maxwell changed her mind, however, after being omitted from a Delta executive board meeting that she thought was in response to her vocal stance regarding the change.[107]

Maxwell's frustration turned into motivation, propelling her to become more involved. In addition to reacting to this exclusion, Maxwell realized that she needed more power to implement structural changes. In 1982, Maxwell decided to run for South Atlantic Regional Director, where she would be an automatic member of the national executive board. Delta Sigma Theta organized collegiate and alumnae chapters into seven geographical regional areas of states and countries: the Central, Eastern, Farwest,[108] Midwest, Southern, South Atlantic, and Southwest. Maxwell's Charlotte Alumnae Chapter was part of the South Atlantic Region. During this period, the South Atlantic regional director managed over sixty Delta undergraduate and alumnae chapters. This campaign would be Maxwell's first successful attempt to win an elective office since her non-election/election as president of Charlotte Alumnae.[109]

Unlike some of Maxwell's other institution-building efforts as the founder of the NCBS or as the co-founder of the Afro-American Cultural Center, Maxwell chose not to delegate Delta leadership to others. Instead, as part of an established organization, Maxwell delved deeper into the fray of the political aspects of the sisterhood because she wanted it to progress. Most Deltas never seek national office, and those that express interest in leadership soon realize that they must run for office and win. Prior to the 1980s, Maxwell was focused on institution building within her profession or as an avocation. Her challenge to the hierarchy afforded her the opportunity to draw upon the skills that she honed as an administrator, cultural institution builder, and a candidate for state office. Despite her initial reluctance, Maxwell was well poised to confront or embrace the intricacies of running for a national office in Delta Sigma Theta. This journey would mark a high point as Maxwell embarked on her campaign for regional director.[110]

8

Bertha's Girls and the Dimensions of a Political Sisterhood

Bertha Maxwell-Roddey[1] often tells the story of when she and two of her fellow national presidents, Mona Bailey and Frankie Freeman, traveled to Dallas, Texas, for a Delta event in the late 1990s. At the end of the evening, the three decided that they wanted to go out on the town to have fun and relax. So, with Oscar Faye Williams, the past president of Delta's Dallas Alumnae Chapter and former Southwest Coordinator for the sorority's Habitat for Humanity program at the wheel, the four women rode to one of Dallas's swankiest hotel clubs to listen to a music performance. Williams later shared her perspective of this eventful evening in an interview. As the women talked and laughed while riding in Williams's car, Williams secretly exclaimed to herself, "I'm driving around three national presidents!"[2]

If Williams expressed private feelings of awe, Maxwell-Roddey had a less reverent recollection. As these women, all adorned in fur, proceeded to enter the venue, Bertha humorously remembered that "Frankie was marching in the front with her big fur coat and I was in the middle wearing my fur, and Mona had a Black silk coat with beautiful fur around the sleeves. We looked like the three bears in our furs. I was Mama Bear, Frankie was Papa Bear, Mona was the baby, and Oscar Faye was Goldilocks!" As they talked and laughed, Bertha, recalled that "we really bonded that night." In later years, as the 20th Past National President shared this funny anecdote, she would reminisce sadly after learning that both Bailey and Freeman had passed away in the same month in January 2018. Though not at the actual Dallas outing, former Delta Midwest Regional Director Roselle Wilson expressed familiarity with Maxwell-Roddey's witty and somewhat preposterous story of Delta Sigma Theta Sorority's most respected leaders reimagined as fuzzy bear characters in a fairy tale because it was actually her fur that Bertha borrowed to wear that evening![3]

If this tale of four women having fun seems innocuous, the repeated recollection reveals Maxwell-Roddey's lack of pretentiousness and irreverent sense of humor. As the leader of Delta Sigma Theta, Bertha often attended meetings and events where sorors literally rolled out red carpets for her. Maxwell-Roddey has interacted with US presidents and leading national figures. Media venues place Delta's national presidents in the company of some of the most powerful Black women in the nation. Yet even as sorors expressed their reverence and respect for their leaders, the women had sisterly fun—including the telling of a joke or two. While this story of the "three bears" evokes laughter, it also offers insight into the inner world of a Black woman leader. Maxwell-Roddey honored Delta's essential role as a sisterhood as she fellowshipped with these women who uniquely understood the magnitude of their positions as Maxwell-Roddey and her peers continued to advise Delta Sigma Theta members and support the service projects and member events. This chapter discusses Maxwell-Roddey's experiences as a leader of Delta Sigma Theta Sorority, Inc., and her dedication to an organization that she committed to serving for most of her adult life.[4]

With a membership of some 185,000 women at the time of her presidency in the early 1990s, it remained no small feat for Maxwell-Roddey to become Delta's president, one of the largest Black women's organizations in the United States. As often the "first" or "only" Black person, Maxwell-Roddey would join a small group of prominent Delta women whose "firsts" involved change on a national level. Some of the past Delta national presidents include Sadie Tanner Mossell Alexander (1898–1989), Delta's first national president from 1919 to 1923, and the first Black woman to receive a PhD in economics and a law degree from the University of Pennsylvania and practice law in Pennsylvania. Active in civil rights in her hometown of Philadelphia, Alexander served on several White House commissions and committees for civil rights and aging under Presidents Truman, Kennedy, and Carter. Dorothy Height (1912–2010) Delta's longest-serving president from 1947 to 1956 and later head of the influential National Council of Negro Women, was often the only woman leader in the room when the male heads of the other major civil rights organizations met.[5]

St. Louis civil rights attorney Frankie Muse Freeman (1916–2018), the 14th National President (1967–1971), successfully led legal actions to desegregate the city's public schools and end discrimination in housing. In 1964, Freeman became the first woman to join President Johnson's US Commission on Civil Rights. National presidents and educators Jeanne Noble (1926–2002) helped to plan the Women's Job Corps and Geraldine Pittman Woods (1921–1999) worked as a consultant for the Head Start Program under President Johnson.

Woods and other Delta presidents often brought civil rights leaders, such as Vernon E. Jordan Jr. to participate in workshops and events at Delta conventions and meetings so that chapters and individual sorors could initiate civil rights projects. They also collaborated with the leaders of the other eight national Greek-letter organizations, often called the "Divine Nine," to support service or educational initiatives.[6]

Becoming South Atlantic Regional Director

In 1982, Bertha Maxwell announced her candidacy for the office of South Atlantic regional director and presented a platform of reform and change as she promised to apply her administrative skills to the position. The past CAC president began her official campaign against a formidable opponent. Constance "Connie" Allen was a popular soror and member of the Norfolk Virginia Alumnae Chapter, Past Chair of Delta's national nominating committee, and a Past President of the Durham NC Alumnae Chapter of Delta Sigma Theta Sorority, Inc. As the head of the powerful national nominating committee, which selected and approved candidates to run for executive office, Allen had name recognition and support from some past regional directors.[7] Even though Maxwell could draw upon her experience after her failed bid for the NC General Assembly, with less recent national leadership experience than Allen, she knew that she needed help.

Maxwell started to build her team by asking sorors from several cities and college chapters to manage her campaign. She first turned to Kay Cunningham, who had recently moved to Charlotte and joined the Charlotte Alumnae Chapter to chair her campaign. Cunningham, a native of Murfreesboro, NC, was not an experienced political operative. Nevertheless, Maxwell knew that the young insurance company executive had strong management skills and, most importantly, an enthusiasm for hard work. She also thought that Cunningham, as a relatively new member of the Charlotte Alumnae Chapter, would have no preset alliances. Cunningham jumped at the opportunity to help because she believed the former chapter president was the right person for the position because of Maxwell's past experiences and character.[8]

Maxwell asked some friends to volunteer for the campaign but other sorors she didn't know joined just because they wished to participate. Maxwell's distinctive personality often resulted in devotion from her fellow faculty, students, and Center staff. This sentiment became even more prevalent when she campaigned for a Delta office. Sorors often supported Maxwell by providing transportation when she traveled to speak to collegiate and alumnae chapters in North Carolina, South Carolina, and Virginia. Reminiscent of traditional political campaigns, running for an elected position in Delta involved organizing campaign support, developing a platform related to service projects and management ideas, and meeting voters. Candidates must raise funds or donate their own money to cover travel costs and supplies.[9]

As the former chapter president, Maxwell knew that she had the backing of the Charlotte Alumnae Chapter. She now had to amass support from Deltas across the entire region. Maxwell's original impetus to run for regional director rose from her experience of being excluded from a national meeting and her outrage because of the elimination of the Heritage and Archives Committee without due process. Maxwell now needed to develop a comprehensive service and management agenda, and she presented a platform of reform and change as she promised to apply her administrative skills to the position which included bringing more organizational structure to the region, increasing soror involvement in local Delta chapters, helping to preserve the history of the South Atlantic Region, and expanding the its service programming. Only a few decades old, the South Atlantic Region was new compared to the powerful Midwest and Eastern Regions that had several influential chapters in major cities. Maxwell's effervescent personality and boundless energy served her well on the campaign trail as she traveled to speak at chapter meetings and events across the region. Whether campaigning for the vote with undergraduate Delta chapters or holding campaign receptions with business, civic, and political leaders like James E. Clyburn, then South Carolina Human Affairs Commissioner, now the third-highest ranking member in the US House of Representatives, Maxwell quickly identified those who were allies and supporters and learned how to work with those who were not, resulting in her successful election![10]

After her installation as regional director during the 1982 Regional Conference in Columbia, South Carolina, Maxwell soon realized how daunting her new position would be and that she needed direction managing it. As a single mother with full-time employment as AAAS director, Maxwell needed help addressing chapters concerns. She first called a meeting at the home of the Immediate Past Regional Director, Norma Sermon, in Pollocksville, North Carolina, inviting other Past South Atlantic Regional Directors and selected chapter presidents to discuss organization concepts and the best ways to transition into the position. In an unprecedented move, Maxwell formed a Regional Council comprised of officers from each chapter in the region, so members of the council could inform her of critical issues that she needed to address. Maxwell also established state meetings for chapters living in the three states of the region so that members could have opportunities to share programming ideas collectively.[11]

As a college administrator, Maxwell worked with young women daily and sensed the need for them to become more involved in the decision-making process and leadership of the sorority. As student uprisings erupted across the nation during the 1960s, Delta had recognized that the organization needed to incorporate the ideas of collegiate sorors in its national policy decisions to continue to be relevant. In the 1960s, during the 13th Delta President Geraldine P. Woods's administration, the sorority held its first Undergraduate Delta Day to include collegiate sorors in national convention activities. In 1969, Frankie Freeman led the sorority to establish the new office of Regional Representative to provide more collegiate representation in the executive leadership.[12] As regional director, Maxwell would introduce strategies that would enable sorors to not only participate but develop effective leadership skills.

After an undergraduate soror mispronounced Socrates when making a presentation, Maxwell started holding mock conventions each spring to help sorors learn how to participate effectively at the national conventions and regional conferences. Cognizant that some collegiate sorors did not have prior experience speaking in front of large crowds, Maxwell instituted training sessions for sorors to learn proper procedures and to gain presentation experience. Even more importantly, she wanted to empower these young women to represent their chapters as delegates, courageously speaking their truth with poise on behalf of their chapters on the floor of the national convention in front of thousands of women.

Just as Maxwell recognized the leadership abilities in her young AAAS students, she identified a willingness to learn and devotion to Delta in Cheryl Hickmon, the brilliant president of Alpha Xi Chapter at South Carolina State University in Orangeburg, SC. Maxwell mentored Hickmon, helping her to learn policies and procedures before and after the collegiate's election to the position of South Atlantic Regional Representative, the undergraduate counterpart to the director's position. Maxwell welcomed the fresh perspective of the bright and determined undergraduate and encouraged Hickmon's proposal to hold the first Collegiate Day to focus on undergraduate sorors' concerns at the regional conference, which was later adopted nationally.[13]

Maxwell had the responsibility of managing and assisting chapters, which included membership intake, holding conferences and meetings, the chartering of new chapters, installing new officers, and traveling to speak across the region. Whether holding mock Delta conventions for sorors, helping to ensure chapter compliance, or preparing advisers during the membership intake process, Maxwell drew from her experiences as a former administrator and institution builder to promote leadership training for women. During her tenure, she worked with sorors on a National Task Force convened by Delta Sigma Theta's National President Mona Bailey and chaired by Jeanne Noble. Established to provide more organization, uniformity, and transparency to the membership intake process, the task force developed standardized policies and procedures to discourage and diminish incidents of favoritism, classism, or colorism.[14]

A New Vision for Membership Intake

Delta promoted academic scholarship and prided itself on its beautiful sisterhood. As a young working college student, Maxwell did not experience the pain of discrimination due to class prejudice or colorism when she sought to join Johnson C. Smith University's Gamma Lambda Chapter. Raised primarily by her grandmother without access to much of the economic definers of a middle-class lifestyle, Maxwell received an invitation to become a member of the chapter based on her merits. Even though Maxwell recalled her initiation experience at Gamma Lambda with affection, as regional director she grew more mindful of the detrimental effects of unfair selection practices on individual members and Delta as an organization. Unfortunately, some sorors, who misunderstood the Delta's purpose and mission, did not treat each other in a loving, sisterly way. The organization and its Greek-letter counterparts had staged a continuous effort to eliminate hazing by suspending or revoking chapters, imposing fines, and, if necessary, expelling individual chapter members. In Delta's revised national Membership Intake Program, developed with Maxwell's guidance as a member of a National Task Force of other regional directors and executive committee members, women invited to become members underwent a prescribed, consistent process to learn more about Delta's history and its rituals and to form bonds with their sorors. It differed from the previous pledge process because each chapter was no longer allowed to develop and utilize its own intake practices.[15]

The origin of hazing can be traced to pre–twentieth century initiation rituals by predominantly white fraternal and Greek-letter organizations. Hazing—inflicting physical or mental abuse as part of initiation processes—grew in intensity as sororities and fraternities expanded nationally. By the 1940s, some members of African American Greek-letter organizations engaged in practices that encouraged initiates to form unbreakable bonds by forcing them to collectively undergo challenges with their fellow pledges. Sometimes this misconception that performing non-Delta-related activities and tasks under the direction of some misguided individual members, reflects the initiates' worthiness and dedication to the sorority has resulted in abusive practices that ironically directly violated Delta's mission and goals.[16]

Though Delta Sigma Theta's executive board previously enacted several measures to stop hazing, including stricter penalties such as suspensions, fines, or expulsion, over the years, growing concerns led the organization to reconsider the ways that women became Deltas. When hazing incidents gained public attention, the resulting negative reactions had the potential to overshadow and taint its prestigious record of public service, diminish the academic achievements of its members, and contradict Delta's historic public reputation as a sisterhood. Fear of hazing sometimes prevented qualified applicants from seeking membership and caused disillusionment among members who left the organization after traumatic initiation experiences. In the occasionally contentious meetings of Delta's National Task Force, some sorors wanted to eliminate the entire intake process. As a former chair of Delta's Heritage and Archives Committee, Maxwell, along with some other members of the task force, disagreed. These members thought that abandoning the intake process in its entirety would deprive initiates' participation in some of Delta Sigma Theta's emotionally moving rituals that reflected its core beliefs and historical legacy. Instead, Maxwell, along with taskforce chairs Jeanne Noble and Nancy Randolph, created and fought to maintain non-hazing bonding rituals.[17]

Maxwell applied some of the concepts that she established as director of UNC Charlotte's AAAS Department, such as human relations workshops and the block program's curricula of self-awareness, to create an event where initiates met in a retreat-like setting to bond with their sisters in a calm and peaceful process of support and discovery. Another issue that emerged was collectively defining hazing beyond instances of physical abuse or verbal harassment. Some time-honored practices, such as learning Delta songs, reciting its history, or collectively dressing in the same outfits, etc. represented treasured traditions. Unfortunately, these established nonviolent activities could be perceived as hazing if done improperly by inconsiderate Deltas. Maxwell and the task force established a standard Membership Intake Program that incorporated leadership training, programs to foster sisterhood, and lessons about Delta's history.

The new membership intake process would be piloted and managed by the regional directors. The task force developed a new manual for inducting women into Delta Sigma Theta, creating instructional modules to train alumnae chapter members to serve as intake advisers to guide collegiate undergraduate chapters and to ensure adherence to the new process. Maxwell selected Durham Alumnae member Ann McMillon, chapter adviser of the Lambda Omega Chapter at Duke University in Durham, NC, to participate in the first pilot program for the new process in the South Atlantic Region. McMillon recalled that some sorors expressed apprehension and resented these changes, but Maxwell worked diligently with McMillon to help sorors adjust. The task force required sorors who wished to participate in the new intake program to first learn the new process.[18]

As regional director, Maxwell promoted positivity, even discouraging undergraduate sorors from doing the widespread practice of humorously insulting other sororities in step (dancing) shows. To the shock of young sorors, she could release a storm of expletives toward a Delta who deliberately broke the rules. Though she sometimes evoked fear among undergraduate sorors, Maxwell also formed close relationships with others to guide their careers both inside and outside Delta. Just as she supported AAAS students by often chastising as well as advocating for them, if the regional director saw signs of remorse in a Delta, she sometimes tempered punishment with compassion. For example, in some instances, Maxwell instructed sorors to make a presentation where they had to memorize Delta's constitution and bylaws or volunteer at a children's camp during the summer, instead of suspending them.[19]

Maxwell worked with the Scholarship and Standards Committee to penalize chapters who hazed, but she wanted to change these sorors' minds by having them undergo a rehabilitation process, which included retraining them and or having them do more public service as an additional penalty. In that way, Maxwell hoped to develop more empathy in these young women. She balanced helping contrite Deltas with the need to enforce severe consequences for those who severely abused their positions of power. Maxwell often told initiates if they experienced hazing to "call 911 first and then contact me."[20]

Honoring the Past, Establishing Policies for the Future

Maxwell strove to establish new traditions, such as revisioning and restructuring the Membership Intake Program and by highlighting past traditions and building upon them. As part of that effort, she and other sorors helped to reinstate the Heritage and Archives Committee as a permanent standing committee. Maxwell encouraged the chronicling and dissemination of Delta Sigma Theta's history by commissioning *From These Roots, A History of the South Atlantic Region*. Created by a committee headed by Lillie Solomon and

Kay Cunningham, *From These Roots* compiled information drawn from early national unpublished histories of Delta Sigma Theta and primary source materials such as regional minutes and media accounts. Maxwell wrote in the foreword, "Thus, we view our role as that of the African griot or storyteller-to tell the story of our glorious sisterhood of Delta Sigma Theta Sorority, Incorporated, in its efforts to help all people understand the importance of our presence in this century and centuries to come." Preparing for the future, Maxwell asserted, "In a century and decade, when the plight of women in America is of primary concern, it is imperative that we help preserve and safeguard the historical documentation of the activities of the Founders and members who chartered the chapters of Delta Sigma Theta, Inc."[21]

Information was compiled for the volume about the sorority's history and biographical information about the founders and national officers. The first publication of its kind, *From These Roots's* other unique contribution to the historical record involved recounting the histories of each Delta chapter in the South Atlantic Region. As Delta Sigma Theta marked historical milestones, it sponsored national histories. As a modern-day race woman, Maxwell thought that including the contributions and efforts of sorors from collegiate and alumnae chapters in their respective regions allowed for greater awareness of the scope and significance of Delta's impact on the lives of African Americans. With a similar sentiment regarding the loss of Charlotte's local African American cultural institutions—that led her and Mary Harper to start the Afro-American Cultural Center—Maxwell wanted to record chapter histories to prevent their loss and eventual erasure from Delta's historical record.[22]

As the new field of African American women's history emerged during the 1980s, the concept that the historical experiences of everyday Black women merited recognition still warranted promotion. Most chapters expressed great interest in participating in the process of compiling local histories. Some chapters needed guidance on how to properly preserve their records and guidelines for preparing a written account. In contrast, the regional director discovered that some skeptical Deltas failed to recognize the historical significance of their chapter's activities and projects and ignored her requests. With possible remorse, they regretted their choice to not participate after the 1984 publication of *From These Roots* when their chapters received little acknowledgment or recognition. After the success of the publication, sorors from other Delta regions published their histories and tribute books. Maxwell directed each Delta chapter's Heritage and Archives Committee to update or submit historical information and to establish its own archives.[23]

Maxwell created new committees and meetings, incorporated collegiate Deltas into regional conferences, and helped to restructure the membership intake process. Even though several of these measures caused controversy, Maxwell's call for Delta chapters to abandon their separate constitutions and adhere to Delta's constitution resulted in heightened criticism claiming that she wanted to start a "new sorority." Maxwell listened to their concerns that eliminating these constitutions diminished each chapter's unique contributions and collective personality. Despite receiving some negative reactions, Maxwell pressed on, stressing that Delta Sigma Theta's National constitution and bylaws should be the sole governing document for the sorority, with each chapter having policies and procedures that pertained to items not addressed in the bylaws, which was eventually accepted and adopted.[24]

Developing Bonds of Friendship through the Sisterhood

When Maxwell became regional director, she thought that one of the core responsibilities of the office included visiting chapters throughout the South Atlantic Region. Reluctant to deplete her Delta stipend of around $1,250, Bertha often used her own funds to pay travel costs to meet with the members of the collegiate and alumnae chapters during the weekends. As Maxwell met with chapters, she frequently stayed with sorors in the area. Bertha looked forward to visiting with sorors to encourage the building of friendships. Maxwell developed several successful programs and established new practices as a leader, but she thought it paramount to create new bonds as sorors. Now, as Maxwell retired from UNC Charlotte and the Afro-American Cultural Center had a new permanent location (moving to the former Little Rock AME Zion Church building in 1986), Maxwell faced new possibilities in her leadership of Delta Sigma Theta.[25]

Maxwell helped cement strong bonds of friendship among Black women in an era where prevalent stereotypes abound that claimed that they were not supportive of each other. As Delta Sigma Theta continued to provide leadership opportunities for its members, it helped Black women to escape family and work pressures by interacting with their sorors. Serving as regional director, Maxwell had the opportunity to meet a multitude of sorors and form lasting friendships. She appreciated their support as they participated in public service efforts and adopted Maxwell's new policies. When they asked Bertha to run for the position of National First Vice President, Maxwell realized that she wanted to help the sorors of the South Atlantic Region and repay the kindness that she received.

A New Love, a New Crisis, and a New Election

Some thirteen years after Bertha's divorce from Horace Maxwell, she met Theodore "Ted" Thomas Roddey Jr., the owner of a bricklaying company, at a friend's family reunion at nearby Rock Hill, South Carolina. After dating the talkative widower, Bertha asked sorors to help test her potential husband's reaction to her prominent status during one of Maxwell's speaking events. She wanted them to observe Ted during her impressive introduction before she spoke and then describe his reaction after hearing accolades describing all her accomplishments to see if he appeared intimidated or resentful. When sorors relayed to Maxwell that Ted listened and smiled with no visible reactions of envy or disrespect, Maxwell knew that her significant other would have no problem being married to a successful, public woman.[26]

Even though Maxwell considered wedding planning a favorite hobby, she wanted a small, intimate wedding. With sorors, community members, UNC Charlotte students and colleagues, and Bertha's friends and family members all desiring invitations, Maxwell became concerned that the potential invitation list would become overwhelming. So, she decided to only invite family and a few close friends, and they hosted a small bridal luncheon for Maxwell. Her daughters Shirley Price Harris served as the matron of honor and the newly married Tawanna Proctor was a bridesmaid. When family friend Reverend Clifford Jones, III, of Friendship Baptist Church finished reciting the vows at Bertha's 1987 wedding, the seasoned couple in their fifties gasped when the minister sarcastically added the directive, "and go forth and multiply!" Bertha and Ted's shocked faces led to an eruption of laughter from the audience.[27]

Only two months after getting married, the now Maxwell-Roddey decided to have her first mammogram. Her doctor had grown to be a friend after Maxwell-Roddey saw how he treated her family during her mother's illness. After neglecting to respond to messages to make an appointment to discuss the test results because she was busy as well as a bit apprehensive, when Bertha finally met with the young physician, he spoke with solemnity instead of his usual comedic disposition. He informed the newlywed that she had a cancerous tumor in the right breast. Stunned, she decided to have a lumpectomy and radiation. As Maxwell-Roddey shared, "The cancer made me stop for a moment and reevaluate everything I was doing. I realized that I could stop and say, I have got this 'cancer' and just sit here and die, or I could continue to go on about my life. I have a great deal of faith."[28]

After surviving breast cancer, Maxwell-Roddey worked to bring more support for breast cancer victims and their families. When speaking at Delta functions, her experience encouraged sorors to get mammograms and asked other breast cancer survivors to stand and be celebrated. At fifty-seven, as Maxwell-Roddey began her new life as a newlywed, she had waged a successful fight against breast cancer. At the same time, her husband, Theodore Roddey Jr., would support her as she embarked on another path: to become the National First Vice President of Delta Sigma Theta.[29]

The Campaign for National First Vice President

If some Deltas engaged in long-range planning or had political ambitions to reach the executive level of Delta Sigma Theta, Maxwell had few aspirations to serve nationally. Instead, she often entered elections to gain the leverage to address a problem or concern. Fabette T. D. Smith, the past co-chair with Ella Goode Johnson of the National Heritage and Archives Committee during Maxwell-Roddey's 1992–1996 presidency, ironically explained, "If people stopped making her mad, she wouldn't run!"[30]

Still reticent about running for a nationally elected office after serving as regional director, an unfortunate incident helped Maxwell to make a final decision. She found out that an elderly Delta national official was left alone without an escort to help her off the dais after an event. Initiated into Delta Sigma Theta in 1917, Ethel Early Pannell chartered the Mu Sigma, later the Norfolk Virginia Alumnae Chapter, in 1929. Recognized and respected by Deltas of every generation, Soror Early Pannell served in the position of sergeant-at-arms at every Delta national convention and regional conferences of her region since she joined. Early Pannell took her responsibilities as sergeant-at-arms so seriously that some thought that she even fined a national president for being late to enter a session! In 1981, Delta Sigma Theta recognized Early Pannell's years of dedicated service and granted her the title of National Honorary Sergeant-at-Arms.[31]

Frustrated, Maxwell-Roddey thought that as national first vice president, she would have the power to enact change and prevent mistakes, such as overlooking the revered sergeant-at-arms and leaving her without help, from occurring in the future. On a broader level, as the sorority continued to expand with over 800 chapters, Maxwell realized that Delta Sigma Theta needed to modernize its organizational structure and that she could provide the necessary leadership in this position. The key reason Maxwell-Roddey considered running for office came from her recognition that sorors from the South Atlantic Region wanted her to do it.[32] As Maxwell-Roddey explained, "Sorors had been so helpful and loving. They would help do whatever I asked them to do." Maxwell-Roddey wanted to satisfy their hopes that a soror from the South Atlantic—a relatively new region—could rise to become the national first vice president. After discussing it with her husband, Ted, she decided to run.[33]

Not just a figurehead, part of Maxwell-Roddey's responsibilities as national first vice president included chairing one of Delta's most critical committees, Scholarship, and Standards. This committee reviews and ensures compliance with the standards and procedures for all collegiate and alumnae chapters. If elected, in most cases, the national first vice president is in direct line to become the president. Maxwell-Roddey faced two formidable and experienced candidates, Nancy Randolph, a former national secretary, chair of National Heritage and Archives, and past president of the Boston Alumnae Chapter and Floraline Stevens, former Farwest regional director and past chapter president of the Los Angeles Alumnae Chapter.[34]

As a candidate from the youngest region in Delta who had little interest in forming strategic political alliances, Maxwell-Roddey faced opponents who had the endorsements of several past national presidents from their regions as well as from other influential figures. As one soror sarcastically warned Maxwell-Roddey, "This candidate is Mona's (Mona Humphries Bailey, 17th National President of Delta Sigma Theta) girl, and this other candidate is Hortense's (Hortense Canady, the 18th National President of Delta Sigma Theta) girl. Bertha, you are nobody's girl!" Undaunted, she grew even more determined to win. Though Maxwell had few influential connections as a so-called outsider, the "nobody's girl" did have the support of hundreds of devoted South Atlantic sorors and soon attracted others outside of the region to her campaign who felt left out of the in-crowd.[35]

In historian Barbara Ransby's groundbreaking biography of civil rights activist and former North Carolina resident Ella Baker, Ransby explained that Baker held an "outsider-within" status. Baker held positions of influence within predominantly male major civil rights organizations, but she never hesitated to confront or challenge other leaders, if necessary, which, along with her gender, often relegated her to an outsider position. As a member of Delta, Maxwell-Roddey's concerns differed from Baker's issues relating to sexism and leadership management. However, as a change advocate who frequently endorsed structural reform and one who openly shared her views with Delta's leadership with a frank honesty, Maxwell-Roddey knew that some sorors might be reluctant to embrace her candidacy. As she entered the election, Maxwell-Roddey parlayed her outsider-within status to build a strong coalition of sorors. These Deltas appreciated Soror Bertha's innovative programming and management perspectives, her devotion to Delta, her charismatic personality, and if needed, her ability to correct a soror with "love."[36]

Each Delta chapter can send one voting delegate to the national convention to represent their chapter's concerns and vote on candidates for elected offices for national offices and to serve on national committees. Even though her South Atlantic Region had a sizable number of active individual Deltas, with its smaller size, the region had a smaller number of alumnae and collegiate chapters and, therefore, fewer voting delegates than the other more established regions with more chapters. As Maxwell-Roddey campaigned by visiting chapters across the nation, the recently retired AAAS director did not always curry favor because of her bold ideas and call for new standards and procedures. Maxwell-Roddey knew that she faced an uphill battle in her first national campaign and recognized the need to expand her support team beyond the South Atlantic's regional boundaries to help manage the campaign and to speak on her behalf to sorors.[37]

As July approached, Maxwell-Roddey faced the final hurdle, as her election team, which included UNC Charlotte's AAAS's own Delta Soror Roberta Duff, South Atlantic sorors, other Deltas, and even a non-Delta, Carolyn Mason, Maxwell-Roddey's trusted assistant from Johnson C. Smith University and the AACC, staged last campaign efforts before the election during the 39th National Convention, held July 8–14, 1988, in San Francisco. Delta Sigma Theta required candidates to display their election materials in a designated Candidates Corner of the convention host hotel, the Hilton. Despite being told that her campaign materials must remain in this one area, Maxwell-Roddey remarked with amusement that my supporters "displayed so much election paraphernalia, and we campaigned so actively that some non-Delta hotel guests questioned if I was running for the actual vice president of the United States!"[38]

Maxwell had another mission at the convention. Mindful that the sorority needed to adopt changes related to procedural issues and transparency in the bylaws before her election to achieve her goals as national first vice president. On the convention floor of the voting delegates, Maxwell-Roddey and her allies developed a secret hand signal system among her supporting delegates to convey the former regional director's approval for passage or disapproval of a particular amendment or bylaw. The casting of ballots closed on Tuesday, July 12, 1988, as Delta Sigma Theta celebrated its 75th Anniversary or Diamond Jubilee in a gala banquet! Maxwell finally saw the benefits of her hard work. This outsider-insider beat the odds and won! With the passage of most of the changes that she wanted, Maxwell-Roddey now faced the daunting responsibility of the tasks ahead.[39]

Maxwell-Roddey as the National First Vice President

Maxwell-Roddey now held the second-highest elected position in Delta Sigma Theta. Her responsibilities included performing the duties of the national president in her absence or due to illness and training regional directors. Maxwell-Roddey now chaired the Scholarship and Standards (S&S) Committee, which interpreted and enforced the sorority's constitution and bylaws. One of Delta's most powerful committees, S&S developed policies and procedures for chapters to implement. It served as a judiciary board arbitrating issues between individual sorors and chapters and internal chapter issues. To provide more transparency, accountability, and equity, the new national first vice president pushed for restructuring the composition of Scholarship and Standards to guarantee representation from each region. So, instead of electing members at the national convention, now each of the seven regions would elect their own members to serve on the National S&S Committee during their regional conventions. By doing this, Maxwell-Roddey wanted to discontinue the uneven practice where some regions had multiple members serve on the committee and consequently gained more opportunities to influence its decisions due to their number of voting delegates. After she lost her election to win a seat on a national committee years before, Maxwell-Roddey knew that sorors from regions with fewer chapter delegates like the South Atlantic had less representation.[40]

Just as she did in her professional roles, Maxwell-Roddey meshed charismatic advocacy with a steely determinism to ensure that sorors adhered to Delta's constitution and bylaws. This position called for her to make unpopular decisions disciplining sorors and chapters who violated Delta's policies that could involve firing and suspending individuals and chapters to harsher measures, such as expulsion. Now granted national authority to sanction chapters, Maxwell-Roddey maintained her philosophy—that she had as a regional director—that chapters that received discipline measures should receive instruction on how to enact reforms. Past Howard University Alpha Chapter President Darlene Jackson-Bowen recalled that during the 1990 Convention in Miami, Maxwell-Roddey showed compassion as they met to develop and finalize plans to help her chapter adopt new membership intake procedures.[41]

In 1990, during Maxwell-Roddey's second term, Delta Sigma Theta and the other eight African American Greek-letter organizations announced the official ending of their traditional pledge processes, directing their organizations to establish new membership programs to prevent hazing. The term "pledge," used as a noun to identify initiates and as a verb, describing the process, no longer officially existed. Maxwell-Roddey now chaired the task force for managing the national implementation of the new Membership Intake Program that she once piloted as regional director of the South Atlantic Region.[42]

Roselle Wilson, then Delta's Midwest Regional Director, recalled flying from Ghana to attend the four-day meeting. Some undergraduate members expressed concerns that initiates would receive less respect and acceptance from other Deltas and members of other Greek-letter organizations because they joined under a more monitored and standardized process. Wilson countered, "They really didn't have a choice. You had to put it on the table and indicate that there really were no exceptions." She elaborated, "Many states were starting to make hazing illegal. We were clear that we were committed. Delta Sigma Theta led the way among the Divine Nine. Every organization committed to no hazing."[43] Melania Page Wicks, then an undergraduate from North Carolina Central University at Durham, North Carolina, who would later serve as Delta Sigma Theta's national second vice president during Maxwell-Roddey's presidency from 1994 to 1996, remembered how conflicted she felt as an undergraduate after joining under the new program. In her position as a representative of undergraduate sorors' concerns, Page Wicks understood their apprehension about the implementation of this new process and how it would affect the sorority's traditions, but as a national officer, she realized the necessity of its implementation.[44]

The Sisterhood and the Presidential Platform

Even though Bertha faced several opponents during her first national election, she ran unopposed in 1990 and continued to focus on completing her goals as national first vice president, serving two terms in the position.[45] Campaigning with the slogan, "Reflect (on) the Past, Revel in the Present, and Rally for the Future," Maxwell-Roddey faced no opponents when she ran, becoming the 20th National President of Delta Sigma Theta, succeeding Alabama State Representative from the 97th District and Bishop State Community College President Yvonne Kennedy. Speaking after her election, Maxwell-Roddey, who decided to use a new abbreviated version of her name, Bertha M. Roddey, during her presidency, shared, "Delta has been, is now, and will continue to be a major factor in the spiritual, intellectual, and cultural life of African American Women throughout the diaspora." She elaborated, "I offer my service to provide leadership and management skills, which will allow Delta to continue as one of the leading volunteer organizations in this nation."[46]

Despite holding positions of prestige and power, most Black women still have few opportunities to gain executive leadership experience in national nonprofit organizations. For some sorors, becoming the national president represented the culmination of a set of goals that they implemented as part of an extensive and detailed long-range plan. However, Bertha M. Roddey's rise reflected more of a reaction to circumstances. As a soror from the youngest region in Delta, she lacked some of the crucial connections that a candidate would have from more established regions. These sorors sometimes relied upon these alliances with Past national presidents or former national executive committee members to form an elite network to help them get votes or connections. Instead, Roddey created an unorthodox network of women who possessed expertise in their careers but didn't have the experience within Delta or the name recognition of other sorors. Some women who didn't consider themselves a part of the Delta elite welcomed new opportunities to serve. Though Roddey valued loyalty, she appointed sorors to influential positions based on their skills and dedication, without seeking approval or subscribing to conventions just as she did as director of AAAS and at the Center. By evoking both devotion and rancor, some sorors considered Roddey a bit of a maverick.[47]

Delta Sigma Theta Sorority's primary objectives include promoting academic excellence and engaging in public service. Over the years, Delta's have done untold hours of community service and donated thousands of dollars to support charitable causes and scholarships. Despite these efforts, Delta and other African American Greek-letter women's organizations often receive criticism for promoting elitism. One of the reasons for these claims may be due to the private nature of sororities. Service remains the foundation of Delta, but it is also a sisterhood of women from diverse backgrounds who share a collective experience. Complicating the stereotype of the independent strong Black woman, participation in a national sisterhood helps African American women practice collective self-care by the simple act of expressing joy. Roddey's hotel suite often served as a meeting place for sorors during national conventions to unwind or humorously reflect on their day. In essence, though Bertha's suite operated as a temporary office, it also became a comfortable space where Deltas could interact with each other, leaving behind family and work responsibilities for just a little while. In a society that often rendered Black women invisible, Delta shined a light on them. Whether receiving recognition at the convention, within the pages of the *Delta Journal,* or at a meeting, the sorority celebrated Black women's successes academically and professionally.[48]

During her presidency and after, Roddey worked and interacted with two US presidents, Jimmy Carter, and Bill Clinton; US Congresspersons Soror Barbara Jordan, John Lewis, and James Clyburn; and Honorary Deltas US Senator Carol Moseley Braun, actress Ruby Dee, Children's Defense Fund Founder Marian Wright Edelman, and entertainers Lena Horne and Nancy Wilson. Some of these national figures even became friends. Roddey cherished her friendship with US Congresswoman and Soror Barbara Jordan. As Delta's president, Roddey sadly presided over her friend's "Omega" "Omega" ceremony, Delta's private memorial ritual for sorors when Jordan passed away in 1996. By placing Roddey within the context of these national figures and some of the Past National Presidents of Delta, it exposes the multilayered leadership efforts of African American women. Roddey often sought the counsel of these leaders as she developed Delta's service platform and policies. Throughout the years, these past leaders continue to advocate for causes or projects under the Five Point Programmatic Thrust and the arts.[49]

One of the central aspects of understanding Delta Sigma Theta as a political sisterhood is to delve deeper into this idea of a political platform. When reviewing United States presidential history, scholars often assess the impact of each president's national agenda. Some of these platforms and resulting legislation or practices, such as the War on Poverty or Reaganomics, continue to have an impact on the lives of American citizens. Others have had a lesser influence. Within Delta, the concept of the political platform has expanded meanings beyond the traditional campaign. A rare and precious opportunity for African American women to exert their collective power as leaders, these national platforms are then implemented and supported by thousands of Deltas in their chapters. With the strength of a national voice, Delta's presidential platforms reflect a response to pressing social, health, social justice, and economic issues affecting Black women and African Americans in general.

As historians examine the experiences of African American women during the latter half of the twentieth century, they sometimes overlook the efforts of Greek-letter organizations such as Delta Sigma Theta to address the pressing needs of the time through public service and the promotion of platforms and resolutions. Based on their priorities and resources available to support their vision, Delta's National Presidents developed platforms that addressed both internal priorities, including operational procedures and processes, and the most extreme inequities affecting African American women, their families, and their communities. In some cases, the impetus and resources emerged from outside the sorority. For example, during the rise of political conservativism in the early 1980s, National President Mona Bailey (1979–1983) sponsored the second National Black Women's Summit since the National Association of Colored Women's meeting in response to the 1896 *Plessy v. Ferguson's* Supreme Court decision. Bailey and other prominent Delta organizers of the Summit included its National Social Action chair, educator Constance Clayton who became the superintendent of Philadelphia's Public Schools in 1982; US Congresswoman and former Democratic presidential primary candidate Shirley Chisholm; and Clark College president Gloria Scott. They led the meeting of Deltas and representatives from sixty women's grassroots and national groups to develop strategies to alleviate the impact of the feminization of poverty in a time of decreasing federal aid and attacks on civil rights. Subscribing to Bailey's platform of self-determination, Chisholm claimed, "We have to look within our own resources. We must come out of any slumber."[50]

Held July 31, 1981, a day before the start of Delta Sigma Theta's 36th National Convention in Washington, DC, (August 1–5), Mona Bailey argued that the two-day Summit held at Howard University's campus was just the beginning. She explained that "America must be turned around from Black oppression . . . from a sophisticated march back to the nineteenth century led by self-proclaimed gatekeepers of the Moral Majority masquerade." Bailey, then the assistant superintendent of Seattle's public schools, elaborated, "We have to talk about plans, move beyond talking. We have to raise issues, identify strategies, and follow-up and monitoring." Local Delta chapters sponsored Black Women's Summits to address issues affecting Black women in their communities. Along with continuing to address the need to revise Delta's Membership Intake Program, Bailey led a campaign to invite Deltas to join local chapters and become active dues-paying participants.[51]

Engulfed in an era where some political leaders blamed the rise in poverty and joblessness on African Americans' lack of personal responsibility, single Black mothers faced an onslaught of criticism that labeled them as irresponsible parents who raised uncontrollable children in "dysfunctional" families. The nation's African American churches and other organizations both internalized and attempted to redirect this discussion by calling for the need to rebuild the Black two-parent heterosexual family. In an intersectional onslaught of racial and gender-based critiques, African American women received directives that stressed the importance of marriage and the integral role of African American fathers in raising Black males. These often obvious suggestions reflected an unfortunate aspect of a reinvented reinterpretation of aspects of the politics of respectability that blamed Black unmarried women for having children or admonished them for failing to stay with their male partners. These women often received repeated mantras that claimed that as single mothers, if they could not provide fathers for their sons who lacked manhood models, their children might resort to dysfunctional or even criminal behavior. As the media promoted the bad Black mother stereotype, popular culture representations continued to stereotype Black fathers as irresponsible and weak. These chastising discussions seldom moved past victim-blaming to examine how systemic racism and gender discrimination in education, employment, and racial disparities in the criminal justice system adversely affected Black families.[52]

In the context of this environment, 18th National President Hortense Canady's (1983–1988) administration called for Deltas to develop programs to address the concerns of African American single mothers as they faced discrimination. In 1984, at Summit II: A Call for Action in Support of Black Single Mothers, Deltas and representatives from other Black organizations met to discuss the underlying causes of the rise of single-parent households, such as loss of employment and the mass incarceration of Black males. Another purpose for the summit involved addressing ways to counter the negative images of Black single mothers in the media; Canady explained, "If you want to discredit a whole family, on the whole, discredit the mother."[53] In 1987, Delta Sigma Theta sponsored Woman to Woman: Single Parenting from a Global Perspective, an international conference in Nassau, Bahamas. Deltas met with global leaders to examine the issues facing Black women as parents from a diasporic perspective.[54]

During Canady's presidency, Delta's international chapters expanded, and the executive board started sponsoring research projects related to the study of women and families in the African diaspora. By formalizing and organizing leadership or human relations development workshops, Canady established the Delta Leadership Academy. To meet the needs of an expanded membership, 19th National President Yvonne Kennedy (1988–1992) launched the "Every Delta in the Delta House" and the "Delshare" fundraising campaigns to raise money through individual soror and chapter donations or purchases to remodel and expand the National Headquarters in Washington, DC. Under Kennedy's administration, Delta Sigma Theta sponsored "Delta Days at the Capitol," where Deltas met with elected officials to share their concerns about policies and issues affecting Black women and families. Local chapters held Delta Days at the state capitols of their respective states. These efforts eventually contributed to Delta Sigma Theta's growing prominence as an influential presence as policy advocates, supporters of candidates, and sponsors of voter registration efforts.[55]

The Roddey Administration

Several of these initiatives continued during Roddey's administration. Some of President Kennedy's additional programs included School America, a national reading program; the Delta Alcohol, Drug Abuse and AIDS Community Education Project to educate Black teenage girls; the Delta Immunization Project; the Seniors Medication and Record Tracking Project, and Summit III: Preparing our Sons for Manhood. Conscious of the importance of historical continuity, one of the first directives that Roddey gave to her new executive board called for each officer and committee to review all past programs. Then they needed to decide whether to continue the initiative as is, modify it, move it to another committee, or discard it as a last resort.[56]

The Membership Intake Program remained an ongoing concern as well. Roddey drew from the earlier efforts of Mona Bailey and past national presidents, such as Jeanne Noble, who helped to redesign the initiation rituals, and Lillian Benbow, whose administration proposed new bylaws in 1973 to impose heavy fines on chapters or individuals who hazed. Benbow exclaimed to Delta's Executive Committee, "We are a sisterhood . . . Some beautiful traditions we had will always be with us. The brutality and harassment we will throw that off. We cannot bear it, my sorors. We cannot bear it!" Roddey worked with the national executive committee and met with chapters across the nation to gain their input regarding the newly revised Membership Intake Program. Delta Sigma Theta, now facing mounting legal and financial repercussions relating to insurability and the threat of potential civil lawsuits, instituted this streamlined and regulated process to openly confirm that Delta Sigma Theta's Executive Committee and its membership intake policies and practices did not sanction or encourage hazing. By the last decades of the twentieth century, Delta and the other Greek-letter organizations have worked on a national level to stop this problem and its emotional, organizational, personal, and legal ramifications.[57]

A Focus on Housing Insecurity

Buying a home was one of the foundational ways to generate wealth in the twentieth century. However, for many decades, redlining, discrimination in mortgage lending, and residential segregation practices often prevented African Americans from securing loans and purchasing homes. Whether on Oprah's television show, which promoted the joy and comfort of the home or encouragement from civil rights leaders who celebrated recent victories to reform racially discriminatory practices in the real estate and mortgage lending industries, the push for African Americans to purchase homes climbed to new heights during the 1990s. After a history of promoting homeownership for families, real estate and related financial industries now encouraged single women to purchase their dream homes. Bombarded with negative welfare queen stereotypes that stressed their dependency on financial assistance, single Black mothers felt a sense of accomplishment and independence when they purchased homes for their families.[58]

Unbeknownst to them, these women became targets, falling prey to unscrupulous lenders. As civil rights leaders and attorneys attacked housing discrimination, they revealed widespread racism in the housing industry that reinforced racial segregation and prevented African Americans from securing mortgages. As historian Keeanga-Yamahtta Taylor described in her award-winning book, *Race to Profit: How Banks and the Real Estate Industry Undermined Black Homeownership,* to address past discriminatory practices such as redlining, realtors and mortgage lenders offered sub-prime mortgages to Black families. Some single mothers, excited to purchase a home for their families, faced dishonest mortgage lenders with loans that contained unexpected fees and payments buried within the fine print. Unable to pay the incredibly unexpected high balloon mortgage interest rates or payments, they lost their homes to bank foreclosure, resulting in increasing rates of homelessness and poverty.[59]

Concurrently, the homeless population continued to remain a mainstay of America's rural and urban landscapes. Adopting the issue of home insecurity as a core component of her national platform, Roddey led Delta Sigma Theta to become the first national African American Greek-letter organization to partner with the prominent nonprofit organization Habitat for Humanity and its founders Millard and Linda Fuller (Degelmann). With this partnership, Roddey wanted Delta Sigma Theta to work with Habitat to help Black families and others to become homeowners without having to interact with discriminatory realtors and mortgage lenders.

The Partnership with Habitat For Humanity

Influenced by Clarence Jordan, a former Southern Baptist preacher who started Koinonia Farm in southwest Georgia in 1965, Millard Fuller adopted Jordan's philosophy of practical Christian discipleship. The successful Montgomery, Alabama, businessman abandoned his comfortable life, gave away most of his wealth, and dedicated his life to Christian service. Fuller's wife, Linda, sensing his dedication to this service mission and eager to rebuild their marriage, agreed to support him. They soon embarked on an extraordinary journey that led them to establish Habitat for Humanity, one of the most influential nonprofit charities of the late twentieth and early twenty-first centuries. In 1973, Millard and Linda Fuller directed a community-development project sponsored by the Disciples of Christ Church to construct houses in Mbandaka, Zaire (now the Democratic Republic of the Congo). After returning to the United States in 1976, the Fullers led a brainstorming session with twenty-seven friends and associates from Koinonia and Zaire to create Habitat for Humanity. This nonprofit, Christian-based organization used potential homeowners and volunteer labor to build homes for low-income families to purchase at low costs.[60]

Millard Fuller described Habitat's philosophy in his 1994 memoir, "The theology of the hammer is that our Christian faith mandates that we do more than just talk about faith and sing about love. We must put faith and love into action to make them real, to make them come alive for people . . . True faith must be acted out." Habitat brought volunteers together to construct homes nationally and internationally to end affordable housing deficits and homelessness. As Habitat formed chapters across the nation, former president Jimmy Carter became an active participant and promoter of the organization, often working on local construction or builds. Habitat for Humanity formed coalitions with construction and other companies and nonprofit organizations and volunteers to purchase the land, select families to be homeowners, and recruit volunteers to construct the homes. The organization later expanded to become Habitat for Humanity International to do builds in other countries.[61]

As Habitat grew to be nationally known, it received sizable financial donations and attracted volunteers from a wide array of architects, construction companies, and corporations, as well as support from churches, universities, and other nonprofit organizations. Although Habitat began to sponsor women-only builds and builds comprised of breast cancer survivors, it had no formal affiliations with any national African American or African American women's organization. Though mourning her seventy-two-year-old father Joe Earle's passing in May, Bertha knew that she had to Roddey meet with fellow supporters to focus on her upcoming platform before Delta's 1992 National Convention in August. At the meeting, one soror suggested rehabbing or renovating houses as a potential national project, but Roddey wanted to do something on a grander scale. After seeing a group of volunteers building a home, she became intrigued by the concept of Deltas volunteering to construct houses for low-income families.[62]

After meeting with Delta and Habitat officials in 1992, Delta Sigma Theta formed a five-year partnership, known as the Habitat Project, with Habitat for Humanity International to raise funds to construct homes and offer financial guidance for potential homeowners. This partnership encouraged Habitat to establish a Diversity Department to develop more partnerships with diverse groups. In describing their partnership, Millard Fuller affirmed, "This is a truly historic partnership between Habitat for Humanity and Delta Sigma Theta Sorority, one of the largest African American organizations in the world." Publicly showing his appreciation at a 1995 Habitat site, Fuller continued to bestow compliments and accolades by adding, "Led by its dynamic president, Dr. Bertha Roddey, this outstanding sorority adopted Habitat for Humanity as a major part of its social action program for the 1990s. Delta Sigma Theta, Dr. Bertha Roddey, and all of her dedicated and talented associates are a wonderful blessing to the growing work of Habitat for Humanity. We thank God for every one of them!"[63]

As the first African American sorority to work with Habitat for Humanity, Roddey expanded Delta Sigma Theta's national presence beyond the traditional African American concerns relating to education, civil rights, and health care. Working with Habitat addressed other Delta service initiatives such as women's economic empowerment and support of Black families when Deltas worked with Habitat to help Black women with children build their own homes. With over 75 percent of Habitat for Humanity homes constructed for and with Black women, a partnership with Habitat, according to national Habitat for Humanity project chair Doris Glymph Greene, "could directly uplift some of the more than 50 percent of African American women-headed households in the United States." The Habitat Project extended Delta's philanthropical reach, expanding its essential role as a provider of scholarships and charitable donations to create a visual image of a collective group of African American women engaged in physical labor to help other Black women. Most homes averaged from $35 to $45 thousand to construct, with homeowners paying a low-interest mortgage of approximately $200 a month. Habitat for Humanity wanted homeowners to have a stake in the construction and buying process. It stressed opportunities for buyers to gain independence.[64]

As sorors finished their meal at the closing event of the 1992 Delta Convention, they waited with anticipation to hear the inaugural address from the first national president from the South Atlantic Region. Dressed in elegant evening attire, some Deltas reacted with astonishment or sat stunned in awkward silence when Roddey boldly announced Delta Sigma Theta's partnership with Habitat for Humanity International to build twenty-two homes, one in each of the seven regions and fifteen in St. Louis, the host city for the 1994 National Convention. Roddey told the audience that "such a project enhances the spiritual and ethical fulfillment of the membership as well as broadens our commitment to public service. We are not content to alert our membership to a problem, we want them to know the problem of poverty housing and to know what they can do about it." Whereas past national presidents have called for Deltas to engage in platforms that addressed issues ranging from educational disparities, civil rights to the Black family, the actual request for Deltas to pick up lumber and hammers to build houses seemed somewhat shocking![65]

Habitat constructed homes for low-income families that often included African Americans, but its organization and leadership had limited African American representation on the executive level. When Roddey decided that Delta would work with Habitat, she brought thousands of African American women to the organization as volunteers. Roddey used the power of her position to persuade Habitat to appoint some of the first African Americans to its management team and to its International Board of Directors. Roddey worked to ensure that Habitat employed women dedicated to supporting Delta's goals. L. Dianne Bennett, a former AAAS student of Roddey, who graduated with a double major, was working and pursuing a doctoral degree when Roddey called her and asked her to work for Habitat for Humanity. Surprised, as she hadn't talked with Bertha in several years, Bennett agreed to leave her job working for the Office of the US Census and serve as the director of diversity for Habitat for Humanity.[66]

Now that she had an advocate working within Habitat, Roddey encouraged Bennett to join Delta Sigma Theta. For Bennett, working with Habitat enabled her to meet Millard Fuller, a southerner, who envisioned Habitat as part of his Christian ethics and ministry. Doris Glymph Greene, a longtime friend and fellow South Atlantic Region soror was the co-chair of Delta's National Housing and Properties Committee along with Jesse Nave-Carpenter of Kansas City, Missouri from the Central Region. Roddey asked Greene, the former president of the Columbia Alumnae Chapter, to serve as the chair of the Habitat for Humanity Project, where she would act as a liaison working with Delta and Habitat for Humanity.[67] Though several Delta chapters were apprehensive to participate at first, Roddey's power as president led chapters to subscribe to the national agenda. After announcing the Habitat Program, Roddey appointed a chairperson from each of Delta's seven regions to work with their local Habitat organization in the area. Habitat coordinators managed local chapter builds, oversaw funding campaigns, and provided support.[68]

After the 1992 Convention, Roddey tapped Oscar Faye Williams, the former president of the Dallas Alumnae Chapter to serve as co-coordinator of the Habitat Project for the Southwest Region after Williams lost an election to be the National Nominating Committee Chair. Though Williams met Roddey previously, the soror from Dallas, Texas, experienced feelings of shock and surprise when the National President requested her service, noting, "If I wanted to be adventurous, then she had something that she needed me to do and if it would sit well with me." Williams's position as co-coordinator took her on a journey that involved working with chapters to fundraise and secure volunteers and visit Habitat construction sites in all the states in her region. Williams even participated in the builds; she revealed, "It was so surprising, and everyone just couldn't believe that we are actually doing this. We happen to sit back at the end of the day and see the progress that we have made." Williams explained that constructing homes took some sorors out of their comfort zones, but she remembered how rewarding it felt, "I mean, even some of these ladies, including myself, had the long fingernails that we always kept manicured and polished. And you are not thinking about your personal life. You're just thinking about the product."[69] Deltas had the rare opportunity to help Black women directly through the partnership with Habitat.

As chair of Delta's Habitat Project and now as a member of Habitat for Humanity International, Doris Glymph Greene expanded her executive leadership skills as she worked with Delta's Habitat regional chairs and local chapters to manage builds and fundraising campaigns and donations from local chapters and the Delta Education and Research Foundation. Along with an entertainment-filled nationwide Delta Christmas Party in 1993—in honor of Delta's 80th anniversary of its founding on January 13, 1913—Roddey deviated from typical fundraising efforts, such as a ball or contest, to raise money for Habitat by establishing Delta's first telethon on January 17, 1993, which aired on local cable access channels across the nation. Individual Delta chapters sponsored viewing parties. An ambitious concept, Roddey's telethon idea, aligned with her focus to expand the sorority's national presence in nontraditional ways.[70]

As part of the Habitat Project, Roddey established two partnerships with Prudential Home Mortgage, working with Walter Sanderson, Vice President of Human Resources, as a liaison. The first was a preferred mortgage relationship to assist sorors with home financing. The mortgage company also worked with Deltas to provide financial advice for Habitat homeowners. Sensing that some sorors flinched at building houses, Roddey worked with Prudential to sponsor a training program for sorors to learn how to provide financial instruction and guidance to Habitat families to help them understand the home buying process, develop a budget, and provide financial planning.[71]

At a 1993 dedication ceremony in Kansas City at the July Central Regional Conference, Bertha M. Roddey personally thanked the volunteers from Delta's Central Region, who volunteered to build homes for Crystal Oates and two other families. Some 200 people gathered in a nearby elementary school to attend the Building Together ceremony. In an emotional response, Oates shared,

"For so long, we were uprooted and had to move from place to place. The Deltas and Habitat have changed that. I want to be self-supporting, and you have made that possible. This has happened because of the grace of God." Oates later received the new keys to her completed home in August. For those Deltas who picked up a nail gun and helped to construct homes and for others who helped the homeowners gain the information to help keep their homes, they gained a new sense of satisfaction when families embraced them with gratitude when they moved into their new residences.[72]

On August 21, 1993, Barbara Lenoir and her family moved into the first Habitat for Humanity house constructed by Deltas. Located in the Lynwood suburb of Los Angeles, California, sorors from the Farwest region worked eleven weeks to construct the Spanish-style home. Delta's Far West Region Habitat coordinators, Jackie Kimbrough and Tressa Latham organized fundraising efforts and recruited volunteers to complete the home. Although working two jobs, Lenoir, a parent of four children, was on the verge of homelessness when she learned about the Habitat Project. During an emotional house dedication ceremony, some 275 Deltas and other volunteers cheered as Lenoir graciously thanked everyone and received the keys to her new $40,000 home. This event recognized construction volunteers, donors, and Lynwood city officials for donating the land.[73]

As Lenoir worked side-by-side with other Black women during the build, this physical act reflected the unique ways in which African American women continued to support each other. As Deltas hammered, taught financial literacy, or sponsored a luncheon for the volunteers, they crossed the hidden class lines among African Americans and especially African American women by working alongside the potential homeowners. Sorors could now see the direct results of their efforts as the Lenoir family no longer faced homelessness. On the other hand, as Deltas engaged in fundraising and working with Habitat officials, they dispelled possible stereotypes of Black women as welfare queens. As donors, Deltas worked with the predominantly white Habitat as fellow philanthropists.[74]

By December of 1993, Delta Sigma Theta had raised over $500,000 from soror donations and in-kind contributions from corporations including Anheuser-Busch and popular figures such as Camille Cosby for the Habitat for Humanity Project. Roddey wanted to expand Delta's efforts with Habitat by asking the leadership of the other eight National Black Greek-letter organizations to join with Delta in working with Habitat for Humanity. In response, L. Diane Bennett recruited Black fraternities including, Kappa Alpha Psi, Inc., Omega Psi Phi, Inc., and Phi Beta Sigma, Inc. to donate funds and volunteer to build houses. Sigma Gamma Rho Sorority, Inc. also donated over $40,000 to Delta's Habitat Project, thus creating a renewed sense of collaboration and strengthening the collective service impact of Greek-letter organizations.[75]

The St. Louis Blitz

As part of Roddey's 1992 Convention pledge, a week before the July 5, 1994, opening of the 42nd National Convention of Delta Sigma Theta, some 4,200 Deltas, and other volunteers gathered for the St. Louis home building blitz. Sorors worked with amateur and professional artisans, other members of Greek-letter organizations, students and employees from Southern Illinois University at Edwardsville, and members of local churches to construct seven homes in the Ville neighborhood on Maffitt Avenue in East St. Louis and eight in the Wellston suburb of St. Louis. Working with local habitat executive director Wilma V. Saunders Schmitz, St. Louis Delta Convention director and head of the St. Louis Blitz, Soror Gloria White had the responsibility of organizing Delta volunteers to build fifteen houses.[76]

Roddey first had the opportunity to talk with White, an administrator at Washington University at St. Louis and the president of the St. Louis Alumnae Chapter, when White picked Roddey up from the airport to facilitate a program. She became impressed by White's no-nonsense manner. Reflecting Roddey's unconventional management style, she overlooked Delta's traditional leadership succession practices of selecting a national executive officeholder to assume such an important position and asked White to oversee the 42nd National Convention in 1994. Roddey turned to White again for help when she asked her to serve as the co-chair of the Habitat St. Louis Blitz Campaign for the Central Region. Despite her apprehension, White agreed. Roddey often relied upon loyal supporters' help, but she sometimes selected women with whom she had little to no personal relationships because she recognized leadership skills and valued their dedication to Delta's goals.[77]

At the 1994 Convention, Roddey announced that Delta had succeeded its original goal and helped to construct some twenty-two homes across the country, as White, Bennett, Greene, Habitat for Humanity's Regional Coordinators, and other officials watched as homeowners received the keys to their new homes.[78] Roddey worked with Prudential executive Walter Sanderson to provide financing to fund the construction of seven Habitat homes in St. Louis, under the direction of Delta Sigma Theta. Prudential later transferred the ownership of an additional home to Habitat, which netted some $54,000 for Habitat after its sale.[79]

In 1995, Roddey traveled to Habitat for Humanity International headquarters in Americus, Georgia, to speak at the annual President Jimmy Carter Weekend. At this event, Roddey presented the organization with a financial donation from Delta and met several Habitat officials, and President Carter invited her to dine with them. Roddey's Habitat Project enabled Delta to broaden its public service efforts beyond traditional African American-centered spaces into national public arenas and opened doors for advancement for African American executives at Habitat.[80]

The Habitat Project Expands to Ghana

As director of the AAAS Department at UNC Charlotte, Bertha Maxwell had the opportunity to take students to visit African countries on a study abroad trip and they could take courses as part of the curriculum. She thought people in African countries should benefit from this program. By directing Delta to work with Habitat to build homes in Ghana, she followed in the ideological and activist tradition of pan-Africanist leaders such as Marcus Garvey, Bethune, and Du Bois, to endorse one of Africana Studies's core tenets: supporting the Africana diaspora. If Garvey promoted Africa for the Africans, Roddey would use Delta's power to provide housing for Ghanaians. Working with Habitat International Director of Africa and the Middle East Director Harrison Goodall Jr. and with the suggestions of King David Amoah, the national coordinator for Ghana, in 1995, Delta Sigma Theta donated $30,000 to construct thirty homes in the rural area of Kwamoso in the Ashanti region and $25,000 to build ten homes in the Adom Habitat Global Village near Acura, Ghana.[81]

Roddey's Habitat campaign in Ghana aligned with Delta Sigma Theta's long tradition of international public service in African countries and the Caribbean. Over the years, the sorority sponsored several international efforts such as funding the Thika Maternity Hospital, now the Mary Help of the Sick Mission Hospital in Thika, Kenya, which opened in 1963. Delta supported an elementary school in Haiti and an orphanage in Swaziland. Even though Delta Sigma Theta advocated for measures to end apartheid, the Habitat for Humanity International/Delta Sigma Theta build in Ghana proved to be one of Delta's most ambitious efforts.[82] In appreciation of the Roddey's, Ghanaian officials offered to donate land to construct a library named in her honor. Although Deltas started donating books to send to the library, according to Oscar Faye

Williams, the sorority's national officers have subsequently chosen to support service projects in other African countries, and construction has yet to start.[83]

Even though Delta Sigma Theta's national partnership with Habitat ended in 1997, Delta chapters across the nation continue to volunteer with Habitat for Humanity helping to construct over 500 homes in the US and Ghana.[84] In 2007, Ken Kendrick, then assistant secretary for the US Department of Housing and Urban Development, commended the sorority during their 18th Delta Days at the National Capitol meeting by stating, "These partnerships are crucial to creating affordable housing and expanding opportunities not only for this nation but the world."[85]

Alliances and Partnerships with African American organizations

Even though Roddey led Delta Sigma Theta on a new path to partner with a predominantly white nonprofit organization, the Black Studies practitioner remained dedicated to honoring the sorority's rich history of alliances and partnerships with African American organizations by maintaining crucial relationships with the Congressional Black Caucus and the National Pan-Hellenic Council of Representatives from nine African American Greek-letter organizations. As Roddey once provided educational materials for her former student Benjamin Chavis Jr. during his internment in jail as part of the Wilmington 10 in the 1970s, she formed a new partnership with the now NAACP chairperson to sponsor voter education, registration, and get out the vote campaigns. Under Roddey's presidency, Delta Sigma Theta sponsored initiatives relating to women and children, including the Children's Defense Fund, the National Council of Negro Women, and the Future Educators of America.[86]

Doing Delta Business

As national president, Roddey worked to provide more transparency and impartiality on national committees and task forces and by ensuring that they included members from each of the seven regions. Reflective of her inability to subscribe to the exclusivity of hierarchal designations, Roddey pushed for the National Headquarters staff to become more involved in decision-making roles on the executive committee. Drawing from her past administrative experiences, after learning that there were few formal processes for managing administrative changes, she formed the Long-Range Planning Committee to develop a five-year plan for the implementation of these measures. Sharing a unique bond, Delta's national presidents often met with each other to provide support and discuss crucial matters. Roddey formalized these interactions by forming the Past Presidents Council of eleven of Delta's leaders, where they would meet in a forum setting to share their experiences. Roddey also asked the council to serve as liaisons working with committees in their area of interest. Frankie Freeman served as a liaison for the Housing and Properties Committee and worked with the Habitat Project.[87]

In addition to Roddey's public service programs, she developed fiscal policies and initiatives to manage the sorority's finances. As a nonprofit organization, dependent upon members' dues and chapter fundraising events to support its financial operational needs, Delta Sigma Theta also sought donations to support its public service or charitable programs. Roddey spearheaded efforts that raised over $1.5 million as part of Delta's partnerships with Habitat for Humanity International and Prudential. The sorority donated an additional $1 million in scholarships to undergraduate and graduate students during Roddey's presidency. She also had the responsibility of developing national fundraising or capital campaigns, such as the Light the Torch: Burn the Mortgage Campaign that sought donations from sorors to pay off the mortgage and remaining renovation costs of the National Headquarters buildings on New Hampshire Avenue Northwest in Washington, DC. Roddey's innovative and prudent fiscal policies enabled the sorority to become more financially independent. Shortly after she left office, the sorority announced that Roddey met her fundraising goal of raising over $2 million![88]

The National Leadership Academy

Roddey expanded on Past National President Hortense Canady and other past national presidents' leadership training programs. Under her direction, Delta established transitional meetings for incoming national officers and orientation meetings for new regional directors to learn budgeting, management, and computer skills. In addition to preparing training materials for chapter and membership intake advisers, during Roddey's presidency, the Leadership Academy transitioned from a nationally led program to one implemented by a cluster of chapters from the same area to improve participation. Chaired by Octavia Gail Matthews and Roddey's former South Atlantic Regional Representative Cheryl Hickmon, Delta's National Leadership Academy topics included training sessions for chapter officers and learning more about Delta protocols and traditions.[89] Roddey suggested that anyone running for executive office undertake leadership training and offered gift incentives in the form of "Delta Dollars." If one earned enough Delta Dollars, they could then spend them on items for sale at the 1996 Convention. Fabette T. D. Smith explained the incentive, "You go to a Leadership Academy Class, you get a Delta Dollar; you go to the Housing and Properties workshop, you get another Delta Dollar. People love to get things."[90]

Promoting and Preserving Delta History

Drawing from her experiences as chair of the Heritage and Archives Committee, Roddey called for the sorority to promote and preserve Delta's history. A supporter of public history exhibits, Roddey asked National Heritage and Archives Committee co-chairs Ella Goode Johnson and Fabette T. D. Smith to work with the regional directors to create traveling region-based historical exhibits for display at their regional conferences. Roddey charged the committee with designing additional public history exhibits for sorors to view at the national conventions.

During her journey with Delta, Roddey met with US presidents and dined with famous entertainers. Albeit a great honor, none of these encounters affected the former little girl who pinned the corsage on Soror Bethune, as much as her interactions with some of Delta's revered founders and national presidents. Roddey hosted several of Delta's founding members, who often served as guests of honor at events. Roddey wanted to formally honor these women and directed the Heritage and Archives Committee to sponsor the Delta Legends Exhibit during the 1994 National Convention.[91] At the following national convention in 1996, Roddey authorized H&A to set up the Heritage and Archives Pavilion, which featured the pictorial history of Delta's national officers and committees.[92]

Delta Sigma Theta used its immense power to promote African American history projects and honor Black achievement. Roddey wanted the organization to fulfill Yvonne Kennedy's vision to continue Jeanne Noble's Project Cherish public history program that asked local chapters to identify African American historic sites in their communities. Delta included written information about these sites in regional guide materials and sponsored tours. Project Cherish endorsed the preservation of African American historical landmarks. Going beyond the promotion of physical landmarks, Roddey wanted the project to acknowledge the achievements of living change agents. During her presidency, the sorority sponsored the first Project Cherish Gala, "Delta's Living Legacies," which honored eighty-one Deltas in the fields of politics, civil rights, government service, and the arts.[93]

Spearheaded by Heritage and Archives co-chair Ella Goode Johnson, the event honored national figures, such as Charlotte Civil Rights Attorney and Chancellor of North Carolina Central University Julius Chambers and Civil Rights Activist Jesse Jackson Sr. Recording Artist Nancy Wilson served as the co-chair. Civil Rights Attorney and Past Delta President Frankie Muse Freemen and Artist Soror Elizabeth Catlett received special recognition. Roddey recalled with astonishment that when Catlett, one of the most respected sculptors in the United States, received a certificate, she seemed so touched. Roddey presented the other recipients with a small sculpture created by Catlett entitled "The Focus of a Woman." Deltas presented awards to outstanding teachers as well.[94]

On Saturday, August 26, 1995, Roddey led the way as over 500 Deltas marched to commemorate the 75th anniversary of the passage of the Nineteenth Amendment by participating in a re-creation of the 1913 National Women's Suffrage March, where twenty-two Deltas decided to take a stand despite criticism from their families and discrimination from white suffragettes. Former Eastern Regional Director Guessippina Bonner recalled how proud she was to see Roddey as Delta's president on the front line of the march.[95]

Expanding Involvement Inside Delta to Further Opportunities Outside Delta

Since Delta's founding in 1913, the international organization has grown to more than 300 thousand initiated members and over 1,000 chapters across the United States and internationally. This impressive 300,000 figure includes both dues-paying and non-financial or inactive Deltas. During the first two years of Roddey's presidency, the sorority reclaimed 36,000 formerly non-financial sorors. As some Deltas seamlessly transitioned from their college chapters to join their alumnae counterparts, other sorors chose not to affiliate with a chapter as an active financial member. Some of the reasons for this include the lack of financial resources, work and family constraints, and disillusionment resulting from a negative experience. Although designated as inactive, these women continue to belong to the sorority. Roddey continued past efforts by former administrations to reclaim these women by encouraging the Membership Services Network Team to produce materials and incentives to invite non-financial sorors to become active members.[96]

With the advent of affirmative action and other civil rights measures, more Black women from diverse economic backgrounds now had the opportunity to attend college and join a sorority. Some of these women may have received Delta scholarships in high school or come from working-class backgrounds.

Participation in Delta then provided opportunities for these women and others to see professional role models and seek mentors. For Melania Page Wicks, involvement as Delta's national second vice president enabled her to travel to Egypt as part of the Delta Delegation to the United Nations.[97]

Despite African American women's unprecedented opportunities to attain higher positions in government and business during the 1980s and 1990s, their numbers in executive positions remained sparse. As Delta's national officers, they had opportunities to interact on the highest levels with leaders in government, business, nonprofit, and the health care professions. Delta and other African American sororities serve as safe spaces for Black women, away from unwelcoming environments as a minority working in predominantly white arenas. Delta enabled these women to use their collective voice to take stands on issues relating to women, health, and race relations. For example, Deltas made resolutions supporting women's reproductive rights, the Million Man March, and promoted AIDS research and education.[98]

The role of the chaplain is integral to Delta Sigma Theta as she offers spiritual guidance to any Delta who seeks her help from chapter members to the executive board. During the national conventions and other meetings at events, chaplains are available to help sorors cope with immediate family crises and/or health emergencies. Juanita Tatum met Bertha in the early 1980s when she was regional director. Roddey asked the former teacher turned hospital chaplain and minister from Winston-Salem, North Carolina, to serve as the chaplain for the South Atlantic Region. Over the years, as Tatum worked to open doors for women chaplains, becoming the first woman pastor of Mt. Moriah Missionary Baptist Church in Winston-Salem, NC. Tatum served as Roddey's spiritual adviser. Seeing a need for more coordination and recognizing that more women now had the opportunity to become ordained ministers, Roddey created a Ministers' Council so that Delta chaplains could support each other and coordinate responsibilities.[99]

The President Emeritus and Bertha's Girls

Having served two two-year terms, in 1996 Bertha M. Roddey now received the title of immediate past national president and attained president emeritus status. National First Vice President Marcia L. Fudge became Delta Sigma Theta's 21st National President, serving from 1996 to 2000. Delta Sigma Theta's past national presidents remain committed to the organization after their tenure, often attending and speaking at events, holding workshops, and serving on the executive board of the organization.[100]

In 2008, Bertha worked with writer and former *Delta Journal* editor Deborah Peaks Coleman to publish *I Remember Nine Precious Pearls.* The publication served as a tribute to some of the Deltas who influenced Roddey's life and work in the sorority and was sold as part of a Delta fundraiser. Due to its successful sales, other chapters and sorors sponsored similar publications.

As scholars often discuss the importance of mentoring for students, participation in African American Greek-letter organizations provided avenues for mentorship apart from traditional educational or professional areas. In *Nine Precious Pearls,* Roddey paid homage to some of her Delta mentors, beginning when she first sought elected office to her presidency. With their guidance, Roddey honed her negotiation skills and developed a model for success as a leader. As a national officer in Delta, she evaluated the merits of past initiatives, such as Project Cherish, and sought to sustain it. Nevertheless, continuing with her motto, "It's better to ask forgiveness than to seek permission," Roddey brought forth original ideas such as forming a partnership with Habitat for Humanity.[101]

As Bertha received guidance from her mentors, she, in turn, became a mentor to other sorors. Former Eastern Regional Director Guessippina Bonner recalls that at one time, she called Roddey almost every morning at 6:30 a.m. to talk and ask for advice.[102] Roddey often served as both mentor and role model for these women as they assumed executive positions in predominantly white work environments of business, education, other nonprofits, and the law. As dedicated volunteers during her presidential campaign or as participants in her projects, these women received the nickname Bertha's Girls (BGs), sometimes in humor and at other times to mock their devotion and to question their validity. The BGs received this critique because Roddey recruited women for leadership through unconventional means. Whereas these women had the skills, they may not have participated in Delta's traditional leadership trajectories of holding continuous office positions. If some sorors snickered when they mentioned the BGs, the Bertha's Girls proudly claimed the title as a badge of honor.[103]

Bertha never severed her relationships with the Bertha's Girls, the group of dedicated women who campaigned for her, served on boards and national committees and commissions, or helped manage the Habitat Initiative. They often met at Delta events and in each other's homes. These relationships epitomize the definition of a Delta soror in the last decades of the twentieth and first decades of the twenty-first centuries. Bertha M. Roddey worked with these women in service projects and in implementing Delta initiatives. They formed a sisterly and sometimes motherly bond with Bertha. Whether working on a national committee or simply helping Bertha maneuver through crowds at national conventions, these women continue to maintain their close connections.[104]

Bertha often considered these women dear friends and colleagues, such as UNC Charlotte's Roberta Duff or students Gaile Dry-Burton and Elaine Nichols. Aside from being close friends, Roddey appreciated their management skills and experience as prominent leaders in Delta in their own right. As members of her team, these women often received calls at 3 or 4 a.m. from Bertha when she had a vision or just wished to brainstorm. Fabette T. D. Smith wittily described receiving one of Bertha's pre-dawn calls to discuss a new idea, "Her vision often became our nightmare." Despite their humorous anecdotes, these women who devoted their time and efforts to helping Bertha campaign or execute policies did so because they thought she could implement positive changes. As sorors, Bertha relied on the BGs for support and advice as she mentored several of them. Their devotion could sometimes seem extreme like when they agreed to drive across Miami at 3 a.m. to look for an open Kinko's Center to make copies for Bertha at the 1990 National Convention. Roddey often reciprocated by including some of the BGs when she met with public figures like US Congressman John Lewis. Bertha's Girls became so dedicated to their friend because they respected Bertha as a leader and innovator and their love for her as a Delta sister. Roddey entrusted these women to help her to fulfill her vision. This dedication led them to form bonds among each other as they worked to assist their national president.[105]

Examining the meanings of a political sisterhood involves exploring the myriad of ways that Bertha, who returned to using the name Maxwell-Roddey after her Delta presidency in other aspects of her life, relied upon Deltas to direct or participate in other organizations and endeavors. Years earlier, in 1964, when Bertha started her first forays into leadership as the president of Delta's Charlotte Alumnae Chapter, she asked several sorors and fellow teachers to form the Charlotte Teachers Corp. In the 1970s, sorors served on the board and volunteered at the Afro-American Cultural Center. Deltas played instrumental roles as chairpersons of Bertha's campaigns both for the North Carolina General Assembly and within Delta during the 1980s and 1990s. Sorors invited Maxwell-Roddey to participate in other women's organizations. Retired educator and CAC Soror Daisy Stroud persistently informed her dear friend that Bertha should join the Charlotte Chapter of The Links, another prestigious international African American women's public service organization. In the 2000s, Deltas served on the board of Maxwell-Roddey's South Carolina-based Theodore and Betha M. Roddey Foundation. As Maxwell-Roddey rose to the top as Delta's national president, she relied on sorors as a creative network of dedicated women who enabled her to succeed as a professional educator and community cultural institution builder.

If the women's movement promoted the concept that the "Personal is Political," this phrase takes on a different meaning in a sisterhood. Maxwell-Roddey's push for more organizational structures and the Habitat Project, which directed sorors to construct homes, caused resistance among some sorors who disagreed with these changes. Nevertheless, Maxwell-Roddey successfully navigated around these challenges to achieve the goals of her presidency. Now, a new cadre of women—Bertha's Girls in-training—serve as her escort, helping her at sorority events. Every year, Delta Sigma Theta sorors gather to meet with their state and nationally elected public officials during Delta Days at the Capitol.

With Deltas serving in the US Congress, the political sisterhood of Delta Sigma Theta now encompasses the realm of national politics. When former US Attorney General Loretta Lynch sat for her confirmation hearings in 2014, Lynch could look out to see a group of women dressed in red, as Deltas sat in silent, but visible support of their soror. As a non-partisan organization, Delta Sigma Theta Sorority makes resolutions regarding policies that affect Black women and families. One of the sorority's core social action thrusts focuses on promoting voter registration. Laying their competitiveness aside, African American sororities share common bonds as public service organizations. When the time arises, they join forces in powerful coalitions to support crucial causes. In 2017, in conjunction with other African American Greek-letter sororities and fraternities, Alabama Deltas engaged in massive voter registration and turnout events. Their actions gained national attention when Doug Jones won the senate race in an upset, defeating Roy Moore. In 2020, Deltas and other African American Greek-letter sororities and fraternities and grassroots voting rights groups turned out again in Georgia. As a result of a massive voter registration and turnout campaign, former vice president Joseph Biden became the first Democrat to win in twenty-eight years in the state and propelled his win to the White House and the successful elections of two Democratic senators, Jon Ossoff and the first African American to be elected to this office from the state, Raphael Warnock.[106]

Delta Sigma Theta's advocacy and growing political influence call for a reconsideration of the role of African American sororities. National politicians now recognize the power of African American Greek-letter women's organizations to shape the political landscape due to their ongoing voter registration programs and advocacy for voting rights. Reflecting upon Maxwell-Roddey's past run for state office, other Deltas continue to engage in the electoral process on all levels of political office from mayoral to the congressional level, including Atlanta, Georgia mayor Keisha Lance Bottoms and St. Louis, Missouri mayor, Tishaura Jones. Past National President Marcia L. Fudge, a former mayor of Warrensville, Ohio, and US Representative from the 11th District of Ohio, now serves as the 18th Secretary of the US Department of Housing and Urban Development. Some Deltas supported Senator Kamala Harris, a member of Alpha Kappa Alpha Sorority, in her historic campaign and election to the office of the vice president of the United States. Maxwell-Roddey's contributions represent efforts to enact change from within the sorority and in the world.[107]

Conclusion

I Am Because We Are

When most people think of the formation of Black Studies, they reflect on the courageous and determined early student activists. These protesters sometimes risked their academic futures to demand that universities and colleges repurpose themselves to acknowledge the worth of non-western bodies of knowledge. Or one remembers the rise of groundbreaking intellectual epistemologies centered on the examination of experiences of people of African descent. As the titles of prominent Black Studies or Africana scholars loom large, in most written histories of Black Studies, Bertha Maxwell-Roddey's name is found in a few paragraphs or pages or only in the footnotes. Her work and the efforts of her administrative peers at first glance appeared to be merely a mundane overview of the boring bureaucratic nuts and bolts of academia. This book hopes to dispel some of these misconceptions. Whether working behind a desk writing a curriculum proposal or sitting in the uncomfortable chairs of a stuffy conference room surrounded by white colleagues arguing for a budget expansion for the Black Studies Program, Black administrators like Maxwell-Roddey welded these nuts and bolts into steel bonds that enabled their programs to endure and thrive in the face of mounting attacks. The importance of understanding their integral role in the development of Black Studies is paramount.

Without the contributions of shrewd administrators like Bertha Maxwell, these programs often failed. The demise of these individual programs eventually marked the potential disintegration of an entire field as a degree-granting curriculum. With no programs, departments, and professors, only the remnants of the dashed dreams of former student activists to make their so-called desegregated universities into a more equitable and inclusive space for Black students remain. Fortunately, with cords of strength and compassion, Maxwell and her AAAS colleagues knit together a foundation that sustained UNC Charlotte's Africana Studies Department, now almost fifty years since its formation and over thirty-six years since Bertha retired.

Administrators as Educational and Cultural Community Advocates

What is the role of a Black Studies administrator? How does one manage a program wrought from the tears and pain of activists' protests to enrich the educational experiences of students once denied the very entry into these institutions? To combat the systemic issues of institutional racism and meet the curricular and programming demands of the student activists who risked their academic careers to fight for educational equity, Bertha Maxwell constructed a model of a program based on management objectives, supported with sound evidence and data and she sought allies from unconventional arenas, regardless of race or gender.

In a 2017 oral history interview, minister and retired UNC Charlotte Administrator Gregory Davis recalled how Maxwell-Roddey taught him how to read when he was in elementary school before he lost his sight due to illness. As a student at the North Carolina School for the Blind, a teacher dismissed his dreams of higher education by stating that as a Black man in the South, the only job he could realistically hope to get was working in a broom factory. With the support of his family, Davis defied his teacher's negative expectations, managing to learn Braille, win scholarships, attend college, and eventually obtain a Master's degree in theology from Duke University and a PhD in education from the Union of Experimenting Colleges and Universities. When Maxwell-Roddey heard of Davis's problems obtaining work, she hired him as a teacher. Impressed by Davis's academic achievements, Maxwell-Roddey recognized that her student's dynamic personality and ability to overcome seemingly impossible obstacles made him the perfect person to inspire her students to achieve. He would continue to support and motivate students at UNC Charlotte for decades in administrative roles and as a member of UNC Charlotte's General Alumni Board where his call for the university to institute a need-based scholarship was created in his honor after his retirement in 2008. UNC Charlotte sponsored its first Green Tie Gala to raise funds for the scholarship.

As the only Black person in her graduate program at UNC Greensboro, Maxwell created a support network that included UNC Greensboro's dean of the College of Education and a domestic worker who graciously let Maxwell stay with her when the dorms refused to admit her with her toddler daughter. Bertha excelled and later applied the pedagogical practices and management techniques that she learned in her graduate program to thrive in diverse situations from the AAAS Department, the NCBS, the Afro-American Cultural Center, and eventually to the national president's office of Delta Sigma Theta Sorority.

Whether starting a free kindergarten program or hiring a vision-impaired graduate student to teach, Maxwell-Roddey worked to expand the parameters of administrative policies created in segregated environments, transforming them to address the needs of Black children and students. Black women, such as Kathleen Crosby and Elizabeth Randolph, took advantage of new professional opportunities. They attempted to make desegregation work by using their newly acquired power to address the educational and cultural needs within their communities.[1]

As the principal of Albemarle Elementary in the late 1960s, Bertha Maxwell created an innovative educational program. She confronted a multitude of problematic issues ranging from racist parents to the complex professional and personal problems affecting faculty. Maxwell knew that for her self-preservation, she needed a change. Yet, the search to find a less stressful work environment became an unattainable goal after becoming the director of UNC Charlotte's Black Studies Program, where she helped Black students succeed at a predominantly white institution. Still teaching, still advocating.[2]

On August 7, 2019, some of her students gathered in the clubhouse of Maxwell-Roddey's townhouse subdivision and reminisced about their experiences as students in the early years of the Black Studies/AAAS, now Africana Studies, Department. In between humorous anecdotes, they stressed how the Black Studies office represented a retreat or home base for them to seek community in a predominantly white university. Bertha, as she allowed students to call her, had fashioned a new model for ensuring the academic success of diverse students by extending her connections beyond traditional academic roles to form an advocacy relationship. In essence, to create a family. Similar to African American teachers' roles during segregation, Bertha Maxwell supported students outside the classroom for many years after they graduated. These relationships often transformed from student/teacher to student/mentor, to colleagues, or just friends.

When Bertha left Albemarle Elementary to work at UNC Charlotte, she joined a faculty to instruct teachers, not be a part of a new Black academic movement. As Maxwell developed the curricula for the Black Studies Program as an administrator, building relationships with students, she implemented, as social scientist James Scott relates in his influential work, *Domination and the Arts of Resistance: Hidden Transcripts,* a hidden transcript of resistance strategies that promoted her students' success.[3] This process required helping students academically; it also demanded that Maxwell serve as a racial protector and advocate for Black Studies by responding to the negative perceptions of colleagues and administrators who refused to acknowledge its merit. As students saw Maxwell hurriedly walking across campus to confront an administrator or fellow professor on behalf of Black Studies students, they knew that she supported them not just as students but as people. Bertha had their back, and now years later, they still have hers.

Almost every Wednesday for several years, David and Jacqueline Stevens Sanders come to their former professor's house to make breakfast, and talk. As one of the early students in the Black Studies Program (BSP), David Sanders challenged Bertha during their first encounter to make a difference in the lives of UNC Charlotte's African American students. She accepted his challenge and has remained a significant figure in his life for decades. Jacqueline, as an original founding member of UNC Charlotte's Iota Rho Chapter of Delta Sigma Theta, became Bertha's soror as well as a friend.

Often a "first" or an "only," Maxwell-Roddey forged a path for subsequent Black administrators by developing a second sense that told her just when and who to sway, such as a stubborn department chair. Or when and who Maxwell-Roddey needed to professionally, or not so professionally, tell off. She became adept at traversing UNC Charlotte's sometimes convoluted administrative waters to advance and sustain a Cultural Nationalist curriculum. The BSP's Block curriculum of courses promoted Black self-identity development, historical awareness, cultural unity, and anti-racist activism within a southern white academic environment. Within that process of bureaucratic hurdle jumping, Maxwell-Roddey established support systems, and she recognized the need for the broader field of Black Studies to gain control over its institutional destiny. In 1975, she created an organization to help Black Studies practitioners come together for mutual support and serve as knowledgeable and non-biased accreditors for Black Studies programs for crucial SACS program assessments.

The National Council for Black Studies

On the sunny Saturday afternoon of March 17, 2016, I moderated a roundtable program on the 40th anniversary of the Africana Studies Department at the University at North Carolina at Charlotte during the Annual Conference of the National Council for Black Studies. Panelists included such respected Black Studies pioneers as Maulana Karenga and Leonard Jeffries, who worked with Maxwell in the early years of the NCBS; Herman Thomas, and Gregory Davis, her AAAS colleagues, and prominent Charlotte civil rights attorney James E. Ferguson II. Even though these men possessed a range of diverse philosophical ideologies regarding the Black experience, they all extolled how Bertha's leadership helped solidify the foundation for NCBS, her local and national impact, and how she influenced their careers. Awarded the Queen Mother Award by the National Council for Black Studies in 1997, the panel claimed that Maxwell deserved this recognition because of her critical role in founding the organization. Though this lofty title seems a bit grand, she did engineer the founding of the NCBS and often provided administrative guidance to other directors in her role as an adviser. After helping to fortify the foundation for the NCBS, Bertha took a step back after her retirement as AAAS director.

Whether Maxwell took command to quiet a raucous discussion between Black Power intellectuals or promised positions of power to Black Studies directors to ensure their support, she did whatever she considered necessary to help the organization progress. Maxwell wanted the NCBS to use its intellectual power and strength to help people learn about Black Studies as children within the public schools, as incarcerated people in jails, and as community members. As the director, Bertha Maxwell used the power of the NCBS to help Black professors challenge racist academic policies that threatened them. Over the years, Africana Studies eventually became less community service–oriented and more akin to a traditional academic field with professors under increased pressure to publish to obtain tenure. As Maxwell's and her peers' unique role as influential administrators lost prominence and attention, Black student unrest continues to erupt in reaction to everything from discriminatory academic practices to state-sanctioned violence, and African American faculty, staff, and administrators remain under siege for promoting anti-racist scholarship, the need for Maxwell's vision of an activist NCBS continues. As the NCBS continues to thrive, it demands that its current members honor and remember the work of the "Queen Mother" and other early Black Studies practitioners who established the foundation of a field. By expanding its current role beyond the sponsorship of academic conferences, NCBS should use its collective power to advocate against injustice toward Africans across the diaspora and for vulnerable professors and students.

Building Cultural Institutions and Institutionalizing Cultural Strategies

The ability to apply the knowledge and experiences that Maxwell gained in one setting to another outwardly different arena remained one of her key strengths. She utilized the management techniques that she learned in graduate school and meshed them with the practical experience she gained as a school administrator to develop programs and policies and establish institutions, like the Afro-American Cultural Center in 1974.[4] On a humid Wednesday evening, on August 20, 2018, hundreds of people gathered at the Harvey B. Gantt Center for African American Culture + Arts in Charlotte to celebrate the naming of the new Harper-Roddey Grand Lobby. As Mary Harper and Bertha Maxwell-Roddey sat in beautifully decorated chairs, former volunteers, staff, donors, and administrative staff all lined up to visit with both women. Some forty-four years ago, Mary Harper sought support from Bertha Maxwell to help her start the Center. Maxwell then proceeded to help the organization establish the foundational pieces to ensure its survival. Maxwell selected a board of directors that helped draft policies and helped with fundraising, as she took on a more silent or sometimes, not so silent partner role. The Center survived despite unstable funding. By serving on several influential nonprofit boards, such as the Charlotte Arts and Science Council, Maxwell worked from inside of the boardroom to construct vital networks among Charlotte's civic and business elite. She then used her growing prominence as a powerful tool to advocate for the Afro-American Cultural Center.

Established initially to counter the negative implications of urban renewal on Charlotte's Black neighborhoods and its residents, the Afro-American Cultural and Service Center, later the Afro-American Cultural Center, eventually served as a physical representation of Black professional success as thousands of African Americans moved to Charlotte to become part of the Black middle class. Although the city's progressive image attracted professional Blacks during the 1970s, Charlotte's forward-thinking reputation masked the systemic problems affecting the city's economically disadvantaged populations and the detrimental impact of the resegregation of the schools on impoverished Black children. As the Center transformed into the Harvey B. Gantt Center in the 2000s, it represents how these urban arts institutions reflected changes within the African American experience as it moved from a gentrification-challenged African American enclave to become part of a tourist-seeking Uptown/Center City urban center. Harper and Maxwell's vision to open a Black center and its later transformation mirrors how African American urban life changed in the latter.

Sisters in Service: Delta Sigma Theta

Seeing a pressing need to support children in Charlotte's vanishing urban neighborhoods, Maxwell established entities like the National Council for Black Studies or the Afro-American Cultural Center. After these organizations gained self-sufficiency in their management and operations, Maxwell moved on; however, with Delta Sigma Theta, she stayed. As Maxwell dedicated her life to educational service as a member of a sisterhood that required a life-long commitment, Maxwell, later Maxwell-Roddey, and Bertha M. Roddey during her presidency, remained to enact change within Delta Sigma Theta.

On a rainy December morning in 2018, several of the Bertha's Girls, or BGs, traveled from across the nation to attend a Christmas gathering to honor the 20th National President of Delta Sigma Theta and their friend Bertha. As they each described how she influenced their lives or what Bertha meant to them, it became less of a tribute to her achievements as president and more of a re-counting of poignant and humorous anecdotes interspersed with sharing tales of sisterly devotion. As Michel Vaughan recalled, "Remember when Bertha tripped at the national convention in Las Vegas and fell into the wading pool, accidentally pulling me in with her? She managed to get up without getting her glasses and hair wet!"[5]

Though one of Delta Sigma Theta's core missions involves engaging in acts of charitable and social service, Bertha's Girls represent how Black women per-formed collegial service by helping each other. Bertha M. Roddey only won her election to Delta's highest elected position with their help and the assistance of her sorors from the South Atlantic Region and the other regions across the country. In turn, they had the opportunity to see the inner world of a leader, a consummate professional who trained them in management or leadership workshops during the day but became a sarcastic and sometimes naughty ("some people are tactful, some people are tactless, and others are just tacky!") jokester in the evening as they all convened in her suite to laugh and have fun.[6]

In 2015, Fabette T. D. Smith, along with some of the other Bertha's Girls, created a mock application for a "Certification Degree" from "The Bertha M. Roddey School of Leadership Studies."[7] The core faculty of BGs in the imag-ined doctoral program included Bertha M. Roddey as "Dean," "Professor of Leadership Studies," and "Queen Mother;" Roselle Wilson as "Provost;" Ber-tha's former UNC Charlotte student Danielle Mathis as chief of staff; and Ann McMillon as executive assistant of propriety and protocol. Several other BGs served as adjunct faculty, including Past Eastern Regional Director Guessip-pina Bonner, Cheryl Hickmon, Past National Heritage and Archives Com-mittee Co-Chair Ella Goode Johnson, 27th National President Cheryl Hick-mon, National Second Vice President and Midwest Regional Director Octavia G. Matthews, Past South Atlantic Regional Director Dorothy C. White, and Past National Heritage and Archives Co-Chair Fabette T. D. Smith, who held the esteemed position of "Adjunct Associate Professor of Humbuggery and Crapola."[8]

With Roddey serving as dean, this mock application for a fictional doctoral program required students to complete fifty-one credit hours in imaginary courses, with subjects ranging from leadership studies to quantitative research; undergo comprehensive exams; and complete a dissertation and a certification exam. While not real, these courses' content reflected over thirty years of real-life lessons that Bertha taught the BGs. After paying the fees with "Delta Dollars," the imaginary program required that the dean interview all applicants. Humorously referring to Bertha's unorthodox selection processes for Delta committees and initiatives, the application stated, "In some cases, said interviews would take place while transporting the Dean to and from airports. Students will be chosen based on performance, recommendations, extracurricular activities, and good intentions."[9]

For applicants to pass the certification exam, they had to show their ability to comprehend Bertha Maxwell-Roddey-like principles, which included, "It is better to ask forgiveness than permission. Everything that can go wrong will go wrong—and at the worst possible time. No one can make you angry, sad, mad, etc.; those are feelings you choose. Keep troublemakers close and surround them with kindness . . . and restraints. Share the credit when things go well; hold onto the blame when things go wrong. Show appreciation and have fun— when you work this hard for no money, that is all the pay you will get." These hilarious assertions caused eruptions of laughter, but beneath the humor, was the serious acknowledgment of the sometimes frustrating situations that these women encountered working alongside sorors who had distinctive personalities. The principles' subtle words of encouragement asked sorors to overlook any perceived slights, to fortify their sisterly bonds, and appreciate each other.[10]

This elaborately detailed irreverent take on a formal doctoral application reflected Smith and the BGs' sense of humor. It exhibited the reverence that these women, some of whom were actual educators, university provosts, business executives, entrepreneurs, lawyers, doctors, and judges, held for Roddey. Why did this group of accomplished women admire her so much? What does it really mean to be in a sisterhood? The BG's devotion represents a reciprocal bond formed over the years. If they gave, she returned their kindness. Bertha could sometimes get some of these women to do outrageous things—like when one BG had to switch suits with her in an elevator when it suddenly became apparent that madam president's too-small outfit might result in possible problems, forcing her to initiate the sudden wardrobe change right before going out to speak to hundreds of sorors.

In return, Roddey embodied the concept of filial love. It's evidenced in her hands-on mentoring role, as she continues to be perfectly willing to answer the phone at any hour or serve as a fierce defender, when necessary, as these women have served in executive leadership positions within Delta and in their professional and personal lives. It's reflected in the BGs' awareness that they experienced the rare opportunity to interact with a true modern-day race woman, one who exudes excellence but seldom reminded you of it: a servant-leader whose expectations of them only reflected her own dedication and work ethic.[11]

In a hilarious tribute at a recent South Atlantic Regional Convention, Fabette T. D. Smith described Roddey as a woman of contrasts. In "The 20th National President/My Friend Bertha," Smith elaborated how "The 20th National President partnered with Habitat to build more than 500 houses. My friend Bertha has an open-door policy at her homes in Charlotte and Catawba. The 20th National President looks very regal in processions. My friend Bertha walks around barefoot, in sweats and a tacky turban." Smith's tongue-in-cheek tribute expressed the admiration of Smith and other sorors from the region that enthusiastically worked so hard to elect a woman to national office, a woman who met with presidents as a national leader while remaining authentically herself.[12]

Despite having unprecedented opportunities to attain higher positions in government and business during the 1980s and 1990s, for Black women intersectional obstacles of racism and sexism persisted. Participation in Delta granted these women opportunities to interact on the most senior levels with leaders in government, business, nonprofit, and the health care professions. Roddey became one of those women as her involvement in Delta enabled her to become a national leader. As membership rolls currently decline in traditional civil rights organizations such as the NAACP, the importance of African American sororities remains more pressing than ever. Thousands of college-educated Black women mobilize to affect the political process from staging voter registration drives and get to the poll events to presenting Delta Sigma Theta's official positions when talking to public officials.

Othermothering and Leadership Development

Black women leaders of social movements are sometimes called "mothers," as in the case of Maxwell-Roddey founding the National Council for Black Studies, but this term sometimes causes controversy because it can potentially diminish the understanding of Black women's leadership. Nevertheless, in Maxwell-Roddey's case, she engaged in what sociologists term as a type of "othermothering," where community members act as mother figures to their non-biological "children." Applying this concept to Maxwell-Roddey's work as an educator and soror, we recognize that as she formed bonds with Deltas or her students, she often supported them later throughout their lives as professionals in a desegregated world.[13] Even though her students, fellow NCBS colleagues, former Center/Gantt staff and volunteers, and sorors considered her a "mother," Bertha treated them as her equals and potential leaders worthy of her respect and deserving of major responsibilities. Maxwell-Roddey relied on proven business management practices. In other words, though her students and colleagues celebrated her as a mother-type figure, she acted as a colleague, and more importantly, a boss.[14]

Melania Page Wicks, now an attorney who resides in London, cherished her experiences working with Maxwell-Roddey during her undergraduate years and their current bond. She described the mentoring friendship that she developed with the past national president. "She's like my grandmother." Early in her leadership career as an adviser or as a regional director, mothers often entrusted Bertha to "take care of their daughters," and she often formed deep bonds with these young women, mentoring and sharing advice as they progressed throughout their careers.[15]

As Delta's president, Maxwell-Roddey established the President's Council of Past national presidents to harness their collective expertise and guidance. Recent National Presidents continue this tradition of mentoring by reflecting on Roddey's administration. Delta's 25th National President Paulette Walker (recalled admiring Roddey's vast knowledge of Delta's history and rituals as she often sought Bertha's advice during Walker's presidency. Their friendship continues as the two call each other weekly to talk about the sorority and the other experiences shaping their lives. Some sorors reacted with skepticism when they learned of Delta's charge to construct homes, but Roddey's Habitat for Humanity Project became the signature program demonstrating her legacy. US Congresswoman Marcia Fudge, the 21st National President, shared that working with Habitat for Humanity "gave us a different perspective as to how we could help people."[16]

Habitat became the project most associated with Roddey's presidency, but past Delta Sigma Theta National Treasurer Deborah Jones-Buggs remembered her inclusive leadership style. "She was not a micro-manager." As a fellow cancer survivor, Jones-Buggs admired how Roddey's openness about her bout with the illness gave other survivors hope and inspiration. "She is definitely a fighter."[17] Delta's 26th National President and CEO Beverly Smith shared that Roddey's focus on leadership development became a part of her legacy. Smith explained that she first became aware of Roddey's strengths after "observing her go out and work with the chapters and talk about leadership development, strengthening their understanding of Delta and their understanding of leadership. I think from the perspective of when I saw her do that, that stuck. Her focus on the development of individuals and her community service through hands-on activity are two of the things that she really pushed and supported."[18]

In 2013, Delta's 24th National President Cynthia Butler-McIntyre spoke to Charlotte and South Atlantic sorors and later walked hand in hand with Bertha as they marched in a parade in Uptown to commemorate Delta Sigma Theta Sorority Inc.'s Centennial.[19] As a small but powerful group of modern-day race women, who once had the power to direct thousands of women to go forth and serve their communities, these past and current national officers celebrated Delta's expansion from the bold concept of twenty-two Howard University college women. Bertha Maxwell-Roddey, a woman who grew up in a small, segregated town in South Carolina and rose to become one of its leaders, embodied both the growth of an African American women's service organization and her personal trajectory of progress as a Black woman living in the desegregated South.

As sororities attempt to counter negative perceptions about Greek-letter organizations, these members' experiences reflect the lesser understood benefits of belonging to a collective sisterhood. As sorors discussed their roles—ranging from serving on committees with Roddey to heading initiatives during her administration or later serving as her escort—they help us to better understand African American women's leadership. Years after the end of her term as president, these women still play key roles in her life, not as supporters, but as sisters. While service remains the foundational purpose of Delta, its unique contribution lies in its concept of sisterhood and empowerment. As Delta and other sororities still grapple with how to eliminate hazing, this issue continues to publicly overshadow and contradict the service organization's core purpose as a loving sisterhood. Delving deeper to examine these relationships explains why the Bertha's Girls dedicated their time and effort to helping Roddey's service goals succeed and continue to support their past national president.[20]

As a woman who dedicated her professional career to educational activism, this mission to serve permeated Bertha Maxwell-Roddey's entire life as she established educational and cultural institutions. As president of one of the most influential Black women's organizations in the nation, Maxwell-Roddey harnessed her power to engage in collective service. She worked with her sorors to address pressing problems within the organization. Maxwell-Roddey did so by promoting the necessity of organization with a sense of humor and charisma. She brushed aside formalities to see past designations based on class or educational attainment.

Charismatic Advocacy as Reconceptualization of Respectability Politics

What does it mean to be a middle-class Black woman in the wake of respectability politics? From a woman who helped to organize a fancy cotillion to celebrate African American beauty, rituals, and young womanhood, to one who espoused African philosophies, promoting Black Cultural Nationalism, Maxwell-Roddey's life journey reconceptualizes past demarcations surrounding respectability politics to expose the complexities of Black women's lives. Roddey embraced respectability's promotion of the promise of academic perseverance, but as a modern-day race woman, she knew that she must confront injustice.

Always an educator, Maxwell-Roddey continued to instruct or help people learn, whether teaching young people within the confines of a traditional school setting, striving to retain and teach aspects of African American history and culture to children in a community center, or serving as a leadership trainer for women. Examining the grassroots efforts that Maxwell-Roddey and other African American women activists performed after the 1970s reveals the often under recognized actions that Black women employed to better the lives of African Americans. Maxwell-Roddey's charismatic advocacy led her to form friendships with whites who sometimes became allies who advocated on her behalf. Adept at negotiating with everyone from educational administrators to nonprofit board directors, to city and corporate leaders, Maxwell-Roddey did so to secure tangible benefits for Blacks and others after the public marches dissipated, and the behind-the-scenes work to ensure that the activists' demands be met, continued.

Abbreviations

AAAS	Afro-American and African Studies Program
AACC	Afro-American Cultural Center
AACSC	Afro-American Cultural and Service Center
AAM	African American Museum of Dallas
ACHR	American Council on Human Rights
AME	AME Zion African Methodist Episcopal Church
ASALH	Association for the Study of African American Life and History
ASC	Arts and Science Council
BGs	Bertha's Girls
BSC	Black Solidarity Committee (Chapter 2)
BSC	Black Studies Committee
BSP	Black Studies Program
BSU	Black Student Union
CAC	Charlotte Alumnae Chapter
CAG	Citizens Advisory Group
CAP	Children's Arts Program
CETA	Comprehensive Employment and Training Act
CLWV	Charlotte League of Women Voters
CMS	Charlotte Mecklenburg Schools
CORE	Congress of Racial Equality
CPCC	Central Piedmont Community College
CTC	Charlotte Teachers Corps
DREF	Delta Research and Education Foundation
DST	Delta Sigma Theta
ESEA	Elementary and Secondary Education Act
ETS	Educational Testing Service
H&A	Heritage and Archives Committee
HDL	College of Human Development and Learning
HEW	Department of Housing, Education, and Welfare

IBW	Institution of the Black World
JCS	Johnson C. Smith University
MBO	Management by Objectives System
MSU	Mississippi State University
N.O.W.	National Organization of Women for Equality in Education
NAACP	National Association for the Advancement of Colored People
NACW	National Association of Colored Women
NACWC	National Association of Colored Women's Clubs
NAESP	National Association of Elementary School Principals
NCAA	National Collegiate Athletic Association
NCBS	National Council for Black Studies
NCNW	National Council of Negro Women
NUL	National Urban League
OCTS	Oconee County Training School
PBS	Public Broadcasting Service
PTA	Parent Teacher Association
QEC	Charlotte Chamber of Commerce Quality Education Committee
ROWP	Rights of White People
SACS	Southern Association of Colleges and Schools
SAFE	Student Advising for Freshmen Excellence
SCLC	Southern Christian Leadership Conference
SNCC	Student Nonviolent Coordinating Committee
SNYC	Southern Negro Youth Congress
SOSID	Show Our Strength in Dollars
UAF	United Arts Fund
UNC at Charlotte	The University of North Carolina at Charlotte
UNCC	The University of North Carolina at Charlotte (no longer used due to rebranding)
UNC Charlotte	The University of North Carolina at Charlotte
UNC Greensboro	The University of North Carolina at Greensboro
USC Lancaster	University of South Carolina at Lancaster
USO	United Service Organizations
WEETAP	Women's Educational Equity Training Project
YMCA	Young Men's Christian Association
YWCA	Young Women's Christian Association

Notes

Preface

1. Paula Giddings, *In Search of Sisterhood: Delta Sigma Theta and the Challenge of the Black Sorority Movement* (New York: William and Morrow Press, 1988), 8, 9.

2. Paula Giddings, *In Search of Sisterhood: Delta Sigma Theta and the Challenge of the Black Sorority Movement,* 9, 10.

3. Paula Giddings, *Where and When I Enter: The Impact of Black Women on Race and Sex in America* (New York: William Morrow, 1984).

Acknowledgments

1. I must also thank the librarians, record keepers, and research assistants at the Charlotte Mecklenburg Schools Board of Education Archives; the David M. Rubenstein Rare Book and Manuscript Library at Duke University; the Louis Round Wilson Library Special Collections at the University of North Carolina at Chapel Hill; former Brooklyn College adjunct professor and research assistant Dane Peters, who conducted research at the Schomburg Center for Research in Black Culture, a research library of The New York Public Library, and Joseph Graham Jr., UNC Charlotte student and Charlotte Research Scholars Program participant.

2. Vanessa Gallman, *Who Am I?: Memoirs of a Transformative Black Studies Program* (Charlotte, North Carolina: Amazon, 2020).

3. I would like to thank the following for serving as interview subjects or shared their information by phone: Lucille Batts, L. Diane Bennett, Phaedra Berry-Holley, Guessippina Bonner, Josephine Brandon McKissack, Elaine Brown, Janeula Burt, Juanita Bynum, Ann C. Carver, Vernetta Conley Foxx, Betty Cunningham, Kay Cunningham, Katherine Crosby, James Culbertson, Humphrey Cummings, Gregory Davis, Jodi Douglas-Turner, Gaile Dry-Burton, Roberta Duff, Shirley Farrar, Kathryn Frye, Marcia Fudge, Vanessa Gallman, Frye Gaillard, Arthur Griffin Jr., Willie Griffin, Doris Glymph Greene, Mary Harper, William Harris, Lena Helton Pickens, Darlene Jackson-Bowen, Susan Jetton, Lyman Johnson, Deborah A. Jones-Buggs, Evadne Jones, Mary Louise Massey Jones, Nikki Keith, Pat Locke Williamson, Carolyn Mason, Mary Maxwell, Bertha Maxwell-Roddey, Hugh McColl Jr., Laura McClettie, Alicia McCullough, Richard McElrath, Ann McMillon, Winnie McNeely Bennett, Dan Morrill, Elaine Nichols, Lorraine Orr, Melania Page Wicks, Frank Parker, Fran Phillips-Calhoun, T.J. Reddy, Harry Robinson Jr., Tommy Robinson, David Sanders, Bernice Sloan Ferguson, Ruth Sloane, Fabette T. D. Smith, Beverly Smith, Terry Smith, Grace Solomon, Brenda Hogue Springs, Jerry Springs, Brenda Steadman, Jacqueline Stevens Sanders, James Stewart, Ger-

aldine Sumter, Juanita Tatum, David R. Taylor, Herman Thomas, Thomas Tillman, James Turner, Michel Vaughan, Paulette Walker, Frank Warren, Sheryl Westmoreland Smith, Oscar Faye Williams, Vivian Williams, and Roselle Wilson.

4. Delta Sigma Theta members who provided information and photos include Gloria Bryan Banks; Guessippina Bonner; Jackie Kimbrough; Kelli James, communication specialist, Delta Sigma Theta Sorority, Inc., National Headquarters; Beulah Moore; Jacqueline Sanders; Past President of Delta Sigma Theta Paulette Walker; and Michel Vaughan.

Introduction

1. The book follows the *Chicago Manual of Style Writing Guide*; however, it will refer to the *2019 Delta Sigma Theta Sorority, Incorporated Writing Style Guide*, which calls for using the numerical version of the year, the capitalization of title "National President," and the term "Past" when referring to the formal title and name of Delta Sigma Theta's national presidents preceding the person's name. For more information see, www.deltasigmatheta.org, accessed December 22, 2021.

2. Eric Clark, "Dr. Bertha M. Roddy [*sic*]: Just a Reluctant Leader Who Takes the Bull By the Horns," *Crisis Magazine,* January 1995, 8, Google Books Database, https://books.google.com/books?id=-lgEAAAAMBAJ&lpg=PA8&dq=Bertha&pg=PA8#v=onepage&q=Bertha&f=false, accessed January 13, 2020.

3. The terms Black and African American are used interchangeably and simultaneously throughout this book.

4. Brenda L. H. Marina and Debora Y. Fontenneau, "Servant Leaders Who Picked Up the Broken Glass," *Journal of Pan African Studies* 5, no. 2 (2012): 67–83, https://jpanafrican.org/docs/vol5no2/5.2Servant.pdf, accessed December 22, 2021; Bertha Maxwell-Roddey, interview by Sonya Ramsey, June 23, 2016, Charlotte, NC, recording in author's possession.

5. For more information on charismatic leadership, see Maximillian Weber, *On Charisma and Institution Building* (Chicago: University of Chicago Press, 1988).

6. For more information about grassroots efforts during the civil rights movement, see Charles M. Payne, *I've Got the Light of Freedom: The Organizing Tradition and the Mississippi Freedom Struggle* (Los Angeles: University of California Press; 2007), originally published, 1995; John Dittmer, *Local People: the Struggle for Civil Rights in Mississippi* (Urbana: University of Illinois Press, 1994).

7. Prudence Cumberbatch, "What 'the Cause' Needs Is a 'Brainy and Energetic Woman': A Study of Female Charismatic Leadership in Baltimore," in *Want to Start a Revolution? Radical Women in the Black Freedom Struggle,* eds. Dayo F. Gore, Jeanne Theoharis, and Komozi Woodard (New York: New York University Press, 2009), 47–69.

8. Jayne Hemphill's first name was also spelled Janye in some records. Robert Greenleaf, *Servant Leadership: A Journey into the Nature of Legitimate Power and Greatness 25th Anniversary Edition* (New York: Paulist Press, 2002); Robert Greenleaf, *Servant Leadership: A Journey into the Nature of Legitimate Power and Greatness, 1st Edition* (Westfield, IN: Greenleaf Center for Servant Leadership, 1970), 31–41, PDF, Squarespace website, https://static1.squarespace.com/static/51473514e4b0090a1cad74f9/t/5194e399e4b0b0879dc2e8ef/1368712089353/Greenleaf+essay+part+one.pdf6, accessed March 12, 2022; Lisa B. Ncube, "Ubuntu: A Trans-

formative Leadership Philosophy," *Journal of Leadership Studies* 4, no. 3 (2010): 2. https://doi.org/10.1002/jls.20182, accessed January 13, 2020.

9. For more biographical information about William Monroe Trotter, see Kerri K. Greenidge, *Black Radical: The Life and Times of William Monroe Trotter* (New York: Liveright Press, 2019) and Hazel V. Carby, *Race Men (W.E.B. Du Bois Lectures)* (Cambridge: Harvard University Press, 1998). For insightful discussions of race in relation to gender and the concept of race women, see Evelyn Brooks Higginbotham, "African-American Women's History and the Metalanguage of Race," *Signs* 17, no. 2 (1992): 251–274 and Gerald Horne, *Race Woman: Shirley Graham Du Bois* (New York: New York University Press, 2002).

10. "100 Most Influential Black Americans and Organizational Leaders," *Ebony Magazine,* May 1995, 44, Google Books, *Ebony Magazine Archives,* https://books.google.com/books?id=JnOSQ7xrcA8C&lpg=PA1&vq=Bertha%20Maxwell-Roddey&pg=PA143#v=onepage&q=Bertha%20Maxwell-Roddey&f=false, accessed June 14, 2019.

11. Jacquelyn Dowd Hall, "The Long Civil Rights Movement and the Political Uses of the Past," *The Journal of American History* 91, no. 4 (2005): 1233–1263.

12. For an assessment of African American historiography, see Joe W. Trotter, "African-American History: Origins, Development, and Current State of the Field," *OAH Magazine of History* 7, no. 4 (1993): 12–18, www.jstor.org/stable/25162906, accessed April 29, 2020.

13. For examples of African American firsts, see Jessie Carney Smith, *Black Firsts: 4,000 Ground-Breaking and Pioneering Historical Events* (Canton, MI: Visible Ink Press, 2012).

14. See Tiyi M. Morris, *Womanpower Unlimited and the Black Freedom Struggle in Mississippi* (Athens: University of Georgia Press, 2015); Bertha Maxwell-Roddey, interview by Sonya Ramsey, June 6, 2016.

15. Guessippina Bonner, interview by Sonya Ramsey, July 12, 2019, Charlotte, NC, recording in author's possession.

16. For more discussion of the intellectual writings and actions of African American race women, see Brittney C. Cooper, *Beyond Respectability: The Intellectual Thought of Race Women* (Champaign-Urbana, Ill: University of Illinois Press, 2017).

17. Katherine Mellen Charron, *Freedom's Teacher: The Life of Septima Clark* (Chapel Hill: University of North Carolina Press, 2012); Joyce A. Hanson, *Mary McLeod Bethune and Black Women's Political Activism* (Columbia: University of Missouri Press, 2003); Barbara Ransby, *Ella Baker and the Black Freedom Movement: A Radical Democratic Vision* (Chapel Hill: University of North Carolina Press, 2003).

18. James Anderson, *The History of African American Education in the South, 1863–1935* (Chapel Hill: University of North Carolina Press, 1988); Adam Fairclough*, A Class of Their Own: Black Teachers in the Segregated South* (Cambridge, MA: Belknap Press, 2007) and *Teaching Equality: Black Schools in the Age of Jim Crow* (Athens: University of Georgia Press, 2001); V.P. Franklin and Carter Julian Savage, eds., *Cultural Capital and Black Education: African American Communities and the Funding of Black Schooling 1865 to the Present* (Greenwich: Information Age Publishing, 2004) and Vanessa Siddle Walker and Ulysses Byas, *Hello Professor: A Black Principal and Professional Leadership in the Segregated South* (Chapel Hill: University of North Carolina Press, 2009).

19. Tondra L. Loder-Jackson, *Schoolhouse Activists: African American Educators and the Long Birmingham Civil Rights Movement* (Albany, NY: State University of New York Press, 2016); Derrick P. Alridge, "Teachers in the Movement: Pedagogy, Activism, and Freedom,"

History of Education Quarterly 60, no. 1 (2020): 1–23, doi:10.1017/heq.2020.6, accessed November 6, 2020. Alridge is the director of the University of Virginia's Curry School of Education and Human Development Project, Teachers in the Movement. For more information about the Teachers in the Movement Civil Rights Oral History Project, see teachersinthemovement.com.

20. Bertha Maxwell-Roddey, interview by Sonya Ramsey, April 29, 2015, Charlotte, NC, recording in author's possession.

21. Paula Giddings, *In Search of Sisterhood: Delta Sigma Theta and the Challenge of the Black Sorority Movement* (New York: William and Morrow Press, 1988).

22. For early histories of Delta Sigma Theta Sorority Inc., see Edna Johnson Morris, "Delta: Its History and Development," and Mary Elizabeth Vroman, *Shaped to Its Purpose: Delta Sigma Theta: The First Fifty Years* (New York: Random House Press, 1965).

23. Kimberlé Crenshaw is a leading scholar of critical race theory whose 1991 article, "Mapping the Margins: Intersectionality, Identity Politics, and Violence Against Women of Color," is one of the foundational works on the subject of the theory of intersectionality. See Kimberlé Crenshaw, "Mapping the Margins: Intersectionality, Identity Politics, and Violence Against Women of Color," *Stanford Law Review* 43, no. 6 (July 1991): 1241–1299, https://doi.org/10.2307/1229039, accessed January 20, 2022. For more information about Black feminist theory, see Patricia Hill Collins, *Black Feminist Thought: Knowledge, Consciousness, and the Politics of Empowerment* (New York: Routledge Press, 1991).

24. Alice Kessler-Harris, "Why Biography?" *The American Historical Review* 114, no. 3 (June 2009): 626, https://www.jstor.org/stable/30223924, accessed June 14, 2019.

25. Bertha Maxwell-Roddey, interview by Sonya Ramsey, March 6, 2011, Charlotte, NC, recording in author's possession. For more information about the rise of the concept of the dysfunctional Black family, see Susan D. Greenbaum, "Kinship and Family Structure: Ethnocentric Myopia," In *Blaming the Poor: The Long Shadow of the Moynihan Report on Cruel Images about Poverty* (New Brunswick, NJ; London: Rutgers University Press, 2015), 46–67, doi:10.2307/j.ctt15sk7xn.6, accessed August 28, 2020.

26. Bertha Maxwell-Roddey, interview by Sonya Ramsey, April 7, 2017, Charlotte, NC, recording in author's possession; Gregory Davis, James Ferguson III, Leonard Jeffries, Maulana Karenga, and Sonya Ramsey, "'We Called Her Queen Mother': The Impact and Legacy of Dr. Bertha Maxwell-Roddey," Roundtable Session Notes, National Council for Black Studies Conference, Charlotte, NC, March 2016.

27. Zandria F. Robinson, *This Ain't Chicago: Race, Class, and Regional Identity in the Post-Soul South* (Chapel Hill: University of North Carolina Press, 2014).

28. For more information about African American museums, see Andrea Burns, *From Storefront to Monument: Tracing the Public History of the Black Museum Movement* (Amherst: University of Massachusetts Press, 2013); Bridget Cook, *Exhibiting Blackness: African Americans and the American Art Museum* (Amherst: University of Massachusetts Press, 2011). For more discussion of the Black Power movement's artistic impact on an urban southern city, see Simon James Smethurst, "The Black Arts Movement in Atlanta," in Peniel E. Joseph, ed. *Neighborhood Rebels: Black Power at the Local Level* (New York: Palgrave Macmillan, 2010), 173–191.

29. Doris Glymph Greene, interview by Sonya Ramsey, Charlotte, NC, May 17, 2017; Fa-

bette T.D. Smith, interview by Sonya Ramsey, December 22, 2018, Charlotte, NC, recording in author's possession.

30. Bertha Maxwell-Roddey, interview by Sonya Ramsey, March 6, 2011, Charlotte, NC, recording in author's possession.

Chapter 1. A "Big Mind," Childhood, and Early Beginnings

1. Bertha Maxwell-Roddey, interview by Sonya Ramsey, March 6, 2011.

2. W. J. Megginson, *African American Life in South Carolina's Upper Piedmont, 1780–1900* (Columbia: University of South Carolina Press, 2006), 314; Fifteenth Census, Population, 1930. South Carolina. Washington, D.C.: [National Archives and Records Administration], 2002, The total population of Seneca in 1930 was 1,929 people; Nora Deniza Nimmons Field, *Seneca Echoes, Oconee County, South Carolina* (Seneca, South Carolina: The Journal Company, 1954), 6. For more information about other African Americans living in South Carolina's Upper Piedmont, see the oral histories contained in William Megginson, The Black Heritage in the Upper Piedmont of South Carolina Project Collection—1982, 1989–1990, Identifier MSS 0282, Special Collections, Clemson University Library, Clemson, SC.

3. After Lillian Lunney's death in 1970, her sister, Myra Mason Lindemann gifted the Lunneys' home to Oconee County to serve as the Lunney Museum. For more information see the Lunney Museum Website, https://www.lunneymuseum.org/blog/2019/1/15/a-brief-history-of-the-lunneys, accessed April 21, 2021. In 2014, Seneca opened the Bertha Lee Strickland Museum in the former home of Bertha Lee Strickland who worked as a domestic worker for the Lunney family and as a caretaker for Lillian Lunney.

4. Bertha Maxwell-Roddey, interview by Sonya Ramsey, April 29, 2015, Charlotte, NC, in author's possession.

5. Hephzibah V. Strmic-Pawl and Phyllis K. Leffler, "Black Families and Fostering of Leadership," *Ethnicities* 11, no. 2 (2011): 139–62, http://www.jstor.org/stable/23890796, accessed September 11, 2020.

6. Hephzibah V. Strmic-Pawl and Phyllis K. Leffler, "Black Families and Fostering of Leadership," 139–62.

7. Ellen Naomi Childers, Willie Cosdena, and Gideon Gunn, *A Journey of Faith: 40 Years of Excellence, 1899–1939: Seneca Institute—Seneca Junior College: Pioneer Institution of Black Education, Seneca, South Carolina* (Seneca, SC: author-published, 2003), 93, 102; James Anderson, *The History of African American Education in the South, 1863–1935* (Chapel Hill: University of North Carolina Press, 1988), 183.

8. Bertha Maxwell-Roddey, interview by Sonya Ramsey, August 9, 2019, Charlotte, NC, recording in author's possession; Childers, Cosdena, and Gunn, *A Journey of Faith: 40 Years of Excellence, 1899–1939: Seneca Institute—Seneca Junior College: Pioneer Institution of Black Education, Seneca, South Carolina*, 32, 93, 95.

9. Childers, Cosdena, and Gunn, *A Journey of Faith: 40 Years of Excellence, 1899–1939: Seneca Institute—Seneca Junior College: Pioneer Institution of Black Education, Seneca, South Carolina*, 12–15.

10. *Plessy v. Ferguson* 163 U.S. 537 (1896).

11. After merging with two other churches and joining the United Methodist Denomination in 1972, St. James Church is now known as New Harmony United Methodist Church.

Seneca City Museum, "New Harmony United Methodist Church" Website https://senecaci-tymuseums.org/background-100s/2020/8/19/s715kzuhhgrapxsqo1bkh8b17eav8b, accessed October 16, 2020; Martha L. Wright, "2011 School Reunion Oconee County Training School and Blue Ridge High School" (Seneca, SC: Unpublished Booklet): 15 in the Private Collection of Betty Cunningham, Charlotte, NC.

12. Betty Cunningham, interview by Sonya Ramsey, August 6, 2018, Charlotte, NC, recording in author's possession; Megginson, 309.

13. Childers, Cosdena, and Gunn, *A Journey of Faith: 40 Years of Excellence, 1899–1939: Seneca Institute—Seneca Junior College: Pioneer Institution of Black Education, Seneca, South Carolina,* 93, 102.

14. James Anderson, *The Education of Blacks in the South, 1860–1935* (Chapel Hill: University of North Carolina Press, 1988; 184.

15. For more information about the experiences of Jeanes Teachers in South Carolina and rural Arkansas, see Courtney Sanabria Woodfaulk, "The Jeanes Teachers of South Carolina: The Emergence, Existence, and Significance of Their Work," PhD, Educational Leadership, and Policy, University of South Carolina, Columbia, 1992, ProQuest Dissertations and Theses Global Database https://uncc.primo.exlibrisgroup.com/permalink/01UNCC_INST/1rqb8fi/cdi_proquest_journals_304025699, accessed June 22, 2021; Cherisse Jones-Branch, "'To Raise Standards Among the Negroes': Jeanes Supervising Industrial Teachers in Rural Jim Crow Arkansas, 1909–1950," *Agricultural History* 412–436, https://doi.org/10.3098/ah.2019.093.3.412, June 22, 2021.

16. For more information about the history of some of the educational philanthropical foundations' impact on African American education, see James Anderson, *The Education of Blacks in the South, 1860–1935* (Chapel Hill: University of North Carolina Press, 1988).

17. For more information about African American communities' efforts to sustain and support schools, see V. P. Franklin and Carter Julian Savage, *Cultural Capital, and Black Education: African American Communities and the Funding of Black Schooling, 1865 to the Present* (Greenwich, Conn: Information Age Publisher, 2004).

18. James Christopher Carbaugh, "The Philanthropic Confluence of the General Education Board and the Jeanes, Slater, and Rosenwald Funds: African-American Education in South Carolina, 1900–1930," PhD, Dissertation, Curriculum, and Instruction (Clemson, SC: Clemson University, ProQuest Dissertations Publishing, 1997), 125, 132, https://uncc.primo.exlibrisgroup.com/permalink/01UNCC_INST/1rqb8fi/cdi_proquest_journals_304341917. For more information about the history of the Rosenwald Schools, see Alfred Perkins, *Edwin Rogers Embree: The Julius Rosenwald Fund, Foundation Philanthropy, and American Race Relations* (Bloomington: Indiana University Press, 2011); and Mary S. Hoffschwelle, *The Rosenwald Schools of the American South* (Gainesville: University Press of Florida, 2006).

19. Wright, "2011 School Reunion Oconee County Training School and Blue Ridge High School," 14–15; South Carolina African American Heritage Commission, "Oconee County," *A Teacher's Guide to African American Historic Places in South Carolina* (Columbia, SC: South Carolina African American Heritage Commission. South Carolina Department of Archives and History, 2015), 77–78, Digital copy, https://scdah.sc.gov/sites/default/files/Documents/Historic%20Preservation%20(SHPO)/Publications/TGAAHPfull.pdf, accessed May 1, 2020; Childers, Cosdena, and Gunn, *A Journey of Faith: 40 Years of Excellence, 1899–1939: Seneca Institute—Seneca Junior College: Pioneer Institution of Black Education, Seneca,*

South Carolina, 102; SC Picture Project, "South Carolina Picture Project: Retreat Rosenwald School," Website, https://www.scpictureproject.org/oconee-county/retreat-rosenwald-school.html, accessed May 1, 2020. For more information about African American schools during segregation, see James Anderson, *The History of African American Education in the South, 1863–1935* (Chapel Hill: University of North Carolina Press, 1988); Vanessa Siddle Walker and Ulysses Byas, *Hello Professor: A Black Principal and Professional Leadership in the Segregated South* (Chapel Hill: University of North Carolina Press, 2009).

20. Bertha Luvenia Lyons Maxwell Roddey, interview by Willie Griffin, May 12, 2008. U-4208, in the Southern Oral History Program Collection, Series U: The Long Civil Rights Movement: The South Since the 1960s, Southern Historical Collection, Wilson Library, University of North Carolina at Chapel Hill, granted authorization for use by Willie Griffin. Correct spelling of Maxwell-Roddey will be used in subsequent citations. Thirteenth Census of the United States, 1910, Rosa Lyons, 1910, Center Oconee, South Carolina, Roll T624, 1469; Page 15B; Enumeration District 0122; FHL microfilm:1375482 (NARA microfilm publication T624, 1,178 rolls); Fifteenth Census of the United States, Population, 1930, South Carolina. Washington, D.C.: [National Archives and Records Administration], 2002, Record Group 29; Wade Lyons, 1930 Census, Seneca, Oconee South Carolina, page 18A. Enumeration District 0008; FHL microfilm: 2341941.Fifteenth Census of the United States, 1930 (NARA microfilm publication T626, 2,667 rolls), Records of the Bureaus of the Census, Record Group 29. National Archives, D.C.

21. Maxwell-Roddey, interview by Willie Griffin, May 12, 2008.

22. Bertha Maxwell-Roddey, interview by Sonya Ramsey, August 9, 2019, Charlotte, NC, recording in author's possession; Maxwell-Roddey, interview by Willie Griffin, May 12, 2008.

23. Leslie Brown, "African American Women and Migration," in *The Practice of U.S. Women's History: Narratives, Intersections, and Dialogues,* eds. Jay S. Kleinberg, Eileen Boris, and Vicki L. Ruiz (New Brunswick, New Jersey; London: Rutgers University Press, 2007). 201–20, http://www.jstor.org/stable/j.ctt5hhxxp.15, accessed September 11, 2020; Bertha Maxwell-Roddey, interview by Sonya Ramsey, August 9, 2019, Charlotte, NC; For more information about the personal reasons related to the avoidance of sexual harassment that motivated some Black women to leave the South, see, Darlene Clark Hine, "Rape and the Inner Lives of Black Women in the Middle West," *Signs* 14, no. 4 (1989): 912–20, http://www.jstor.org/stable/3174692, accessed May 10, 2021.

24. Bertha Maxwell-Roddey, interview by Sonya Ramsey, August 9, 2019, Charlotte, NC.

25. Bertha Maxwell-Roddey, interview by Sonya Ramsey, August 11, 2016, Charlotte, NC, recording in author's possession, "Matthews Prattville, Joe Earle Obituary," *Alabama Journal,* May 25, 1992, 27, Newspapers.com Database, https://www.newspapers.com/image/467026295/?article=f19633ed-9795-4f7d-b83f-3ad9c6b30901&focus=0.50608367,0.48066148,0.6626944, 0.58435565&xid=3355&_ga=2.52116768.861939853.1642703042-2002418683.1640217921#:~:text=https%3A//www.newspapers.com/clip/93059017/, accessed December 22, 2021.

26. For more discussion of African American male expressive culture through dress, see Shane White and Graham White, *Stylin': African-American Expressive Culture, from Its Beginnings to the Zoot Suit* (Ithaca, NY: Cornell University Press, 1998).

27. Maxwell-Roddey, interview by Willie Griffin, May 12, 2008.

28. Maxwell-Roddey, interview by Sonya Ramsey, April 29, 2015. Ancestry.com, 1940 United States Federal Census [database on-line]. Provo, UT, USA: Ancestry.com Operations,

Inc., 2012: Original data: United States of America, Bureau of the Census. Sixteenth Census of the United States, 1940. Washington, D.C.: National Archives and Records Administration, 1940. T627, 4,643 rolls. https://search.ancestry.com/cgi-bin/sse.dll?db=1940usfedcen&indiv =try&h=138420143, accessed May 4, 2020.

29. Maxwell-Roddey, interview by Sonya Ramsey, April 29, 2015.

30. Maxwell-Roddey, interview by Sonya Ramsey, August 11, 2016; Maxwell-Roddey, interview by Willie Griffin, May 12, 2008.

31. Maxwell-Roddey, interview by Sonya Ramsey, August 11, 2016; Maxwell-Roddey, interview by Willie Griffin, May 12, 2008; For more information about the practice of elocution among African Americans, see Susan Kates, "The Embodied Rhetoric of Hallie Quinn Brown," *College English* 59, no. 1 (1997): 59–71; For more information about the role of the Black church in African American life, see C. Eric (Charles Eric) Lincoln and Lawrence H. Mamiya, *The Black Church in the African-American Experience* (Durham: Duke University Press, 1990).

32. For more information about the role of elocution in African American education see, Arthur L. Smith, "Socio-historical Perspectives of Black Oratory," *Quarterly Journal of Speech* 56:3, 1970, 264–269, Taylor and Francis Online, DOI: 10.1080/00335637009383010, accessed December 22, 2021; Maxwell-Roddey, interview by Sonya Ramsey, August 11, 2016; Maxwell-Roddey, interview by Sonya Ramsey, August 9, 2019.

33. Bertha Maxwell-Roddey, interview by Sonya Ramsey, April 29, 2015, Charlotte, NC, recording in author's possession; For more information about the experiences of African American domestic workers during segregation, see Elizabeth Clark-Lewis, *Living In, Living Out: African American Domestics in Washington, D.C., 1910–1940* (Washington: Smithsonian Institution Press, 1994).

34. Maxwell-Roddey, interview by Sonya Ramsey, August 11, 2016; Lori K. Tate, "True Convictions: Educator, Activist Bertha Maxwell Roddey Believes in Taking a Stand—and Her Life Reflects it," *Pride Magazine*, March 2009: 7. For more discussion of how Black and white children learned about race during segregation, see Jennifer Ritterhouse, *Growing Up Jim Crow: How Black and White Southern Children Learned Race* (Chapel Hill: The University of North Carolina Press, 2006).

35. Waldo Martin, "A Dream Deferred": The Southern Negro Youth Congress, The Student Nonviolent Coordinating Committee, and the Politics of Historical Memory," *South Carolina State Souvenir Journal* 9, no. 26 (2016), 4, https://ediscplinas.usp.br/pluginfile. php/1017528/mod_resource/content/1/Waldo%20Martin%20A%20Dream%20Deferred%20 -%20SNYC%20SNCC%20and%20the%20Politics%20of%20Historical%20Memory.pdf, accessed July 6, 2021; South Carolina Progressive Network, "History Lost and Found: Lessons from the Southern Negro Youth Congress," www.scpronet.com, Website, August 28, 2016, https://www.scpronet.com/wordpress/2016/09/28/history-lost-and-found-the-lessons-of-modjeska-simkins-the-southern-negro-youth-congress-and-the-bleaching-of-south-carolinas-history/, accessed Oct. 27, 2020.

36. Erik Gellman, *Death Blow to Jim Crow: The National Negro Congress and the Rise of Militant Civil Rights* (Chapel Hill: University of North Carolina Press, 2012), 216, 234; Bertha Maxwell-Roddey, interview by Sonya Ramsey, August 31, 2017, Charlotte, NC, recording in author's possession. For more information about African American women and Commu-

nism, see Erik S. McDuffie, *Sojourning for Freedom: Black Women, American Communism, and the Making of Black Left Feminism* (Durham: Duke University Press, 2011).

37. Bertha Maxwell-Roddey, interview by Sonya Ramsey, September 19, 2020, Charlotte, NC, recording in author's possession; Gellman, 69.

38. Bertha Maxwell-Roddey, interview by Sonya Ramsey, September 19, 2020.

39. Bertha was in the eleventh grade during her senior year. The school added the twelfth grade the next year. Bertha Maxwell-Roddey, interview by Willie Griffin, May 12, 2008; South Carolina State Department of Education, "School Directory of South Carolina 1947–1949," (PDF Document: South Carolina State Library Digital Collections), 45, https://dc.statelibrary.sc.gov/handle/10827/4023, accessed May 1, 2020.

40. Maxwell-Roddey, interview by Sonya Ramsey, August 11, 2016.

41. South Carolina Department of Archives and History, "South Carolina Death Records, Columbia, South Carolina, Year Range, 1925–1949, Death County or Certificate Range; Oconee," Columbia, SC: South Carolina Department of Archives and History, Ancestry.com, https://search.ancestry.com/cgi-bin/sse.dll?db=1940usfedcen&indiv=try&h=138420143, l; Maxwell-Roddey, interview by Sonya Ramsey, June 9, 2013.

42. For more information about the history of Black migration rural areas to urban southern cities, see Bernadette Pruitt, *The Other Great Migration: The Movement of Rural African Americans to Houston, 1900–1941* (College Station, TX: Texas A&M University Press, 2017); Luther Adams, *Way Up North in Louisville: African American Migration in the Urban South, 1930–1970* (Chapel Hill: University of North Carolina Press, 2010); Leslie Brown, "African American Women and Migration," in *The Practice of U.S. Women's History: Narratives, Intersections, and Dialogues,* eds., Jay S. Kleinberg, Eileen Boris, and Vicki L. Ruiz (New Brunswick, New Jersey; London: Rutgers University Press, 2007), 206, http://www.jstor.org/stable/j.ctt5hhxxp.15, accessed September 15, 2020.

43. Bertha Maxwell-Roddey interview by Sonya Ramsey, June 9, 2013.

44. Maxwell-Roddey, interview April 29, 2015; "The Racial Record of Johns Hopkins University," *The Journal of Blacks in Higher Education* no. 25 (1999): 42–43; https://doi.org/10.2307/2999371, accessed December 22, 2021; "Alumni Profiles: She Had a Dream," *John Hopkins Nursing Magazine,* Fall/Winter 2009, John Hopkins School of Nursing Website, https://web.jhu.edu/jhnmagazine/fall2009/vigilando/alumni.html, accessed December 22, 2021. For a complex discussion of race, segregation, and geography, Stephen A. Berrey, *The Jim Crow Routine: Everyday Performances of Race, Civil Rights, and Segregation in Mississippi* (Chapel Hill: University of North Carolina Press, 2015).

45. Johnson C. Smith University, "The Golden Bull Yearbook," Digital Yearbooks Collection, Johnson C. Smith University, 37, DigitalNC Database, https://lib.digitalnc.org/record/28325#?c=0&m=0&s=0&cv=0&r=0&xywh=-1762%2C-177%2C5803%2C3526, accessed September 16, 2020.

46. Johnson C. Smith University, "Our History," https://www.jcsu.edu/about/our_university/history/, accessed February 19, 2020; For more information about the history of Johnson C. Smith University, see Henry Lawrence McCrorey, *A Brief History of Johnson C. Smith University* (Charlotte, NC: Johnson C. Smith University, 1935) in the Special Collections and Archives, J. Murrey Atkins Library, University of North Carolina at Charlotte, Charlotte, NC; Arthur Allen George and Arthur H. (Henry) George, *100 Years, 1867–1967: Salient Factors in the Growth and Development of Johnson C. Smith University, Charlotte, N.C.: a History*

(Charlotte, N.C.: Johnson C. Smith University, 1968); For more information about historically Black colleges and universities, see Bobby L. Lovett, *America's Historically Black Colleges: A Narrative History, 1837–2009* (Macon, GA: Mercer University Press, 2011).

47. Maxwell-Roddey, interview by Sonya Ramsey, August 17, 2017, Charlotte, NC, recording in author's possession; Johnson C. Smith University, "Johnson C. Smith University Bulletin 1954," Inez Moore Parker Archives, James B. Duke Memorial Library, Johnson C. Smith
University DigitalNC Database, https://lib.digitalnc.org/record/39848?ln=en#?c=0&m=0&s
=0&cv=0&r=0&xywh=-807%2C-168%2C3528%2C3344, accessed July 30, 2019.

48. Bertha Lyons will now be referenced as Bertha Maxwell, due to her marriage.

49. Maxwell-Roddey interview by Sonya Ramsey, April 29, 2015; Maxwell-Roddey, interview by Willie Griffin, May 12, 2008.

50. Maxwell-Roddey, interview by Sonya Ramsey, April 29, 2015; For more information about Charlotte civil rights activist Reginald Hawkins, see Michael B. Richardson,
"Not Gradually . . . But Now": Reginald Hawkins, Black Leadership, and Desegregation in
Charlotte, North Carolina," *The North Carolina Historical Review* 82, no. 3 (2005): 347–79,
doi:10.5406/jcivihumarigh.5.2.0068, accessed July 24, 2020, and Evan Faulkenbury, "Reginald Hawkins, the 1968 North Carolina Democratic Primary, and the Future of Black Political Participation," *Journal of Civil and Human Rights* 5, no. 2 (2019): 68–88, www.jstor.org/
stable/23523030, accessed July 24, 2020; For more information about the role of the development of the Charlotte Douglas International Airport and its impact on the development of
Charlotte, see Wilber C. Rich, *The Transformative City: Charlotte's Takeoffs and Landings*
(Athens: University of Georgia Press, 2020).

51. Robin Kelley, "'We Are Not What We Seem': Rethinking Black Working-Class Opposition in the Jim Crow South," *Journal of American History* 80, no. 1 (June 1, 1993): 75–112,
http://search.proquest.com/docview/224917635/, accessed January 14, 2020; For more information about the murder of Emmett Till and its impact on race relations, see Timothy B.
Tyson, *The Blood of Emmett Till* (New York: Simon and Schuster Press, 2017).

52. Maxwell-Roddey, interview by Sonya Ramsey, August 9, 2019; Maxwell-Roddey, interview by Willie Griffin, May 12, 2008.

Chapter 2. "It Was like Putting Diapers on Gnats"

1. Charlotte's school system was known as the Charlotte City Schools before the City of
Charlotte and its surrounding Mecklenburg County merged their school systems in 1960 to
form the Charlotte Mecklenburg Schools System or CMS.

2. Charlotte Mecklenburg Public Library, "Principals: African American Album: The
Black Experience in Charlotte and Mecklenburg County," vol. 2., Digital Exhibit (Charlotte,
NC. Public Library of Charlotte and Mecklenburg County, 1998), https://www.cmstory.org/
exhibits/african-american-album-volume-2/principals, accessed April 15, 2020.

3. "199 New Teachers Hired in Charlotte System," *Charlotte Observer*, September 2, 1954,
15, NewsBank: Access World News—Historical and Current, https://infoweb-NewsBank-com.
eu1.proxy.openathens.net/apps/news/document-view?p=WORLDNEWS&docref=image/
v2%3A11260DC9BB798E30%40WHNPX-15E24F048044F281%402434988-
15F4C1D82E439383%4014-15F4C1D82E439383%40, accessed September 16, 2020.

4. Bertha Maxwell-Roddey, interview by Sonya Ramsey, March 6, 2011, Charlotte, NC,

in author's possession; Interactive Knowledge, Inc. and Kathryn Frye, *An African American Album Vol. 2: The Black Experience in Charlotte and Mecklenburg County* Online Exhibit on Compact Disc," (Charlotte, NC: Public Library of Charlotte and Mecklenburg County, 1997), in the Private Collection of Kathryn Frye, Charlotte, NC.

5. Thomas Hanchett, *Sorting Out the New South City: Race, Class, and Urban Development in Charlotte, 1875–1975* (Chapel Hill: University of North Carolina Press, 1998), 121–127.

6. Bertha Maxwell-Roddey, interview by Sonya Ramsey, March 6, 2011, Charlotte, NC; "199 New Teachers in Charlotte System," 15.

7. Josephine Brandon McKissack, Bernice Sloan Ferguson, and Bertha Maxwell-Roddey, interview by Sonya Ramsey, September 17, 2015, Charlotte NC, written notes in author's possession; Bertha Maxwell-Roddey, interview by Sonya Ramsey, September 17, 2015, Charlotte NC, written notes in author's possession; Bertha Maxwell-Roddey, interview by Sonya Ramsey, April 20, 2020, Charlotte NC, recoding in author's possession; State Superintendent of Public Instruction, "Educational Directory of North Carolina, 1953–1954," (Raleigh, N.C., State Board of Education Publisher, 1953–1954), 17, in the Digital Collections, North Carolina State Archives, North Carolina State Library, Raleigh, North Carolina, https://digital.ncdcr. gov/digital/collection/p249901coll22/id/259256/rec/1, archived, May 4, 2020.

8. "Mrs. Sasso, Teacher, Principal," *Charlotte Observer,* February 9, 1970, 28, NewsBank: Access World News—Historical and Current, https://infoweb-NewsBank-com.eu1.proxy.openathens. net/apps/news/document-view?p=WORLDNEWS&docref=image/v2:11260DC9BB798E30@ WHNPX-15E2507DFAFDFD03@2440627-15E24EE2AD3D70E7@27-15E24EE2AD3D70E7@, accessed March 4, 2020; "Biddleville School Wins Two Awards in One Year," *Charlotte Observer,* November 20, 1932, 57, NewsBank: Access World News—Historical and Current, https://infoweb-NewsBank-com.eu1.proxy.openathens.net/apps/news/document-view?p=WORLDNEWS&docref=image/v2:11260DC9BB798E30@WHNPX-1518363ED706925C@2427032-151741BD7116B744@56-151741BD7116B744@, accessed March 4, 2020.

9. John Summersette, "Fairview School: A Shrine of Black Education," *Charlotte Observer,* July 2, 1970, 6, Newspapers.com Database; "Head of Negro School is Dead: Mrs. Maria (sp) Gaston Davis, Principal at Fairview, Dies in Hospital," *Charlotte Observer,* May 21, 1945, 7, Newspaper.com Database, accessed May 4, 2020; "Friday Services Planned for Mrs. Jayne Hemphill, 77," *Charlotte News,* March 19, 1975, 16, NewsBank: Access World News—Historical and Current; Judy Gaultney, "Providing Good Education Yearly Theme to Principal," *Charlotte News,* August 28, 1981, 8, NewsBank: Access World News—Historical and Current; "Service of Witness to the Resurrection for Gwendolyn Davidson Cunningham, February 12, 1919-July 2, 2013," Unpublished Funeral Program, https://mccrorey. historysouth.org/wp-content/uploads/2014/02/Cunningham_Gwendolyn_Davidson.pdf, 2, accessed March 4, 2020; State Superintendent of Public Instruction, "Educational Directory of North Carolina, 1953–1954," (Raleigh, N.C., State Board of Education, 1953–1954), 17, in the Digital Collections, North Carolina State Archives, North Carolina State Library, Raleigh, North Carolina, https://digital.ncdcr.gov/digital/collection/p249901coll22/ id/259256/rec/1, archived, May 4, 2020; "Mrs. Moore," *The Charlotte News,* September 11, 1965, 42, Newspapers.com Database, https://www.newspapers.com/image/618264561/?ter ms=%22Beulah%2BD.%2BMoore%22, accessed May 4, 2020; "Isabella Butler Wyche," Find a Grave Website, https://www.findagrave.com/memorial/180015702/isabella-wyche, ac-

cessed May 4, 2020; For a brief history of North Carolina's public schools and colleges, see Glenda Elizabeth Gilmore, "Educational Capital and Human Flourishing: North Carolina's Public Schools and Universities, 1865–2015," in *New Voyages to Carolina: Reinterpreting North Carolina History,* Larry E. Tise and Jeffrey J. Crow, eds. (Chapel Hill: University of North Carolina Press, 2017), 194–216, http://www.jstor.org/stable/10.5149/9781469634609_crow.12, accessed May 10, 2021.

10. Ann Doss Helms, "She Broke a Racial Barrier at CMS. Now the Community Says Thanks," *Charlotte Observer,* February 16, 2017, 1A, *Charlotte Observer* Website. http://www.charlotteobserver.com/news/local/education/article133131684.html, accessed January 14, 2020. For a visual image and more information about Elizabeth Randolph, see https://foundation.cmlibrary.org/news/honoring-elizabeth-s-randolph/, accessed January 20, 2022.

11. Kathleen Crosby, interview by Sonya Ramsey, Charlotte, NC, June 9, 1993, from *Behind the Veil: Documenting African-American Life in the Jim Crow South,* in Center for Documentary Studies at Duke University, David M. Rubenstein Rare Book and Manuscript Library, Duke University, https://library.duke.edu/digitalcollections/behindtheveil_btvnco2011/, accessed January 14, 2020; Ricki Morrell, "Outspoken Educator Official to End 40-Year Career with No Regrets," *Charlotte Observer,* November 22, 1986, 1A; "Kathleen Crosby Obituary," November 22, 2012, NewsBank: Access World News—Historical and Current, https://infoweb-NewsBank-com.eu1.proxy.openathens.net/apps/news/document-view?p=WORLDNEWS&docref=news/142C0B9857A471C8, accessed January 14, 2020.

12. Elizabeth Randolph, interview by Rhonda Mawhood, July 5, 1993, Charlotte, NC, located in Behind the Veil: Documenting African-American Life in the Jim Crow South. Center for Documentary Studies at Duke University. David M. Rubenstein Rare Book and Manuscript Library, Duke University, https://library.duke.edu/digitalcollections/behindtheveil_btvnco2044/, accessed January 14, 2020.

13. Beulah D. Moore retired in 1963. Bertha Maxwell-Roddey, interview by Sonya Ramsey, April 10, 2016, Charlotte, NC, recording in author's possession; For more information about the role of African American educators during segregation, see James D. Anderson, *The Education of Blacks in the South, 1860–1935* (Chapel Hill: University of North Carolina Press, 1988); Adam Fairclough, *A Class of Their Own: Black Teachers in the Segregated South* (Cambridge: Harvard University Press, 2007); Vanessa Siddle Walker, *Their Highest Potential: An African American School Community in the Segregated South* (Chapel Hill: University of North Carolina Press, 1996).

14. Maxwell-Roddey interview by Sonya Ramsey, April 10, 2016; For more information about the experiences of Black principals during segregation, see Vanessa Siddle Walker, *Hello Professor: A Black Principal and Professional Leadership in the Segregated South* (Chapel Hill, University of North Carolina Press, 2009).

15. Elizabeth Randolph, interview by Rhonda Mawhood, July 5, 1993, located in *Behind the Veil: Documenting African-American Life in the Jim Crow South,* Center for Documentary Studies at Duke University, David M. Rubenstein Rare Book & Manuscript Library, Duke University, July 5, 1993, https://library.duke.edu/digitalcollections/behindtheveil_btvnco2044/, accessed January 14, 2020; Kathleen Crosby, interview by Sonya Ramsey, Charlotte, NC, June 9, 1993.

16. Elizabeth Randolph, interview by Rhonda Mawhood, Charlotte, NC.

17. Kathleen Crosby, interview by Melinda H. Desmarais, October 1, 2001, Charlotte, NC in Special Collections, J. Murrey Atkins Library, University North Carolina at Charlotte, Charlotte, NC.

18. Kathleen Crosby, interview by Melinda H. Desmarais, October 1, 2001, Charlotte, NC.

19. Kathleen Crosby, interview by Sonya Ramsey, Charlotte, NC, June 9, 1993.

20. For more information about Black professional women and teachers, see, Ann Short Chirhart, *Torches of Light: Georgia Teachers & the Coming of the Modern South* (Athens: University of Georgia Press, 2005); Tamara Beauboeuf-Lafontant, "Womanist Lessons for Reinventing Teaching," *Journal of Teacher Education* 56, no. 5 (November 2005): 441; Stephanie Shaw, *What a Woman Ought to Be and to Do: Black Professional Workers in the Age of Jim Crow* (Chicago: University of Chicago Press, 1996); Valinda W. Littlefield, "A Yearly Contract With Everybody and His Brother: Durham County, North Carolina Black Female Public School Teachers 1885–1927," *The Journal of Negro History* 79, no. 1, 1994: 37–53, https://doi.org/10.2307/2717666, accessed May 10, 2021; Adah L. Ward Randolph, "'It Is Better to Light a Candle Than to Curse the Darkness': Ethel Thompson Overby and Democratic Schooling in Richmond, Virginia, 1910–1958," *Educational Studies* 48, no. 3 (2012): 220–243, doi. 10.1080/00131946.2012.660795, accessed May 10, 2021.

21. Frye Gaillard, interview by Sonya Ramsey, October 10, 2014, Charlotte, NC, recording in author's possession.

22. Davison Douglas, *Reading, Writing and Race: The Desegregation of Charlotte Schools* (Chapel Hill: University of North Carolina Press; 1995), 72, 73.

23. Douglas, *Reading, Writing and Race: The Desegregation of Charlotte Schools,* 72, 73.

24. Douglas, *Reading, Writing and Race: The Desegregation of Charlotte Schools,* 72, 73, 76, 77.

25. Maxwell-Roddey interview, July 17, 2017, The University of North Carolina at Charlotte, Professional Data for Dr. Bertha L Maxwell-Roddey, "Assistant Professor of Education, Director of Black Studies," Document, located in the African American Studies Collection, Box 3, Folder 5, Special Collections, J. Murrey Atkins Library, University of North Carolina at Charlotte, Charlotte, NC.

26. Bertha Maxwell-Roddey, interview by Sonya Ramsey, May 16, 2016, Charlotte, NC, recording in author's possession.

27. For more information about Bank Street College of Education, see Elsbeth Pfeiffer, "The Special Teaching Program of the Bank Street College of Education," *The Phi Delta Kappan,* 55, no. 8 (1974): 553–555, www.jstor.org/stable/20297671, accessed January 14, 2020.

28. Crosby, interview by Sonya Ramsey, June 9, 1993; Morrell, "Outspoken Educator Official to End 40-Year Career with No Regrets," 1986; Maxwell-Roddey, interview by Sonya Ramsey, March 6, 2011.

29. Bertha Maxwell-Roddey, interview by Sonya Ramsey, May 16, 2016, Charlotte, NC, recording in author's possession.

30. Bertha Maxwell-Roddey, interview by Sonya Ramsey, May 16, 2016, Charlotte, NC.

31. For more information about the experiences of Black principals during segregation, see Vanessa Siddle Walker and Ulysses Byas, *Hello Professor: A Black Principal and Professional Leadership in the Segregated South* (Chapel Hill: University of North Carolina Press, 2009). For more information about African American women in educational leadership, see Sonya Douglass Horsford and Linda C Tillman, "Inventing Herself: Examining the Inter-

sectional Identities and Educational Leadership of Black Women in the USA," *International Journal of Qualitative Studies in Education: Emerging African American Women Scholars* 25, no. 1 (February 1, 2012): 1–9, Taylor and Francis Database http://www.tandfonline.com/doi/abs/10.1080/09518398.2011.647727, accessed May 17, 2020.

32. For more information about the recent debates surrounding intersectionality, see Ange-Marie Hancock, *Intersectionality: An Intellectual History* (New York: Oxford University Press, 2016) and Jennifer Nash, "Re-thinking Intersectionality," *Feminist Review* 89, no. 1 (June 2008): 1–15, https://doi.org/10.1057/fr.2008.4, accessed January 20, 2022.

33. Harvey Kantor, "Education, Social Reform, and the State: ESEA and Federal Education Policy in the 1960s," *American Journal of Education* 100, no. 1 (1991): 60, https://www.jstor.org/stable/1085652, accessed May 17, 2020.

34. Martha J. Bailey and Sheldon Danziger, eds., *Legacies of the War on Poverty* (New York: Russell Sage Foundation, 2013), 7.

35. Several scholars and policy makers have discussed poverty and the impact of the Moynihan Report, including Daniel Geary, *The Moynihan Report* (Philadelphia: University of Pennsylvania Press, 2015); Michael B. Katz, *The Undeserving Poor: From the War on Poverty to Welfare* (New York: Pantheon Books, 1989); and William Julius Wilson, *More Than Just Race: Being Black and Poor in the Inner City* (New York: W. W. Norton and Company, 2009).

36. Kantor, "Education, Social Reform, and the State: ESEA and Federal Education Policy in the 1960s," 55; Bertha Maxwell-Roddey, interview by Sonya Ramsey, March 6, 2011, Charlotte NC, recording in author's possession; Celeste Smith, "Teachers Gave Kids Head Start 35 Years Ago," *Charlotte Observer,* August 26, 1999, 1A, NewsBank: Access World News—Historical and Current, https://infoweb-NewsBank-com.eu1.proxy.openathens.net/apps/news/document-view?p=WORLDNEWS&docref=news/0EB6D75749E795C4, accessed January 14, 2020; Kathleen Crosby, interview by Sonya Ramsey, Charlotte, NC, June 9, 1993, located in *Behind the Veil: Documenting African-American Life in the Jim Crow South,* Center for Documentary Studies at Duke University, David M. Rubenstein Rare Book & Manuscript Library, Duke University from Behind the Veil: Documenting African-American Life in the Jim Crow South, https://library.duke.edu/digitalcollections/behindtheveil_btvnc02011/, accessed January 14, 2020.

37. Bertha Maxwell-Roddey, interview by Sonya Ramsey, August 29, 2015, Charlotte, NC.

38. Bertha Maxwell-Roddey, interview by Sonya Ramsey, August 4, 2016, Charlotte, NC, recording in author's possession; Social Security Applications and Claims, 1936–2007 located in Ancestry.com, U.S. Social Security Applications and Claims Index, 1936–2007 [database on-line]. Provo, UT, USA: Ancestry.com Operations, Inc., 2015; "Shirley P. Harris Obituary," *Charlotte Observer,* April 7, 2006, NewsBank: Access World News—Historical and Current, https://infoweb-NewsBankcom.eu1.proxy.openathens.net/apps/news/document-view? p=WORLDNEWS&docref=news/110E6C2C82E17CE, accessed December 15, 2019.

39. Maxwell-Roddey, interview, August 4, 2016.

40. "Teacher Corps Gets Needed Aid," *Charlotte Observer,* June 6, 1964, NewsBank: Access World News—Historical and Current, https://infoweb-NewsBank-com.eu1.proxy.openathens.net/apps/news/document-view?p=WORLDNEWS&docref=image/v2:11260DC9BB798E30@WHNPX-15E24FE298126D66@2438553-15E34703A8C4F6E5@16-15E34703A8C4F6E5@, accessed September 9, 2019.

41. William Delaney, "Youngsters Get First Look at Farm: They're Seeing Unfamiliar Sights

They'll Read About in School," *Charlotte Observer,* June 26, 1964, B1, NewsBank: Access World News—Historical and Current, https://infoweb-NewsBank-com.eu1.proxy.openathens.net/apps/news/document-view?p=WORLDNEWS&docref=image/v2:11260DC9BB798E30@WHNPX-15E24FE2998C17DC@2438573-15E347040FCBC691@34-15E347040FCBC691@, accessed September 9, 2019.

42. William Delaney, "Youngsters Get First Look at Farm: They're Seeing Unfamiliar Sights They'll Read About in School," June 26, 1964, B1.

43. William Delaney, "Youngsters Get First Look at Farm: They're Seeing Unfamiliar Sights They'll Read About in School," June 26, 1964, B1.

44. Robert Hummerstone, "These 85 'Unfolded' Like Flowers," *Charlotte Observer,* November 27, 1964, 61, NewsBank: Access World News—Historical and Current, https://infoweb-NewsBank-com.eu1.proxy.openathens.net/apps/news/document-view?p=WORLDNEWS&docref=image/v2:11260DC9BB798E30@WHNPX-15E24FC007898301@2438727-15E34721C260D307@60-15E34721C260D307@, accessed January 14, 2020.

45. "Teachers Corps Gets Needed Aid;" Hummerstone, "These 85 'Unfolded' Like Flowers," 61. For more information about the growth of the federal government, see Ballard C. Campbell, in *The Growth of American Government: Governance from the Cleveland Era to the Present* (Bloomington, IN, Indiana University Press, 2015).

46. Kay Miles, *Something Better for My Children: The History and People of Head Start* (New York: Penguin Books, 1998), 75; For more information about the impact of the War on Poverty programs and the struggle for civil rights in Mississippi, see Françoise N. Hamlin, "It Was a Peaceful Revolution: Johnson's Great Society And Economic Justice In Coahoma County," In *Crossroads at Clarksdale: The Black Freedom Struggle in the Mississippi Delta after World War II* (University of North Carolina Press, 2012), 209–243.

47. For more information about the Head Start Program in Mississippi, see Crystal Saunders, *A Chance for Change, Head Start and the Black Freedom Struggle in Mississippi* (Chapel Hill, University of North Carolina Press, 2016).

48. Bernice Sloan Ferguson, Josephine Brandon McKissack, Lena Helton Pickens, Bertha Maxwell-Roddey, interview notes: Celeste Smith, "Teachers Gave Kids Head Start 35 Years Ago, 1A.

49. Celeste Smith, "Teachers Gave Kids Head Start 35 Years Ago, 1A."

50. Wingate Main, "Children Have Head Start in Learning," *Charlotte Observer,* August 4, 1966, 29, NewsBank: Access World News – Historical and Current, https://infoweb-newsbank-com.eu1.proxy.openathens.net/apps/news/document-view?p=WORLDNEWS&docref=image/v2%3A11260DC9BB798E30%40WHNPX-15E2503D791FD57A%402439342-15E24C412ECC073C%4028-15E24C412ECC073C%40, accessed March 30, 2022. John Goodwin, "CAF Will Seek $420,000 For Head Start Program," *Charlotte News,* December 16, 1967: 48. NewsBank: Access World News—Historical and Current, https://infoweb-NewsBank-com.eu1.proxy.openathens.net/apps/news/document-view?p=WORLDNEWS&docref=image/v2%3A112616783138096o%40WHNPX-16F72F7A2E3288B3%402439841-16F72E3B524A374A%4047-16F72E3B524A374A%40, accessed May 10, 2020.

51. Bob Smith, "For a Head Start," *Charlotte News,* August 5, 1965, 28, NewsBank: Access World News—Historical and Current, https://infoweb-NewsBank-com.eu1.

proxy.openathens.net/apps/news/document-view?p=WORLDNEWS&docref=image/ v2:1126167831380960@WHNPX-16F53FBA2C17EC5A@2438978-16F4367BD2EE306A@27- 16F4367BD2EE306A@, accessed March 3, 2020. For more information about the North Carolina Fund, the Charlotte Area Fund, and War on Poverty efforts in North Carolina, see, Robert Korstad, Robert Rodgers, Billy E. Barnes, and James L. Leloudis, *To Right These Wrongs The North Carolina Fund and the Battle to End Poverty and Inequality in 1960s America* (Chapel Hill: University of North Carolina Press, 2010), 102, 103, 105, 128, 174–175.

52. Maxwell-Roddey, interview, May 16, 2016; Crosby Interview by Sonya Ramsey, 1993; Minutes of the Charlotte Mecklenburg County Board of Education, March 1967, Charlotte Mecklenburg County Board of Education, Charlotte, NC.

53. For more information about public school desegregation in Charlotte, see Davison Douglas, *Reading, Writing and Race: The Desegregation of Charlotte Schools* (Chapel Hill: University of North Carolina Press; 1995); Frye Gaillard, *The Dream Long Deferred: The Landmark Struggle for Desegregation in Charlotte, North Carolina* (Columbia: University of South Carolina Press, 2006), first edition, 1988; Matthew Lassiter, *Silent Majority: Suburban Politics in the Sunbelt South* (Princeton, NJ: Princeton University Press, 2007); Bernard Schwartz, *Swann's Way: The School Busing Case and the Supreme Court* (New York: Oxford University Press, 1986), and Stephen Samuel Smith, *Boom for Whom? Education, Desegregation, and Development* (Albany, NY: State University of New York Press, 2004); Swann v. Charlotte-Mecklenburg Board of Education, 402 U.S. 1, 91 S. Ct. 1267, 28 L. Ed. 2d 554 (U.S. 1971).

54. Douglas, *Reading, Writing and Race: The Desegregation of Charlotte Schools*, 113.

55. Bertha Maxwell-Roddey, interview by Sonya Ramsey, March 6, 2011.

56. Lisa Smulyan, *Balancing Acts: Women Principals at Work* (Albany: State University of New York Press, 2000), 10.

57. Smulyan, *Balancing Acts: Women Principals at Work,* 10.

58. Smulyan, *Balancing Acts: Women Principals at Work,* 22; Lorraine Orr, Frederick Warren, and Bertha Maxwell-Roddey, interview by Sonya Ramsey, April 12, 2016, Sonya Ramsey, Charlotte, NC, recording in author's possession.

59. Maxwell-Roddey, interview by Sonya Ramsey, March 6, 2011; Michael Ervin, "Public Order Is Even More Important Than the Rights of Negroes': Race and Recreation in Charlotte, North Carolina, 1927–1973," MA thesis, History (University of North Carolina at Charlotte, 2015), Charlotte, NC.

60. " The Charlotte-Mecklenburg School System: Analysis and Recommendations 1969," Julius L. Chambers Papers, Desegregation Plans, Series 6, Folder 1, Special Collections and Archives, J. Murrey Atkins Library, Atkins Library Website https://repository.charlotte.edu/ islandora/object/mss%3A63267, accessed December 22, 2021; Douglas, *Reading, Writing and Race: The Desegregation of Charlotte Schools,* 156, 157.

61. Douglas, *Reading, Writing and Race: The Desegregation of Charlotte Schools,* 217; Maxwell-Roddey, interview by Sonya Ramsey, August 16, 2016. For an in-depth discussion of how desegregation affected West Charlotte High School, see Pamela Grundy, *Color and Character: West Charlotte High and the American Struggle over Educational Equality* (Chapel Hill: University of North Carolina Press, 2017).

62. Douglas, *Reading, Writing and Race: The Desegregation of Charlotte Schools,* 156–157; Maxwell-Roddey, interview by Sonya Ramsey, August 16, 2016.

63. "Desegregating the Faculty," *Charlotte News,* 18 August 1965, 14A; NewsBank:

Access World News—Historical and Current, https://infoweb-NewsBank-com.eu1. proxy.openathens.net/apps/news/document-view?p=WORLDNEWS&docref=image/ v2:1126167831380960@WHNPX-16F53FC4C02A0D0C@2438991-16F4368AA9AAE428@13- 16F4368AA9AAE428@, accessed January 14, 2020; *Green v. County School Board of New Kent County* (No. 695) 391 U.S. 430, 1968; Nora Carroll, "In the Classroom: Charlotte-Mecklenburg School Desegregation: 1969–1975," Unpublished MA thesis manuscript (Vassar College, Department of History, 2004), 24 in J. Murrey Atkins Library, UNC Charlotte, Charlotte, NC; Nancy Brachey, "Pupils Faculty Included," *Charlotte Observer,* April 24, 1969, 1A, 4A, Julius L. Chambers Papers, Goldmine Digital Collection 1969–2004, Series 3, Clippings 5, Special Collections, J. Murrey Atkins Library, UNC Charlotte, Charlotte, NC, https://repository.charlotte. edu//islandora/object/mss:57095?ui=embed, accessed December 22, 2021; "Most Teachers Oppose Integration Transfers," *Charlotte Observer,* May 25, 1969, 28, NewsBank: Access World News—Historical and Current, https://infoweb-NewsBank-com.eu1.proxy.openathens.net/ apps/news/document-view?p=WORLDNEWS&docref=image/v2:11260DC9BB798E30@ WHNPX-15E2504DDC66EBC5@2440367-15E24ED27AE0F3FB@27-15E24ED27AE- 0F3FB@, accessed January 14, 2020; Kay Reimler, "Polled Teachers Touchy on Transfers," *Charlotte News,* May 24, 1969, 1B, NewsBank: Access World News—Historical and Current, https://infoweb-NewsBank-com.eu1.proxy.openathens.net/apps/news/ document-view?p=WORLDNEWS&docref=image/v2:1126167831380960@WHNPX- 16F6CB2D0B261664@2440366-16F687F64034DC8B@12-16F687F64034DC8B@, accessed October 27, 2020.

64. Linda C. Tillman, "(Un)Intended Consequences? The Impact of the Brown v. Board of Education Decision on the Employment Status of Black Educators," *Education and Urban Society* 36, no. 3 (May 2004): 280–303, https://uncc.primo.exlibrisgroup.com/ permalink/01UNCC_INST/1rqb8fi/sage_s10_1177_0013124504264360, accessed May 15, 2020; Linda C. Tillman, "African American Principals and the Legacy of Brown," *Review of Research in Education* 28 (2004): 112, http://www.jstor.org/stable/3568137, accessed January 14, 2020; Jeffrey Lyons, and Joanne Chesney, "Fifty Years After Brown: the Benefits and Tradeoffs for African American Educators and Students," *The Journal of Negro Education* 73, no. 3 (Summer 2004): 302, http://www.jstor.org/stable/4129613, accessed January 14, 2020; Gerry Hostetler, "Pioneer 'Jennye' Shadd Never Too Busy for Kids," *The Charlotte Observer,* May 3, 1996, 2C, NewsBank: Access World News—Historical and Current, https://infoweb- NewsBank-com.eu1.proxy.openathens.net/apps/news/document-view?p=WORLDNEW S&docref=news/0F2447122B4D28D2, accessed January 14, 2020; Charlotte Mecklenburg Board of Education, "Desegregation Planning Documents, 1965, April, May," File—Box: 7 [F09.136.04.01], Folder: 3, Julius Chambers Papers, Manuscript Collections, J. Murrey Atkins Library Special Collections and University Archives, UNC Charlotte, Charlotte, North Carolina.

65. Maxwell-Roddey, interview by Sonya Ramsey, May 6, 2016, Charlotte, NC, recording in author's possession; "You Were Born to Serve," *Tuesday Morning Breakfast Forum: Charlotte News: 3 Female Firsts,* March 13, 2007, 1, http://www.tuesdayforumcharlotte.org/ NewsPages/07Q1NewsPages/Roddy.htm, accessed January 14, 2020.

66. Maxwell-Roddey, interview by Sonya Ramsey, March 6, 2011; Tillman, "African American Principals and the Legacy of Brown," 101–146; "County School Desegregation Up," *Charlotte Observer* (Charlotte, North Carolina) 79, September 5, 1964, 3. News-

Bank: Access World News—Historical and Current, https://infoweb-NewsBank-com.eu1.proxy.openathens.net/apps/news/document-view?p=WORLDNEWS&docref=image/v2%3A1126oDC9BB798E30%40WHNPX-15E24FBF26079390%402438644-15E34718B5B8FD9B%402-15E34718B5B8FD9B%40, accessed May 15, 2020. From 1964 to 1968, Natalie C. Holmes served as principal of Wesley Heights Elementary School, a formerly all-white school that had transformed to an all-Black school by 1964, when she was appointed principal. In 1968, Natalie C. Holmes became principal of Wilmore Elementary, a predominantly white elementary school with a small Black student population. Maxwell was the first African American woman to be appointed to a newly constructed all-white school, with fewer than five Black students.

67. Maxwell-Roddey, interview by Sonya Ramsey, March 6, 2011.

68. Carol F. Karpinski, "Bearing the Burden of Desegregation," *Urban Education,* 41, no. 3 (May 2006): 237–276, DOI: 10.1177/0042085905284961, accessed January 14, 2020; Maxwell-Roddey, interview by Sonya Ramsey, May 16, 2016.

69. *Charlotte Observer* Staff, "She Brought Innovation in Education to All Students," *Charlotte Observer,* February 17, 2002, 9A, NewsBank: Access World News—Historical and Current, https://infoweb-NewsBank-com.eu1.proxy.openathens.net/apps/news/document-view?p=WORLDNEWS&docref=news/0F1C2D9E893848B1, accessed January 14, 2020; Maxwell-Roddey, interview by Sonya Ramsey, August 16, 2016.

70. Maxwell-Roddey, interview by Sonya Ramsey, August 16, 2016; "Negro Principals Expect Minimal Race Problems," *Charlotte News,* April 24, 1968, 27, Newspapers.com Database, https://www.newspapers.com/image/621243052/?terms=Bertha%20Maxwell&match=1, accessed January 21, 2022.

71. Maxwell-Roddey, interview by Sonya Ramsey, July 17, 2017; Warren King, "Black Principal's Ideal Shattered," *Charlotte Observer,* July 3, 1970, 16, NewsBank: Access World News—Historical and Current, https://infoweb-NewsBank-com.eu1.proxy.openathens.net/apps/news/document-view?p=WORLDNEWS&docref=image/v2:1126oDC9BB798E30@WHNPX-15E2509105EB6BF2@2440771-15E24ED9F567FEC4@15-15E24ED9F567FEC4@, accessed October 14, 2019.

72. Maxwell-Roddey, interview by Sonya Ramsey, August 16, 2016.

73. Maxwell-Roddey, interview by Sonya Ramsey, August 16, 2016.

74. King, "Black Principal's Ideal Shattered," 16.

75. Maxwell-Roddey, Interview by Sonya Ramsey, August 29, 2015.

76. Maxwell-Roddey, Interview by Sonya Ramsey, August 29, 2015.

77. For more information about the theory of intersectionality, see Kimberlé Crenshaw, "Demarginalizing the Intersection of Race and Sex: A Black Feminist Critique of Antidiscrimination Doctrine, Feminist Theory and Antiracist Politics," *University of Chicago Legal Forum* 149 (1989): 139–167, https://chicagounbound.uchicago.edu/uclf/vol1989/iss1/8, accessed January 14, 2020; Patricia Hill Collins, *Black Feminist Thought: Knowledge, Consciousness, and the Politics of Empowerment* (New York: Routledge University Press, 2000); Kathleen Crosby, interview by Sonya Ramsey, June 9, 1993; Maxwell-Roddey, interview by Sonya Ramsey, March 6, 2011.

78. Maxwell-Roddey, interview by Sonya Ramsey, May 16, 2016.

79. Tillman, "African American Principals and the Legacy of Brown," 112.

80. Crosby, interview by Melinda H. Desmarais, October 1, 2001; C. Vanessa Baxter, inter-

view by Mary Metzger, December 21, 2004; Charlotte, NC, in the Before Brown Collection, Special Collections, J. Murrey Atkins Library, University of North Carolina at Charlotte.

81. Gaillard, *The Dream Long Deferred: The Landmark Struggle for Desegregation in Charlotte, North Carolina*, 106–121; Douglas, *Reading, Writing and Race: The Desegregation of Charlotte Schools,* 236.

82. Douglas, *Reading, Writing and Race: The Desegregation of Charlotte Schools,* 226.

83. Douglas, *Reading, Writing and Race: The Desegregation of Charlotte Schools,* 111; Swann v. Charlotte-Mecklenburg Board of Education, 402 U.S. 1, 91 S. Ct. 1267, 28 L. Ed. 2d 554 (US 1971); Crosby, interview by Sonya Ramsey, June 9, 1993.

84. Gaillard, *The Dream Long Deferred: The Landmark Struggle for Desegregation in Charlotte, North Carolina,* 82; Carroll, "In the Classroom: Charlotte-Mecklenburg School Desegregation: 1969–1975," 33.

85. Claudia Levin Productions, "Educating to End Inequity," in *Only a Teacher: The Impact of Teachers on American Public Education, Educating to End Inequity, Desegregation* (New York, N.Y: Infobase, 2005), J. Murrey Atkins library link, https://uncc.primo.exlibrisgroup.com/discovery/fulldisplay?docid=alma991010992054104091&context=L&vid=01UNCC_INST:01UNCC_INST&lala=en&search_scope=MyInst_and_CI&adaptor=Local%20Search%20Engine&tab=Everything&query=any,contains,educating%20to%20end%20inequiin&offset=, accessed April 3, 2017.

86. Crosby interview by Melinda H. Desmarais, October 1, 2001; Gaillard, *The Dream Long Deferred: The Landmark Struggle for Desegregation in Charlotte, North Carolina,* 82; Ricki Morrell, "Outspoken Educator Official to End 40-Year Career with No Regrets," 1A.

87. Crosby, interview by Sonya Ramsey, June 9, 1993.

88. Crosby, interview by Sonya Ramsey, June 9, 1993; Morrell, "Outspoken Educator Official to End 40-Year Career with No Regrets," 1A.

89. Davison Douglas, *Reading, Writing and Race: The Desegregation of Charlotte Schools,* 111.

90. Gaillard, *The Dream Long Deferred: The Landmark Struggle for Desegregation in Charlotte, North Carolina,* 204; Ann Doss Helms, "She Broke a Racial Barrier at CMS. Now the Community Says Thanks," *Charlotte Observer,* February 16, 2017, 1A.

91. Maxwell-Roddey, interview by Sonya Ramsey, August 16, 2016.

92. Maxwell-Roddey, interview by Sonya Ramsey, August 16, 2016.

93. Elizabeth S. Randolph, interview by Jennifer Greeson, July 13, 1993, Charlotte, NC: J. Murrey Atkins Library Special Collections and University Archives, University of North Carolina at Charlotte.

94. Crosby, interview by Sonya Ramsey, June 9, 1993; Maxwell-Roddey, interview by Sonya Ramsey, April 29, 2015.

95. Beauboeuf-Lafontant, "Womanist Lessons for Reinventing Teaching," 442; Morrell, "Outspoken Educator Official to End 40-Year Career with No Regrets," 1A; Rick Morrell, "Officials Honor, Roast Kat Crosby at Banquet," *Charlotte Observer,* December 12, 1986: 3B. NewsBank: Access World News—Historical and Current. https://infoweb-NewsBankcom.eu1.proxy.openathens.net/apps/news/document-view?p=WORLDNEWS&docref=news/0EB6C12B933567A7, accessed June 22, 2021; Crosby, interview by Sonya Ramsey, June 9, 1993.

Chapter 3. Planting the Seed

1. This term "planting the seed" is paraphrased from the title of a section of Bertha Maxwell's dissertation, Bertha Maxwell, "Black Studies: Paradox with a Promise?" PhD Dissertation, Educational Administration, Tampa, FL: Union Graduate School, 1974.

2. For more information about the history of the University of North Carolina at Charlotte, see Ken Sanford, *Charlotte and UNC Charlotte Growing Up Together* (Charlotte: University of North Carolina at Charlotte Press, 1996); For more information about the history of Charlotte, North Carolina, see Thomas W. Hanchett, *Sorting Out the New South City: Race, Class, and Urban Development, 1875–1975* (Chapel Hill: University of North Carolina Press, 1998).

3. "History and Traditions," The University of North Carolina at Chapel Hill Website, https://www.unc.edu/about/history-and-traditions/; Sanford, *Charlotte and UNC Charlotte Growing Up Together*, 76.

4. UNC Charlotte Department of Institutional Research Analytics, "Quick Facts, Fall 2021," UNC Charlotte website, https://ir-analytics.charlotte.edu/tableau/quick-facts, accessed March 7, 2022; Sanford, *Charlotte and UNC Charlotte Growing Up Together*, 8.

5. UNC Charlotte, Department of Institutional Research Analytics, "Official Degree Credit Enrollment by Level, 2018," https://ir-analytics.uncc.edu/tableau/fact-book-enrollment-summary-dashboard, accessed May 25, 2018; Sanford, *Charlotte and UNC Charlotte Growing Up Together*, 8.

6. Bonnie Cone, interview by Lynn Haessly, January 7, 1986, Southern Oral History Collection #4007, Wilson Library, University of North Carolina at Chapel Hill, Chapel Hill, North Carolina.

7. Sanford, *Charlotte and UNC Charlotte Growing Up Together*, 25.

8. Laura McAuliffe, "Bonnie E. Cone," Howard Covington Jr. and Marion A. Ellis, eds., *The North Carolina Century: Tar Heels Who Made a Difference* (Charlotte, NC: Levine Museum of the New South Publisher, 2002), 217–220.

9. Laura McAuliffe, "Bonnie E. Cone," Howard Covington Jr. and Marion A. Ellis, eds., *The North Carolina Century: Tar Heels Who Made a Difference*, 217–220; Sanford, *Charlotte and UNC Charlotte Growing Up Together*, 31.

10. Mary Snead Boger, *Charlotte 23* (Basset Virginia: Bassett Printing Corporation, 1972), 59; Sanford, *Charlotte, and UNC Charlotte Growing Up Together*, 31.

11. Sanford, *Charlotte and UNC Charlotte Growing Up Together*, 3; Richard Maschal, "Orphan Then, Ghost Now-Segregated Carver College," *Charlotte Observer*, November 21, 1999, 1C, NewsBank: Access World News—Historical and Current, https://infoweb-NewsBank-com.eu1.proxy.openathens.net/apps/news/document-view?p=WORLDNEWS&docref=news/0F244A875F7E8626, accessed May 17, 2020; Maxwell-Roddey, Dissertation, *Black Studies: Paradox with a Promise?* 5; "NAACP to Seek Non-Segregated Junior College," *Charlotte Observer*, August 13, 1949, 3, Newsbank: Access World News-Historical and Current database, https://infoweb-newsbank-com.eu1.proxy.openathens.net/apps/news/document-view?p=WORLDNEWS&docref=image/v2%3A11260DC9BB798E30%40WHNPX-15E24FAAB656BB02%402433142-15FEE7C4D0C45D07%402-15FEE7C4D0C45D07%40, accessed March 3, 2022.

12. Sanford, *Charlotte, and UNC Charlotte Growing Up Together*, 31, 34; Louis R. Wilson,

The University of North Carolina Under Consolidation, 1931–1963 History and Appraisal (Chapel Hill: The University of North Carolina Consolidated Office, 1964), 469.

13. Bonnie Cone, interview by Lynn Haessly, January 7, 1986.

14. L. M. Wright, "Charlotte Builds Two Community Colleges; No Racial Restrictions," *Southern School News,* May 1, 1961, 9, Georgia Historic Newspapers of Georgia Website, https://gahistoricnewspapers.galileo.usg.edu/lccn/sn59049440/1961-05-01/ed-1/seq-9/, accessed October 27, 2020.

15. For more information about the desegregation of southern public universities, see, Charles W. Eagles, *The Price of Defiance: James Meredith and the Integration of Ole Miss* (Chapel Hill: University of North Carolina Press, 2014); B. J. Hollars, *Opening the Doors: The Desegregation of the University of Alabama and the Fight for Civil Rights in Tuscaloosa* (University of Alabama Press, 2013); Robert Pratt, *We Shall Not Be Moved: The Desegregation of the University of Georgia* (Athens: University of Georgia Press, 2002). Eddie R. Cole, *The Campus Color Line: College Presidents and the Struggle for Black Freedom* (Princeton, NJ: Princeton University Press, 2020).

16. Sanford, *Charlotte and UNC Charlotte Growing Up Together,* 48; Kays Gary, "'No Doors Closed,' Negroes Assured," *Charlotte Observer,* March 30, 1957, 13, 15, Newspapers. com website, https://www.newspapers.com/image/619923668, accessed March 2, 2022.

17. Sanford, *Charlotte and UNC Charlotte Growing Up Together,* 48.

18. Richard Maschal, "Orphan Then, Ghost Now-Segregated Carver College," 1C, News-Bank: Access World News—Historical and Current, https://infoweb-NewsBank-com.eu1. proxy.openathens.net/apps/news/document-view?p=WORLDNEWS&docref=news/0F244 A875F7E8626, accessed May 17, 2020; Maxwell-Roddey, dissertation, 5.

19. L. M. Wright, "Charlotte Builds Two Community Colleges; No Racial Restrictions," *Southern School News,* May 1, 1961, 9, Georgia Historic Newspapers of Georgia Website, https://gahistoricnewspapers.galileo.usg.edu/lccn/sn59049440/1961-05-01/ed-1/seq-9/, accessed October 27, 2020.

20. Wynn v. Trustees of Charlotte Community College System, 255 N.C. 594, 122 S.E.2d 404, 1961 N.C. in Addison H. Reese Papers, Charlotte Community College System—Wynn v. Charlotte Community College System, 1958—1961, Box 1, Folder 13, Special Collections and Archives, J. Murrey Atkins Library, UNC Charlotte, Charlotte, NC; "Court Asked to Halt Construction on One of Two Charlotte College Units," *Southern School News,* June 1, 1961, 5, Georgia Historic Newspapers Database, https://gahistoricnewspapers.galileo.usg. edu/lccn/sn59049440/1961-06-01/ed-1/seq-5/print/image_555x817_from_0,2_to_3538,5204/; L. M. Wright, "Charlotte Builds Two Community Colleges; No Racial Restrictions," *Southern School News,* May 1, 1961, 9; "State Supreme Court Upholds Separate Charlotte Campuses," *Southern School News,* December 1, 1961, 5, Historic Georgia Newspapers Database, https://gahistoricnewspapers.galileo.usg.edu/lccn/sn59049440/1961-12-01/ed-1/seq-5/print/ image_549x817_from_0,0_to_3507,5211/, accessed December 22, 2021.

21. Bertha Maxwell, interview by Robert Rieke, February 27, 1974, Box 1, Folder 1 in Special Collections and University Archives, J. Murrey Atkins Library, UNC Charlotte, Charlotte, NC.

22. Sanford, *Charlotte and UNC Charlotte Growing Up Together,* 31; Maxwell interview by Robert Rieke, February 27, 1974.

23. Jack Clairborne quoted in William Thomas Jeffers, *Jewel in the Crown: Bonnie Cone*

and the Founding of UNC Charlotte (Charlotte, NC: J. Murrey Atkins Library at UNC Charlotte Press, 2021), 22.

24. Sanford, *Charlotte and UNC Charlotte Growing Up Together,* 57, 58; Wynn v. Trustees of Charlotte Community College System, 255 N.C. 594, 122 S.E.2d 404, 1961 N.C. LEXIS 654 N.C. (January 1, 1961), Charlotte Community College System—Wynn v. Charlotte Community College System, 1958–1961, Addison H. Reese papers, Manuscript Collections, Special Collections, J. Murrey Atkins Library Special Collections and University Archive, UNC Charlotte; Wilson, 475.

25. Sanford, *Charlotte and UNC Charlotte Growing Up Together,* 57, 58.

26. David Hunter, interview by Ebony J. Grisom, October 2, 1996, Charlotte, NC, recording in Special Collections, J. Murrey Atkins Library, University of North Carolina at Charlotte, Charlotte, NC; David Hunter, interview by Debbie Howard, April 4, 2005, Charlotte, NC, recording in Special Collections, J. Murrey Atkins Library, University of North Carolina at Charlotte, Charlotte, NC.

27. Sanford, *Charlotte and UNC Charlotte Growing Up Together,* 76, 81–83; "CC Becomes UNC at Charlotte," *UNC-C News,* July 1965, 2, in Subject files, Bonnie Ethel Cone papers, Manuscript Collections, J. Murrey Atkins Library Special Collections and University Archives, UNC Charlotte, Charlotte, NC; "The School Miss Bonnie Built," *Time Magazine,* July 16, 1965, no page number given, in Subject files, Bonnie Ethel Cone papers, Manuscript Collections, J. Murrey Atkins Library Special Collections and University Archives, UNC Charlotte, Charlotte, NC.

28. Wilson, *The University of North Carolina Under Consolidation, 1931–1963 History and Appraisal,* 471, 472, 475, and 476.

29. McAuliffe, "Bonnie E. Cone," Howard Covington Jr. and Marion A. Ellis, eds., *The North Carolina Century: Tar Heels Who Made a Difference,* 217–220; For more information about Dean W. Colvard's experiences at Mississippi State University, see, Dean W. Colvard, *Mixed Emotions: As Racial Barriers Fell, A University President Remembers* (Danville, Illinois: The Interstate Printers and Publishers, 1985); Marion A. Ellis, *Dean W. Colvard: Quiet Leader* (Charlotte: University of North Carolina at Charlotte Publisher, 2004).

30. William C. Friday, "Letter to Bonnie E. Cone," January 25, 1966, in Subject files. Bonnie Ethel Cone papers, Manuscript Collections, J. Murrey Atkins Library Special Collections and University Archive, UNC Charlotte, Charlotte, NC; Thomas Jeffers, *Jewel in the Crown: Bonnie Cone and the Founding of UNC Charlotte,* 37. For an informational online exhibit featuring a visual images of Bonnie Cone, see https://bonniecone.uncc.edu/exhibits/show/vision/university, accessed July 12, 2021.

31. Sanford, Charlotte and UNC Charlotte Growing Up Together, 95; McAuliffe, "Bonnie E. Cone," Howard Covington Jr. and Marion A. Ellis, eds., *The North Carolina Century: Tar Heels Who Made a Difference,* 219.

32. Maxwell, interview by Lynn Haessly, January 7, 1986.

33. For more information about Charlotte's public zoning regulations and segregation, see, Michael Ervin, "'Public Order is Even More Important than the Rights of Negroes': Race and Recreation in Charlotte, North Carolina, 1927–1973," MA thesis, History (University of North Carolina at Charlotte, ProQuest Dissertations Publishing, 2015).

34. For more information about Charlotte's development as a New South city, see, Thomas W. Hanchett, *Sorting Out the New South City: Race, Class, and Urban Development, 1875–1975*

(Chapel Hill: University of North Carolina Press, 1998); For more information about the rise of New South cities in the region, see, David Goldfield, *Cotton Fields and Skyscrapers: Southern City and Region* (Baton Rouge, LA, Louisiana University Press, 1982). See chapter 6 for more discussion.

35. Bertha Maxwell, "Report, The Black Action Design Program Study," Departments—Afro-American and African Studies, 1977–1980, College of Humanities records, UNC Charlotte Departments—Afro-American and African Studies, 1977–1980, Box 1, Folder 4, J, Murrey Atkins Library Special Collections and University Archives, University of North Carolina at Charlotte, Charlotte, NC; Sanford, *Charlotte and UNC Charlotte Growing Up Together,* 132.

36. "New Buildings, Courses at UNC-C," *Charlotte News,* September 6, 1969, 26, NewsBank: Access World News—Historical and Current, https://infoweb-NewsBank-com.eu1.proxy.openathens.net/apps/news/document-view?p=WORLDNEWS&docref=image/v2%3A1126167831380960%40WHNPX-16F5944A56D6AFF4%402440471-16F476A1A61470BD%4025-16F476A1A61470BD%40, accessed May 30, 2020.

37. Sanford, *Charlotte and UNC Charlotte Growing Up Together,* 182; William D. Snider, *Light on the Hill: A History of the University of North Carolina at Chapel Hill* (Chapel Hill: University of North Carolina Press, 1992), 307; Joseph Califano Jr., "The HEW-UNC Struggle," *Charlotte Observer,* June 21, 1981, B1, NewsBank: Access World News—Historical and Current, https://infoweb-NewsBank-com.eu1.proxy.openathens.net/apps/news/document-view?p=WORLDNEWS&docref=image/v2:11260DC9BB798E30@WHNPX-15FAAD8F37A67A21@2444777-15E3478435434D1E@29-15E3478435434D1E@, accessed January 15, 2020; Katherine White, "Judge Oks UNC Plan to Integrate," *The Charlotte Observer,* July 18, 1981, B1, NewsBank: Access World News—Historical and Current, https://infoweb-NewsBank-com.eu1.proxy.openathens.net/apps/news/document-view?p=WORLDNEWS&docref=image/v2:11260DC9BB798E30@WHNPX-15FAAD93F8BE655A@2444804-15E3479366EA6B0A@62-15E3479366EA6B0A@, accessed January 15, 2020; Herman Thomas, interview by Sonya Ramsey, July 7, 2011, Charlotte, NC, recording in author's possession; Clifford P. Harbour, "Dominant and Shadow Narratives Regarding the Desegregation of North Carolina Public Higher Education," *Community College Review* 48, 2 (April 2020): 156–172, DOI: 10.1177/0091552119893768, JSTOR Database, accessed June 22, 2021.

38. Dan Morrill, interview by Sonya Ramsey, August 6, 2013, Charlotte, NC, recording in author's possession; Frank Parker, interview by Sonya Ramsey, July 6, 2018, Charlotte, NC, recording in author's possession.

39. Humphrey S. Cummings and Victor Pollack, "Report of Black Studies Subcommittee on Faculty and Staff Recruitment," April 20, 1972, Committees—Black Studies, 1969–1971, Student Affairs Vice Chancellor (Bonnie Cone) Records, University Archives, Box 5, Folder, 148, J. Murrey Atkins Library Special Collections and University Archives, The University of North Carolina at Charlotte, Charlotte, NC; Humphrey S. Cummings, interview by Sonya Ramsey, September 19, 2017, Charlotte, NC, phone recording in author's possession; For more information about the history of African American women in higher education, see Linda Perkins, "'Bound to Them by a Common Sorrow': African American Women, Higher Education, and Collective Advancement," *The Journal of African American History* 100, no. 4, African American Education, Civil Rights, and Black Power (Fall

2015): 721–747, https://www.jstor.org/stable/10.5323/jafriamerhist.100.4.072, accessed June 22, 2021.

40. For more information about the intellectual history of Black Studies, see Shirley Moody-Turner and James Stewart, "Gendering Africana Studies: Insights from Anna Julia Cooper," *African American Review* 43, no. 1 (2009): 35–44, http://www.jstor.org/stable/27802557, accessed June 22, 2021; James B. Stewart, "Black/Africana Studies, Then and Now: Reconstructing a Century of Intellectual Inquiry And Political Engagement, 1915–2015," *The Journal of African American History* 100, no. 1 (Winter 2015): 87–118, https://www.jstor.org/stable/10.5323/jafriamerhist.100.1.0087, accessed January 15, 2020.

41. For more information about southern student movements, see, Jeffrey A. Turner, *Sitting in and Speaking Out: Student Movements in the American South, 1960–1970* (Athens: University of Georgia Press, 2010).

42. Constance L. Hays, "How an Era Empowered Students," *The New York Times,* January 8, 1989, A4, New York Times Digital Article, https://www.nytimes.com/1989/01/08/education/how-an-era-empowered-students.html, accessed November 9, 2020; James Turner, interview by Sonya Ramsey, February 26, 2012, Charlotte, NC, phone recording in author's possession.

43. Hays, "How an Era Empowered Students," *The New York Times,* January 8, 1989, A4; Turner, interview by Sonya Ramsey, February 26, 2012. For more discussion of the rise of the Black student movement at historically Black colleges and universities, see Jelani M. Favors, *Shelter in a Time of Storm: How Black Colleges Fostered Generations of Leadership and Activism* (Chapel Hill: University of North Carolina Press, 2019); Joy Ann Williamson, *Radicalizing the Ebony Tower: Black Colleges and the Black Freedom Struggle in Mississippi* (New York: Teachers College Press, 2008).

44. Stefan M. Bradley, *Harlem vs. Columbia University: Black Student Power in the Late 1960s* (Urbana and Chicago: University of Illinois Press, 2009), 13, 111, 112.

45. Noliwe M. Rooks, *White Money/Black Power: The Surprising History of African American Studies and the Crisis of Race in Higher Education* (Boston MA: Beacon Press, 2006), 20.

46. Ibram X. Kendi, *The Black Campus Movement: Black Students and the Racial Reconstruction of Higher Education, 1965–1972* (New York: Palgrave Macmillan Press, 2012), 3.

47. Kendi, *The Black Campus Movement: Black Students and the Racial Reconstruction of Higher Education, 1965–1972,* 3.

48. Philip T. K. Daniel and Asmasu Zike, "Black Studies Four-Year College and University Survey," (Sample Survey Results, Center for Minority Studies, Northern Illinois University, May 1983) cited in Carlos A. Brossard, "Classifying Black Studies Programs," *The Journal of Negro Education* 53, no. 3 (Summer 1984): 280.

49. Peniel Joseph, "Black Studies, Student Activism, and the Black Power Movement," *The Black Power Movement, Rethinking the Civil Rights Black Power Era,* Peniel Joseph ed. (New York: Routledge Press, 2006), 252.

50. For more discussion of the Black Student and Anti-War Movements in the South, see Joy Ann Williamson-Lott, *Jim Crow Campus: Higher Education and the Struggle for a New Southern Social Order* (New York, NY: Teachers College Press, 2018).

51. Benjamin Chavis Jr., interview by Bridgette Sanders and Lois Stickel, February 7, 2005, Charlotte, NC, recording in the Oral History, UNC Charlotte Civil Rights Series, J Murrey Atkins Library, University of North Carolina at Charlotte, Charlotte, NC.

52. T. J. (Thomas James) Reddy, interview by Sonya Ramsey, June 22, 2018, Charlotte, NC, recording in author's possession.

53. Kendi, *The Black Campus Movement: Black Students and the Racial Reconstruction of Higher Education*, 68.

54. Humphrey Cummings, interview by Bridgette Sanders and Lois Stickel, December 14, 2004, Charlotte, NC, in the New South Voices Oral History Civil Rights Series, J Murrey Atkins Library, University of North Carolina at Charlotte, Charlotte, NC.

55. Humphrey Cummings, interview by Sonya Ramsey, September 19, 2017, Charlotte, NC, recording in author's possession; David Sanders, interview by Sonya Ramsey, June 27, 2018, Charlotte, NC, recording in author's possession.

56. Ray Holton, "Students Take Over Fayetteville College," *Charlotte Observer,* April 5, 1968, 17A, NewsBank: Access World News—Historical and Current, https://infoweb-NewsBank-com.eu1.proxy.openathens.net/apps/news/document-view?p=WORLDNEWS&docref=image/v2:11260DC9BB798E30@WHNPX-15E2500A4F4AFF47@2439952-15E24C3B4C3989F6@16-15E24C3B4C3989F6@, accessed January 15, 2020; "The Black Student Movement's 23 Demands: December 1968," The Carolina Story: A Virtual Museum of University History, University of North Carolina Chapel Hill, https://museum.unc.edu/items/show/1803, accessed May 29, 2018; Gale Jensen and Anne Newman, "Black Thursday at Duke, 1969: Students Seize Allen Building," *The Chronicle: Duke University* 71, no. 7 (September 8, 1975), 1, in Black History at Duke Reference Collection, Duke University Archives, Black Studies Program Clippings 1969–1983, Box 1, Folder 10, David M. Rubenstein Rare Book and Manuscript Library, Duke University, Durham, NC.

57. Kimberley Stahler, "Three Dead in South Carolina: Student Radicalization and the Forgotten Orangeburg Massacre," MA Thesis, History, Kent State University (ProQuest Dissertations Publishing, 2018), ProQuest Dissertations and Theses Global Database, https://uncc.primo.exlibrisgroup.com/permalink/01UNCC_INST/1rqb8fi/cdi_proquest_journals_2056876412, accessed October 20, 2020.

58. Jennifer Howe, "Paul Hemphill, '72: Reflections from the First President of the Black Student Union," *Alumni News,* UNC Charlotte, February 23, 2021, digital article, https://49eralumni.uncc.edu/s/1721/m19/interior.aspx?sid=1721&gid=2&pgid=3526&cid=7630&ecid=7630&crid=0&calpgid=2094&calcid=5617, accessed May 10, 2021; Paul E. Hemphill, interview by Alyson Finch Wilson, January 7, 2021, video file, located in Charlotte, J. Murrey Atkins Library, Special Collections and University Archives, UNC Charlotte, Charlotte, NC; "Statement from the Black Student Union," in William King, "The Early Years of Three Major Professional Black Studies Organizations," *Out of the Revolution: The Development of Africana Programs,* Delores Aldridge and Carlene Young, eds. (Lanham, MD: Lexington Books, 2000), 126.

59. "BSU Celebrates 14th Anniversary," in *Black Perspective, The Struggle Continues, II,* Newspaper, no II (February 28, 1983): 3, Departments—Afro-American and African Studies, 1977–1980, College of Humanities records, Box 1, Folder 4, J. Murrey Atkins Library, University of North Carolina at Charlotte, Charlotte, NC; For a visual image of the student protesters and more information about Black student activism at UNC Charlotte, see this link, https://inside.uncc.edu/news-features/2021-02-23/uplifting-uniting-and-empowering-black-community-unc-charlotte-origins-and, accessed July 16, 2021.

60. "BSU Celebrates 14th Anniversary," in *Black Perspective, The Struggle Continues, II, Newspaper,* no II (February 28, 1983): 3.

61. Jennifer Howe, "Paul Hemphill, '72: Reflections from the First President of the Black Student Union," *Alumni News,* UNC Charlotte, February 23, 2021; T. J. Reddy, interview by Sonya Ramsey, June 22, 2008.

62. Benjamin Chavis Jr., interview by Bridgette Sanders and Lois Stickel, February 7, 2005; Ronald Caldwell, interview by Lois Stickel and Bridgette Sanders, May 31, 2005, Charlotte, NC, recording in New South Voices Oral History Civil Rights Series, J Murrey Atkins Library, University of North Carolina at Charlotte, Charlotte, NC; Thomas Jeffers, *Jewel in the Crown: Bonnie Cone and the Founding of UNC Charlotte,* 43.

63. Benjamin Chavis Jr., interview by Bridgette Sanders and Lois Stickel, February 7, 2005.

64. T. J. Reddy, interview by Sonya Ramsey, June 22, 2008.

65. Maxwell, "Black Studies: Paradox with a Promise?," 16.

66. Nick Aaron Ford, *Black Studies: Threat or Challenge* (Port Washington, NY: National University Publications Kennikat Press, 1973), 4.

67. Ford, Black Studies: Threat or Challenge, 43.

68. Ford, Black Studies: Threat or Challenge, 43.

69. David Sanders, interview by Sonya Ramsey, June 27, 2018, Charlotte, NC, recording in author's possession, Charlotte, NC

70. Ann C. Carver, interview by Sonya Ramsey, October 18, 2015, Charlotte, NC, recording in author's possession.

71. "James Farmer to Speak March 5," *The Carolina Journal,* February 19, 1969: 1; "If We Are Not for Ourselves, Who Will Be For Us? James Farmer Stresses Black Identity in Talk at UNC-C," *The Carolina Journal,* March 12, 1969: 19, Special Collections and University Archives, J. Murrey Atkins Library, University of North Carolina at Charlotte, Charlotte, NC.

72. Jennifer Howe, "Paul Hemphill, '72: Reflections from the First President of the Black Student Union, *"Alumni News,* UNC Charlotte, February 23, 2021, digital article, https://49eralumni.uncc.edu/s/1721/m19/interior.aspx?sid=1721&gid=2&pgid=3526&cid=7630&ecid=7630&crid=0&calpgid=2094&calcid=5617, accessed May 10, 2021. Paul E. Hemphill, interview by Alyson Finch Wilson, January 7, 2021, video file, located in Charlotte, Special Collections, J. Murrey Atkins Library, Charlotte, NC.

73. Bertha Maxwell-Roddey, interview by Sonya Ramsey, July 5, 2010, Charlotte, NC, recording in author's possession.

74. Ann Carver, "Letter to W. Hugh McEniry," April 8, 1971, document, Committees—Black Studies, 1969–1971, Student Affairs Vice Chancellor (Bonnie Cone) Records, University Archives, Box 5, Folder 148, J. Murrey Atkins Library Special Collections and University Archives, UNC Charlotte, Charlotte, NC.

75. Benjamin Chavis Jr., interview by Bridgette Sanders and Lois Stickel, February 7, 2005.

76. Maxwell-Roddey, interview by Sonya Ramsey, July 5, 2010.

77. Ford, *Black Studies: Threat or Challenge,* 182.

78. Maxwell-Roddey quoted in Deborah F. Atwater and La Verne Gyant, in "A Woman of Vision; Dr. Bertha Maxwell Roddy [sic]," *International Journal of Africana Studies: The Journal of the National Council for Black Studies* I no. 10 (Spring 2004): 121; T. J. Reddy, interview by Sonya Ramsey, June 22, 2018.

79. David Sanders, interview by Sonya Ramsey, June 27, 2018; Bertha Maxwell-Roddey, interview by Sonya Ramsey, July 9, 2013, Charlotte, NC, recording in author's possession.

80. Frank Parker, interview by author, July 6, 2018; Maxwell, dissertation, 31; Bertha Maxwell-Roddey, interview by Sonya Ramsey, March 6, 2012, Charlotte, NC, recording in author's possession.

81. For more information about the impact of the Institute of the Black World on Black Studies, see Derrick E. White, "An Independent Approach to Black Studies: The Institute of the Black World (IBW) and Its Evaluation and Support of Black Studies," *Journal of African American Studies* 16, no. 1 (2012): 70–88, www.jstor.org/stable/43525475, accessed June 22, 2020.

82. Bertha Maxwell-Roddey, interview by Sonya Ramsey, April 29, 2015, Charlotte, NC, recording in author's possession.

83. Bertha Luvenia Lyons Maxwell Roddey, interview by Willie Griffin, May 18, 2008. U-4209, in the Southern Oral History Program Collection, Series U: The Long Civil Rights Movement: The South Since 1960s, Southern Historical Collection, Wilson Library, University of North Carolina at Chapel Hill. (Correct spelling of Maxwell-Roddey will be used in subsequent citations).

84. Perry Hall, *In the Vineyard: Working in African American Studies* (Knoxville: University of Tennessee Press, 1999), 34.

85. Maxwell, "Black Studies: Paradox with a Promise?" 20.

86. Amanda Chan, "Jim Polk," *Charlotte Observer,* July 30, 2010, NewsBank: Access World News—Historical and Current, https://infoweb-NewsBank-com.eu1.proxy.openathens.net/apps/news/document-view?p=WORLDNEWS&docref=news/1314C2DAE4480278, accessed January 15, 2020; Ann Doss, "James Ross," *Charlotte Observer,* July 10, 2012, NewsBank Database, https://infoweb.NewsBank.com/apps/news/document-view?p=WORLDNEWS&docref=news/13FF89A6C8EEAEA0, accessed January 15, 2020; David Sanders, interview by Sonya Ramsey, June 27, 2018.

87. T. J. Reddy, interview by Sonya Ramsey, June 22, 2018.

88. Rhett Jones, "From Ideology to Institution: The Evolution of Africana Studies," in Johnella E. Butler, ed., *Colorline to Borderlands: The Matrix of American Ethnic Studies* (Seattle: University of Washington Press, 2001), 126.

89. Mary Turner Harper, "Beyond Act I: A Transdisciplinary and Experiential Approach to Afro-American Literature and Culture," (Dissertation, English, Union Graduate School for Experimenting Colleges and Universities, Yellow Springs, Ohio, 1975): 76–106, https://librarylink.uncc.edu/login?url=https://search-proquest-com.librarylink.uncc.edu/docview/302808053?accountid=14605, accessed October 21, 2020.

90. University of North Carolina at Charlotte Black Studies Program, "Appendix: Freshman Program in Black Studies, University of North Carolina at Charlotte, 16, in Black Studies Program, 1969–1974," Document, Student Affairs Vice Chancellor (Bonnie Cone) Records, University Archives, Box 3, Folder 83, J. Murrey Atkins Library Special Collections and University Archives, UNC Charlotte; Bertha Maxwell, interview by Sonya Ramsey, January 7, 2017, Charlotte, NC, recording in author's possession.

91. Larry Neal, "The Black Arts Movement," *The Drama Review* 12, no. 4 (1968): 28–39. JSTOR, doi:10.2307/1144377, accessed June 10, 2020. For more information about the concept of the Black aesthetic, see Gayle Addison, *The Black Aesthetic,* 1st ed. (Garden City, N.Y:

Doubleday, 1971; Maxwell-Roddey, interview by Sonya Ramsey, May 16, 2016. For more information about one of the key figures of the Black Arts Movement, see Jonathan Fenderson, *Building the Black Arts Movement: Hoyt Fuller and the Cultural Politics of the 1960s* (Champaign Urbana: University of Illinois Press, 2019).

92. Neal, "The Black Arts Movement," *The Drama Review* 12, no. 4 (1968): 28–39; Ann C. Carver, interview by Sonya Ramsey, October 18, 2015; Humphrey Cummings, interview by Sonya Ramsey, September 19, 2017.

93. Ann C. Carver, interview by Sonya Ramsey, October 18, 2015, Charlotte, NC, phone recording in author's possession.

94. Bertha Maxwell-Roddey, interview by Sonya Ramsey, July 18, 2018, Charlotte, NC, recording in author's possession.

95. Dorothy Dae, interview by Bridgette Sanders and Lois Stickel, October 11, 2004, Charlotte, NC, New South Voices Oral History Civil Rights Series, J Murrey Atkins Library, University of North Carolina at Charlotte.

96. Maxwell-Roddey, interview by Sonya Ramsey, January 7, 2017; Bertha Maxwell, "The Black Action Design Program Study," document in Black Studies Program, 1969–1974. Student Affairs Vice Chancellor (Bonnie Cone) Records, Box 3, Folder 83, Special Collections and University Archives, J. Murrey Atkins Library, UNC Charlotte, Charlotte, North Carolina.

97. Carole Moore, "Queens Series: The Future and Black Women," *Charlotte News*, October 19, 1971, 7, NewsBank: Access World News—Historical and Current, https://infoweb-NewsBank-com.eu1.proxy.openathens.net/apps/news/document-view?p=WORLDNEWS&docref=image/v2:1126167831380960@WHNPX-16F6854E1C139141@2441244-16F6011C95C3B5AC@6, accessed January 14, 2020.

98. Maxwell, *Black Studies: Paradox with a Promise?* 47; Bertha Maxwell-Roddey, interview by Sonya Ramsey, May 16, 2018, Charlotte, NC, recording in author's possession.

99. William E. Cross Jr., *Shades of Blackness: Diversity in African American Identity* (Philadelphia, PA: Temple University Press, 1991), 174; Kristine S. Lewis, and Stephanie C. McKissic, "Drawing Sustenance at the Source: African American Students' Participation in the Black Campus Community as an Act of Resistance," *Journal of Black Studies* 41, no. 2 (2010): 264–80, accessed May 10, 2021. http://www.jstor.org/stable/25780776; Hall, *In the Vineyard: Working in African American Studies* 123; Maxwell-Roddey, interview by Sonya Ramsey, January 7, 2017.

100. Ann C. Carver, "Letter to US Senator Ted Kennedy of Massachusetts," December 5, 1969, Black Studies Program, 1969–1974, Box 3, Folder 83, Student Affairs Vice Chancellor (Bonnie Cone) Records, University Archives, J. Murrey Atkins Library Special Collections and University Archives, UNC Charlotte, Charlotte, NC.

101. University of North Carolina at Charlotte, *Rouge and Rascals, UNC Charlotte Yearbook*, 1974 and the *University of North Carolina at Charlotte Course Catalog, 1975* in Digital Collections, J. Murrey Atkins Library Special Collections and University Archives, UNC Charlotte and Digital NC, https://library.digitalnc.org/cdm/ref/collection/yearbooks/id/742, accessed January 15, 2020; Bertha Maxwell-Roddey interview by Sonya Ramsey, January 7, 2017.

102. Roberta Duff, interview by Sonya Ramsey, September 20, 2017.

103. Roberta Duff, interview by Sonya Ramsey, September 20, 2017; Maxwell-Roddey, interview by Sonya Ramsey, March 7, 2012.

104. James B. Stewart, "Bridging Time, Space, and Technology: Challenges Confronting Black Cultural Centers in the 21st Century," in Haki R. Madubuti and Fred Hord, *Black Cultural Centers: Politics of Survival and Identity* (Chicago: Third World Press, Association of Black Culture Centers, 2005), 76.

105. Herman Thomas, interview by Sonya Ramsey, July 27, 2017, Charlotte, NC, phone recording in author's possession.

106. Roberta Duff, interview by Sonya Ramsey, September 20, 2017, Gastonia, NC, recording in author's possession; Bertha Maxwell-Roddey, interview by Sonya Ramsey, April 6, 2017.

107. Bertha Maxwell-Roddey, interview by Sonya Ramsey, April 6, 2017, Charlotte, NC, recording in author's possession. Martha Biondi, *The Black Revolution on Campus* (Berkley: University of California Press, 2012), 187–189.

108. Edwin Cody, "Grant Gives UNC-C Black Professorship," *Charlotte Observer,* July 26, 1969, Document, "UNCC Gifts, 1967–1978, 1990," in Dean W. Colvard papers, Box 8, Manuscript Collections, J. Murrey Atkins Library Special Collections and University Archive, UNC Charlotte.

109. Bertha Maxwell-Roddey, interview by Sonya Ramsey, July 18, 2018, Charlotte, NC, recording author's possession.

110. Sheryl Westmoreland Smith, interview by Sonya Ramsey, March 8, 2016, recording in author's possession.

111. David Sanders, interview by Sonya Ramsey, June 27, 2018, Charlotte, NC, recording in author's possession, Charlotte, NC; Bertha Maxwell-Roddey, interview by Sonya Ramsey, July 9, 2013, Charlotte, NC, recording in author's possession; Beverly Ford, conversation with Sonya Ramsey, December 9, 2021, Charlotte NC, notes in author's possession.

112. Winnie McNeely Bennett, conversation with Sonya Ramsey, August 17, 2019, Charlotte NC. notes in author's possession. Brenda Stedman, conversation with Sonya Ramsey, August 17, 2019, Charlotte, NC, notes in author's possession.

113. Pat Borden, "Black Studies: UNCC Has a Fresh Approach," *Charlotte Observer,* September 22, 1974, E1, NewsBank: Access World News—Historical and Current, https://infoweb-NewsBank-com.eu1.proxy.openathens.net/apps/news/document-view?p=WORLDNEWS&docref=image/v2:11260DC9BB798E30@WHNPX-15FAAD55B4C2C7A2@2442313-16067768829FEA94@88-16067768829FEA94@, accessed January 15, 2020; *Black Studies: The Invisible Man Confronts the American Dream, A Documentary on the Black Studies Program at UNCC,* Transcript, Black Studies Program, 1969–1974, Student Affairs Vice Chancellor (Bonnie Cone) Records, Box 3, Folder 83, University Archives, J. Murrey Atkins Library Special Collections and University Archives, UNC Charlotte; Terry Smith, interview by Sonya Ramsey, May 12, 2018, Charlotte, NC, phone recording in author's possession.

114. Bertha Maxwell-Roddey, interview by Sonya Ramsey, April 6, 2017, Charlotte, NC, recording in author's possession; Elaine Nichols, interview by Sonya Ramsey, August 15, 2017, phone recording in author's possession.

115. Borden, "Black Studies: UNCC Has a Fresh Approach," *Charlotte Observer,* 3E.

116. L. Diane Bennett, PhD, interview by Sonya Ramsey, May 17, 2017, Charlotte, NC, digital phone recording in author's possession.

117. Sheryl Westmoreland Smith, interview by Sonya Ramsey, March 8, 2016.

118. Phaedra Berry-Holley, conversation with Sonya Ramsey, August 17, 2019; written notes in author's possession.

119. L. Dianne Bennett, interview by Sonya Ramsey, April 27, 2017.

120. L. Dianne Bennett, interview by Sonya Ramsey, April 27, 2017

121. Tondra L. Loder-Jackson, *Schoolhouse Activists: African American Educators and the Long Birmingham Civil Rights Movement* (Albany, NY: State University of New York Press, 2016), 8.

122. Kenneth Robert Janken, *The Wilmington 10: Violence, Injustice, and the Rise of Black Politics in the 1970s* (Chapel Hill, N.C.: University of North Carolina Press, 2015).

123. Phaedra Berry-Holley, conversation with Sonya Ramsey, August 17, 2019; written notes in author's possession; Westmoreland Smith, interview by Sonya Ramsey, March 8, 2016.

124. Janken, *The Wilmington 10: Violence, Injustice, and the Rise of Black Politics in the 1970s*, 1.

125. James Cuthbertson, "Convicts Find Freedom in Studies," *Charlotte News,* September 25, 1974, 12, NewsBank: Access World News—Historical and Current, https://infoweb-NewsBank-com.eu1.proxy.openathens.net/apps/news/document-view?p=WORLDNEWS&docref=image/v2%3A1126167831380960, accessed May 27, 2020; For more information about the Attica prison uprising, see Heather Thompson, *Blood in the Water: The Attica Prison Uprising of 1971 and Its Legacy* (New York: Pantheon, 2016).

126. Cuthbertson, "Convicts Find Freedom in Studies," *Charlotte News,* September 25, 1974, 12, Newspaper.com Database, https://www.newspapers.com/image/622659953, accessed December 22, 2021. Greg Davis, who is cited in this article is not the same person as UNC Charlotte faculty member, Gregory Davis.

127. Roberta Duff, interview by Sonya Ramsey, September 20, 2017.

128. Bertha Maxwell-Roddey, interview, July 18, 2018, Charlotte, NC, recording in author's possession.

129. Bertha Maxwell-Roddey, interview July 19, 2017, Charlotte, NC, recording in author's possession; Carver, interview by Sonya Ramsey, October 18, 2015; Roberta Duff, interview by Sonya Ramsey, September 20, 2017; Ann Carver, interview by Christina Wright, Charlotte, NC, February 22, 2018, J. Murrey Atkins Library Special Collections and University Archives, UNC Charlotte, Charlotte, NC.

130. Sheryl Westmoreland Smith, interview by Sonya Ramsey, March 8, 2016; "BSU Protests Sanskrit Article," *The Journal* ix, no. 23 (May 20,1974), in Black Studies Program, 1969–1974, Student Affairs Vice Chancellor (Bonnie Cone) Records, Box 3, folder 83, University Archives, J. Murrey Atkins Library Special Collections and University Archives, UNC Charlotte, Charlotte, NC.

131. Sheryl Westmoreland Smith, interview by Sonya Ramsey, March 8, 2016; Humphrey Cummings, interview by Sonya Ramsey, September 19, 2017; Maxwell-Roddey, interview of Robert Albright, by Konya Owens, Charlotte, NC, August 8, 1992, Levine Museum of the New South, Local History Series, in Special Collections, J. Murrey Atkins Library, University of North Carolina at Charlotte, Charlotte, NC

132. T. J. Reddy, interview by Sonya Ramsey, June 22, 2018, Charlotte, NC, recording in author's possession.

Chapter 4. Aluta Continua! The Struggle Continues! Looking Outward to Strengthen Within

1. Bertha Maxwell-Roddey interview by Sonya Ramsey, June 15, 2020, Charlotte, NC, recording in author's possession.

2. Beverly Ford, conversation with Sonya Ramsey, December 9, 2021, Charlotte, NC, notes in author's possession.

3. Ken Sanford, *Charlotte and UNC Charlotte Growing Up Together* (Charlotte: University of North Carolina at Charlotte Press, 1996), 99; Malcolm Scully, "$275,000 Gift Benefits UNC-C Negro Students," *Charlotte Observer,* May 21, 1967, A1, A3; Charles, Lockheart, and Eheller Law Firm, "Letter to Alice Tate," May 15, 1969, in Alice Lindsay Tate Papers, Box 6, Folder 3, J. Murrey Atkins Library Special Collections, University of North Carolina at Charlotte, Charlotte, NC; Bertha Maxwell-Roddey, interview by Sonya Ramsey, September 9, 2016, Charlotte, NC, recording in author's possession.

4. Alice Tate, "Letter to Bertha Maxwell," October 20, 1973, in the Alice Lindsay Tate Papers, Box 6, Folder 3. J. Murrey Atkins Library Special Collections, University of North Carolina at Charlotte; Bertha Maxwell-Roddey, interview by Sonya Ramsey, September 9, 2016.

5. Alice Tate, "Letter to Thomas Ashe Lockheart," November 30, 1968; Bertha Maxwell, "Letter to Alice Tate," September 16, 1972; Alice Tate, "Letter to Bertha Maxwell," July 28, 1976; located in the Alice Lindsay Tate Papers, J. Murrey Atkins Library Special Collections, University of North Carolina at Charlotte, Box 6, Folder 3; Maxwell-Roddey interview, September 9, 2016.

6. Bertha Maxwell-Roddey interview by Sonya Ramsey, September 9, 2016, Charlotte, NC, recording in author's possession; Martin Luther King Jr., "Letter to Alice Tate," July 5, 1966, in the Alice Lindsay Tate Papers, Box 6, Folder 3, J. Murrey Atkins Library Special Collections, University of North Carolina at Charlotte.

7. For more information on the funding for Black Studies programs, see Noliwe M. Rooks, *White Money Black Power: The Surprising History of African American Studies and the Crisis of Race in Higher Education* (Boston Mass: Beacon Press, 2006).

8. State Superintendent of Education, "Bertha Maxwell-Roddey, PhD" in *The 2019 South Carolina African American History Calendar,"* (Columbia, SC: South Carolina Department of Education, 2019); Jacquelyn Dowd Hall, "The Long Civil Rights Movement and the Political Uses of the Past," *Journal of American History* 91, no. 4 (March 2005): 1233–1263.

9. Charlotte League of Women Voters, "Historical Note," Document in Charlotte League of Women Voters Records, 1920–2004, Finding Guide, in Robinson-Spangler Carolina Room, Charlotte Mecklenburg Library, Charlotte, NC; Dorothy Osborne, "Women's Clubs Lower Color Bar Slowly," *Charlotte Observer,* December 29, 1968, 53, NewsBank: Access World News—Historical and Current, https://infoweb-NewsBank-com.eu1.proxy.openathens.net/apps/news/document-view?p=WORLDNEWS&docref=image/v2:11260DC9BB798E30@WHNPX-15E2502E1AC450CC@2440220-15E24EB43756441F@52, accessed January 14, 2020.

10. Membership Roster, Document in Charlotte League of Women Voters Records, 1920–2004, Box 1, Folder 2; Box 5, Folder 7, in Robinson-Spangler Carolina Room, Charlotte Mecklenburg Library, Charlotte, NC; Rodney Clare, "The Activist Non-Partisans: The North Carolina League of Women Voters, 1947–1979," (Dissertation, Duke University, 2001),

ProQuest Dissertations Publishing, 2001, http://search.proquest.com/docview/304692202/, accessed January 14, 2020.

11. Howard Maniloff, "Education Panel Gets Head," *Charlotte Observer,* March 26, 1972, 29, NewsBank: Access World News—Historical and Current, https://infoweb-NewsBank-com. eu1.proxy.openathens.net/apps/news/document-view?p=WORLDNEWS&docref=image/ v2:11260DC9BB798E30@WHNPX-15FAAD0CB1BC4FD5@2441403-15E33B-73FAFE44C2@28, accessed September 3, 2019; Emery Wister, "Schools Said Now Ready for Climate of Learning," *Charlotte Observer,* September 19, 1972, 20, NewsBank: Access World News—Historical and Current, https://infoweb-NewsBank-com.eu1.proxy.openathens.net/ apps/news/document-view?p=WORLDNEWS&docref=image/v2:1126167831380960@WH-NPX-16F621B2F76A60D0@2441580-16F47EAFA5E7EEE2@19, accessed January 14, 2020.

12. Wister, "Schools Said Now Ready for Climate of Learning," *Charlotte Observer,* September 19, 1972, 20.

13. Howard Maniloff, "Parent Conference A Success," *Charlotte Observer,* March 26, 1972, 29–30, NewsBank: Access World News—Historical and Current, https://infoweb-NewsBank-com. eu1.proxy.openathens.net/apps/news/document-view?p=WORLDNEWS&docref=image/ v2:11260DC9BB798E30@WHNPX-15FAAD0CB1BC4FD5@2441403-15E33B-73FAFE44C2@28, accessed January 14, 2020; Bob Bestler, "I Don't Talk Black On Commission Now," *Charlotte Observer,* September 9 and 21, 1970: 27, 29, NewsBank: Access World News—Historical and Current. https://infoweb-NewsBank-com.eu1. proxy.openathens.net/apps/news/document-view?p=WORLDNEWS&docref=image/ v2%3A11260DC9BB798E30%40WHNPX-15E25098E051A9F3%402440851-15E24EDE9D7D163F%4028-15E24EDE9D7D163F%40; Charlotte Mecklenburg Library Foundation Website, "Honoring Elizabeth Randolph," February 19, 2018, https://foundation. cmlibrary.org/news/honoring-elizabeth-s-randolph/ document, accessed June 22, 2021.

14. "Black Studies: Catalyst for Change, February 21–23, 1973," Document in *Black Studies Program, 1969–1974,* Student Affairs Vice Chancellor (Bonnie Cone) Records, Box 3, Folder 83, University Archives, J. Murrey Atkins Library Special Collections and University Archives, UNC Charlotte.

15. "Black Studies: Catalyst for Change, February 21–23, 1973," Document in *Black Studies Program, 1969–1974,* Student Affairs Vice Chancellor (Bonnie Cone) Records, Box 3, Folder 83, University Archives, J. Murrey Atkins Library Special Collections and University Archives, UNC Charlotte, Charlotte North Carolina.

16. Benjamin Chavis Jr., interview by Bridgette Sanders and Lois Stickel, February 7, 2005.

17. Bertha Maxwell, "Black Studies: Paradox with a Promise?" PhD Dissertation (Tampa, FL: Union Graduate School, Educational Administration, 1974), 40.

18. Borden, "Black Studies: UNCC Has a Fresh Approach;" Terry Smith, interview by Sonya Ramsey, May 12, 2018.

19. Bertha Maxwell-Roddey, interview by Sonya Ramsey, April 6, 2017, Charlotte, NC, recording in author's possession.

20. Bertha Maxwell-Roddey, interview by Sonya Ramsey, April 6, 2017.

21. Maxwell quoted in the "Black Studies: The Invisible Man Confronts the American Dream, A Documentary on the Black Studies Program at UNCC," Produced and Written by Carol Won Savage and John Steed, Special Consultant, Bertha Maxwell; Produced by WBTV-Charlotte, January 1974, in Black Studies Program, 1969–1974, Student Affairs Vice

Chancellor (Bonnie Cone) Records, Box 3, Folder 83, J. Murrey Atkins Library Special Collections and University Archives, UNC Charlotte, NC.

22. For more information on the history of SACS, see George Jackson Allen Jr., "A History of the Commission on Colleges of The Southern Association of Colleges and Schools, 1949–1975" (dissertation, Georgia State University, 1978), ProQuest Dissertations and Theses Global Database, https://librarylink.uncc.edu/login?url=https://search.proquest.com/docview/302877197?accountid=14605, accessed January 14, 2020.

23. Bertha Maxwell-Roddey, interview by Sonya Ramsey, July 9, 2013.

24. Bertha Maxwell-Roddey, interview by Sonya Ramsey, July 9, 2013.

25. Abdul Alkalimat, *The History of Black Studies* (London: Pluto Press, 2021), 272; Charles P. Henry, *Black Studies and the Democratization of Higher Education* (Cham, Switzerland: Palgrave Macmillan Publishers, 2017), 96; William King, "The Early Years of Three Major Professional Black Studies Organizations," in *Out of the Revolution: The Development of Africana Programs,* eds., Delores Aldridge and Carlene Young (Lanham, MD: Lexington Books, 2000), 128; Jonathan Fenderson, James B. Stewart, and Kabria Baumgartner, "Expanding the History of the Black Studies Movement: Some Prefatory Notes," *Journal of African American History* 16 (2012): 15, DOI 10.1007/s12111-011-9200-3, accessed January 14, 2020; Bertha Maxwell-Roddey, interview by Sonya Ramsey, March 7, 2012, Charlotte, NC, recording in author's possession.

26. Delores Aldridge and Carlene Young, eds., *Out of the Revolution: The Development of Africana Studies;* Claudrena N. Harold, "Of the Wings of Atalanta": The Struggle for African American Studies at the University of Virginia, 1969–1995," *Journal of African American Studies* 16, no.1 (2012): 41–69 JSTOR Database, http://www.jstor.org/stable/43525474, accessed January 14, 2020.

27. Milton Jordan, "Black Studies Here to Stay," *The Charlotte Observer,* March 21, 1975, B1, NewsBank: Access World News—Historical and Current, https://infoweb-NewsBank-com.eu1.proxy.openathens.net/apps/news/document-view?p=WORLDNEWS&docref=image/v2:11260DC9BB798E30@WHNPX-15FAAD57D3ECBCE9@2442493-1606776 36D245591@24-160677636D245591@, accessed January 15, 2020; Bertha Maxwell-Roddey, interview by Sonya Ramsey, July 18, 2018, Charlotte, NC, recording in author's possession; "North Carolina Conference on Black Studies," Flier, in *Black Studies Program, 1969–1974,* Student Affairs Vice Chancellor (Bonnie Cone) Records, Box 3, Folder 83, Special Collections and University Archives, J. Murrey Atkins Library, UNC Charlotte, Charlotte, NC.

28. Karanja Keita Carroll and senior editor Itibari M. Zulu, "Dr. William M. King, interviewed: National Council for Black Studies Founding Member," *The Journal of Pan African Studies* 3, no. 1 (September 2009): 24, Ebsco Database, http://search.ebscohost.com/login.aspx?direct=true&db=a9h&AN=44369513&authtype=shib&site=ehost-live&scope=site, accessed January 14, 2020.

29. Bertha Maxwell, "National Conference for Black Studies," Announcement, *Black World Magazine* (March 1975), 50 Negro Digest/Google Books Database, https://books.google.com/books?id=eLIDAAAAMBAJ&lpg=PA3&dq=march%201975&pg=PA14#v=onepage&q=Charlotte&f=false; "Flyer, North Carolina Conference on Black Studies," Flier, in Department of Africana Studies records (RG 80, RG 81, RG 24–09–01), College of Humanities Records, 1967–1980 in Special Collections, University of North Carolina at Charlotte,

Box 1, Charlotte, NC; Bertha Maxwell-Roddey, interview by Sonya Ramsey, April 6, 2017, Charlotte, NC, recording in author's possession.

30. Charles P. Henry, *Black Studies and the Democratization of Higher Education* (Cham, Switzerland: Palgrave Macmillian Publishers, 2017), 96; William King, "The Early Years of Three Major Professional Black Studies Organizations, in *Out of the Revolution: The Development of Africana Programs,* eds., Delores Aldridge and Carlene Young (Lanham, MD: Lexington Books, 2000), 128.

31. Bertha Maxwell-Roddey, interview by Sonya Ramsey, April 6, 2017, Charlotte, NC, recording in author's possession.

32. William Harris, interview by Sonya Ramsey, September 11, 2017, Charlotte, NC, recording in author's possession.

33. James Turner, interview by Sonya Ramsey, February 26, 2012, phone recording in author's possession.

34. James B. Stewart, interview by Sonya Ramsey, February 22, 2017, phone recording in author's possession.

35. Bertha Maxwell-Roddey, interview by Sonya Ramsey, April 6, 2017; Bertha Luvenia Lyons Maxwell Roddey, interview by Willie Griffin, May 19, 2008. U-4209, in the Southern Oral History Program Collection, Series U: The Long Civil Rights Movement: The South Since 1960s, Southern Historical Collection, Wilson Library, University of North Carolina at Chapel Hill. (Correct spelling of Maxwell-Roddey will be used in subsequent citations).

36. James B. Stewart, "Black/Africana Studies, Then and Now: Reconstructing a Century of Intellectual Inquiry and Political Engagement, 1915–2015," *The Journal of African American History* 100, no. 1 "Centennial Perspectives, 1915–2015" (Winter 2015): 103, DOI: 10.5323/jafriamerhist.100.1.0087, accessed January 14, 2020.

37. Joseph Russell, "Strides Toward Organization," 18, Document, *Constitution of the National Council for Black Studies, July-7-9 1976,* 1, in Box 1, in National Council for Black Studies records, Schomburg Center for Research in Black Culture, The New York Public Library, New York, NY.

38. Russell, "Strides Toward Organization," 97.

39. Stewart, "Black/Africana Studies Then and Now," 103; Moses Massenburg, "Documenting the Contributions Made by Black Women to Carter G. Woodson's Early Black History Movement: Mary McLeod Bethune and Zora Neale Hurston," *Black History Bulletin* 81, no. 1 (2018): 28–32, https://doi.org/10.5323/blachistbull.81.1.0028, accessed December 22, 2021.

40. Maxwell, Dissertation, 47; Bertha Maxwell-Roddey, interview by Sonya Ramsey, May 16, 2018, Charlotte, NC, recording author's possession.

41. "3 Students Will Study in Africa," *Charlotte Observer,* June 22, 1976, 7B, NewsBank: Access World News—Historical and Current, https://infoweb-NewsBank-com.eu1.proxy.openathens.net/apps/news/document-view?p=WORLDNEWS&docref=image/v2%3A11260DC9BB798E30%40WHNPX-15FAAD5C779AACDE%402442952-16067780E6F09D44%4022-16067780E6F09D44%40, accessed May 25, 2020.

42. University of North Carolina Charlotte, University of North Carolina at Charlotte Undergraduate Catalogs, 1975–1979: 45, Digital NC Database, https://lib.digitalnc.org/record/33562?ln=en#?c=0&m=0&s=0&cv=0&r=0&xywh=-1556%2C-138%2C4534%2C2755, accessed September 19, 2020.

43. Beverly Ford, "Letter to Dean W. Colvard," March 23, 1976, in Departments—Afro-

American and African Studies, 1977–1980, College of Humanities records, University Archives, J. Murrey Atkins Library Special Collections and University Archives, UNC Charlotte.

44. Bertha Maxwell-Roddey, interview by Sonya Ramsey, January 7, 2017, Charlotte, NC, recording in author's possession; John W. Blassingame, "Black Studies: An Intellectual Crisis," *The American Scholar* 38, No. 4 (Autumn, 1969): 54, JSTOR Database, https://www.jstor.org/stable/41209695, accessed May 20, 2021.

45. Timothy Stanton, Dwight E. Giles Jr., and Nadine I. Cruz, *Service-Learning: A Movement's Pioneers Reflect on Its Origins, Practice, and Future* (New York: Josey Bass Publishers, 1999), 2, 250.

46. For more about the changes in Black Studies, see Stewart, "Black Studies: Then and Now."

47. For more discussion about the role of service-learning in Africana Studies see, Ibram X. Kendi, "Required Service-Learning Courses: A Disciplinary Necessity to Preserve the Decaying Social Mission of Black Studies," *Journal of Black Studies* 40, no. 6 (July 2010): 1119–1135, http://www.jstor.org/stable/25704079, accessed January 14, 2020; Bertha Maxwell-Roddey, interview by Sonya Ramsey, April 21, 2016, Charlotte, NC, recording in author's possession.

48. Maxwell-Roddey interview by Sonya Ramsey, April 21, 2016; Maxwell-Roddey interview by Sonya Ramsey, January 7, 2017.

49. Roberta Duff, interview by Sonya Ramsey, September 20, 2017, Charlotte, NC, recording in author's possession; Elaine Nichols, interview by Sonya Ramsey, August 15, 2017, Charlotte, NC, recording in author's possession; Sheryl Westmoreland Smith, interview by Sonya Ramsey, March 8, 2016, Charlotte, NC, recording in author's possession.

50. Maxwell-Roddey, interview by Sonya Ramsey, January 7, 2017.

51. Bertha Maxwell-Roddey, interview by Sonya Ramsey, May 17, 2017, Charlotte, NC, recording in author's possession; Vanessa Gallman, "Double Jeopardy: Black and Female: UNCC Course to Profile Outstanding Black Women," *Charlotte Observer,* September 29, 1976, 8, NewsBank: Access World News—Historical and Current, https://infoweb-NewsBank-com.eu1.proxy.openathens.net/apps/news/document-view?p=WORLDNEWS&docref=image/v2:11260DC9BB798E30@WHNPX-15FAAD60C40741B3@2443051-1606779168686E6C@7-1606779168686E6C@, accessed January 14, 2020; Vernetta Conley Foxx, conversation with Sonya Ramsey, August 18, 2019, notes in author's possession. For more discussion of Black Women's Studies see, Beverly Guy-Sheftall, "Black Women's Studies: The Interface of Women's Studies and Black Studies," *Phylon (1960-)* 49, no. 1/2 (1992): 33–41, doi:10.2307/3132615, accessed May 10, 2021.

52. Maxwell-Roddey, interview by Sonya Ramsey, April 6, 2017.

53. Ann C. Carver, interview by Sonya Ramsey, October 18, 2015.

54. Deborah Stanley, "It's Good to be Back," *Charlotte Post,* October 19, 1978, DigitalNC.org Database, North Carolina Newspapers, North Carolina Digital Heritage Center, https://newspapers.digitalnc.org/lccn/sn88063138/1978-10-19/ed-1/seq-3/, accessed December 22, 2021; Mary Maxwell, interview by Sonya Ramsey, July 10, 2018, Charlotte, NC, recording in author's possession.

55. For more information about Parker and the Management by Objectives (MBO) process, see Peter Drucker, *Peter Drucker on the Profession of Management* (Boston, Mass: Har-

vard Business School Press, 1998). Carolyn Mason, interview by Sonya Ramsey, June 10, 2018, Charlotte, NC, phone recording in author's possession.

56. Office of Alumni Affairs, Johnson C. Smith University, "Dr. Bertha Maxwell-Roddey Appointed Vice President of Administrative Affairs," *Johnson C. Smith University Newsletter* (Winter 1977), 3 in University Publications, Series 1, Box 8, Folder 3, Inez Moore Parker Archives, James B. Duke Memorial Library, Johnson C. Smith University, Charlotte, NC Digital Smith Website, https://cdm16324.contentdm.oclc.org/digital/collection/p15170coll7/id/83/rec/67; Bertha Maxwell-Roddey, interview, May 26, 2017, Charlotte, NC, recording in author's possession; "Bertha Maxwell Leaves University," *UNCC* (Winter, 1977), no page number, in Departments—Afro-American and African Studies, 1977–1980. College of Humanities records, Box 1, Folder 4, University Archives, J. Murrey Atkins Library Special Collections and University Archives, UNC Charlotte; "UNCC's Maxwell Takes Job as VP at JCSU," *Charlotte Observer*, December 7, 1976, 23, NewsBank: Access World News—Historical and Current, https://infoweb-NewsBank-com.eu1.proxy.openathens.net/apps/news/document-view?p=WORLDNEWS&docref=image/v2:1126oDC9BB798E30@WH-NPX-15FAAD61D02E9ED2@2443120-1605D720320BFEF8@22-1605D720320BFEF8@, accessed January 15, 2020; Milton Jordan, "Charting the Future, Johnson C. Smith University Gets Civic Leaders to Help Plan Growth," *Charlotte Observer*, March 30, 1977, 42, News-Bank: Access World News—Historical and Current, https://infoweb-NewsBank-com.eu1.proxy.openathens.net/apps/news/document-view?p=WORLDNEWS&docref=image/v2:1126oDC9BB798E30@WHNPX-15FAAD64521182E6@2443233-1606777E5C13F2B2@41-1606777E5C13F2B2@, accessed January 15, 2020; "Dr. Bertha Maxwell Speaks to Long Range Planning," *The Johnson C. Smith Newsletter* (Winter 1977) (Charlotte, NC: Johnson C. Smith University, Office of Public Affairs, 1977), 5, in JCSU Publications, Inez Moore Parker Archives, Johnson C. Smith University, Digital Smith Database, https://cdm16324.contentdm.oclc.org/digital/collection/p15170coll7/search/searchterm/Bertha%20Maxwell/field/all/mode/all/conn/and, accessed January 14, 2020.

57. Maxwell-Roddey, interview by Sonya Ramsey, June 2, 2017, Charlotte, NC, recording in author's possession.

58. Maxwell-Roddey, interview by Sonya Ramsey, June 2, 2017, Charlotte, NC; Beverly Ford, conversation with Sonya Ramsey, December 9, 2021, Charlotte NC, notes in author's possession.

59. Bertha Maxwell-Roddey, interview by Sonya Ramsey, June 26, 2017. Mary Maxwell, interview by Sonya Ramsey, July 10, 2018; Loretta Manago Stanley, "Dr. Maxwell Is an Inspiration to Young Blacks," *Charlotte Post,* September 20, 1984, 2B, http://newspapers.digitalnc.org/lccn/sn88063138/1984–09–20/ed-1/seq-22/print/image_681x814_from_0,0_to_3396,4063/, accessed May 25, 2020. For more sources describing the role of gender on Black college campuses see Marybeth Gasman, "Swept under the Rug? A Historiography of Gender and Black Colleges," *American Educational Research Journal* 44, no. 4 (2007): 760–805, http://www.jstor.org/stable/30069414, accessed May 10, 2021; Carolyn Mason, interview by Sonya Ramsey, June 10, 2018.

60. Bertha Maxwell-Roddey, interview by Sonya Ramsey, August 31, 2018, Charlotte, NC, recording in author's possession.

61. Sanford, *Charlotte and UNC Charlotte Growing Up Together,* 149, 178.

62. Bertha Maxwell, "Response to Chancellor E. (Elbert) K. Fretwell Memo," Nov. 23,

1982, Departments—Afro-American and African Studies, 1980–1983, File—Box 2, Folder 69, J. Murrey Atkins Library Special Collections and University Archives, University of North Carolina at Charlotte, Charlotte, NC.

63. Gregory Davis, interview by Sonya Ramsey, February 16, 2016, Harrisburg, NC, recording in author's possession.

64. Gregory Davis, interview by Sonya Ramsey, February 16, 2016.

65. Lyman Johnson, interview by Sonya Ramsey, December 30, 2007, Charlotte, NC, recording in author's possession.

66. Mary Minchin, "She Had So Much Love to Give," *The Daily Tar Heel,* September 17, 1992, 1, DigitalNC Database, http://newspapers.digitalnc.org/lccn/sn92073228/1992-09-17/ed-1/seq-1/, accessed January 14, 2020.

67. Beverly Ford, conversation with Sonya Ramsey, December 9, 2021, Charlotte NC, notes in author's possession; Bertha Maxwell-Roddey, interview by Sonya Ramsey, August 31, 2018.

68. Black Student Movement Letter to the Office of the Chancellor of the University of North Carolina at Chapel Hill, "Black Student Movement Demands, 1979," in the Nelson Ferebee Taylor Records #40023, University Archives, Wilson Library, University of North Carolina at Chapel Hill, December 3, 1979, Reclaiming the University of the People, Racial Justice Movements at the University Of North Carolina At Chapel Hill Website, https://uncofthepeople.com/2018/05/01/black-student-movement-demands-1979/, accessed December 9, 2021; Minchin, "She Had So Much Love to Give," *The Daily Tar Heel,* September 17, 1992, 1.

69. Nancy Faires Conklin, Brenda McCallum, and Marcia Wade, "The Culture of Southern Black Women: Approaches and Materials Curriculum Guide," Unpublished Document, in the Special Collections, University Archive of American Minority Cultures and the Women's Studies Program, University of Alabama, Sponsored by the Department of Education, Fund for the Improvement of Post-Secondary Education, 1983.

70. "Dr. Bertha Maxwell Participates in Conference," *Charlotte Post,* November 5, 1981, 6, http://newspapers.digitalnc.org/lccn/sn88063138/1981-11-05/ed-1/seq-6/print/image_521x817_from_1016,0_to_5280,6676/, accessed June 15, 2020.

71. Peter St. Onge, "Bertha Maxwell-Roddey," *Charlotte Observer,* March 5, 2005, 6, NewsBank: Access World News—Historical and Current, https://infoweb-NewsBank-com.eu1.proxy.openathens.net/apps/news/document-view?p=WORLDNEWS&docref=news/108B01AC645E8F2E, accessed September 19, 2020.

72. "Council Approves Women's Studies Program to Begin in Spring," *The 49er Times,* December 3, 1983, 5, Box 24, Folder 267, Student Publications—49er Times, 1983–1985, Student Affairs Vice Chancellor Records, University Archives, J. Murrey Atkins Library Special Collections and University Archives, UNC Charlotte, Charlotte, NC; UNCC News Release, "Council Approves Women's Studies," *The 49er Times,* January 16, 1984, 1, Box 24, Folder 267, Student Publications—49er Times, 1983–1985, Student Affairs Vice Chancellor Records, University Archives, J. Murrey Atkins Library Special Collections and University Archives, UNC Charlotte, Charlotte, NC.

73. Kim Urquhart, "Making 'Herstory,'" *Emory Report* 59, no 3 (March 19, 2007), http://www.emory.edu/EMORY_REPORT/erarchive/2007/March/March%2019/Profile_Delores%20Aldridge.htm, accessed January 15, 2020; Henry, 104; Laverne Gyant, "The Missing

Link: Women in Black/Africana Studies," in *Out of the Revolution: The Development of Africana Programs*, eds., Delores Aldridge and Carlene Young (Lanham, MD: Lexington Books, 2000), 182.

74. Bertha Maxwell-Roddey, interview by Sonya Ramsey, August 31, 2018; Edward B. Fiske, "The State of Black Studies: A Remarkable Impact, But the Growth Has Ended," *The Charlotte Observer* January 16, 1983, 29, NewsBank: Access World News—Historical and Current, https://infoweb-NewsBank-com.eu1.proxy.openathens.net/apps/news/document-view?p=WORLDNEWS&docref=image/v2:11260DC9BB798E30@WHNPX-15E3F197514764A7@2445351-15E348391D65E9DC@28-15E348391D65E9DC@, accessed September 9, 2019.

75. Charles E. Jones and Nafeesa Muhammed, "Town and Gown: Reaffirming Social Responsibility in Africana Studies," in *African American Studies*, ed. by Jeanette R. Davidson (Edinburgh, Scotland: Edinburgh University Press, 2010), 64.

76. Myriette Guinyard Ekechukwu, 1981, "Africa Day Planning Notes," Box: 1, Folder,43. Department of Africana Studies records, UA0104. University Archives, J. Murrey Atkins Library Special Collections and University Archives, UNC Charlotte, Charlotte, NC; "Local African Students Share Their Culture," *Charlotte Post*, October 29, 1981, DigitalNC Database, http://newspapers.digitalnc.org/lccn/sn88063138/1981-10-29/ed-1/seq-14/print/image_535x817_from_0,0_to_4380,6686/, accessed June 15, 2020.

77. Bertha Maxwell-Roddey, interview by Sonya Ramsey, March 9, 2018, Charlotte, NC, recording in author's possession.

78. Gregory Davis, interview by Sonya Ramsey, February 16, 2016, recording in author's possession; "Black Studies Director Returns to UNCC," *Charlotte Observer*, June 12, 1978, 7, NewsBank: Access World News—Historical and Current, https://infoweb-NewsBank-com.eu1.proxy.openathens.net/apps/news/document-view?p=WORLDNEWS&docref=image/v2:11260DC9BB798E30@WHNPX-15FAAD69F37E73E4@2443672-1605D74583F9F1A2@6-1605D74583F9F1A2@, accessed January 15, 2020.

79. Bertha Maxwell-Roddey, interview by Sonya Ramsey, April 6, 2017, Charlotte, NC, recording in author's possession.

80. Herman Thomas, interview by Sonya Ramsey, July 7, 2017; Herman Thomas Curriculum Vitae. Unpublished Online Document, https://www.hoodseminary.edu/storage/components/Thomas,%20Herman%20(C.V.).pdf, accessed January 14, 2020.

81. Gregory Davis, "Curriculum Vitae," Bellefonte Church Website, Harrisburg, NC, Website inactive, paper copy in author's possession; Gregory Davis, interview by Sonya Ramsey, February 16, 2016.

82. University of North Carolina at Charlotte Africana Studies Department, "Akinwumi Ogundiran Faculty Page," No Page Number, in The University of North Carolina at Charlotte, Department of Africana Studies, College of Liberal Arts and Sciences Website, https://clas-pages.uncc.edu/akinwumi-ogundiran, accessed June 1, 2018.

83. University of North Carolina at Charlotte Africana Studies Department, "Akinwumi Ogundiran Faculty Pages," No Page Number in The University of North Carolina at Charlotte; Gregory Davis, interview by Sonya Ramsey, February 16, 2016.

84. Bertha Maxwell-Roddey, interview by Sonya Ramsey, April 29, 2018, Charlotte, NC, recording in author's possession.

85. Bertha Maxwell-Roddey, interview by Sonya Ramsey, May 25, 2018, Charlotte, NC, recording in author's possession.

86. Arthur Griffin Jr., interview by Sonya Ramsey, July 13, 2017, Charlotte, NC, recording in author's possession; Arthur Griffin Jr., interview by Pamela Grundy, May 7, 1999, Southern Oral History Program, #4007, University of North Carolina at Chapel Hill; Bob Edwards, "Analysis: School Desegregation Being Re-Examined," *Morning Edition [NPR] (USA),* February 9, 1999, transcript, Morning Edition [NPR] (USA), February 9, 1999, NewsBank: Access World News—Historical and Current. https://infoweb-NewsBank-com.eu1.proxy. openathens.net/apps/news/document-view?p=WORLDNEWS&docref=news/1577CFDA8 FBCA408, accessed November 19, 2019; Thomas Bradbury, "Preamble," *Charlotte Observer,* February 22, 1997, 16A, NewsBank: Access World News—Historical and Current. https:// infoweb-NewsBank-com.eu1.proxy.openathens.net/apps/news/document-view?p=WORLD NEWS&docref=news/0EB6D413515D1EBB, accessed January 14, 2020.

87. Abdul Alkalimat, Ronald Bailey, Sam Byndom, Desiree McMillion, LaTasha Nesbitt, Kate Williams, and Brian Zelip, "African American Studies 2013: A National Web-Based Survey," (Urbana-Champaign: University of Illinois at Urbana-Champaign Department of African American Studies, 2013), 6.

88. James Turner, interview by Sonya Ramsey, September 8, 2013, Charlotte, NC, phone recording in author's possession.

Chapter 5. Retrieving What Was Lost, Building New Beginnings

1. Charlotte's downtown area is called Uptown. The name, Afro-American Cultural and Service Center was later changed to the Afro-American Cultural Center in 1984. For clarity, the abbreviated name, "the Center" and the initials AACC will be used in this book.

2. Mark Washburn, "Gantt Praised at Center's Opening," *Charlotte Observer,* Web Edition Articles (NC), October 24, 2009, no page number, NewsBank: Access World News—Historical and Current, https://infoweb-NewsBank-com.eu1.proxy.openathens.net/apps/news/ document-view?p=WORLDNEWS&docref=news/158A5204B6507310, accessed July 7, 2020.

3. Mark Washburn, "Gantt Praised at Center's Opening," *Charlotte Observer, Web Edition Articles (NC),* October 24, 2009.

4. Mary Turner Harper, "Beyond Act I: A Transdisciplinary and Experiential Approach to Afro-American Literature and Culture," PhD Dissertation, English (Union Graduate School for Experimenting Colleges and Universities, Yellow Springs, Ohio, 1975), 76–106, https:// librarylink.uncc.edu/login?url=https://search-proquest-com.librarylink.uncc.edu/docview/ 302808053?accountid=14605, accessed July 20, 2020.

5. See Mary Turner Harper, "Beyond Act I: A Transdisciplinary and Experiential Approach to Afro-American Literature and Culture," 1; Bertha Maxwell-Roddey, interview by Sonya Ramsey, December 28, 2017, Charlotte, NC, recording in author's possession.

6. Rhett Jones, "From Ideology to Institution: The Evolution of Africana Studies," in *Color-line to Borderlands: The Matrix of American Ethnic Studies,* ed. Johnella E. Butler (Seattle: University of Washington Press, 2001), 138.

7. Andrea A. Burns, *From Storefront to Monument: Tracking the Public History of the Black Museum Movement* (Amherst: University of Massachusetts Press, 2013), 4, 24, 25.

8. Alice Walker, *In Search of Our Mothers' Gardens* (New York: Harcourt Press, 1983), xii;

For more information about womanism and womanist theory, see Clenora Hudson Weems, *Africana Womanism: Reclaiming Ourselves* (New York: Bedford Press, 1993); and Layli Phillips, ed., *The Womanist Reader* (New York: Routledge Press, 2006); For more information about current issues relating to the theory of intersectionality, see, Ange-Marie Hancock, *Intersectionality: an Intellectual History* (New York: Oxford University Press, 2016).

9. "About ULCC, Agency History," Urban League of Central Carolina's, Inc. Website, https://www.urbanleaguecc.org/about-2/history/, accessed March 12, 2022; "Kathleen Crosby Obituary," November 22, 2012, NewsBank: Access World News—Historical and Current, https://infoweb-NewsBank-com.eu1.proxy.openathens.net/apps/news/document-view ?p=WORLDNEWS&docref=news/142C0B9857A471C8, accessed January 14, 2020; Charlene Price Patterson, "Charlotte Public Health Pioneer Tells Her Story," *Charlotte Observer,* digital article, no page number, https://www.charlotteobserver.com/news/local/community/university-city/article9101864.html, accessed July 3, 2020; Melissa Hankins, "Miss Sarah's Breakfast Club," *Charlotte Magazine,* October 14, 2014, digital article, no page number, https://www.charlottemagazine.com/ms-sarahs-breakfast-club/, accessed July 3, 2020; Jim Morrill, "Phyllis Lynch, 'Teacher of Leaders' in Area Politics Dies," *Charlotte Observer,* December 20, 2007; 1, 10, https://www.newspapers.com/image/632548815/?terms=%22Phyllis%2BLynch%22, accessed July 3, 2020; James Alexander, "Third Ward's Overseer Works Nonstop," *Charlotte Observer,* July 11, 1982, 24, 25, Newspapers.com Database, https://www.newspapers.com/image/623654158/?terms=%22Mildred%2BBaxter%2BDavis%22#, accessed July 3, 2020.

10. Thomas W. Hanchett, *Sorting Out the New South City: Race, Class, and Urban Development in Charlotte, 1875–1975* (Chapel Hill: University of North Carolina Press; 1997, 127–134; Khalid Hijazi, "The Effects of Urban Renewal on African Americans in Charlotte, North Carolina, the case of the Brooklyn Neighborhood: 1960–1997," MA Thesis, History (University of North Carolina at Charlotte, Ann Arbor, MI: ProQuest LLC, 2014), ProQuest Dissertations and Theses Global Database, https://uncc.primo.exlibrisgroup.com/permalink/01UNCC_INST/1rqb8fi/cdi_proquest_journals_1706350423, accessed December 22, 2021; Pamela Grundy, "Black History of Charlotte Part 2: The Building of Brooklyn, A Community to Call Their Own," *Queen City Nerve: Charlotte's Alternative Newspaper,* August 13, 2020, QCnerve.com Website, https://qcnerve.com/black-history-of-charlotte-part-2-the-building-of-brooklyn/, accessed October 23, 2020.

11. Bertha Maxwell-Roddey, interview by Sonya Ramsey, July 24, 2017.

12. Bob Meadows, "Pivotal Black-Community Events: A Conversation," *Charlotte Observer,* February 23, 1997, 3B, NewsBank: Access World News—Historical and Current, https://infoweb-NewsBank-com.eu1.proxy.openathens.net/apps/news/document-view?p= WORLDNEWS&docref=news/0EB6D41407C958DD, accessed September 9, 2019.

13. Thomas Hanchett, "The Center City: The Business District and the Original Four Wards," *Charlotte Historical Landmarks Commission, no date,* http://landmarkscommission. org/wp-content/uploads/2016/11/THE-CENTER-CITY.pdf, accessed July 20, 2020.

14. Charlotte Redevelopment Commission, "Charlotte's Inner City Urban Renewal Area" *Redevelopment Commission of the City of Charlotte:* 2 (Charlotte: *Charlotte Redevelopment Commission,* 1970): 2. Charlotte Redevelopment Commission Records, Goldmine Planning and Development Collection, in the Digitized Collections, J. Murrey Atkins Library Special Collections and University Archives, University of North Carolina at Charlotte. Here is a link to a map of urban renewal efforts in Charlotte: https://repository.uncc.edu/islandora/object/

mss%3A73083, in Charlotte Redevelopment Commission Records, Goldmine Planning and Development Collection, Digitized Collections, J. Murrey Atkins Library Special Collections and University Archives, University of North Carolina at Charlotte, accessed July 15, 2021.

15. Ruth L. Pace and Lynn Egoe, "A Better Charlotte Through Urban Renewal, The Brooklyn Story" Redevelopment Commission of the City of Charlotte: 1, Charlotte Redevelopment Commission Records, Goldmine Planning and Development Collection, Digitized Collections, J. Murrey Atkins Library Special Collections and University Archives, University of North Carolina at Charlotte.

16. Rhonda Y. Williams, "Welcome Back, Greenville Once Flattened by Bulldozers, Neighborhood Savors Revival," *Charlotte Observer,* August 2, 1992, 1. NewsBank: Access World News—*Historical and Current,* https://infoweb-NewsBank-com.eu1.proxy.openathens. net/apps/news/document-view?p=WORLDNEWS&docref=news/0EB6C9BF152F1825, accessed July 28, 2020; Jim Morrill, "Phyllis Lynch, 'Teacher of Leaders' in Area Politics Dies," *Charlotte Observer,* December 20, 2007; 1, 10, https://www.newspapers.com/image/6325488 15/?terms=%22Phyllis%2BLynch%22, accessed July 3, 2020; James Alexander, "Third Ward's Overseer Works Nonstop," *Charlotte Observer,* July 11, 1982, 24, 25, https://www.newspapers. com/image/623654158/?terms=%22Mildred%2BBaxter%2BDavis%22#, accessed July 3, 2020.

17. Jalyne Strong, "Center Is Proud Achievement," *Charlotte Post,* January 26, 1989, 4A, DigitalNC Database, http://newspapers.digitalnc.org/lccn/sn88063138/1989-01-26/ed-1/ seq-4/print/image_494x817_from_0,0_to_3490,5764/, accessed July 17, 2020.

18. For more information about public school desegregation in Charlotte, see Davison Douglas, *Reading, Writing and Race: The Desegregation of Charlotte Schools* (Chapel Hill: University of North Carolina Press; 1995); Frye Gaillard, *The Dream Long Deferred: The Landmark Struggle for Desegregation in Charlotte, North Carolina* (Columbia: University of South Carolina Press, 2006, Third Edition, First Edition 1988); Matthew Lassiter, *Silent Majority: Suburban Politics in the Sunbelt South* (Princeton, NJ: Princeton University Press, 2007); Bernard Schwartz, *Swann's Way: The School Busing Case and the Supreme Court* (New York: Oxford University Press, 1986); and Stephen Samuel Smith, *Boom for Whom? Education, Desegregation, and Development* (Albany, NY: State University of New York Press, 2004).

19. Bob Meadows, "Pivotal Black-Community Events: A Conversation" *Charlotte Observer,* February 23, 1997, 3B, NewsBank: Access World News—Historical and Current, https://infoweb-NewsBank-com.eu1.proxy.openathens.net/apps/news/document-view?p= WORLDNEWS&docref=news/0EB6D41407C958DD, accessed September 9, 2019.

20. Mary Turner Harper, "Beyond Act I: A Transdisciplinary and Experiential Approach to Afro-American Literature and Culture," dissertation, 40.

21. Afro-American Cultural Center, "Board of Directors List, 1976–1982," Afro-American Cultural Center, Vertical File Collection, Box: 1 [F09.147.01.01], Manuscript Collections, J. Murrey Atkins Library Special Collections and University Archives, UNC Charlotte; "Editor Says Blacks Face Grave Crisis," *Charlotte Observer,* September 10, 1976, 2C, NewsBank: Access World News—Historical and Current, https://infoweb-NewsBank-com. eu1.proxy.openathens.net/apps/news/document-view?p=WORLDNEWS&docref=image/ v2:1126oDC9BB798E30@WHNPX-15FAAD60C31F4B14@2443032-16067791108F80F4@31, accessed January 2020.

22. Bertha Maxwell-Roddey, interview by Sonya Ramsey, August 2, 2017, Charlotte, NC,

recording in author's possession; Mary Maxwell, interview by Sonya Ramsey, May 21, 2018, Charlotte, NC, recording in author's possession.

23. Bertha Maxwell-Roddey, interview by Sonya Ramsey, August 2, 2017; Elaine Nichols, interview by Sonya Ramsey, August 25, 2017; Humphrey Cummings, interview by Sonya Ramsey, September 19, 2017, Charlotte, NC, recording in author's possession; and Brenda Springs and Jerry Springs, interview by Sonya Ramsey, August 5, 2018, Charlotte, NC, recording in author's possession.

24. Brenda Springs and Jerry Springs, interview by Sonya Ramsey, August 5, 2018; Elaine Nichols, interview by Sonya Ramsey, August 25, 2017.

25. Clara Williams, interview by Dwana Waugh, May 22, 2008, recording in the Southern Oral History Program #U-0366, Southern Historical Collection Manuscripts Department, Wilson Library, The University of North Carolina at Chapel Hill, Chapel Hill, NC.

26. Sylvia McGriff, "Soul Stirring Choir Highlights Black Fest," *Charlotte Observer,* September 1, 1974, C1, NewsBank: Access World News—Historical and Current, https://infoweb-NewsBank-com.eu1.proxy.openathens.net/apps/news/document-view?p=WORLDNEWS&docref=image/v2:11260DC9BB798E30@WHNPX-15FAAD55B3951AB7@2442292-160677681A2FB422@38, accessed July 20, 2017; Tommy Robinson, interview by Sonya Ramsey, July 6, 2018, Charlotte, NC. phone recording in author's possession.

27. Bertha Maxwell-Roddey, interview, December 28, 2017; see Harper dissertation, 40.

28. Elaine Nichols, interview by Sonya Ramsey, August 25, 2017, Charlotte, NC. phone recording in author's possession; Tommy Robinson, interview by Sonya Ramsey, July 6, 2018.

29. Bertha Maxwell-Roddey, interview by Sonya Ramsey, June 24, 2018, Charlotte, NC, recording in author's possession.

30. Bertha Maxwell-Roddey, interview by Sonya Ramsey, September 27, 2018, Charlotte, NC, recording in author's possession; "Charlotte North Carolina," *Charlotte Observer,* December 11, 1973, 23, NewsBank: Access World News—Historical and Current, https://infoweb-NewsBank-com.eu1.proxy.openathens.net/apps/news/document-view?p=WORLDNEWS&docref=image/v2:1126167831380960@WHNPX-16F87D8099585407@2442028-16F6DDC6E44574D4@22-16F6DDC6E44574D4@, accessed September 9, 2019.

31. Bertha Maxwell-Roddey, interview by Sonya Ramsey, September 27, 2018; Jim Morrill, "Phyllis Lynch, 'Teacher of Leaders' in Area Politics Dies," 1A, Historical and Current, https://infoweb-NewsBank-com.eu1.proxy.openathens.net/apps/news/document-view?p=WORLDNEWS&docref=news/0EB6C1DF5DF228B4, accessed September 30, 2019.

32. Bertha Maxwell-Roddey, interview by Sonya Ramsey, September 27, 2018; John Vaughn, "Yolanda King to Bring Civil Rights Message to Charlotte," *Charlotte Observer,* June 18, 1987, 5C, NewsBank: Access World News—Historical and Current, https://infoweb-NewsBank-com.eu1.proxy.openathens.net/apps/news/document-view?p=WORLDNEWS&docref=news/0EB6C1DF5DF228B4, accessed September 30, 2019.

33. Mary Turner Harper, "Beyond Act I: A Transdisciplinary and Experiential Approach to Afro-American Literature and Culture," Dissertation, 40; William H. Williamson, III, "Cultural Action Plan for Charlotte/Mecklenburg," June 19, 1975, 19, 26, 28 in United Arts Council Archives, United Arts Council, Charlotte, NC.

34. William H. Williamson, III, "Cultural Action Plan for Charlotte/Mecklenburg," 28; Bertha Maxwell-Roddey, interview by Sonya Ramsey, September 27, 2018.

35. Pat Locke Williamson, interview by Sonya Ramsey, June 24, 2018, Charlotte, NC, recording in author's possession; Bertha Maxwell-Roddey, interview by Sonya Ramsey, December 28, 2017, Charlotte, NC, recording in author's possession.

36. Dick Banks, "$122,000 U.S. Grant Eases Cultural Pains for 12 Arts Groups," *Charlotte Observer,* Sat. Oct. 18, 1975, 2B, *Charlotte Observer* (Charlotte, North Carolina), October 18, 1975, 16, NewsBank: Access World News—*Historical and Current,* https://infoweb-NewsBank-com. eu1.proxy.openathens.net/apps/news/document-view?p=WORLDNEWS&docref=image/ v2%3A11260DC9BB798E30%40WHNPX-15FAAD5F0123472D%402442704- 16067753398BF467%4015-16067753398BF467%40, accessed October 28, 2020.

37. William H. Williamson, III, United Arts Council, "Cultural Action Plan for Charlotte/ Mecklenburg," June 19, 1975, 19, 26, 28.

38. Bertha Maxwell-Roddey, interview by Sonya Ramsey, September 27, 2018; Miriam Murff, "Spirit Square Comes Alive, Oct. 2," *Charlotte Observer,* September 19, 1976, 88, NewsBank: Access World News—Historical and Current, https://infoweb-NewsBank-com. eu1.proxy.openathens.net/apps/news/document-view?p=WORLDNEWS&docref=image/ v2%3A11260DC9BB798E30%40WHNPX-15FAAD60C38FC369%402443041- 1606779140DF3AAA%4087, accessed October 28, 2020.

39. Bertha Maxwell-Roddey, interview by Sonya Ramsey, September 27, 2018; Charles Hardy, "Black Culture Booming," *Charlotte Observer,* July 13, 1976, 42, NewsBank: Access World News—Historical and Current, https://infoweb-NewsBank-com.eu1.proxy.openathens.net/ apps/news/document-view?p=WORLDNEWS&docref=image/v2:11260DC9BB798E30@ WHNPX-15FAAD64AA221A45@2442973-16067785E6ED7271@41-16067785E6ED7271@, accessed January 14, 2020.

40. Hardy, "Black Culture Booming," *Charlotte Observer,* July 13, 1976, 42.

41. "Kids Culture," *Charlotte Observer,* November 12, 1976, 56, Newspapers.com Database, https://www.newspapers.com/image/622838651, accessed July 7, 2020; "Black Art Exhibit Opens This Week," *Charlotte Observer,* February 13, 1978, 79, Newspapers.com Database, https://www.newspapers.com/image/622837741, accessed July 7, 2020; Sheliah Vance, "Brooklyn Lost Community Lives in Memories," *Charlotte News,* July 18, 1977, 15, Newspapers.com Database, https://www.newspapers.com/image/622843225, accessed July 7, 2020; Patrice Carter, "60s Black Power Advocate Urges Students to Help Each Other," *Charlotte Observer,* February 11, 1978, 23, Newspapers.com Database, https://www.newspapers.com/ image/623522664, accessed July 7, 2020.

42. T. J. Reddy, interview by Sonya Ramsey, June 22, 2018, Charlotte, NC, recording in author's possession.

43. Jim Morrill, "Charlotte Three Case: A Twisted Path Through Tense Times," *Charlotte Observer,* February 27, 2015, Web Edition, No Page Number, https://www.charlotteobserver. com/news/local/article11252768.html, accessed July 7, 2020; J. Christopher Schutz, "The Burning of America: Race, Radicalism, and the 'Charlotte Three' Trial in 1970s North Carolina," *The North Carolina Historical Review* 76, no. 1 (1999): 43–65, accessed May 10, 2021. http://www.jstor.org/stable/23522170.

44. Herman Thomas, "Curriculum Vitae," Unpublished Document, https://www.hoodseminary.edu/storage/components/Thomas,%20Herman%20(C.V.).pdf, accessed January 14, 2020.

45. Shirley Farrar, interview by Sonya Ramsey, October 20, 2018, Charlotte, NC, recording in author's possession; Maxwell-Roddey, interview by Sonya Ramsey, July 24, 2017.

46. Beth Rodgers, "Arts Program to Fill Saturday Mornings Full of Learning, Games, *Charlotte News,* October 30, 1984, 26, NewsBank: Access World News—Historical and Current, https://infoweb-NewsBank-com.eu1.proxy.openathens.net/apps/news/document-view?p=WORLDNEWS&docref=image/v2%3A1126167831380960%40WHNPX-16F718C2E056A36F%402446004-16F717AA698317AF%4025-16F717AA698317AF%40, accessed July 1, 2020.

47. "George Robert Lyons Obituary," *Charlotte Observer,* April 6, 1979, 36, NewsBank: Access World News—Historical and Current, https://infoweb-NewsBank-com.eu1.proxy.openathens.net/apps/news/document-view?p=WORLDNEWS&docref=image/v2:1126167831380960@WHNPX-16F6CA978BED3AAB@2443970-16F61CB3A7E4E530@6-16F61CB3A7E4E530@, accessed September 2, 2019.

48. "Leroy Baxter Obituary," *Charlotte Observer,* October 25, 1963, 78, NewsBank: Access World News—Historical and Current, https://infoweb-NewsBank-com.eu1.proxy.openathens.net/apps/news/document-view?p=WORLDNEWS&docref=image/v2:1126oDC9BB798E30@WHNPX-15E24FDB14CDDB91@2438328-15E3470FF59608FD@9-15E3470FF59608FD@, accessed September 2, 2019.

49. Henry Scott, "Council Gets Chance to Avoid Fights With Planners," *Charlotte Observer,* July 11, 1978, 17, NewsBank: Access World News—Historical and Current, https://infoweb-NewsBank-com.eu1.proxy.openathens.net/apps/news/document-view?p=WORLDNEWS&docref=image/v2:1126oDC9BB798E30@WHNPX-15FAAD6EE136D59E@2443700-1605D748BB81A228@16, accessed September 9, 2019.

50. "University BOG to Meet Friday Morning," *Daily Tar Heel,* July 10, 1980, 4, DigitalNC Database, http://newspapers.digitalnc.org/lccn/sn92073228/1980-07-10/ed-1/seq-4/, accessed January 14, 2020.

51. Doug Smith and Lu Stanton, "Can Any Democrat Unseat Martin?" *Charlotte News,* January 17, 1980: 2, NewsBank: Access World News—Historical and Current, https://infoweb-NewsBank-com.eu1.proxy.openathens.net/apps/news/document-view?p=WORLDNEWS&docref=image/v2:1126167831380960@WHNPX-16F8E89071DE589B@2444256-16F819516C67E7EF@1-16F819516C67E7EF@, accessed September 9, 2019; Charlotte Douglas Airport Weather History, Weatherunderground.com. https://www.wunderground.com/history/daily/KCLT/date/1980-1-25?req_city=&req_state=&req_statename=&reqdb.zip=&reqdb.magic=&reqdb.wmo=, accessed January 14, 2020.

52. Bertha Maxwell-Roddey, interview by Sonya Ramsey, June 23, 2016, Charlotte, NC, recording in author's possession; Carolyn Sandford, "'Uphill Battle' Ahead for Dr. Bertha Maxwell as She Files to Run for a Seat in State House," *Charlotte News,* January 26, 1980, 10, NewsBank: Access World News—Historical and Current, https://infoweb-NewsBank-com.eu1.proxy.openathens.net/apps/news/document-view?p=WORLDNEWS&docref=image/v2:1126167831380960@WHNPX-16F8E8B9C4BA5DCC@2444265-16F819603B7F9388@, accessed September 9, 2019.

53. "21 Candidates Endorsed," *The Charlotte News,* April 18, 1980, 9, NewsBank: Access World News—Historical and Current, https://infoweb-NewsBank-com.eu1.proxy.openathens.net/apps/news/document-view?p=WORLDNEWS&docref=image/

v2:1126167831380960@WHNPX-16F8FB4832F929AC@2444348-16F8196F224AE8EE@8-16F8196F224AE8EE@9, accessed September 9, 2019.

54. Lu Stanton, "House Newcomers Maxwell, Black Join Incumbents," *Charlotte News,* May 7, 1980, 26, NewsBank: Access World News—Historical and Current, https://infoweb-NewsBank-com.eu1.proxy.openathens.net/apps/news/document-view?p=WORLDNEWS&docref=image/v2:1126167831380960@WHNPX-16F8EBEFB4C80B60@2444367-16F8195D87514CE6@25, accessed December 29, 2019.

55. "Fraternal Order of Police Endorses 17," *Charlotte News,* November 1, 1980, 4A, NewsBank: Access World News—Historical and Current, https://infoweb-NewsBank-com.eu1.proxy.openathens.net/apps/news/document-view?p=WORLDNEWS&docref=image/v2:1126167831380960@WHNPX-16FADF1F31A70DDF@2444545-16F8199B03176392@3, accessed September 9, 2019.

56. Wilson Sayre, "Smoldering Liberty City: Remembering the McDuffie Riots," *National Public Radio, NPR,* transcript of broadcast, May 17, 2015, https://www.wlrn.org/post/smoldering-liberty-city-remembering-mcduffie-riots, accessed July 7, 2020; Patsy Daniels, "Chief Goodman Wants Police to Improve Rapport with Blacks," *Charlotte Observer,* June 4, 1980, 21, NewsBank: Access World News—Historical and Current, https://infoweb-NewsBank-com.eu1.proxy.openathens.net/apps/news/document-view?p=WORLDNEWS&docref=image/v2:11260DC9BB798E30@WHNPX-15FAAD79B863ADFD@2444395-1605D78353330B12@20-1605D78353330B12@, accessed January 14, 2020.

57. Vanessa Gallman and Patsy Daniels, "Riots Can Occur, Black Leaders Warn at Meeting," *Charlotte Observer,* June 6, 1980, 19, NewsBank: Access World News—Historical and Current, https://infoweb-NewsBank-com.eu1.proxy.openathens.net/apps/news/document-view?p=WORLDNEWS&docref=image/v2:11260DC9BB798E30@WHNPX-15FAAD79B882492B@2444397-1605D7835EFBFC35@18-1605D7835EFBFC35@, accessed January 14, 2020; Doug Waller and Ted DeAdwyler, "Black Leaders: After the Talks, What?" *Charlotte News,* June 6, 1980; 1, NewsBank: Access World News—Historical and Current, https://infoweb-NewsBank-com.eu1.proxy.openathens.net/apps/news/document-view?p=WORLDNEWS&docref=image/v2:1126167831380960@WHNPX-16F8EBFD935504A1@2444397-16F81974DBD15A91@0, accessed September 9, 2019.

58. Doug Waller and Ted DeAdwyler, "Black Leaders: After the Talks, What?" 1.

59. Gaile Dry-Burton, interview by Sonya Ramsey, August 8, 2018, Charlotte, NC, phone recording in author's possession; Wendy Fox, "National Black Leaders Helping Charlotte Woman's Assembly Bid," *Charlotte Observer,* October 8, 1980, 21, NewsBank: Access World News—Historical and Current, https://infoweb-NewsBank-com.eu1.proxy.openathens.net/apps/news/document-view?p=WORLDNEWS&docref=image/v2%3A11260DC9BB798E30%40WHNPX-15FAAD7F56FAE77C%402444521-15E34790177BEA9D%4020-15E34790177BEA9D%40, accessed July 12, 2021; Wendy Fox, "Jackson Puts Sparkle in Candidate's Rally," *Charlotte Observer,* Oct 9, 1980, 62, NewsBank: Access World News—Historical and Current, https://infoweb-NewsBank-com.eu1.proxy.openathens.net/apps/news/document-view?p=WORLDNEWS&docref=image/v2:11260DC9BB798E30@WHNPX-15FAAD7F5708DCC6@2444522-15E347901EDAFF59@61-15E347901EDAFF59@, accessed January 14, 2020.

60. Wendy Fox, "National Politicians Helping Charlotte Woman's Assembly Bid;" Milton

Jordan, "Black Legislators: From Political Novelty to Political Force," *North Carolina Insight*, Sponsored by the North Carolina Center for Public Policy Research 50, no. 1 (1999): 40–58, NCPPR.org/EdNC.org Website, https://nccppr.org/wp-content/uploads/2017/02/Black_Legislators-From_Political_Novelty_to_Political_Force.pdf, accessed January 14, 2020.

61. Wendy Fox, "Jackson Puts Sparkle in Candidate's Rally," *Charlotte Observer*, Oct 9, 1980, 62, NewsBank: Access World News—Historical and Current, https://infoweb-NewsBank-com.eu1.proxy.openathens.net/apps/news/document-view?p=WORLDNEWS&docref=image/v2:11260DC9BB798E30@WHNPX-15FAAD7F5708DCC6@2444522-15E347901EDAFF59@61-15E347901EDAFF59@, accessed January 14, 2020; "Disco Dance Sunday at Excelsior Club," *Charlotte News*, August 29, 1980, 37, NewsBank: Access World News—Historical and Current, https://infoweb-NewsBank-com.eu1.proxy.openathens.net/apps/news/document-view?p=WORLDNEWS&docref=image/v2:112616783138096o@WHNPX-16F981F15A9ABAB8@2444481-16F819ADDDAC9E0C@36, accessed September 22, 2017; Bertha Maxwell-Roddey, interview by Sonya Ramsey, July 28, 2018, Charlotte, NC, recording in author's possession.

62. John York, "Mrs. Luellar Baxter, Mother of Dr. Bertha Maxwell Dies," *Charlotte Observer*, October 21, 1980, 6A, NewsBank: Access World News—Historical and Current, https://infoweb-NewsBank-com.eu1.proxy.openathens.net/apps/news/document-view?p=WORLDNEWS&docref=image/v2:11260DC9BB798E30@WHNPX-15FAAD7F57A3AF7D@2444534-15E34790832CB1F1@5-15E34790832CB1F1@, accessed September 17, 2019.

63. "These Eight for the NC House," *Charlotte Observer*, October 24, 1980, 18, News-Bank: Access World News—Historical and Current, https://infoweb-NewsBank-com.eu1.proxy.openathens.net/apps/news/document-view?p=WORLDNEWS&docref=image/v2:11260DC9BB798E30@WHNPX-15FAAD7F57D08066@2444537-15E34790982956CB@17-15E34790982956CB@, accessed June 18, 2018.

64. "These Eight for the NC House," *Charlotte Observer*, October 24, 1980, 18.

65. "Economos Wins Election," *Charlotte Observer*, November 7, 1980, 21, NewsBank: Access World News—Historical and Current, https://infoweb-NewsBank-com.eu1.proxy.openathens.net/apps/news/document-view?p=WORLDNEWS&docref=image/v2:11260DC9BB798E30@WHNPX-15FAAD6F39916788@2444551-1605D78E048A25B1@20, accessed January 14, 2020.

66. Wendy Fox, "Black Attributes N.C. House Victory to High Visibility," *Charlotte Observer*, November 5, 1980, 29, NewsBank: Access World News—Historical and Current, https://infoweb-NewsBank-com.eu1.proxy.openathens.net/apps/news/document-view?p=WORLDNEWS&docref=image/v2:11260DC9BB798E30@WHNPX-15FAAD6F3AFBD893@2444549-1605D78DF36803A1@28-1605D78DF36803A1@; Associated Press and Charlotte Observer Reports, "All But Two Incumbents Do Well In House Races, Black Attributes Victory to Visibility, *Charlotte Observer*, 34C, NewsBank: Access World News—Historical and Current, https://infoweb-NewsBank-com.eu1.proxy.openathens.net/apps/news/document-view?p=WORLDNEWS&docref=image/v2:11260DC9BB798E30@WHNPX-15FAAD6F3AFBD893@2444549-1605D78DF3AA5DA3@33, accessed September 9, 2019. After his election in 1980, Jim Black served eleven terms in the NC General Assembly and became speaker of the House from 1999–2006. He resigned in 2007 after he was found guilty of taking $25,000 in bribes from three chiropractors and served three years in

prison. In later years, Maxwell-Roddey remarked that prior to his conviction, Black sarcastically alluded to her that she might have been better off by not winning. Rob Christensen, "Former House Speaker Jim Black's Law Finds New Life," *Raleigh News and Observer,* May 9, 2015, no page number, *Raleigh News and Observer* Website, https://www.newsobserver.com/news/politics-government/politics-columns-blogs/rob-christensen/article20609109.html, accessed November 2, 2020; Maxwell-Roddey, interview by Sonya Ramsey, June 23, 2016.

67. Alfreda Johnson Webb and Annie Brown Kennedy were the first Black women appointed to serve in the NC General Assembly. Milton C. Jordan, "Black Legislatures from Political Novelty to Political Force," *North Carolina Insight,* December 1989, 52, 40–58, https://nccppr.org/Black-legislators-from-political-novelty-to-political-force/, accessed January 14, 2020; Lisa Song, "Monday Numbers: A Closer Look at Women Serving in the NC General Assembly," August 8, 2018, 1 http://www.ncpolicywatch.com/2018/08/27/monday-number-a-closer-look-at-the-history-of-women-serving-in-the-nc-general-assembly/, accessed January 14, 2020.

68. Farrar, interview by Sonya Ramsey, October 20, 2018; Maxwell-Roddey, interview by Sonya Ramsey, July 24, 2017.

69. Farrar, interview by Sonya Ramsey, October 20, 2018; Maxwell-Roddey, interview by Sonya Ramsey, July 24, 2017.

70. Maxwell-Roddey, interview by Sonya Ramsey, July 24, 2017; Farrar, interview by Sonya Ramsey, October 20, 2018.

71. For more information about the history and impact of the mass incarnation of African Americans, see James Foreman, *Locking Up Our Own: Crime and Punishment in Black America* (New York: Farrar, Straus and Giroux Press, 2018); Michelle Alexander, *The New Jim Crow : Mass Incarceration in the Age of Colorblindness* (New York: The New Press, 2020), 10th Anniversary Edition.

72. Karen R. Lacy, *Blue-Chip Black: Race, Class, and Status in the New Black Middle Class* (University of California Press, 2007), 173.

73. Lacy, *Blue-Chip Black: Race, Class, and Status in the New Black Middle Class,* 173.

74. Lacy, *Blue-Chip Black: Race, Class, and Status in the New Black Middle Class,* 156; Patricia A. Banks, "Cultural Socialization in Black Middle-Class Families," *Cultural Sociology,* 6, no. 1 (March 2012): 61–73, https://doi.org/10.1177/1749975511427646, accessed October 20, 2020; Janita Poe, "Jack and Jill Fights Label of Black Elite," *Chicago Tribune,* November 27, 1992, no page number, *Chicago Tribune* Website, https://www.chicagotribune.com/news/ct-xpm-1992-11-27-9204180518-story.html; For a more comprehensive examination of Jack and Jill of America, Inc., see Melanie Lavern Sloan, "The Acquisition of Cultural and Social Capital in the Black Middle Class: an Analysis of Jack and Jill of America," MA Thesis, Department of Sociology, Anthropology, and Social Work (University of North Carolina at Charlotte, 2001), https://uncc.primo.exlibrisgroup.com/permalink/01UNCC_INST/14gt3pp/alma991009732439704091, accessed September 20, 2020.

75. Farrar, interview by Sonya Ramsey, October 20, 2018; Dean Smith, "Arts," *Charlotte Observer,* February 3, 1991, 1F, NewsBank: Access World News—Historical and Current, https://infoweb-NewsBank-com.eu1.proxy.openathens.net/apps/news/document-view?p=WORLDNEWS&docref=news/0EB6C76A05B82D0C, accessed September 20, 2020.

76. Shirley Farrar, "AACC Past Executive Directors," *Charlotte Post,* January 26, 1989, 7D,

http://newspapers.digitalnc.org/lccn/sn88063138/1989-01-26/ed-1/seq-35/, accessed January 14, 2020.

77. Rosalyn Gist, "Black Arts Groups Seeking More Support," *Charlotte News,* February 2, 1980, 8, NewsBank: Access World News—Historical and Current, https://infoweb-NewsBank-com. eu1.proxy.openathens.net/apps/news/document-view?p=WORLDNEWS&docref=image/ v2%3A1126167831380960%40WHNPX-16F8ECFAAB248DBE%402444272-16F8193CF8752417%407-16F8193CF8752417%40, accessed July 15, 2020.

78. Charlotte City Council Minutes, Charlotte, NC, June 10, 1980, Budget Hearing, Book 73: 438, Charlotte City Council Minutes Website, https://codelibrary.amlegal.com/codes/ CharlotteNC/latest/m/1980/6/10, accessed January 2022.

79. Charlotte City Council Minutes, Charlotte, NC, June 8, 1981, Budget Hearing, Book 76: 93, 94, Charlotte City Council Minutes, https://codelibrary.amlegal.com/codes/Charlot-teNC/latest/m/1981/6/8, accessed January 2022; Charlotte City Council Minutes, October 27, 1981, Book 77: 21, Charlotte City Council Minutes Website, https://codelibrary.amlegal.com/ codes/CharlotteNC/latest/m/1981/10/26, accessed January 20, 2022.

80. Mary Maxwell, interview by Sonya Ramsey, May 21, 2018, Charlotte, NC, recording in author's possession.

81. Deborah Gates, "Afro-American Center to Launch Search for Funds," *Charlotte News,* July 24, 1979, 5, NewsBank: Access World News—Historical and Current, https://infoweb-NewsBank-com.eu1.proxy.openathens.net/apps/news/ document-view?p=WORLDNEWS&docref=image/v2:1126167831380960@WHNPX-16F6A5F5763ACB8E@2444079-16F6183CA267781C@4, accessed September 9, 2019.

82. Maxwell-Roddey, interview by Sonya Ramsey, August 2, 2017; Kathy Haight, "Friends of the Arts in Charlotte," *Charlotte Observer,* August 12, 1984, 87, NewsBank: Access World News—Historical and Current, https://infoweb-NewsBank-com.eu1.proxy.openathens.net/ apps/news/document-view?p=WORLDNEWS&docref=image/v2:1160DC9BB798E30@ WHNPX-15E3F1C04A2BF814@2445925-15E48EBB9C048456@96, accessed June 11, 2018.

83. Maxwell-Roddey, interview by Sonya Ramsey, July 24, 2017; Ryanne Persinger, "Jazzy Holiday Tradition—Annual Luncheon Supports the Arts in Charlotte, Honors Philanthropy," *Charlotte Post,* November 25, 2010: 6B. NewsBank: Access World News—Historical and Current, https://infoweb-NewsBank-com.eu1.proxy.openathens.net/apps/news/document-view ?p=WORLDNEWS&docref=news/133BB24D4D20FE10, accessed July 20, 2020.

84. Farrar, interview by Sonya Ramsey, October 20, 2018; Maxwell-Roddey, interview by Sonya Ramsey, July 24, 2017; "Harvey Gantt Biography,"(Lyceum Announcement, published by Johnson C. Smith University), 2012, https://www.jcsu.edu/happenings/lyceum-series/ jcsu-lyceum-lecture-series/schedule/harvey-gantt, accessed June 29, 2020; Harvey Gantt, interview by Lynn Haessly, January 6, 1986, #4077, Transcript, Southern Oral History Program, University of North Carolina at Chapel Hill, Chapel Hill, North Carolina.

85. "Septima Poinsette Clark," *The Martin Luther King Jr. Research and Education Institute,* Stanford University, https://kinginstitute.stanford.edu/encyclopedia/clark-septima-poinsette, accessed July 6, 2020; "Septima Clark," *Digital SNCC Gateway* webpage, https:// snccdigital.org/people/septima-clark/, accessed July 6, 2020; Katherine Mellen Charron, *Freedom's Teacher: The Life of Septima Clark* (Chapel Hill: University of North Carolina Press, 2012), 169–170, 302, 345.

86. "Rights Activist Septima Clark to Visit Charlotte," *Charlotte Observer,* February 19, 1982,

16, NewsBank: Access World News—Historical and Current, https://infoweb-NewsBank-com. eu1.proxy.openathens.net/apps/news/document-view?p=WORLDNEWS&docref=image/ v2:11260DC9BB798E30@WHNPX-15E3F12296D7A830@2445020-15E347CC3727E896@15- 15E347CC3727E896@, accessed January 14, 2020; Farrar, interview by Sonya Ramsey, October 20, 2018.

87. Associated Press, "Teacher Fired for NAACP Role Gets $3600," *Charlotte Observer,* July 15, 1976, South Carolina Edition, 107, NewsBank: Access World News—Historical and Current, https://infoweb-NewsBank-com.eu1.proxy.openathens.net/apps/news/ document-view?p=WORLDNEWS&docref=image/v2:11260DC9BB798E30@WHNPX- 15FAAD64AA3C7166@2442975-16067785EFBFF1E2@106-16067785EFBFF1E2@, accessed September 26, 2019.

88. For more information about the life of Rosa Parks, see Jeanne Theoharis, *The Rebellious Life of Rosa Parks* (New York: Beacon Press, 2015).

89. "Septima Clark: A Worthy Appeal," *Charlotte Observer,* February 25, 1985, no page number, in WBTV Corporate Records, Box 1, Folder 3, Special Collections, J. Murrey Atkins Library, University of North Carolina at Charlotte Library, Charlotte, NC.

90. "Septima Clark: A Worthy Appeal," *Charlotte Observer,* February 25, 1985, no page number.

91. Jim Walser, "Fundraisers to Honor Civil Rights Pioneer," *Charlotte Observer,* March 16, 1985, 18, Newspapers.com https://www.newspapers.com/image/623908672, accessed March 2, 2022; Linda Brown, "Civil Rights Pioneer Honored At Luncheon," *Charlotte Observer,* March 22, 1985, 36, Newspapers.com, https://www.newspapers.com/image/623932909, accessed March 2, 2022.

92. *"The Town Is It Up or Down?" Charlotte Observer,* November 21,1974, 16, News-Bank: Access World News—Historical and Current, https://infoweb-NewsBank-com.eu1. proxy.openathens.net/apps/news/document-view?p=WORLDNEWS&docref=image/ v2:11260DC9BB798E30@WHNPX-15FAAD5669570661@2442373-1606776E3AF67613@15, accessed January 14, 2020; David Wagner, "Uptown? Downtown: or What?" *Charlotte Observer,* March 16, 1993, Editorial Page, NewsBank: Access World News—Historical and Current, https://infoweb-NewsBank-com.eu1.proxy.openathens.net/apps/news/documentview? p=WORLDNEWS&docref=news/0EB6CAA44C88104D, accessed October 7, 2019; For more information about Charlotte's development, see William Graves and Heather Smith, *Charlotte, NC: The Global Evolution of a New South City* (Athens: University of Georgia Press, 2012).

93. Maxwell-Roddey, interview by Sonya Ramsey, August 2, 2017.

94. Mary Turner Harper, "Beyond Act I: A Transdisciplinary and Experiential Approach to Afro-American Literature and Culture," Dissertation, 40; Lawrence Toppman, "Afro-American Cultural Center Raising Money to Renovate Church as Part of Its Expansion Plan," Charlotte Observer, 1C, May 29, 1984, 9, NewsBank: Access World News—*Historical and Current,* https://infoweb-NewsBank-com.eu1.proxy.openathens.net/apps/news/docu-ment-view?p=WORLDNEWS&docref=image/v2%3A11260DC9BB798E30%40WHNPX- 1736734DA8594FDE%402445850-17351EE5CF1031C9%408-17351EE5CF1031C9%40, accessed July 6, 2020.

95. Hugh McColl Jr., interview by Sonya Ramsey, May 26, 2016, Charlotte, NC, recording in author's possession, Charlotte, NC.

96. For a discussion of the history of Charlotte after the 1980s, see David Goldfield, "A Place to Come Home To," in *Charlotte, NC: The Global Evolution of a New South City,* eds., William Graves, and Heather A. Smith, eds. (Athens: University of Georgia Press, 2010); McColl Jr., interview by Sonya Ramsey, May 26, 2016.

Chapter 6. Charlotte's Afro-American Cultural Center and the Rise of the New South, Post-Soul City

1. Eric Avila, and Mark H. Rose, "Race, Culture, Politics, and Urban Renewal: An Introduction," *Journal of Urban History* 35, no. 3 (March 2009): 335–347, DOI, 10.1177/0096144208330393, accessed January 14, 2020.

2. For more information about the history of Charlotte prior to 1980, see David Goldfield, *Region, Race, and the Urban South* (Baton Rouge: Louisiana State University Press, 1997); Thomas W. Hanchett, *Sorting Out the New South City: Race, Class, and Urban Development in Charlotte, 1875–1975* (Chapel Hill: University of North Carolina Press, 1997); Gerald L. Ingalls and Isaac Heard Jr., "Developing a Typology of African American Neighborhoods in the American South," in William Graves and Heather A. Smith, eds. *Charlotte, NC: The Global Evolution of a New South City* (Athens: University of Georgia Press, 2010); Steven Samuel Smith, "The Development and the Politics of School Desegregation and Resegregation," in *Charlotte, NC: The Global Evolution of a New South City,* William Graves and Heather A. Smith, eds. (University of Georgia Press, 2010).

3. For more information about reverse migration and the Post-Soul South, see Carol B. Stack, *Call to Home: African Americans Reclaim the Rural South* (New York: Basic Books, 1996): Zandria F. Robinson*, This Ain't Chicago: Race, Class, and Regional Identity in the Post-Soul South* (Chapel Hill: University of North Carolina Press, 2014); William H. Frey, *Diversity Explosion: How New Racial Demographics are Remaking America* (Washington, DC: Brookings Institution Press, 2015); William H. Frey, "The New Great Migration: Black Americans' Return to the South, 1965–2000" (Washington, DC: Center on Urban and Metropolitan Policy, the Brookings Institution, 2004), http://www.brookings.edu/~/media/research/files/reports/2004/5/demographics-frey/20040524_frey.pdf, accessed January 14, 2020; Noah Goyke and Puneet Dwivedi, "Going South or Going Home? Trends in "Concurrent Streams of African American Migrants to the US South Over Four Decades," *Southeastern Geographer* 58, no. 3 (October 1, 2018): 282–299, http://search.proquest.com/docview/2161056396/, accessed January 14, 2020. For more information about immigration to Charlotte during this period, see Michael Jones-Correa, "The Kindness of Strangers:" Ambivalent Reception in Charlotte, North Carolina," in *Unsettled Americans: Metropolitan Context and Civic Leadership for Immigrant Integration,* edited by John Mollenkopf and Manuel Pastor (Cornell University Press, 2016), 163–188, accessed May 10, 2021, http://www.jstor.org/stable/10.7591/j.ctt18kr61m.10.

4. Patricia A. Banks, *Represent: Art and Identity Among the Black Upper-Middle Class* (New York: Taylor & Francis Group, 2009), 51–53; For more information about interpretations of Blackness among African American suburban residents, see Lori Latrice Martin, "Strategic Assimilation or Creation of Symbolic Blackness: Middle-Class Blacks in Suburban Contexts," *Journal of African American Studies* 14, no. 2 (2010): 234–46, http://www.jstor.org/stable/41819248, accessed May 10, 2021.

5. Zandria Robinson, *This Ain't Chicago: Race, Class, and Regional Identity in the Post-Soul South,* 83; Eric Frazier, "Southern Appeal-Influx of Blacks to 'New South' Accelerates Particularly in N.C. and Mecklenburg County," *Charlotte Observer,* August 6, 2006, 1A, NewsBank: Access World News—Historical and Current, https://infoweb-NewsBank-com.eu1.proxy.openathens.net/apps/news/document-view?p=WORLDNEWS&docref=news/1135B9D628288098, accessed January 14, 2020.

6. Bernadette Pruitt, *The Other Great Migration: The Movement of Rural African Americans to Houston, 1900–1941* (Commerce, TX: Texas A&M University Press, 2017); Luther Adams, *Way Up North in Louisville: African American Migration in the Urban South, 1930–1970* (Chapel Hill, University of North Carolina Press, 2010).

7. For more discussion of the post-soul concept, see Nelson George, *Post-Soul Nation: The Explosive, Contradictory, Triumphant, and Tragic, 1980s as Experienced by African Americans (Previously Known as Blacks and Before that, Negroes)* (New York: Penguin Books, 2004); Mark Anthony Neal, *Soul Babies: Black Popular Culture and the Post-Soul Aesthetic* (New York: Routledge Press, 2002), and Zandria Robinson*, This Ain't Chicago: Race, Class, and Regional Identity in the Post-Soul South.*

8. African American Museum of Dallas, "History," The African American Museum of Dallas Website. http://www.aamdallas.org/history.html, accessed July 30, 2020.

9. Harry Robinson Jr., interview by Sonya Ramsey, July 5, 2018, Charlotte, NC, phone recording in author's possession; Rhett Jones, 138; For more information about the rise of the African American Museum Movement, see Andrea Burns, *From Storefront to Monument: Tracking the Public History of the Black Museum Movement* (Amherst: University of Massachusetts Press, 2013).

10. Maxwell-Roddey, interview by Sonya Ramsey, August 2, 2017; Deborah Gates, "Organization Seek City Funds to Save Mount Carmel Baptist," *Charlotte News,* April 11, 1979, 5, NewsBank: Access World News—Historical and Current, https://infoweb-NewsBank-com.eu1.proxy.openathens.net/apps/news/document-view?p=WORLDNEWS&docref=image/v2%3A1126167831380960%40WHNPX-16F6A91C75B02A64%402444194-16F61869D216397E%404-16F61869D216397E%40, accessed July 6, 2020; Charlotte City Council Minutes, Minute Book 71, July 2, 1979, 232–234, Charlotte City Council Minutes Website, https://codelibrary.amlegal.com/codes/CharlotteNC/latest/m/1979/7/2, accessed December 22, 2021; "An Historical Brief on the AACC," *Charlotte Post,"* January 26, 1989; 3D, DigitalNC Database, http://newspapers.digitalnc.org/lccn/sn88063138/1989-01-26/ed-1/seq-31/, accessed January 14, 2020.

11. Charlotte City Council Minutes, Minute Book 71, July 2, 1979, 232–234; Maxwell-Roddey, interview by Sonya Ramsey, August 2, 2017; Dean Smith, "Savoring Success—The Afro-American Cultural Center Celebrates 20 Years of Overcoming Hardships," *Charlotte Observer,* October 9, 1994, 1F, NewsBank: Access World News—Historical and Current, https://infoweb-NewsBank-com.eu1.proxy.openathens.net/apps/news/document-view?p=WORLDNEWS&docref=news/0F24464DC8CE28D4, accessed October 27, 2020.

12. Dan Morrill, "Little Rock A.M.E. Zion Church Application," Charlotte Mecklenburg Historic Commission, February 4, 1981; Charlotte City Council Minutes, Book 77, February 22, 1982: 322, Charlotte City Council Minutes Website, https://codelibrary.amlegal.com/codes/CharlotteNC/latest/m/1982/2/22, accessed January 20, 2022.

13. Charlotte City Council Minutes, Book 79, October 25, 1982: 74–80, Charlotte

City Council Minutes Website, https://codelibrary.amlegal.com/codes/CharlotteNC/latest/m/1982/10/25, accessed January 20, 2022; Charlotte City Council Minutes, Book 87, November 24, 1986: 226, Charlotte City Council Minutes Website, https://codelibrary.amlegal.com/codes/CharlotteNC/latest/m/1986/11/24, accessed January 20, 2022; Maxwell-Roddey, interview by Sonya Ramsey, August 2, 2017; Herman Thomas, interview by Sonya Ramsey, January 8, 2019, Charlotte, NC, notes in author's possession; Dan Morrill, interview by Sonya Ramsey, September 9, 2013, Charlotte, NC, recording in author's possession.

14. Herman Thomas, interview by Sonya Ramsey, January 8, 2019; Dan Morrill, interview by Sonya Ramsey, September 9, 2013.

15. La Fleur Paysour, "Afro American Cultural Center Expands, Renews," *Charlotte Observer,* March 9, 1986, 1F, NewsBank: Access World News—Historical and Current, https://infoweb-NewsBank-com.eu1.proxy.openathens.net/apps/news/document-view?p=WORLDNEWS&docref=news/0EB6C0224E7E0908, accessed January 14, 2020; Herman Thomas, interview by Sonya Ramsey, January 8, 2019.

16. "AACC Past Directors," *Charlotte Post,* January 26, 1989; 7D, NewsBank: Access World News—Historical and Current, https://infoweb-NewsBank-com.eu1.proxy.openathens.net/apps/news/document-view?p=WORLDNEWS&docref=news/0EB6C0224E7E0908, accessed January 14, 2020.

17. Paysour, "Afro American Cultural Center Expands, Renews," 1F; Thomas, interview by Sonya Ramsey, July 27, 2017; "A Cultural Bridge for Charlotte," *Charlotte Observer,* August 8, 1984, 10; NewsBank: Access World News—Historical and Current, https://infoweb-NewsBank-com.eu1.proxy.openathens.net/apps/news/document-view?p=WORLDNEWS&docref=image/v2%3A11260DC9BB798E30%40WHNPX-15E3F1C049F79ADF%402445921-15E48EBB7828B555%409-15E48EBB7828B555%40, accessed July 16, 2020.

18. "AACC Past Directors," *Charlotte Post,* January 26, 1989; 7D, NewsBank: Access World News—Historical and Current, https://infoweb-NewsBank-com.eu1.proxy.openathens.net/apps/news/document-view?p=WORLDNEWS&docref=news/0EB6C0224E7E0908, accessed January 14, 2020.

19. Paysour, "Afro American Cultural Center Expands, Renews," 1F; Carolyn Mason, interview by Sonya Ramsey, July 10, 2018; Charlotte, NC, recording in author's possession; Lawrence Toppman, "Black Theater Starts Formal Season Again," *Charlotte Observer,* March 15, 1986: 11A, NewsBank *Access World news*—Historical and Current, https://infoweb-NewsBank-com.eu1.proxy.openathens.net/apps/news/document-view?p=WORLDNEWS&docref=news/0F2443BD66910DD9, accessed September 20, 2020; April Turner, "Defoy Glenn Returns to Charlotte Stage With 'A Month of Sundays,'" *Charlotte Post,* March 13, 2008, 2D, NewsBank: Access World News—Historical and Current, https://infoweb-NewsBank-com.eu1.proxy.openathens.net/apps/news/document-view?p=WORLDNEWS&docref=news/11FB99921833BD60, accessed January 14, 2020.

20. LaFleur Paysour, "Afro-American Cultural Center Gets New Home," *Charlotte Observer,* March 16, 1986, 1A, reprinted in the *Afro-American Cultural Center Brochure,* Afro-American Cultural Center, Vertical File Collection, Box: 1, Folder 3, Manuscript Collections, J. Murrey Atkins Library Special Collections and University Archives, UNC Charlotte.

21. Maxwell-Roddey, interview by Sonya Ramsey, August 2, 2017; Ruth Sloane, interview by Sonya Ramsey, July 26, 2018; Charlotte, NC, recording in author's possession.

22. Maxwell-Roddey, interview by Sonya Ramsey, August 2, 2017; Ruth Sloane, interview by Sonya Ramsey, July 26, 2018, Charlotte, NC.

23. Maxwell-Roddey, interview by Sonya Ramsey, August 2, 2017. For more information about the leadership philosophy of Ella Baker, see Barbara Ransby, *Ella Baker, and the Black Freedom Movement: A Radical Democratic Vision* (Chapel Hill: University of North Carolina Press, 2003).

24. Maxwell-Roddey, interview by Sonya Ramsey, August 2, 2017; Paysour, "Afro-American Cultural Center Gets New Home," 1A; Lawrence Toppman, "Arts and Science Council Distributes Grants," *Charlotte Observer,* May 29, 1986, 6B, NewsBank: Access World News— Historical and Current, https://infoweb-NewsBank-com.eu1.proxy.openathens.net/apps/news/document-view?p=WORLDNEWS&docref=news/0EB6C069039CC27D, accessed September 26, 2019; Richard Haag, "Commitment Afro American Center Sets Sights Higher," *Charlotte Observer,* June 17, 1987, 1, NewsBank: Access World News—Historical and Current, https://infoweb-NewsBank-com.eu1.proxy.openathens.net/apps/news/document-view?p=WORLDNEWS&docref=news/0EB6C1DEF3135598, accessed January 14, 2020.

25. For more information about reverse migration, see Larry L. Hunt, Matthew O. Hunt and William W. Falk, "Who Is Headed South? U.S. Migration Trends in Black and White, 1970–2000," *Social Forces* 87, no. 1 (September 2008): 95–119, JSTOR Database, www.jstor.org/stable/20430851, accessed January 14, 2020; Eric Frazier, "Southern Appeal-Influx of Blacks to 'New South' Accelerates Particularly in N.C. and Mecklenburg County," *Charlotte Observer,* August 6, 2006, 1A, NewsBank: Access World News—Historical and Current, https://infoweb-NewsBank-com.eu1.proxy.openathens.net/apps/news/document-view?p=WORLDNEWS&docref=news/1135B9D628288098, accessed January 14, 2020.

26. Robert M. Adelman, Chris Morett, and Stewart E. Tolnay, "Homeward Bound: The Return Migration of Southern-Born Black Women, 1940 to 1990," *Sociological Spectrum* 20, no. 4 (2000): 438, https://doi.org/10.1080/02732170050122639, accessed January 14, 2020.

27. Robinson, *This Ain't Chicago: Race, Class, and Regional Identity in the Post-Soul* South, 189.

28. John Vaughn, "Yolanda King to Bring Civil Rights Message to Charlotte," *Charlotte Observer,* June 18, 1987, 5C, NewsBank: Access World News—Historical and Current, https://infoweb-NewsBank-com.eu1.proxy.openathens.net/apps/news/document-view?p=WORLDNEWS&docref=news/0EB6C1DF5DF228B4, accessed September 30, 2019.

29. Laura McClettie, interview by Sonya Ramsey, June 20, 2018; Charlotte, NC, recording in author's possession; Jalyne Strong, "Who Will Be Crowned Queen of the Nile?" *Charlotte Post,* April 16, 1987, B1, DigitalNC Database, http://newspapers.digitalnc.org/lccn/sn88063138/1987-04-16/ed-1/seq-9/, accessed July 19, 2020.

30. Strong, "Who Will Be Crowned Queen of the Nile?" "Queen of the Nile Was Huge Success for AACC," May 21, 1997, 9A, DigitalNC Database, http://newspapers.digitalnc.org/lccn/sn88063138/1987-05-21/ed-1/seq-9/, accessed July 19, 2020.

31. Jalyne Strong, "Hindsight Is 20–20: A Glance Back on the Events of 1987," *Charlotte Post,* December 31, 1987; 8A, DigitalNC Database, http://newspapers.digitalnc.org/lccn/sn88063138/1987-12-31/ed-1/seq-8/, accessed October 27, 2020.

32. Herman Thomas correspondence to Sonya Ramsey, October 21, 2020; Richard Haag, "3 Shotgun Houses Targeted for Saving," *Charlotte Observer,* Nov. 13, 1985, 8, NewsBank: Access World News—Historical and Current, https://infoweb-NewsBank-com.eu1.proxy.ope-

nathens.net/apps/news/document-view?p=WORLDNEWS&docref=news/0EB6BFBE35BE A32A, accessed January 14, 2020; Thomas, interview by Sonya Ramsey, July 27, 2017; Valca Valentine, "Historic Houses at Cultural Center Get Second Chance," *Charlotte Observer*, January,15, 1992, 1C, NewsBank: Access World News—Historical and Current, https://infoweb-NewsBank-com.eu1.proxy.openathens.net/apps/news/document-view?p=WORLDNEWS& docref=news/0EB6C8DB8E2A86F7, accessed January 14, 2020; Dan L. Morrill, "*Survey and Research Report on Representative Shotgun Houses*," Charlotte Afro-American Cultural Center, Charlotte Mecklenburg Historical Properties Commission, May 8, 1985, 1–13, Special Collections and University Archives, J. Murrey Atkins Library, University of North Carolina at Charlotte, Charlotte, North Carolina.

33. Thomas, correspondence to Sonya Ramsey, October 21, 2020; Thomas, interview by Sonya Ramsey, July 27, 2017.

34. Tony Brown, "New Director," *Charlotte Observer*, May 24, 1989, 1D, NewsBank: Access World News—Historical and Current, https://infoweb-NewsBank com.eu1.proxy.openathens.net/apps/news/document-view?p=WORLDNEWS&docref=news/0EB6C4776FEA A77C, accessed September 20, 2020; Dean Smith, "Arts," *Charlotte Observer*, February 3, 1991, 1F, NewsBank: Access World News—Historical and Current, https://infoweb-NewsBankcom.eu1.proxy.openathens.net/apps/news/document-view?p=WORLDNEWS&docref =news/0F244B686C81183B, accessed July 15, 2020.

35. Lowell Gaston Foxx, "Membership Drive, New Programs and Groups," *The Charlotte Post*, January 26, 1989, 6D, DigitalNC Database, https://newspapers.digitalnc.org/lccn/ sn88063138/1989-01-26/ed-1/seq-34/print/image_674x817_from_707,392_to_2575,2653/, accessed September 20, 2020.

36. Foxx, Membership Drive, New Programs and Groups, *The Charlotte Post;* Tony Brown, "New Director," *Charlotte Observer*, May 24, 1989, 1D.

37. Dean Smith, "'Sick' Center on Road to Recovery Director Slashes Expenses, Beefs Up Programming," *Charlotte Observer*, February 3, 1991, 2F, NewsBank: Access World News, https://infoweb-NewsBank-com.eu1.proxy.openathens.net/apps/news/document-view?p=A WNB&docref=news/0EB6C76A03FA92B6, accessed October 30, 2020.

38. Smith, "'Sick' Center on Road to Recovery Director Slashes Expenses, Beefs Up Programming," 2F; Herman Thomas correspondence to Sonya Ramsey, October 21, 2020

39. Dean Smith, "Arts," *Charlotte Observer*, February 3, 1991, 2F.

40. Smith, "Arts," *Charlotte Observer*, February 3, 1991, 2F.

41. Smith, "'Sick' Center on Road to Recovery Director Slashes Expenses, Beefs Up Programming," 2F; Tommy Robinson, interview by Sonya Ramsey, July 6, 2018; Charlotte, NC, recording in author's possession; Geraldine Sumter, Interview by Sonya Ramsey, October 17, 2017, Charlotte, NC, recording in author's possession.

42. Geraldine Sumter, Interview by Sonya Ramsey, October 17, 2017, Charlotte, NC; Maxwell-Roddey, interview by Sonya Ramsey, June 25, 2017; Maxwell interview, June 25, 2018.

43. Dean Smith, "Savoring Success—The Afro-American Cultural Center Celebrates 20 Years of Overcoming Hardships," *Charlotte Observer*, October 9, 1994, 1F, NewsBank: Access World News—Historical and Current, https://infoweb-NewsBank-com.eu1.proxy.openathens. net/apps/news/document-view?p=WORLDNEWS&docref=news/0F24464DC8CE28D4.

44. Mae Israel and Tammy Joyner, "In Public Lives, New Barriers Impede Equality Blacks Push to Breakthrough Invisible Corporate Ceilings," *Charlotte Observer*, October 6, 1987, 1A,

NewsBank: Access World News—Historical and Current, https://infoweb-NewsBank-com. eu1.proxy.openathens.net/apps/news/document-view?p=WORLDNEWS&docref=news/0E B6C24E7025C34E, accessed July 19, 2020.

45. Dean Smith, "Savoring Success—The Afro-American Cultural Center Celebrates 20 Years Of Overcoming Hardships," 1F, NewsBank: Access World News, https://infoweb-News-Bank-com.eu1.proxy.openathens.net/apps/news/document-view?p=AWNB&docref=news/ 0F24464DC8CE28D4, accessed September 20, 2020; Dean Smith, "The House That Wanda Montgomery Built," *Charlotte Observer,* December 21, 1997, 1B, NewsBank: Access World News*,* https://infoweb-NewsBank-com.eu1.proxy.openathens.net/apps/news/document-vie w?p=AWNB&docref=news/0EB6D4F9E79A65D8, accessed September 20, 2020.

46. Dean Smith, "Arts Endowment: $26.161 Million—Success Puts City in Spotlight," *Charlotte Observer,* April 1, 1995, 1C, NewsBank: Access World News—Historical and Current, https://infoweb-NewsBank-com.eu1.proxy.openathens.net/apps/news/document-view ?p=WORLDNEWS&docref=news/0F2447D88897F7CE, accessed July 19, 2020.

47. *Charlotte Magazine* Staff, "Where Are They Now?" *Charlotte Magazine,* July 21, 2010, Website Article https://www.charlottemagazine.com/where-are-they-now-the-group/, accessed September 20, 2020.

48. Hugh McColl Jr. interview by Sonya Ramsey, May 25, 2016, Charlotte, NC, recording in author's possession; Dean Smith, "Bank Buys Art for Cultural Center—Donation of 58 Works by 20 Black Americans Stuns Arts Watchers," *Charlotte Observer,* July 8, 1998, 1A. NewsBank: Access World News—Historical and Current, https://infoweb-NewsBank-com. eu1.proxy.openathens.net/apps/news/document-view?p=WORLDNEWS&docref=news/0F 244DCF03D26EE7, accessed July 20, 2020.

49. Charlotte City Council Minutes, March 23, 1998, Book 112: 80, Charlotte City Council Minutes Website, https://codelibrary.amlegal.com/codes/CharlotteNC/latest/m/1998/3/23, accessed January 20, 2022.

50. Tommy Robinson, interview by Sonya Ramsey, July 6, 2018; Charlotte, NC, recording in author's possession; Geraldine Sumter, interview by Sonya Ramsey, October 17, 2017, Charlotte, NC, recording in author's possession.

51. Michel Vaughan, interview by Sonya Ramsey, February 25, 2018; Charlotte, NC, recording in author's possession.

52. Maxwell-Roddey, interview by Sonya Ramsey, August 2, 2018; Charlotte, NC, recording in author's possession. Carolyn Mason, interview by Sonya Ramsey, July 10, 2018, phone recording in author's possession.

53. Maxwell-Roddey, interview by Sonya Ramsey, August 2, 2017; David Taylor, interview by Sonya Ramsey, July 23, 2018; Charlotte, NC, recording in author's possession; Geraldine Sumter, interview by Sonya Ramsey, October 17, 2017.

54. *Charlotte Magazine* Staff, "Where Are They Now?" *Charlotte Magazine,* July 20, 2010.

55. Harry Robinson Jr., interview by Sonya Ramsey, July 5, 2018; Betty Cunningham, interview by Sonya Ramsey, July 16, 2020, Charlotte, N.C.; recording in author's possession.

56. Harry Robinson Jr., interview by Sonya Ramsey, July 5, 2018.

57. Brian D. Behnken, "The 'Dallas Way': Protest, Response, and the Civil Rights Experience in Big D and Beyond," *The Southwestern Historical Quarterly* 111, no. 1 (2007): 7, 8, http:// www.jstor.com/stable/40495679, accessed July 20, 2020.

58. Behnken, "The 'Dallas Way': Protest, Response, and the Civil Rights Experience in Big D and Beyond," 25.

59. Betty Cunningham, interview by Sonya Ramsey, July 16, 2020, Charlotte, N.C, notes in author's possession.

60. Richard Rubin, "Arts Plan Down, But Not Out-City Council Wants Time," *Charlotte Observer,* May 30, 2004, 1B, NewsBank: Access World News—Historical and Current, https:// infoweb-NewsBank-com.eu1.proxy.openathens.net/apps/news/document-view?p=WORLD NEWS&docref=news/102EB5D1A154E0F8, accessed January 14, 2020.

61. Christina Rexrode, "Wachovia Project: Arts Funding Secure-City of Charlotte, Which Is Paying Much of the Bill for Uptown Arts Facilities, Is Expressing Confidence," *Charlotte Observer,* August 1, 2008, 1D, NewsBank: Access World News, https://infoweb-NewsBank-com.eu1.proxy.openathens.net/apps/news/document-view?p=AWNB&docref=news/122501 8725ABEBCo, accessed September 20, 2020.

62. Kathy Haight, "A Day Full of Art, 1,500 Turn Out for the Fun at Harvey B. Gantt Center," *Charlotte Observer,* September 12, 2010, 1B, NewsBank: Access World News—Historical and Current, https://infoweb-NewsBank-com.eu1.proxy.openathens.net/apps/news/ document-view?p=WORLDNEWS&docref=news/132639D31EA28B68, accessed September 20, 2020.

63. The AACC executive director is now known as the president and CEO. David Taylor, interview by Sonya Ramsey, July 24, 2018; Charlotte City Council Minutes, Book 28: 844, April 27, 2009, Charlotte City Council Minutes Website, https://codelibrary.amlegal. com/codes/CharlotteNC/latest/m/2009/4/27, accessed January 20, 2022; Ely Portillo, "Lighting a Fire of Renewal for Uptown Church—Little Rock A.M.E. Zion Bought Back What It Once Sold, Launches a New Community Center," *Charlotte Observer,* December 14, 2009, 1B, NewsBank Access World News, https://infoweb-NewsBank-com.eu1.proxy.openathens. net/apps/news/document-view? p=AWNB&docref=news/12C99D78AC473098, accessed September 20, 2020.

64. Katy Stafford, "Arts Plan Drives New Tax-Car Rental Levy Now 16% Proceeds to Help Pay for Cultural Center Charlotte's Car Rental Tax Now Higher Than in Los Angeles and New York, Still Lower Than In Chicago, Las Vegas," *Charlotte Observer,* December 3, 2006, 1B, NewsBank: Access World News—Historical and Current, https://infoweb-NewsBank-com.eu1. proxy.openathens.net/apps/news/document-view?p=WORLDNEWS&docref=news/115CF603 AF9F19E0, accessed January 14, 2020; David Taylor, interview by Sonya Ramsey, July 24, 2018.

65. Thomas, interview by Sonya Ramsey, July 27, 2017; Taylor, interview by Sonya Ramsey, July 24, 2018; Zandria Robinson, 189.

66. Charlotte City Council Minutes, April 23, 2007, Book 125: 635, Charlotte City Council minutes, https://codelibrary.amlegal.com/codes/CharlotteNC/latest/m/2007/4/23, accessed January 20, 2022.

67. Taylor, interview by Sonya Ramsey, July 24, 2018; Thomas, interview by Sonya Ramsey, July 27, 2017; Geraldine Sumter, interview by Sonya Ramsey, October 17, 2017; Maxwell-Roddey, interview by Sonya Ramsey, June 24, 2017.

68. The Harvey B. Gantt Center for African American Art + Culture will be called the Gantt Center in this book.

69. Hugh McColl Jr., interview by Sonya Ramsey, May 25, 2016, Charlotte, NC; Mark Washburn, "Vivian and John Hewitt Built the Art Collection that Led to the Building of

Harvey B. Gantt Center," *Charlotte Observer,* October 25, 2009, 1A, NewsBank: Access World News—Historical and Current, https://infoweb-NewsBank-com.eu1.proxy.openathens.net/apps/news/document-view?p=WORLDNEWS&docref=news/12B9742B89499040, accessed Oct. 7, 2019; For more information about museums and the presence of Black artists, see Susan Cahan, *Mounting Frustration: the Art Museum in the Age of Black Power* (Durham: Duke University Press, 2016).

70. Mark Washburn, "Vivian and John Hewitt Built the Art Collection that Led to the Building of Harvey B. Gantt Center," 1A; Taylor, interview by Sonya Ramsey, July 24, 2018; Geraldine Sumter, interview by Sonya Ramsey, October 17, 2017.

71. Maxwell-Roddey, interview by Sonya Ramsey, June 24, 2018; Geraldine Sumter, interview by Sonya Ramsey, October 17, 2017; T. J. Reddy, interview by Sonya Ramsey, June 2, 2018.

72. Raj Chetty, Nathaniel Hendren, Patrick Kline, and Emmanuel Saez, "Where is the Land of Opportunity? The Geography of Intergenerational Mobility in the United States?" Study Sponsored by National Science Foundation, the Lab for Economic Applications and Policy at Harvard, the Center for Equitable Growth at UC-Berkeley, and the Laura and John Arnold Foundation, *Quarterly Journal of Economics* 129, no. 4. (2014): 1553–1623, in Opportunity Insights Website, https://opportunityinsights.org/paper/land-of-opportunity/, accessed January 14, 2020.

73. Capacchione v. Charlotte-Mecklenburg Schools 80 F. Supp. 2d 557 (W.D.N.C. 1999); Jim Morrill, "Ruling May Keep McColl Off Stand—Banker Likely Won't Testify for School System," *Charlotte Observer,* May 1, 1999, 1C, NewsBank: Access World News—Historical and Current, https://infoweb-NewsBank-com.eu1.proxy.openathens.net/apps/news/document-view?p=WORLDNEWS&docref=news/0F244A66E40F0B41, accessed July 20, 2020; Stephen Samuel Smith, "The Price of Success: The Political Economy of Education, Desegregation and Development in Charlotte," in *Yesterday, Today, and Tomorrow: School Desegregation and Resegregation in Charlotte,* eds., Roslyn Arlin Mickelson, Stephen Samuel Smith, and Amy Hawn Nelson (Cambridge, MA: Harvard Education Press, 2015), 25–35; David Goldfield, "A Place to Come Home To," in *Charlotte, NC: The Global Evolution of a New South City* (Athens: University of Georgia Press, 2012, eds., William Graves and Heather A. Smith, 10–24; Stephen Samuel Smith, *Boom For Whom? Education, Desegregation and Development in Charlotte* (Albany, NY: State University of New York Press, 2002), 224; James E. Ferguson II, interview by Melinda H. Desmarais, November 28, 2001, Charlotte, NC, J. Murrey Atkins Library Special Collections, University of North Carolina at Charlotte.

74. On June 2020, Charlotte mayor Vi Lyles created a fifteen-member Legacy Commission, comprised of historians and diverse group of Charlotte residents to identify, remove, and rename Charlotte's city streets, monuments, and other entities that honored slave holders, Confederate officers, and segregation-era white supremacists. After sponsoring a city-wide poll to encourage resident participation, the commission has renamed several of streets after influential Black Charlotteans. Stonewall Street is expected to be renamed by June 2022. See "City of Charlotte, About the Legacy Commission," City of Charlotte Website, https://charlottenc.gov/Mayor/Legacy-Commission/Pages/About-The-Legacy-Commission.aspx, accessed January 22, 2022; Devna Bose, "Charlotte Renames Street That Honored President of the Confederacy," *Charlotte Observer,* September 26, 2021, 1A. NewsBank: Access World News—Historical and Current. https://infoweb-NewsBank-com.eu1.proxy.openathens.net/

apps/news/document-view?p=WORLDNEWS&docref=news/18544816594F04E8, accessed
January 22, 2022.

75. Maxwell-Roddey, interview by Sonya Ramsey June 24, 2018; Brandon Lunsford,
"Good Samaritan Hospital," (Charlotte, NC: The Charlotte Museum of History), Charlotte
Museum of History Website, https://charlottemuseum.org/good-samaritan-hospital/, ac-
cessed October 27, 2020.

Chapter 7. What Does It Mean to Be a Delta?

1. Bertha Maxwell-Roddey, interview by Sonya Ramsey, April 29, 2015, Charlotte, NC,
recording in author's possession.

2. Bertha Maxwell-Roddey, interview, April 29, 2015, Official Website of Delta Sigma
Theta Sorority, https://www.deltasigmatheta.org/Incorporated, accessed July 3, 2019.

3. "Jabberwock History and Mission," Richland County Alumnae Chapter of Delta Sigma
Theta, Columbia, South Carolina Website, https://www.richlandcountydeltas.org/jabber-
wock-scholarship-pageant, accessed June 30, 2021.

4. Merriam Webster Dictionary, https://www.merriam-webster.com/dictionary/sister,
accessed July 1, 2019; Delta Sigma Theta Grand Chapter, "Constitution and Bylaws," 2.D;
Clarenda M. Phillips, "Sisterly Bonds: African American Sororities Rising to Overcome Ob-
stacles," in *African American Fraternities and Sororities: The Legacy and the Vision,* Tamara L.
Brown, Gregory S. Parks, and Clarenda M. Phillips, eds. (Lexington: University of Kentucky
Press, 2005), 345.

5. Delta Sigma Theta Grand Chapter, "Constitution and Bylaws," 43–45, 60–61.

6. Delta Sigma Theta Grand Chapter, "Constitution and Bylaws," 43.

7. Bertha Maxwell-Roddey, interview by Sonya Ramsey, June 28, 2019, Charlotte, NC,
recording in author's possession.

8. For more information about the establishment of the National Association of Colored
Women, see Stephanie Shaw, "Black Club Women and the Creation of the National Asso-
ciation of Colored Women," *Journal of Women's History* 3, no. 2 (1991): 11–25, Project Muse
Datebase, http://doi.org/10.1353/jowh.2010.0065, accessed January 20, 2022.

9. For more information about the politics of respectability, see Evelyn Brooks Higginbotham, *Righteous Discontent: The Women's Movement in the Black Baptist Church* (Cambridge
MA: Harvard University Press, 1993); For more information about Ida B. Wells Barnett see,
Mia Bay, *To Tell the Truth Freely: The Life of Ida B. Wells* (New York: Hill and Wang Publishers, 2009) and Paula J. Giddings, *Ida: A Sword Among Lions: Ida B. Wells and the Campaign
Against Lynching* (New York: Amistad Press, 2009. Even though Higginbotham's arguments
emanated from her analysis of African American church women across class lines within a
segregated society, some scholars, activists, and others have de-emphasized the politics of
respectability's complicated impact as a strategy for African American women's self-identity
formation as a sole effort for empowerment and neglected to recognize these women's other
social justice endeavors. In a modern-day critique by some scholars, activists, and others, the
derived and reinterpreted phrase, "respectability politics," now denotes a class-distinctive,
gender-neutral, misguided, and powerless endeavor to stem racial discrimination by African Americans. For an analysis of current scholarship on the politics of respectability, For
an analysis of current scholarship on the politics of respectability, see Ralina L. Joseph and

Jane Rhodes, "Guest Editors' Notes," *Souls: A Critical Journal of Black Politics, Culture, and Society* 18, no. 2–4 African American Representation and the Politics of Respectability (2016): 187–191, DOI: 10.1080/10999949.2016.1233032, accessed January 20, 2022. As Black people continue to encounter senseless acts of state-sponsored violence, some activists and scholars debate the usefulness and impact of what they deem "respectability politics." For a discussion of the impact of respectability politics, see Carol Anderson, "Respectability Will Not Save Us: On the History of Respectability Politics and their Failure to Keep Black Americans Safe," *Literary Hub,* August 9, 2017, Literary Hub Website, https://lithub.com/respectability-will-not-save-us/, accessed December 9, 2019.

10. For more information about the history of African American Greek-letter organizations, see Lawrence Gross Jr., *The Divine Nine: The History of African American Fraternities and Sororities* (New York: Kensington Books, 2000).

11. Craig L. Torbenson, "The Origin and Evolution of College Fraternities and Sororities," in *African American Fraternities and Sororities: The Legacy and the Vision,* Tamara Brown, Gregory S. Parks, and Clarenda Williams, eds. (Lexington, KY: The University Press of Kentucky, 2005), 37–67.

12. For more information about the history of African American Greek-letter organizations, see Andrew Mackenzie, "In the Beginning: The Early History of the Divine Nine," Tamara Brown, Gregory S. Parks, and Clarenda Williams, *African American Fraternities and Sororities: The Legacy and the Vision* (Lexington, KY: The University Press of Kentucky, 2008), 181–199. For more information about the history of Black women in higher education, see Linda M. Perkins, ""Bound to Them by a Common Sorrow": African American Women, Higher Education, and Collective Advancement," *The Journal of African American History* 100, no. 4 (2015): 721–47, doi:10.5323/jafriamerhist.100.4.0721, accessed May 10, 2021; For more history about the founders of Sigma Gamma Rho Sorority, see Bernadette Pruitt, Caryn E. Neumann, and Katrina Hamilton, "Seven Schoolteachers Challenge the Klan: The Founders of Sigma Gamma Rho Sorority," in *Black Greek-letter Organizations in the Twenty-First Century: Our Fight Has Just Begun,* Gregory S. Parks, Julianne Malveaux, and Marc H. Morial eds. (Lexington: University Press of Kentucky, 2008), 125–40; Matthew W. Hughey, "Constitutionally Bound: The Founders of Phi Beta Sigma Fraternity and Zeta Phi Beta Sorority," in *Black Greek-letter Organizations in the Twenty-First Century: Our Fight Has Just Begun,* edited by Gregory S. Parks, Julianne Malveaux, and Marc H. Morial (Lexington: University Press of Kentucky, 2008), 95–114; For more information about early African American women educational leaders in higher education see, Stephanie Evans, *Black Women in the Ivory Tower, 1850–1954: An Intellectual History* (Gainesville: University Press of Florida, 2007).

13. Paula Giddings, *In Search of Sisterhood: Delta Sigma Theta and the Challenge of the Black Sorority Movement* (New York: William and Morrow Press, 1988), 43.

14. For recent studies of Black Greek-letter organizations, see Theda Skocpol, *Black Greek-letter Organizations 2.0: New Directions in the Study of African American Fraternities and Sororities* (Jackson, MS: Univ. Univ. Press of Mississippi, 2011).

15. Pero Gaglo Dagbovie, "Black Women Historians from the Late 19th Century to the Dawning of the Civil Rights Movement," *The Journal of African American History* 89, no. 3 (2004): 255, doi:10.2307/4134077, accessed May 10, 2021.

16. Helen G. Edmonds, "The History of Delta Sigma Theta, 1954," unpublished manu-

script, 29, private collection of Fabette T. D. Smith, Raleigh, NC; Fabette T. D. Smith, interview by Sonya Ramsey, December 22, 2018, Charlotte, NC, recording in author's possession. For more information about the experiences of Black women historians, see Pero Gaglo Dagbovie, "Black Women Historians from the Late 19th Century to the Dawning of the Civil Rights Movement," *The Journal of African American History* 89, no. 3 (2004): 255, doi:10.2307/4134077, accessed May 10, 2021.

17. Fabette T. D. Smith, interview by Sonya Ramsey, December 22, 2018, Charlotte, NC, recording in author's possession; "Helen G. Edmonds," Funeral Program, R. Kelly Bryant Papers and Obituary Collection, North Carolina Collection, Durham County Library, 1995, in DigitalNC Database, https://lib.digitalnc.org/record/24011?ln=en, accessed October 20, 2020.

18. Deborah Gray White, *Too Heavy a Load: Black Women in Defense of Themselves, 1884–1994* (New York: W. W. Norton Publishing, 1999); Paula Giddings, *In Search of Sisterhood: Delta Sigma Theta and the Challenge of the Black Sorority Movement* (New York: William and Morrow Press, 1988).

19. For more information about the history of Greek-letter organizations see Walter M. Kimbrough, *Black Greek 101: The Culture, Customs, and Challenges of Black Fraternities and Sororities* (Farleigh Dickinson University Press, 2003); Tamara L. Brown, Gregory S. Parks, and Clarenda Williams, eds., *African American Fraternities and Sororities: The Legacy and the Vision* (Lexington, KY: The University Press of Kentucky, 2005); and Gregory S. Parks, ed. *Black Greek-letter Organizations in the Twentieth-Century: Our Fight Has Just Begun* (Lexington: University of Kentucky Press, 2008).

20. Gross Jr., *The Divine Nine: The History of African American Fraternities and Sororities,* 3–45; Alpha Kappa Alpha Sorority National Website, "History," http://aka1908.com/about/history, accessed May 14, 2019.

21. Grand Chapter, "Delta Sigma Theta Sorority, Inc. a Public Service Sorority, Heritage and Archives Resource Manual, 1993," 200.1; Unpublished Booklet in the Private Collection of Bertha Maxwell-Roddey, Charlotte, NC; Giddings, *In Search of Sisterhood: Delta Sigma Theta and the Challenge of the Black Sorority Movement,* 51–54; Helen G. Edmonds, "The History of Delta Sigma Theta, 1954," Unpublished Manuscript, 29, in the Private Collection of Fabette T. D. Smith, Raleigh, NC; Fabette T. D. Smith, interview by Sonya Ramsey, phone interview, September 5, 2020, notes in author's possession.

22. Beverly Smith, "How Beverly E. Smith Made Her Sorority a Lifetime Commitment," *Atlanta Journal and Constitution,* January 12, 2016, *Atlanta Journal and Constitution* Website, https://www.ajc.com/news/local-education/delta-sigma-theta-spoke/DvfbohjuoYRHpmVz-VCAeoO, accessed January 15, 2020. For more biographical information about Delta Sigma Theta Sorority's founders, see Jessica Harris, "Women of Vision, Catalysts for Change: The Founders of Delta Sigma Theta Sorority," in *Black Greek-letter Organizations in the Twenty-First Century: Our Fight Has Just Begun,* eds., Gregory S. Parks, Julianne Malveaux, and Marc H. Morial (Lexington: University Press of Kentucky, 2008), 75–95.

23. Marjorie H. Parker, *The History of Alpha Kappa Alpha, 1908–1999* (Washington, D.C.: Alpha Kappa Alpha, Sorority, Inc., 1999), 21; Stephanie Y. Evans, "The Vision of Virtuous Women: The Twenty Pearls of Alpha Kappa Alpha Sorority," in *Black Greek-letter Organizations in the Twenty-First Century: Our Fight Has Just Begun,* eds., Gregory S. Parks, Julianne Malveaux Julianne, and Marc H. Morial (Lexington: University Press of Kentucky, 2008), 41–66, accessed May 10, 2021. http://www.jstor.org/stable/j.ctt2jcrs6.8; Janeula

Burt, "Alpha Chapter, Delta Sigma Theta," January 13, 2022, https://www.facebook.com/groups/149104751799660, accessed January 14, 2022.

24. Grand Chapter, "Delta Sigma Theta Sorority, Inc. a Public Service Sorority, Heritage and Archives Resource Manual, 1993," 200.1; Unpublished booklet in the Private Collection of Bertha Maxwell-Roddey, Charlotte, NC; Giddings, *In Search of Sisterhood: Delta Sigma Theta and the Challenge of the Black Sorority Movement,* 51–54; Helen G. Edmonds, "The History of Delta Sigma Theta, 1954," Unpublished manuscript, 29, in the Private Collection of Fabette T. D. Smith, Raleigh, NC; Fabette T. D. Smith, phone conversation by Sonya Ramsey, September 5, 2020, written notes in author's possession.

25. Elsa Barkley Brown, "To Catch the Vision of Freedom: Reconstructing Southern Black Women's Political History, 1865–1880," in *Unequal Sisters: An Inclusive Reader in U.S. Women's History,* 4th ed., eds., Vicki Ruiz and Ellen Carol DuBois (New York: Routledge, 2008), 77–83. For more information about African American women's struggle for voting rights, see Rosalyn Terborg-Penn, *African American Women in the Struggle for the Vote, 1850–1920* (Bloomington, IN: Indiana University Press, 1998); Martha S. Jones, *Vanguard, How Black Women Broke Barriers, Won the Vote, and Insisted on Equality for All* (New York: Basic Books, 2020).

26. Giddings, *In Search of Sisterhood: Delta Sigma Theta and the Challenge of the Black Sorority Movement,* 57; Angelette L. Arias, "Delta Sigma Theta Enjoys a Rich Legacy: Sorority Played Role in Women's Suffrage," *News Press, Fort Myers Florida,"* February 1, 2002, 151, Newspapers.com Database, https://www.newspapers.com/image/217911292, accessed January 30, 2018; "T. Montgomery Gregory Dead: Retired Educator in Jersey, 84," *New York Times,* November 25, 1971, 40, N*ew York Times* Website, https://www.nytimes.com/1971/11/25/archives/t-montgomery-gregory-dead-retired-educator-in-jersey-84.html, accessed June 28, 2021. For biographical information about Mary Church Terrell, see Allison Parker, *Unceasing Militant: The Life of Mary Church Terrell* (Chapel Hill: University of North Carolina Press, 2020); Martha S. Jones, *Vanguard: How Black Women Broke Barriers, Won the Vote, and Insisted on Equality for All,* 164–165.

27. Parker, *Unceasing Militant: The Life of Mary Church Terrel*l, 126, 127.

28. Roddey is the name used when attributing quotes made during her presidency. Bertha Maxwell-Roddey, "President's Message: The Delta Legacy: A Journey of Historical Significance," *Delta Journal* (Spring, 1996), 3, National Headquarters Archives of Delta Sigma Theta Sorority, Inc., Washington, DC; Treva Lindsey, *Colored Women No More: Reinventing Black Womanhood* (Champaign Urbana: University of Illinois Press, 2017), 105–106.

29. Grand Chapter, "Delta Sigma Theta Sorority, Inc. a Public Service Sorority, Heritage and Archives Resource Manual, 1993," 200.3.

30. Delta Sigma Theta Grand Chapter, "Constitution and Bylaws," 7.

31. Phillips, "Sisterly Bonds: African American Sororities Rising to Overcome Obstacles," 354.

32. Fabette T. D. Smith, interview by Sonya Ramsey, phone interview, September 5, 2020, notes in author's possession.

33. Rachel Crouch, "Join the Delta Girls," paraphrased song excerpt performed by members of the Alpha Chapter, Delta Sigma Theta, Proselyte Show, Alpha Chapter, Howard University, 2011, Posted to YouTube, January 27, 2013, https://youtu.be/b4AmMJRPczA, accessed January 14, 2020.

34. For more information about the social welfare and social action activities of members of Greek-letter organizations, see Gregory S. Parks and Matthew W. Hughey, *A Pledge with Purpose: Black Sororities and Fraternities and the Fight for Equality* (New York: New York University Press, 2020).

35. Gregory S. Parks, Marcia Hernandez, "Fortitude in the Face of Adversity: Delta Sigma Theta's History of Racial Uplift," *Hastings Race and Law Journal* 13, 2 (Summer 2016): 290, UC Hastings Law School Website, https://repository.uchastings.edu/hastings_race_poverty_law_journal/vol13/iss2/2, accessed June 21, 2021.

36. Giddings, *In Search of Sisterhood: Delta Sigma Theta and the Challenge of the Black Sorority Movement,* 195; Charlotte Alumnae Chapter, Delta Sigma Theta, "Honoring the Past, Celebrating the Present, Embracing the Future, 75th Anniversary Booklet," *2017 Souvenir Booklet,* in the Private Collection of Bertha Maxwell-Roddey, Charlotte, NC, 4.

37. "Clothing Articles Given to Hospital, *Charlotte News,* February 26, 1954, in "Charlote Alumnae Chapter, Delta Sigma Theta Sorority Souvenir Booklet, 2017," in the Private Collection of the Charlotte Alumnae Chapter of Delta Sigma Theta Sorority, Inc., and the *Charlotte News,* NewsBank: Access World News—Historical and Current Database, https://www.newspapers.com/image/618394063/?terms=delta%20sigma%20theta&match=1, accessed December 22, 2021; Maxwell-Roddey, Interview by Sonya Ramsey, April 6, 2017, Charlotte, recording in author's possession.

38. Giddings, *In Search of Sisterhood: Delta Sigma Theta and the Challenge of the Black Sorority Movement,* 201–202, 208.

39. Harris, "Women of Vision, Catalysts for Change: The Founders of Delta Sigma Theta Sorority," in Black Greek-letter Organizations in the Twenty-First Century: Our Fight Has Just Begun, 84; Virginia Culver, "Denver Educator Gladys Bates, 90, Was A Tireless Fighter for Civil Rights," *Denver Post,* no page number, *Denver Post* Website, https://www.denverpost.com/2010/10/23/denver-educator-gladys-bates-90-was-a-tireless-fighter-for-civil-rights/, accessed June 22, 2021. John A. Kirk, "The NAACP Campaign for Teachers' Salary Equalization: African American Women Educators and the Early Civil Rights Struggle," *Journal of African American History* 94, no. 4 (Fall 2009): 535, https://www.jstor.org/stable/25653977, accessed July 10, 2021.

40. Giddings, *In Search of Sisterhood: Delta Sigma Theta and the Challenge of the Black Sorority Movement,* 219–220.

41. Bertha Maxwell-Roddey, interview by Sonya Ramsey, April 29, 2016, recording in author's possession; Johnson C. Smith University, "Golden Bull Yearbook," 1951–1953, DigitalNC Database, https://lib.digitalnc.org/search?ln=en&p=691%3A%22Johnson%20C.%20Smith%20University%22+AND+collectioninformation%3A%22North+Carolina+College+and+University+Yearbooks%22+AND+year%3A1951&sf=year&so=a, accessed May 23, 2019; Mary Louise Massey Jones, interview by Sonya Ramsey, March 7, 2012, Charlotte, NC, recording in author's possession.

42. Mary Elizabeth Vroman, *Shaped to Its Purpose: Delta Sigma Theta: The First Fifty Years* (New York: Random House Press, 1965), 25; Bertha Maxwell-Roddey, interview by Sonya Ramsey, April 29, 2016, Charlotte, NC, recording in author's possession.

43. Bertha Maxwell-Roddey, interview by Sonya Ramsey, April 29, 2016.

44. Jasmine Sanders, "A Black Legacy Wrapped Up in Fur," *The New York Times,* Janu-

ary 31, 2019, *New York Times* Website; https://www.nytimes.com/2019/01/31/style/fur-black-women-history.html, accessed June 11, 2019.

45. Robert H. Harris Jr., "Lobbying Congress for Civil Rights: The American Council on Human Rights, 1948–1963," in *African American Fraternities and Sororities: The Legacy and the Vision,* eds., Tamara Brown, Gregory S. Parks, and Clarenda Williams (Lexington, KY: The University Press of Kentucky, 2005), 211–213; Gregory S. Parks and Matthew W. Hughey, *A Pledge with Purpose: Black Sororities and Fraternities and the Fight for Equality,* 142.

46. Giddings, *In Search of Sisterhood: Delta Sigma Theta and the Challenge of the Black Sorority Movement,* 244.

47. Giddings, *In Search of Sisterhood: Delta Sigma Theta and the Challenge of the Black Sorority Movement,* 218–219.

48. Dorothy Counts-Scoggins desegregated Charlotte's Harding High School in 1957. She later became a member of the Charlotte Alumnae Chapter of Delta Sigma Theta; Giddings, *In Search of Sisterhood: Delta Sigma Theta and the Challenge of the Black Sorority Movement,* 208, 244–245.

49. Giddings, *In Search of Sisterhood: Delta Sigma Theta and the Challenge of the Black Sorority Movement,* 257; "17 Women's Groups Organize to Combat School Segregation," *The New York Times,* January 19, 1960, 31, Proquest.com Database, https://librarylink.uncc.edu/login?url=https://search-proquest-com.librarylink.uncc.edu/docview/115210358?accoun tid=14605, accessed May 23, 2019.

50. "17 Women's Groups Organize to Combat School Segregation," *The New York Times,* January 19, 1960, 31. For more information about Wednesdays in Mississippi and its efforts, see Debbie Harwell, *Wednesdays in Mississippi: Proper Ladies Working for Radical Change, Freedom Summer 1964* (Jackson: University Press of Mississippi, 2014). For more information about the civil rights activism of the National Council of Negro Women, see Rebecca Tuuri, *Strategic Sisterhood: The National Council of Negro Women in the Black Freedom Struggle* (Chapel Hill: University of North Carolina Press, 2018).

51. "Russell Says Groups in North Foment Riots to Push Rights Bill," *St. Louis Post-Dispatch,* February 28, 1960, 33; Newspapers.com Database, https://www.newspapers.com/ima ge/139114944/?terms=National%2BOrganization%2Bof%2BWomen%2Bfor%2BEquality%2B in%2BEducation, accessed June 18, 2019; "Many Southern Students Approve of Integration," *Kingsport Times,* February 17, 1960, 11, Newspapers.com Database, https://www.newspapers. com/image/592313220/?terms=National%2BOrganization%2Bof%2BWomen%2Bfor%2BEqu ality%2Bin%2BEducation, accessed June 17, 2019.

52. The South Atlantic Region, Delta Sigma Theta Sorority, Incorporated, "From These Roots: Violets and Pearls, 3rd Edition, 60th Anniversary, 1960–2020," (Unpublished Booklet of the South Atlantic Region, 2020): 15; Giddings, *In Search of Sisterhood: Delta Sigma Theta and the Challenge of the Black Sorority Movement,* 253. In addition to the South Atlantic, the six regions of Delta Sigma Theta include the following states, islands, and countries: Central (Colorado, Iowa, Kansas, Missouri, Nebraska, Oklahoma, and Wyoming); Eastern (Connecticut, Delaware, Maine, Massachusetts, New Hampshire, New Jersey, New York, Pennsylvania, Rhode Island, Vermont, Washington, DC, Germany, US Virgin Islands, and the Arabian Gulf-including Bahrain, Kuwait, Oman, Qatar, Saudi Arabia, and the United Arab Emirates); Farwest (Alaska, Arizona, California, Hawaii, Idaho, Oregon, Nevada, Utah, Washington, Japan, and the Republic of Korea); Midwest (Kentucky, Illinois, Indiana, Michigan, Minnesota,

Ohio, West Virginia, Wisconsin, and Canada); Southern (Alabama, Georgia, Florida, Mississippi, Tennessee, Virginia, the Bahamas, Southwest Arkansas, Louisiana, New Mexico, Texas, and Jamaica); the Southern Africa Alumnae Chapter (Angola, Eswatini, Kenya, Lesotho, and South Africa); and the West Africa Alumnae Chapter (Benin, Burkina Faso, Cape Verde, Côte d'Ivoire, The Gambia, Ghana, Guinea, Guinea-Bissau, Liberia, Mali, Niger, Nigeria, Senegal, Sierra Leone, and Togo); "Regional Leadership," Delta Sigma Theta Sorority, Inc., https://www.deltasigmatheta.org/regional-leadership, accessed October 23, 2020.

53. Giddings, *In Search of Sisterhood: Delta Sigma Theta and the Challenge of the Black Sorority Movement,* 253; "Jeanne L. Noble, 76, Pioneer in Education," *New York Times,* November 2, 2002, B76, Proquest, Inc. Database, https://librarylink.uncc.edu/login?url=https://search-proquest-com.librarylink.uncc.edu/docview/92158364?accountid=14605, accessed January 14, 2020; Vroman, *Delta Sigma Theta: The First Fifty Years,* 162–163, 178–179, Giddings, *In Search of Sisterhood: Delta Sigma Theta and the Challenge of the Black Sorority Movement,* 263; Bertha Maxwell-Roddey, interview by Sonya Ramsey, November 29, 2018, Charlotte, NC, recording in author's possession.

54. Delta Sigma Theta, "To Strive and Attain for Delta," Delta Corporate Report, 1977–1979, The Official Publication of Delta Sigma Theta, Inc. A Public Service Organization, vol 66, no. 5 (1979): 36.

55. For more information about the experiences of Blacks who migrated to southern urban enclaves, see Bernadette Pruitt, *The Other Great Migration: The Movement of Rural African Americans to Houston, 1900–1941* (College Station, Texas: A&M University Press, 2013).

56. Attend Merry Makers' Luncheon Card Party," *Charlotte Post,* April 3, 1975, 8, DigitalNC Database, http://newspapers.digitalnc.org/lccn/sn88063138/1975-04-03/ed-1/seq-8/, accessed September 20, 2020.

57. Bertha Maxwell-Roddey, interview by Sonya Ramsey, November 29, 2018, Charlotte, NC, recording in author's possession.

58. Grace Solomon, interview by Sonya Ramsey, September 21, 2017, Charlotte, NC, recording in author's possession.

59. Caryn E. Neumann, "Black Feminist Thought in Black Sororities," in *Black Greek-letter Organizations in the Twenty-First Century: Our Fight Has Just Begun,* Gregory S. Parks ed. (Lexington: University of Kentucky Press, 2008), 181.

60. "Debutante is Crowned," *Charlotte News,* April 20, 1964, 25, NewsBank: Access World News—Historical and Current, https://infoweb-NewsBank-com.eu1.proxy.openathens.net/apps/news/document-view?p=WORLDNEWS&docref=image/v2:1126167831380960@WHNPX-16F6C9BDCFE1500A@2438506-16F6C8D0961F2564@24, accessed January 14, 2020.

61. Neumann, "Black Feminist Thought in Black Sororities," in *Black Greek-letter Organizations in the Twenty-First Century: Our Fight Has Just Begun,* 181.

62. See Hilton Kelly, "'The Way We Found Them to Be': Remembering E. Franklin Frazier and the Politics of Respectable Black Teachers," *Urban Education* 45.2 (2010): 142–165, Urban Education Database, https://doi.org/10.1177%2F0042085908322726, accessed August 10, 2020.

63. For more discussion of the portrayal of African American women in the media, see Marian Meyers, *African American Women in the News: Gender, Race, and Class in Journalism* (New York: Routledge, Taylor & Francis Group, 2013).

64. Bertha Maxwell-Roddey, interview by Sonya Ramsey, August 16, 2016, Charlotte, NC, recording in author's possession; Bertha Maxwell-Roddey, interview by Sonya Ramsey, December 7, 2019, Charlotte, NC, recording in author's possession.

65. Maxwell-Roddey, interview by Sonya Ramsey, July 3, 2018; Vroman, *Delta Sigma Theta: The First Fifty Years,* 107, 108.

66. "Delta Sigma Theta Boast Five Point Program for Civic Work," *Charlotte Observer,* October 15, 1965, 21C, NewsBank: Access World News—Historical and Current, https://infoweb-NewsBank-com.eu1.proxy.openathens.net/apps/news/document-view?p=WORLDNEWS&docref=image/v2:11260DC9BB798E30@WHNPX-15E24FCB2A2D2F26@2439039-15E346F6033F095B@52-15E346F6033F095B@, accessed January 14, 2020.

67. Maxwell-Roddey, interview by Sonya Ramsey, July 3, 2018; Bertha Maxwell-Roddey, "President's Message," *Delta Journal* (Winter, 1992–1993): 2, in the National Archives of Delta Sigma Theta Sorority Inc., Washington, D.C.

68. "Three-State Meeting Set," *Charlotte Observer,* February 25, 1966, 46, NewsBank: Access World News—Historical and Current, https://infoweb-NewsBank-com.eu1.proxy.openathens.net/apps/news/document-view?p=WORLDNEWS&docref=image/v2%3A11260DC9BB798E30%40WHNPX-15E2501CA765980E%402439182-15E24D418517C95F%4045-15E24D418517C95F%40, accessed January 14, 2020; "Anna M. Earls (misspelled) Anna M. Brewer, South Carolina Department of Archives and History; Columbia, South Carolina; South Carolina Death Records; Year Range: 1962–1965; Death County or Certificate Range: 020124–020765, Ancestry.com. South Carolina, U.S., Death Records, 1821–1969 Database, https://www.ancestry.com/discoveryui-content/view/1697554:8741, accessed December 22, 2022.

69. Erika N. Duckworth, "Delta Sigma Theta, A Legacy of Strength," *St. Petersburg Times,* July 19, 1996, 1D, NewsBank: Access World News, https://infoweb-NewsBank-com.eu1.proxy.openathens.net/apps/news/document-view?p=AWNB&docref=news/0EB52E25B231AFE5, accessed January 14, 2020.

70. Duckworth, "Delta Sigma Theta, A Legacy of Strength," July 19, 1996, 1D.

71. Bertha Maxwell-Roddey, interview by Sonya Ramsey, February 15, 2019, Charlotte, NC, recording in author's possession.

72. Giddings, *In Search of Sisterhood: Delta Sigma Theta and the Challenge of the Black Sorority Movement,* 257, 263.

73. Giddings, *In Search of Sisterhood: Delta Sigma Theta and the Challenge of the Black Sorority Movement,* 257, 263, 266–267; Tiyi Makeda Morris, *Womanpower Unlimited and the Black Freedom Struggle in Mississippi* (Athens: The University of Georgia Press, 2014), 77, 133–134.

74. Giddings, *In Search of Sisterhood: Delta Sigma Theta and the Challenge of the Black Sorority Movemen*t, 266–267; Delta Sigma Theta Sorority, Incorporated, Photo of Martin Luther King with Delta Presidents Geraldine Woods and Past National President Dorothy Height at the 28th National Convention of Delta Sigma Theta, 1965, Facebook, https://www.facebook.com/dstinc1913/photos/with-3-more-days-until-the-formal-opening-of-dstvegas-we-are-reminiscing-on-some/1127703070665165/, accessed June 30, 2021; Bertha Maxwell-Roddey, interview by Sonya Ramsey, July 3, 2018, Charlotte, NC, recording in author's possession.

75. Bertha Maxwell-Roddey, interview by Sonya Ramsey, February 15, 2019, Charlotte, NC, recording in author's possession.

76. Joe Duster, "Anti-Poverty War Called Successful," *Charlotte Observer,* October 25, 1965, C1, NewsBank: Access World News—Historical and Current, https://infoweb-NewsBank-com.eu1.proxy.openathens.net/apps/news/document-view?p=WORLDNEWS&docref=image/v2:11260DC9BB798E30@WHNPX-15E24FCB2B9CEB7A@2439059-15E346F662B503D4@24-15E346F662B503D4@, accessed January 14, 2020.

77. "Anti-Terrorism Fund Passes $8,000 Mark," *Charlotte Observer,* December 4, 1965, 42, NewsBank: Access World News—Historical and Current, https://infoweb-NewsBank-com.eu1.proxy.openathens.net/apps/news/document-view?p=WORLDNEWS&docref=image/v2:11260DC9BB798E30@WHNPX-15F66151183A3326@2439099-15F6083450F73A4D@44-15F6083450F73A4D@, accessed January 14, 2020.

78. "Branton Speaks on Voting Rights at Delta Regional," *Carolina Times,* April 16, 1966, 3A, http://newspapers.digitalnc.org/lccn/sn83045120/1966-04-16/ed-1/seq-3/, accessed January 15, 2020.

79. Lena Horne and Richard Schickel, *Lena* (Garden City, NY, Doubleday Press, 1965).

80. Maxwell-Roddey, interview by Sonya Ramsey, July 3, 2018.

81. "Branton Speaks on Voting Rights at Delta Regional," April 16, 1966, 3A; Maxwell-Roddey, interview by Sonya Ramsey, July 3, 2018.

82. Charlotte Alumnae Chapter, "Past Presidents of the Charlotte Alumnae Chapter: Bertha Maxwell-Roddey," Charlotte Alumnae Chapter of Delta Sigma Theta, Inc. Official Website, http://www.charlottedst.org/aboutus/pastpresidents.html, accessed January 15, 2020.

83. Maxwell-Roddey, interview by Sonya Ramsey, July 3, 2018.

84. Gamma Chapter Delta Sigma Theta Sorority, Incorporated, "The History of Gamma Chapter, University of Pennsylvania" Website, https://www.dstgamma.com/new-page, accessed July 15, 2021; Jacqueline Stevens Sanders, interview by Sonya Ramsey, June 27, 2018, recording in author's possession.

85. Jacqueline Stevens Sanders, interview by Sonya Ramsey, June 27, 2018.

86. The Kappa Kappa Chapter of Alpha Kappa Alpha Sorority was started in 1976; Jacqueline Stevens Sanders, interview by Sonya Ramsey, June 27, 2018; Bertha Maxwell-Roddey, interview by Sonya Ramsey, April 6, 2017, Charlotte, NC, recording in author's possession.

87. Maxwell-Roddey, interview by Sonya Ramsey, July 3, 2018.

88. Giddings, *In Search of Sisterhood: Delta Sigma Theta and the Challenge of the Black Sorority Movement,* 274–277.

89. Jacqueline Stevens Sanders, "The Chartering of Iota Rho Chapter: Delta Sigma Theta Sorority, Incorporated," Unpublished Document; in the Private Collection of Jacqueline Stevens Sanders, Charlotte, NC.

90. Jacqueline Stevens Sanders, interview by Sonya Ramsey, June 27, 2018.

91. North Carolina Deaths, 1997–2004, North Carolina State Center for Health Statistics, Raleigh, North Carolina, https://search.ancestry.com/cgi-bin/sse.dll?dbid=8908&h=4684355&indiv=try&o_vc=Record:OtherRecord&rhSource=3693, accessed September 20, 2020.

92. Giddings, *In Search of Sisterhood: Delta Sigma Theta and the Challenge of the Black Sorority Movement,* 280.

93. Giddings, *In Search of Sisterhood: Delta Sigma Theta and the Challenge of the Black

Sorority Movement, 281. For more information about the style of Black college women, see Tanisha C. Ford, *Liberated Threads: Black Women, Style, and the Global Politics of Soul* (Chapel Hill: University of North Carolina Press, 2015), 95–122.

94. Giddings, *In Search of Sisterhood: Delta Sigma Theta and the Challenge of the Black Sorority Movement,* 282–289; Fabette T. D. Smith, "National Presidents," Unpublished notes, in the Private Collection of Fabette T. D. Smith, Raleigh, NC. DST is a Latin alphabet version of the Greek letters, Delta Sigma Theta. *Countdown at Kusini* (1976) is an American-Nigerian action drama, directed by Ossie Davis and produced by Ladi Ladebo and DST Telecommunications.

95. Giddings, *In Search of Sisterhood: Delta Sigma Theta and the Challenge of the Black Sorority Movement,* 294–296.

96. Delta Sigma Theta, Inc., "I Will Not Shrink from Undertaking What Seems Wise and Good," *Delta Corporate Report, 1977–1979, The Official Publication of Delta Sigma Theta, Inc. A Public Service Organization* (Washington, DC: Delta Sigma Theta Inc.), 66, 5 (1979): 6, 11, in the Private Collection of Bertha Maxwell-Roddey, Charlotte, NC; Giddings, *In Search of Sisterhood: Delta Sigma Theta and the Challenge of the Black Sorority Movement,* 294–296. For a visual image of Fortitude see, Delta Sigma Theta, Inc., "And High Ideals Preserve Monument to Founders," Delta Corporate Report, 1977–1979, The Official Publication of Delta Sigma Theta, Inc. A Public Service Organization (Washington, DC: Delta Sigma Theta, Inc.) 66, no. 5 (1979): 3, Private Collection of Bertha Maxwell-Roddey, Charlotte, NC; Aeja O. Washington, "Lady Fortitude," *The Hilltop,* October 26, 2004, Website article, no page number, http://www.howard.edu/library/imagesofthecapstone/Lady_Fortitude.htm, accessed August 21, 2020.

Delta Sigma Theta, Inc., "And High Ideals Preserve: Monument to Founders," *Delta Corporate Report, 1977–1979, The Official Publication of Delta Sigma Theta, Inc. A Public Service Organization* (Washington, DC: Delta Sigma Theta, Inc.) 66, no. 5 (1979): 3, Private Collection of Bertha Maxwell-Roddey, Charlotte, NC; For more information about "Lady Fortitude," and a visual image see, Aeja O. Washington, "Lady Fortitude," *The Hilltop,* October 26, 2004, no page number, Howard University Library Website, http://www.howard.edu/library/imagesofthecapstone/Lady_Fortitude.htm, accessed August 21, 2020.

97. Fabette T. D. Smith, "National Presidents;" Charles C. Hardy, "Conference Sets Equal Rights Goals," *Charlotte Observer,* February 11, 1979, 22A, NewsBank: Access World News—Historical and Current, https://infoweb-NewsBank-com.eu1.proxy.openathens.net/apps/news/document-view?p=WORLDNEWS&docref=image/v2:11260DC9BB798E30@WHNPX-15FAAD6B056185F8@2443916-1605D7650D382B20@22-1605D7650D382B20@, accessed January 15, 2020.

98. Hardy, "Conference Sets Equal Rights Goals," *Charlotte Observer,* February 11, 1979, 22A; "Next Saturday, WEETAP Workshop," *Charlotte Observer,* February 3, 1979, 22, NewsBank: Access World News—Historical and Current, https://infoweb-NewsBank-com.eu1.proxy.openathens.net/apps/news/document-view?p=WORLDNEWS&docref=image/v2:11260DC9BB798E30@WHNPX-15FAAD6B04EF5B27@2443908-1605D764E7C9A2E5@21-1605D764E7C9A2E5@, accessed January 15, 2020; Bertha Maxwell-Roddey, interview by Sonya Ramsey, July 3, 2018.

99. Lucille Batts, interview by Sonya Ramsey, June 26, 2018, Charlotte, NC, recording in

author's possession; Gaile Dry-Burton, interview by Sonya Ramsey, August 18, 2018, Charlotte, NC, recording in author's possession.

100. Grand Chapter, Delta Sigma Theta Sorority, Incorporated, "Constitution and Bylaws" (Washington, D.C.), *Private Collection of Bertha Maxwell-Roddey, Charlotte, NC, 2013.

101. Delta Sigma Theta Sorority, Incorporated, Grand Chapter, "Constitution and Bylaws" (Washington, D.C.), Private Collection of Bertha Maxwell-Roddey, Charlotte, NC, 2013.

102. Delta Sigma Theta Sorority Incorporated, A Public Service Sorority, "The Heritage and Archives Committee Presents, Delta's Heritage: The First Decade: 1913–1923," Booklet Private Collection of Bertha Maxwell-Roddey, Charlotte, NC., August 1, 1981, 4; Fabette T. D. Smith, interview by Sonya Ramsey, December 22, 2018, Charlotte, NC, recording in author's possession.

103. Bertha Maxwell-Roddey, interview by Sonya Ramsey, June 23, 2016, Charlotte, NC, recording in author's possession. The other members of the Heritage and Archives Committee were Margaret Carson, Donna P. Charles, Allie Miller Holley, Jean Hudson, Pearl McCleese, Edna Johnson Morris, Danielle P. Smith, Ruth Starke, and Grace White-Ware.

104. Fabette T. D. Smith, "Bertha M. Roddey, Highlights of One Delta's Journey of Historical Significance, 2011" Unpublished Document, Private Collection of Fabette T. D. Smith, Raleigh, NC.

105. Maxwell-Roddey, interview by Sonya Ramsey, June 23, 2016; Fabette T. D. Smith, interview by Sonya Ramsey, December 22, 2018.

106. Fabette T. D. Smith, interview by Sonya Ramsey, December 22, 2018.

107. Bertha Maxwell-Roddey, interview by Sonya Ramsey, June 23, 2016.

108. Farwest is the sorority's spelling.

109. "Regional Leadership," Delta Sigma Theta Sorority, Inc.

110. "Branton Speaks on Voting Rights at Delta Regional," *Carolina Times,* April 16, 1966, 3A, DigitalNC Database, http://newspapers.digitalnc.org/lccn/sn83045120/1966-04-16/ed-1/seq-3/, accessed January 15, 2020; Maxwell-Roddey, interview by Sonya Ramsey, July 3, 2016.

Chapter 8. Bertha's Girls and the Dimensions of a Political Sisterhood

1. Bertha Maxwell-Roddey abbreviated her name to Bertha M. Roddey during her tenure as the 20th National President of Delta Sigma Theta Sorority, Inc. and for other occasions relating to her presidency. For clarity, this chapter will use "Roddey." In later years, she would use Bertha Maxwell-Roddey.

2. Bertha Maxwell-Roddey, interview by Sonya Ramsey, March 9, 2018, Charlotte, NC, recording in author's possession; Oscar Faye Williams, interview by Sonya Ramsey, December 20, 2018, Charlotte, NC, recording in author's possession

3. Bertha Maxwell-Roddey, interview by Sonya Ramsey, March 9, 2018; Roselle Wilson, interview by Sonya Ramsey, December 12, 2018, Charlotte, NC, recording in author's possession.

4. "100 Most Influential Black Americans and Organizational Leaders," *Ebony Magazine* (May 1996): 130–132, Google Books Database, https://books.google.com/books?id=yFETn aIR808C&lpg=PA132&dq=ebony%20magazine%20%22Bertha%20M.%20Roddey%22&pg=

PA131#v=onepage&q=ebony%20magazine%20%22Bertha%20M.%20Roddey%22&f=false, accessed October 27, 2020.

5. Paula Giddings, *In Search of Sisterhood: Delta Sigma Theta and the Challenge of the Black Sorority Movement* (New York: William Morris, 1988), 71–73 and 216–221.

6. Letter from Vernon E. Jordan Jr. to Geraldine P. Woods, Voter Education Project Organizational Records, Special Collections, Robert W. Woodruff Library, Atlanta University Center Website, http://hdl.handle.net/20.500.12322/auc.076:0102, accessed December 22, 2021; Giddings, *In Search of Sisterhood: Delta Sigma Theta and the Challenge of the Black Sorority Movement,* 71–73, 216–221, 217–275, 244, 249–251, 214–242.

7. Maxwell-Roddey, interview by Sonya Ramsey, June 18, 2019, Charlotte, NC, recording in author's possession.

8. Gaile Dry-Burton, Bertha Maxwell-Roddey, and Kay Cunningham, interview by Sonya Ramsey, June 23, 2018, Charlotte, NC, recording in author's possession.

9. Bertha Maxwell-Roddey, interview by Sonya Ramsey, July 3, 2018, Charlotte, NC, recording in author's possession.

10. Maxwell-Roddey, interview by Sonya Ramsey, July 3, 2018.

11. Maxwell-Roddey, Gaile Dry-Burton, and Kay Cunningham, interview by Sonya Ramsey, June 23, 2018; Ann McMillion, interview by Sonya Ramsey, July 30, 2019; Charlotte, NC, recording in author's possession. The members of the 1982–86 South Atlantic Regional Council are Lucille Batts, Linda Brown, Mamie H. Brown, Kay Cunningham, Demetrice Davis, Roberta Duff, Andrea Fulton, Doris Greene, Carroll Hardy, Cheryl A. Hickmon, Sarah Johnson, Pearl McCleese, Iris Officer, Brandoyn C. Pinkston, Sharon Reed, Louise Riddick, Cynthia Roddey, Norma Sermon-Boyd, Juanita Sheppard, Fabette T. D. Smith, Lillie Solomon, Mudy Stone, Genevieve Swinton, Mary Sutton, Carolyn Taylor, Shelia Taylor, Edythe Tweedy, Carla Watson, Kaye R. Webb, Dorothy C. White, and Leila White.

12. Fabette T. D. Smith, interview by Sonya Ramsey, December 22, 2018; Maxwell-Roddey, interview by Sonya Ramsey, July 3, 2018.

13. Since her graduation, Cheryl A. Hickmon has epitomized Delta's philosophy of lifetime membership and service by participating in almost every aspect of the sorority and holding influential chapter, regional, and national offices. After forty years of dedication and service, one of Maxwell-Roddey's original BGs, friend, and mentee, Cheryl A. Hickmon was elected the 27th National President of Delta Sigma Theta Sorority, Inc. at the national convention in November 2021. Tragically, after holding office for only a few months, she died after succumbing to a recent illness in January 2022. Maxwell-Roddey, interview by Sonya Ramsey, July 3, 2018; Fabette T. D. Smith, "Bertha M. Roddey, Highlights of One Delta's Journey of Historical Significance," 2011, 1, Unpublished Document, Private Collection of Fabette T. D. Smith, Charlotte, NC.

14. Maxwell-Roddey, interview by Sonya Ramsey, July 3, 2018.

15. Maxwell-Roddey, interview by Sonya Ramsey, July 3, 2018.

16. For a recent exploration of the subject of Black sororities and hazing, see Walter Kimbrough, *Black Greek 101: The Culture, Customs, and Challenges of Black Fraternities and Sororities* (Madison, Teaneck, NJ: Fairleigh Dickinson University Press, 2003).

17. Maxwell-Roddey, interview by Sonya Ramsey, July 3, 2018.

18. Fabette T. D. Smith, interview by Sonya Ramsey, December 22, 2018; Maxwell-Roddey, interview by Sonya Ramsey, July 3, 2018.

19. Maxwell-Roddey, interview by Sonya Ramsey, July 3, 2018.

20. Ann C. McMillon, interview by Sonya Ramsey, December 12, 2018, Charlotte, NC, phone recording in author's possession; Fabette T. D. Smith, interview by Sonya Ramsey, December 22, 2018.

21. Bertha Maxwell-Roddey, "Forward," *From These Roots, A History of the South Atlantic Region,* edited by Lillie Solomon and Kaye Cunningham. (Charlotte, NC: Delmar Printing, 1984), 8.

22. Bertha Maxwell-Roddey interview by Sonya Ramsey, December 28, 2017, Charlotte, NC, recording in author's possession.

23. For more information about the field of Black Women's History see, Leslie M. Alexander, "The Challenge of Race: Rethinking the Position of Black Women in the Field of Women's History." *Journal of Women's History* 16, no. 4 (2004): 50–60. doi:10.1353/jowh.2004.0074, accessed January 22, 2022; Daina Ramey Berry and Kali Nicole Gross, "Black Women's History in the US: Past & Present," April 24, 2020, *Not Even Past,* Digital Magazine, Department of History University of Texas at Austin, Austin, TX, https://notevenpast.org/black-womens-history-in-the-us-past-present/, accessed December 22, 2021; Maxwell-Roddey interview by Sonya Ramsey, December 28, 2017.

24. Fabette T. D. Smith, interview by Sonya Ramsey, December 22, 2018; Fabette T. D. Smith, interview by Sonya Ramsey, June 30, 2019.

25. Bertha Maxwell-Roddey interview by Sonya Ramsey, September 4, 2020, phone audio recording, Charlotte, NC, recording in author's possession.

26. Bertha Maxwell-Roddey interview by Sonya Ramsey, December 28, 2017.

27. Bertha Maxwell-Roddey interview by Sonya Ramsey, December 28, 2017.

28. Bertha M. Roddey, "Love After Breast Cancer," in *Celebrating Life: African American Women Speak Out About Breast Cancer,* Sylvia Dunnavant, and Sharon Egiebor, eds. (Dallas, TX: USFI, Inc., Press, 1995), 67; Ryanne Persinger, "Full Life for 2-Time Survivor," *Charlotte Post,* October 20, 2011, no page number *Charlotte Post* Website, http://www.thecharlottepost.com/news/2011/10/20/life-and-religion/full-life-for-2-time-survivor/, accessed December 30, 2019.

29. After thirty-four years of marriage to Bertha Maxwell-Roddey, Theodore Thomas Roddey Jr., age 95, passed away on September 5, 2021. See "Theodore Thomas Roddey Jr. 1926–2021," *The Herald,* September 8, 2021, *The Herald* Website, https://www.legacy.com/us/obituaries/heraldonline/name/theodore-roddey-obituary?id=18783137, accessed January 20, 2022.

30. Fabette T. D. Smith, correspondence to Sonya Ramsey, April 22, 2020, in author's possession.

31. Bertha Maxwell-Roddey, interview by Sonya Ramsey, June 18, 2019, Charlotte, NC, recording in author's possession.

32. Bertha Maxwell-Roddey, interview by Sonya Ramsey, June 18, 2019; Fabette T. D. Smith, correspondence to Sonya Ramsey, April 22, 2020, in author's possession.

33. Smith, correspondence to Sonya Ramsey, April 22, 2020

34. Delta Sigma Theta Sorority, Inc., "40th National Convention Workbook," 1988 (Washington, DC: Delta Sigma Theta, 1992), 68, in the National Archives of Delta Sigma Theta Sorority, Inc., Washington, D.C.

35. Bertha Maxwell-Roddey, interview by Sonya Ramsey, June 18, 2019.

36. Barbara Ransby, *Ella Baker and the Black Freedom Movement: A Radical Democratic Vision* (Chapel Hill: University of North Carolina Press, 2003), 4; Maxwell-Roddey, interview by Sonya Ramsey, June 18, 2019.

37. Delta Sigma Theta Sorority, Inc., "39th National Convention Workbook," San Francisco, CA, July 8–14, 1988, 9, The 39th National Convention Folder, National Archives of Delta Sigma Theta Sorority Inc., Washington, DC; Maxwell-Roddey, interview by Sonya Ramsey, June 18, 2019.

38. Delta Sigma Theta Sorority, Inc., "39th National Convention Workbook, San Francisco, CA, July 8–14, 1988," 9, The 39th National Convention Folder, National Archives of Delta Sigma Theta Sorority Inc., Washington, DC; Maxwell-Roddey, interview by Sonya Ramsey, June 18, 2019. The members of the 1988–92 Scholarship and Standards Committee are Carolyn V. Atkins, Doris Jackson Britt, Mamie H. Brown, Jessie Nave Carpenter, Elsie Cooke-Homes, Yvonne Kennedy, Sharon J. Lettman, Octavia G. Matthews, Yvonne McGhee, Claudia L. McKoin, Deborah Carol Thomas, and Thyra L. White-Austin.

39. Smith notes to Sonya Ramsey, October 9, 2020, Charlotte, NC, in author's possession.

40. Bertha Maxwell-Roddey, "Statement from the National First Vice-President," in *Delta Sigma Theta Sorority, Incorporated, "The Corporate Report,* July 1990," (Washington, DC: Delta Sigma Theta Sorority, Inc., 1990), 6, National Archives of Delta Sigma Theta Sorority, Inc.; Bertha Maxwell-Roddey, interview by Sonya Ramsey, June 14, 2017, Charlotte, NC, recording in author's possession.

41. Darlene Jackson-Bowen, interview by Sonya Ramsey, October 18, 2020, Charlotte, NC, notes in author's possession.

42. Marcia Fudge, "Report of the First Vice President of Delta Sigma Theta," *The Corporate Report,* July 1992, National Archives of Delta Sigma Theta Sorority, Inc., Washington, DC.

43. Roselle Wilson, interview by Sonya Ramsey, December 12, 2018, Charlotte, NC, recording in author's possession. The Divine Nine is the title for the nine African American Greek-letter organizations.

44. Melania Page Wicks, interview by Sonya Ramsey, January 4, 2019, Charlotte, NC, recording in author's possession.

45. Delta Sigma Theta Sorority, Inc. *Delta Sigma Theta Sorority, Inc. The Delta Launch 2000: A New Leadership for a New Century, 41st National Convention Workbook,* Baltimore, Maryland, July 10–15, 1992 (Washington, DC: Delta Sigma Theta Sorority, Inc., 1992), 68–69; Private Collection of Bertha Maxwell-Roddey, Charlotte, NC.

46. Delta Sigma Theta Sorority, Inc., *Souvenir Journal, Delta Sigma Theta, Sisterhood: A Global Connection, 41st National Convention Program, Baltimore, Maryland, July 10–15, 1992* (Washington, DC: Delta Sigma Theta Sorority, Inc., 1992), 101, Private Collection of Bertha Maxwell-Roddey, Charlotte, NC; Delta Sigma Theta Sorority, Inc., *Delta Sigma Theta Sorority, Inc. The Delta Launch 2000: A New Leadership for a New Century, 41st National Convention Workbook,* 68; "Bertha Maxwell-Roddey Elected Delta Sigma Theta President," *New York Amsterdam News,* August 15, 1992, 18, ProQuest Historical Newspapers Database https://librarylink.uncc.edu/login?url=https://search-proquest-com.librarylink.uncc.edu/docview/226435439?accountid=14605, accessed May 23, 2019.

47. The 1992–96 Delta Sigma Theta Executive Board members were Louise L. Alexander, Gloria B. Banks, Valerie D. Baston, Tamara M. Brown, Guessippina Bonner, Akilah A. Campbell, Jessie Nave Carpenter, Sharon J. Chapman, Sheila Wheatley Clark, Jolene L. Cook,

Minnie Cook, Pamela Y. Cook, Barbara F. Curtis, Barbara Moseley Davis, Bobbie J. Ewing, Nettie D. Faulcon, Dwala N. Foster, Khadija A. Fredericks, Shirley Ann Fridia, Marcia L. Fudge, Lois J. Gilder, Wilhelmina D. Goff, Annie C Goodson, Doris G. Greene, Jacqueline B. Hairston, Alison J. Harmon, Cheryl A. Hickmon, Pamela D. Jackson, Ella Goode Johnson, Gloria E. Johnson, Ruth Tamar Jones, Yvonne Kennedy, Milele L. Kudumu, Octavia G. Matthews, Veleter Mazyck, Ruth J. McClendon, Betty A. McGill, Kelley K. McKeever, Vashti McKenzie, Claudia L. McKoin, Roseline McKinney, Deanna L. Mills, Melania Page, Marion Phillips, Brandolyn C. Pinkston, Carol S. Puryear, Louise A. Rice, Neeka L. Sanders, Delores Sennette, Sara Howell Smalley, Fabette T. D. Smith, Floraline I. Stevens, Rose Marie D. Swanson, Adrienne Brooks Taylor, Lynette Taylor, Deborah Carol Thomas, Gladys Gary Vaughn, Angela D. Watson, Erika L. Watson, Avril Weathers, Kaye R. Webb, Dorothy C. White, Gloria W. White, Tessa H. Wilbert, Ada Williams and Gloria L. Williams.

48. L. Diane Bennett, interview by Sonya Ramsey, May 4, 2017, Charlotte, NC, recording in author's possession; Darlene Clark Hine, African American Women and Their Communities in the Twentieth Century: The Foundation and Future of Black Women's Studies," *Black Women, Gender + Families* 1, no. 1 (Spring 2007): 1–23, https://www.jstor.org/stable/10.5406/blacwomegendfami.1.1.0001, accessed January 20, 2022.

49. Bertha Maxwell-Roddey, interview by Sonya Ramsey, April 4, 2019, Charlotte, NC, recording in author's possession.

50. Jacqueline Trescott, "Summit Politics: Black Women's Summit," *The Washington Post,* July 31, 1981, no page number, *Washington Post* Website, https://www.washingtonpost.com/archive/lifestyle/1981/07/31/summit-politics-black-womens-summit/efc7397e-5753-4d13-ab2f-cc6245c04ebd/, accessed August 18, 2020; Fabette T. D. Smith, unpublished notes, in author's possession, April 20, 2020.

51. "National President Speaks: Deltas' Black Women's Summit Challenges Sorors to 'Break the Chains of Denial,'" *Indianapolis Recorder,* March 21, 1981, 4, https://newspapers.library.in.gov/cgi-bin/indiana?a=d&d=INR19810321-01.1.4&e=-------en-20--1--txt-txIN-------, accessed October 27, 2020.

52. "National President Speaks: Deltas' Black Women's Summit Challenges Sorors to 'Break the Chains of Denial,'" 4. For a discussion of Black families, see Robert Staples and Leanor Boulin Johnson, *Black Families at the Crossroads: Challenges and Prospects* Revised edition (San Francisco, CA: Jossey-Bass, a Wiley Imprint, 2005).

53. Giddings, *In Search of Sisterhood: Delta Sigma Theta and the Challenge of the Black Sorority Movement,* 298; Donna Franklin, *Enduring Inequality: The Structural Transformation of the African American Family* (New York: Oxford Press, 1997), 236.

54. Giddings, *In Search of Sisterhood: Delta Sigma Theta and the Challenge of the Black Sorority Movement,* 299.

55. Fabette T. D. Smith and Ann McMillon, interview by Sonya Ramsey, June 30, 2019, Charlotte, NC, recording in author's possession; Delta Sigma Theta Sorority, Incorporated, "The Corporate Report" (Washington, DC: Delta Sigma Theta Sorority, Inc.), July 1992, National Archives of Delta Sigma Theta Sorority, Inc., Washington, DC.

56. Smith and Ann McMillon, interview by Sonya Ramsey, June 30, 2019; Giddings, *In Search of Sisterhood: Delta Sigma Theta and the Challenge of the Black Sorority Movement,* 299–302.

57. Giddings, *In Search of Sisterhood: Delta Sigma Theta and the Challenge of the Black*

Sorority Movement, 285; Bertha M. Roddey, "Delta Sigma Theta Seal of the President: Report of the National President to the Regions of the Grand Chapter," June 1993 (Washington, DC: Delta Sigma Theta Sorority, Inc. 1993), Private Collection of Bertha Maxwell-Roddey, Charlotte, NC.

58. For more information about women and homeownership, see Anita Hill, *Reimagining Equality: Stories of Race, Gender, and Finding Home* (New York: Beacon Press, 2011).

59. For more information about the history of African Americans and homeownership after World War II, see Keeanga-Yamahtta Taylor, *Race for Profit: How Banks and the Real Estate Industry Undermined Black Homeownership* (Chapel Hill, NC; University of North Carolina Press, 2019).

60. Frye Gaillard, *If I Were a Carpenter: Twenty Years of Habitat for Humanity* (Winston-Salem, NC: J. F. Blair Publishing, First Edition, 1996), 5–27.

61. Millard Fuller, *The Theology of the Hammer* (Macon, GA: Smyth and Helwys Publishing, 1996), 2, 7.

62. Bertha Maxwell-Roddey, interview by Sonya Ramsey, September 18, 2018, Charlotte, NC, recording in author's possession.

63. Fuller, *The Theology of the Hammer,* 94, 95; Joe Earle, Social Security Administration; Washington D.C., USA; Social Security Death Index, Master File, Ancestry.com, US Social Security Death Index, 1935–2014 Database, https://search.ancestry.com/collections/3693/records/17127902/printer-friendly?o_vc=Record%3aOtherRecord&rhSource=61843, accessed Dec. 22, 2021.

64. Doris Glymph Greene, "Delta Habitat for Humanity Committee Report, 1994," in *Delta Sigma Theta Sorority Inc. Corporate Report: Delta Launch 2000: A New Leadership for a New Century* (Washington, DC: Delta Sigma Theta Sorority, Inc., July 1994), 28, National Archives of Delta Sigma Theta Sorority Inc., Washington, D.C.

65. Doris Glymph Greene, "Delta Sigma Theta Sorority and Habitat for Humanity International Share Global Vision," *Delta Journal* (Winter 1992) 8, in the National Archives of Delta Sigma Theta Sorority Inc., Washington, D.C.

66. Greene, "Delta Sigma Theta Sorority and Habitat for Humanity International Share Global Vision," 28.

67. Bertha Maxwell-Roddey, interview by Sonya Ramsey, September 18, 2018.

68. Danon Carter, "'We Did It:' Sorority Builds 22 Delta Habitat Houses," *Delta Journal* (Fall–Winter, 1994), 4–6, in the National Archives of Delta Sigma Theta, Washington, DC.

69. Oscar Faye Williams, interview by Sonya Ramsey, Dec. 20, 2018, Charlotte, NC, recording in author's possession.

70. Delta Sigma Theta, "Delta Update Delta Sigma Theta Sorority, Inc.: *Delta Sigma Theta,* Special Telethon Edition," vol 2, no. 1 (January 1993), in the private collection of Roberta Duff, Gastonia, NC.

71. L. Diane Bennett, interview by Sonya Ramsey, May 4, 2017, Charlotte, NC, recording in author's possession; Bertha M. Roddey, "Letter to Carol Freeland," May 10, 1995, Habitat for Humanity International Records, MMS 3786, Hargrett Rare Book and Manuscript Library, The University of Georgia Libraries, Athens, GA; Bertha Maxwell-Roddey, interview by Sonya Ramsey, Charlotte, NC, April 4, 2019, recording in author's possession.

72. Carmen Jones, "Partners Delta Sigma Theta and Habitat for Humanity Dedicate Crystal Oates House," *Kansas City Call,* July 23, 1993; Habitat for Humanity International Records, MSS

3786, Hargrett Rare Book and Manuscript Library, The University of Georgia Libraries, Athens, GA. The Central Region of Delta Sigma Theta now includes the states of Colorado, Kansas, Iowa, Missouri, Montana, Nebraska North Dakota, Oklahoma, South Dakota, and Wyoming.

73. Jackie Kimbrough and Tressa Latham, "Farwest Region is First to Complete Delta Habitat House," *Delta Journal* (Spring 1994), 10, in the National Archives of Delta Sigma Theta Sorority, Inc., Washington, DC.

74. Jackie Kimbrough and Tressa Latham, "Farwest Region is First to Complete Delta Habitat House," 10.

75. Doris Glymph Greene, Delta Habitat Committee Report, 28, in the National Archives of Delta Sigma Theta, Washington, DC; Delta Sigma Theta Sorority Corporate Report, July 1994, 28; in the National Archives of Delta Sigma Theta Sorority Inc., Washington, DC.; Dr. Bertha M. Roddey, David Snell, L. Diane Bennett, "Habitat for Humanity International and Delta Sigma Theta Sorority, Inc. Biennial Report, October, 1992—October 1994:" 19, in the Personal Collection of Fabette T. D. Smith, Raleigh, NC.; Doris Glymph Greene, interview by Sonya Ramsey, Charlotte, NC, May 17, 2017; L. Diane Bennett, interview by Sonya Ramsey, May 4, 2017.

76. Joan Foster Dames, "Volunteers to Build 15 Homes: Sorority Expects 4,200 Workers to Pitch in for 3-Day Blitz Here," *St. Louis Post Dispatch,* April 3, 1994, 7E, NewsBank: Access World News—Historical and Current, https://infoweb-NewsBank-com.eu1.proxy.openathens.net/apps/news/document-view?p=WORLDNEWS&docref=news/0EB04E8504 2FA72F, accessed June 16, 2019; Cynthia Todd, "Housing Group Builds Support, Not Fear," *St. Louis Post Dispatch,* July 17, 1994; 8D.

77. Fabette T. D. Smith and Ann McMillon, interview by Sonya Ramsey, June 30, 2019.

78. Doris Glymph Greene, *Delta Journal* (Spring 1996), in the National Archives of Delta Sigma Theta Sorority, Inc., Washington, DC.

79. L. Diane Bennett, interview by Sonya Ramsey, May 4, 2017, Charlotte, NC, recording in author's possession; Bertha M. Roddey, "Letter to Carol Freeland," May 10, 1995, Habitat for Humanity International Records, MS 3786, Hargrett Rare Book and Manuscript Library, The University of Georgia Libraries. Bertha Maxwell-Roddey, interview by Sonya Ramsey, Charlotte, NC, April 4, 2019, recording in author's possession.

80. Millard Fuller, "Letter from Millard Fuller to Bertha Maxwell-Roddey," April 25, 1995, see paper for comments; Habitat for Humanity International Records, MS 3786, Hargrett Rare Book and Manuscript Library, The University of Georgia Libraries, Athens, GA.

81. Harrison Goodall Jr., "Letter to Bertha M. Roddey," October 12, 1995, Habitat for Humanity International Records, MS 3786, Hargrett Rare Book and Manuscript Library, The University of Georgia Libraries, Athens, GA.

82. Delta Sigma Theta Sorority, Inc., *Delta Sigma Theta Media Kit, 2018* (Washington, DC: Delta Sigma Theta Sorority, Inc., 2018), 2, in the National Archives of Delta Sigma Theta Sorority, Inc., Washington, DC.

83. Oscar Faye Williams, interview by Sonya Ramsey, Dec. 20, 2018.

84. Doris Glymph Greene, interview by Sonya Ramsey, Charlotte, NC, May 17, 2017; Fabette T. D. Smith, "Bertha M. Roddey, Highlights of One Delta's Journey of Historical Significance, 2011," Unpublished Document, Private Collection of Fabette T. D. Smith, Raleigh, NC.

85. Claudia Washington, "Sorority Works Toward Ending Home Ownership Gap," *Washington Informer,* April 17, 2007, 17, ProQuest Dissertations and Theses Global Database,

https://librarylink.uncc.edu/login?url=https://search-proquest-com.librarylink.uncc.edu/docview/367459328?accountid=14605, accessed May 23, 2019.

86. Cynthia Todd, "Chavis Calls on Blacks to Spend with Blacks," *St. Louis Post Dispatch,* July 19, 1994: 3B, NewsBank: Access World News—Historical and Current, https://infoweb-NewsBank-com.eu1.proxy.openathens.net/apps/news/document-view?p=WORLDNEWS&docref=news/0EB04EA8947AAA8C, accessed January 22, 2022; "DST-NAACP Partnership for Change," *Delta Journal* (Fall/Winter 1994–1995), 19, in the National Archives of Delta Sigma Theta, Washington, DC; *Delta Sigma Theta Sorority Corporate Report,* July 1994, 8–30; in the National Archives of Delta Sigma Theta Sorority Inc., Washington, DC.

87. Fabette T. D. Smith, "Bertha M. Roddey, Highlights of One Delta's Journey of Historical Significance, 1;" Delta Sigma Theta, "Past Presidents' Council," Delta Sigma Theta Sorority Corporate Report, July 1994, 46; National Archives of Delta Sigma Theta Sorority Inc., Washington, DC.

88. National Heritage and Archives Committee, Delta Sigma Theta Sorority, Inc., "Heritage Movements: Habitat for Humanity," November 18, 2020, Facebook Post, https://www.facebook.com/search/top/?q=DSTHeritagemoment%20, accessed December 22, 2021; "Society World Cocktail Chit Chat," *Jet Magazine,* August 3, 1992, 82 (no. 15): 20, https://books.google.com/books?id=yMEDAAAAMBAJ&lpg=PA29&vq=society&pg=PA30#v=snippet&q=society&f=false, accessed January 14, 2020; Delta Sigma Theta, "Update," Special Telethon Edition 2, no. 1, January 1993, pamphlet, Private Collection of Bertha Maxwell-Roddey, Charlotte, NC; Bertha M. Roddey and David Snell, "Letter to L. Diane Bennett," *Habitat for Humanity International and Delta Sigma Theta Sorority, Inc. Biennial Report, October 1992–October 1994,* 121, in the private collection of Fabette T. D. Smith, Raleigh, NC; Cynthia Todd, "Housing Group Builds Support, Not Fear," *St. Louis Post Dispatch,* July 17, 1994; 8D.

89. Octavia Matthews, "Leadership Academies Report," *Delta Sigma Theta Sorority Corporate Report,* July 1994, 8–30, National Archives of Delta Sigma Theta Sorority Inc., Washington, DC; Bertha Maxwell-Roddey, interview by Sonya Ramsey, April 4, 2019.

90. Fabette T. D. Smith and Ann McMillon, interview by Sonya Ramsey, June 30, 2019.

91. Ella Goode Johnson, "Report of the Heritage and Archives Committee," *Delta Sigma Theta Sorority Corporate Report,* July 1994, 8–30; National Archives of Delta Sigma Theta Sorority Inc., Washington, DC.

92. Smith, "Bertha M. Roddey, "Highlights of One Delta's Journey of Historical Significance "Highlights, 1."

93. Goode Johnson, "Report of the Heritage and Archives Committee."

94. Goode Johnson, "Report of the Heritage and Archives Committee;" Maxwell-Roddey, interview by Sonya Ramsey, April 4, 2019.

95. Anna Borgman, "In Their Foremothers Footsteps: Women March to Honor 75 Years of Women's Suffrage," *Washington Post,* August 27, 1995, B1, *Washington* Post Digital Archives, https://www.washingtonpost.com/archive/local/1995/08/27/in-their-foremothers-footsteps/49b0fddd-e844-4d6e-9ad7-be7cb31a7e86/, accessed October 27, 2020; Guessippina Bonner, interview by Sonya Ramsey, July 12, 2019, Charlotte, NC, recording in author's possession.

96. Barbara F. Curtis, "Membership Services Committee Report," *Delta Sigma Theta Sorority Corporate Report,* July 1994, 8–30; in the National Archives of Delta Sigma Theta Sorority Inc., Washington, DC.

97. Melania Page Wicks, interview by Sonya Ramsey, January 4, 2019, Charlotte, NC, recording in author's possession.

98. Delta Sigma Theta, Delta Sigma Theta Sorority, Inc., *The Delta Launch 2000: A New Leadership for a New Century, 41st National Convention Workbook* (Washington, D.C.: Delta Sigma Theta, 1992), National Archives of Delta Sigma Theta Sorority Inc., Washington, DC.

99. Juanita Tatum, interview by Sonya Ramsey, Dec. 18, 2018, Charlotte, NC, recording in author's possession; Vashti Turly Murphy, "Chaplin's Report," *Delta Sigma Theta Sorority Corporate Report,* July 1994, 48–49, in the National Archives of Delta Sigma Theta Sorority Inc., Washington, DC.

100. Talis Shelbourne, "Paying Homage: Congresswoman Inspires Sisters on Delta Sigma Theta's Founders Day," *Milwaukee Journal Sentinel,* February 15, 2020, *Milwaukee Journal Sentinel* Website, https://www.jsonline.com/story/news/local/milwaukee/2020/02/15/congresswoman-marcia-fudge-delta-sigma-theta-founders-day/4771351002/, accessed September 24, 2020.

101. Deborah Peaks Coleman and Bertha Maxwell-Roddey, *I Remember Nine Precious Pearls: Reflections of Servant Ladies of Delta Sigma Theta Sorority, Inc.* (Charlotte, NC: Brown Angel Publishing, 2008).

102. Guessippina Bonner, interview, July 12, 2019, Charlotte, NC, recording in author's possession.

103. Wilson, interview by Sonya Ramsey, December 12, 2018; Fabette T. D. Smith and Ann McMillon, interview by Sonya Ramsey, June 30, 2019.

104. Melania Page Wicks, interview by Sonya Ramsey, January 4, 2019; Fabette T. D. Smith, interview by Sonya Ramsey, June 30, 2019; Wilson, interview by Sonya Ramsey, December 12, 2018.

105. Fabette T. D. Smith and Ann McMillon, interview by Sonya Ramsey, June 30, 2019.

106. Theodore Johnson, "The Political Power of the Black Sorority," *Atlantic Magazine,* April 15, 2015, *Atlantic Magazine* Website, https://www.theatlantic.com/politics/archive/2015/04/loretta-lynch-and-the-political-power-of-the-black-sorority/391385/, accessed January 14, 2020; 11 News Team, "Historically Black Sororities in Atlanta Unite for 'Stroll to the Polls' Video, Images, Now Viral," WXIA Television Website, https://www.11alive.com/article/news/local/atlanta-stroll-to-the-polls-video-images-go-viral/85-b8541896-40d5-40c3-8a32-81d3982b6324, accessed July 12, 2021.

107. "Delta Sigma Theta Sorority, Community Partners Work to Get Out the Vote for Runoff Election," December 3, 2020, On Common Ground (OCG) News, OCG News Website, https://ocgnews.com/delta-sigma-theta-sorority-community-partners-work-to-get-out-the-vote-for-runoff-election/, accessed July 12, 2021.

Conclusion: I Am Because We Are

1. Gregory Davis, interview by Sonya Ramsey, February 16, 2016, Harrisburg, NC, recording in author's possession.

2. Bertha Maxwell-Roddey, interview by author, March 6, 2011, Charlotte, NC, recording in author's possession.

3. See James Scott, *Domination and the Arts of Resistance: Hidden Transcripts* (New Haven, CT: Yale University Press, Revised edition, 1992).

4. Bertha Maxwell-Roddey, interview by Sonya Ramsey, March 9, 2018, Charlotte, NC, recording in author's possession.

5. Michel Vaughan, interview by Sonya Ramsey, February 25, 2018; Charlotte, NC, recording in author's possession.

6. Bertha Maxwell-Roddey, interview by Sonya Ramsey, March 9, 2018, Charlotte, NC.

7. Fabette T. D. Smith and Roselle Wilson, "The Bertha M. Roddey School of Leadership Studies Application for Certification Program Admission, 2015" Unpublished Document, in the Private Collection of Fabette T. D. Smith, Raleigh, NC.

8. Delta Sigma Theta's 27th National President, the late Cheryl Hickmon's positions were too numerous to list in this section; however, they included the positions of national secretary and national first vice president. Fabette T. D. Smith and Roselle Wilson, "The Bertha M. Roddey School of Leadership Studies Application for Certification Program Admission, 2015."

9. Fabette T. D. Smith and Roselle Wilson, "The Bertha M. Roddey School of Leadership Studies Application for Certification Program Admission, 2015."

10. Fabette T. D. Smith and Roselle Wilson, "The Bertha M. Roddey School of Leadership Studies Application for Certification Program Admission, 2015."

11. Fabette T. D. Smith and Roselle Wilson, "The Bertha M. Roddey School of Leadership Studies Application for Certification Program Admission, 2015."

12. Fabette T. D. Smith, "The 20th National President/My Friend Bertha," 1996, Unpublished Document, in the Private Collection of Fabette T. D. Smith, Raleigh, North Carolina.

13. For more information on the concept of "othermothering" or other mothering, see Patricia Hill Collins, *Black Feminist Thought: Knowledge, Consciousness, and the Politics of Empowerment* (New York: Routledge, 1990); Wanda Thomas Bernard, Sasan Issari, Jamel Moriah, Marok Njiwaji, Princewill Obgan, and Althea Tolliver, "Othermothering in the Academy: Using Maternal Advocacy for Institutional Change," *Journal of the Motherhood Initiative* 3, no: 2, 2012: 102–120, https://jarm.journals.yorku.ca/index.php/jarm/article/view/36305, accessed July 12, 2021; Karen Case "African American Other Mothering in the Urban Elementary School," *The Urban Review* 29, no. 1 (1997): 25–39, DOI http://dx.doi.org/10.1023/A:1024645710209, accessed January 14, 2020.

14. Maxwell-Roddey, interview by Sonya Ramsey, September 18, 2018, Charlotte, NC, recording in author's possession; Melania Page Wicks, interview by Sonya Ramsey, January 4, 2019; Fabette T. D. Smith, interview by Sonya Ramsey, Dec. 22, 2018, Raleigh, NC, recording in author's possession.

15. Melania Page Wicks, interview by Sonya Ramsey, January 4, 2019, Charlotte, NC, recording in author's possession.

16. Marcia Fudge, interview by Sonya Ramsey, March 5, 2019, Charlotte, NC, phone recording in author's possession. Charlotte, NC.

17. Deborah Jones-Buggs, interview by Sonya Ramsey, August 18, 2018, Charlotte, NC, phone recording in author's possession.

18. Beverly Smith, interview by Sonya Ramsey, Oct 25, 2018, Charlotte, NC, phone recording, in author's possession.

19. Paulette Walker, Interview by Sonya Ramsey, 2018, Charlotte, NC, phone recording in author's possession.

20. Beverly Guy Shetfall quoted in the transcript of *The Black Sorority Project: The Exodus,*

directed by Derek Fordjour and Jamar White, written by Rosalyn White, Derek Fordjour, and Jamar White, Documentary (Derek and Jamar Productions, 2006); The producers of the film were Mayam Myika Day, Derek Fordjour, Jay-Z, LaChanze, Jamar White, and Craig T. Williams. In 2006, Delta Sigma Theta Sorority filed a lawsuit seeking monetary relief against Derek and Jamar Productions for trademark infringement under federal and district law. All parties came to an agreement and settled the case in 2007. See Delta Sigma Theta Sorority, Inc. v. Derek and Jamar Production, LLC, No. 1:2006cv01993, Document 12 (D.D.C. 2007), Justia US Database, https://law.justia.com/cases/federal/district-courts/district-of-columbia/dcdce/1:2006cv01993/123284/12/, accessed October 20, 2020; For more information about Black women and sisterhood, see Katrina McDonald, *Embracing Sisterhood: Class, Identity, and Contemporary Black Women,* (New York: Rowman and Littlefield Publishers, 2007).

Index

Page numbers in *italics* refer to illustrations.

Bottoms, Keisha Lance, 270
Bracey, John H., Jr., 112, 224
Bradley, Deon, 191
Branton, Wiley A., 222
Braun, Carol Moseley, 250
Brewington, Mamie, 147, 151
Bridges, Kenneth, 183
Britt, Doris Jackson, 354n38
Britt, William, 146
Brooklyn Presbyterian Church (Charlotte, NC), 112
Brookshire, Stanford (Stan), 76, 221
Brown, Charlotte Hawkins, 27
Brown, Cheryl L., 124
Brown, Edward, 70
Brown, Linda, 352n11
Brown, Mamie H., 352n11, 354n38
Brown, Tamara M., 355n47
Brown v. Board of Education, 9, 34, 40, 53, 67, 71, 74, 208, 211–13
Brown v. Board of Education II, 211
Bryant, Carolyn, 32
Building Bridges Program, 154, 163, 183, 185
Burch, James T., 52, 88, 92–93
Burroughs, Nannie Helen, 199, 201
Burson, Sherman, Jr., 121
Butler-McIntyre, Cynthia, 281
Butler University (Indianapolis, IN), 200

Caldwell, Octavia Walker, 140
Caldwell, Ronald R., 83, 140
Cameron, Chris, 127
Campbell, Akilah A., 355n47
Campbell, Peggy, 183
Canady, Hortense, 135, 245, 252, 263
Capacchione v. Charlotte-Mecklenburg Schools, 193
Carmichael, Stokely, 152
Carolina Israelite, 149
Carolina Journal, 126
Carson, Margaret, 351n103
Carter, Jimmy, 137, 234, 249, 255, 261
Carter, Rosalynn, 137
Carver, Ann C., 133, 153; biography, 84; and BSC, 84–85, 86; as BSP faculty, 90, 92, 93, 95, 98–99, 102–3; Women's Studies Program, founding of, 10, 118, 124
Carver, George Washington, 70
Carver College, 66, 67, 68, 69–70, 71–73. See also Central Piedmont Community College (CPCC); Mecklenburg College

Catlett, Elizabeth, 186, 265
Central Piedmont Community College (CPCC), 67, 74–75, 77, 99, 122, 152, 221. See also Carver College; Mecklenburg College
Chambers, Julius, 60, 64, 77, 107, 115, 221, 228, 265
Chapman, Sharon J., 355n47
Charismatic advocacy, 5, 97, 201, 247, 281–82
Charismatic leadership, 2, 7, 46, 201, 209
Charles, Donna P., 351n103
Charles H. Wright Museum of African American History (Detroit, MI), 142
Charlotte Advancement Center, 98
Charlotte Alumnae Chapter of Delta Sigma Theta Sorority (CAC), 194, 213, 227, 235, 268, 346n48; as Beta Xi Sigma, 208, 211, 214; fundraising, 214–16, 218, 222; and Iota Rho, 224, 225, 229; Maxwell-Roddey as president of, 13–14, 106, 198, 214–23, 228–29, 231, 235–36, 268; social action, 13, 217–18, 220–22
Charlotte Area Fund, 49, 221
Charlotte Chamber of Commerce Quality Education Committee (QEC), 106
Charlotte City Council, 69, 147, 150–53, 164–65, 167, 190, 221
Charlotte City Planning Commission, 155
Charlotte City Schools. See Charlotte Mecklenburg Schools System (CMS)
Charlotte College, 66, 69–75. See also Carver College; University of North Carolina at Charlotte (UNC Charlotte)
Charlotte League of Women Voters (CLWV), 105–6
Charlotte-Mecklenburg Council on Human Relations, 72
Charlotte-Mecklenburg Historic Landmarks Commission, 175
Charlotte-Mecklenburg Parents Commission, 71, 73
Charlotte-Mecklenburg PTA Council, 61, 143
Charlotte Mecklenburg Schools System (CMS), 88, 92, 128, 180, 220, 221, 228; and AACC, 150, 161, 163, 177, 178; as Charlotte City Schools system, xxii, 34–35, 40, 41, 68–69, 73, 294n1; desegregation, 9, 37, 41–44, 48–55, 60–65, 106, 145, 193; and Elizabeth Randolph, 9, 36, 49, 52, 59, 62–65, 107; and Head Start, 47–48; and Kathleen Crosby, 9, 36–37, 42, 59–65, 107, 118, 143; and Maxwell-Roddey, 41, 42, 47, 50–52, 54–55, 58, 63–65, 106; merger, xxii, 41, 294n1; and UNC Charlotte, 77, 78, 86

220; Height, Dorothy, *140,* 208–9, 210–14, 234; Five Point Programmatic Thrust, 208, 211, 216–18, 221–22, 226, 229, 250; Habitat for Humanity, partnership with, 14, *137,* 233, 254–63, 267, 269, 279–80; hazing, 197, 238–39, 240, 247–48, 253, 281; Heritage and Archives Committee (H&A), 198, 228–31, 236, 239–41, 244, 264, 277, 351n103; history of, 6–7, 195–204, 205–9; Iota Rho Chapter (UNCC), xi, *139,* 222, 224–26, 228, 229, 274; Maxwell-Roddey, CAC president of, 13, 106, 198, 214–23, 228–29, 231, 235–36, 268; Maxwell-Roddey, campaign for national president of, 2, 13, *136,* 198, 234, 248; Maxwell-Roddey, campaign for state office, support of, 158, 228; Maxwell-Roddey, Gamma Lambda member & adviser, 13, 106, *131,* 160, 195, 209–10, 223; Maxwell-Roddey, as National First Vice President of, 184, 242, 244–48; Maxwell-Roddey, as national president of, 3, 14, 129, 167, 184, 249–50, 252–66, 272, 352n1;Maxwell-Roddey, as regional director, 12–13, 198, 231–32, 235–42, 244, 266, 280; Maxwell-Roddey, sisters' support of, 8, 13, 46, 276–81; National Library Project, 207; President's Council of Past National Presidents, 280; public service of, 13–14, 197, 207–10, 221, 249; Shirley Price Harris, member of, 46; social action of, 13, 204, 207–220, 221–22, 224–27, 251–70; stereotypes about, 7, 13, 197, 206–8, 218, 249; Terrell, Mary Church, honorary member of, 199, 204, 209, 214

Denney, Mary, 77

Dent, Jessie McGuire, 208

Department of Health, Education, and Welfare, (HEW), 52, 77, 83, 149

Department of Vocational Rehabilitation, 98

Diamond, Alice, *132*

Diamond, Patrick, 191

Dickson, R. S., 71

Dillard, Geraldine, 92

Disciples of Christ Church, 255

Division of Negro Affairs of the National Youth Administration, 208

Dolby, Edward, 186

Downs, Mae Wright (Mae W. Peck-Williams), 208

Drenan, Naomi, 169

Drucker, Peter, 119

Dry-Burton, Gaile, 157, 268

Du Bois, W.E.B., 2, 27, 78, 84, 93, 108, 199–200, 261

Duff, Roberta, *132,* 246, 268, 352n11; at BSP, 93, 99, 111, 117; at CMS, 92–93

Duke Power, 70, 188

Duke University, xi, 68, 81, 93, 240

Dusable Museum of African American History, 142

Earle, Anna Brewer, 17, 21, 22, *130,* 218

Earle, Joseph (Joe), 15, 17, 22, 28, 255

Earle, Joseph Jr., 22

Earle, Lula Austin, 15

Earle, Monroe, 17, 22–24, 159

Earth Wind and Fire, 189

Ebony, 3

Ebony Players, 152, 164, 165

Economos, Gus, 159

Edelman, Marian Wright, 250

Edmonds, Helen G., 201–2

Edmundson, Valerie, 124

Efird's Department Store, 166

Eisenhower, Dwight D., 201

Ekechukwu, Myriette, 125

Elder, Thereasea, 105, 143, 145

Elementary and Secondary Education Act (ESEA), 36, 43–44, 49, 50

Elnora (Maxwell-Roddey's sibling), 22

Elouise (Maxwell-Roddey's great-aunt), 210

Elston, Gerald, 35

Emory, Frank, Jr., 186

Evers, Medgar, 220

Evers, Myrlie, 220

Ewing, Bobbie J., 355n47

Fairview School (Charlotte, NC), 36

Fanon, Frantz, 108

Farmer, James, 83

Farrar, Shirley, 153–54, 161, 163–65, 168, 169, 175, 176

Faulcon, Nettie D., 355n47

Fayetteville State University, 79, 124

Federal Higher Education Act, 74

Ferguson, Barbara, 178

Ferguson, Bernice Sloan, 46

Ferguson, James E., II, 64, 77, 274

Fifteenth Amendment, 204

First Baptist Church-West (Charlotte, NC), 46, 151, 160, 169, 183

First Union Bank, 188

First United Presbyterian (Charlotte, NC), 31

First Ward Urban Renewal Area Plan, 175

Fisk University (Nashville, TN), 78

Flood, Dudley, 90
Flowers, Robert (Bobby), 115
Folk, Chris, 62
Ford, Beverly (Bev) Odom, 108, 223; as counselor, 90–91, 92, 94, 95; and AAAS internship program, 115–16; and AACC, 146; at JCSU, 119, 120; higher education of, 95, 103, 122; and NCBS, 111, 123
Ford, Nick Aaron, 111
Ford Foundation, 104
Fordjour, Derek, 361n20
Foster, Dwala N., 355n47
Four Tops, 189
Foxx, Laura, 186
Frank (Maxwell-Roddey's sibling), 22
Fraternal Order of Police, 156
Frazier, Vonda, 181
Fredericks, Khadija A., 355n47
Freedmen's College of North Carolina, 30–31. *See also* Johnson C. Smith University
Freeman, Frankie Muse, *135, 136,* 224–25, 233, 234, 237, 263
Freeman, O. N., 49, 220
Fretwell, E. K., Jr., 121
Fridia, Shirley Ann, 355n47
Friendship Missionary Baptist Church (Charlotte, NC), 21, 31, *140,* 160, 183, 243
Frye, David, 92, 146
Frye, Gaillard, 40, 60, 62
Fudge, Marcia L., 266, 270, 280, 355n47
Fuller, Millard, 254–57
Fuller (Degelmann), Linda, 254–55
Fulton, Andrea, 352n11
Future Educators of America, 262

Gallman, Vanessa, 118
Gantt, Harvey Bernard, 141, 147, 159, 166–67, 175–76, 179–80, 182, 192
Gantt, Sonja, 182
Garibaldi, Linn D., 71
Garinger, Elmer H., 68–69
Garvey, Marcus, 261
Geraldine (teacher), 57
Ghana, 14, 115, 248, 261–62
Giddings, Paula, xii, 7, 202
Gilder, Lois J., *138,* 355n47
Glenn, Defoy, 178
Goff, Wilhelmina D., 355n47
Golden, Harry, 149
Goodall, Harrison, Jr., 261

Goode Johnson, Ella, *138,* 244, 264, 277, 355n47
Goodman, J. C., 156–57
Good Samaritan Hospital (Charlotte, NC), 193–94, 208
Goodson, Annie C., 355n47
Grant, Jim, 152–53
Graves, Carrie, *132*
Gray, Helen, 26
Greene, Doris Glymph, *138,* 256, 257, 258, 260, 352n11, 355n47
Greene, Vanessa, 182–84
Greenfield, Wilbert, 119
Greenleaf, Robert, 2
Gregory, T. Montgomery, 204
Griffin, Arthur, Jr., xiv, 128
Guinier, Ewart, 112

Habitat for Humanity, 14, *137,* 233, 254–63, 267, 269, 279–80
Hagemeyer, Richard, 75
Hairston, Jacqueline B., 355n47
Haiti, 209, 261
Hall, Pamela, *135*
Hall, Perry, 88, 112
Hall of Negro Life (Dallas, TX), 173, 189
Hammond House Museum (Atlanta, GA), 173
Hansberry, William Leo, 78
Harding, Vincent, 87–88
Hardy, Carroll, 352n11
Hare, Nathan, 79
Harmon, Alison J., 355n47
Harper, Mary, *135,* 223, 276; AACC, founding of, xiii, 1, 11–12, 141–50, 152, 169–70, 241; and AACC changes after, 161, 163, 171, 174, 178, 182–83, 185, 191–93; at BSP, 90–91, 92, 122, 142; higher education of, 122; and NCBS, 111
Harris, Kamala, 270
Harris, Shirley Price, 45–46, 243
Harris, William, 112
Harris, William T., 64, 76
Harrison, Dorothy, 211
Harrison, Henry, 185
Harshaw, Julia, *132*
Harvey B. Gantt Center for African-American Arts + Culture, xxi, 129, *134,* 173, 279, 340n68; building of, 191, 192; change since AACC, xiii, 1, 11–12, 141, 192–94, 276; grand opening, 141; Harper-Roddey Grand Lobby, *135,* 276; and Harvey B. Gantt, 141, 147, 166–67, 175–76, 182, 192. *See also* Afro-American Cultural Center (AACC)

McGhee, Yvonne, 354n38
McGill, Betty A., 355n47
McGlohon, Loonis, 151, 166, 167, 168–69
McKeever, Kelley K., 355n47
McKenzie, Vashti, 355n47
McKinney, Roseline, 355n47
McKoin, Claudia L., *138*, 354n38, 355n47
McLain, Mary, 73
McLean, Mabel, 118
McMillian, James B., 53, 60
McMillon, Ann, *138*, 240, 277
McNeely Bennett, Winnie, 95
Mecklenburg College, 67, 74–75. *See also* Carver College; Central Piedmont Community College (CPCC)
Merry Makers, 214
Middleton, Jimmie Bugg, 217–18, 222
Milholland, Inez, 205
Miller, Paul, 84
Mills, Deanna L., 355n47
Mint Museum of Craft + Design (Charlotte, NC), 141, 186, 190, 191
Miracle Voices, 148
Mississippi State University (MSU), 75
Mitchell, Clarence, Jr., 219
Mitchell, Juanita Jackson, 2
Mitchell, Steve, 98
Mobley, Charlotte, 70
Montgomery, Wanda, 185–86
Moore, Beulah D., 36, 296n13
Moore, Roy, 269
Morehouse College, 17, 84, 158
Moreland, William Howard (W. H.), 34
Morgan State University, 200
Morrill, Dan, 175
Morris, Charles, 72
Morris, Edna Johnson, 201, 351n103
Motley, Constance Baker, 213
Mount Carmel Baptist Church, 175, 176
Moynihan, Patrick, 44
Muhammad, Nafeesa, 125
Murphy, Dee Dee, 176
Murphy, Skip, 182
Myers, W. R., 31
Myrick, Sue, 182

National Association for the Advancement of Colored People (NAACP), 2, 200; and Benjamin Chavis Jr., 82; and Black sororities, 202, 208, 212–13, 217, 219, 228, 262; Carver College,

opposition to, 69, 72, 73; and desegregation of schools, 40, 41, 53; and desegregation of universities, 30, 71, 73, 77; and Jayne Wallace Hemphill, 37; Maxwell-Roddey, endorsement of, 156; and Modjeska Simkins, 26; and Septima Poinsette Clark, 167, 168; and Sonja Hayes Stone, 123
National Association of Colored Women (NACW). *See* National Association of Colored Women's Clubs (NACWC)
National Association of Colored Women's Clubs (NACWC), 3, 20, 199–200, 204, 213, 250
National Association of Elementary School Principals (NAESP), 58, 63
National Campaign to Oppose Bank Loans to South Africa, 125
National Collegiate Athletic Association (NCAA), 75
National Council for Black Studies (NCBS), xiv, xxii, 124, 125–26, 194, 272, 279; Maxwell-Roddey, founding by, xiii, 10, 14, 110–14, 129, 146, 224, 231, 274–75; and Sonja Hayes Stone, 122–23
National Council of Negro Women (NCNW), 164, 195, 208–10, 212–13, 234, 262
National Football League (NFL), 188, 193
National League of Women Voters, 105
National March on Washington for Jobs and Freedom, 213
National Negro Congress, 26
National Organization of Women (NOW), 212–13
National Urban League (NUL), 143, 212
National Women's Studies Association, 124
NationsBank, 186
Nave-Carpenter, Jessie, 257, 354n38, 255n47
Neal, Larry, 89
Neill, Rolfe, 176, 178, 188
Nelson, William, Jr., 114
New Harmony United Methodist Church, 289n11. *See also* St. James Methodist Church
Nichols, Elaine, 96, 148–49, 178, 268
Nigeria, 226, 350n94
Nivens, Vivian, 176–77, 178, 181, 182
Noble, Jeanne, *135*, 212, 213, 222, 234, 238, 239, 253, 264
Noel Bates, Gladys, 208
Norrel Boarding School (Seneca, SC), 18
North Carolina Agricultural and Technical State University, 78, 79
North Carolina Association of Educators, 156

North Carolina Central University (Durham, NC), 79, 82, 201, 248, 265
North Carolina Council for the Arts, 152
North Carolina National Bank, 119
Northwestern University, 79

Oates, Crystal, 258–59
Oconee County Training School (OCTS), 19, 20
Officer, Iris, 352n11
Ogundiran, Akinwumi, 127
Omega Psi Phi Fraternity, 200, 209, 260
Operation PUSH (People United to Save Humanity), 157
Optimist Club, 47
Orr, James, 23
Orr, Lorraine, 51
Ossoff, Jon, 269
Owens, Bill, 158
Owens, Gwennie Mae, 22

Palmer Memorial Institute, 27
Pan Africanism, 112, 261
Pannell, Ethel Early, 244
Parker, Charles, 152–53
Parker, Frank, 77, 87
Parker, Henry C., 31–33
Parks, Rosa, 129, 156, 167, 168
Paul, Alice, 204–5
Peabody, George, 19
Peace Corps, 116
Peck-Williams, Mae W. See Downs, Mae Wright
Penn (White), Madre, 202–3
Pereira, Malin, 127
Performing Arts Ensemble, PAGE, 164
Perry, Catherine, 17
Phi Beta Sigma Fraternity, 200, 260
Phi Delta Kappa Sorority, 210
Phillips, Craig, 42, 63
Phillips, John, 47, 50, 63, 220
Phillips, Marion, 355n47
Pickens, William (Bill), 183
Pine Street Graded School (Seneca, SC), 18
Pinkston, Brandolyn C., 352n11, 355n47
Pleasant Hill Baptist Church (Oconee County, SC), 19
Plessy v. Ferguson, 18, 250
Politics of respectability, 199, 220, 224, 251, 281–82, 342n9
Polk, Jim, 88
Poor People's Campaign, 224

Porter, Billy, 154
Porter, Michael, 166
Price, Shirley. See Harris, Shirley Price
Prince, Cecil, 71
Proctor, Tawanna, 42, 120, 216, 219, 243
Puryear, Carol S., 355n47
Pyles, Julian, 77, 85, 122

Quander, Nellie, 203
Queens University, 118, 128

Race women, 3, 5–6, 9, 11, 143, 281
Randolph, Elizabeth (Libby) Schmoke, xi, 273; biography, 36–37, 38–39, 41, 61; at CMS, 9, 36–38, 49, 52–53, 58–59, 62–65, 107; and Head Start, 36, 49–50; as principal, 41, 51, 62, 63–64
Randolph, Nancy, 239, 245
Ray, Margaret, 60, 65
Reagon, Bernice Johnson, 167
Red Cross, 47, 217
Reddick, Louise, 223
Reddy, Thomas James (T. J.), 80–84, 89, 100, 104, 140, 152–54, 178, 225
Reed, Sharon, 352n11
Reese, Addison H., 71
Reginald F. Lewis Museum of African American History and Culture (Baltimore), 142
Reinhart, Mrs. (teacher), 57
Remmers, H. H., 212
Reverse migration, xiii, 12, 172, 174, 192
Rice, Louise A., 355n47
Rieke, Robert, 73
Rights of White People (ROWP), 97
Rippy, Almeda, 78
Roberts, Gus, 40
Robeson, Paul, 27
Robinson, Ethel, 202
Robinson, Harry, Jr., 12, 173, 188–89, 190
Robinson, Tommy, 148, 178, 184
Roddey, Bertha M. See Maxwell-Roddey, Bertha
Roddey, Cynthia, 352n11
Roddey, Theodore (Ted) Thomas, Jr., xxi, 137, 243, 244, 245, 354n29
Roosevelt, Eleanor, 212
Rosemond, James R., 18
Rosenwald, Julius, 19
Rosenwald Fund, 19, 60
Ross, Calvene, 169
Ross, James, 88
Rowe, Oliver R., 71

Talladega College (Alabama), 95
Tanner, Henry O., 186
Tate, Alice Lindsay, 102, 103–5, 115, 168
Tate, Thad, 144
Tatum, Juanita, 266
Taylor, Adrienne Brooks, 355n47
Taylor, Andress, 109
Taylor, Carolyn, 352n11
Taylor, David R., 141, 183, 190–91
Taylor, Lynette, 355n47
Taylor, Shelia, 352n11
Taylor-Burroughs, Margaret, 142
Terrell, Mary Church, 3, 20–21, 199–201, 204–5, 209, 213, 214
Terrell, Robert, 204
Theodore and Bertha M. Roddey Foundation, xiii, 268
Thomas, Deborah Carol, 354n38, 355n47
Thomas, Delores, 227
Thomas, Herman, *139*; and AACC, 146, 150, 153–54, 164, 175, 177, 186–87; biography, 92, 93, 126, 153, 177; at BSP, 92–93, 95–96, 153; minister, 92, 153, 160; and NCBS, 111, 117, 129, 274; and Shotgun Restoration Committee, 181–82, 183; at University Transitions Opportunities Program, 126
Thomas, W. J., 17, 18
Thompson v. Gibbs, 167
Thornton, Sharman, 186
Tidwell, Isaiah, 180, 183–85
Till, Emmett, 32
Tindall, Connie, 97
Trotter, William Monroe, 2–3
Truman, Harry S., 234
Tryon, William, 193
Ture, Kwame, 152
Turner, James, 10, 112, 113, 125, 129
Tuskegee Institute, 19
Tweedy, Edythe, 352n11

Ubuntu, 2, 13
Uchenger, Justin, 77, 94
Umoja Sasa (Unity Now), 184–85
Union of Experimenting College and Universities, 109, 122, 142
United Arts Fund (UAF). *See* Arts and Science Council (ASC) (Charlotte, NC)
United Nations, 209, 266
United Negro College Fund, 165, 227
United Services Organizations (USO), 208

University of Alabama (Tuscaloosa, AL), 71, 123
University of Connecticut, 127
University of North Carolina at Asheville, 75
University of North Carolina at Charlotte (UNC Charlotte), 63, 272; College of Human Development and Learning, 57–58, 66, 77–78, 86–87, 102, 106, 110; history of, 9, 66, 69–75; Iota Rho, xi, *139,* 222, 224–26, 228, 229, 274. *See also* African American and African Studies (AAAS) (UNC Charlotte); Africana Studies Department (UNC Charlotte); Black Studies Program (BSP) (UNC Charlotte); Women's Studies Program (UNC Charlotte)
University of North Carolina at Greensboro, 67, 74, 78, 81; Maxwell-Roddey degree, 3, 42–43, 50, 54, 214, 219–20, 272; Shirley Price Harris degree, 46
University of North Carolina at Wilmington, 75
University of North Carolina Chapel Hill, xii, 41, 67–69, 74, 81, 122–23, 127
University of Notre Dame, 127
University of Pennsylvania, 223, 234
University of South Carolina at Lancaster, xiii, xiv, 15, 127–29, 187
University of the District of Columbia, 109
Urban League of the Carolinas, 181
US Department of Education, 123, 227
US Department of Labor, 157

Vaughan, Michel Denise, *138,* 187, 277
Vaughn, Gladys Gary, 355n47
Volunteers in Service to America (VISTA), 116
Voting Rights Act of 1965, 50, 217, 222
Vroman, Mary Elizabeth, 202

Wachovia Bank, 184, 188, 190–91
Waddell, E. E. (Edwin Elbert), 177–78
Walker, Alice, 143
Walker, Paulette, 218, 280
Wallace, Robert, 84
Walter Reed General Hospital, 30
Walton, Jay, 175
Warnock, Raphael, 269
War on Poverty, 9, 43, 47–48, 61, 213, 220–21, 250
Warren, Frederick, 51
Washington, Barbara A., *139*
Washington, Booker T., 18, 19, 108, 199
Washington University at St. Louis, 260
Waters, Sharon, 181
Watson, Angela D., 355n47

SONYA Y. RAMSEY (pronouns she/her/hers) is associate professor of history and women's and gender studies and is the director of the Women's and Gender Studies Program at the University of North Carolina at Charlotte. She is the author of *Reading, Writing, and Segregation: A Century of Black Women Teachers in Nashville*. She lives in Charlotte, North Carolina.